A-Z MINI ...

CO...

REFERENCE

Motorway	**M1**
A Road	**A2**
B Road	**B519**
Dual Carriageway	
One-way	
Traffic flow on A Roads is indicated by a heavy line on the driver's left.	
All one-way streets are shown on Large Scale Pages 4-27	
Junction Names	MARBLE ARCH
Pedestrianized Road	
Restricted Access	
Railway	Tunnel / Level Crossing
Stations:	
National Rail Network	
Docklands Light Railway	**DLR**
Underground Station	is the registered trade mark of Transport for London
Congestion Charging Zone	● ●
Large Scale Pages only.	
Map Continuation	84 Large Scale City Centre 8

Car Park Selected	P
Church or Chapel	†
Fire Station	■
Hospital	H
House Numbers A & B Roads only	40 23
Information Centre	i
National Grid Reference	539
Police Station	▲
Post Office	★
Toilet	▽
with facilities for the Disabled	▽
Educational Establishment	
Hospital or Hospice	
Industrial Building	
Leisure & Recreational Facility	
Place of Interest	
Public Building	
Shopping Centre or Market	
Other Selected Building	

SCALE

Map Pages 28-125	Map Pages 4-11
1:21477 Approx. 3 inches to 1 mile	1:10560 6 inches to 1 mile
0 ⅛ ¼ Mile	0 1/16 ⅛ Mile
0 100 200 300 Metres	0 100 200 Metres
4.66 cm to 1km 7.49 cm to 1 mile	9.47 cm to 1km 15.24 cm to 1 mile

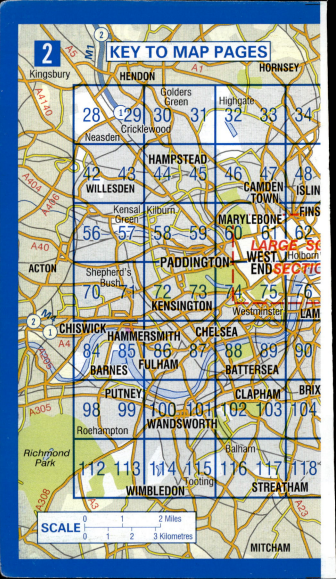

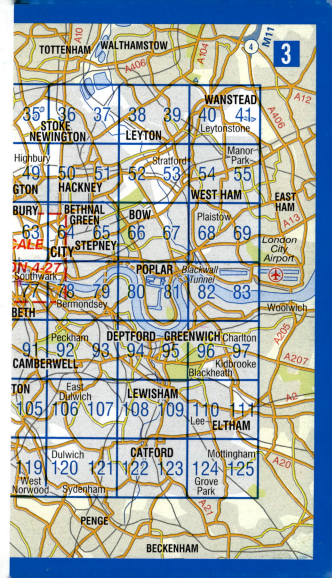

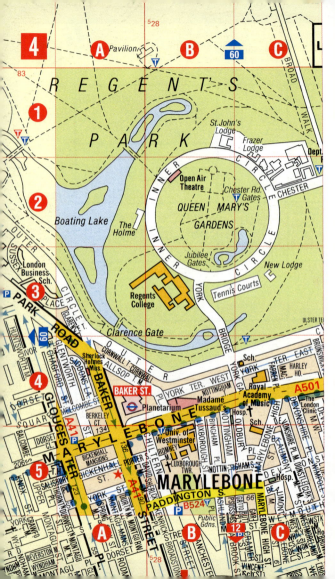

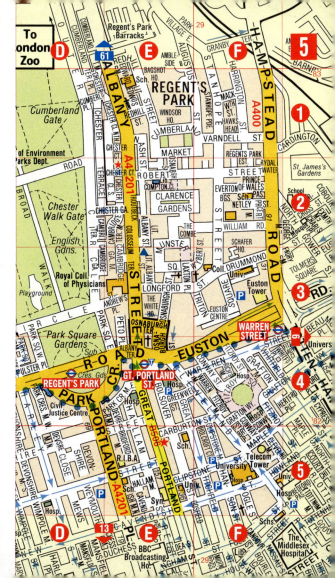

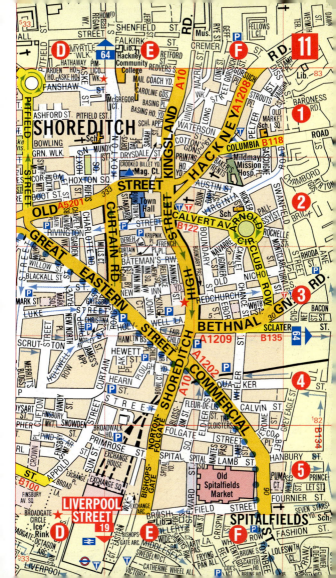

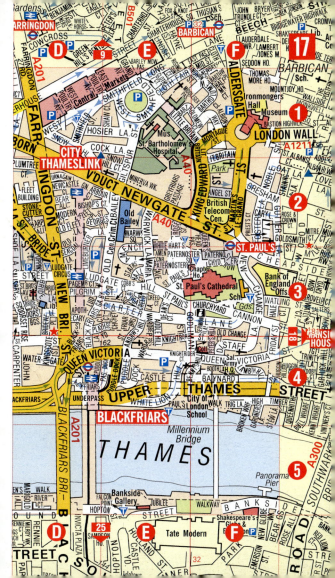

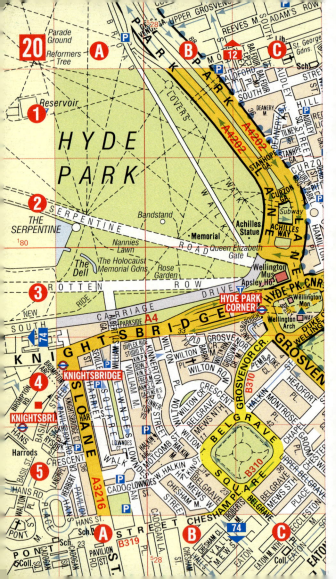

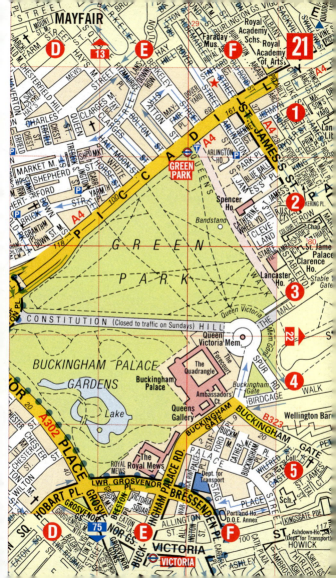

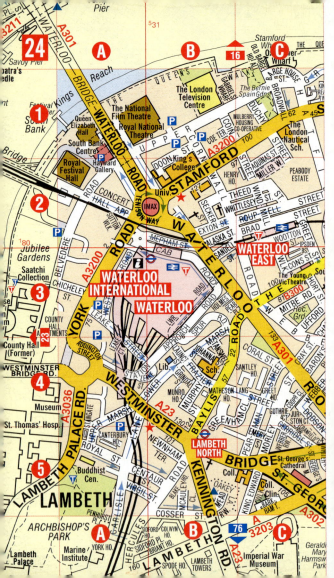

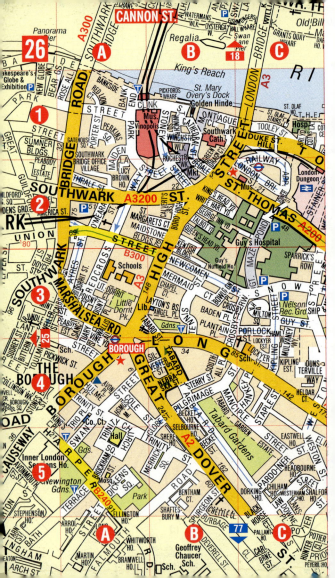

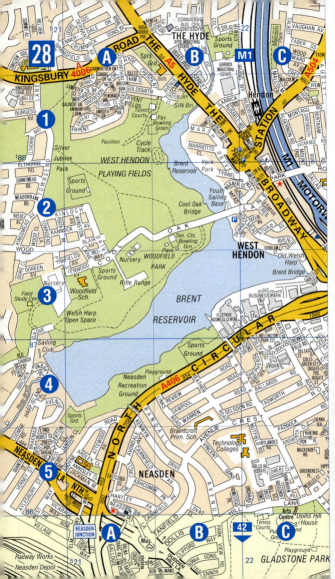

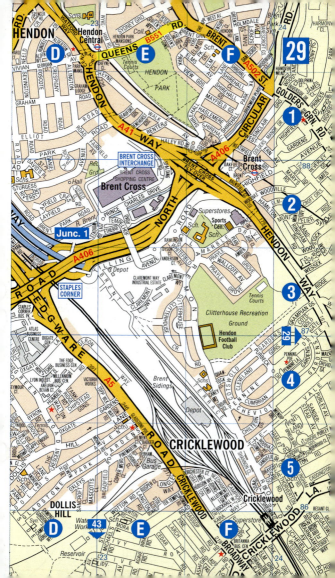

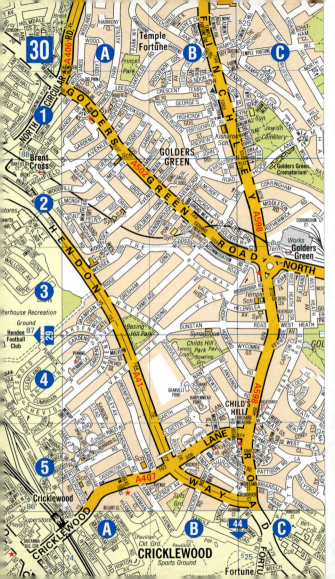

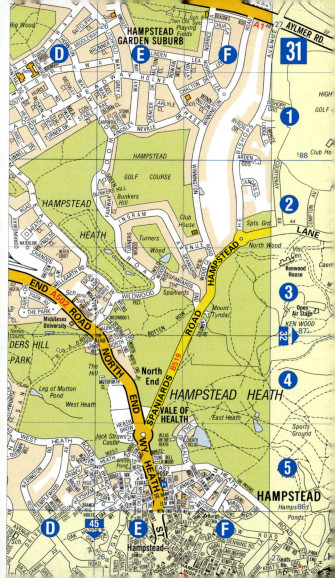

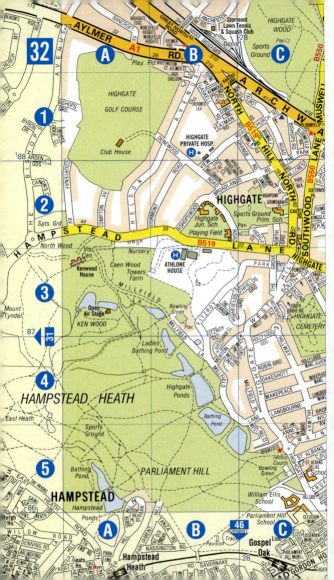

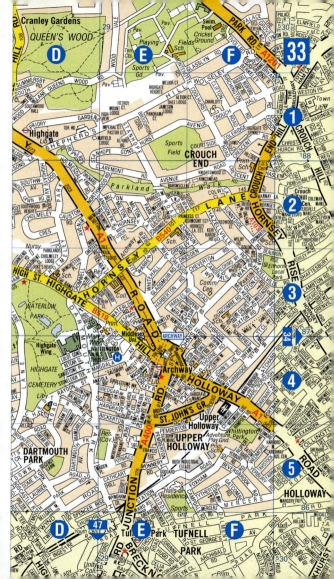

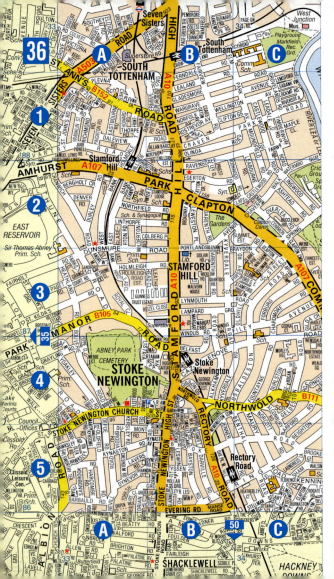

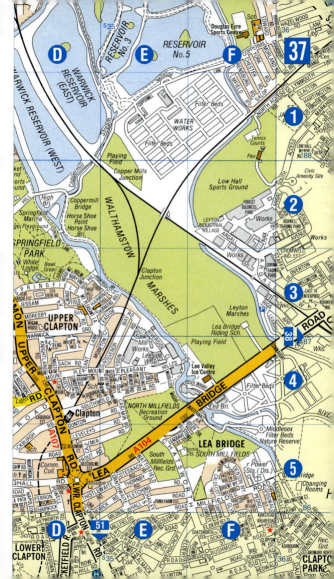

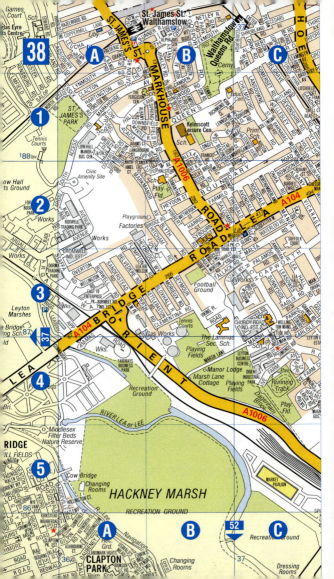

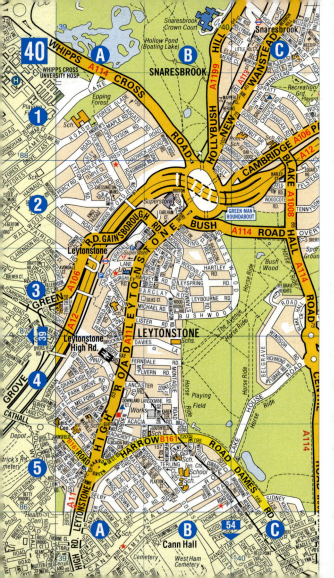

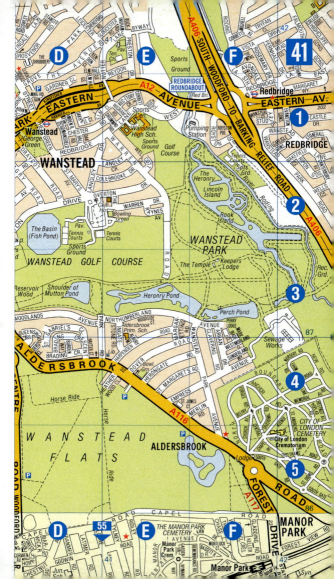

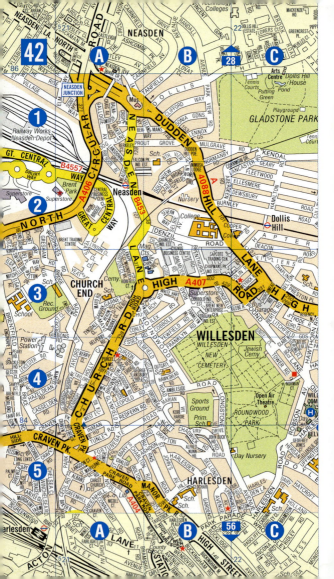

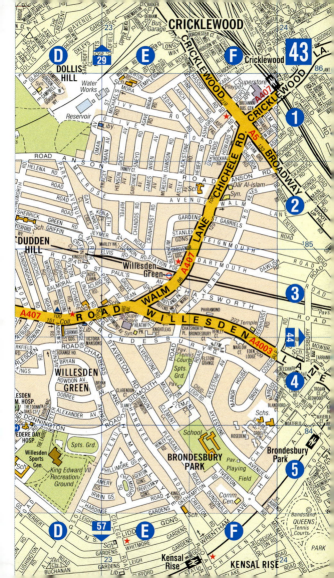

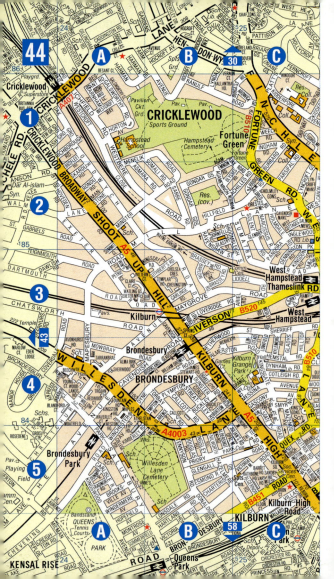

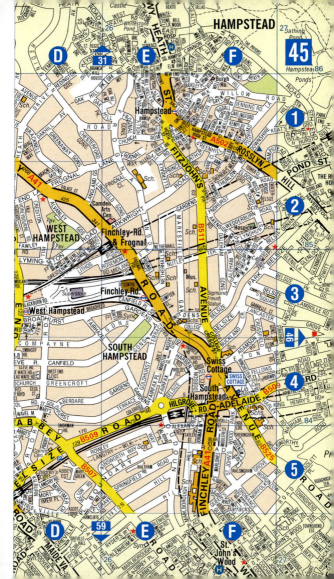

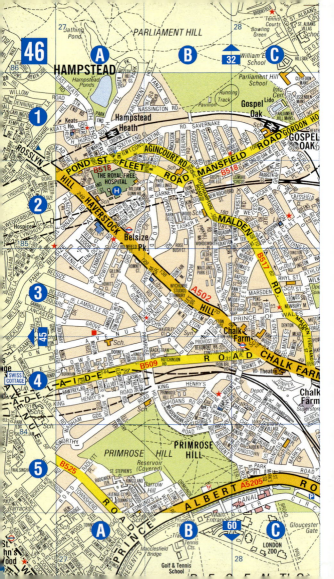

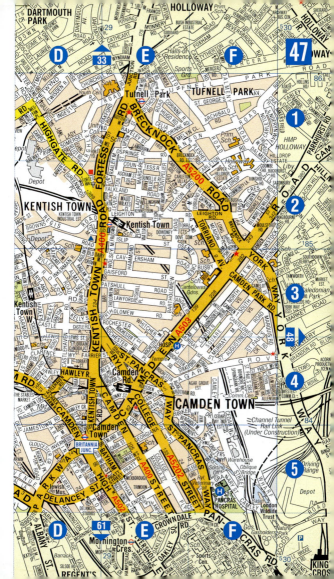

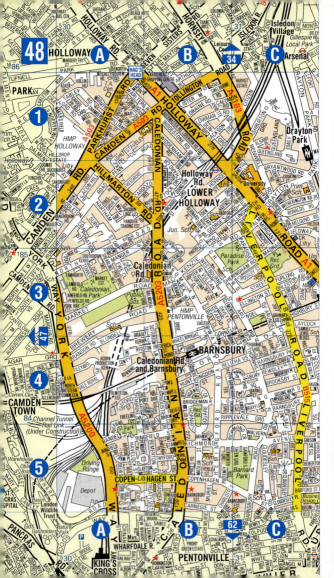

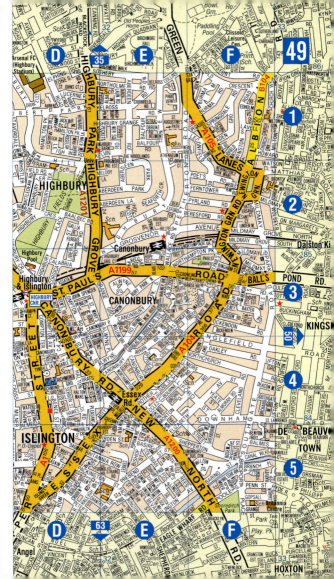

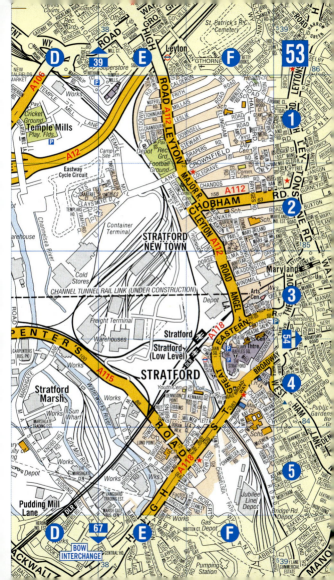

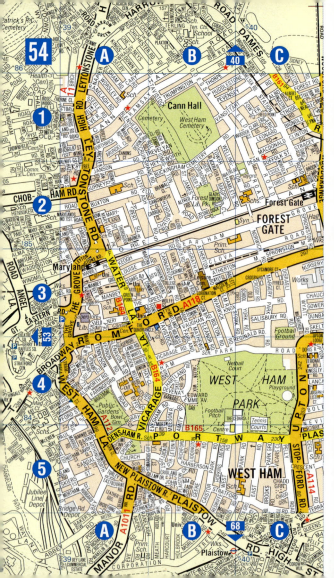

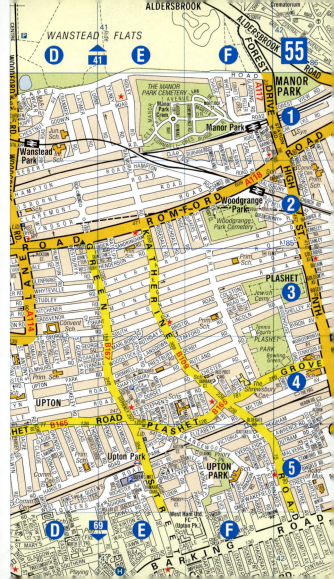

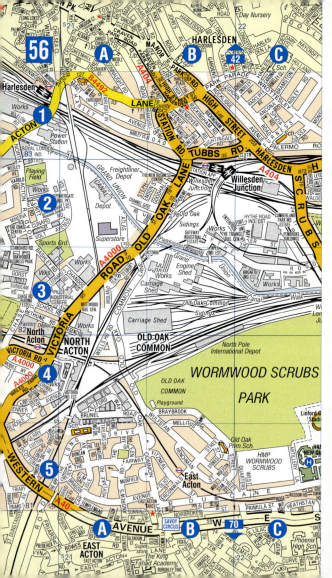

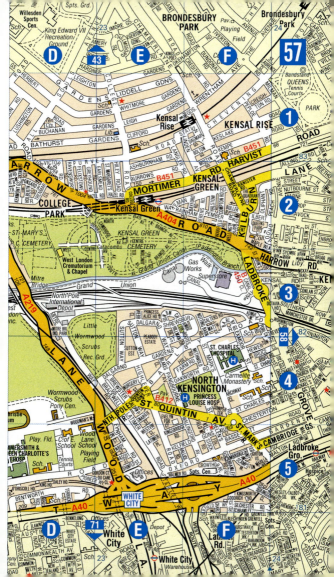

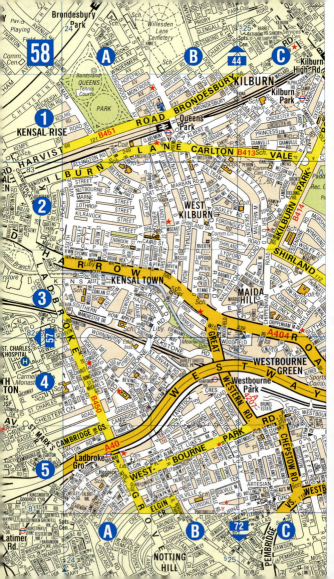

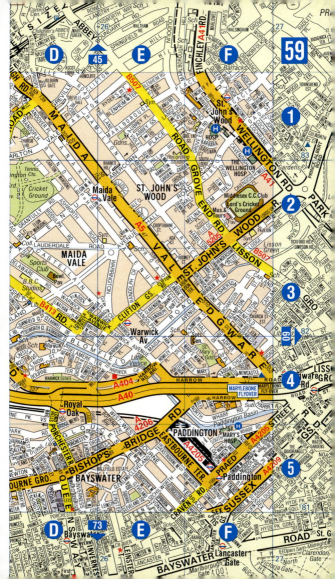

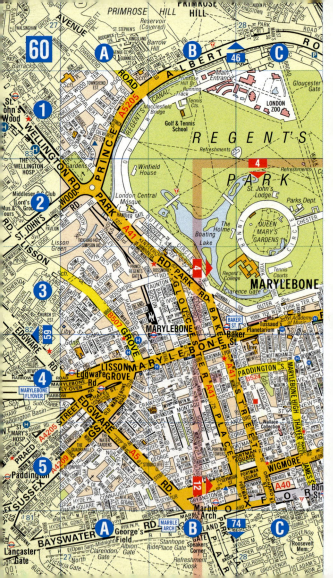

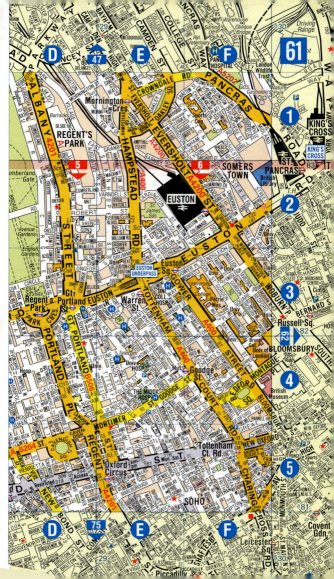

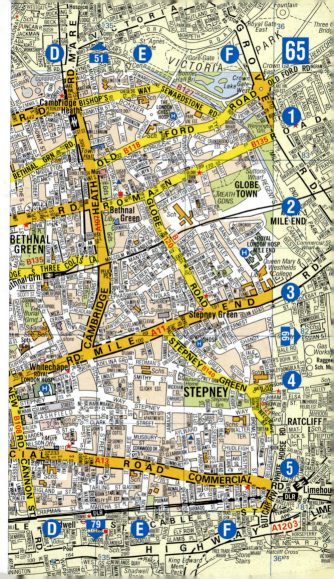

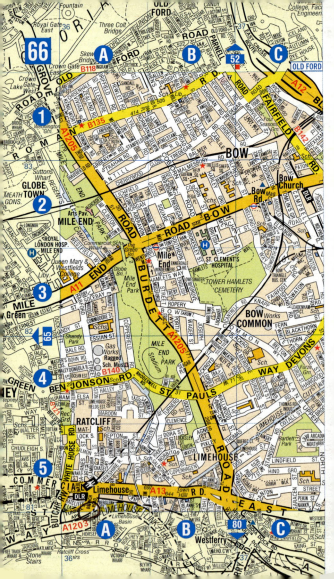

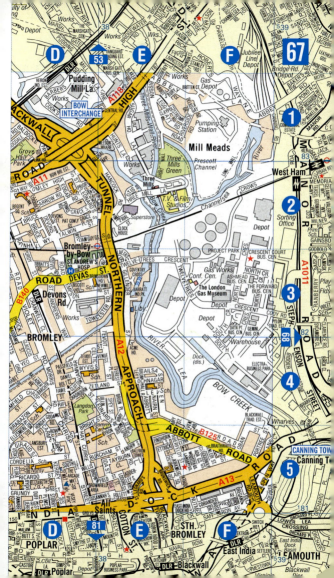

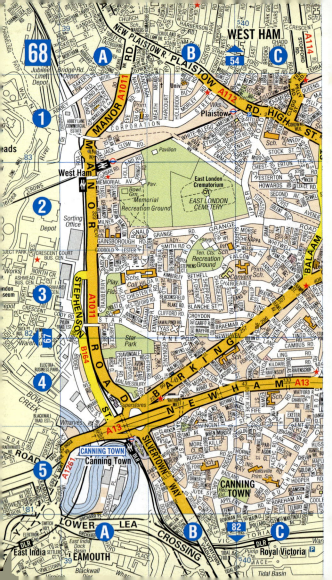

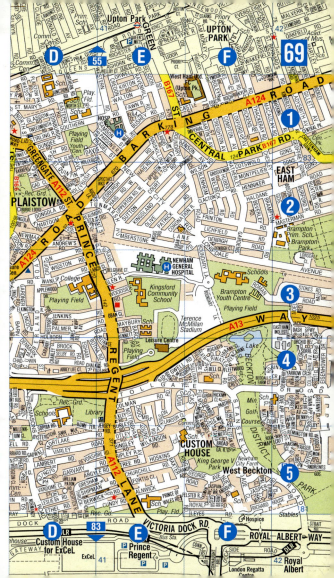

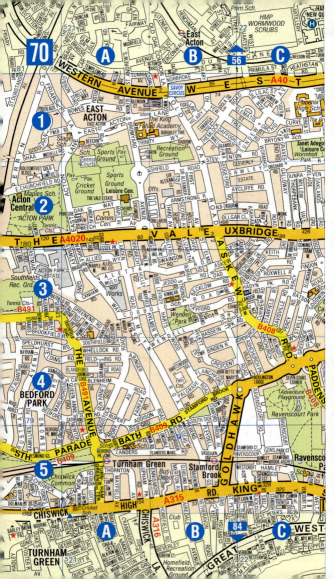

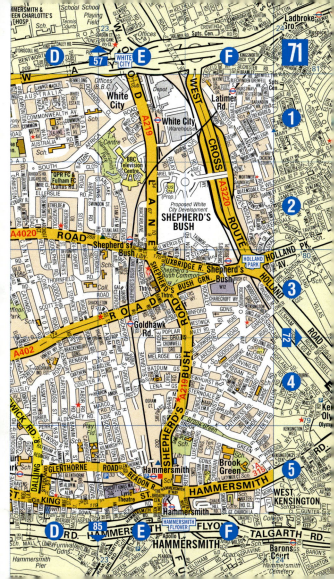

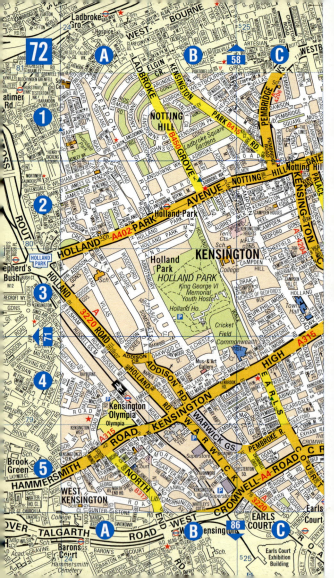

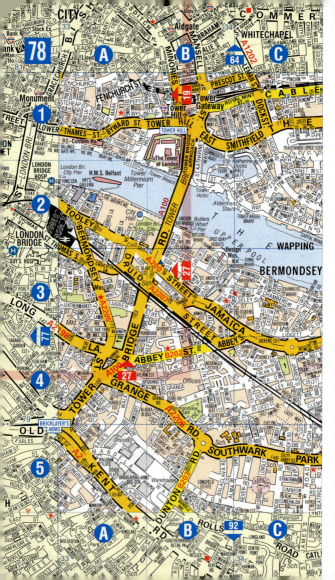

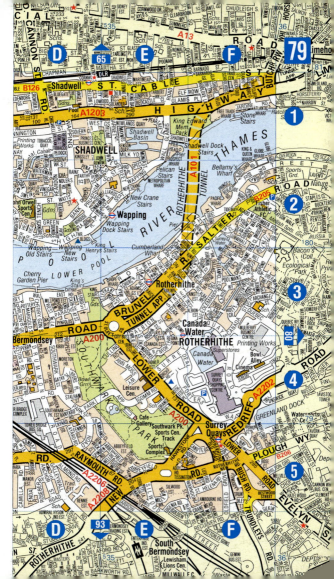

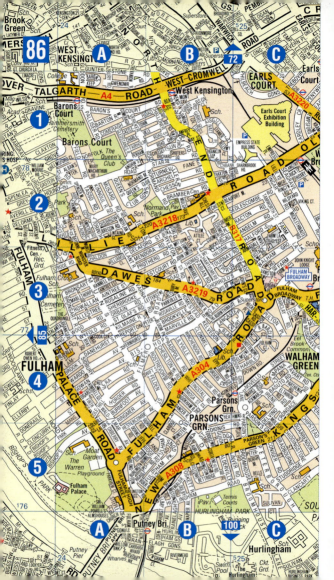

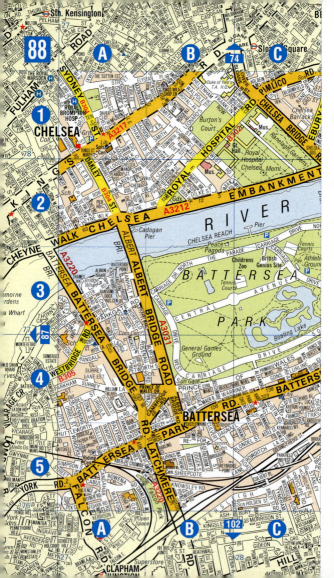

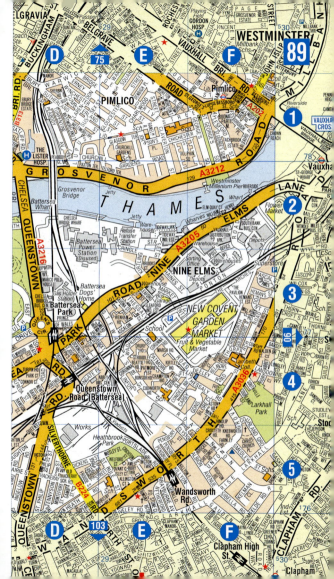

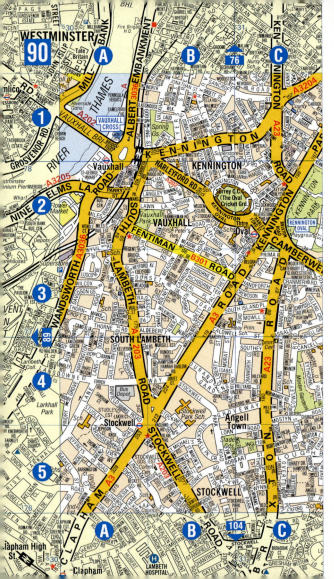

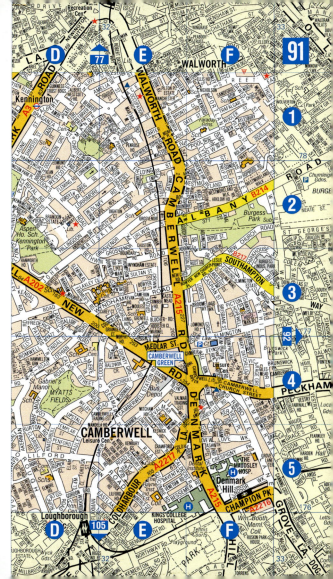

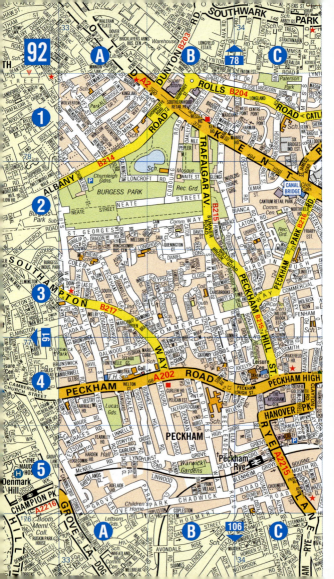

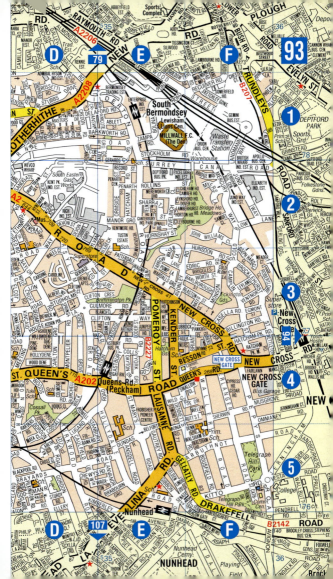

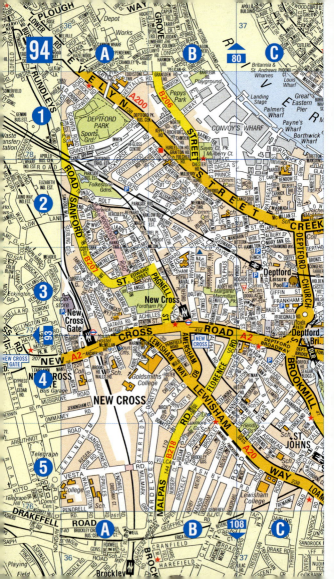

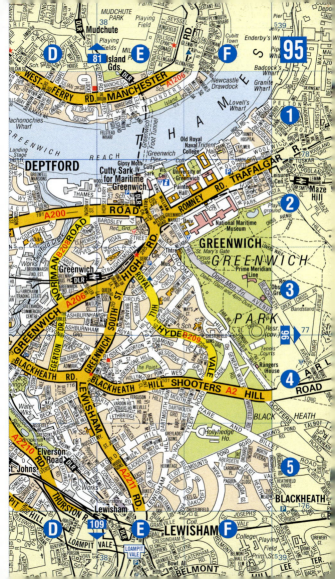

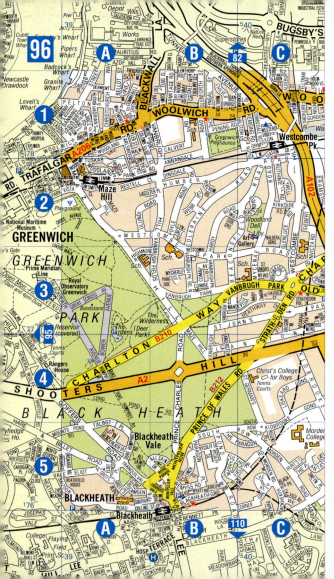

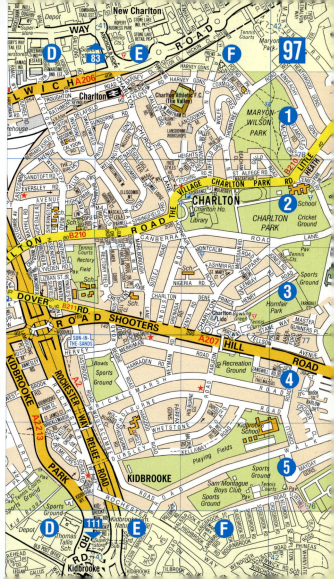

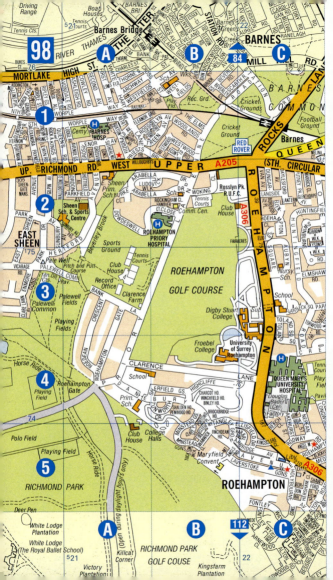

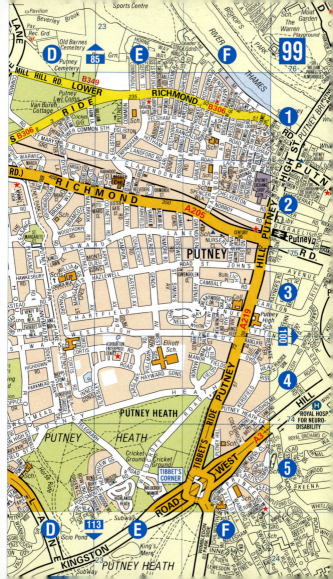

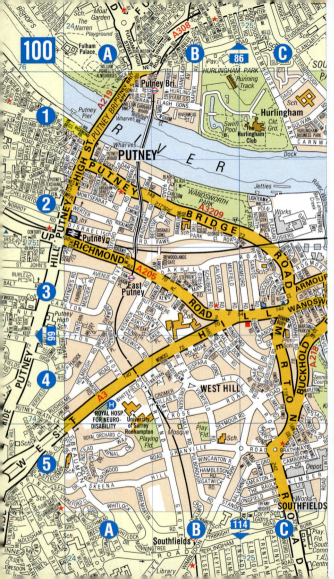

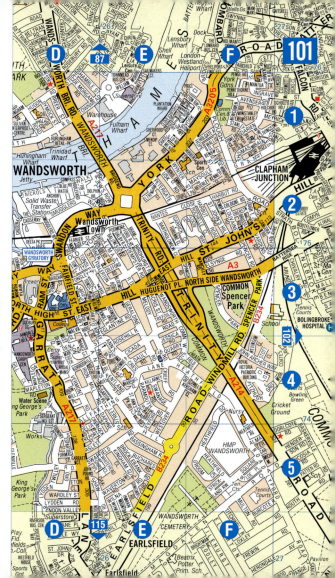

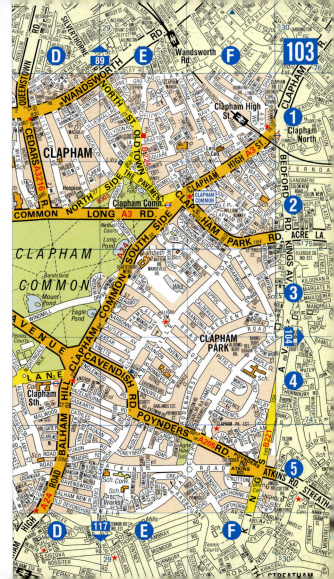

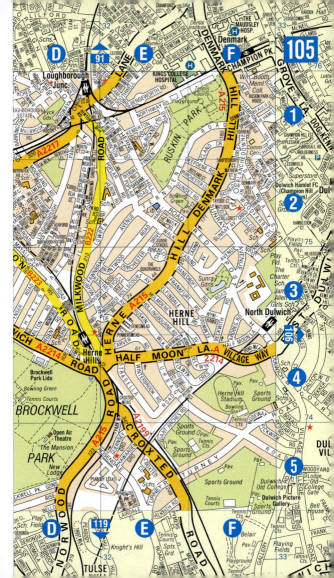

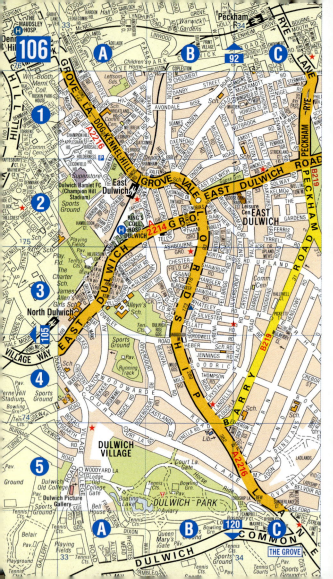

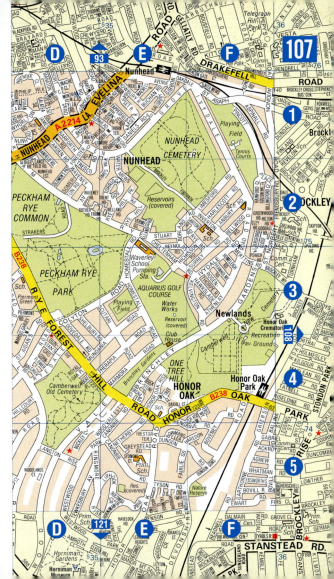

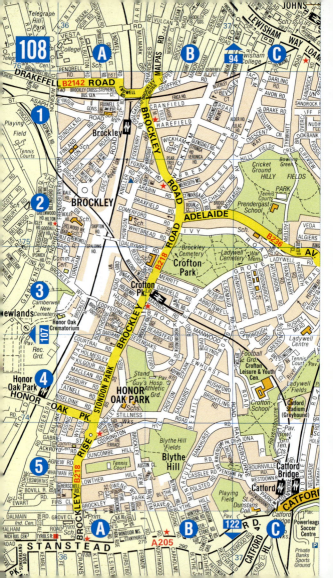

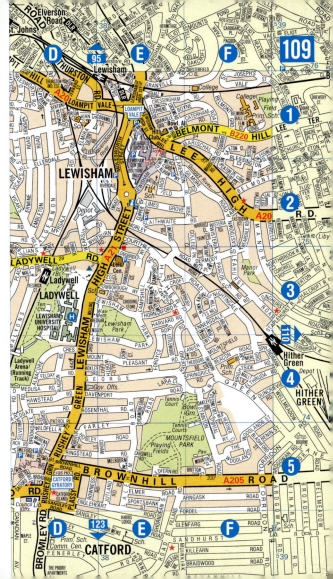

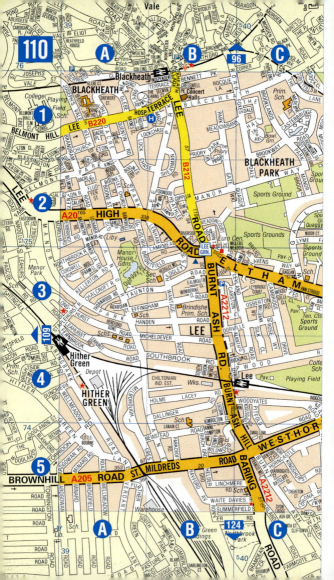

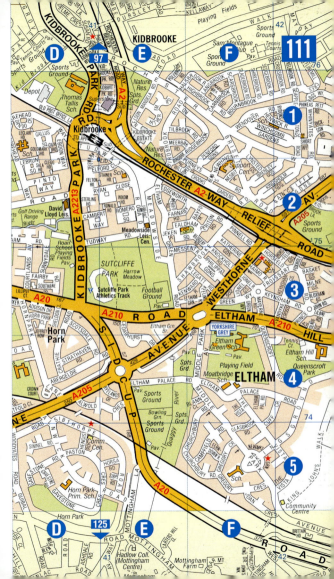

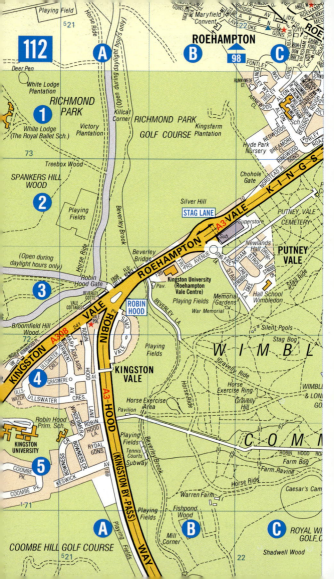

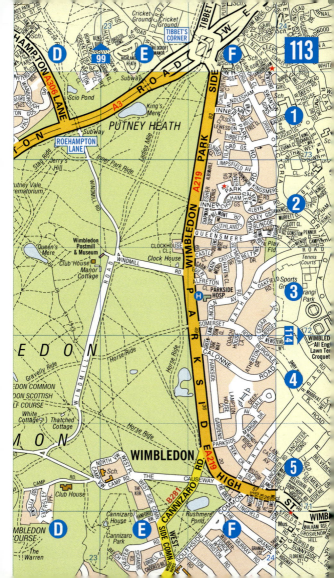

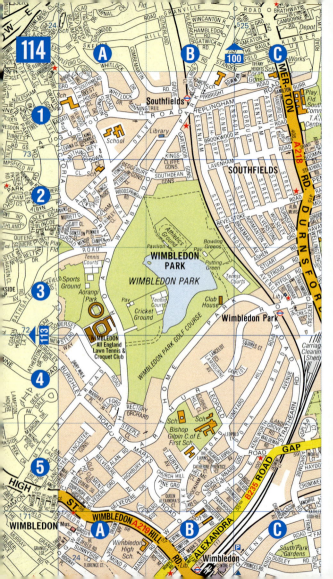

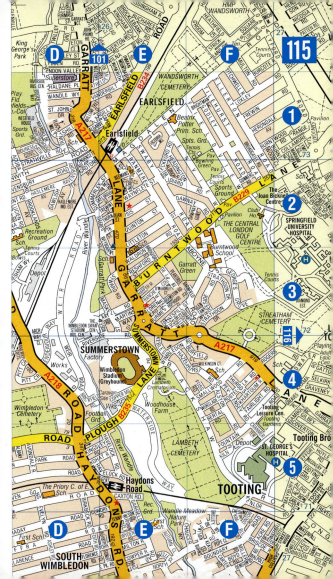

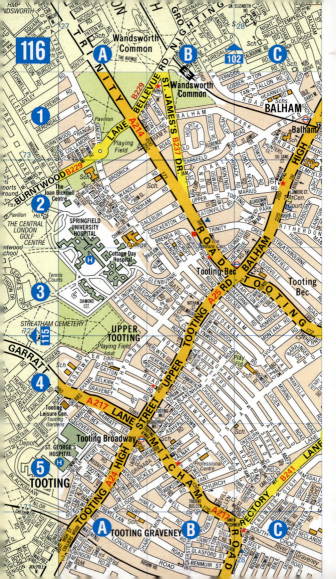

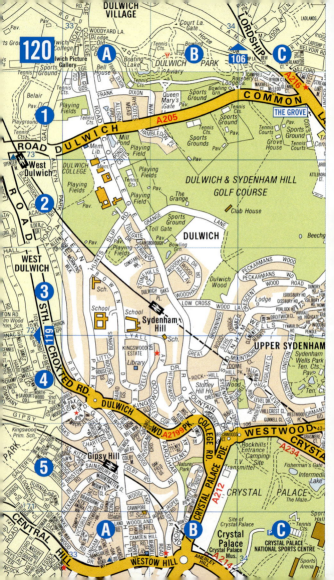

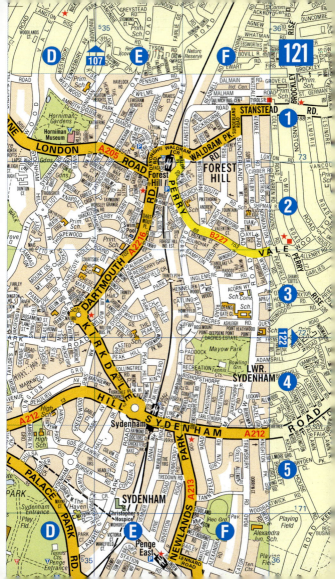

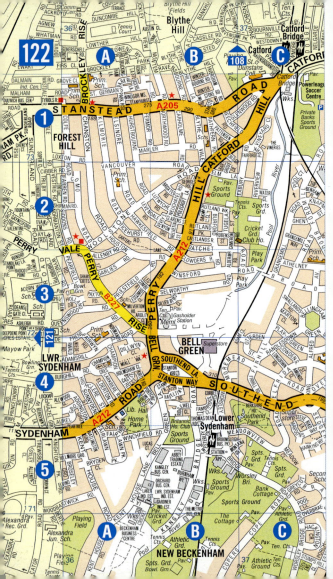

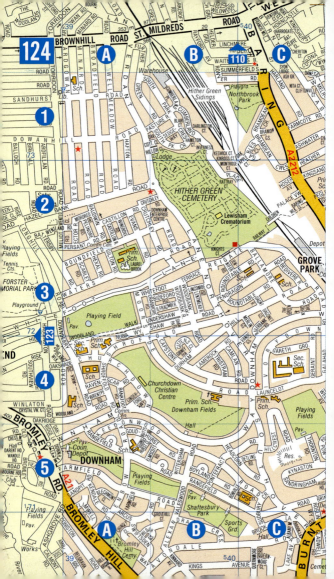

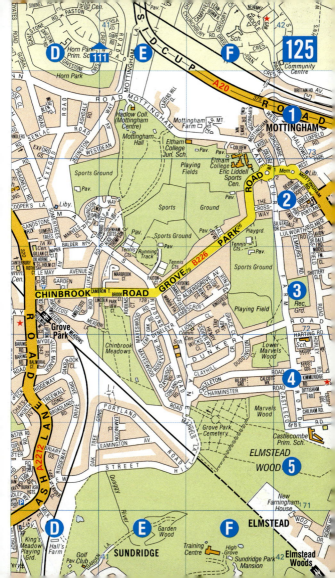

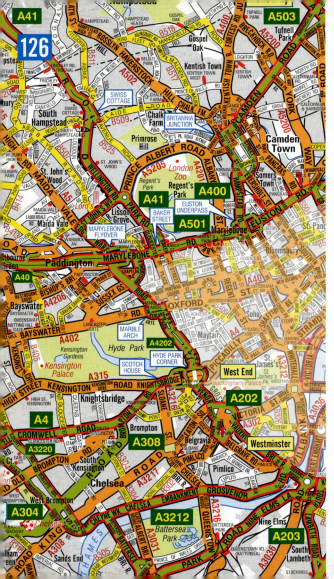

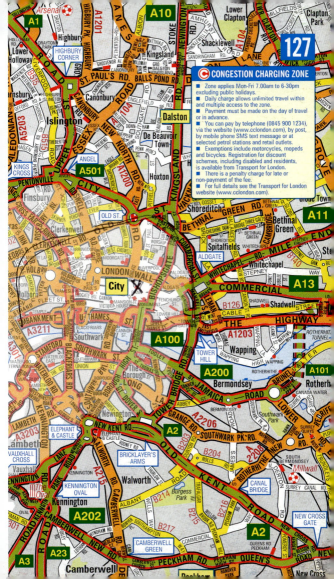

127

CONGESTION CHARGING ZONE

- Zone applies Mon-Fri 7.00am to 6-30pm excluding public holidays.
- Daily charge allows unlimited travel within and multiple access to the zone.
- Payment must be made on the day of travel or in advance.
- You can pay by telephone (0845 900 1234), via the website (www.cclondon.com), by post, by mobile phone SMS text message or at selected petrol stations and retail outlets.
- Exemptions include motorcycles, mopeds and bicycles. Registration for discount schemes, including disabled and residents, is available from Transport for London.
- There is a penalty charge for late or non-payment of the fee.
- For full details see the Transport for London website (www.cclondon.com).

INDEX

Including Streets, Places & Areas, Industrial Estates,
Selected Flats & Walkways, Junction Names and
Selected Places of Interest.

HOW TO USE THIS INDEX

1. Each street name is followed by its Postcode District (or, if outside the London Postcodes, by its Locality Abbreviation(s)) and then by its map reference;
e.g. **Abbess Cl.** SW2 . . . .1D **119** is in the SW2 Postcode District and is to be found in square 1D on page **119**. The page number is shown in bold type.

2. A strict alphabetical order is followed in which Av., Rd., St., etc. (though abbreviated) are read in full and as part of the street name; e.g. **Abbotstone Rd.** appears after **Abbots Ter.** but before **Abbot St.**

3. Streets and a selection of flats and walkways too small to be shown on the maps, appear in the index with the thoroughfare to which it is connected shown in brackets;
e.g. **Abady Ho.** SW1 . . . .5F **75** *(off Page St.)*

4. Addresses that are in more than one part are referred to as not continuous.

5. Places and areas are shown in the index in BLUE TYPE and the map reference is to the actual map square in which the town centre or area is located and not to the place name shown on the map; e.g. ALDERSBROOK 4D **41**

6. An example of a selected place of interest is Albert Memorial 3F **73**

7. Junction names are shown in the index in **BOLD TYPE**; e.g. **ANGEL** 1D **63**

8. Map references shown in brackets; e.g. **Abbey Orchard St.** SW1 . . . .4F **75** (5B **22**) refer to entries that also appear on the large scale pages **4-27.**

GENERAL ABBREVIATIONS

All. : Alley	**Emb.** : Embankment	**Nth.** : North
App. : Approach	**Ent.** : Enterprise	**No.** : Number
Arc. : Arcade	**Est.** : Estate	**Pal.** : Palace
Av. : Avenue	**Ests.** : Estates	**Pde.** : Parade
Bk. : Back	**Fld.** : Field	**Pk.** : Park
Blvd. : Boulevard	**Flds.** : Fields	**Pas.** : Passage
Bri. : Bridge	**Gdn.** : Garden	**Pav.** : Pavilion
B'way. : Broadway	**Gdns.** : Gardens	**Pl.** : Place
Bldg. : Building	**Gth.** : Garth	**Pct.** : Precinct
Bldgs. : Buildings	**Ga.** : Gate	**Prom.** : Promenade
Bungs. : Bungalows	**Gt.** : Great	**Quad.** : Quadrant
Bus. : Business	**Grn.** : Green	**Res.** : Residential
Cvn. : Caravan	**Gro.** : Grove	**Ri.** : Rise
C'way. : Causeway	**Hgts.** : Heights	**Rd.** : Road
Cen. : Centre	**Ho.** : House	**Rdbt.** : Roundabout
Chu. : Church	**Ho's.** : Houses	**Shop.** : Shopping
Chyd. : Church Yard	**Ind.** : Industrial	**Sth.** : South
Circ. : Circle	**Info.** : Information	**Sq.** : Square
Cir. : Circus	**Intl.** : International	**Sta.** : Station
Cl. : Close	**Junc.** : Junction	**St.** : Street
Coll. : College	**La.** : Lane	**Ter.** : Terrace
Comn. : Common	**Lit.** : Little	**Twr.** : Tower
Cnr. : Corner	**Lwr.** : Lower	**Trad.** : Trading
Cott. : Cottage	**Mnr.** : Manor	**Up.** : Upper
Cotts. : Cottages	**Mans.** : Mansions	**Va.** : Vale
Ct. : Court	**Mkt.** : Market	**Vw.** : View
Cres. : Crescent	**Mdw.** : Meadow	**Vs.** : Villas
Cft. : Croft	**Mdws.** : Meadows	**Vis.** : Visitors
Dpt. : Depot	**M.** : Mews	**Wlk.** : Walk
Dr. : Drive	**Mt.** : Mount	**W.** : West
E. : East	**Mus.** : Museum	**Yd.** : Yard

Beck : Beckenham
Brom : Bromley
Chst : Chislehurst

Ilf : Ilford
King T : Kingston Upon Thames

Lon : London
Rich : Richmond

---

02 Centre NW3 . . . . 3E **45**
101 Bus. Units SW11 . .1B **102**
198 Gallery **4D 105**
   (off Railton Rd.)

A

Abady Ho. SW1. . . . . . . 5F **75**
   (off Page St.)
Abberley M. SW4. . . . 1D **103**
Abbess Cl. SW2 . . . . . . 1D **119**
Abbeville M. SW4. . . . 2F **103**
Abbeville Rd. SW4 . . . . 4E **103**
Abbey Bus. Cen. SW8 . . 4E **89**
Abbey Cl. E5. . . . . 1C **50**
  SW8 . . . . 4F **89**
Abbey Ct. NW8 . . . . 1E **59**
   (off Abbey Rd.)
  SE17 . . . . 1E **91**
   (off Macleod St.)
Abbey Dr. SW17. . . . . 5C **116**
Abbey Est. NW8 . . . . . . 5D **45**
Abbeyfield Est. SE16 . . . 5E **79**
Abbeyfield Rd. SE16 . . . 5E **79**
   (not continuous)
Abbey Gdns. NW8 . . . . . 1E **59**
  SE16 . . . . 5C **78**
  W6 . . . . 2A **86**
Abbey Ho. E15 . . . . 1A **68**
   (off Baker's Row)
  NW8 . . . . 2E **59**
   (off Garden Rd.)
Abbey La. E15 . . . . 1E **67**
Abbey La. Commercial Est.
  E15 . . . . 1A **68**
Abbey Life Ct. E16 . . . . 4D **69**
Abbey Lodge NW8 . . . . . 2A **60**
   (off Park Rd.)
Abbey M. E17. . . . . 1C **38**
Abbey Orchard St.
  SW1 . . . . . . 4F **75** (5B **22**)
Abbey Orchard St. Est.
  SW1 . . . . . . 4F **75** (5C **22**)
   (not continuous)
Abbey Rd. E15 . . . . 1F **67**
  NW6 . . . . 4D **45**
Abbey St. E13. . . . . 3C **68**
  SE1 . . . . . . 4A **78** (5E **27**)
Abbey Trad. Est.
  SE26. . . . . 5B **122**
Abbot Ct. SW8 . . . . 3A **90**
   (off Hartington Rd.)
Abbot Ho. E14 . . . . 1D **81**
   (off Smythe St.)
Abbotsbury Cl. E15. . . . 1E **67**
  W14 . . . . 3A **72**
Abbotsbury M. SE15. . . 1E **107**
Abbotsbury Rd. W14 . . . 3A **72**
Abbotshade Rd. SE16. . . 2F **79**
Abbotshall Rd. SE6. . . . 1F **123**

Abbot's Ho. W14 . . . . . . 4B **72**
   (off St Mary Abbots Ter.)
Abbots La. SE1. . 2A **78** (2E **27**)
Abbotsleigh Rd. SW16. . 4E **117**
Abbots Mnr. SW1. . . . . . 5D **75**
Abbots Pk. SW2 . . . . . 1C **118**
Abbot's Pl. NW6. . . . . . . 5D **45**
Abbot's Rd. E6 . . . . 5F **55**
Abbots Ter. N8 . . . . 1A **34**
Abbotstone Rd. SW15 . . 1E **99**
Abbot St. E8 . . . . 3B **50**
Abbots Wlk. W8 . . . . . . 4D **73**
Abbotswell Rd. SE4. . . 3B **108**
Abbotswood Rd.
  SE22. . . . . 2A **106**
  SW16 . . . . 3F **117**
Abbott Rd. E14 . . . . 4E **67**
   (not continuous)
Abbotts Cl. N1 . . . . 3E **49**
Abbotts Ho. SW1 . . . . . . 1F **89**
   (off Aylesford St.)
Abbotts Pk. Rd. E10. . . . 2E **39**
Abbotts Wharf E14 . . . . 5C **66**
   (off Stainsby Pl.)
Abchurch La.
  EC4. . . . . 1F **77** (4C **18**)
   (not continuous)
Abchurch Yd.
  EC4. . . . . 1F **77** (4B **18**)
Abdale Rd. W12. . . . . . . 2D **71**
Abel Ho. SE11 . . . . 2C **90**
   (off Kennington Rd.)
Aberavon Rd. E3 . . . . . . 2A **66**
Abercorn Cl. NW8 . . . . . 2E **59**
Abercorn Ho. SE10 . . . . 3D **95**
   (off Tarves Way)
Abercorn Mans. NW8. . . 1E **59**
   (off Abercorn Pl.)
Abercorn Pl. NW8 . . . . . 2E **59**
Abercorn Way SE1 . . . . 1C **92**
Abercrombie St. SW11. . 5A **88**
Aberdale Ct. SE16 . . . . . 3F **79**
   (off Garter Way)
Aberdare Gdns. NW6. . . 4D **45**
Aberdeen Ct. W9 . . . . . . 3E **59**
   (off Lanark Pl.)
Aberdeen La. N5 . . . . . . 2E **49**
Aberdeen Mans. WC1 . . . 3D **7**
   (off Kenton St.)
Aberdeen Pk. N5 . . . . . . 2E **49**
Aberdeen Pl. NW8 . . . . . 3F **59**
Aberdeen Rd. N5 . . . . . . 1E **49**
  NW10. . . . . 2B **42**
Aberdeen Sq. E14. . . . . . 2B **80**
Aberdeen Ter. SE3 . . . . . 5F **95**
Aberdeen Wharf E1 . . . . 2D **79**
   (off Wapping High St.)
Aberdour St. SE1. . . . . . 5A **78**
Aberfeldy Ho. SE5 . . . . . 3D **91**
Aberfeldy St. E14. . . . . . 4E **67**
   (not continuous)
Aberford Gdns. SE18 . . . 4F **97**
Abergeldie Rd. SE12. . . 4D **111**
Abernethy Rd. SE13. . . . 2A **110**
Abersham Rd. E8. . . . . . 2B **50**

Abingdon W14 . . . . 5B **72**
   (off Kensington Village)
Abingdon Cl. NW1 . . . . . 3F **47**
  SE1. . . . . 5B **78**
   (off Bushwood Dr.)
Abingdon Ct. W8 . . . . . . 4C **72**
   (off Abingdon Vs.)
Abingdon Gdns. W8. . . . 4C **72**
Abingdon Ho. E2. . . . . . . 3F **11**
   (off Boundary St.)
Abingdon Lodge W8. . . . 4C **72**
Abingdon Rd. W8 . . . . . . 4C **72**
Abingdon St.
  SW1. . . . . . . 4A **76** (5D **23**)
Abingdon Vs. W8 . . . . . . 4C **72**
Abinger Gro. SE8 . . . . . . 2B **94**
Abinger Ho. SE1. . . . . . . 4B **26**
   (off Gt. Dover St.)
Abinger M. W9. . . . . 3C **58**
Abinger Rd. W4 . . . . 4A **70**
Ablett St. SE16. . . . . 1E **93**
Abney Gdns. N16. . . . . . 4B **36**
Aboyne Rd. NW10 . . . . . 5A **28**
  SW17 . . . . 3F **115**
Abyssinia Cl. SW11 . . . 2A **102**
Abyssinia Ct. N8 . . . . . . 1B **34**
Abyssinia Rd. SW11 . . . 2A **102**
Acacia Bus. Cen. E11 . . 5A **40**
Acacia Cl. SE8 . . . . 5A **80**
Acacia Gdns. NW8 . . . . . 1F **59**
Acacia Gro. SE21 . . . . . 2F **119**
Acacia Pl. NW8 . . . . 1F **59**
Acacia Rd. E11. . . . . 4A **40**
  E17. . . . . 1A **38**
  NW8 . . . . 1F **59**
Academy Apartments
  E8. . . . . 2D **51**
   (off Dalston La.)
  E8. . . . . 2D **51**
   (off Institute Pl.)
Academy Bldgs. N1. . . . 1D **11**
   (off Fanshaw St.)
Academy Ct. E2 . . . . 2E **65**
   (off Kirkwall Pl.)
Academy Ho. E3 . . . . . . 4D **67**
   (off Violet Rd.)
Acanthus Dr. SE1 . . . . . 1C **92**
Acanthus Rd. SW11. . . . 1C **102**
Acfold Rd. SW6 . . . . 4D **87**
Achilles Cl. SE1. . . . . . . 1C **92**
Achilles Ho. E2 . . . . 1D **65**
   (off Old Bethnal Grn. Rd.)
Achilles Rd. NW6. . . . . . 2C **44**
Achilles Statue. . 2C **74** (2C **20**)
Achilles St. SE14 . . . . . . 3A **94**
Achilles Way W1. .2C **74** (2C **20**)
Acklam Rd. W10 . . . . . . 4A **58**
   (not continuous)
Ackmar Rd. SW6 . . . . . . 4C **86**
Ackroyd Dr. E3 . . . . 4B **66**
Ackroyd Rd. SE23. . . . . 5F **107**
Acland Cres. SE5 . . . . . 1F **105**
Acland Ho. SW9. . . . . . . 4B **90**
Acland Rd. NW2 . . . . . . 3D **43**
Acme Ho. E14. . . . . 4E **67**

Acol Ct. NW6 . . . . 4C **44**
Acol Rd. NW6 . . . . 4C **44**
Acorn Ct. E6 . . . . 4F **55**
Acorn Gdns. W3 . . . . . . 4A **56**
Acorn Pde. SE15 . . . . . . 3D **93**
Acorn Production Cen.
  N7 . . . . 4A **48**
Acorn Wlk. SE16 . . . . . . 2A **80**
Acorn Way SE23 . . . . . . 3F **121**
Acre Dr. SE22 . . . . 2C **106**
Acre La. SW2 . . . . 2A **104**
Acre Rd. SW19 . . . . 5F **115**
Acris St. SW18 . . . . 3E **101**
Acton Ho. E8 . . . . 5B **50**
  (off Lee St.)
Acton La. NW10 . . . . . . 1A **56**
Acton M. E8 . . . . 5B **50**
Acton Pk. Est. W3 . . . . 3A **70**
Acton St. WC1 . . 2B **62** (2F **7**)
Acton Va. Ind. Pk. W3 . 2B **70**
Acuba Rd. SW18 . . . . . . 2D **115**
Ada Ct. N1 . . . . 5E **49**
  (off Packington St.)
NW8 . . . . 2E **59**
Ada Gdns. E14 . . . . 5F **67**
  E15 . . . . 5B **54**
Ada Ho. E2 . . . . 5C **50**
  (off Ada Pl.)
Adair Rd. W10 . . . . 3A **58**
Adair Twr. W10 . . . . 3A **58**
  (off Appleford Rd.)
Ada Kennedy Ct. SE10 . 3E **95**
  (off Greenwich Sth. St.)
Adam & Eve Ct. W1 . . . 2A **14**
Adam & Eve M. W8 . . . 4C **72**
Adam Cl. SE6 . . . . 4B **122**
Adam Ct. SE11 . . . . 5D **77**
  (off Opal St.)
  SW7 . . . . 5E **73**
  (off Gloucester Rd.)
Adams Ct. E17 . . . . 1A **38**
  EC2 . . . . 5A **64** (2C **18**)
Adams Gdns. Est. SE16 . 3E **79**
Adams Ho. E14 . . . . 5F **67**
  (off Aberfeldy St.)
Adamson Rd. E16 . . . . . 5C **68**
  NW3 . . . . 4F **45**
Adams Pl. E14 . . . . 2D **81**
  (off Nth. Colonnade, The)
  N7 . . . . 2B **48**
Adamsrill Rd. SE26 . . . . 4F **121**
Adam's Row W1 . . 1C **74** (5C **12**)
Adam St. WC2 . . . 1A **76** (4E **5**)
Adam Wlk. SW6 . . . . . . 3E **85**
Ada Pl. E2 . . . . 5C **50**
Adare Wlk. SW16 . . . . . 3B **118**
Ada Rd. SE5 . . . . 3A **92**
Adastral Ho. WC1 . . . . . 5F **7**
  (off New Nth. St.)
Ada St. E8 . . . . 5D **51**
Ada Workshops E8 . . . . 5D **51**
Adderley Gro. SW11 . . . 3C **102**
Adderley St. E14 . . . . . . 5E **67**
Addey Ho. SE8 . . . . 3B **94**
Addington Ct. SW14 . . . 1A **98**
Addington Gro. SE26 . . . 4A **122**
Addington Ho. SW9 . . . 5B **90**
  (off Stockwell Rd.)
Addington Rd. E16 . . . . 3A **68**
  E3 . . . . 2C **66**

Addington Rd. N4 . . . . . 1C **34**
Addington Sq. SE5 . . . . 2F **91**
  (not continuous)
Addington St.
  SE1 . . . . 3B **76** (4A **24**)
Addis Ho. E1 . . . . 4E **65**
  (off Lindley St.)
Addisland Ct. W14 . . . . 3A **72**
  (off Holland Vs. Rd.)
Addison Av. W11 . . . . . 2A **72**
Addison Bri. Pl. W14 . . 5B **72**
Addison Cres. W14 . . . . 4A **72**
Addison Dr. SE12 . . . . . 3D **111**
Addison Gdns. W14 . . . 4F **71**
Addison Gro. W4 . . . . . 4A **70**
Addison Ho. NW8 . . . . . 2F **59**
  (off Grove End Rd.)
Addison Pk. Mans. W14 . 4F **71**
  (off Richmond Way)
Addison Pl. W11 . . . . . . 2A **72**
Addison Rd. E11 . . . . . . 1C **40**
  W14 . . . . 3A **72**
Addle Hill EC4 . . 5D **63** (3E **17**)
Addlestone Ho. W10 . . . 4E **57**
  (off Sutton Way)
Addle St. EC2 . . 5E **63** (2A **18**)
Addy Ho. SE16 . . . . 5E **79**
Adela Ho. W6 . . . . 1E **85**
  (off Queen Caroline St.)
Adelaide Av. SE4 . . . . . 2B **108**
Adelaide Cl. SW9 . . . . . 2C **104**
Adelaide Ct. NW8 . . . . . 1E **59**
  (off Abercorn Pl.)
Adelaide Gro. W12 . . . . 2C **70**
Adelaide Ho. E15 . . . . . 1B **68**
  SE5 . . . . 5A **92**
  W11 . . . . 5B **58**
  (off Portobello Rd.)
Adelaide Rd. E10 . . . . . 5D **39**
  NW3 . . . . 4F **45**
  SW18 . . . . 3C **100**
Adelaide St.
  WC2 . . . . 1A **76** (5D **15**)
Adela St. W10 . . . . 3A **58**
Adelina Gro. E1 . . . . . . 4E **65**
Adelina M. SW12 . . . . . 1F **117**
Adeline Pl. WC1 . 4F **61** (1C **14**)
Adelphi Ct. E8 . . . . 4B **50**
  (off Celandine Dr.)
  SE16 . . . . 3F **79**
  (off Garter Way)
  W4 . . . . 2A **84**
Adelphi Ter.
  WC2 . . . . 1A **76** (5E **15**)
Adelphi Theatre 5E **15**
  (off Strand)
Adeney Cl. W6 . . . . 2F **85**
Aden Gro. N16 . . . . 1F **49**
Aden Ho. E1 . . . . 4F **65**
  (off Duckett St.)
Adenmore Rd. SE6 . . . . 5C **108**
Aden Ter. N16 . . . . 1F **49**
Adeyfield Ho. EC1 . . . . . 2C **10**
  (off Cranwood St.)
Adie Rd. W6 . . . . 4E **71**
Adine Rd. E13 . . . . 3D **69**
Adler St. E1 . . . . 5C **64**
Adley St. E5 . . . . 2A **52**
Admiral SW10 . . . . 4E **87**
  (off Admiral Sq.)

Admiral Ct. W1 . . . . 1B **12**
  (off Blandford St.)
Admiral Ho. SW1 . . . . . 5E **75**
  (off Willow Pl.)
Admiral Hyson Ind. Est.
  SE16 . . . . 1D **93**
Admiral M. W10 . . . . . . 3F **57**
Admiral Pl. SE16 . . . . . 2A **80**
Admirals Ct. SE1 . . . . . 2F **27**
  (off Horselydown La.)
Admiral's Ga. SE10 . . . . 4D **95**
Admiral Sq. SW10 . . . . 4E **87**
Admiral St. SE8 . . . . . . 5C **94**
Admirals Wlk. NW3 . . . 5E **31**
Admirals Way E14 . . . . 3C **80**
Admiralty Arch. . 2F **75** (1C **22**)
Admiralty Cl. SE8 . . . . . 3C **94**
Admiral Wlk. W9 . . . . . 4C **58**
Adolf St. SE6 . . . . 4D **123**
Adolphus Rd. N4 . . . . . 4D **35**
Adolphus St. SE8 . . . . . 3B **94**
Adpar St. W2 . . . . 4F **59**
Adrian Boult Ho. E2 . . . 2D **65**
  (off Mansford St.)
Adrian Ho. N1 . . . . 5B **48**
  (off Barnsbury Est.)
  SW8 . . . . 3A **90**
  (off Wyvil Rd.)
Adrian M. SW10 . . . . . . 2D **87**
Adriatic Bldg. E14 . . . . 1A **80**
  (off Horseferry Rd.)
Adriatic Ho. E1 . . . . 3F **65**
  (off Ernest St.)
Adron Ho. SE16 . . . . . . 5E **79**
  (off Millender Wlk.)
Adstock Ho. N1 . . . . . . 4D **49**
  (off Sutton Est., The)
Advance Rd. SE27 . . . . 4E **119**
Adventurers Ct. E14 . . . 1F **81**
  (off Newport Av.)
Adys Lawn NW2 . . . . . 3D **43**
Ady's Rd. SE15 . . . . . . 1B **106**
Aegon Ho. E14 . . . . 4D **81**
  (off Lanark Sq.)
Affleck St. N1 . . . 1B **62** (1F **7**)
Afghan Rd. SW11 . . . . . 5A **88**
Afsil Ho. EC1 . . . . 1C **16**
  (off Viaduct Bldgs.)
Agamemnon Rd. NW6 . . 1B **44**
Agar Gro. NW1 . . . . 4E **47**
Agar Gro. Est. NW1 . . . 4F **47**
Agar Pl. NW1 . . . . 4E **47**
Agar St. WC2 . . . 1A **76** (5D **15**)
Agate Cl. E16 . . . . 5F **69**
Agate Rd. W6 . . . . 4E **71**
Agatha Cl. E1 . . . . 2D **79**
Agave Rd. NW2 . . . . . . 1E **43**
Agdon St. EC1 . . 3D **63** (3D **9**)
Agincourt Rd. NW3 . . . 1B **46**
Agnes Ho. W11 . . . . . . 1F **71**
  (off St Ann's Rd.)
Agnes Rd. W3 . . . . 2B **70**
Agnes St. E14 . . . . 5B **66**
Agnew Rd. SE23 . . . . . 5F **107**
Aigburth Mans. SW9 . . 3C **90**
  (off Mowll St.)
Aileen Wlk. E15 . . . . . . 4B **54**
Ailsa St. E14 . . . . 4E **67**
Ainger M. NW3 . . . . . . 4B **46**
  (off Ainger Rd., not cont.)

Ainger Rd. NW3 . . . . . . 4B 46
Ainsdale NW1 . . . . 1F 5
(off Harrington St.)
Ainsdale Dr. SE1 . . . . . 1C 92
Ainsley St. E2 . . . . 2D 65
Ainslie Wlk. SW12 . . 5D 103
Ainsty Est. SE16 . . . . . . 3F 79
Ainsty St. SE16 . . . . 3E 79
Ainsworth Cl. NW2 . . . . 5C 28
SE15 . . . . 5A 92
Ainsworth Ho. NW8 . . . 5D 45
(off Ainsworth Way)
Ainsworth Rd. E9 . . . . . 4E 51
Ainsworth Way NW8 . . . 5E 45
Aintree Av. E6 . . . . 5F 55
Aintree Est. SW6 . . . . . 3A 86
(off Aintree St.)
Aintree St. SW6 . . . . . . 3A 86
Aird Ho. SE1 . . . . 5F 25
(off Rockingham St.)
Airdrie Cl. N1 . . . . 4B 48
Airedale Av. W4 . . . . . . 5B 70
Airedale Av. Sth. W4 . . 1B 84
Airedale Rd. SW12 . . . 5B 102
Airlie Gdns. W8 . . . . . . 2C 72
Air St. W1 . . . . . 1E 75 (5A 14)
Aisgill Av. W14 . . . . 1B 86
(not continuous)
Aislibie Rd. SE12 . . . . . 2A 110
Aiten Pl. W6 . . . . 5C 70
Aithan Ho. E14 . . . . 5B 66
(off Copenhagen Pl.)
Aitken Cl. E8 . . . . 5C 50
Aitken Rd. SE6 . . . . 2D 123
Ajax Ho. E2 . . . . 1D 65
(off Old Bethnal Grn. Rd.)
Ajax Rd. NW6 . . . . 1B 44
Akbar Ho. E14 . . . . 5D 81
(off Cahir St.)
Akehurst St. SW15 . . . . 4C 98
Akenside Rd. NW3 . . . . 2F 45
Akerman Rd. SW9 . . . . 5D 91
Akintaro Ho. SE8 . . . . . 2B 94
(off Alverton St.)
Alamaro Lodge SE10 . . 4B 82
Aland Ct. SE16 . . . . 4A 80
Alan Hocken Way E15 . 1A 68
Alan Preece Ct. NW6 . . 4F 43
Alan Rd. SW19 . . . . 5A 114
Alanthus Cl. SE12 . . . . 4C 110
Alaska Bldgs. SE1 . . . . 4A 78
Alaska St. SE1 . . 2C 76 (2B 24)
Alastor Ho. E14 . . . . 4E 81
(off Strattondale St.)
Albacore Cres. SE13 . . 4D 109
Alba M. SW19 . . . . 2C 114
Alban Highwalk EC2 . . . 2A 18
(not continuous)
Albany W1 . . . . 1E 75 (5F 13)
Albany Ct. E10 . . . . 2C 38
NW8 . . . . 1F 59
(off Abbey Rd.)
NW10 . . . . 2D 57
(off Trenmar Gdns.)
Albany Courtyard
W1 . . . . 1E 75 (5A 14)
Albany Mans. SW11 . . . 3A 88
Albany M. BR1: Brom. . 5C 124
N1 . . . . 4C 48
SE5 . . . . 2E 91

Albany Pl. N7 . . . . 1C 48
Albany Rd. E10 . . . . 2C 38
E12 . . . . 1F 55
E17 . . . . 1A 38
N4 . . . . 1C 34
SE5 . . . . 2F 91
SW19 . . . . 5D 115
Albany St. NW1 . . 1D 61 (1D 5)
Albany Ter. NW1 . . . . . . 4E 5
Alba Pl. W11 . . . . 5B 58
Albatross Way SE16 . . . 3F 79
Albemarle SW19 . . . . . 2F 113
Albemarle Ho. SE8 . . . . 5B 80
(off Foreshore)
SW9 . . . . 1C 104
Albemarle St.
W1 . . . . 1D 75 (5E 13)
Albemarle Way
EC1 . . . . 3D 63 (4D 9)
Alberta Est. SE17 . . . . . 1D 91
(off Alberta St.)
Alberta Ho. E14 . . . . 2E 81
(off Gaselee St.)
Alberta St. SE17 . . . . . . 1D 91
Albert Av. SW8 . . . . 3B 90
Albert Barnes Ho. SE1 . 4E 77
(off New Kent Rd.)
Albert Bigg Point E15 . . 1E 67
(off Godfrey St.)
Albert Bri. SW3 . . . . 2A 88
SW11 . . . . 2A 88
Albert Bri. Rd. SW11 . . . 3A 88
Albert Carr Gdns.
SW16 . . . . 5A 118
Albert Cl. E9 . . . . 5D 51
Albert Cotts. E1 . . . . 4C 64
(off Deal St.)
Albert Ct. E7 . . . . 1C 54
SW7 . . . . 4F 73
Albert Ct. Ga. SW7 . . . . 3B 74
(off Knightsbridge)
Albert Dr. SW19 . . . . . . 2A 114
Albert Emb. SE1 . . . . . . 4B 76
(Lambeth Pal. Rd.)
SE1 . . . . 1A 90
(Vauxhall Bri.)
Albert Gdns. E1 . . . . . . 5F 65
Albert Ga. SW1 . . 3B 74 (3A 20)
Albert Gray Ho. SW10 . 3F 87
(off Worlds End Est.)
Albert Hall Mans. SW7 . 3F 73
(not continuous)
Albert Memorial 3F 73
Albert M. E14 . . . . 1A 80
(off Northey St.)
N4 . . . . 3B 34
SE4 . . . . 2A 108
W8 . . . . 4E 73
Albert Pal. Mans.
SW11 . . . . 4D 89
(off Lurline Gdns.)
Albert Pl. W8 . . . . 4D 73
Albert Rd. E10 . . . . 4E 39
E16 . . . . 2F 83
E17 . . . . 1C 38
N4 . . . . 3B 34
N15 . . . . 1A 36
NW6 . . . . 1B 58
Albert Sq. E15 . . . . 2A 54
SW8 . . . . 3B 90

Albert Starr Ho. SE8 . . . 5F 79
(off Bush Rd.)
Albert St. NW1 . . . . 5D 47
Albert Studios SW11 . . . 4B 88
Albert Ter. NW1 . . . . . . 5C 46
Albert Ter. M. NW1 . . . . 5C 46
Albert Way SE15 . . . . . 3D 93
Albert Westcott Ho.
SE1 . . . . 1D 91
Albery Ct. E8 . . . . 4B 50
(off Middleton Rd.)
Albery Theatre 4D 15
(off St Martin's La.)
Albion Av. SW8 . . . . 5F 89
Albion Cl. W2 . . . . 1A 74
Albion Ct. W6 . . . . 5D 71
(off Albion Pl.)
Albion Dr. E8 . . . . 4B 50
Albion Est. SE16 . . . . . 3F 79
Albion Gdns. W6 . . . . . 5D 71
Albion Ga. W2 . . . . 1A 74
(off Albion St., not continuous)
Albion Gro. N16 . . . . . . 1A 50
Albion Ho. SE8 . . . . 3C 94
(off Watsons St.)
Albion M. N1 . . . . 5C 48
W2 . . . . 1A 74
W6 . . . . 5D 71
Albion Pl. EC1 . . 4D 63 (5D 9)
EC2 . . . . 4F 63 (1C 18)
W6 . . . . 5D 71
Albion Rd. N16 . . . . 1F 49
Albion Sq. E8 . . . . 4B 50
(not continuous)
Albion St. SE16 . . . . . . 3E 79
W2 . . . . 5A 60
Albion Ter. E8 . . . . 4B 50
Albion Vs. Rd. SE26 . . . 3E 121
Albion Way EC1 . 4E 63 (1F 17)
SE13 . . . . 2E 109
Albion Wharf SW11 . . . 3A 88
Albion Yd. N1 . . . . 1A 62
Albrighton Rd. SE22 . . 1A 106
Albury Ho. SE1 . . . . 4E 25
(off Boyfield St.)
Albury M. E12 . . . . 4E 41
Albury St. SE8 . . . . 2C 94
Albyn Rd. SE8 . . . . 4C 94
Alcester Cres. E5 . . . . . 4D 37
Alconbury Rd. E5 . . . . . 4C 36
Aldam Pl. N16 . . . . 4B 36
Aldbourne Rd. W12 . . . 2B 70
(not continuous)
Aldbridge St. SE17 . . . 1A 92
Aldburgh M. W1 . . 5C 60 (2C 12)
(not continuous)
Aldbury Ho. SW3 . . . . . 5A 74
(off Ixworth Pl.)
Aldebert Ter. SW8 . . . . 3A 90
Aldeburgh Cl. E5 . . . . . 4D 37
Aldeburgh St. SE10 . . . 1C 96
Alden Av. E15 . . . . 2B 68
Aldenham Ho. NW1 . . . 1A 6
(off Aldenham St.)
Aldenham St.
NW1 . . . . 1E 61 (1A 6)
Alden Ho. E8 . . . . 5D 51
(off Duncan Rd.)
Aldensley Rd. W6 . . . . . 4D 71
Alderbrook Rd. SW12 . . 4D 103

Alderbury Rd. SW13 . . . 2C **84**
Alder Cl. SE15 . . . . 2B **92**
Alder Gro. NW2 . . . . 4C **28**
Alder Ho. NW3 . . . . 3B **46**
  SE4. . . . . 1C **108**
  SE15. . . . . (off Alder Cl.)
Alder Lodge SW6 . . . . . . 4E **85**
Aldermanbury
  EC2 . . . . 5E **63** (2A **18**)
Aldermanbury Sq.
  EC2 . . . . 4E **63** (1A **18**)
Aldermans Wlk.
  EC2 . . . . 4A **64** (1D **19**)
Alder M. N19 . . . . 4E **33**
Aldermoor Rd. SE6 . . . 3B **122**
Alderney Ho. *N1 . . . . . . 3E **49**
  (off Arran Wlk.)
Alderney Rd. E1 . . . . . . 3F **65**
Alderney St. SW1 . . . . . 5D **75**
ALDERSBROOK **4D 41**
Aldersbrook Rd. E11 . . . 4D **41**
  E12 . . . . 4D **41**
Alders Cl. E11 . . . . 4D **41**
Aldersford Cl. SE4 . . . . 3F **107**
Aldersgate St.
  EC1 . . . . 4E **63** (5F **9**)
Aldersgrove Av. SE9 . . . 3F **125**
Aldershot Rd. NW6 . . . . 5B **44**
Alderson St. W10 . . . . . 3A **58**
Alders, The SW16 . . . . 4E **117**
Alderton Cl. NW10 . . . . 5A **28**
Alderton Rd. SE24 . . . . 1E **105**
Alderville Rd. SW6 . . . . 5B **86**
Alderwick Ct. *N7 . . . . . 3B **48**
  (off Cornelia St.)
Aldford Ho. *W1 . . . . . . 1B 20*
  (off Park St.)
Aldford St. W1. . 2C **74** (1C **20**)
Aldgate *E1* 5B **64**
  (off Whitechapel High St.)
  EC3 . . . . 5A **64** (3E **19**)
Aldgate Av. E1 . . 5B **64** (2F **19**)
Aldgate Barrs E1 . . . . . 2F **19**
Aldgate High St.
  EC3. . . . . 5B **64** (3F **19**)
Aldgate Triangle *E1* . . . 5C **64**
  (off Coke St.)
Aldham Ho. *SE4 . . . . . . 5B 94*
  (off Malpas Rd.)
Aldine Ct. *W12 . . . . 3E 71*
  (off Aldine St.)
Aldine Pl. W12 . . . . 3E **71**
Aldine St. W12 . . . . 3E **71**
Aldington Ct. *E8 . . . . . . 4C 50*
  (off London Flds. W. Side)
Aldington Rd. SE18 . . . . 4F **83**
Aldis M. SW17 . . . . 5A **116**
Aldis St. SW17 . . . . 5A **116**
Aldred Rd. NW6 . . . . . . 2C **44**
Aldren Rd. SW17 . . . . . 3E **115**
Aldrich Ter. SW18 . . . . 2E **115**
Aldrick Ho. *N1 . . . . 5B 48*
  (off Barnsbury Est.)
Aldridge Rd. Vs. W11 . . 4B **58**
Aldrington Rd. SW16 . . 5E **117**
Aldsworth Cl. W9 . . . . . . 3D **59**
Aldworth Gro. SE13 . . . 4E **109**
Aldworth Rd. E15 . . . . . 4A **54**
Aldwych WC2 . . . 5B **62** (4F **15**)

Aldwych Ct. *E8 . . . . 4B 50*
  (off Middleton Rd.)
Aldwych Theatre *3F 15*
  (off Aldwych)
Aldwyn Ho. *SW8 . . . . . . 3A 90*
  (off Davidson Gdns.)
Alestan Beck Rd. E16 . . 5F **69**
Alexa Cl. W8 . . . . 5C **72**
Alexander Av. NW10 . . . 4D **43**
Alexander Evans M.
  SE23 . . . . 2F **121**
Alexander Fleming Mus.
  . . . . *5F 59*
  (off Praed St.)
Alexander Ho. *E14. . . . . 4C 80*
  (off Tiller Rd.)
Alexander M. W2. . . . . . 5D **59**
Alexander Pl. SW7 . . . . 5A **74**
Alexander Rd. N19 . . . . 5A **34**
Alexander Sq. SW3 . . . 5A **74**
Alexander St. W2 . . . . . 5C **58**
Alexander Studios
  SW11 . . . . 2F 101
  (off Haydon Way)
Alexandra Av. SW11 . . . 4C **88**
  W4 . . . . 3A **84**
Alexandra Cl. SE8 . . . . 2B **94**
Alexandra Cotts. SE14 . . 4B **94**
Alexandra Ct. *SW7. . . . . 4E 73*
  (off Queen's Ga.)
  W2 . . . . 1D 73
  (off Moscow Rd.)
  W9 . . . . 3E 59
  (off Maida Va.)
Alexandra Cres.
  BR1: Brom 5B **124**
Alexandra Dr. SE19 . . . 5A **120**
Alexandra Gdns. W4 . . . 3A **84**
Alexandra Gro. N4 . . . . 3D **35**
Alexandra Ho. *E16. . . . . 1D 83*
  (off Wesley Av.)
  W6 . . . . 1E 85
  (off Queen Caroline St.)
Alexandra Mans. *SW3 . . 2F 87*
  (off Moravian Cl.)
Alexandra M. SW19 . . . 5B **114**
Alexandra Pl. NW8 . . . . 5E **45**
Alexandra Rd. E10 . . . . 5E **39**
  E17 . . . . 1B **38**
  NW8 . . . . 5E **45**
  SE26 . . . . 5F **121**
  SW14 . . . . 1A **98**
  SW19 . . . . 5B **114**
  W4 . . . . 3A **70**
Alexandra St. E16 . . . . . 4C **68**
  SE14 . . . . 3A **94**
Alexandra Ter. *E14. . . . . 1D 95*
  (off Westferry Rd.)
Alexandra Wlk. SE19 . . 5A **120**
Alexandra Yd. E9 . . . . . 5F **51**
Alexis St. SE16 . . . . . . 5C **78**
Alfearn Rd. E5 . . . . 1E **51**
Alford Ct. *N1 . . . . 1A 10*
  (off Shepherdess Wlk.)
Alford Ho. N6 . . . . 1E **33**
Alford Pl. N1 . . . 1E **63** (1A **10**)
  (not continuous)
Alfreda St. SW11 . . . . . 4D **89**
Alfred Ho. *E9 . . . . 2A 52*
  (off Homerton Rd.)

Alfred Ho. *E12 . . . . 4F 55*
  (off Tennyson Av.)
Alfred M. W1 . . . 4F **61** (5B **6**)
Alfred Nunn Ho. NW10. . 5B **42**
Alfred Pl. WC1 . . 4F **61** (5B **6**)
Alfred Rd. E15 . . . . 2B **54**
  W2 . . . . 4C **58**
Alfred St. E3 . . . . 2B **66**
Alfreton Cl. SW19 . . . . 3F **113**
Alfriston Rd. SW11 . . . 3B **102**
Algar Ho. SE1 . . . . 4D **25**
Algarve Rd. SW18 . . . 1D **115**
Algernon Rd. NW6 . . . . 5C **44**
  SE13 . . . . 2D **109**
Algiers Rd. SE13 . . . . . 2C **108**
Alice Gilliatt Ct. *W14. . . 2B 86*
  (off Star Rd.)
Alice La. E3 . . . . 5B **52**
Alice Owen Technology Cen.
  EC1. . . . . 1D 9
  (off Goswell Rd.)
Alice Shepherd Ho. *E14. .3E 81*
  (off Manchester Rd.)
Alice St. SE1. . . 4A **78** (5D **27**)
  (not continuous)
Alice Thompson Cl.
  SE12 . . . . 2E **125**
Alice Walker Cl. SE24. . 2D **105**
Alie St. E1 . . . . 5B **64** (3F **19**)
Alison Ct. SE1 . . . . 1C **92**
Aliwal Rd. SW11 . . . . . 2A **102**
Alkerden Rd. W4 . . . . . 1A **84**
Alkham Rd. N16 . . . . . . 4B **36**
Allan Barclay Cl. N15 . . 1B **36**
Allanson Ct. *E10 . . . . . 4C 38*
  (off Leyton Grange Est.)
Allard Gdns. SW4 . . . . 3F **103**
Allardyce St. SW4 . . . . 2B **104**
Allcott Ho. *W12 . . . . . . 5D 57*
  (off Du Cane Rd.)
Allcroft Rd. NW5 . . . . . 2C **46**
Allenby Rd. SE23 . . . . . 3A **122**
Allen Ct. *E17 . . . . 1C 38*
  (off Yunus Khan Cl.)
Allendale Cl. SE5 . . . . . 5F **91**
  SE26 . . . . 5F **121**
Allen Edwards Dr. SW8. . 4A **90**
Allenford Ho. *SW15. . . . 4B 98*
  (off Tunworth Cres.)
Allen Rd. E3 . . . . 1B **66**
  N16 . . . . 1A **50**
Allensbury Pl. NW1 . . . 4F **47**
Allen St. W8 . . . . 4C **72**
Allerford Rd. SE6 . . . . 3D **123**
Allerton Ho. *N1 . . . . . . 1B 10*
  (off Fairbank Est.)
Allerton Rd. N16 . . . . . 4E **35**
Allerton St. N1. . 2F **63** (1B **10**)
Allerton Wlk. N7 . . . . . . 4B **34**
Allestree Rd. SW6 . . . . 3A **86**
Alleyn Cres. SE21 . . . . 2F **119**
Alleyn Ho. *SE1 . . . . . . 5C 26*
  (off Burbage Cl.)
Alleyn Pk. SE21 . . . . . . 2F **119**
Alleyn Rd. SE21 . . . . . 3F **119**
Allfarthing La. SW18 . . 4D **101**
Allgood St. E2 . . . . 1B **64**
Allhallows La.
  EC4. . . . . 1F **77** (5B **18**)
Allhallows Rd. E6. . . . . 4F **69**

Amyruth Rd. SE4 . . . . . 3C **108**	ANGEL 1D **63**
Amy's Cl. E16 . . . . 1D **83**	Angela Davies Ind. Est.
(off Pankhurst Av.)	SE24 . . . . 2D **105**
Anatola Rd. N19 . . . . . . 4D **33**	Angel All. E1 . . . . 5B **64**
Anchor SW18 . . . . 2D **101**	(off Whitechapel High St.)
Anchorage Cl. SW19 . . 5C **114**	Angel Cen., The N1 . . . 1C **62**
Anchorage Ho. E14 . . . . 1F **81**	Angel Ct. EC2 . . 5F **63** (2C **18**)
(off Clove Cres.)	SW1 . . . . . . 2E **75** (2A **22**)
Anchorage Point E14 . . . 3B **80**	Angel Ga. EC1 . . . . 1E **9**
(off Cuba St.)	(not continuous)
Anchorage Point Ind. Est.	Angelina Ho. SE15 . . . . . 4C **92**
SE7 . . . . 4E **83**	(off Goldsmith Rd.)
Anchor & Hope La. SE7 . . 4D **83**	Angel La. E15 . . . . 3F **53**
Anchor Brewhouse	Angell Pk. Gdns. SW9 . . 1C **104**
SE1 . . . . 2B **78** (2F **27**)	Angell Rd. SW9 . . . . . . 1C **104**
(off Vauxhall Bri. Rd.)	ANGELL TOWN 4C **90**
Anchor Ct. SW1 . . . . 5F **75**	Angell Town Est. SW9 . . 5C **90**
(off Vauxhall Bri. Rd.)	Angel M. E1 . . . . 1D **79**
Anchor Ho. E16 . . . . 4B **68**	N1 . . . . 1C **62**
(off Barking Rd.)	SW15 . . . . 5C **98**
E16 . . . . 5E **69**	Angel Pas. EC4 . . 1F **77** (5B **18**)
(off Prince Regent La.)	Angel Pl. SE1 . . 3F **77** (3B **26**)
EC1 . . . . 3F **9**	Angel Sq. N1 . . . . 1C **62**
(off Old St.)	Angel St. EC1 . . 5E **63** (2F **17**)
Anchor M. SW12 . . . . . . 4D **103**	Angel Wlk. W6 . . . . 5E **71**
Anchor Rd. E12 . . . . 4F **41**	Angel Yd. N6 . . . . 3C **32**
Anchor St. SE16 . . . . . . 5D **79**	Angerstein Bus. Pk.
Anchor Ter. E1 . . . . 3C **65**	SE10 . . . . 5C **82**
Anchor Wharf E3 . . . . . 4D **67**	Angerstein La. SE3 . . . . 4B **96**
(off Yeo St.)	Anglebury W2 . . . . 5C **58**
Anchor Yd. EC1 . . 3E **63** (3A **10**)	(off Talbot Rd.)
Ancill Cl. W6 . . . . 2A **86**	Angler's La. NW5 . . . . . . 3D **47**
Ancona Rd. NW10 . . . . 1C **56**	Anglesey Ho. E14 . . . . . 5C **66**
Andalus Rd. SW9 . . . . 1A **104**	(off Lindfield St.)
Andaman Ho. E1 . . . . . . 4A **66**	Angles Rd. SW16 . . . . . 4A **118**
(off Duckett St.)	Anglia Ho. E14 . . . . 5A **66**
Anderson Cl. W3 . . . . . . 5A **56**	(off Salmon La.)
Anderson Cl. NW2 . . . . . 3E **29**	Anglian Rd. E11 . . . . . . 5F **39**
Anderson Ho. E14 . . . . . . 1E **81**	Anglo Rd. E3 . . . . 1B **66**
(off Woolmore St.)	Angrave Ct. E8 . . . . 5B **50**
W12 . . . . 5D **57**	(off Scriven St.)
(off Du Cane Rd.)	Angrave Pas. E8 . . . . . . 5B **50**
Anderson Rd. E9 . . . . . . 3F **51**	Angus Ho. SW2 . . . . . . 5F **103**
Anderson Sq. N1 . . . . . . 5D **49**	Angus Rd. E13 . . . . 2E **69**
(off Gaskin St.)	Angus St. SE14 . . . . . . 3A **94**
Anderson St. SW3 . . . . 1B **88**	Anhalt Rd. SW11 . . . . . . 3A **88**
Anderton Cl. SE5 . . . . . 1F **105**	Anley Rd. W14 . . . . 3F **71**
Andover Av. E16 . . . . . . 5F **69**	Annabel Cl. E14 . . . . . . 5D **67**
Andover Pl. NW6 . . . . . 1D **59**	Anna Cl. E8 . . . . 5B **50**
Andover Rd. N7 . . . . . . 4B **34**	Annandale Rd. SE10 . . . 2B **96**
Andoversford Ct. SE15 . . 2A **92**	W4 . . . . 1A **84**
(off Bibury Cl.)	Anna Neagle Cl. E7 . . . 1C **54**
Andre St. E8 . . . . 2C **50**	Anne Compton M.
Andrew Borde St.	SE12 . . . . 5B **110**
WC2 . . . . 5F **61** (2C **14**)	Anne Goodman Ho. E1 . . 5E **65**
Andrew Ct. SE23 . . . . . 2F **121**	(off Jubilee St.)
Andrewes Gdns. E6 . . . 5F **69**	Annesley Cl. NW10 . . . 5A **28**
Andrewes Highwalk	Annesley Ho. SW9 . . . . 4C **90**
EC2 . . . . 1A **18**	Annesley Rd. SE3 . . . . . 4D **97**
Andrewes Ho. EC2 . . . . 1A **18**	Annesley Wlk. N19 . . . . 4E **33**
Andrew Pl. SW8 . . . . . . 3F **89**	Anne St. E13 . . . . 3C **68**
Andrews Crosse WC2 . . 3B **16**	Annette Rd. N7 . . . . 5B **34**
Andrews Ho. NW3 . . . . . 4B **46**	(not continuous)
(off Fellows Rd.)	Annetts Cres. N1 . . . . . 4E **49**
Andrew's Rd. E8 . . . . . . 5D **51**	Annie Besant Cl. E3 . . . 5B **52**
Andrews Wlk. SE17 . . . 2D **91**	Anning St. EC2 . . 3A **64** (3E **11**)
Anerley Hill SE19 . . . . . 5B **120**	Annis Rd. E9 . . . . 3A **52**
Aneurin Bevan Ct.	Ann La. SW10 . . . . 2F **87**
NW2 . . . . 4D **29**	Ann Moss Way SE16 . . . 4E **79**
Anfield Cl. SW12 . . . . . 5E **103**	

Ann's Cl. SW1 . . . . 4A **20**
Ann's Pl. E1 . . . . 1F **19**
Ann Stroud Ct. SE12 . . 3C **110**
Ansar Gdns. E17 . . . . . 1B **38**
Ansdell Rd. SE15 . . . . . 5E **93**
Ansdell St. W8 . . . . 4D **73**
Ansdell Ter. W8 . . . . . . 4D **73**
Ansell Ho. E1 . . . . 4E **65**
(off Mile End Rd.)
Ansell Rd. SW17 . . . . . 3A **116**
Anselm Rd. SW6 . . . . . 2C **86**
Ansford Rd.
BR1: Brom 5E **123**
Ansleigh Pl. W11 . . . . . . 1F **71**
Anson Ho. E1 . . . . 3A **66**
(off Shandy St.)
SW1 . . . . 2E **89**
(off Churchill Gdns.)
Anson Rd. N7 . . . . 1E **47**
NW2 . . . . 1D **43**
Anstey Ho. E9 . . . . 5E **51**
(off Templecombe Rd.)
Anstey Rd. SE15 . . . . . 1C **106**
Anstice Cl. W4 . . . . 3A **84**
Antenor Ho. E2 . . . . 1D **65**
(off Old Bethnal Grn. Rd.)
Anthony Cope Ct. N1 . . 1C **10**
(off Chart St.)
Anthony Ho. NW1 . . . . . 3A **60**
(off Ashbridge St.)
Anthony St. E1 . . . . 5D **65**
Antigua Wlk. SE19 . . . . 5F **119**
Antilles Bay E14 . . . . . . 3E **81**
Antill Rd. E3 . . . . 2A **66**
Antill Ter. E1 . . . . 5F **65**
Anton St. E8 . . . . 2C **50**
Antony Ho. SE14 . . . . . . 3F **93**
(off Barlborough St.)
SE16 . . . . 5E **79**
(off Raymouth Rd.)
Antrim Gro. NW3 . . . . . 3B **46**
Antrim Ho. E3 . . . . 5B **52**
(off Birdsfield La.)
Antrim Rd. NW3 . . . . . . 3B **46**
Apex Ind. Est. NW10 . . 3B **56**
Aphrodite Ct. E14 . . . . . 5C **80**
(off Homer Dr.)
Apollo Bldg. E14 . . . . . 5C **80**
Apollo Bus. Cen. SE8 . . 1F **93**
Apollo Ct. E1 . . . . 1C **78**
(off Thomas More St.)
SW9 . . . . 4C **90**
(off Southey Rd.)
Apollo Ho. E2 . . . . 1D **65**
(off St Jude's St.)
N6 . . . . 2B **32**
SW10 . . . . 3F **87**
(off Riley St.)
Apollo Pl. E11 . . . . 5A **40**
SW10 . . . . 3F **87**
Apollo Theatre 4B **14**
(off Shaftesbury Av.)
Apollo Victoria Theatre
. . . . 4E **75**
(off Wilton Rd.)
Apothecary St.
EC4 . . . . 5D **63** (3D **17**)
Appach Rd. SW2 . . . . . 3C **104**
Apple Blossom Ct. SW8 . 3F **89**
(off Pascal St.)

Armadale Rd. SW6 . . . . . 3C **86**
Armada St. SE8 . . . . 2C **94**
   (off McMillan St.)
Armagh Rd. E3 . . . . 5B **52**
Arminger Rd. W12 . . . . . 2D **71**
Armitage Rd. NW11 . . . 3A **30**
SE10 . . . . 1B **96**
Armour Cl. N7 . . . . 3B **48**
Armoury Rd. SE8 . . . . . . 5D **95**
SE13 . . . . 5D **95**
Armoury Way SW18 . . 3C **100**
Armsby Ho. E1 . . . . 4E **65**
   (off Stepney Way)
Armstrong Rd. SW7 . . . 4F **73**
W3 . . . . 2B **70**
Arnal Cres. SW18 . . . . . 5A **100**
Arncliffe NW6 . . . . 1D **59**
Arncliffe Cl. N11 . . . . . . 1B **34**
Arndale Wlk. SW18 . . 3D **101**
Arne Ho. SE11 . . . . 1B **90**
   (off Worgan St.)
Arne St. WC2 . . 5A **62** (3E **15**)
Arne Wlk. SE3 . . . . 2B **110**
Arneway St. SW1 . . . . . . 4F **75**
Arnewood Cl. SW15 . . . 1C **112**
Arngask Rd. SE6 . . . . . . 5F **109**
Arnhem Pl. E14 . . . . 4C **80**
Arnhem Way SE22 . . . . 3A **106**
Arnhem Wharf E14 . . . . 4B **80**
Arnold Cir. E2 . . . 2B **64** (2F **11**)
Arnold Est. SE1 . . . . 3B **78**
   (not continuous)
Arnold Ho. SE3 . . . . 3E **97**
   (off Shooters Hill Rd.)
SE17 . . . . 1D **91**
   (off Doddington Gro.)
Arnold Mans. W14 . . . . 2B **86**
   (off Queen's Club Gdns.)
Arnold Rd. E3 . . . . 2C **66**
Arnot Ho. SE5 . . . . 3E **91**
   (off Comber Gro.)
Arnott Cl. W4 . . . . 5A **70**
Arnould Av. SE5 . . . . . . 2F **105**
Arnside St. SE17 . . . . . . 2F **91**
Arnulf St. SE6 . . . . 4D **123**
Arnulls Rd. SW16 . . . . 5D **119**
Arodene Rd. SW2 . . . . . 4B **104**
Aragon Rd. E6 . . . . 5F **55**
SW18 . . . . 1C **114**
Arran Ct. NW10 . . . . . . 5A **28**
Arran Dr. E12 . . . . 3F **41**
Arran Ho. E14 . . . . 2E **81**
   (off Raleana Rd.)
Arran Rd. SE6 . . . . 2D **123**
Arran Wlk. N1 . . . . 4E **49**
Arrol Ho. SE1 . . 4E **77** (5A **26**)
Arrow Ct. SW5 . . . . 5C **72**
   (off W. Cromwell Rd.)
Arrowhead Ct. E11 . . . . 1F **39**
Arrow Rd. E3 . . . . 2D **67**
Arrows Ho. SE14 . . . . . . 3E **93**
   (off Clifton Way)
Arrowsmith Ho. SE11 . . 1B **90**
   (off Wickham St.)
Arsenal F.C. (Highbury)
   . . . . 5D **35**
Artemis Ct. E14 . . . . 5C **80**
   (off Homer Dr.)
Artesian Cl. NW10 . . . . 4A **42**
Artesian Rd. W2 . . . . . . 5C **58**

Artesian Wlk. E11 . . . . . 5A **40**
Arthingworth St. E15 . . 5A **54**
Arthur Ct. SW11 . . . . . . 4C **88**
W2 . . . . 5D **59**
   (off Queensway)
W10 . . . . 5F **57**
   (off Silchester Rd.)
Arthur Deakin Ho. E1 . . 4C **64**
   (off Hunton St.)
Arthurdon Rd. SE4 . . . 3C **108**
Arthur Henderson Ho.
   SW6 . . . . 5B **86**
   (off Fulham Rd.)
Arthur Horsley Wlk.
   E7 . . . . 2B **54**
   (off Twr. Hamlets Rd.)
Arthur Rd. N7 . . . . 1B **48**
SW19 . . . . 5B **114**
Arthur St. EC4 . . 1F **77** (4C **18**)
Artichoke Hill E1 . . . . . . 1D **79**
Artichoke M. SE5 . . . . . 4F **91**
   (off Artichoke Pl.)
Artichoke Pl. SE5 . . . . . 4F **91**
Artillery Ho. E15 . . . . . . 3A **54**
Artillery La. E1 . . 4A **64** (1E **19**)
W12 . . . . 5C **56**
Artillery Pas. E1 . . . . . . 1F **19**
Artillery Pl.
   SW1 . . . . . . 4F **75** (5B **22**)
Artillery Row
   SW1 . . . . . . 4E **75** (5B **22**)
Artizan St. E1 . . . . 2F **19**

Arts Theatre 4D **15**
   (off St Martin's St.)

Arundel Bldgs. SE1 . . . . 4A **78**
   (off Swan Mead)
Arundel Cl. E15 . . . . 1A **54**
SW11 . . . . 3A **102**
Arundel Ct. SE16 . . . . . . 1D **93**
   (off Varcoe Rd.)
SW3 . . . . 1A **88**
   (off Jubilee Pl.)
SW13 . . . . 2D **85**
   (off Arundel Ter.)
Arundel Gdns. W11 . . . 1B **72**
Arundel Gt. Ct.
   WC2 . . . . . . 1B **76** (4A **16**)
Arundel Gro. N16 . . . . . 2A **50**
Arundel Mans. SW6 . . . 4B **86**
   (off Kelvedon Rd.)
Arundel Pl. N1 . . . . 3C **48**
Arundel Sq. N7 . . . . 3C **48**
Arundel St.
   WC2 . . . . . . 1B **76** (4A **16**)
Arundel Ter. SW13 . . . . 2D **85**
Arvon Rd. N5 . . . . 2C **48**
   (not continuous)
Asbridge Ct. W6 . . . . . . 4D **71**
   (off Dalling Rd.)
Ascalon Ho. SW8 . . . . . 3E **89**
   (off Thessaly Rd.)
Ascalon St. SW8 . . . . . . 3E **89**
Ascham St. NW5 . . . . . . 2E **47**
Ascot Ct. NW8 . . . . 2F **59**
   (off Grove End Rd.)
Ascot Ho. NW1 . . . . 1E **5**
   (off Redhill St.)
W9 . . . . 3C **58**
   (off Harrow Rd.)
Ascot Lodge NW6 . . . . . 5D **45**

Ascot Rd. N15 . . . . 1F **35**
SW17 . . . . 5C **116**
Ashbee Ho. E2 . . . . 2E **65**
   (off Portman Pl.)
Ashbourne Ct. E5 . . . . . 1A **52**
Ashbourne Gro. SE22 . . 2B **106**
W4 . . . . 1A **84**
Ashbridge Rd. E11 . . . . 2A **40**
Ashbridge St. NW8 . . . 3A **60**
Ashbrook Rd. N19 . . . . 3F **33**
Ashburn Gdns. SW7 . . . 5E **73**
Ashburnham Gro.
   SE10 . . . . 3D **95**
Ashburnham Mans.
   SW10 . . . . 3E **87**
   (off Ashburnham Rd.)
Ashburnham Pl.
   SE10 . . . . 3D **95**
Ashburnham Retreat
   SE10 . . . . 3D **95**
Ashburnham Rd.
   NW10 . . . . 2E **57**
   SW10 . . . . 3E **87**
Ashburnham Twr.
   SW10 . . . . 3F **87**
   (off Worlds End Est.)
Ashburn Pl. SW7 . . . . . . 5E **73**
Ashburton Ent. Cen.
   SW15 . . . . 4F **99**
Ashburton Gro. N7 . . . . 1C **48**
Ashburton Ho. W9 . . . . 3B **58**
   (off Fernhead Rd.)
Ashburton Rd. E16 . . . . 5C **68**
Ashburton Ter. E13 . . . . 1C **68**
Ashbury Pl. SW19 . . . . . 5E **115**
Ashbury Rd. SW11 . . . . 1B **102**
Ashby Ct. NW8 . . . . 3F **59**
   (off Pollitt Dr.)
Ashby Gro. N1 . . . . 4E **49**
   (not continuous)
Ashby Ho. N1 . . . . 4E **49**
   (off Essex Rd.)
SW9 . . . . 5D **91**
Ashby M. SE4 . . . . 5B **94**
SW2 . . . . 3A **104**
   (off Prague Pl.)
Ashby Rd. SE4 . . . . 5B **94**
Ashby St. EC1 . . 2D **63** (2E **9**)
Ashchurch Gro. W12 . . 4C **70**
Ashchurch Pk. Vs.
   W12 . . . . 4C **70**
Ashchurch Ter. W12 . . . 4C **70**
Ashcombe Ho. NW2 . . . 5A **28**
Ashcombe Rd. SW19 . . 5C **114**
Ashcombe St. SW6 . . . . 5D **87**
Ash Ct. NW5 . . . . 2E **47**
Ashcroft Ho. SW8 . . . . . 4E **89**
   (off Wadhurst Rd.)
Ashcroft Rd. E3 . . . . 2A **66**
Ashcroft Sq. W6 . . . . . . 5E **71**
Ashdale Ho. N4 . . . . 2F **35**
Ashdale Rd. SE12 . . . . . 1D **125**
Ashdene SE15 . . . . 3D **93**
Ashdon Rd. NW10 . . . . 5B **42**
Ashdown Cres. NW5 . . . 2C **46**
Ashdown Ho. SW1 . . . . 4E **75**
   (off Victoria St.)
Ashdown Wlk. E14 . . . . 5C **80**
   (off Copeland Dr.)
Ashdown Way SW17 . . 2C **116**

Atlantic Rd. SW9 . . . . 2C **104**
Atlantic Wharf E1 . . . . . 1F **79**
 (off Jardine Rd.)
Atlas Bus. Cen. NW2 . . 3D **29**
Atlas Gdns. SE7 . . . . 5E **83**
Atlas M. E8 . . . . 3B **50**
 N7 . . . . 3B **48**
Atlas Rd. E13 . . . . 1C **68**
 NW10 . . . . 2A **56**
Atlas Wharf E9 . . . . 3C **52**
Atley Rd. E3 . . . . 5C **52**
Atney Rd. SW15 . . . . 2A **100**
Atterbury Rd. N4 . . . . 1C **34**
Atterbury St. SW1 . . . . . . 5A **76**
Attewood Av. NW10 . . . 5A **28**
Attilburgh Ho. SE1 . . . . . 5F **27**
 (off Abbey St.)
Attleborough Ct. SE26 . . 2C **120**
Attneave St. WC1 . . 2C **62 (2B 8)**
Atwater Cl. SW2 . . . . 1C **118**
Atwell Cl. E10 . . . . 1D **39**
Atwell Rd. SE15 . . . . 5C **92**
Atwood Ho. W14 . . . . 5B **72**
 (off Beckford Cl.)
Atwood Rd. W6 . . . . 5D **71**
Aubert Ct. N5 . . . . 1D **49**
Aubert Pk. N5 . . . . 1D **49**
Aubert Rd. N5 . . . . 1D **49**
Aubrey Beardsley Ho.
 SW1 . . . . 5E **75**
 (off Vauxhall Bri. Rd.)
Aubrey Mans. NW1 . . . . 4A **60**
 (off Lisson St.)
Aubrey Moore Point
 E15 . . . . 1E **67**
 (off Abbey La.)
Aubrey Pl. NW8 . . . . 1E **59**
Aubrey Rd. N8 . . . . 1A **34**
 W8 . . . . 2B **72**
Aubrey Wlk. W8 . . . . 2B **72**
Auburn Cl. SE14 . . . . 3A **94**
Aubyn Hill SE27 . . . . 4E **119**
Aubyn Sq. SW15 . . . . . . 3C **98**
Auckland Hill SE27 . . . . . 4E **119**
Auckland Ho. W12 . . . . . 1D **71**
 (off White City Est.)
Auckland Rd. E10 . . . . . . 5D **39**
 SW11 . . . . 2A **102**
Auckland St. SE11 . . . . . 1B **90**
Auden Pl. NW1 . . . . 5C **46**
 (not continuous)
Audley Cl. SW11 . . . . . . 1C **102**
Audley Dr. E16 . . . . 2D **83**
Audley Rd. NW4 . . . . 1C **28**
Audley Sq. W1 . . 2C **74 (1C 20)**
Audrey St. E2 . . . . 1C **64**
Augurs La. E13 . . . . 2D **69**
Augusta St. E14 . . . . 5D **67**
Augustine Rd. W14 . . . . . 4F **71**
Augustus Cl. W12 . . . . . 3D **71**
Augustus Ct. SW16 . . . . 2F **117**
Augustus Ho. NW1 . . . . 1F **5**
 (off Augustus St.)
Augustus Rd. SW19 . . . 1F **113**
Augustus St. NW1 . .1D **61 (1E 5)**
Aulton Pl. SE11 . . . . 1C **90**
Auriga M. N1 . . . . 2F **49**
Auriol Ho. W12 . . . . 2D **71**
 (off Ellerslie Rd.)
Auriol Rd. W14 . . . . 5A **72**

Aurora Ho. E14 . . . . 5D **67**
 (off Kerbey St.)
Austen Ho. NW6 . . . . 2C **58**
 (off Cambridge Rd.)
Austin Cl. SE23 . . . . 5A **108**
Austin Ct. E6 . . . . 5E **55**
 SE15 . . . . 1C **106**
 (off Philip Wlk.)
Austin Friars
 EC2 . . . . 5F **63 (2C 18)**
 (not continuous)
Austin Friars Pas. EC2 . . 2C **18**
Austin Friars Sq. EC2 . . 2C **18**
Austin Ho. SE14 . . . . 3B **94**
 (off Achilles St.)
Austin Rd. SW11 . . . . . . 4C **88**
Austin St. E2 . . . 2B **64 (2F 11)**
Austin Ter. SE1 . . . . 4C **24**
 (off Morley St.)
Australia Rd. W12 . . . . . . 1D **71**
Austral St. SE11 . . . . 5D **77**
Autumn Cl. SW19 . . . . . 5E **115**
Autumn St. E3 . . . . 5C **52**
Avalon Rd. SW6 . . . . 4D **87**
Avarn Rd. SW17 . . . . . . 5B **116**
Avebury Ct. N1 . . . . 5F **49**
 (off Imber St.)
Avebury Rd. E11 . . . . 3F **39**
Avebury St. N1 . . . . 5F **49**
Aveline St. SE11 . . . . . . 1C **90**
Ave Maria La.
 EC4 . . . . 5D **63 (3E 17)**
Avenell Rd. N5 . . . . 5D **35**
Avenfield Ho. W1 . . . . . . 4A **12**
 (off Park La.)
Avening Rd. SW18 . . . . 5C **100**
Avening Ter. SW18 . . . . 5C **100**
Avenons Rd. E13 . . . . . . 3C **68**
Avenue Cl. NW8 . . . . . . 5A **46**
Avenue Ct. NW2 . . . . 5B **30**
 SW3 . . . . 5B **74**
 (off Draycott Av.)
Avenue Gdns. SW14 . . 1A **98**
Avenue Ho. NW8 . . . . . . 1A **60**
 (off Allitsen Rd.)
 NW10 . . . . 1D **57**
 (off All Souls Av.)
Avenue Lodge NW8 . . . . 4F **45**
 (off Avenue Rd.)
Avenue Mans. NW3 . . . . 2D **45**
 (off Finchley Rd.)
Avenue Pk. Rd. SE27 . . 2D **119**
Avenue Rd. E7 . . . . 1D **55**
 N6 . . . . 2E **33**
 N15 . . . . 1F **35**
 NW3 . . . . 4F **45**
 NW10 . . . . 1B **56**
Avenue, The E11 . . . . . . 1D **41**
 NW6 . . . . 5F **43**
 SE10 . . . . 3F **95**
 SW4 . . . . 3C **102**
 SW18 . . . . 5A **102**
 W4 . . . . 4A **70**
Averill St. W6 . . . . 2F **85**
Avery Farm Row SW1 . . 5C **74**
Avery Row W1 . . 1D **75 (4D 13)**
Aviary Cl. E16 . . . . 4B **68**
Avignon Rd. SE4 . . . . . . 1F **107**
Avington Ct. SE1 . . . . 5A **78**
 (off Old Kent Rd.)

Avis Sq. E1 . . . . 5F **65**
Avoca Rd. SW17 . . . . . . 4C **116**
Avocet Cl. SE1 . . . . 1C **92**
Avon Ct. W9 . . . . 4C **58**
 (off Elmfield Way)
Avondale Av. NW2 . . . . . 5A **28**
Avondale Ct. E11 . . . . . . 3A **40**
 E16 . . . . 4A **68**
Avondale Cres. IG4: Ilf . . 1F **41**
Avondale Ho. SE1 . . . . . 1C **92**
 (off Avondale Sq.)
Avondale Pk. Gdns.
 W11 . . . . 1A **72**
Avondale Pk. Rd. W11 . . 1A **72**
Avondale Ri. SE15 . . . . 1B **106**
Avondale Rd.
 BR1: Brom 5B **124**
 E16 . . . . 4A **68**
 E17 . . . . 2C **38**
 N15 . . . . 1D **35**
 SE9 . . . . 2F **125**
 SW14 . . . . 1A **98**
 SW19 . . . . 5D **115**
Avondale Sq. SE1 . . . . . 1C **92**
Avon Ho. W8 . . . . 4C **72**
 (off Allen St.)
 W14 . . . . 5B **72**
 (off Kensington Village)
Avonhurst Ho. NW2 . . . . 4A **44**
Avonley Rd. SE14 . . . . . 3E **93**
Avonmore Gdns. W14 . . 5B **72**
Avonmore Pl. W14 . . . . . 5A **72**
Avonmore Rd. W14 . . . . 5A **72**
Avonmouth St.
 SE1 . . . . 4E **77 (5F 25)**
Avon Pl. SE1 . . . 3E **77 (4A 26)**
Avon Rd. SE4 . . . . 1C **108**
Avro Ho. SW8 . . . . 3D **89**
 (off Havelock Ter.)
Axminster Rd. N7 . . . . . . 5A **34**
Aybrook St. W1 . . 4C **60 (1B 12)**
Aycliffe Rd. W12 . . . . . . 2C **70**
Ayerst Ct. E10 . . . . 2E **39**
Aylesbury Cl. E7 . . . . . . 3B **54**
Aylesbury Ho. SE15 . . . 2C **92**
 (off Friary Est.)
Aylesbury Rd. SE17 . . . 1F **91**
Aylesbury St.
 EC1 . . . . 3D **63 (4D 9)**
 NW10 . . . . 5A **28**
Aylesford Ho. SE1 . . . . . 4C **26**
 (off Long La.)
Aylesford St. SW1 . . . . . 1F **89**
Aylesham Cen., The
 SE15 . . . . 4C **92**
Aylestone Av. NW6 . . . . 4F **43**
Aylmer Ct. N2 . . . . 1B **32**
Aylmer Ho. SE10 . . . . . . 1F **95**
Aylmer Pde. N2 . . . . 1B **32**
Aylmer Rd. E11 . . . . 3B **40**
 N2 . . . . 1A **32**
 W12 . . . . 3B **70**
Aylton Est. SE16 . . . . . . 3E **79**
Aylward Rd. SE23 . . . . . 2F **121**
Aylward St. E1 . . . . 5E **65**
 (Jamaica St.)
 E1 . . . . 5E **65**
 (Jubilee St.)
Aylwin Est.
 SE1 . . . . 4A **78 (5E 27)**

Aynhoe Mans. *W14*. 5F **71**
  (off Aynhoe Rd.)
Aynhoe Rd. W14. . . . . 5F **71**
Ayres Cl. E13 . . . . 2C **68**
Ayres Rd. SE1. . . . 3E **77** (3A **26**)
Ayrsome Rd. N16. . . . . . . 5A **36**
Ayrton Gould Ho. *E2*. . . . 2F **65**
  (off Roman Rd.)
Ayrton Rd. SW7 . . . . 4F **73**
Aysgarth Rd. SE21. . . . . 5A **106**
Ayshford Ho. *E2*. 2D **65**
  (off Viaduct St.)
Ayston Ho. SE16. . . . . 5F **79**
  (off Plough Way)
Ayton Ho. *SE5*. 3F **91**
  (off Edmund St.)
Aytoun Pl. SW9 . . . . 5B **90**
Aytoun Rd. SW9. . . . . 5B **90**
Azalea Ho. *SE14*. 3B **94**
  (off Achilles St.)
Azania M. NW5 . . . . 3D **47**
Azenby Rd. SE15 . . . . 5B **92**
Azof St. SE10 . . . . 5A **82**
Azov Ho. *E1* 3A **66**
  (off Commodore St.)

B

Baalbec Rd. N5 . . . . 2D **49**
Babington Ct. WC1 . . . . . . 5F **7**
Babington Ho. *SE1*. 3A **26**
  (off Disney St.)
Babington Rd. SW16 . . . 5F **117**
Babmaes St.
  SW1 . . . . 1F **75** (5B **14**)
Bacchus Wlk. *N1* 1A **64**
  (off Regan Way)
Bache's St. N1 . . 2F **63** (1C **10**)
Back All. EC3 . . . . 3E **19**
Bk. Church La. E1 . . . . . . 5C **64**
Back Hill EC1. . . . 3C **62** (4C **8**)
Backhouse Pl. SE17. . . . . 5A **78**
Back La. N8 . . . . 1A **34**
  NW3 . . . . 1E **45**
Bacon Gro. SE1 . . . . 4B **78**
Bacons La. N6 . . . . 3C **32**
Bacon St. E1 . . . . 3B **64** (3F **11**)
Bacton St. E2 . . . . 2E **65**
Baddesley Ho. *SE11*. . . . 1B **90**
  (off Jonathan St.)
Baddow Wlk. *N1*. 5E **49**
  (off New Nth. Rd.)
Baden Pl. SE1 . . . 3F **77** (3B **26**)
Baden Powell Ho. SW7. . . 5E **73**
  (off Queens Ga.)
Badger Ct. NW2 . . . . 5E **29**
Badminton M. E16 . . . . . . 2C **82**
Badminton Rd. SW12. . . 4C **102**
Badsworth Rd. SE5. . . . . . 4E **91**
Baffin Way E14 . . . . 2E **81**
Bagley's La. SW6 . . . . 4D **87**
Bagnigge Ho. *WC1*. 2B **8**
  (off Margery St.)
Bagshot Ho. NW1 . . . . 1E **5**
Bagshot St. SE17 . . . . . . 1A **92**
Baildon *E2*. 1E **65**
  (off Cyprus St.)
Baildon St. SE8 . . . . 3B **94**
Bailey M. SW2 . . . . 3C **104**

Bailey Pl. SE26 . . . . 5F **121**
Bainbridge St.
  WC1 . . . . 5F **61** (2C **14**)
Baird Cl. E10 . . . . 3C **38**
Baird Gdns. SE19. . . . . . 4A **120**
Baird Ho. *W12*. 1D **71**
  (off White City Est.)
Baird St. EC1 . . . 3E **63** (3A **10**)
Baizdon Rd. SE3 . . . . 5A **96**
Baker Ho. *WC1*. 4E **7**
  (off Colonnade)
Baker Pas. NW10 . . . . 5A **42**
Baker Rd. NW10 . . . . 5A **42**
Bakers Av. E17. . . . . 1D **39**
Baker's Fld. N7 . . . . 1A **48**
Bakers Hall Ct. EC3. . . . . 5D **19**
Bakers Hill E5. . . . . 3E **37**
Bakers La. N6 . . . . 1B **32**
Baker's M. W1. . 5C **60** (2B **12**)
Bakers Pas. NW3 . . . . 1E **45**
  (off Heath St.)
Baker's Rents E2. 2B **64** (2F **11**)
Baker's Row E15 . . . . 1A **68**
  EC1 . . . . 3C **62** (4B **8**)
BAKER ST. 3B **60** (4A **4**)
BAKER STREET 3B **60**
Baker St. NW1 . . 3B **60** (4A **4**)
  W1. . . . . 4B **60** (5A **4**)
Baker's Yd. EC1 . . . . 4B **8**
Bakery Cl. SW9 . . . . 3B **90**
Bakery Pl. SW11 . . . . 2B **102**
Balaam Leisure Cen. . . 3C **68**
Balaam St. E13 . . . . 3C **68**
Balaclava Rd. SE1 . . . . . . 5B **78**
Bala Grn. NW9 . . . . 1A **28**
  (off Ruthin Cl.)
Balchen Rd. SE3. . . . . . . 5F **97**
Balchier Rd. SE22 . . . . . 4D **107**
Balcombe Ho. NW1 . . . . . 3A **60**
  (off Taunton Pl.)
Balcombe St.
  NW1. . . . . 3B **60** (5A **4**)
Balcorne St. E9 . . . . 4E **51**
Balder Ri. SE12 . . . . 2D **125**
Balderton Flats *W1* 3C **12**
  (off Balderton St.)
Balderton St.
  W1. . . . . 5C **60** (3C **12**)
Baldock St. E3 . . . . 1D **67**
Baldrey Ho. SE10. . . . . . . 1B **96**
  (off Blackwall La.)
Baldwin Cres. SE5 . . . . . . 4E **91**
Baldwin Ho. SW2. . . . . . 1C **118**
Baldwins Gdns.
  EC1 . . . . 4C **62** (5B **8**)
Baldwin St. EC1. . 2F **63** (2B **10**)
Baldwin Ter. N1 . . . . 1E **63**
Bale Rd. E1 . . . . 4A **66**
Balfern Gro. W4. . . . . 1A **84**
Balfern St. SW11. . . . . . . 5A **88**
Balfe St. N1 . . . . 1A **62**
Balfour Ho. *W10*. 4F **57**
  (off St Charles Sq.)
Balfour M. W1. . 2C **74** (1C **20**)
Balfour Pl. SW15. . . . . . . 2D **99**
  W1. . . . . 1C **74** (5C **12**)
Balfour Rd. N5. . . . . 1E **49**
Balfour St. SE17. . . . . 5F **77**
Balfron Twr. E14. . . . . . . 5E **67**
BALHAM 1C **116**

Balham Continental Mkt.
  SW12 . . . . 1D **117**
  (off Shipka Rd.)
Balham Gro. SW12 . . . . . 5C **102**
Balham High Rd.
  SW12 . . . . 1C **116**
  SW17 . . . . 3C **116**
Balham Hill SW12. . . . . . 5D **103**
Balham New Rd.
  SW12 . . . . 5D **103**
Balham Pk. Rd. SW12. . 1B **116**
Balham Sta. Rd.
  SW12 . . . . 1D **117**
Balin Ho. *SE1*. 3B **26**
  (off Long La.)
Balkan Wlk. E1 . . . . 1D **79**
Balladier Wlk. E14. . . . . . 4D **67**
Ballamore Rd.
  BR1: Brom 3C **124**
Ballance Rd. E9 . . . . 3F **51**
Ballantine St. SW18. . . . . 2E **101**
Ballantrae Ho. NW2. . . . . 1B **44**
Ballard Ho. *SE10*. 2D **95**
  (off Thames St.)
Ballards Rd. NW2 . . . . . . 4C **28**
Ballast Quay SE10 . . . . . . 1F **95**
Ballater Rd. SW2. . . . . . . 2A **104**
Ball Ct. *EC3* 3C **18**
  (off Cornhill)
Ballina St. SE23 . . . . 5F **107**
Ballin Ct. *E14*. 3E **81**
  (off Stewart St.)
Ballingdon Rd. SW11 . . 4C **102**
Balliol Rd. W10 . . . . 5E **57**
Balloch Rd. SE6 . . . . 1F **123**
Ballogie Av. NW10. . . . . . 1A **42**
Ballow Cl. SE5 . . . . 3A **92**
Ball's Pond Pl. N1 . . . . . . 3F **49**
Balls Pond Rd. N1 . . . . . . 3F **49**
Balman Ho. *SE16*. 5F **79**
  (off Rotherhithe New Rd.)
Balmer Rd. E3 . . . . 1B **66**
Balmes Rd. N1 . . . . 5F **49**
Balmoral Cl. SW15. . . . . . 4F **99**
Balmoral Ct. SE12 . . . . . 4D **125**
  SE16. . . . . 2F **79**
  (off King & Queen Wharf)
  SE27. . . . . 4E **119**
Balmoral Gro. N7. . . . . . . 3B **48**
Balmoral Ho. E14 . . . . . . 4D **81**
  (off Lanark Sq.)
  E16. . . . . 1D **83**
  (off Keats Av.)
  W14 . . . . 5A **72**
  (off Windsor Way)
Balmoral M. W12. . . . . . . 4B **70**
Balmoral Rd. E7. . . . . 1E **55**
  E10. . . . . 4D **39**
  NW2 . . . . 3D **43**
Balmore St. N19 . . . . 4D **33**
Balmuir Gdns. SW15. . . . 2E **99**
Balnacraig Av. NW10. . . . 1A **42**
Balniel Ga. SW1. . . . . 1F **89**
Balsam Ho. *E14* 1D **81**
  (off E. India Dock Rd.)
Baltic Ct. SE16. . . . . 3F **79**
Baltic Ho. SE5 . . . . 5E **91**
Baltic Pl. N1 . . . . 5A **50**
Baltic St. E. EC1. . 3E **63** (4F **9**)
Baltic St. W. EC1. . 3E **63** (4F **9**)

Baltimore Ho. *SE11* *1C 90*
  (off Hotspur St.)
Balvaird Pl. SW1 . . . . . . 1F 89
Balvernie Gro. SW18 . . 5B 100
Balvernie M. SW18 . . . . 5C 100
Bamber Rd. SE15 . . . . . 4B 92
Bamborough Gdns. W12. .3E 71
Bamford Ct. *E15* *2D 53*
  (off Clays La.)
Bamford Rd.
  BR1: Brom 5E 123
Bampton Rd. SE23 . . 3F 121
Banbury Ct. WC2 . . . . 4D 15
Banbury Ho. E9 . . . . . . 4F 51
Banbury Rd. E9 . . . . . . 4F 51
Banbury St. SW11 . . . . 5A 88
Banchory Rd. SE3 . . . . 3D 97
Bancroft Av. N2 . . . . . . 1A 32
Bancroft Ct. *SW8* *3A 90*
  (off Allen Edwards Dr.)
Bancroft Ho. *E1* *3E 65*
  (off Cephas St.)
Bancroft Rd. E1 . . . . . 2E 65
Banfield Rd. SE15 . . 1D 107
Bangalore St. SW15. . . 1E 99
Banim St. W6. . . . . . . 5D 71
Banister Ho. E9. . . . . . 2F 51
  SW8 . . . . *4E 89*
  (off Wadhurst Rd.)
  W10 . . . . *2A 58*
  (off Bruckner St.)
Banister Rd. W10 . . . . 2F 57
Bank End SE1 . . 2E 77 (1A 26)
Bankfoot Rd.
  BR1: Brom 4A 124
Bankhurst Rd. SE6 . . 5B 108
Bank La. SW15. . . . . 3A 98
Bank of England
  . . . . **5F 63 (3B 18)**
Bank of England Mus. . . **3C 18**
Bank of England Offices
  EC4 . . . . 3F 17
Banks Ho. *SE1* *5F 25*
  (off Rockingham St.)
Bankside SE1 . . 1E 77 (5F 17)
  (not continuous)
Bankside Art Gallery
  . . . . **1D 77 (5E 17)**
Bankside Way SE19 . . 5A 120
Bank, The N6 . . . . 3D 33
Bankton Rd. SW2 . . . . 2C 104
Bankwell Rd. SE13. . . 2A 110
Bannerman Ho. SW8 . . 2B 90
Banner St. EC1 . . 3E 63 (4A 10)
Banning St. SE10 . . . . 1A 96
Bannister Cl. SW2 . . . 1C 118
Bannister Ho. *SE14* . . . *2F 93*
  (off John Williams Cl.)
Banqueting House
  . . . . **2A 76 (2D 23)**
Banstead St. SE15 . . 1E 107
Banting Ho. NW2 . . . . 5C 28
Bantock Ho. *W10* *2A 58*
  (off Third Av.)
Bantry Ho. *E1* *3F 65*
  (off Ernest St.)
Bantry St. SE5. . . . . . 3F 91
Banyard Rd. SE16 . . . 4D 79
Baptist Gdns. NW5. . . 3C 46
Barandon Rd. W11 . . . 1F 71

Barandon Wlk. W11 . . . 1F 71
Barbanel Ho. *E1*. *3E 65*
  (off Cephas St.)
Barbara Brosnan Ct.
  NW8 . . . . 1F 59
Barbauld Rd. N16 . . . 5A 36
Barber Beaumont Ho.
  E1 . . . . *2F 65*
  (off Bancroft Rd.)
Barbers All. E13. . . . . 2D 69
Barbers Rd. E15. . . . . 1D 67
Barbican Arts Cen.
  . . . . **4E 63 (5A 10)**
Barbican Theatre **5A 10**
  (off Barbican)
Barb M. W6 . . . . 4E 71
Barbon Cl. WC1. . 4B 62 (5E 7)
Barchard St. SW18 . . 3D 101
Barchester St. E14. . . 4D 67
Barclay Cl. SW6. . . . . 3C 86
Barclay Ho. *E9* *4E 51*
  (off Well St.)
Barclay Path E17 . . . . 1E 39
Barclay Rd. E11. . . . . 3B 40
  (not continuous)
  E13 . . . . 3E 69
  E17 . . . . 1E 39
  SW6 . . . . 3C 86
Barcombe Av. SW2 . . 2A 118
Bardell Ho. *SE16* *3C 78*
  (off Dickens Est.)
Bardolph Rd. N7 . . . . 1A 48
Bard Rd. W10 . . . . . . 1F 71
Bardsey Pl. *E1* *3E 65*
  (off Mile End Rd.)
Bardsey Wlk. *N1* *3E 49*
  (off Douglas Rd. Nth.)
Bardsley Ho. *SE10* . . . *2E 95*
  (off Bardsley La.)
Bardsley La. SE10 . . . 2E 95
Barents Ho. *E1* *3F 65*
  (off White Horse La.)
Barfett St. W10 . . . . 3B 58
Barfield Rd. E11. . . . . 3B 40
Barfleur Ho. SE8 . . . . 1B 94
Barford St. N1 . . . . . . 5C 48
Barforth Rd. SE15 . . 1D 107
Barge Ho. St.
  SE1 . . . . . . 2C 76 (1C 24)
Bargery Rd. SE6 . . . 1D 123
Bargrove Cres. SE6 . . 2B 122
Barham Ho. *SE17*. . . . *1A 92*
  (off Kinglake St.)
Baring Cl. SE12 . . . . 2C 124
Baring Ho. *E14*. *5C 66*
  (off Canton St.)
Baring Rd. SE12. . . . 5C 110
Baring St. N1 . . . . . . 5F 49
Barker Dr. NW1 . . . . . 4E 47
Barker M. SW4 . . . . . 2D 103
Barkers Arc. W8. . . . . 3D 73
Barker St. SW10. . . . . 2E 87
Barker Wlk. SW16 . . . 3F 117
Barkham Ter. SE1. . . . 5C 24
Barking Rd E6. . . . . . 1F 69
Barking Rd. E13 . . . . 1E 69
  E16 . . . . 4B 68
  (not continuous)
Bark Pl. W2 . . . . 1D 73
Barkston Gdns. SW5 . . 5D 73

Barkway Ct. N4. . . . . . 4E 35
Barkwith Ho. *SE14* . . . *2F 93*
  (off Cold Blow La.)
Barkworth Rd. SE16. . . 1D 93
Barlborough St. SE14. . 3F 93
Barlby Gdns. W10 . . . 3F 57
Barlby Rd. W10 . . . . . 4E 57
Barleycorn Way E14. . . 1B 80
Barley Mow Pas. EC1. . 5E 9
  W4 . . . . 1A 84
Barley Shotts Bus. Pk.
  W10 . . . . 4B 58
Barling *NW1*. *3D 47*
  (off Castlehaven Rd.)
Barlings Ho. *SE4* *2F 107*
  (off Frendsbury Rd.)
Barlow Dr. SE18 . . . . 4F 97
Barlow Ho. *N1* *1B 10*
  (off Fairbank Est.)
  SE16. . . . . *5D 79*
  (off Rennie Est.)
  W11 . . . . *1A 72*
  (off Walmer Rd.)
Barlow Pl. W1. . 1D 75 (5E 13)
Barlow Rd. NW6 . . . . 3B 44
Barlow St. SE17 . . . . 5F 77
Barmeston Rd. SE6 . . 2D 123
Barmouth Rd. SW18 . . 4E 101
Barnabas Rd. E9. . . . 2F 51
Barnaby Ct. *SE16*. . . . *3C 78*
  (off Scott Lidgett Cres.)
Barnaby Pl. *SW7* *5F 73*
  (off Brompton Rd.)
Barnard Gro. E15. . . . 4B 54
Barnard Ho. *E2* *2D 65*
  (off Ellsworth St.)
Barnard Lodge *W9*. . . . *4C 58*
  (off Admiral Wlk.)
Barnard M. SW11 . . . 2A 102
Barnardo Gdns. E1. . . 1F 79
Barnardo St. E1 . . . . 5F 65
Barnard Rd. SW11. . . 2A 102
Barnards Ho. *SE16*. . . *3B 80*
  (off Wyatt Cl.)
Barnard's Inn EC4 . . . 1C 16
  (not continuous)
Barnbrough *NW1* *5E 47*
  (off Camden St.)
Barnby Sq. E15 . . . . . 5A 54
Barnby St. E15. . . . . . 5A 54
  NW1. . . . . . . 1E 61 (1A 6)
Barn Cl. *NW5* *2F 47*
  (off Torriano Av.)
Barn Elms Pk. SW15 . . 1E 99
BARNES **5B 84**
Barnes Av. SW13 . . . . 3C 84
Barnes Cl. E12 . . . . . 1F 55
Barnes Ct. E16 . . . . . 4E 69
  N1. . . . . 4C 48
Barnes High St. SW13. . 5B 84
Barnes Ho. *SE14* *2F 93*
  (off John Williams Cl.)
Barnes St. E14 . . . . . 5A 66
Barnes Ter. SE8 . . . . 1B 94
Barnet Gro. E2 . . . . . 2C 64
Barnett St. E1. . . . . . 5D 65
Barney Cl. SE7 . . . . . 1E 97
Barn Fld. NW3 . . . . . 2B 46
Barnfield Cl. N4 . . . . . 2A 34
  SW17 . . . . 3F 115

Barnfield Pl. E14 . . . . . . 5C 80
Barnham St.
　SE1 . . . . 3A 78 (3E 27)
BARNSBURY 4B 48
Barnsbury Est. N1 . . . . . 5B 48
　(not continuous)
Barnsbury Gro. N7 . . . . . 4B 48
Barnsbury Ho. SW4 . . 4F 103
Barnsbury Pk. N1 . . . . . 4C 48
Barnsbury Rd. N1 . . . . . 1C 62
Barnsbury Sq. N1 . . . . . 4C 48
Barnsbury St. N1 . . . . . 4C 48
Barnsbury Ter. N1 . . . . . 4C 48
Barnsdale Av. E14 . . . . . 5D 81
Barnsdale Rd. W9 . . . . . 3B 58
Barnsley St. E1 . . . . 3D 65
Barnstable La. SE13. . 2E 109
Barnstaple Ho. SE10 . . 3D 95
　(off Devonshire St.)
　SE12 . . . . 3B 110
　(off Taunton Rd.)
Barnston Wlk. N1 . . . . . 5E 49
　(off Popham St.)
Barn St. N16. . . . . 4A 36
Barnwell Ho. SE5 . . . . . 4A 92
　(off St Giles Rd.)
Barnwell Rd. SW2 . . . 3C 104
Barnwood Cl. W9. . . . . 3D 59
Baroness Rd.
　E2 . . . . 2B 64 (1F 11)
Baronsclere Ct. N6 . . . . 2E 33
BARONS COURT 1A 86
Baron's Ct. Rd. W14 . . 1A 86
Barons Court Theatre . . 1A 86
　(off Comeragh Rd.)
Barons Keep W14 . . . . . 1A 86
Baronsmead Rd. SW13. . 4C 84
Baron's Pl.
　SE1 . . . . 3C 76 (4C 24)
Baron St. N1 . . . . 1C 62
Baron Wlk. E16 . . . . . . 4B 68
Barque M. SE8 . . . . 2C 94
Barratt Ho. N1 . . . . 4D 49
　(off Sable St.)
Barratt Ind. Pk. E3 . . . 3E 67
Barret Ho. NW6 . . . . . . 5C 44
　SW9 . . . . 1B 104
　(off Benedict Rd.)
Barrett Ho. SE17 . . . . . . 1E 91
　(off Browning St.)
Barrett's Gro. N16 . . . . . 2A 50
Barrett St. W1 . . 5C 60 (3C 12)
Barrhill Rd. SW2 . . . . . 2A 118
Barriedale SE14 . . . . . . 5A 94
Barrie Est. W2 . . . . 1F 73
Barrie Ho. W2 . . . . 1E 73
　(off Lancaster Ga.)
Barrier App. SE7 . . . . . . 4F 83
Barrier Point Rd. E16. . 2E 83
Barringer Sq. SW17. . 4C 116
Barrington Cl. NW5 . . . 2C 46
Barrington Rd. NW5 . . . 2C 46
　SW4 . . . . 5A 90
Barrington Rd. SW9. . 1D 105
Barrow Ct. SE6 . . . . . . 1B 124
　(off Cumberland Pl.)
Barrowgate Rd. W4 . . . 1A 84
Barrow Hill Est. NW8. . 1A 60
　(off Barrow Hill Rd.)
Barrow Hill Rd. NW8 . . 1A 60

Barrow Rd. SW16. . . . . 5F 117
Barry Av. N15 . . . . 1B 36
Barry Ho. SE16 . . . . 5D 79
　(off Rennie Est.)
Barry Rd. SE22. . . . . . 4C 106
Barset Rd. SE15 . . . . . . 1E 107
　(not continuous)
Barston Rd. SE27. . . . 3E 119
Barstow Cres. SW2 . . 1B 118
Barter St. WC1. . 4A 62 (1E 15)
Bartholomew Cl.
　EC1. . . . . 4E 63 (1E 17)
　(not continuous)
　SW18 . . . . 2E 101
Bartholomew Ct. E14 . . 1F 81
　(off Newport Av.)
　EC1 . . . . 3A 10
　(off Old St.)
Bartholomew La.
　EC2. . . . . 5F 63 (3C 18)
Bartholomew Pl. EC1 . . 1F 17
Bartholomew Rd. NW5. . 3E 47
Bartholomew Sq. E1 . . 3D 65
　EC1 . . . . 3E 63 (3A 10)
Bartholomew St. SE1 . . 4F 77
Bartholomew Vs. NW5. . 3E 47
Bartle Rd. W11 . . . . 5A 58
Bartlett Cl. E14. . . . . . . 5C 66
Bartlett Ct. EC4 . . 5C 62 (2C 16)
Bartletts Pas. EC4 . . . . 2C 16
　(off Fetter La.)
Barton Cl. E9 . . . . 2E 51
　SE15 . . . . 1D 107
Barton Ct. W14. . . . . . . 1A 86
　(off Baron's Ct. Rd.)
Barton Ho. N1 . . . . 4D 49
　(off Sable St.)
　SW6 . . . . 1D 101
　(off Wandsworth Bri. Rd.)
Barton Rd. W14 . . . . . . 1A 86
Barton St.
　SW1. . . . . 4A 76 (5D 23)
Bartonway NW8 . . . . . . 5F 45
　(off Queen's Ter.)
Bartram Rd. SE4 . . . . . 3A 108
Bartrip St. E9 . . . . 3B 52
Barville Cl. SE4 . . . . . . 2A 108
Barwell Ho. E2. . . . . 3C 64
　(off Menotti St.)
Barwick Rd. E7 . . . . . . 1D 55
Bascombe St. SW2 . . 4C 104
Basevi Way SE8. . . . . . 2C 94
Bashley Rd. NW10. . . . 3A 56
Basildon Ct. W1. . . . . . . 5C 4
　(off Devonshire St.)
Basil Gdns. SE27 . . . . 5E 119
Basil Ho. SW8 . . . . 3A 90
　(off Wyvil Rd.)
Basil St. SW3 . . 4B 74 (5A 20)
Basin App. E14. . . . . . . 5A 66
Basing Ct. SE15. . . . . . 4B 92
Basingdon Way SE5 . . 2F 105
Basinghall Av.
　EC2. . . . . 5F 63 (2B 18)
Basinghall St.
　EC2. . . . . 5F 63 (2B 18)
Basing Hill NW11. . . . . 3B 30
Basing Ho. Yd.
　E2. . . . . 2A 64 (1E 11)
Basing Pl. E2. . . 2A 64 (1E 11)

Basing St. W11 . . . . 5B 58
Basire St. N1 . . . . 5E 49
Baskerville Gdns.
　NW10 . . . . 1A 42
Baskerville Rd. SW18. . 5A 102
Basket Gdns. SE9 . . . . 3F 111
Baslow Wlk. E5 . . . . 1F 51
Basnett Rd. SW11 . . . 1C 102
Basque Ct. SE16. . . . . . 3F 79
　(off Garter Way)
Bassano St. SE22. . . . 3B 106
Bassein Pk. Rd. W12. . 3B 70
Bassett Rd. E7 . . . . 1F 55
　W10. . . . . 5F 57
Bassett St. NW5. . . . . . 3C 46
Bassingbourn Ho. N1. . 4C 48
　(off Sutton Est., The)
Bassingham Rd. SW18. . 5E 101
Bassishaw Highwalk
　EC2 . . . . 1A 18
Basswood Cl. SE15 . . 1D 107
Basterfield Ho. EC1 . . . 4F 9
　(off Golden La. Est.)
Bastion Highwalk EC2 . . 1F 17
Bastion Ho. EC2 . . . . . . 1A 18
　(off London Wall)
Bastwick St. EC1. . 3E 63 (3F 9)
Basuto Rd. SW6. . . . . . 4C 86
Batavia Ho. SE14 . . . . . 3A 94
　(off Batavia Rd.)
Batavia M. SE14 . . . . . 3A 94
Batavia Rd. SE14 . . . . . 3A 94
Batchelor St. N1 . . . . . . 5C 48
Bateman Ho. SE11. . . . 2D 91
　(off Otto St.)
Bateman's Bldgs. W1 . . 3B 14
Bateman's Row
　EC2 . . . . 3A 64 (3E 11)
Bateman St. W1. . 5F 61 (3B 14)
Bates Point E13 . . . . 5C 54
　(off Pelly Rd.)
Bate St. E14 . . . . 1B 80
Bath Cl. SE15. . . . . 3D 93
Bath Ct. EC1 . . . . 2B 10
　(off St Lukes Est.)
　SE26 . . . . 3C 120
　(off Droitwich Cl.)
Bathgate Rd. SW19 . . 3F 113
Bath Gro. E2. . . . . 1C 64
　(off Horatio St.)
Bath Ho. E2 . . . . 3C 64
　(off Ramsey St.)
　SE1 . . . . 5A 26
　(off Bath Ter.)
Bath Pl. EC2 . . 2A 64 (2D 11)
　W6 . . . . 1E 85
　(off Peabody Est.)
Bath Rd. E7. . . . . 3F 55
　W4 . . . . 5A 70
Baths App. SW6. . . . . . 3B 86
Bath St. EC1 . . 2E 63 (2A 10)
Bath Ter. SE1 . . 4E 77 (5F 25)
Bathurst Gdns.
　NW10 . . . . 1D 57
Bathurst Ho. W12 . . . . . 1D 71
　(off White City Est.)
Bathurst M. W2 . . . . . . 5F 59
Bathurst St. W2 . . . . . . 1F 73
Batley Pl. N16 . . . . 5B 36
Batley Rd. N16. . . . . . . 5B 36

Batman Cl. W12 . . . . .2D **71**
Batoum Gdns. W6 . . . . .4E **71**
Batson Rd. E1. . . . . .5C **64**
 (off Fairclough St.)
Batson St. W12 . . . . .3D **70**
Battenberg Wlk. SE19. .5A **120**
Batten Ho. SW4 . . . . . . .3E **103**
 W10 . . . . .2A **58**
 (off Third Av.)
Batten St. SW11 . . . . . .1A **102**
Battersby Rd. SE6. . . . . .2F **123**
BATTERSEA **4C 88**
Battersea Bri. SW3. . . . . .3F **87**
 SW11 . . . . .3A **88**
Battersea Bri. Rd.
 SW11 . . . . .3A **88**
Battersea Bus. Cen.
 SW11 . . . . .1C **102**
Battersea Chu. Rd.
 SW11 . . . . .4F **87**
Battersea Dogs' Home
 . . . .**3D 89**
Battersea High St.
 SW11 . . . . .4F **87**
 (not continuous)
Battersea Pk. **3B 88**
Battersea Pk. Children's Zoo
 . . . .**3C 88**
Battersea Pk. Rd.
 SW8 . . . . .4C **88**
 SW11 . . . . .5A **88**
Battersea Ri. SW11 . .3A **102**
Battersea Sq. SW11 . . . .4F **87**
Battishill St. N1. . . . . . . .4D **49**
Battlebridge Ct. *N1* . . .1A **62**
 (off Wharfdale Rd.)
Battle Bri. Rd. NW1 . . .1A **62**
Battle Cl. SW19 . . . . . . .5E **115**
Battledean Rd. N5 . . . . .2D **49**
Battle Ho. *SE15* 2C **92**
 (off Haymerle Rd.)
Batty St. E1. . . . . .5C **64**
Baudwin Rd. SE6 . . . . .2A **124**
Baulk, The SW18 . . . . . .5C **100**
Bavaria Rd. N19. . . . . . . .4A **34**
 (not continuous)
Bavent Rd. SE5 . . . . .5E **91**
Bawdale Rd. SE22 . . . .3B **106**
Bawtree Rd. SE14 . . . . . .3A **94**
Baxendale St. E2 . . . . . . .2C **64**
Baxter Rd. E16 . . . . .5E **69**
 N1 . . . . .3F **49**
Bay Ct. *E1* 3F **65**
 (off Frimley St.)
Bayer Ho. *EC1*. 4F **9**
 (off Golden La. Est.)
Bayes Ct. *NW3* 4B **46**
 (off Primrose Hill Rd.)
Bayfield Ho. *SE4*. 2F **107**
 (off Coston Wlk.)
Bayfield Rd. SE9. . . . . .2F **111**
Bayford Ho. *N8*. 4D **51**
 (off Bayford St.)
Bayford Rd. NW10 . . . . .2F **57**
Bayford St. E8 . . . . .4D **51**
Bayford St. Bus. Cen.
 E8. . . . . .4D **51**
 (off Sidworth St.)

Bayham Pl. NW1 . . . . . . .5E **47**
Bayham Rd. W4 . . . . . . .4A **70**
Bayham St. NW1 . . . . . . .5E **47**
Bayley St. WC1. .4F **61** (1B **14**)
Baylis Rd. SE1. .3C **76** (4B **24**)
Baynes M. NW3 . . . . . . .3F **45**
Baynes St. NW1 . . . . . . .4E **47**
Bayonne Rd. W6 . . . . . . .2A **86**
Bays Cl. SE26. . . . . . . .5E **121**
Bayston Rd. N16 . . . . . . .5B **36**
BAYSWATER **1E 73**
Bayswater Rd. W2. . . . . .1D **73**
Baythorne St. E3 . . . . . .4B **66**
Bayton Ct. *E8* 4C **50**
 (off Lansdowne Dr.)
Baytree Cl. SW2. . . . . . .2B **104**
Baytree Rd. SW2 . . . . . .2B **104**
Bazalgette Ho. *NW8* . . .3F **59**
 (off Orchardson St.)
Bazeley Ho. *SE1* 4D **25**
 (off Library St.)
Bazely St. E14 . . . . .1E **81**
BBC Broadcasting House
 . . . .**4D 61** (1E **13**)
Beacham Cl. SE7 . . . . . .1F **97**
Beachborough Rd.
 BR1: Brom 4E **123**
Beachcroft Rd. E11 . . . . .5A **40**
Beachcroft Way N19. . . .3F **33**
Beach Ho. *SW5* 1C **86**
 (off Philbeach Gdns.)
Beachy Rd. E3 . . . . .4C **52**
Beacon Ga. SE14 . . . . .1F **107**
Beacon Hill N7 . . . . .2A **48**
Beacon Ho. *E14* 1D **95**
 (off Burrells Wharf Sq.)
 SE5 . . . . .3A **92**
 (off Southampton Way)
Beacon Rd. SE13 . . . . . .4F **109**
Beaconsfield Cl. SE3 . . .2C **96**
Beaconsfield Rd. E10. . .4E **39**
 E16 . . . . .3B **68**
 E17 . . . . .1B **38**
 NW10 . . . . .3B **42**
 SE3 . . . . .3B **96**
 SE9 . . . . .2F **125**
 SE17 . . . . .1F **91**
Beaconsfield Ter. Rd.
 W14 . . . . .4A **72**
Beaconsfield Wlk. SW6. .4B **86**
Beacontree Rd. E11 . . . .3B **40**
Beadman St. SE27 . . . .4D **119**
Beadnell Rd. SE23 . . . .1F **121**
Beadon Rd. W6 . . . . . . .5E **71**
Beak St. W1 . . .1E **75** (4A **14**)
Beale Pl. E3 . . . . .1B **66**
Beale Rd. E3 . . . . .5B **52**
Beaminster Ho. SW8. .3B **90**
 (off Dorset Rd.)
Beamish Ho. *SE16*. 5D **79**
 (off Rennie Est.)
Beanacre Cl. E9 . . . . . . .3B **52**
Bear All. EC4 . .5D **63** (2D **17**)
Beardell St. SE19 . . . . .5B **120**
Beardsfield E13 . . . . .1C **68**
Bear Gdns. SE1. .2E **77** (1F **25**)
Bear La. SE1. . .2D **77** (1F **25**)
Bearstead Ri. SE4 . . . . .3B **108**
Bear St. WC2. . .1F **75** (4C **14**)
Beaton Cl. SE15. . . . . . .4B **92**

Beatrice Cl. E13. . . . . . .3C **68**
Beatrice Ho. *W6*. 1E **85**
 (off Queen Caroline St.)
Beatrice Pl. W8 . . . . . . .4D **73**
Beatrice Rd. E17 . . . . . . .1C **38**
 N4. . . . . .2C **34**
 SE1 . . . . .5C **78**
Beatrix Ho. *SW5* 1D **87**
 (off Old Brompton Rd.)
Beatson Wlk. SE16 . . . .2A **80**
 (not continuous)
Beattie Ho. SW8. . . . . . .4E **89**
Beatty Ho. *E14*. 3C **80**
 (off Admirals Way)
 NW1 . . . . .3E **61** (3F **5**)
 SW1 . . . . .1E **89**
 (off Dolphin Sq.)
Beatty Rd. N16. . . . . .1A **50**
Beatty St. NW1 . . . . .1E **61**
Beauchamp Pl. SW3 . . .4A **74**
Beauchamp Rd. E7 . . . .4D **55**
 SW11 . . . . .2A **102**
Beauchamp St.
 EC1 . . . . .4C **62** (1B **16**)
Beauchamp Ter. SW15. .1D **99**
Beauclerc Rd. W6 . . . . . .4D **71**
Beauclerk Ho. SW16. . .3A **118**
Beaufort Cl. SW15. . . . . .5D **99**
Beaufort Ct. *E14*. 3C **80**
 (off Admirals Way)
Beaufort Gdns. NW4 . . .1E **29**
 SW3 . . . . .4A **74**
Beaufort Ho. *E16* 1D **83**
 (off Fairfax M.)
 SW1 . . . . .1F **89**
 (off Aylesford St.)
Beaufort M. SW6 . . . . . .2B **86**
Beaufort St. SW3 . . . . . .2F **87**
Beaufort Ter. *E14* 1E **95**
 (off Ferry St.)
Beaufoy Ho. SE27 . . . .3D **119**
 SW8 . . . . .3B **90**
 (off Rita Rd.)
Beaufoy Wlk. SE11 . . . .5B **76**
Beaulieu Av. E16 . . . . . .2D **83**
 SE26. . . . . .4D **121**
Beaulieu Cl. SE5 . . . . . .1F **105**
Beaulieu Lodge *E14*. . . .4F **81**
 (off Schooner Cl.)
Beaumaris Grn. NW9. . . .1A **28**
Beaumont *W14*. 5B **72**
 (off Kensington Village)
Beaumont Av. W14 . . . . .1B **86**
Beaumont Bldgs. *WC2*. .3E **15**
 (off Martlett Ct.)
Beaumont Ct. E5 . . . . . .5D **37**
 W1 . . . . .5C **4**
 (off Beaumont St.)
Beaumont Cres. W14. . . .1B **86**
Beaumont Gdns. NW3 . .5C **30**
Beaumont Gro. E1 . . . . .3F **65**
Beaumont Ho. E10. . . . .2D **39**
 E15. . . . . .5B **54**
 (off John St.)
Beaumont Lodge *E8*. . . .3C **50**
 (off Greenwood Rd.)
Beaumont M.
 W1. . . . . .4C **60** (5C **4**)
Beaumont Pl.
 W1 . . . . .3E **61** (3A **6**)

Beaumont Ri. N19 . . . . . 3F **33**
Beaumont Rd. E10. . . . 2D **39**
    (not continuous)
E13. . . . . 2D **69**
SW19 . . . . 5A **100**
Beaumont Sq. E1 . . . . 4F **65**
Beaumont St.
  W1. . . . . 4C **60** (5C **4**)
Beaumont Ter. SE13. . . 5A **110**
    (off Wellmeadow Rd.)
Beaumont Wlk. NW3 . . 4B **46**
Beauvale NW1 . . . . 4C **46**
    (off Ferdinand St.)
Beauval Rd. SE22 . . . . 4B **106**
Beaux Arts Building N7. . 5A **34**
Beavor Gro. W6 . . . . . . 1C **84**
    (off Beavor La.)
Beavor La. W6 . . . . 1C **84**
Beccles St. E14 . . . . . . 5B **66**
Bechervaise Ct. E10. . . 3D **39**
    (off Leyton Grange Est.)
Bechtel Ho. W6. . . . . . . 5F **71**
    (off Hammersmith Rd.)
Beck Cl. SE13. . . . . 4D **95**
Beckenham Bus. Cen.
  BR3: Beck. 5A **122**
Beckenham Hill Est.
  BR3: Beck. 5D **123**
Beckenham Hill Rd.
  BR3: Beck. 5D **123**
  SE6. . . . . 5D **123**
Beckers, The N16. . . . . 1C **50**
Becket Ho. E16. . . . . . . 1D **83**
    (off Constable Av.)
SE1 . . . . 4B **26**
Becket St. SE1 . 4F **77** (5B **26**)
Beckett Cl. NW10. . . . . 3A **42**
  SW16 . . . . 2F **117**
Beckett Ho. E1 . . . . 4E **65**
    (off Jubilee St.)
SW9 . . . . 5A **90**
Beckfoot NW1 . . . . 1A **6**
    (off Ampthill Est.)
Beckford Cl. W14. . . . . 5B **72**
Beckford Ho. N16. . . . . 2A **50**
Beckford Pl. SE17. . . . . 1E **91**
Becklow Gdns. W12. . . 3C **70**
    (off Becklow Rd.)
Becklow M. W12 . . . . . 3C **70**
    (off Becklow Rd.)
Becklow Rd. W12 . . . . . 3B **70**
    (not continuous)
Beck Rd. E8 . . . . 5D **51**
Beckton Rd. E16. . . . . . 4B **68**
Beckway St. SE17 . . . . 5A **78**
    (not continuous)
Beckwith Rd. SE24 . . . . 3F **105**
Beclands Rd. SW17. . . 5C **116**
Becmead Av. SW16 . . . 4F **117**
Becondale Rd. SE19 . . 5A **120**
Becquerel Ct. SE10 . . . 4B **82**
Bective Pl. SW15 . . . . . 2B **100**
Bective Rd. E7 . . . . 1C **54**
  SW15 . . . . 2B **100**
Bedale St. SE1. . 2F **77** (2B **26**)
Beddalls Farm Ct. E6 . . 4F **69**
Bedefield WC1. . . 2A **62** (2E **7**)
Bede Ho. SE4 . . . . 4B **94**
    (off Clare Rd.)

Bedford Av.
  WC1. . . . . 4F **61** (1C **14**)
Bedfordbury
  WC2. . . . . 1A **76** (4D **15**)
Bedford Cl. W4. . . . . . . 2A **84**
Bedford Cnr. W4. . . . . . 5A **70**
    (off South Pde.)
Bedford Ct.
  WC2. . . . . 1A **76** (5D **15**)
    (not continuous)
Bedford Ct. Mans.
  WC1 . . . . 1C **14**
Bedford Gdns. W8 . . . . 2C **72**
Bedford Hill SW12. . . 1D **117**
  SW16 . . . . 1D **117**
Bedford Ho. SW4 . . . . 2A **104**
    (off Solon New Rd. Est.)
Bedford M. SE6 . . . . . 2D **123**
BEDFORD PARK 4A **70**
Bedford Pk. Cnr. W4 . . 5A **70**
Bedford Pk. Mans. W4. . 5A **70**
Bedford Pas. SW6 . . . . 3A **86**
    (off Dawes Rd.)
W1. . . . . 4E **61** (5A **6**)
Bedford Pl.
  WC1. . . . . 4A **62** (5D **7**)
Bedford Rd. N8. . . . . . . 1F **33**
SW4 . . . . 2A **104**
W4 . . . . 4A **70**
Bedford Row
  WC1. . . . . 4B **62** (5A **8**)
Bedford Sq.
  WC1. . . . . 4F **61** (1C **14**)
Bedford St.
  WC2. . . . . 1A **76** (4D **15**)
Bedford Ter. SW4. . . . 3A **104**
Bedford Way
  WC1. . . . . 3F **61** (4C **6**)
Bedgebury Gdns.
  SW19 . . . . 2A **114**
Bedgebury Rd. SE9 . . . 2F **111**
Bedivere Rd.
  BR1: Brom 3C **124**
Bedlam M. SE11 . . . . . . 5C **76**
    (off Walnut Tree Wlk.)
Bedmond Ho. SW3. . . . 1A **88**
    (off Ixworth Pl.)
Bedser Cl. SE11. . . . . . 2B **90**
Bedwell Ho. SW9. . . . . 5C **90**
Beeby Rd. E16 . . . . 4D **69**
Beech Av. W3. . . . . 2A **70**
Beech Cl. SE8 . . . . 2C **94**
  SW15 . . . . 5C **98**
  SW19 . . . . 5E **113**
Beech Ct. W9 . . . . 4C **58**
    (off Elmfield Way)
Beech Cres. Ct. N5 . . . 1D **49**
Beechcroft Av. NW11. . 2B **30**
Beechcroft Cl.
  SW16 . . . . 5B **118**
Beechcroft Ct. NW11. . 2B **30**
    (off Beechcroft Av.)
Beechcroft Rd. SW17. . 3A **116**
Beechdale Rd. SW2. . . 4B **104**
Beechdene SE15 . . . . . 4D **93**
    (off Carlton Gro.)
Beechen Pl. SE23. . . . 2F **121**
Beeches Rd. SW17 . . . 3A **116**
Beechey Ho. E1 . . . . . . 2D **79**
    (off Watts St.)

Beechfield Rd. N4 . . . . 1E **35**
SE6. . . . . 1B **122**
Beech Gdns. EC2 . . . . . 5F **9**
    (off Beech St.)
Beech Ho. SE16 . . . . . . 3E **79**
    (off Ainsty Est.)
Beechmont Cl.
  BR1: Brom 5A **124**
Beechmore Rd. SW11 . 4B **88**
Beecholme Est. E5. . . . 5D **37**
Beech St. EC2 . . 4E **63** (5F **9**)
Beech Tree Cl. N1 . . . . 4C **48**
Beechwood Gro. W3 . . 1A **70**
Beechwood Ho. E2. . . . 1C **64**
    (off Teale St.)
Beechwood Rd. E8. . . . 3B **50**
Beechwoods Ct. SE19. . 5B **120**
Beechworth NW6 . . . . . 4A **44**
Beechworth Cl. NW3 . . 4C **30**
Beecroft La. SE4 . . . . 3A **108**
Beecroft M. SE4 . . . . . 3A **108**
Beecroft Rd. SE4 . . . . 3A **108**
Beehive Cl. E8 . . . . 4B **50**
Beehive Pl. SW9 . . . . . 1C **104**
Beemans Row SW18 . . 2E **115**
Bee Pas. EC3. . . . . 3D **19**
    (off Lime St.)
Beeston Cl. E8. . . . . . . 2C **50**
Beeston Ho. SE1 . . . . . 5B **26**
Beeston Pl.
  SW1. . . . . 4D **75** (5E **21**)
Beethoven St. W10 . . . 2A **58**
Begbie Rd. SE3 . . . . . . 4E **97**
Begonia Wlk. W12. . . . 5B **56**
Beira St. SW12 . . . . . 5D **103**
Bekesbourne St. E14 . . 5A **66**
Beldanes Lodge NW10. . 4C **42**
Belfast Rd. N16. . . . . . 4B **36**
Belfont Wlk. N7 . . . . . . 1A **48**
    (not continuous)
Belford Ho. E8 . . . . 5B **50**
Belfort Rd. SE15. . . . . . 5E **93**
Belfry Cl. SE16. . . . . . . 1D **93**
Belfry Rd. E12 . . . . 4F **41**
Belgrade Rd. N16 . . . . 1A **50**
Belgrave Ct. E13 . . . . . 3E **69**
E14 . . . . 1B **80**
    (off Westferry Cir.)
SW8 . . . . 3E **89**
    (off Ascalon St.)
Belgrave Gdns. NW8 . . 5D **45**
Belgrave Hgts. E11 . . . 3C **40**
Belgrave Ho. SW9 . . . . 3C **90**
Belgrave M. Nth.
  SW1. . . . . 3C **74** (4B **20**)
Belgrave M. Sth.
  SW1. . . . . 4C **74** (5C **20**)
Belgrave M. W.
  SW1. . . . . 4C **74** (5B **20**)
Belgrave Pl.
  SW1. . . . . 4C **74** (5C **20**)
Belgrave Rd. E10. . . . . 3E **39**
E11 . . . . 4C **40**
E13 . . . . 3E **69**
E17 . . . . 1C **38**
SW1 . . . . 5D **75**
SW13 . . . . 3B **84**
Belgrave Sq.
  SW1. . . . . 4C **74** (5B **20**)
Belgrave St. E1. . . . . . . 4F **65**

Belgrave Yd. SW1 . . . . . .5D **21**
BELGRAVIA **4C 74**
Belgravia Ct. *SW1* 4D **75**
(off Ebury St.)
Belgravia Gdns.
BR1: Brom 5A **124**
Belgravia Ho. *SW1*. *5B* **20**
(off Halkin Pl.)
SW4 . . . . .4F **103**
Belgravia Workshops
N19 . . . .*4A* **34**
(off Marlborough Rd.)
Belgrove St.
NW1 . . . . .2A **62** (1E **7**)
Belham Wlk. SE5 . . . . . .4F **91**
Belinda Rd. SW9 . . . . . .1D **105**
Belitha Vs. N1 . . . . .4B **48**
Bellamy Cl. E14 . . . . . . .3C **80**
W14 . . . . .1B **86**
Bellamy's Ct. *SE16* *2F* **79**
(off Abbotshade Rd.)
Bellamy St. SW12 . . . . .5D **103**
Bellasis Av. SW2 . . . . . .2A **118**
Bell Dr. SW18. . . . . .5A **100**
Bellefields Rd. SW9. . . . .1B **104**
Bellenden Rd. SE15. . . . .4B **92**
Belleville Rd. SW11. . . . .3A **102**
Bellevue Pl. E1. . . . . . . .3E **65**
Bellevue Rd. SW13 . . . . .5C **84**
SW17 . . . . .1A **116**
Bellew St. SW17 . . . . . .3E **115**
Bellflower Ct. E6. . . . . . .4F **69**
Bell Gdns. *E10* *3C* **38**
(off Church Rd.)
Bellgate M. NW5 . . . . . .1D **47**
BELL GREEN **4A 122**
Bell Grn. SE26 . . . . .4B **122**
Bell Grn. La. SE26 . . . . .5B **122**
Bell Ho. *SE10* *2E* **95**
(off Haddo St.)
Bellina M. NW5 . . . . . . .1D **47**
BELLINGHAM **3C 122**
Bellingham Grn. SE6 . . . .3C **122**
Bellingham Rd. SE6. . . . .3D **123**
Bellingham Trad. Est.
SE6. . . . . .3D **123**
Bell Inn Yd. EC3. .5F **63** (3C **18**)
Bell La. E1. . . . . .4B **64** (1F **19**)
E16 . . . . .2B **82**
Bellmaker Ct. E3 . . . . . .4C **66**
Bell Mdw. SE19 . . . . . . .5A **120**
Bell Moor *NW3* *5E* **31**
(off E. Heath Rd.)
Bello Cl. SE24 . . . . .5D **105**
Bellot Gdns. *SE10* *1A* **96**
(off Bellot St.)
Bellot St. SE10 . . . . .1A **96**
Bells All. SW6 . . . . .5C **86**
Bell St. NW1 . . . . .4A **60**
SE18 . . . . .4F **97**
Belltrees Gro. SW16 . . . .5B **118**
Bell Wharf La.
EC4 . . . . .1E **77** (5A **18**)
Bellwood Rd. SE15. . . . .2F **107**
Bell Yd. WC2. . . .5C **62** (3B **16**)
Belmont Cl. SW4 . . . . . .1E **103**
Belmont Ct. N5 . . . . .1E **49**
NW11 . . . . .1B **30**
Belmont Gro. SE13 . . . . .1F **109**
W4 . . . . .5A **70**

Belmont Hall Ct. SE13. . .1F **109**
Belmont Hill SE13 . . . . .1E **109**
Belmont M. SW19 . . . . .2F **113**
Belmont Pde. NW11 . . . .1B **30**
Belmont Pk. SE13. . . . . .2F **109**
Belmont Pk. Cl. SE13. .2A **110**
Belmont Pk. Rd. E10. . . .1D **39**
Belmont Rd. SW4. . . . . .1E **103**
Belmont St. NW1 . . . . . .4C **46**
Belmore La. N7 . . . . . . .2F **47**
Belmore St. SW8 . . . . . .4F **89**
Beloe Cl. SW15 . . . . . . .2C **98**
Belsham St. E9. . . . . . . .3E **51**
Belsize Av. NW3 . . . . . . .3F **45**
Belsize Ct. NW3 . . . . . . .2F **45**
Belsize Ct. Garages
NW3 . . . .*2F* **45**
(off Belsize La.)
Belsize Cres. NW3 . . . . .2F **45**
Belsize Gro. NW3. . . . . .3A **46**
Belsize La. NW3 . . . . . . .3F **45**
Belsize M. NW3 . . . . . . .3F **45**
Belsize Pk. NW3 . . . . . . .3F **45**
Belsize Pk. Gdns.
NW3 . . . . .3F **45**
Belsize Pk. M. NW3 . . . .3F **45**
Belsize Pl. NW3 . . . . . . .2F **45**
Belsize Rd. NW6 . . . . . . .5D **45**
Belsize Sq. NW3 . . . . . . .3F **45**
Belsize Ter. NW3 . . . . . .3F **45**
Beltane Dr. SW19 . . . . .3F **113**
Belthorn Cres. SW12 . . .5E **103**
Belton Rd. E7 . . . . .4D **55**
E11 . . . . .1A **54**
NW2 . . . . .3C **42**
Belton Way E3 . . . . .4C **66**
Beltran Rd. SW6 . . . . . . .5D **87**
Belvedere Av. SW19 . . . .5A **114**
Belvedere Bldgs.
SE1 . . . . .3D **77** (4E **25**)
Belvedere Ct. *NW2* *3F* **43**
(off Willesden La.)
SW15 . . . . .2E **99**
Belvedere Dr. SW19. . . . .5A **114**
Belvedere Gro. SW19. .5A **114**
Belvedere M. SE3 . . . . . .3D **97**
SE15 . . . . .1E **107**
Belvedere Pl.
SE1 . . . . .3D **77** (4E **25**)
SW2 . . . . .2B **104**
Belvedere Rd. E10. . . . . .3A **38**
SE1 . . . . .2B **76** (3A **24**)
Belvedere Sq. SW19 . . . .5A **114**
Belvedere, The *SW10* . . .*4E* **87**
(off Chelsea Harbour)
Belvoir Rd. SE22 . . . . . .5C **106**
Bembridge Cl. NW6. . . . .4A **44**
Bembridge Ho. *SE8* *5B* **80**
(off Longshore)
Bemersyde Point *E13* . .*2D* **69**
(off Dongola Rd. W.)
Bemerton Est. N1. . . . . .4A **48**
Bemerton St. N1 . . . . . . .5B **48**
Bemish Rd. SW15 . . . . . .1F **99**
Benbow Cl. *W6*. *4E* **71**
(off Benbow Rd.)
Benbow Ho. *SE8* *2C* **94**
(off Benbow St.)
Benbow Rd. W6 . . . . . . .4D **71**
Benbow St. SE8 . . . . . . .2C **94**

Benbury Cl.
BR1: Brom 5E **123**
Bence Ho. *SE8* *5A* **80**
(off Rainsborough Av.)
Bendall M. *NW1*. *4A* **60**
(off Bell St.)
Bendemeer Rd. SW15 . . .1F **99**
Benden Ho. *SE13* *3E* **109**
(off Monument Gdns.)
Bendish Rd. E6 . . . . .4F **55**
Bendon Valley SW18. .5D **101**
Benedict Rd. SW9 . . . . .1B **104**
Ben Ezra Ct. *SE17* *5E* **77**
(off Asolando Dr.)
Benfleet Ct. E8. . . . . . . .5B **50**
Bengal Ct. *EC3*. *3C* **18**
(off Birchin La.)
Bengal Ho. *E1*. *4F* **65**
(off Duckett St.)
Bengeworth Rd. SE5 . .1E **105**
Benham Cl. SW11 . . . . .1F **101**
Benham's Pl. NW3. . . . . .1E **45**
Benhill Rd. SE5 . . . . .3F **91**
Benhurst Ct. SW16. . . . .5C **118**
Benhurst La. SW16 . . . .5C **118**
Benin St. SE13 . . . . .5F **109**
Benjamin Cl. E8. . . . . . .5C **50**
Benjamin Franklin House
. . . .**1D 23**
(off Craven St.)
Benjamin St.
EC1. . . . . .4D **63** (5D **9**)
Ben Jonson Ct. N1 . . . . .1A **64**
Ben Jonson Ho. EC2 . . . .5A **10**
Ben Jonson Pl. EC2 . . . .5A **10**
Ben Jonson Rd. E1. . . . . .4F **65**
Benledi St. E14. . . . . . . .5F **67**
Bennelong Cl. W12 . . . . .1D **71**
Bennerley Rd. SW11 . .3A **102**
Bennet's Hill
EC4. . . . . .1E **77** (4E **17**)
Bennet St. SW1. . .2E **75** (1F **21**)
Bennett Cl. N7 . . . . .5B **34**
Bennett Gro. SE13 . . . . .4D **95**
Bennett Ho. *SW1* *5F* **75**
(off Page St.)
Bennett Pk. SE3 . . . . . . .1B **110**
Bennett Rd. E13. . . . . . . .3E **69**
N16. . . . . .1A **50**
Bennetts Copse
BR7: Chst 5F **125**
Bennett St. W4 . . . . .2A **84**
Bennett's Yd.
SW1 . . . . .4F **75** (5C **22**)
Benn St. E9 . . . . .3A **52**
Bensbury Cl. SW15 . . . . .5D **99**
Ben Smith Way SE16. . .4C **78**
Benson Av. E6 . . . . .1E **69**
Benson Ho. *E2* *3F* **11**
(off Ligonier St.)
SE1. . . . .*2C* **24**
(off Hatfields)
Benson Quay E1. . . . . . .1E **79**
Benson Rd. SE23 . . . . . .1E **121**
Bentfield Gdns. SE9 . . .3F **125**
Benthal Rd. N16. . . . . . .4C **36**
Bentham Ct. *N1* *4E* **49**
(off Ecclesbourne Rd.)
SE1 . . . . .5B **26**
Bentham Rd. E9 . . . . . . .3F **51**

Bentinck Cl. NW8 . . . . . . 1A **60**
Bentinck Ho. W12 . . . . . 1D **71**
   (off White City Est.)
Bentinck M. W1. . 5C **60** (2C **12**)
Bentinck St.
  W1. . . . . 5C **60** (2C **12**)
Bentley Dr. NW2 . . . . . . 5B **30**
Bentley Ho. SE5 . . . . . . 4A **92**
   (off Peckham Rd.)
Bentley Rd. N1 . . . . 3A **50**
Bentons La. SE27 . . . . 4E **119**
Benton's Ri. SE27 . . . . 5F **119**
Bentworth Cl. W12 . . . . . 5D **57**
   (off Bentworth Rd.)
Bentworth Ct. E2 . . . . . . 3C **64**
   (off Granby St.)
Bentworth Rd. W12 . . . . 5D **57**
Benville Ho. SW8 . . . . . 3B **90**
   (off Oval Pl.)
Benwell Rd. N7 . . . . 1C **48**
Benwick Cl. SE16 . . . . . 5D **79**
Benworth St. E3 . . . . . . 2B **66**
Benyon Ct. N1 . . . . 5A **50**
   (off De Beauvoir Est.)
Benyon Ho. EC1 . . . . 1C **8**
   (off Myddelton Pas.)
Benyon Rd. N1 . . . . 5F **49**
Berberis Ho. E3 . . . . . . 4C **66**
   (off Gale St.)
Berber Pl. E14 . . . . 1C **80**
Berber Rd. SW11 . . . . . 3B **102**
Berenger Twr. SW10 . . . 3F **87**
   (off Worlds End Est.)
Berenger Wlk. SW10 . . . 3F **87**
   (off Worlds End Est.)
Berens Rd. NW10 . . . . . 2F **57**
Beresford Ho. N5 . . . . . 2F **49**
Beresford Ter. N5 . . . . . 2E **49**
Berestede Rd. W6 . . . . . 1B **84**
Bere St. E1 . . . . 1F **79**
Bergen Ho. SE5 . . . . . . 5E **91**
   (off Carew St.)
Bergen Sq. SE16 . . . . . 4A **80**
Berger Rd. E9 . . . . 3F **51**
Berghem M. W14 . . . . . 4F **71**
Bergholt Cres. N16 . . . . 2A **36**
Bergholt M. NW1 . . . . . 4E **47**
Berglen Ct. E14 . . . . . . 5A **66**
Bering Sq. E14 . . . . . . 1C **94**
Bering Wlk. E16 . . . . . . 5F **69**
Berisford M. SW18 . . . 4E **101**
Berkeley Cl. NW1 . . . . . . 4A **4**
  NW10 . . . . 1A **42**
  NW11 . . . . 2B **30**
   (off Ravenscroft Av.)
Berkeley Gdns. W8 . . . . 2C **72**
Berkeley Ho. SE8 . . . . . 1B **94**
   (off Grove St.)
Berkeley M.
  W1. . . . . 5B **60** (3A **12**)
Berkeley Rd. E12 . . . . . 2F **55**
  N8 . . . . 1F **33**
  N15 . . . . 1F **35**
  SW13 . . . . 4C **84**
Berkeley Sq.
  W1. . . . . 1D **75** (5E **13**)
Berkeley St.
  W1. . . . . 1D **75** (5E **13**)
Berkeley Twr. E14 . . . . . 2B **80**
   (off Westferry Cir.)

Berkeley Wlk. N7 . . . . . . 4B **34**
   (off Durham Rd.)
Berkley Gro. NW1 . . . . . 4C **46**
Berkley Rd. NW1 . . . . . 4B **46**
Berkshire Ho. SE6 . . . . 4C **122**
Berkshire Rd. E9 . . . . . 3B **52**
Bermans Way NW10 . . . 1A **42**
BERMONDSEY **3C 78**
Bermondsey Sq.
  SE1 . . . . 4A **78** (5E **27**)
Bermondsey St.
  SE1 . . . . 2A **78** (2D **27**)
Bermondsey Trad. Est.
  SE16 . . . . 1E **93**
Bermondsey Wall E.
  SE16 . . . . 3C **78**
Bermondsey Wall W.
  SE16 . . . . 3C **78**
Bernard Angell Ho.
  SE10 . . . . 2F **95**
   (off Trafalgar Rd.)
Bernard Ashley Dr.
  SE7 . . . . 1D **97**
Bernard Cassidy St.
  E16 . . . . 4B **68**
Bernard Gdns. SW19 . . . 5B **114**
Bernard Mans. WC1 . . . . 4D **7**
   (off Bernard St.)
Bernard Rd. N15 . . . . . 1B **36**
Bernard Shaw Ct. NW1. . 4E **47**
   (off St Pancras Way)
Bernard St.
  WC1 . . . . 3A **62** (4D **7**)
Bernard Sunley Ho.
  SW9 . . . . 3C **90**
   (off Sth. Island Pl.)
Bernays Gro. SW9 . . . . 2B **104**
Berners Ho. N1 . . . . . . 1C **62**
   (off Barnsbury Est.)
Berners M.
  W1. . . . . 4E **61** (1A **14**)
Berners Pl.
  W1. . . . . 5E **61** (2A **14**)
Berners Rd. N1 . . . . . . 5D **49**
Berners St.
  W1. . . . . 4E **61** (1A **14**)
Berner Ter. E1 . . . . 5C **64**
   (off Fairclough St.)
Bernhardt Cres. NW8 . . . 3A **60**
Berridge M. NW6 . . . . . 2C **44**
Berridge Rd. SE19 . . . . 5F **119**
Berriman Rd. N7 . . . . . 5B **34**
Berry Cl. NW10 . . . . . . 4A **42**
Berryfield Rd. SE17 . . . . 1D **91**
Berry Ho. E1 . . . . 3D **65**
   (off Headlam St.)
Berry La. SE21 . . . . . . 4F **119**
Berryman's La. SE26 . . . 4F **121**
Berry Pl. EC1 . . . . 2D **63** (2E **9**)
Berry St. EC1 . . . . 3D **63** (3E **9**)
Bertal Rd. SW17 . . . . . 4F **115**
Berthon St. SE8 . . . . . . 3C **94**
Bertie Rd. NW10 . . . . . 3C **42**
  SE26 . . . . 5F **121**
Bertram Rd. NW4 . . . . . 1C **28**
Bertram St. N19 . . . . . . 4D **33**
Bertrand Ho. SW16 . . . . 3A **118**
   (off Leigham Av.)
Bertrand St. SE13 . . . . 1D **109**
Berwick Rd. E16 . . . . . . 5D **69**

Berwick St. W1. . 5E **61** (2A **14**)
Berwyn Rd. SE24. . . . . 1D **119**
Beryl Rd. W6 . . . . 1F **85**
Besant Cl. NW2 . . . . . . 5A **30**
Besant Ct. N1 . . . . 2F **49**
Besant Ho. NW8 . . . . . . 5E **45**
   (off Boundary Rd.)
Besant Pl. SE15 . . . . . 2B **106**
Besant Rd. NW2 . . . . . 1A **44**
Besant Wlk. N7 . . . . . . 4B **34**
Besford Ho. E2 . . . . . . 1C **64**
   (off Pritchard's Rd.)
Besley St. SW16 . . . . . 5E **117**
Bessborough Gdns.
  SW1 . . . . 1F **89**
Bessborough Pl. SW1 . . 1F **89**
Bessborough Rd.
  SW15 . . . . 1C **112**
Bessborough St. SW1 . . 1F **89**
Bessemer Ct. NW1 . . . . 4E **47**
   (off Rochester Sq.)
Bessemer Rd. SE5 . . . . 5E **91**
Bessingham Wlk. SE4. . 2F **107**
   (off Aldersford Cl.)
Besson St. SE14. . . . . . 4E **93**
Bessy St. E2 . . . . 2E **65**
Bestwood St. SE8 . . . . . 5F **79**
Beswick M. NW6 . . . . . 3D **45**
Beta Pl. SW9 . . . . 2B **104**
Bethal St. SE1 . . . . 2E **27**
Bethell Av. E16 . . . . . . 3B **68**
Bethersden Ho. SE17 . . 1A **92**
   (off Kinglake St.)
Bethlehem Ho. E14 . . . . 1B **80**
   (off Limehouse C'way.)
BETHNAL GREEN **2D 65**
Bethnal Green Mus. of
  Childhood **2E 65**
Bethnal Grn. Rd.
  E1. . . . . 3B **64** (3F **11**)
Bethune Cl. N16 . . . . . . 3A **36**
Bethune Rd. N16 . . . . . 2F **35**
  NW10 . . . . 3A **56**
Bethwin Rd. SE5 . . . . . 3D **91**
Betsham Ho. SE1 . . . . . 3B **26**
   (off Newcomen St.)
Betterton Ho. WC2 . . . . 3E **15**
   (off Betterton St.)
Betterton St.
  WC2. . . . . 5A **62** (3D **15**)
Bettons Pk. E15 . . . . . . 5A **54**
Bettridge Rd. SW6 . . . . 5B **86**
Betts Ho. E1 . . . . 1D **79**
   (off Betts St.)
Betts M. E17 . . . . 1B **38**
Betts Rd. E16 . . . . 1D **83**
Betts St. E1 . . . . 1D **79**
Betty Brooks Ho. E11 . . 5F **39**
Betty May Gray Ho.
  E14 . . . . 5E **81**
   (off Pier St.)
Beulah Hill SE19 . . . . . 5D **119**
Beulah Rd. E17 . . . . . . 1D **39**
Bevan Ho. WC1 . . . . 5E **7**
   (off Boswell St.)
Bevan St. N1 . . . . 5E **49**
Bev Callender Cl.
  SW8 . . . . 1D **103**
Bevenden St. N1. . 2F **63** (1C **10**)
Beveridge Rd. NW10 . . . 4A **42**

Beverley Cl. SW11 . . . . . 2F **101**
SW13 . . . . 5C **84**
Beverley Cotts. SW15. . 3A **112**
Beverley Ct. SE4 . . . . . 1B **108**
(not continuous)
Beverley Gdns. NW11 . . 2A **30**
SW13 . . . . 1B **98**
Beverley Ho.
*BR1: Brom 5F **123**
(off Brangbourne Rd.)*
Beverley La. SW15 . . . . 3B **112**
Beverley Path SW13 . . . 5B **84**
Beverley Rd. E6 . . . . 2F **69**
SW13 . . . . 1B **98**
W4 . . . . 1B **84**
Beversbrook Rd. N19 . . . 5F **33**
Beverstone Rd. SW2 . . 3B **104**
Beverston M. *W1 . . . . . 1A **12***
(off Up. Montagu St.)
Bevill Allen Cl. SW17. . 5B **116**
Bevin Cl. SE16 . . . . 2A **80**
Bevin Cl. WC1 . . . 2B **62** (1A **8**)
Bevington Path *SE1 . . . 4F **27***
(off Tanner St.)
Bevington Rd. W10 . . . . 4A **58**
Bevington St. SE16 . . . . 3C **78**
Bevin Ho. *E2 . . . . 2E **65***
(off Butler St.)
Bevin Sq. SW17 . . . . . . 3B **116**
Bevin Way WC1 . . 1C **62** (1B **8**)
Bevis Marks EC3. . 5A **64** (2E **19**)
Bew Ct. SE22 . . . . 5C **106**
Bewdley St. N1 . . . . 4C **48**
Bewick M. SE15. . . . . . . 3D **93**
Bewick St. SW8 . . . . 5D **89**
Bewley Ho. *E1 . . . . 1D **79***
(off Bewley St.)
Bewley St. E1 . . . . 1E **79**
Bewlys Rd. SE27 . . . . . 5D **119**
Bexhill Rd. SE4 . . . . . . 4B **108**
Bexhill Wlk. E15. . . . . . . 5A **54**
Bexley Ho. SE4. . . . . . . 2A **108**
Bianca Rd. SE15 . . . . . . 2C **92**
Bibury Cl. SE15 . . . . 2A **92**
Bickenhall Mans. NW1 . . 5A **4**
(not continuous)
Bickenhall St. W1 . .4B **60** (5A **4**)
Bickersteth Rd. SW17. . 5B **116**
Bickerton Rd. N19 . . . . . 4E **33**
Bickley Rd. E10 . . . . 2D **39**
Bickley St. SW17 . . . . . 5A **116**
Bicknell Ho. *E1. . . . . . . 5C **64***
(off Ellen St.)
Bicknell Rd. SE5. . . . . . 1E **105**
Bidborough St.
WC1 . . . . 2A **62** (2D **7**)
Biddenham Ho. *SE16 . . 5F **79***
(off Plough Way)
Bidder St. E16 . . . . 3A **68**
(not continuous)
Biddesden Ho. *SW3. . . 5B **74***
(off Cadogan St.)
Biddestone Rd. N7 . . . . 1B **48**
Biddulph Mans. *W9 . . . 2D **59***
(off Elgin Av.)
Biddulph Rd. W9 . . . . . . 2D **59**
Bideford Rd.
*BR1: Brom 3B **124***
Bidwell St. SE15 . . . . . . 4D **93**

Big Ben 3A **76** (4E **23**)
Biggerstaff Rd. E15 . . . . 5E **53**
Biggerstaff St. N4 . . . . . 4C **34**
Biggs Row SW15 . . . . . . 1F **99**
Big Hill E5 . . . . 3D **37**
Bigland St. E1 . . . . 5D **65**
Bignold Rd. E7. . . . . 1C **54**
Bigwood Ct. NW11. . . . . 1D **31**
Bigwood Rd. NW11 . . . . 1D **31**
Bilberry Ho. *E3. . . . . 4C **66***
(off Watts Gro.)
Billingford Cl. SE4 . . . . . 2F **107**
Billing Ho. *E1 . . . . 5F **65***
(off Bower St.)
Billingley *NW1 . . . . 5E **47***
(off Pratt St.)
Billing Pl. SW10 . . . . . . 3D **87**
Billing Rd. SW10. . . . . . 3D **87**
Billing St. SW6 . . . . 3D **87**
Billington Rd. SE14 . . . . 3F **93**
Billiter Sq. EC3. . . . . 3E **19**
Billiter St. EC3. . 5A **64** (3E **19**)
Billson St. E14 . . . . 5E **81**
Bilsby Gro. SE9 . . . . . . 4F **125**
Bilton Towers *W1 . . . . . 3A **12***
(off Gt. Cumberland Pl.)
Bina Gdns. SW5 . . . . . . 5E **73**
Binbrook Ho. *W10 . . . . . 4E **57***
(off Sutton Way)
Binden Rd. W12. . . . . . . 4B **70**
Binfield Rd. SW4 . . . . . . 4A **90**
SW8 . . . . 4A **90**
Bingfield St. N1 . . . . 5A **48**
(not continuous)
Bingham Ct. *N1 . . . . 4D **49***
(off Halton Rd.)
Bingham Pl. W1. .4C **60** (5B **4**)
Bingham St. N1 . . . . 3F **49**
Bingley Rd. E16 . . . . 5E **69**
Binley Ho. SW15 . . . . . . 4B **98**
Binney St. W1 . . 5C **60** (3C **12**)
Binnie Ct. *SE10 . . . . . . 3D **95***
(off Greenwich High Rd.)
Binnie Ho. *SE1 . . . . 5F **25***
(off Bath Ter.)
Binns Rd. W4 . . . . 1A **84**
Binns Ter. W4 . . . . 1A **84**
Bircham Path *SE4. . . . . 2F **107***
(off Aldersford Cl.)
Birch Cl. E16 . . . . 4A **68**
N19. . . . . 4E **33**
*SE15 . . . . 5C **92***
(off Bournemouth Cl.)
Birchdale Rd. E7 . . . . . . 2E **55**
Birchen Cl. NW9 . . . . . . 4A **28**
Birchen Gro. NW9 . . . . . 4A **28**
Birches, The E12 . . . . . . 1F **55**
SE7. . . . . 2D **97**
Birchfield Ho. *E14 . . . . . 1C **80***
(off Birchfield St.)
Birchfield St. E14. . . . . . 1C **80**
Birch Gro. E11 . . . . 1A **54**
SE12. . . . . 5B **110**
Birch Ho. SE14. . . . . . . 4B **94**
*SW2 . . . . 4C **104***
(off Tulse Hill)
*W10 . . . . 3A **58***
(off Droop St.)
Birchington Ct. *NW6 . . . 5D **45***
(off W. End La.)

Birchington Ho. E5. . . . . 2D **51**
Birchington Rd. N8. . . . . 1F **33**
NW6 . . . . 5C **44**
Birchin La.
EC3. . . . . 5F **63** (3C **18**)
Birchlands Av. SW12 . . 5B **102**
Birchmere Lodge
*SE16. . . . . 1D **93***
(off Sherwood Gdns.)
Birchmere Row SE3 . . . 5B **96**
Birchmore Hall N5 . . . . . 5E **35**
Birchmore Wlk. N5. . . . . 5E **35**
Birch Va. Ct. *NW8 . . . . . 3F **59***
(off Pollitt Dr.)
Birchwood Dr. NW3 . . . . 5D **31**
Birchwood Rd. SW17. . . 5D **117**
Birdbrook Ho. *N1 . . . . . 4E **49***
(off Popham Rd.)
Birdbrook Rd. SE3 . . . . 2E **111**
Birdcage Wlk.
SW1 . . . . 3E **75** (4F **21**)
Birdhurst Rd. SW18. . . 3E **101**
Bird in Bush Rd. SE15 . . 3C **92**
Bird-in-Hand Pas.
SE23 . . . . 2E **121**
Bird in Hand Yd. *NW3 . . 1E **45***
(off Holly Bush Va.)
NW3 . . . . 1E **45**
Birdlip Cl. SE15 . . . . 2A **92**
Birdsall Ho. SE5. . . . . . 1A **106**
Birdsfield La. E3 . . . . . . 5B **52**
Bird St. W1 . . . 5C **60** (3C **12**)
Birkbeck College
. . . . 4F **61** (5C **6**)
Birkbeck Hill SE21 . . . . 1D **119**
Birkbeck M. E8 . . . . 2B **50**
Birkbeck Pl. SE21 . . . . . 2E **119**
Birkbeck Rd. E8 . . . . . . 2B **50**
SW19 . . . . 5D **115**
Birkbeck St. E2 . . . . 2D **65**
Birkdale Cl. SE16. . . . . . 1D **93**
Birkenhead St.
WC1 . . . . 2A **62** (1E **7**)
Birkhall Rd. SE6 . . . . . . 1F **123**
Birkwood Cl. SW12 . . . 5F **103**
Birley Lodge *NW8 . . . . . 1F **59***
(off Acacia Rd.)
Birley St. SW11 . . . . 5C **88**
Birnam Rd. N4 . . . . 4B **34**
Birrell Ho. *SW9 . . . . 5B **90***
(off Stockwell Rd.)
Birse Cres. NW10 . . . . . 5A **28**
Birstall Rd. N15 . . . . 1A **36**
Biscay Ho. *E1 . . . . 3F **65***
(off Mile End Rd.)
Biscay Rd. W6 . . . . 1F **85**
Biscoe Way SE13 . . . . . 1F **109**
Biscott Ho. E3 . . . . 3D **67**
Bisham Gdns. N6. . . . . . 3C **32**
Bishop King's Rd.
W14 . . . . 5A **72**
Bishop's Av. E13 . . . . . . 5D **55**
SW6 . . . . 5F **85**
Bishops Av., The N2 . . . 1F **31**
Bishop's Bri. Rd. W2. . . 5D **59**
Bishop's Cl. N19. . . . . . . 5E **33**
Bishop's Ct. EC4 . . . . . . 2D **17**
WC2 . . . . 2B **16**
Bishops Ct. *W2 . . . . . . 5D **59***
(off Bishop's Bri. Rd.)

Bishopsdale Ho. *NW6* . . *5C 44*
  (off Kilburn Va.)
Bishopsgate
  EC2 . . . . 5A 64 (3D 19)
Bishopsgate Arc. EC2. . . 1E 19
Bishopsgate Chyd.
  EC2 . . . . 4A 64 (2D 19)
Bishopsgate Institute &
  Libraries **1E 19**
Bishops Gro. N2. . . . . . . 1A 32
Bishops Ho. *SW8* *3A 90*
  (off S. Lambeth Rd.)
Bishop's Mans. SW6 . . 5F 85
  (not continuous)
Bishops Mead *SE5* *3E 91*
  (off Camberwell Rd.)
Bishop's Pk. Rd. SW6 . . 5F 85
Bishops Rd. N6 . . . . 1C 32
  SW6 . . . . 4A 86
Bishop's Rd. SW11 . . . . 3A 88
Bishop's Ter. SE11 . . . . 5C 76
Bishopsthorpe Rd.
  SE26 . . . . 4F 121
Bishop St. N1. . . . . 5E 49
Bishop's Way E2. . . . . . 1D 65
Bishopswood Rd. N6 . . 2B 32
Bishop Way NW10 . . . . 4A 42
Bishop Wilfred Wood Cl.
  SE15 . . . . 5C 92
Bishop Wilfred Wood Ct.
  E13 . . . . *1E 69*
  (off Pragel St.)
Bissextile Ho. SE8 . . . . 5D 95
  SE13. . . . . 5D 95
Bisson Rd. E15 . . . . 1E 67
Bittern Ct. SE8 . . . . 2C 94
Bittern Ho. *SE1* *4F 25*
  (off Gt. Suffolk St.)
Bittern St. SE1 . . 3E 77 (4F 25)
Blackall St. EC2. 3A 64 (3D 11)
Blackbird Yd. E2 . . . . . . 2B 64
Black Boy La. N15 . . . . 1E 35
Blackburne's M.
  W1 . . . . 1C 74 (4B 12)
Blackburn Rd. NW6 . . 3D 45
Blackett St. SW15 . . . . 1F 99
Blackford's Path SW15. . 5C 98
Blackfriars Bri.
  SE1 . . . . 1D 77 (5D 17)
Blackfriars Ct. EC4. . . . 4D 17
Black Friars La.
  EC4 . . . . 5D 63 (4D 17)
  (not continuous)
Blackfriars Pas.
  EC4 . . . . 1D 77 (4D 17)
Blackfriars Rd.
  SE1 . . . . 3D 77 (1D 25)
Blackfriars Underpass
  EC4 . . . . 1C 76 (4D 17)
BLACKHEATH **5B 96**
Blackheath Av. SE10. . 3F 95
Blackheath Bus. Est.
  SE10 . . . . *4E 95*
  (off Blackheath Hill)
Blackheath Concert Halls
  . . . . **1B 110**
Blackheath Gro. SE3 . . 5B 96
Blackheath Hill SE10 . . 4E 95
BLACKHEATH PARK . . . **2C 110**
Blackheath Pk. SE3 . . 1B 110

Blackheath Ri. SE13 . . 5E 95
  (not continuous)
BLACKHEATH VALE . . **5B 96**
Blackheath Va. SE3 . . 5A 96
Blackheath Village
  SE3 . . . . 5B 96
Black Horse Ct. SE1 . . 5C 26
Blackhorse Rd. SE8 . . 2A 94
Blacklands Rd. SE6 . . 4E 123
Blacklands Ter. SW3 . . 5B 74
Black Lion La. W6 . . . . 5C 70
Black Lion M. W6 . . . . 5C 70
Blackmans Yd. *E2* *3C 64*
  (off Grimsby St.)
Blackmore Ho. *N1* . . . *5B 48*
  (off Barnsbury Est.)
Black Path E10. . . . . . . 2A 38
Blackpool Rd. SE15. . . . 5D 93
Black Prince Rd. SE1. . 5B 76
Blackshaw Rd. SW17. . 4E 115
Blacks Rd. W6 . . . . 1E 85
Blackstock M. N4. . . . . 4D 35
Blackstock Rd. N4 . . . . 4D 35
  N5. . . . . 4D 35
Blackstone Est. E8 . . . 4C 50
Blackstone Ho. *SW1* . . *1E 89*
  (off Churchill Gdns.)
Blackstone Rd. NW2 . . 2E 43
Black Swan Yd.
  SE1 . . . . 3A 78 (3E 27)
Blackthorn Ct. *E11* *1F 53*
  (off Hall Rd.)
Blackthorne Ct. *SE15*. . *3B 92*
  (off Cator St.)
Blackthorn St. E3 . . . . 3C 66
Blacktree M. SW9 . . . . 1C 104
BLACKWALL **2E 81**
Blackwall La. SE10 . . 1A 96
Blackwall Trad. Est.
  E14 . . . . 4F 67
Blackwall Tunnel E14 . . 2F 81
  (not continuous)
Blackwall Tunnel App.
  E14 . . . . 5E 67
Blackwall Tunnel
  Northern App. E14 . . 3E 67
  E3. . . . . 1C 66
Blackwall Tunnel
  Southern App. SE10. . 4A 82
Blackwall Way E14. . . . 2E 81
Blackwater Ct. E7. . . . 1B 54
Blackwater Ho. *NW8* . . *4F 59*
  (off Church St.)
Blackwater St. SE22 . . 3B 106
Blackwell Cl. E5. . . . . . 1F 51
Blackwell Ho. SW4. . . . 4F 103
Blackwood Ho. *E1* *3D 65*
  (off Collingwood St.)
Blackwood St. SE17 . . 1F 91
Blade M. SW15 . . . . . . 2B 100
Bladen Ho. *E1*. *5F 65*
  (off Dunelm St.)
Blades Ct. SW15 . . . . 2B 100
  W6 . . . . 1D 85
  (off Lower Mall)
Blades Ho. *SE11* *2C 90*
  (off Kennington Rd.)
Bladon Ct. SW16 . . . . 5A 118
Blagdon Rd. SE13 . . . 4D 109

Blagrove Rd. W10 . . . . 4A 58
Blair Av. NW9. . . . . 2A 28
Blair Cl. N1. . . . . 3E 49
Blair Ct. NW8 . . . . 5F 45
  SE6. . . . . 1B 124
Blairderry Rd. SW2 . . 2A 118
Blair Ho. SW9 . . . . 5B 90
Blair St. E14. . . . . 5E 67
Blake Ct. *NW6* *2C 58*
  (off Malvern Rd.)
  SE16. . . . . *1D 93*
  (off Stubbs Dr.)
Blake Gdns. SW6. . . . . 4D 87
Blake Hall Cres. E11 . . 3C 40
Blake Hall Rd. E11. . . . 2C 40
Blake Ho. *E14* *3C 80*
  (off Admirals Way)
  SE1 . . . . 4C 76 (5B 24)
  SE8. . . . . *2C 94*
  (off New King St.)
Blakeley Cotts. SE10 . . 3F 81
Blakemore Rd.
  SW16 . . . . 3A 118
Blakeney Cl. E8 . . . . . . 2C 50
  NW1 . . . . 4F 47
Blakenham Rd. SW17. . 4B 116
Blaker Ct. SE7 . . . . . . 3E 97
  (not continuous)
Blake Rd. E16 . . . . 3B 68
Blaker Rd. E15. . . . . . . 1E 67
Blakes Cl. W10 . . . . . . 4E 57
Blake's Rd. SE15 . . . . 3A 92
Blanchard Way E8 . . . . 3C 50
Blanch Cl. SE15 . . . . . 3E 93
Blanchedowne SE5. . . 2F 105
Blanche St. E16 . . . . . 3B 68
Blandfield Rd. SW12 . . 5C 102
Blandford Ct. *E8*. *4A 50*
  (off St Peter's Way)
  NW6 . . . . 4F 43
Blandford Ho. *SW8* . . *3B 90*
  (off Richborne Ter.)
Blandford Rd. W4 . . . . 4A 70
Blandford Sq. NW1 . . 3A 60
Blandford St.
  W1 . . . . 5B 60 (2A 12)
Bland Ho. *SE11* *1B 90*
  (off Vauxhall St.)
Bland St. SE9 . . . . 2F 111
Blann Cl. SE9 . . . . 4F 111
Blantyre St. SW10 . . . . 3F 87
Blantyre Twr. *SW10* . . . *3F 87*
  (off Blantyre St.)
Blantyre Wlk. *SW10*. . . *3F 87*
  (off Worlds End Est.)
Blashford *NW3*. *4B 46*
  (off Adelaide Rd.)
Blashford St. SE13 . . 5F 109
Blasker Wlk. E14. . . . . 1D 95
Blaxland Ho. *W12* *1D 71*
  (off White City Est.)
Blazer Ct. *NW8* *2F 59*
  (off St John's Wood Rd.)
Blechynden Ho. W10 . . 1F 71
  (off Kingsdown Cl.)
Blechynden St. W10. . . 1F 71
Bledlow Ho. *NW8*. *3F 59*
  (off Capland St.)
Bleeding Heart Yd.
  EC1 . . . . 1C 16

Blegborough Rd.
SW16 . . . . 5E 117
Blemundsbury WC1 . . . . . 5F 7
(off Dombey St.)
Blendon Row SE17 . . . . . . 5F 77
(off Townley St.)
Blenheim Cl. SE12 . . . . 1D 125
Blenheim Ct. N19 . . . . . 4A 34
SE16 . . . . 2F 79
(off King & Queen Wharf)
Blenheim Cres. W11 . . . 1A 72
Blenheim Gdns. NW2 . . 3E 43
SW2 . . . . 4B 104
Blenheim Gro. SE15 . . . 5C 92
Blenheim Ho. E16 . . . . . 1D 83
(off Constable Av.)
Blenheim Pas. NW8 . . . . 1E 59
(not continuous)
Blenheim Rd. E6 . . . . . 2F 69
E15 . . . . 1A 54
NW8 . . . . 1E 59
W4 . . . . 4A 70
Blenheim St.
W1 . . . . 5D 61 (3D 13)
Blenheim Ter. NW8 . . . . 1E 59
Blenkarne Rd. SW11 . . 4B 102
Blessington Cl. SE13 . . 1F 109
Blessington Rd. SE13 . . 1F 109
Bletchley Ct. N1 . . . . 1B 10
(not continuous)
Bletchley St.
N1 . . . . 1F 63 (1A 10)
Bletsoe Wlk. N1 . . . . . . 1E 63
Blick Ho. SE16 . . . . 4E 79
(off Neptune St.)
Blincoe Cl. SW19 . . . . 2F 113
Bliss Cres. SE13 . . . . . 5D 95
Blissett St. SE10 . . . . . 4E 95
Bliss M. W10 . . . . 2A 58
Blisworth Ho. E2 . . . . . 5C 50
(off Whiston Rd.)
Blithfield St. W8 . . . . . . 4D 73
Bloemfontein Av. W12 . 2D 71
Bloemfontein Rd. W12 . 1D 71
Bloemfontein Way
W12 . . . . 2D 71
Blomfield Ct. W9 . . . . . . 3E 59
(off Maida Va.)
Blomfield Mans. W12 . . 2E 71
(off Stanlake Rd.)
Blomfield Rd. W9 . . . . 4D 59
Blomfield St.
EC2 . . . . 4F 63 (1C 18)
Blomfield Vs. W2 . . . . . 4D 59
Blondel St. SW11 . . . . . 5C 88
Blondin St. E3 . . . . 1C 66
Bloomburg St. SW1 . . . 5F 75
Bloomfield Ct. N6 . . . . . 1C 32
Bloomfield Ho. E1 . . . . . 4C 64
(off Old Montague St.)
Bloomfield Pl. W1 . . . . 4E 13
Bloomfield Rd. N6 . . . . 1C 32
Bloomfield Ter. SW1 . . 1C 88
Bloom Gro. SE27 . . . . 3D 119
Bloomhall Rd. SE19 . . . 5F 119
Bloom Pk. Rd. SW6 . . . 3B 86
BLOOMSBURY . . 4A 62 (5D 7)
Bloomsbury St. WC1 . . 1E 15
Bloomsbury Ho.
SW4 . . . . 4F 103

Bloomsbury Pl.
SW18 . . . . 3E 101
WC1 . . . . 4A 62 (5E 7)
Bloomsbury Sq.
WC1 . . . . 4A 62 (1E 15)
Bloomsbury St.
WC1 . . . . 4F 61 (1C 14)
Bloomsbury Theatre 3B 6
Bloomsbury Way
WC1 . . . . 4A 62 (1D 15)
Blore Cl. SW8 . . . . 4F 89
Blore Ct. W1 . . . . 3B 14
Blossom St.
E1 . . . . 3A 64 (4E 11)
Blount Ho. E14 . . . . 4A 66
(off Maroon St.)
Blount St. E14 . . . . 5A 66
Bloxam Gdns. SE9 . . . . 3F 111
Bloxhall Rd. E10 . . . . . 1D 38
Blucher Rd. SE5 . . . . . . 3E 91
Blue Anchor La. SE16 . . 5C 78
Blue Anchor Yd. E1 . . . 1C 78
Blue Ball Yd.
SW1 . . . . 2E 75 (2F 21)
Bluebell Av. E12 . . . . . . 2F 55
Bluebell Cl. E9 . . . . 5E 51
SE26 . . . . 4B 120
Blue Elephant Theatre
. . . . 3E 91
Bluegate M. E1 . . . . . . 1D 79
Blue Lion Pl.
SE1 . . . . 4A 78 (5D 27)
Blue Water SW18 . . . . 2D 101
Blundell Cl. E8 . . . . 2C 50
Blundell St. N7 . . . . 4A 48
Blurton Rd. E5 . . . . 1E 51
Blyth Cl. E14 . . . . 5F 81
Blythe Cl. SE6 . . . . 5B 108
Blythe Hill SE6 . . . . . . 5B 108
Blythe Hill La. SE6 . . . 5B 108
Blythe Hill Pl. SE23 . . 5A 108
Blythe Ho. SE11 . . . . . . 2C 90
Blythe M. W14 . . . . 4F 71
Blythendale Ho. E2 . . . 1C 64
(off Mansford St.)
Blythe Rd. W14 . . . . . . 4F 71
(not continuous)
Blythe St. E2 . . . . 2D 65
Blythe Va. SE6 . . . . . . 1B 122
Blyth Hill Pl. SE23 . . . 5A 108
(off Brockley Pk.)
Blyth Rd. E17 . . . . 2B 38
Blyth's Wharf E14 . . . . 1A 80
Blythwood Rd. N4 . . . . 2A 34
Boades M. NW3 . . . . . . 1F 45
Boadicea St. N1 . . . . . . 5B 48
Boardwalk Pl. E14 . . . . 2E 81
Boarley Ho. SE17 . . . . . 5A 78
(off Massinger St.)
Boathouse Cen., The
W10 . . . . 3F 57
(off Canal Cl.)
Boathouse Wlk. SE15 . . 3B 92
(not continuous)
Boat Lifter Way SE16 . . 5A 80
Bob Anker Cl. E13 . . . . 2C 68
Bobbin Cl. SW4 . . . . . 1E 103
Bob Marley Way
SE24 . . . . 2C 104

Bocking St. E8 . . . . 5D 51
BOC Mus. 1C 14
(off Bedford Sq.)
Boddicott Cl. SW19 . . . 2A 114
Boddington Ho. SE14 . . 4E 93
(off Pomeroy St.)
SW13 . . . . 2D 85
(off Wyatt Dr.)
Boddy's Bri. SE1 . . . . . 2C 76
(off Hatfields)
Bodeney Ho. SE5 . . . . . 4A 92
(off Peckham Rd.)
Boden Ho. E1 . . . . 4C 64
(off Woodseer St.)
Bodington Ct. W12 . . . . 3F 71
Bodley Mnr. Way SW2 . 5C 104
Bodmin Pl. SE27 . . . . 4D 119
Bodmin St. SW18 . . . . 1C 114
Bodney Rd. E8 . . . . 2D 51
Bogart Ct. E14 . . . . 1C 80
(off Premiere Pl.)
Bohemia Pl. E8 . . . . . . 3E 51
Bohn Rd. E1 . . . . 4A 66
Boileau Rd. SW13 . . . . 3C 84
Boisseau Ho. E1 . . . . . 4E 65
(off Stepney Way)
Bolden St. SE8 . . . . . . 5D 95
Boldero Pl. NW8 . . . . . 3A 60
(off Gateforth St.)
Boleyn Ho. E16 . . . . . . 1C 82
(off Southey M.)
Boleyn Rd. E6 . . . . 1F 69
E7 . . . . 4C 54
N16 . . . . 2A 50
Bolina Rd. SE16 . . . . . . 1E 93
Bolingbroke Gro.
SW11 . . . . 2A 102
Bolingbroke Rd. W14 . . 4F 71
Bolingbroke Wlk.
SW11 . . . . 4F 87
Bolney Ga. SW7 . . . . . . 3A 74
Bolney St. SW8 . . . . . . 3B 90
Bolsover St. W1 . 3D 61 (4E 5)
Bolt Ct. EC4 . . . . 5C 62 (3C 16)
Bolton Cres. SE5 . . . . . 3D 91
Bolton Gdns. NW10 . . . 1F 57
SW5 . . . . 1D 87
Bolton Gdns. M. SW10 . 1E 87
Bolton Ho. SE10 . . . . . . 1A 96
(off Trafalgar Rd.)
Bolton Pl. NW8 . . . . . . 5D 45
(off Bolton Rd.)
Bolton Rd. E15 . . . . . . 3B 54
NW8 . . . . 5D 45
NW10 . . . . 5A 42
Boltons Cl. SW5 . . . . . 1D 87
(off Old Brompton Rd.)
Boltons Pl. SW5 . . . . . 1E 87
Boltons, The SW10 . . . 1E 87
Bolton St. W1 . . 2D 75 (1E 21)
Bolton Studios SW10 . . 1E 87
Bolton Wlk. N7 . . . . . . 4B 34
(off Durham Rd.)
Bombay St. SE16 . . . . . 5D 79
Bomore Rd. W11 . . . . . 1A 72
Bonar Rd. SE15 . . . . . . 3C 92
Bonchurch Rd. W10 . . . 4A 58
Bond Ct. EC4 . . . 1F 77 (4B 18)
Bond Ho. NW6 . . . . 1B 58
(off Rupert Rd.)

Bond Ho. *SE14* 3A *94*
  (off Goodwood Rd.)
Bonding Yd. Wlk.
  SE16 . . . . 4A **80**
Bond St. E15 . . . . 2A **54**
  W4 . . . . 5A **70**
Bondway SW8 . . . . 2A **90**
Bonfield Rd. SE13 . . . . 2E **109**
Bonham Rd. SW2 . . . . 3B **104**
Bonheur Rd. W4 . . . . . . 3A **70**
Bonhill St. EC2 . . 3F **63** (4C **10**)
Bonita M. SE4 . . . . 1F **107**
Bon Marche Ter. M.
  SE27 . . . . 4A **120**
Bonner Rd. E2 . . . . 1E **65**
Bonner St. E2 . . . . 1E **65**
Bonneville Gdns.
  SW4 . . . . 4E **103**
Bonnington Ho. N1 . . . . 1B **62**
Bonnington Sq. SW8 . . 2B **90**
Bonny St. NW1 . . . . 4E **47**
Bonsor Ho. SW8 . . . . . . 4E **89**
Bonsor St. SE5 . . . . 3A **92**
Bonville Rd.
  BR1: Brom 5B **124**
Booker Cl. E14 . . . . 4B **66**
Boones Rd. SE13 . . . . . 2A **110**
Boone St. SE13 . . . . . . 2A **110**
Boord St. SE10 . . . . 4A **82**
Boothby Rd. N19 . . . . . . 4F **33**
Booth Cl. E9 . . . . 5D **51**
Booth La. EC4 . . . . 4F **17**
Booth's Pl. W1 . . 4E **61** (1A **14**)
Boot St. N1 . . . . 2A **64** (2D **11**)
Border Cres. SE26 . . . . 5D **121**
Border Rd. SE26 . . . . . . 5D **121**
Bordon Wlk. SW15 . . . . 5C **98**
Boreas Wlk. N1 . . . . 1E **9**
Boreham Av. E16 . . . . . 5C **68**
Boreham Cl. E11 . . . . . . 3E **39**
Boreman Ho. *SE10* 2E *95*
  (off Thames St.)
Borland Rd. SE15 . . . . 2E **107**
Borneo St. SW15 . . . . . 1E **99**
Borough High St.
  SE1 . . . . . . 3E **77** (4A **26**)
Borough Rd.
  SE1 . . . . 4D **77** (5E **25**)
Borough Sq. SE1 . . . . . . 4F **25**
BOROUGH, THE
  . . . . 3F **77** (4A **26**)
Borrett Cl. SE17 . . . . . . 1E **91**
Borrodaile Rd. SW18 . . 4D **101**
Borrowdale *NW1* *2F 5*
  (off Robert St.)
Borthwick M. E15 . . . . . 1A **54**
Borthwick Rd. E15 . . . . 1A **54**
  NW9 . . . . 1B **28**
Borthwick St. SE8 . . . . . 1C **94**
Bosbury Rd. SE6 . . . . . 3E **123**
Boscastle Rd. NW5 . . . . 5D **33**
Boscobel Ho. E8 . . . . . . 3D **51**
Boscobel Pl. SW1 . . . . . 5C **74**
Boscobel St. NW8 . . . . . 3F **59**
Boscombe Av. E10 . . . . 2F **39**
Boscombe Cl. E5 . . . . . . 2A **52**
Boscombe Rd. SW17 . . 5C **116**
  W12 . . . . 2C **70**
Boss Ho. *SE1* 3F *27*
  (off Boss St.)

Boss St. SE1 . . . 3B **78** (3F **27**)
Boston Gdns. W4 . . . . . 2A **84**
Boston Pl. NW1 . . . . 3B **60**
Boston Rd. E6 . . . . 2F **69**
  E17 . . . . 1C **38**
Bosun Cl. E14 . . . . 3C **80**
Boswell Ct. *W14* 4F *71*
  (off Blythe Rd.)
  WC1 . . . . 4A **62** (5E **7**)
Boswell Ho. *WC1* *5E 7*
  (off Boswell St.)
Boswell St.
  WC1 . . . . 4A **62** (5E **7**)
Bosworth Ho. *W10* 3A *58*
  (off Bosworth Rd.)
Bosworth Rd. W10 . . . . 3A **58**
Botha Rd. E13 . . . . 4D **69**
Bothwell Cl. E16 . . . . . . 4B **68**
Bothwell St. W6 . . . . . . 2F **85**
Botolph All. EC3 . . . . . . 4D **19**
Botolph La.
  EC3 . . . . 1A **78** (5D **19**)
Botts M. W2 . . . . 5C **58**
Boughton Ho. *SE1* 3B *26*
  (off Tennis St.)
Boulcott St. E1 . . . . 5F **65**
Boulevard, The SW17. . 2C **116**
  SW18 . . . . 2D **101**
Boulogne Ho. *SE1* 5F *27*
  (off Abbey St.)
Boulter Ho. *SE14* 4E *93*
  (off Kender St.)
Boundaries Rd. SW12. . 2B **116**
Boundary Av. E17 . . . . . 2B **38**
Boundary Ho. SE5 . . . . 3E **91**
Boundary La. E13 . . . . . 2F **69**
  SE5 . . . . 2F **91**
Boundary M. *NW8* 5E *45*
  (off Boundary Rd.)
Boundary Pas.
  E1 . . . . 3B **64** (3F **11**)
Boundary Rd. E13 . . . . 1E **69**
  E17 . . . . 2B **38**
  NW8 . . . . 5D **45**
  SW19 . . . . 5F **115**
Boundary Row
  SE1 . . . . 3D **77** (3D **25**)
Boundary St.
  E2 . . . . 2B **64** (2F **11**)
Boundfield Rd. SE6 . . . 3A **124**
Bourbon Ho. SE6 . . . . . 5E **123**
Bourchier St.
  W1 . . . . 1F **75** (4B **14**)
  (not continuous)
Bourdon Pl. W1 . . . . . . 4E **13**
Bourdon St.
  W1 . . . . 1D **75** (5D **13**)
Bourke Cl. NW10 . . . . . 3A **42**
  SW4 . . . . 4A **104**
Bourlet Cl. W1 . . 4E **61** (1F **13**)
Bournbrook Rd. SE3 . . . 1F **111**
Bourne Est. EC1 . . 4C **62** (5B **8**)
Bourne M. W1 . . 1C **60** (3C **12**)
Bournemouth Cl. SE15 . . 5C **92**
Bournemouth Rd. SE15. . 5C **92**
Bourne Pl. W4 . . . . 1A **84**
Bourne Rd. E7 . . . . 5B **40**
  N8 . . . . 1A **34**
Bournes Ho. *N15* 1A *36*
  (off Chisley Rd.)

Bourneside Gdns.
  SE6 . . . . 5E **123**
Bourne St. SW1 . . . . . . 5C **74**
Bourne Ter. W2 . . . . 4D **59**
Bournevale Rd. SW16. . 4A **118**
Bournville Rd. SE6 . . . . 5C **108**
Bousfield Rd. SE14 . . . . 5F **93**
Boutflower Rd. SW11. . 2A **102**
Boutique Hall SE13 . . . 2E **109**
Bouverie M. N16 . . . . . . 4A **36**
Bouverie Pl. W2 . . . . . . 5F **59**
Bouverie Rd. N16 . . . . . 3A **36**
Bouverie St.
  EC4 . . . . 5C **62** (3C **16**)
Boveney Rd. SE23 . . . . 5F **107**
Bovill Rd. SE23 . . . . 4E **107**
Bovingdon Cl. N19 . . . . 4E **33**
Bovingdon Rd. SW6 . . . 4D **87**
BOW **2B 66**
Bowater Ho. SW2 . . . . 4A **104**
Bowater Ho. *EC1* *4F 9*
  (off Golden La. Est.)
Bowater Pl. SE3 . . . . . . 3D **97**
Bowater Rd. SE18 . . . . 4F **83**
Bow Bri. Est. E3 . . . . . . 2D **67**
Bow Brook, The *E2* 1F *65*
  (off Mace St.)
Bow Chyd. EC4 . . . . 3A **18**
BOW COMMON **4C 66**
Bow Comn. La. E3 . . . . 3B **66**
Bowden St. SE11 . . . . . 1C **90**
Bowditch SE8 . . . . 5B **80**
  (not continuous)
Bowdon Rd. E17 . . . . . . 2C **38**
Bowen Dr. SE21 . . . . . . 3A **120**
Bowen St. E14 . . . . 5D **67**
Bower Av. SE10 . . . . . . 4A **96**
Bowerdean St. SW6 . . . 4D **87**
Bower Ho. *SE14* 4F *93*
  (off Besson St.)
Bowerman Av. SE14 . . . 2A **94**
Bowerman Ct. *N19* 4F *33*
  (off St John's Way)
Bower St. E1 . . . . 5F **65**
Bowes-Lyon Hall *E16* . . *2C 82*
  (off Wesley Av.)
Bowes Rd. W3 . . . . 1A **70**
Bowfell Rd. W6 . . . . 2E **85**
Bowhill Cl. SW9 . . . . . . 3C **90**
Bowie Cl. SW4 . . . . 5F **103**
Bow Ind. Pk. E15 . . . . . 4C **52**
BOW INTERCHANGE . . 1D **67**
Bowland Rd. SW4 . . . . . 2F **103**
Bowland Yd. SW1 . . . . . 4A **20**
Bow La. EC4 . . . 5E **63** (3A **18**)
Bowl Ct. EC2 . . 3A **64** (4E **11**)
Bowles Rd. SE1 . . . . . . 2C **92**
Bowley Cl. SE19 . . . . . . 5B **120**
Bowley Ho. SE16 . . . . . 4C **78**
Bowley La. SE19 . . . . . 5B **120**
Bowling Grn. Cl.
  SW15 . . . . 5D **99**
Bowling Grn. La.
  EC1 . . . . 3C **62** (3C **8**)
Bowling Grn. Pl.
  SE1 . . . . 3F **77** (3B **26**)
Bowling Grn. St. SE11. . 2C **90**
Bowling Grn. Wlk.
  N1 . . . . 2A **64** (1D **11**)
Bowman Av. E16 . . . . . 1B **82**

Bramwell M. N1 . . . . . . 5B 48
Brancaster Ho. E1 . . . . . 2F 65
  (off Moody St.)
Brancaster Rd. SW16 . . 3A 118
Branch Hill NW3 . . . . . . 5E 31
Branch Hill Ho. NW3 . . . 5D 31
Branch Pl. N1 . . . . 5F 49
Branch St. SE5 . . . . 3A 92
Brandlehow Rd. SW15 . . 2B 100
Brandon Est. SE17 . . . . . 2D 91
Brandon Ho.
  BR3: Beck. 5D 123
  (off Beckenham Hill Rd.)
Brandon Mans. W14 . . . . 2A 86
  (off Queen's Club Gdns.)
Brandon M. EC2 . . . . . . 1B 18
Brandon Rd. N7 . . . . 4A 48
Brandon St. SE17 . . . . . . 5E 77
  (not continuous)
Brandram M. SE13 . . . . 2A 110
  (off Brandram Rd.)
Brandram Rd. SE13 . . . 1A 110
Brandreth Rd. SW17 . . 2D 117
Brand St. SE10 . . . . 3E 95
Brangbourne Rd.
  BR1: Brom 5E 123
Brangton Rd. SE11 . . . . 1B 90
Brangwyn Ct. W14 . . . . . 4A 72
  (off Blythe Rd.)
Branksea St. SW6 . . . . . 3A 86
Branksome Ho. SW8 . . . 3B 90
  (off Meadow Rd.)
Branksome Rd. SW2 . . 3A 104
Branscombe NW1 . . . . . 5E 47
  (off Plender St.)
Branscombe St. SE13 . . 1D 109
Bransdale Cl. NW6 . . . . . 5C 44
Brantwood Ho. SE5 . . . . 3E 91
  (off Wyndam Est.)
Brantwood Rd. SE24 . . 3E 105
Brasenose Dr. SW13 . . 2E 85
Brassett Point E15 . . . . 5A 54
  (off Abbey Rd.)
Brassey Ho. E14 . . . . . . 5D 81
  (off Cahir St.)
Brassey Rd. NW6 . . . . . 3B 44
Brassey Sq. SW11 . . . . 1C 102
Brassie Av. W3 . . . . 5A 56
Brass Talley All. SE16 . . 3F 79
Brasted Cl. SE26 . . . . . 4E 121
Brathay NW1 . . . . 1A 6
  (off Ampthill Est.)
Brathway Rd. SW18 . . . 5C 100
Bratley St. E1 . . . . 3C 64
Bravington Pl. W9 . . . . . 3B 58
Bravington Rd. W9 . . . . 1B 58
Brawne Ho. SE17 . . . . . . 2D 91
  (off Brandon St.)
Braxfield Rd. SE4 . . . . 2A 108
Braxted Pk. SW16 . . . . 5B 118
Bray NW3 . . . . 4A 46
Brayards Rd. SE15 . . . . 5D 93
Brayards Rd. Est. SE15 . 5E 93
  (off Brayards Rd.)
Braybrook St. W12 . . . . 4B 56
Brayburne Av. SW4 . . . . 5E 89
Bray Ct. SW16 . . . . . . 5A 118
Bray Cres. SE16 . . . . . . 3F 79

Braydon Rd. N16 . . . . . 3C 36
Bray Dr. E16 . . . . 1B 82
Brayfield Ter. N1 . . . . . . 4C 48
Brayford Sq. E1 . . . . 5E 65
Bray Pas. E16 . . . . 1C 82
Bray Pl. SW3 . . . . 5B 74
Bread St. EC4 . . 5E 63 (3A 18)
  (not continuous)
Breakspears M. SE4 . . . 5B 94
Breakspears Rd. SE4 . . 2B 108
Breamore Cl. SW15 . . 1C 112
Breamore Ho. SE15 . . . 3C 92
  (off Friary Est.)
Bream's Bldgs.
  EC4 . . . . 5C 62 (2B 16)
Bream St. E3 . . . . 4C 52
Breasley Cl. SW15 . . . . 2D 99
Brechin Pl. SW7 . . . . . . 5E 73
Breckenhock Rd. N7 . . . 2F 47
  N19 . . . . 1E 47
Brecknock Rd. Est. N19 . 1E 47
Brecon Grn. NW9 . . . . . 1A 28
Brecon Ho. W2 . . . . 5E 59
  (off Hallfield Est.)
Brecon M. NW5 . . . . 2F 47
Brecon Rd. W6 . . . . 2A 86
Bredel Ho. E14 . . . . 4C 66
  (off St Paul's Way)
Bredgar SE13 . . . . 3D 109
Bredgar Rd. N19 . . . . . . 4E 33
Bredhurst Cl. SE20 . . . 5E 121
Bredin Ho. SW10 . . . . . 3D 87
  (off Coleridge Gdns.)
Breer St. SW6 . . . . 1D 101
Breezers Ct. E1 . . . . 1C 78
  (off Highway, The)
Breezer's Hill E1 . . . . . . 1C 78
Bremner Rd. SW7 . . . . . 4E 73
Brenchley Gdns. SE23 . . 4E 107
Brenda Rd. SW17 . . . . 2B 116
Brendon Av. NW10 . . . . 1A 42
Brendon St. W1 . . . . . . 5A 60
Brenley Gdns. SE9 . . . 2F 111
Brenley Ho. SE1 . . . . . . 3B 26
  (off Tennis St.)
Brennand Ct. N19 . . . . . 5E 33
Brent Ct. NW11 . . . . . . 2F 29
BRENT CROSS 2E 29
Brent Cross Fly-Over
  NW2 . . . . 2F 29
  NW4 . . . . 2F 29
Brent Cross Gdns. NW4 . 1F 29
BRENT CROSS INTERCHANGE
  . . . . 1E 29
Brent Cross Shop. Cen.
  NW4 . . . . 2E 29
Brentfield Gdns. NW2 . . 2F 29
Brentfield Ho. NW10 . . 4A 42
Brentfield Rd. NW10 . . 3A 42
Brent Grn. NW4 . . . . . . 1E 29
Brent Ho. E9 . . . . 3E 51
  (off Frampton Pk. Rd.)
Brenthouse Rd. E9 . . . . 4E 51
Brenthurst Rd. NW10 . . 3B 42
Brentmead Pl. NW4 . . . 1F 29
  NW11 . . . . 1F 29
Brent New Ent. Cen.
  NW10 . . . . 3A 42
Brenton St. E14 . . . . . . 5A 66
Brent Pk. Rd. NW4 . . . . 2D 29

Brent Rd. E16 . . . . 5C 68
Brent St. NW4 . . . . 1F 29
Brent Ter. NW2 . . . . 3E 29
  (not continuous)
Brent Trad. Cen. NW10 . 2A 42
Brent Vw. Rd. NW9 . . . . 1C 28
Brentwood Ho. SE18 . . . 3F 97
  (off Portway Gdns.)
Brentwood Lodge NW4 . 1F 29
  (off Holmdale Gdns.)
Bressenden Pl.
  SW1 . . . . 4D 75 (5E 21)
Breton Highwalk EC2 . . 5A 10
  (off Golden La.)
Breton Ho. EC1 . . . . 4A 10
  SE1 . . . . 5F 27
  (off Abbey St.)
Brett Cl. N16 . . . . 4A 36
Brettell St. SE17 . . . . . . 1F 91
Brett Ho. Cl. SW15 . . . . 5F 99
Brettinghurst SE1 . . . . . 1C 92
  (off Avondale Sq.)
Brett Pas. E8 . . . . 2D 51
Brett Rd. E8 . . . . 2D 51
Brewer's Grn. SW1 . . . . 5B 22
Brewer's Hall Gdn. EC2 . 1A 18
  (off London Wall)
Brewer St. W1 . . 1E 75 (4A 14)
Brewery Ind. Est., The
  N1 . . . . 1A 10
  (off Wenlock Rd.)
Brewery Rd. N7 . . . . 4A 48
Brewery Sq. SE1 . . . . . . 2F 27
Brewhouse La. E1 . . . . . 2D 79
  SW15 . . . . 1A 100
Brewhouse Wlk. SE16 . . 2A 80
Brewhouse Yd.
  EC1 . . . . 3D 63 (3D 9)
Brewster Gdns. W10 . . . 4E 57
Brewster Ho. E14 . . . . . 1B 80
  (off Three Colt St.)
  SE1 . . . . 5B 78
  (off Dunton Rd.)
Brewster Rd. E10 . . . . . 3D 39
Briant Ho. SE1 . . . . 5B 24
Briant St. SE14 . . . . 4F 93
Briar Ct. SW15 . . . . 2D 99
Briardale Gdns. NW3 . . 5C 30
Briar Rd. NW2 . . . . 1E 43
Briar Wlk. SW15 . . . . . . 2D 99
  W10 . . . . 3A 58
Briarwood Rd. SW4 . . . 3F 103
Briary Cl. NW3 . . . . 4A 46
Briary Ct. E16 . . . . 5B 68
Briary Gdns.
  BR1: Brom 5D 125
Brickbarn Cl. SW10 . . . 3E 87
  (off King's Barn)
Brickfield Rd. SW19 . . 4D 115
Brick La. E2 . . . 2B 64 (2F 11)
Brick Lane Music Hall . . 2E 11
  (off Curtain Rd.)
BRICKLAYER'S ARMS . . 5F 77
Bricklayers Arms Bus. Cen.
  SE1 . . . . 5A 78
Brick St. W1 . . 2D 75 (2D 21)
Brickwood Cl. SE26 . . 3D 121
Brideale Cl. SE15 . . . . . 2B 92
Bride Ct. EC4 . . . . 3D 17

Broadfield Cl. NW2 . . . . 5E 29
Broadfield La. NW1 . . . . 4A 48
Broadfield Rd. SE6. . . . 5A 110
Broadfields Way
 NW10 . . . . 2B 42
Broadford Ho. E1 . . . . . . 3A 66
 (off Commodore St.)
Broadgate EC2 . . . . 1D 19
Broadgate Circ.
 EC2 . . . . 4A 64 (1D 19)
Broadgate Rd. E16 . . . . . 5F 69
Broadgates Ct. SE11 . . 1C 90
 (off Cleaver St.)
Broadgates Rd.
 SW18 . . . . 1F 115
Broadhinton Rd.
 SW4 . . . . 1D 103
Broadhurst Cl. NW6 . . . . 3E 45
Broadhurst Gdns.
 NW6 . . . . 3D 45
Broadlands Av. SW16.. 2A 118
Broadlands Cl. N6 . . . . . 2C 32
 SW16 . . . . 2A 118
Broadlands Lodge N6. . 2B 32
Broadlands Rd.
 BR1: Brom 4D 125
 N6 . . . . 2B 32
Broad La. EC2. . 4A 64 (5D 11)
 (not continuous)
Bradley St. NW8 . . . . . . 4F 59
Broadley Ter. NW1 . . . . 3A 60
Broadmayne SE17 . . . . . 1F 91
 (off Portland St.)
Broadmead SE6 . . . . . . 3C 122
 W14 . . . . 5B 72
Broadoak Ct. SW9 . . . . 1C 104
Broadoak Ho. NW6 . . 5D 45
 (off Mortimer Cres.)
Broad Sanctuary
 SW1 . . . . 3F 75 (4C 22)
Broadstone Ho. SW8 . . 3B 90
 (off Dorset Rd.)
Broadstone Pl.
 W1. . . . . 4C 60 (1B 12)
Broad St. Av.
 EC2 . . . . 4A 64 (1D 19)
Broad St. Pl. EC2 . . . . . 1C 18
Broad Wlk.
 NW1 . . . . 5C 46 (1C 4)
 SE3 . . . . 5E 97
 W1 . . . . 1B 74 (5A 12)
Broadwalk Cl. E14 . . . 2E 81
 (off Broadwalk Pl.)
Broadwalk Ct. W8 . . . 2C 72
 (off Palace Gdns. Ter.)
Broadwalk Ho.
 EC2 . . . . 3A 64 (5D 11)
 SW7 . . . . 3E 73
 (off Hyde Pk. Ga.)
Broad Wlk. La.
 NW11 . . . . 2B 30
Broad Wlk., The W8 . . 2D 73
Broadwall SE1 . . 2C 76 (1C 24)
Broadwater Rd.
 SW17 . . . . 4A 116
Broadway E13 . . . . 1D 69
 E15 . . . . 4F 53
 SW1 . . . . 4F 75 (4B 22)
Broadway Arc. W6 . . . 5E 71
 (off Hammersmith B'way.)

Broadway Cen., The
 W6 . . . . 5E 71
Broadway Chambers
 W6 . . . . 5E 71
 (off Hammersmith B'way.)
Broadway Ho.
 BR1: Brom 5F 123
 (off Bromley Rd.)
 E8 . . . . 5D 51
Broadway Mkt. E8 . . . . 5D 51
 SW17 . . . . 4B 116
Broadway Mkt. M. E8 . . 5C 50
Broadway M. N16 . . . . . 2B 36
Broadway Pde. N8 . . . . 1A 34
Broadway Shop. Mall
 SW1 . . . . 4F 75 (5B 22)
Broadway, The N8 . . . . 1A 34
 NW9 . . . . 1B 28
 SW14 . . . . 5A 84
Broadwick St.
 W1 . . . . 1E 75 (4A 14)
Broadwood Ter. W14 . . 5B 72
 (off Warwick Rd.)
Broad Yd. EC1 . . 3D 63 (4D 9)
Brocas Cl. NW3 . . . . . . 4A 46
Brockbridge Ho. SW15. 4B 98
Brocket Ho. SW8 . . . . . 5F 89
Brockham Cl. SW19. . 5B 114
Brockham Dr. SW2. . . 5B 104
Brockham Ho. NW1 . . . 5E 47
 (off Bayham St.)
 SW2 . . . . 5B 104
 (off Brockham Dri.)
Brockham St.
 SE1 . . . . 4E 77 (5A 26)
Brockill Cres. SE4 . . . . 2A 108
Brocklebank Ind. Est.
 SE7 . . . . 5C 82
Brocklebank Rd. SE7. . 5D 83
 SW18 . . . . 5E 101
Brocklehurst St. SE14 . . 3F 93
BROCKLEY 2F 107
Brockley Cross SE4 . . 1A 108
Brockley Cross Bus. Cen.
 SE4 . . . . 1A 108
Brockley Footpath SE4 . 3A 108
 (not continuous)
 SE15 . . . . 2E 107
Brockley Gdns. SE4 . . . 5B 94
Brockley Gro. SE4 . . . . 3B 108
Brockley Hall Rd. SE4. . 3A 108
Brockley M. SE4. . . . . . 3A 108
Brockley Pk. SE23 . . . . 5A 108
Brockley Ri. SE23 . . . . 1A 122
Brockley Rd. SE4. . . . . 1B 108
Brockley Vw. SE23. . . . 5A 108
Brockley Way SE4 . . . . 3F 107
Brockman Ri.
 BR1: Brom 4F 123
Brockmer Ho. E1 . . . . . 1D 79
 (off Crowder St.)
Brock Pl. E3 . . . . 3D 67
Brock Rd. E13 . . . . 4D 69
Brock St. SE15 . . . . . . 1E 107
Brockway Cl. E11. . . . . 4A 40
Brockweir E2 . . . . 1E 65
 (off Cyprus St.)
Brockwell Ct. SW2 . . . 3C 104
Brockwell Ho. SE11. . . 2B 90
 (off Vauxhall St.)

Brockwell Pk. Gdns.
 SE24 . . . . 1C 104
Brockwell Pk. Row
 SW2 . . . . 5C 104
Brodia Rd. N16 . . . . . . 5A 36
Brodie Ho. SE1. . . . . . . 1B 92
 (off Cooper's Rd.)
Brodie St. SE1 . . . . 1B 92
Brodlove La. E1 . . . . . . 1F 79
Brodrick Rd. SW17 . . . 2A 116
Broken Wharf
 EC4 . . . . 1E 77 (4F 17)
Brokesley St. E3. . . . . . 2B 66
Broke Wlk. E8 . . . . 5B 50
Bromar Rd. SE5 . . . . . 1A 106
Bromell's Rd. SW4. . . . 2E 103
Bromfelde Rd. SW4 . . 1F 103
Bromfelde Wlk. SW4 . . 5F 89
Bromfield St. N1 . . . . . 5C 48
Bromhead Rd. E1. . . . . 5E 65
 (off Jubilee St.)
Bromhead St. E1 . . . . . 5E 65
Bromleigh Ct. SE23 . . 2C 120
Bromleigh Ho. SE1. . . . 5F 27
 (off Abbey St.)
BROMLEY 2D 67
Bromley Hall Rd. E14 . . 4E 67
Bromley High St. E3 . . 2D 67
Bromley Hill
 BR1: Brom 5A 124
Bromley Pl. W1 . . 4E 61 (5F 5)
Bromley Rd.
 BR1: Brom 1D 123
 E10 . . . . 1D 39
 SE6 . . . . 1D 123
Bromley St. E1 . . . . 4F 65
BROMPTON 4A 74
Brompton Arc. SW1 . . 4A 20
Brompton Oratory . . . 4A 74
Brompton Pk. Cres.
 SW6 . . . . 2D 87
Brompton Pl. SW3 . . . . 4A 74
Brompton Rd.
 SW3 . . . . 5A 74 (4A 20)
Brompton Sq. SW3 . . . 4A 74
Bromwich Av. N6 . . . . . 4C 32
Bromyard Av. W3. . . . . 1A 70
Bromyard Ho. SE15. . . 3D 93
 (off Commercial Way)
Bron Ct. NW6 . . . . 5C 44
BRONDESBURY 4B 44
Brondesbury Ct. NW2. . 3F 43
Brondesbury M. NW6. . 4C 44
BRONDESBURY PARK . . 5A 44
Brondesbury Pk. NW2. . 3D 43
Brondesbury Rd. NW6 . 1B 58
Brondesbury Vs. NW6 . 1B 58
Bronsart Rd. SW6 . . . . 3A 86
Bronte Cl. E7 . . . . 1C 54
Bronte Ct. W14 . . . . . . 4F 71
 (off Girdler's Rd.)
Bronte Ho. N16 . . . . . . 2A 50
 NW6 . . . . 2C 58
 SW4 . . . . 5E 103
Bronti Cl. SE17. . . . . . . 1E 91
Bronwen Ct. NW8. . . . . 2F 59
 (off Grove End Rd.)
Bronze St. SE8 . . . . 3C 94
Brookbank Rd.
 SE13 . . . . 1C 108

Brook Cl. SW17 . . . . 2C 116
Brook Ct. E11 . . . . 5A 40
E15 . . . . 2D 53
  (off Clays La.)
SE12 . . . . 3E 125
Brookdale Rd. SE6 . . . . 5D 109
  (not continuous)
Brook Dr. SE11 . . . . 4C 76
Brooke Ho. SE14 . . . . . . 4A 94
Brookehowse Rd. SE6 . . 2C 122
Brooke Rd. E5 . . . . 5C 36
N16 . . . . 5B 36
Brooke's Ct. EC1 . 4C 62 (1B 16)
Brooke's Mkt. EC1 . . . . . 5C 8
Brooke St. EC1 . 4C 62 (1B 16)
Brookfield N6 . . . . 5C 32
Brookfield Pk. NW5 . . . . 5D 33
Brookfield Rd. E9 . . . . . . 3A 52
W4 . . . . 3A 70
Brook Gdns. SW13 . . . . . 1B 98
Brook Ga. W1 . 1B 74 (5A 12)
BROOK GREEN 5F 71
Brook Grn. W6 . . . . 4F 71
Brook Grn. Flats W14 . . . 4F 71
  (off Dunsany Rd.)
Brook Ho's. NW1 . . . . . . 1E 61
  (off Cranleigh St.)
Brook Ho. W6 . . . . 5E 71
  (off Shepherd's Bush Rd.)
Brooking Rd. E7 . . . . 2C 54
Brooklands Av. SW19 . . 2D 115
Brooklands Ct. NW6 . . . 4B 44
Brooklands Pk. SE3 . . . 1C 110
Brooklands Pas. SW8 . . 4F 89
Brook La. BR1: Brom . . 5C 124
  (not continuous)
SE3 . . . . 5D 97
Brookmarsh Ind. Est.
SE8 . . . . 3D 95
SE10 . . . . 3D 95
Brook M. WC2 . 5F 61 (3C 14)
Brook M. Nth. W2 . . . . . 1E 73
Brookmill Rd. SE8 . . . . . 4C 94
Brook Rd. NW2 . . . . 4B 28
Brooksbank St. E9 . . . . . 3E 51
Brooksby M. N1 . . . . 4C 48
Brooksby St. N1 . . . . . . 4C 48
Brooksby's Wlk. E9 . . . . 2F 51
Brooks Ct. SW8 . . . . 3E 89
Brookside Rd. N19 . . . . . 4E 33
NW11 . . . . 1A 30
Brooks Lodge N1 . . . . . 1A 64
  (off Hoxton St.)
Brooks M. W1 . 1D 75 (4D 13)
Brook Sq. SE18 . . . . 4F 97
Brooks Rd. E13 . . . . 5C 54
Brook St. W2 . . . . 1F 73
W1 . . . . 1D 75 (4D 13)
Brooksville Av. NW6 . . . 5A 44
Brookview Rd. SW16 . . . 5E 117
Brookville Rd. SW6 . . . . 3B 86
Brookway SE3 . . . . 1C 110
Brookwood Av. SW13 . . 5B 84
Brookwood Ho. SE1 . . . 4E 25
  (off Webber St.)
Brookwood Rd. SW18 . . 1B 114
Broome Way SE5 . . . . . . 3F 91
Broomfield E17 . . . . 2B 38
NW1 . . . . 4C 46
  (off Ferdinand St.)

Broomfield Ct. SE16 . . . 4C 78
  (off Ben Smith Way)
Broomfield Ho. SE17 . . . 5A 78
  (off Massinger St.)
Broomfield St. E14 . . . . 4C 66
Broomgrove Rd. SW9 . . 5B 90
Broomhill Rd. SW18 . . . 3C 100
Broomhouse La. SW6 . . 5C 86
  (not continuous)
Broomhouse Rd. SW6 . . 5C 86
Broomsleigh Bus. Pk.
SE26 . . . . 5B 122
Broomsleigh St. NW6 . . 2B 44
Broomwood Rd. SW11 . . 4B 102
Broseley Gro. SE26 . . . 5A 122
Brougham Rd. E8 . . . . . . 5C 50
Brougham St. SW11 . . . 5B 88
Brough Cl. SW8 . . . . 3A 90
Broughton Dr. SW9 . . . . 2C 104
Broughton Gdns. N6 . . . 1E 33
Broughton Rd. SW6 . . . . 5D 87
Broughton St. SW8 . . . . 5C 88
Broughton St. Ind. Est.
SW11 . . . . 5C 88
Browne Ho. SE8 . . . . 3C 94
  (off Deptford Chu. St.)
Brownfield Area E14 . . . 5D 67
Brownfield St. E14 . . . . 5D 67
Brown Hart Gdns.
W1 . . . . 1C 74 (4C 12)
Brownhill Rd. SE6 . . . . . 5D 109
Browning Cl. W9 . . . . . . 3E 59
Browning Ho. SE14 . . . . 4A 94
  (off Loring Rd.)
W12 . . . . 5E 57
  (off Wood La.)
Browning M. W1 . . 4D 61 (1C 12)
Browning Rd. E11 . . . . . 2B 40
Browning St. SE17 . . . . 1E 91
Brownlow Ho. SE16 . . . . 3C 78
  (off George Row)
Brownlow M.
WC1 . . . . 3B 62 (4A 8)
Brownlow Rd. E7 . . . . . . 1C 54
E8 . . . . 5B 50
NW10 . . . . 4A 42
Brownlow St.
WC1 . . . . . . 4B 62 (1A 16)
Browns Arc. W1 . . . . . . 5A 14
  (off Regent St.)
Brown's Bldgs.
EC3 . . . . . . 5A 64 (3E 19)
Browns La. NW5 . . . . . . 2D 47
Brown St. W1 . . . . 5B 60
BROWNSWOOD PARK . . 4D 35
Brownswood Rd. N4 . . . 5D 35
Broxash Rd. SW11 . . . . 4C 102
Broxbourne Rd. E7 . . . . 5C 40
Broxholme Ho. SW6 . . . 4D 87
  (off Harwood Rd.)
Broxholm Rd. SW16 . . . 3C 118
Broxted Rd. SE6 . . . . . . 2B 122
Broxwood Way NW8 . . . 5A 46
Bruce Cl. W10 . . . . 4F 57
Bruce Hall M. SW17 . . . 4C 116
Bruce Ho. W10 . . . . 4F 57
Bruce Rd. E3 . . . . 2D 67
NW10 . . . . 4A 42
Bruckner St. W10 . . . . . 2A 58
Brudenell Rd. SW17 . . . 3B 116

Bruges Pl. NW1 . . . . 4E 47
  (off Randolph St.)
Brune Ho. E1 . . . . 1F 19
Brunel Est. W2 . . . . 4C 58
Brunel Ho. E14 . . . . 1D 95
  (off Ship Yd.)
Brunel Rd. E17 . . . . 1A 38
SE16 . . . . 3E 79
W3 . . . . 4A 56
Brunel St. E16 . . . . 5B 68
Brune St. E1 . . 4B 64 (1F 19)
Brunlees Ho. SE1 . . . . . 5F 25
  (off Bath Ter.)
Brunner Cl. NW11 . . . . . 1D 31
Brunner Ho. SE6 . . . . . . 4E 123
Brunner Rd. E17 . . . . . . 1A 38
Brunswick Cen.
WC1 . . . . 3A 62 (3D 7)
Brunswick Cl. Est.
EC1 . . . . 2D 63 (2D 9)
Brunswick Ct. EC1 . . . . . 2D 9
  (off Tompion St.)
SE1 . . . . 3A 78 (4E 27)
SW1 . . . . 5F 75
  (off Regency St.)
Brunswick Gdns. W8 . . . 2C 72
Brunswick Ho. E2 . . . . . 1B 64
  (off Thurtle Rd.)
SE16 . . . . 4A 80
  (off Brunswick Quay)
Brunswick Mans. WC1 . . 3E 7
  (off Handel St.)
Brunswick M. SW16 . . . 5F 117
W1 . . . . 5B 60 (2A 12)
Brunswick Pk. SE5 . . . . 4A 92
Brunswick Pl.
N1 . . . . 2F 63 (2C 10)
NW1 . . . . 3C 60 (4C 4)
  (not continuous)
Brunswick Quay SE16 . . 4F 79
Brunswick Rd. E10 . . . . 3E 39
E14 . . . . 5E 67
Brunswick Sq.
WC1 . . . . 3A 62 (3E 7)
Brunswick Vs. SE5 . . . . 4A 92
Brunton Pl. E14 . . . . 5A 66
Brushfield St.
E1 . . . . 4A 64 (5E 11)
EC2 . . . . 4A 64
Brussels Rd. SW11 . . . . 2F 101
Bruton La. W1 . 1D 75 (5E 13)
Bruton Pl. W1 . 1D 75 (5E 13)
Bruton St. W1 . 1D 75 (5E 13)
Brutus Ct. SE11 . . . . 5D 77
  (off Kennington La.)
Bryan Av. NW10 . . . . . . 4D 43
Bryan Ho. NW10 . . . . . . 4D 43
SE16 . . . . 3B 80
Bryan Rd. SE16 . . . . 3B 80
Bryan's All. SW6 . . . . . . 5D 87
Bryanston Cl. W1 . . . . . . 2A 12
  (not continuous)
Bryanstone Rd. N8 . . . . 1F 33
Bryanston Mans. W1 . . . 5A 4
  (off York St.)
Bryanston M. E.
W1 . . . . 4B 60 (1A 12)
Bryanston M. W.
W1 . . . . 4B 60 (2A 12)

Bryanston Pl. W1 . . . . . 4B **60**
Bryanston Sq.
 W1 . . . . 5B **60** (2A **12**)
Bryanston St.
 W1 . . . . 5B **60** (3A **12**)
Bryant Ct. E2 . . . . 1B **64**
 (off Whiston Rd.,
 not continuous)
Bryant St. E15 . . . . 4F **53**
Bryantwood Rd. N7 . . 2C **48**
Bryce Ho. SE14 . . . . 2F **93**
 (off John Williams Cl.)
Brydale Ho. SE16 . . . . . 5F **79**
 (off Rotherhithe New Rd.)
Bryden Cl. SE26 . . . . . 5A **122**
Brydges Pl.
 WC2 . . . . 1A **76** (5D **15**)
Brydges Rd. E15 . . . . . 2F **53**
Brydon Wlk. N1 . . . . . . 5A **48**
Bryer Ct. EC2 . . . . 5F **9**
Bryet Rd. N7 . . . . 5A **34**
Bryher Ct. SE11 . . . . . . 1C **90**
 (off Sancroft St.)
Brymay Cl. E3 . . . . 1C **66**
Brynmaer Rd. SW11 . . 4B **88**
Bryony Rd. W12 . . . . . . 1C **70**
Buccleugh Ho. E5 . . . . 2C **36**
Buchanan Ct. SE16 . . . 5F **79**
 (off Worgan St.)
Buchanan Gdns.
 NW10 . . . . 1D **57**
Buchan Rd. SE15 . . . . 1E **107**
Bucharest Rd. SW18 . 5E **101**
Buckden Cl. SE12 . . . . 4C **110**
Buckfast St. E2 . . . . . . 2C **64**
Buck Hill Wlk. W2 . . . . 1F **73**
Buckhold Rd. SW18 . . 4C **100**
Buckhurst Ho. N7 . . . . 2F **47**
Buckhurst St. E1 . . . . . 3D **65**
Buckingham Arc.
 WC2 . . . . 5D **15**
Buckingham Chambers
 SW1 . . . . 5E **75**
 (off Greencoat Pl.)
Buckingham Ga.
 SW1 . . . . 4E **75** (5F **21**)
Buckingham La. SE23 . 5A **108**
Buckingham Mans. NW6 2D **45**
 (off W. End La.)
Buckingham M. N1 . . . 3A **50**
 NW10 . . . . 1B **56**
 SW1 . . . . 5F **21**
Buckingham Palace
 . . . . 3D **75** (4E **21**)
Buckingham Pal. Rd.
 SW1 . . . . 5D **75** (5E **21**)
Buckingham Pl.
 SW1 . . . . 4E **75** (5F **21**)
Buckingham Rd. E10 . . 5D **39**
 E11 . . . . 1E **41**
 E15 . . . . 2B **54**
 N1 . . . . 3A **50**
 NW10 . . . . 1B **56**
Buckingham St.
 WC2 . . . . 1A **76** (1E **23**)
Buckland Ct. N1 . . . . . . 1A **64**
 (off St John's Est.)
Buckland Cres. NW3 . . 4F **45**
Buckland Rd. E10 . . . . 4E **39**
Buckland St. N1 . . . . . . 1F **63**

Bucklebury NW1 . . . . . . 3F **5**
 (off Stanhope St.)
Bucklers All. SW6 . . . . 2B **86**
 (not continuous)
Bucklersbury EC2 . . . . 3B **18**
Bucklersbury Pas.
 EC2 . . . . 5F **63** (3B **18**)
Buckle St. E1 . . . . 5B **64**
Buckley Cl. SE23 . . . . 5D **107**
Buckley Ho. NW6 . . . . . 4B **44**
Buckley Rd. NW6 . . . . . 4B **44**
Buckmaster Cl. SW9 . 1C **104**
 (off Stockwell Pk. Rd.)
Buckmaster Ho. N7 . . . 1B **48**
Buckmaster Rd.
 SW11 . . . . 2A **102**
Bucknall St. WC1 . . . . . 5A **62**
 WC2 . . . . 5A **62** (2C **14**)
Bucknell Cl. SW9 . . . . 2B **104**
Buckner Rd. SW2 . . . . 2B **104**
Buckhill Ho. SW1 . . . . . 1D **89**
 (off Ebury Bri. Rd.)
Buckridge Ho. EC1 . . . . 5B **8**
 (off Portpool La.)
Buckstone Cl. SE23 . . 4E **107**
Buck St. NW1 . . . . 4D **47**
Buckters Rents SE16 . . 2A **80**
Buckthorne Rd. SE4 . . 3A **108**
Bude Cl. E17 . . . . 1B **38**
Budge Row EC4 . 1F **77** (4B **18**)
Budge's Wlk. W2 . . . . . 2E **73**
Budleigh Ho. SE15 . . . 3C **92**
 (off Bird in Bush Rd.)
Buer Rd. SW6 . . . . 5A **86**
Bugsby's Way SE7 . . . 5B **82**
 SE10 . . . . 5B **82**
Bugsby's Way Retail Est.
 SE7 . . . . 5C **82**
Bulbarrow NW8 . . . . . . 5D **45**
 (off Abbey Rd.)
Bulinga St. SW1 . . . . . . 5A **76**
 (off John Islip St.)
Bullace Row SE5 . . . . . 4F **91**
Bullard's Pl. E2 . . . . . . 2F **65**
Bulleid Way SW1 . . . . 5D **75**
Bullen Ho. E1 . . . . 3D **65**
 (off Collingwood St.)
Bullen St. SW11 . . . . . . 5A **88**
Buller Cl. SE15 . . . . . . 3C **92**
Buller Rd. NW10 . . . . . 2F **57**
Bullingham Mans. W8 . 3C **72**
 (off Pitt St. La.)
Bull Inn Ct. WC2 . . . . . 5E **15**
Bullivant St. E14 . . . . . 1E **81**
Bull Rd. E15 . . . . 1B **68**
Bulls Gdns. SW3 . . . . . 5A **74**
 (not continuous)
Bulls Head Pas. EC3 . . 3D **19**
Bull Wharf La.
 EC4 . . . . 1E **77** (4A **18**)
Bull Yd. SE15 . . . . 4C **92**
Bulmer M. W11 . . . . . . 1C **72**
Bulmer Pl. W11 . . . . . . 2C **72**
Bulow Est. SW6 . . . . . . 4D **87**
 (off Pearscroft Rd.)
Bulstrode Pl.
 W1 . . . . 4C **60** (1C **12**)
Bulstrode St.
 W1 . . . . 5C **60** (2C **12**)

Bulwer Ct. E11 . . . . . . 3F **39**
Bulwer Ct. Rd. E11 . . . 3F **39**
Bulwer Rd. E11 . . . . . . 2F **39**
Bulwer St. W12 . . . . . . 2E **71**
Bunbury Ho. SE15 . . . . 3C **92**
 (off Fenham Rd.)
Bungalows, The E10 . . 1E **39**
Bunhill Row EC1 . 3F **63** (3B **10**)
Bunhouse Pl. SW1 . . . 1C **88**
Bunkers Hill NW11 . . . 2E **31**
Bunning Way N7 . . . . . 4A **48**
Bunsen Ho. E3 . . . . 1A **66**
 (off Grove Rd.)
Bunsen St. E3 . . . . 1A **66**
Bunyan Ct. EC2 . . . . 5F **9**
 (off Beech St.)
Buonaparte M. SW1 . . 1F **89**
Burbage Cl. SE1 4F **77** (5B **26**)
Burbage Ho. N1 . . . . . . 5F **49**
 (off Poole St.)
 SE14 . . . . 2F **93**
 (off Samuel Cl.)
Burbage Rd. SE21 . . . 4E **105**
 SE24 . . . . 4E **105**
Burcham St. E14 . . . . . 5D **67**
Burchell Ho. SE11 . . . . 1B **90**
 (off Jonathan St.)
Burchell Rd. E10 . . . . . 3D **39**
 SE15 . . . . 4D **93**
Burcote Rd. SW18 . . . 5F **101**
Burden Ho. SW8 . . . . . 3A **90**
 (off Thorncroft St.)
Burden Way E11 . . . . . 4D **41**
Burder Cl. N1 . . . . 3A **50**
Burder Rd. N1 . . . . 3A **50**
Burdett M. NW3 . . . . . . 3F **45**
 W2 . . . . 5D **59**
Burdett Rd. E3 . . . . 3A **66**
Burfield Cl. SW17 . . . . 4F **115**
Burford Rd. E6 . . . . 2F **69**
 E15 . . . . 5F **53**
 SE6 . . . . 2B **122**
Burford Wlk. SW6 . . . . 3E **87**
Burge Rd. E7 . . . . 1F **55**
Burges Gro. SW13 . . . 3D **85**
Burgess Av. NW9 . . . . 1A **28**
Burgess Hill NW2 . . . . 1C **44**
Burgess Ind. Pk. SE5 . 3F **91**
Burgess Pk. **2A 92**
Burgess Rd. E15 . . . . . 1A **54**
Burgess St. E14 . . . . . 4C **66**
Burge St. SE1 . 4F **77** (5C **26**)
Burgh House **1F 45**
Burghill Rd. SE26 . . . 4A **122**
Burghley Hall Cl.
 SW19 . . . . 1A **114**
Burghley Rd. E11 . . . . 3A **40**
 NW5 . . . . 1D **47**
 SW19 . . . . 4F **113**
Burghley Twr. W3 . . . . 1B **70**
Burgh St. N1 . . . . 1D **63**
Burgon St. EC4 . 5D **63** (3E **17**)
Burgos Gro. SE10 . . . . 4D **95**
Burgoyne Rd. N4 . . . . 1D **35**
 SW9 . . . . 1B **104**
Burke Cl. SW15 . . . . . . 2A **98**
Burke Lodge E13 . . . . 2D **69**
Burke St. E16 . . . . 4B **68**
 (not continuous)
Burland Rd. SW11 . . . . 3B **102**

Burleigh Ho. *SW3*. 2F **87**
 (off Beaufort St.)
W10 . . . . 4A **58**
 (off St Charles Sq.)
Burleigh Pl. SW15 . . . . . . 3F **99**
Burleigh St. WC2. .1B 76 (4F **15**)
Burleigh Wlk. SE6 . . . . 1E **123**
Burley Ho. *E1* 5F **65**
 (off Chudleigh St.)
Burley Rd. E16 . . . . 5E **69**
Burlington Arc.
 W1 . . . . 1E 75 (5F **13**)
Burlington Cl. W9. . . . . . . 3C **58**
Burlington Gdns. SW6 . . 5A **86**
 W1 . . . . 1E 75 (5F **13**)
Burlington La. W4 . . . . . . 3A **84**
Burlington M. SW15. . . 3B **100**
Burlington Pl. SW6 . . . . . 5A **86**
Burlington Rd. SW6 . . . . 5A **86**
Burma M. N16 . . . . 1F **49**
Burma Rd. N16 . . . . 1F **49**
Burma Ter. SE19. . . . . . . 5A **120**
Burmester Rd. SW17 . . 3E **115**
Burnaby St. SW10 . . . . . . 3E **87**
Burnand Ho. *W14*. 4F **71**
 (off Redan St.)
Burnard Pl. N7 . . . . 2B **48**
Burnaston Ho. E5 . . . . . . 5C **36**
Burnbury Rd. SW12 . . 1E **117**
Burne Jones Ho.
 W14 . . . . 5A **72**
 (off Abingdon Cl.)
Burnell Wlk. *SE1* 1B **92**
 (off Abingdon Cl.)
Burness Cl. N7 . . . . 3B **48**
Burne St. NW1 . . . . 4A **60**
Burnett Cl. E9 . . . . 2E **51**
Burnett Ho. *SE13* 5E **95**
 (off Lewisham Hill)
Burney St. SE10 . . . . 3E **95**
Burnfoot Av. SW6. . . . . . 4A **86**
Burnham NW3 . . . . 4A **46**
Burnham Cl. SE1 . . . . 5B **78**
Burnham Ct. *W2*. 1D **73**
 (off Moscow Rd.)
Burnham Est. *E2*. 2E **65**
 (off Burnham St.)
Burnham St. E2 . . . . 2E **65**
Burnham Way SE26 . . 5B **122**
Burnley Rd. NW10 . . . . . . 2B **42**
 SW9 . . . . 5B **90**
Burnsall St. SW3 . . . . 1A **88**
Burns Cl. SW19 . . . . . . 5F **115**
Burns Ho. *E2*. 2E **65**
 (off Cornwall Av.)
 SE17. . . . . 1D **91**
 (off Doddington Gro.)
Burnside Cl. SE16. . . . . . 2F **79**
Burns Rd. NW10. . . . . 5B **42**
 SW11 . . . . 5B **88**
Burnt Ash Hgts.
 BR1: Brom 5D **125**
Burnt Ash Hill SE12 . . 4B **110**
 (not continuous)
Burnt Ash La.
 BR1: Brom 5C **124**
Burnt Ash Rd. SE12 . . 3B **110**
Burnthwaite Rd. SW6. . 3B **86**
Burntwood Cl. SW18 . . 1A **116**
Burntwood Grange Rd.
 SW18 . . . . 1F **115**

Burntwood La. SW17 . . 3E **115**
Burntwood Vw. SE19 . . 5B **120**
Buross St. E1. . . . . 5D **65**
Burrage Ct. *SE16* 5F **79**
 (off Worgan St.)
Burrard Rd. E16. . . . . 5D **69**
 NW6. . . . . 2C **44**
Burr Cl. E1 . . . . 2C **78**
Burrell St. SE1 . .2D 77 (1D **25**)
Burrells Wharf Sq. E14. . 1C **94**
Burrell Towers E10. . . . . 2C **38**
Burrhill Ct. *SE16*. 4F **79**
 (off Worgan St.)
Burroughs Cotts. *E14*. . . 4A **66**
 (off Halley St.)
Burrow Ho. *SW9* 5C **90**
 (off Stockwell Pk. Rd.)
Burrow Rd. SE22 . . . . . . 2A **106**
Burrows M.
 SE1 . . . . .3D 77 (3D **25**)
Burrows Rd. NW10. . . . . 2E **57**
Burrow Wlk. SE21 . . . . . 5E **105**
Burr Rd. SW18. . . . . 1C **114**
Bursar St. SE1. . 2A 78 (2D **27**)
Burslem St. E1 . . . . 5C **64**
Burstock Rd. SW15 . . . 2A **100**
Burston Rd. SW15 . . . . . 3F **99**
Burtley Cl. N4. . . . . 3E **35**
Burton Bank *N1*. 4F **49**
 (off Yeate St.)
Burton Ct. *SW3* 1B **88**
 (off Turks Row, not cont.)
Burton Gro. SE17 . . . . . . 1F **91**
Burton Ho. *SE16* 3D **79**
 (off Cherry Garden St.)
Burton La. SW9 . . . . 5C **90**
 (not continuous)
Burton M. SW1. . . . . 5C **74**
Burton Pl. WC1 . .2F 61 (2C **6**)
Burton Rd. NW6. . . . . 4B **44**
 SW9 . . . . 5D **91**
 (Akerman Rd.)
 SW9 . . . . 5C **90**
 (Evesham Wlk.)
Burton St. WC1 . .2F 61 (2C **6**)
Burtonwood Ho. N4 . . . . 2F **35**
Burt Rd. E16. . . . . 2E **83**
Burtt Ho. *N1*. 1D **11**
 (off Aske St.)
Burtwell La. SE27. . . . . 4F **119**
Burwash Ho. *SE1*. 4C **26**
 (off Kipling Est.)
Burwell Cl. E1 . . . . 5D **65**
Burwell Rd. E10. . . . . 3A **38**
Burwell Rd. Ind. Est.
 E10. . . . . 3A **38**
Burwell Wlk. E3. . . . . 3C **66**
Burwood Ho. SW9 . . . . 2D **105**
Burwood Pl. W2. . . . . 5A **60**
Bury Cl. SE16 . . . . 2F **79**
Bury Ct. EC3 . . .5A 64 (2E **19**)
Bury Pl. WC1 . .4A 62 (1D **15**)
Bury Sq. WC1 . . . . 4A **62**
Bury St. EC3 . . .5A 64 (3E **19**)
 SW1. . . . . . .2E 75 (1A **22**)
Bury Wlk. SW3. . . . . 5A **74**
Busbridge Ho. *E14*. 4C **66**
 (off Brabazon St.)
Busby M. NW5 . . . . 3F **47**
Busby Pl. NW5 . . . . 3F **47**

Bushbaby Cl.
 SE1 . . . . .4A 78 (5D **27**)
Bushberry Rd. E9. . . . . . 3A **52**
Bush Cotts. SW18 . . . 3C **100**
Bush Ct. W12 . . . . 3F **71**
Bushell Cl. SW2. . . . . . 2B **118**
Bushell St. E1 . . . . 2C **78**
Bushey Down SW12. . 2D **117**
Bushey Hill Rd. SE5. . . . 4A **92**
Bushey Rd. E13 . . . . 1E **69**
 N15. . . . . 1A **36**
Bush Ind. Est. N19. . . . . 5E **33**
Bush La. EC4 . .1F 77 (4B **18**)
Bushnell Rd. SW17 . . 2D **117**
Bush Rd. E8 . . . . 5D **51**
 E11. . . . . 2B **40**
 SE8 . . . . 5F **79**
Bushwood E11 . . . . 3B **40**
Bushwood Dr. SE1 . . . . 5B **78**
Butcher Row E1 . . . . 5F **65**
 E14. . . . . 1F **79**
Butchers Rd. E16. . . . . . 5C **68**
Bute Gdns. W6 . . . . 5F **71**
Bute St. SW7 . . . . 5F **73**
Bute Wlk. N1 . . . . 3F **49**
Butfield Ho. *E9*. 3E **51**
 (off Stevens Av.)
Butler Ho. *E2* 2E **65**
 (off Bacton St.)
 E14. . . . . 5B **66**
 (off Burdett St.)
 SW9 . . . . 4D **91**
 (off Lothian Rd.)
Butler Pl. SW1 . . . . 5B **22**
Butler Rd. NW10 . . . . . . 4B **42**
Butlers & Colonial Wharf
 SE1 . . . . 3F **27**
 (off Shad Thames)
Butler St. E2 . . . . 2E **65**
Butlers Wharf *SE1* 3F **27**
 (off Gainsford St.)
Butley Ct. *E3* 1A **66**
 (off Ford St.)
Butterfield Cl. SE16. . . . 3D **79**
Butterfields E17 . . . . 1E **39**
Butterfly Wlk. *SE5* 5F **91**
 (off Denmark Hill)
Buttermere *NW1*. 1E **5**
 (off Augustus St.)
Buttermere Cl. E15. . . . . 1F **53**
 SE1 . . . . 5B **78**
Buttermere Ct. *NW8*. . . 5F **45**
 (off Boundary Rd.)
Buttermere Dr. SW15. . 3A **100**
Buttermere Wlk. E8 . . . . 3B **50**
Butterwick W6 . . . . 5F **71**
Buttesland St.
 N1 . . . . .2F 63 (1C **10**)
Butts Rd. BR1: Brom . . 5A **124**
Buxhall Cres. E9 . . . . . . 3B **52**
Buxted Rd. E8 . . . . 4B **50**
 SE22 . . . . 2A **106**
Buxton Cl. E11. . . . . 2B **40**
 N1. . . . . 1A **10**
Buxton Rd. E6. . . . . 2F **69**
 E15. . . . . 2A **54**
 N19. . . . . 3F **33**
 NW2 . . . . 3D **43**
 SW14 . . . . 1A **98**
Buxton St. E1 . . . . 3B **64**

Byam St. SW6 . . . . .5E **87**
Byards Ct. *SE16* 5F **79**
    (off Worgan St.)
Byelands Cl. SE16 . . . .2F **79**
Bye, The W3. . . . . .5A **56**
Byfield Gdns. SW13 . . . .4C **84**
Byfield Cl. SE16 . . . . . .3B **80**
Byford Cl. E15 . . . . . . .4A **54**
Bygrove St. E14 . . . . . . .5D **67**
    (not continuous)
Byne Rd. SE26 . . . . . . .5E **121**
Byng Pl. WC1 . . .3F **61** (4C **6**)
Byng St. E14. . . . . .3C **80**
Byrne Rd. SW12. . . . . .1D **117**
Byron Av. E12 . . . . .3F **55**
Byron Cl. E8 . . . . .5C **50**
  SE26 . . . . .4A **122**
  SW16 . . . . .5A **118**
Byron Ct. NW6 . . . . . . .4E **45**
    (off Fairfax Rd.)
  SE22 . . . . .1C **120**
  W9 . . . .*3C* **58**
    (off Lanhill Rd.)
  WC1 . . . . .3F **7**
    (off Mecklenburgh Sq.)
Byron Dr. N2 . . . . .1F **31**
Byron M. NW3 . . . . . . .2B **46**
  W9 . . . . .3C **58**
Byron Rd. E10 . . . . . . .3D **39**
  NW2 . . . . .4D **29**
Byron St. E14 . . . . .5E **67**
Bythorn St. SW9. . . . . .1B **104**
Byton Rd. SW17 . . . . . .5B **116**
Byward St.
  EC3 . . . . . . .1A **78** (5E **19**)
Bywater Ho. SE18. . . . . .4F **83**
Bywater Pl. SE16 . . . . . .2A **80**
Bywater St. SW3 . . . . . .1B **88**
Byway E11 . . . . .1E **41**
Bywell Pl. W1 . . . . .1F **13**
Byworth Wlk. N19 . . . . .3A **34**

C

Cabbell St. NW1 . . . . . .4A **60**
Cabinet War Rooms
  . . . . .3F **75** (3C **22**)
Cable Ho. *WC1* *1B* **8**
    (off Gt. Percy St.)
Cable Pl. SE10 . . . . . . .4E **95**
Cable St. E1 . . . . .1C **78**
Cable Trade Pk. SE7. . . .5E **83**
Cabot Ct. *SE16* *5F* **79**
    (off Worgan St.)
Cabot Sq. E14. . . . . . . .2C **80**
Cabot Way E6 . . . . .5F **55**
Cab Rd. SE1 . . . . .3B **24**
Cabul Rd. SW11. . . . . . .5A **88**
Caci Ho. *W14* *5B* **72**
    (off Avonmore Rd.)
Cactus Cl. SE15 . . . . . .5A **92**
Cactus Wlk. W12 . . . . . .5B **56**
Cadbury Way SE16. . . . .4B **78**
    (not continuous)
Caddington Rd. NW2 . . .5A **30**
Cadell Cl. E2 . . . . .1B **64**
Cade Rd. SE10 . . . . . . .4F **95**
Cader Rd. SW18. . . . . . .4E **101**
Cadet Dr. SE1 . . . . .5B **78**

Cadet Pl. SE10. . . . . . . .1A **96**
Cadiz St. SE17 . . . . . . .1E **91**
Cadley Ter. SE23 . . . . . .2E **121**
Cadman Cl. SW9 . . . . . .3D **91**
Cadmore Ho. *N1* *4D* **49**
    (off Sutton Est., The)
Cadmus Cl. SW4 . . . . . .1F **103**
Cadmus Ct. *SW9* *4C* **90**
    (off Southey Rd.)
Cadnam Lodge *E14* *4E* **81**
    (off Schooner Cl.)
Cadogan Cl. E9 . . . . . . .4B **52**
Cadogan Ct. *SW3*. *5B* **74**
    (off Draycott Av.)
Cadogan Gdns. SW3 . . . .5B **74**
Cadogan Ga. SW1 . . . . . .5B **74**
Cadogan Ho. *SW3* *2F* **87**
    (off Beaufort St.)
Cadogan La.
  SW1 . . . . .4C **74** (5B **20**)
Cadogan Mans. *SW3* . . .*5B* **74**
    (off Cadogan Gdns.)
Cadogan Pl.
  SW1 . . . . .4B **74** (5A **20**)
Cadogan Sq.
  SW1 . . . . .4B **74** (5A **20**)
Cadogan St. SW3 . . . . . .5B **74**
Cadogan Ter. E9 . . . . . . .3B **52**
Cadoxton Av. N15 . . . . . .1B **36**
Caedmon Rd. N7 . . . . . .1B **48**
Caernarvon Ho. *E16*. . . .*1D* **83**
    (off Audley Dr.)
  W2 . . . .*5E* **59**
    (off Hallfield Est.)
Café Gallery 4E **79**
Cahill St. EC1 . . .3E **63** (4A **10**)
Cahir St. E14 . . . . .5D **81**
Caird St. W10. . . . . .2A **58**
Cairncross M. *N8*. *1A* **34**
    (off Felix Av.)
Cairnfield Av. NW2 . . . . .5A **28**
Cairns Rd. SW11 . . . . . .3A **102**
Caister Ho. N7 . . . . .3B **48**
Caistor Ho. *E15* *5B* **54**
    (off Caistor Pk. Rd.)
Caistor M. SW12 . . . . . .5D **103**
Caistor Pk. Rd. E15 . . . .5B **54**
Caistor Rd. SW12 . . . . . .5D **103**
Caithness Ho. *N1*. *5B* **48**
    (off Twyford St.)
Caithness Rd. W14. . . . .4F **71**
Calabria Rd. N5. . . . . . .3D **49**
Calais Ga. SE5. . . . . . . .4D **91**
Calais St. SE5 . . . . .4D **91**
Calbourne Rd. SW12. . . .5B **102**
Calcott Ct. *W14* *4A* **72**
    (off Blythe Rd.)
Calcott Wlk. SE9. . . . . . .4F **125**
Calcraft Ho. *E2*. *1E* **65**
    (off Bonner Rd.)
Caldecot Rd. SE5 . . . . . .5E **91**
Caldecott Way E5 . . . . . .5F **37**
Calder Ct. SE16 . . . . . . .2B **80**
Calderon Ho. *NW8* *1A* **60**
    (off Townshend Est.)
Calderon Pl. W10. . . . . .4E **57**
Calderon Rd. E11. . . . . .1E **53**
Caldervale Rd. SW4. . . .3F **103**
Caldew St. SE5. . . . . . . .3F **91**
Caldicot Grn. NW9 . . . . .1A **28**

Caldwell Ho. *SW13* *3E* **85**
    (off Trinity Chu. Rd.)
Caldwell St. SW9. . . . . .3B **90**
Caldy Wlk. N1 . . . . .4E **49**
Caleb St. SE1. . .3E **77** (3F **25**)
Caledonia Ho. *E14*. *5A* **66**
    (off Salmon La.)
Caledonian Rd.
  N1 . . . . .1A **62** (1E **7**)
  N7 . . . . .1B **48**
Caledonian Wharf E14 . . .5F **81**
Caledonia St.
  N1 . . . . .1A **62** (1E **7**)
Cale St. SW3 . . . . .1A **88**
Caletock Way SE10 . . . .1B **96**
Calgarth *NW1* *1A* **6**
    (off Ampthill Est.)
Calgary Ct. *SE16* *3E* **79**
    (off Canada Est.)
Caliban Twr. *N1* *1A* **64**
    (off Arden Est.)
Calico Ho. *EC4*. *3A* **18**
    (off Well Ct.)
Calico Row SW11. . . . . .1E **101**
Calidore Cl. SW2 . . . . . .4B **104**
Callaby Ter. N1. . . . . . . .3F **49**
Callaghan Cl. SE13 . . . .2A **110**
Callahan Cotts. *E1*. *4E* **65**
    (off Lindley St.)
Callander Rd. SE6 . . . . .2D **123**
Callcott Ct. NW6 . . . . . .4B **44**
Callcott Rd. NW6. . . . . .4B **44**
Callcott St. W8. . . . . . . .2C **72**
Callendar Rd. SW7. . . . .4F **73**
Callingham Cl. E14 . . . .4B **66**
Callis Rd. E17 . . . . .1B **38**
Callow St. SW3 . . . . . . .2F **87**
Calmington Rd. SE5. . . .2A **92**
Calmont Rd.
  BR1: Brom 5F **123**
Calonne Rd. SW19. . . . .4F **113**
Calshot Ho. *N1*. *1B* **62**
    (off Calshot St.)
Calshot St. N1 . . .1B **62** (1F **7**)
Calstock *NW1* *5E* **47**
    (off Royal College St.)
Calstock Ho. *SE11* *1C* **90**
    (off Kennings Way)
Calthorpe St.
  WC1 . . . . .3B **62** (3A **8**)
Calton Av. SE21 . . . . . . .4A **106**
Calverley Cl.
  BR3: Beck. 5D **123**
Calverley Gro. N19. . . . .3F **33**
Calvert Av. E2 . .2A **64** (2E **11**)
Calvert Ho. *W12* *1D* **71**
    (off White City Est.)
Calverton *SE17*. *2A* **92**
    (off Albany Rd.)
Calvert Rd. SE10 . . . . . .1B **96**
Calvert's Bldgs.
  SE1. . . . . . . .2F **77** (2B **26**)
Calvert St. NW1 . . . . . . .5C **46**
Calvin St. E1 . . .3B **64** (4F **11**)
Calydon Rd. SE7 . . . . . .1D **97**
Calypso Cres. SE15 . . . .3B **92**
Calypso Way SE16. . . . .4B **80**
Cambalt Rd. SW15. . . . .3F **99**
Cambay Ho. *E1* *3A* **66**
    (off Harford St.)

Carker's La. NW5 . . . . 2D 47
Carleton Gdns. N19 . . . . 2E 47
Carleton Rd. N7 . . . . 2F 47
Carleton Vs. NW5 . . . . 2E 47
Carlingford Rd. NW3 . . . 1F 45
Carlisle Av.
  EC3 . . . . 5B 64 (3F 19)
  W3 . . . . 5A 56
Carlisle Gdns.
  IG1: Ilf 1F 41
Carlisle La.
  SE1 . . . . 4B 76 (5A 24)
Carlisle Mans. SW1 . . . . . 5E 75
  (off Carlisle Pl.)
Carlisle Pl.
  SW1 . . . . . . 4E 75 (5F 21)
Carlisle Rd. E10 . . . . . . 3C 38
  N4 . . . . 2C 34
  NW6 . . . . 5A 44
Carlisle St. W1 . . 5F 61 (3B 14)
Carlisle Wlk. E8 . . . . 3B 50
Carlisle Way SW17 . . 5C 116
Carlos Pl. W1 . . 1C 74 (5C 12)
Carlow St. NW1 . . . . 1E 61
Carlson Ct. SW15 . . . . 2B 100
Carlton Cl. NW3 . . . . . . 4C 30
Carlton Ct. SW9 . . . . . . 4D 91
  W9 . . . . 1D 59
  (off Maida Va.)
Carlton Dr. SW15 . . . . . 3F 99
Carlton Gdns.
  SW1 . . . . . . 2F 75 (2B 22)
Carlton Hill NW8 . . . . . 1D 58
Carlton Ho. NW6 . . . . . . 1C 58
  (off Canterbury Ter.)
  SE16 . . . . 3F 79
  (off Wolfe Cres.)
Carlton Ho. Ter.
  SW1 . . . . . . 2F 75 (2B 22)
Carlton Lodge N4 . . . . . . 2C 34
  (off Carlton Rd.)
Carlton Mans. NW6 . . . . 4C 44
  (off W. End La.)
  W9 . . . . 2D 59
Carlton M. NW6 . . . . . . 2C 44
  (off West Cotts.)
  NW6 . . . . 2C 58
Carlton Rd. E11 . . . . . . 3B 40
  E12 . . . . 1F 55
  N4 . . . . 2C 34
Carlton Sq. E1 . . . . 3F 65
  (not continuous)
Carlton St.
  SW1 . . . . . . 1F 75 (5B 14)
Carlton Ter. SE26 . . . . . 3E 121
Carlton Ter. St. E7 . . . . . 4E 55
Carlton Twr. Pl.
  SW1 . . . . . . 4B 74 (5A 20)
Carlton Va. NW6 . . . . . . 1B 58
Carlwell St. SW17 . . . . 5A 116
Carlyle Cl. N2 . . . . 1E 31
  NW10 . . . . 5A 42
Carlyle Ct. SW6 . . . . 4D 87
  (off Imperial Rd.)
  SW10 . . . . 4E 87
  (off Chelsea Harbour Dr.)
Carlyle M. E1 . . . . 3F 65
Carlyle Pl. SW15 . . . . . 2F 99

Carlyle Rd. E12 . . . . 1F 55
Carlyle's House **2A 88**
  (off Cheyne Row)
Carlyle Sq. SW3 . . . . 1F 87
Carmalt Gdns. SW15 . . 2E 99
Carmarthen Grn. NW9 . . 1A 28
Carmarthen Pl.
  SE1 . . . . 3A 78 (3D 27)
Carmel Ct. W8 . . . . 3D 73
  (off Holland St.)
Carmelite St.
  EC4 . . . . 1C 76 (4C 16)
Carmen St. E14 . . . . 5D 67
Carmichael Cl. SW11 . . 1F 101
Carmichael Ct. SW13 . . 5B 84
  (off Grove Rd.)
Carmichael Ho. E14 . . . . 1E 81
  (off Poplar High St.)
Carmichael M. SW18 . . 5F 101
Carminia Rd. SW17 . . . 2D 117
Carnaby St. W1 . . 5E 61 (3F 13)
Carnac St. SE27 . . . . . . 4F 119
Carnarvon Rd. E10 . . . . . 1E 39
  E15 . . . . 3B 54
Carnbrook Rd. SE3 . . . . 1F 111
Carnegie Pl. SW19 . . . . 3F 113
Carnegie St. N1 . . . . . . 5B 48
Carnie Hall SW17 . . . . . 3D 117
Carnival Ho. SE1 . . . . . . 3F 27
  (off Gainsford St.)
Carnoustie Dr. N1 . . . . . 4B 48
  (not continuous)
Carnwath Rd. SW6 . . . . 1C 100
Carolina Cl. E15 . . . . . . 2A 54
Caroline Cl. SW16 . . . . 3B 118
  W2 . . . . 1D 73
  (off Bayswater Rd.)
Caroline Cl. SE6 . . . . . . 4F 123
Caroline Gdns.
  E2 . . . . 2A 64 (1E 11)
  SE15 . . . . 3D 93
Caroline Ho. W6 . . . . 1E 85
  (off Queen Caroline St.)
Caroline Pl. SW11 . . . . . 5C 88
  W2 . . . . 1D 73
Caroline Pl. M. W2 . . . . 1D 73
Caroline St. E1 . . . . 5F 65
Caroline Ter. SW1 . . . . . 5C 74
Caroline Wlk. W6 . . . . . . 2A 86
  (off Lillie Rd.)
Carol St. NW1 . . . . 5E 47
Caronia St. SE16 . . . . . . 5A 80
  (off Plough Way)
Carpenter Ho. E14 . . . . . 4C 66
  (off Burgess St.)
  NW11 . . . . 1E 31
Carpenters Bus. Pk.
  E15 . . . . 4D 53
Carpenters Ct. NW1 . . . . 5E 47
  (off Pratt St.)
Carpenters M. N7 . . . . . 2A 48
Carpenters Pl. SW4 . . . 2F 103
Carpenter's Rd. E15 . . . 3C 52
Carpenter St.
  W1 . . . . 1D 75 (5D 13)
Carradale Ho. E14 . . . . . 5E 67
  (off St Leonard's Rd.)
Carrara Cl. SE24 . . . . . . 2C 104
Carrara M. E8 . . . . 3C 50
Carrara Wharf SW6 . . . 1A 100

Carriage Dr. E. SW11 . . 3C 88
Carriage Dr. Nth.
  SW11 . . . . 3B 88
  (Carriage Dr. W.,
    not continuous)
Carriage Dr. Nth.
  SW11 . . . . 2C 88
  (Carriage Dr. E.)
Carriage Dr. Sth.
  SW11 . . . . 4B 88
  (not continuous)
Carriage Dr. W. SW11 . . 3B 88
Carriage Pl. N16 . . . . . . 5F 35
  SW16 . . . . 5E 117
Carrick Ho. N7 . . . . 3B 48
  (off Caledonian Rd.)
  SE11 . . . . 1C 90
Carrick M. SE8 . . . . 2C 94
Carrington Ct. SW11 . . 2A 102
  (off Barnard Rd.)
Carrington Gdns. E7 . . . 1C 54
Carrington Ho. W1 . . . . 2D 21
  (off Carrington St.)
Carrington St.
  W1 . . . . 2D 75 (2D 21)
Carrol Cl. NW5 . . . . 1D 47
Carroll Cl. E15 . . . . 2B 54
Carroll Ho. W2 . . . . 1F 73
  (off Craven Ter.)
Carron Cl. E14 . . . . 5D 67
Carroun Rd. SW8 . . . . . 3B 90
Carr St. E14 . . . . 4A 66
Carslake Rd. SW15 . . . . 4E 99
Carson Rd. E16 . . . . 3C 68
  SE21 . . . . 2F 119
Carstairs Rd. SE6 . . . . . 3E 123
Carston Cl. SE12 . . . . . 3B 110
Carswell Rd. SE6 . . . . . 5E 109
Carter Cl. EC4 . . . . 3D 17
Carteret Ho. W12 . . . . . 1D 71
  (off White City Est.)
Carteret St.
  SW1 . . . . . . 3F 75 (4B 22)
Carteret Way SE8 . . . . . 5A 80
Carter Ho. E1 . . . . 1F 19
Carter La. EC4 . . 5D 63 (3E 17)
Carter Pl. SE17 . . . . . . 1E 91
Carter Rd. E13 . . . . 5D 55
  SW19 . . . . 5F 115
Carters Cl. NW5 . . . . . . 2F 47
  (off Torriano Av.)
Carters Hill Cl. SE9 . . . 1E 125
Carters La. SE23 . . . . . 2A 122
Carter St. SE17 . . . . . . 2E 91
Carter's Yd. SW18 . . . . 3C 100
Carthew Rd. W6 . . . . . . 4D 71
Carthew Vs. W6 . . . . . . 4D 71
Carthusian St.
  EC1 . . . . 4D 63 (5F 9)
Cartier Circ. E14 . . . . . . 2D 81
Carting La.
  WC2 . . . . 1A 76 (5E 15)
Cartmel NW1 . . . . 1F 5
  (off Hampstead Rd.)
Carton Ho. SE16 . . . . . . 4C 78
  (off Marine St.)
  W11 . . . . 2F 71
  (off St Ann's Rd.)
Cartwright Gdns.
  WC1 . . . . 2A 62 (2D 7)

Cartwright Ho. *SE1* 4E **77**
(off County St.)
Cartwright St. E1 . . . . . . 1B **78**
Cartwright Way SW13 . . 3D **85**
Carvel Ho. *E14* *1E 95*
(off Manchester Rd.)
Carver Rd. SE24 . . . . . . 4E **105**
Cary Rd. E11 . . . . 1A **54**
Carysfort Rd. N16 . . . . . . 5F **35**
Casby Ho. *SE16* *4C 78*
(off Marine St.)
Cascades Twr. E14 . . . . . . 2B **80**
Casella Rd. SE14 . . . . 3F **93**
Casewick Rd. SE27 . . . 5C **118**
Casimir Rd. E5 . . . . 4E **37**
Casino Av. SE24 . . . . . . 3E **105**
Caspian Ho. *E1* *4F 65*
(off Shandy St.)
Caspian St. SE5 . . . . 3F **91**
Caspian Wlk. E16 . . . . . . 5F **69**
Casselden Rd. NW10 . . 4A **42**
Cassell Ho. *SW9* *5A 90*
(off Stockwell Gdns. Est.)
Cassidy Rd. SW6 . . . . . . 3C **86**
(not continuous)
Cassiobury Rd. E17 . . . 1A **38**
Cassland Rd. E9 . . . . 4F **51**
Casslee Rd. SE6 . . . . . . 5B **108**
Casson Ho. *E1* *4C 64*
(off Spelman St.)
Casson St. E1 . . . . 4C **64**
Castalia Sq. E14 . . . . 3E **81**
Castellain Mans. *W9* . . *3D 59*
*(off Castellain Rd.,
not continuous)*
Castellain Rd. W9 . . . . . 3D **59**
Castell Ho. SE8 . . . . 3C **94**
Castello Av. SW15 . . . . 3E **99**
CASTELNAU **2D 85**
Castelnau SW13 . . . . . . 4C **84**
Castelnau Gdns.
SW13 . . . . 2D **85**
Castelnau Mans.
SW13 . . . . *2D 85*
(off Castelnau, not continuous)
Castelnau Row
SW13 . . . . 2D **85**
Casterbridge NW6 . . . . *5D 45*
(off Abbey Rd.)
Casterbridge W11 . . . . *5B 58*
(off Dartmouth Clo.)
Casterbridge Rd. SE3 . . 1C **110**
Casterton St. E8 . . . . 3D **51**
Castillon Rd. SE6 . . . . . . 2A **124**
Castlands Rd. SE6 . . . . . 2B **122**
Castleacre *W2* *5A 60*
(off Hyde Pk. Cres.)
Castle Baynard St.
EC4 . . . . 1D **77** (4E **17**)
Castlebrook Ct. SE11 . . 5D **77**
Castle Climbing Cen., The
. . . . **4E 35**
Castle Cl. E9 . . . . 2A **52**
SW19 . . . . 3F **113**
Castlecombe Dr. SW19. . 5F **99**
Castlecombe Rd. SE9 . . 4F **125**
Castle Ct. *EC3* *3C 18*
(off Birchin La.)
SE26 . . . . 4A **122**
Castle Dr. IG4: Ilf 1F **41**

Castleford Ct. NW8 . . . . *3F 59*
(off Henderson Dr.)
Castlehaven Rd. NW1 . . 4D **47**
Castle Ho. *SE1* *5E 77*
(off Walworth Rd.)
SW8 . . . . *3A 90*
(off S. Lambeth Rd.)
Castle Ind. Est. SE17 . . . 5E **77**
Castle La. SW1 . . 4E **75** (5A **22**)
Castlemaine SW11 . . . . . 5B **88**
Castle Mead SE5 . . . . . . 3E **91**
Castle M. NW1 . . . . 3D **47**
Castle Pl. NW1 . . . . 3D **47**
W4 . . . . 5A **70**
Castle Point *E13* *1E 69*
(off Boundary Rd.)
Castlereagh St. W1 . . . . 5B **60**
Castle Rd. NW1 . . . . 3D **47**
Castle St. E6 . . . . 1E **69**
Castleton Ho. *E14* *5E 81*
(off Pier St.)
Castleton Rd. SE9 . . . . . 4F **125**
Castletown Rd. W14 . . . 1A **86**
Castleview Cl. N4 . . . . . . 4E **35**
Castle Way SW19 . . . . . . 3F **113**
Castle Wharf *E14* *1A 82*
(off Orchard Pl.)
Castlewood Rd. N15 . . . 1C **36**
N16 . . . . 1C **36**
Castle Yd. N6 . . . . 2C **32**
SE1 . . . . 2D **77** (1E **25**)
Castor La. E14 . . . . 1D **81**
Caterham Rd. SE13 . . 1F **109**
Catesby Ho. *E9* *4E 51*
(off Frampton Pk. Rd.)
Catesby St. SE17 . . . . . . 5F **77**
CATFORD **5D 109**
Catford B'way. SE6 . . 5D **109**
CATFORD GYRATORY
. . . . **5D 109**
Catford Hill SE6 . . . . . . 1B **122**
Catford Island SE6 . . . 5D **109**
Catford M. SE6 . . . . . . 5D **109**
Catford Rd. SE6 . . . . . . 5C **108**
Catford Stadium (Greyhound)
. . . . **4C 108**
Catford Trad. Est. SE6. . 2D **123**
Cathall Leisure Cen. . . **4A 40**
Cathall Rd. E11 . . . . 4F **39**
Cathay Ho. SE16 . . . . . . 3D **79**
Cathay St. SE16 . . . . 3D **79**
Cathcart Hill N19 . . . . . . 5E **33**
Cathcart Rd. SW10 . . . . 2D **87**
Cathcart St. NW5 . . . . . . 3D **47**
Cathedral Lodge *EC1* . . . *5F 9*
(off Aldersgate St.)
Cathedral Mans. *SW1* . . 5E **75**
(off Vauxhall Bri. Rd.)
Cathedral Piazza
SW1 . . . . . . 4E **75** (5F **21**)
Cathedral St.
SE1 . . . . 2F **77** (1B **26**)
Catherall Rd. N5 . . . . . . 5E **35**
Catherine Ct. SW19 . . 5B **114**
Catherine Griffiths Ct.
EC1 . . . . *3C 8*
(off Northampton St.)
Catherine Gro. SE10 . . 4D **95**
Catherine Ho. *N1* *5A 50*
(off Whitmore Est.)

Catherine Pl.
SW1 . . . . . . 4E **75** (5F **21**)
Catherine St.
WC2 . . . . . . 1B **76** (4F **15**)
Catherine Wheel All.
EC2 . . . . 4A **64** (1E **19**)
(not continuous)
Catherine Wheel Yd.
SW1 . . . . 2F **21**
Catherwood Ct. N1 . . . . 1B **10**
(not continuous)
Cathles Rd. SW12 . . . . 4D **103**
Cathnor Rd. W12 . . . . . . 3D **71**
Catling Cl. SE23 . . . . . . 3E **121**
Catlin St. SE16 . . . . 1C **92**
Cato Rd. SW4 . . . . 1F **103**
Cator Rd. SE26 . . . . 5F **121**
Cator St. SE15 . . . . 3B **92**
(E. Surrey Gro.)
SE15 . . . . 2B **92**
(Ebley Cl.)
Cato St. W1 . . . . 4A **60**
Catton St. WC1 . . 4B **62** (1F **15**)
Caudwell Ter. SW18 . . . 4F **101**
Caughley Ho. *SE11* *4C 76*
(off Lambeth Wlk.)
Caulfield Rd. SE15 . . . . 5D **93**
Causeway, The SW18 . 3D **101**
(not continuous)
SW19 . . . . 5E **113**
Causton Cotts. E14 . . . 5A **66**
Causton Ho. SE5 . . . . . . 2E **91**
Causton Rd. N6 . . . . 2D **33**
Causton St. SW1 . . . . . . 5F **75**
Cautley Av. SW4 . . . . . . 3E **103**
Cavalry Gdns. SW15 . . 3B **100**
Cavan Ho. E3 . . . . 5B **52**
Cavaye Pl. SW10 . . . . . . 1E **87**
Cavell Ho. *N1* *5A 50*
(off Colville Est.)
Cavell St. E1 . . . . 4D **65**
Cavendish Av. NW8 . . . 1F **59**
Cavendish Cl. NW6 . . . 3B **44**
NW8 . . . . 2F **59**
Cavendish Ct. EC3 . . . . 2E **19**
Cavendish Dr. E11 . . . . 3F **39**
Cavendish Gdns. SW4. . 4E **103**
Cavendish Ho. *NW8* . . . *1F 59*
(off Wellington Rd.)
Cavendish Mans. *EC1* . . *4B 8*
(off Rosebery Av.)
NW6 . . . . 2C **44**
Cavendish M. Nth.
W1 . . . . 4D **61** (5E **5**)
Cavendish M. Sth.
W1 . . . . 4D **61** (1E **13**)
Cavendish Pde.
SW12 . . . . *4D 103*
(off Clapham Comn. Sth. Side)
Cavendish Pl. SW4 . . . . 3F **103**
W1 . . . . 5D **61** (2E **13**)
Cavendish Rd. N4 . . . . . 1D **35**
NW6 . . . . 4A **44**
SW12 . . . . 4D **103**
Cavendish Sq.
W1 . . . . 5D **61** (2E **13**)
Cavendish St. N1 . . . . . 1F **63**
Cave Rd. E13 . . . . 2D **69**
Caversham Ho. *SE15* . . *2C 92*
(off Haymerle Rd.)

Caversham Rd. NW5 . . . . 3E **47**
Caversham St. SW3 . . . . 2B **88**
Caverswall St. W12 . . . . 5E **57**
Cavour Ho. *SE17* *1D 91*
    (off Alberta Est.)
Cawnpore St. SE19 . . . . 5A **120**
Caxton Cl. SW11 . . . . . . 5A **88**
Caxton Gro. E3 . . . . 2C **66**
Caxton Rd. SW19 . . . . . . 5E **115**
    W12 . . . . 3F **71**
Caxton St. SW1. . 4E **75** (5B **22**)
Caxton St. Nth. E16 . . . 5B **68**
Caxton Wlk.
    WC2 . . . . 5F **61** (3C **14**)
Cayton Pl. EC1 . . . . 2B **10**
Cayton St. EC1. . 2F **63** (2B **10**)
Cazenove Rd. N16 . . . . . 4B **36**
Cearns Ho. E6. . . . . 5F **55**
Cecil Ct. NW6. . . . . 4D **45**
    SW10 . . . . *2E 87*
    (off Fawcett St.)
    WC2 . . . . 1A **76** (5D **15**)
Cecile Pk. N8 . . . . 1A **34**
Cecilia Rd. E8 . . . . 2B **50**
Cecil Rhodes Ho. *NW1* . *1F 61*
    (off Goldington St.)
Cecil Rd. E11 . . . . 5B **40**
    E13 . . . . 5C **54**
    NW10 . . . . 5A **42**
Cedar Cl. E3 . . . . 5B **52**
    SE21 . . . . 1E **119**
Cedar Ct. N1 . . . . 4E **49**
    SE7 . . . . 2E **97**
    SW19 . . . . 3F **113**
Cedar Hgts. NW2 . . . . . . 3B **44**
Cedar Ho. *E14* *3E 81*
    (off Manchester Rd.)
    SE14 . . . . 4F **93**
    SE16 . . . . *3F 79*
    (off Woodland Cres.)
    W8 . . . . *4D 73*
    (off Marloes Rd.)
Cedarhurst Dr. SE9. . . . 3E **111**
Cedar Mt. SE9. . . . . 1F **125**
Cedarne Rd. SW6 . . . . . 3D **87**
Cedar Pl. SE7 . . . . 1E **97**
Cedar Rd. NW2 . . . . 1E **43**
Cedars Av. E17 . . . . 1C **38**
Cedars Cl. SE13 . . . . . . 1F **109**
Cedars M. SW4 . . . . 2D **103**
    (not continuous)
Cedars Rd. E15 . . . . 3A **54**
    SW4 . . . . 1D **103**
    SW13 . . . . 5C **84**
Cedars, The E15 . . . . . . 4B **54**
Cedar Tree Gro. SE27. . 5D **119**
Cedar Way NW1 . . . . 4F **47**
Cedar Way Ind. Est.
    NW1 . . . . 4F **47**
Cedra Ct. N16 . . . . 3C **36**
Celandine Cl. E3 . . . . . . 4C **66**
Celandine Dr. E8 . . . . . . 4B **50**
Celandine Way E15 . . . . 2A **68**
Celbridge M. W2 . . . . . . 5D **59**
Celestial Gdns. SE13 . . 2F **109**
Celia Ho. *N1*. *1A 64*
    (off Arden Est.)
Celia Rd. N19 . . . . 1E **47**
Celtic St. E14 . . . . 4D **67**
Cemetery La. SE7. . . . . . 2F **97**

Cemetery Rd. E7 . . . . . . 2B **54**
Cenacle Cl. NW3 . . . . . . 5C **30**
Cenotaph . . . . **3A 76 (3D 23)**
Centaur St.
    SE1 . . . . 4B **76** (5A **24**)
Central Av. E11. . . . . 4F **39**
    E12 . . . . 5F **41**
    SW11 . . . . 3B **88**
Central Bus. Cen.
    NW10 . . . . 2A **42**
Central Cir. NW4 . . . . . . 1D **29**
Central Criminal Court
    (Old Bailey). . **5D 63 (2E 17)**
Central Hill SE19 . . . . . 5E **119**
Central Ho. E15 . . . . 1E **67**
Central Mans. *NW4* *1D 29*
    (off Watford Way)
Central Markets (Smithfield)
    . . . . **1D 17**
Central Pk. Rd. E6 . . . . . 1F **69**
Central Sq. NW11 . . . . . 1D **31**
Central St. EC1 . . 2E **63** (1F **9**)
Centre Av. NW10 . . . . . . 2E **57**
    W3 . . . . 2A **70**
Centre Ct. Shop. Cen.
    SW19 . . . . 5B **114**
Centre Dr. E7 . . . . 1E **55**
Cen. for the Magic Arts, The
    . . . . *3A 6*
    (off Stephenson Way)
Centre Hgts. *NW3*. *4F 45*
    (off Finchley Rd.)
Centre Point SE1 . . . . . . 1C **92**
Centrepoint WC2 . . . . . . 2C **14**
Centre Point Ho. *WC2* . . *2C 14*
    (off St Giles High St.)
Centre Rd. E7. . . . . 4D **41**
    E11. . . . . 4C **40**
Centre St. E2 . . . . 1D **65**
Centric Cl. NW1 . . . . 5C **46**
Centurion Cl. N7 . . . . . . 4B **48**
Centurion La. E3 . . . . . . 5B **52**
Century Cl. NW4 . . . . . . 1F **29**
Century Ho. SW15 . . . . . 2F **99**
Century M. E5. . . . . 1E **51**
Century Yd. SE23 . . . . . 2E **121**
Cephas Av. E1 . . . . 3E **65**
Cephas Ho. *E1* *3E 65*
    (off Doveton St.)
Cephas St. E1. . . . . 3E **65**
Cerise Rd. SE15. . . . . . . 4C **92**
Cerney M. W2. . . . . 1F **73**
Cervantes Ct. W2. . . . . . 5D **59**
Cester St. E2 . . . . 5C **50**
Ceylon Rd. W14 . . . . 4F **71**
Chadacre Ct. *E15* *5C 54*
    (off Vicars Cl.)
Chadacre Ho. *SW9* . . . *2D 105*
    (off Loughborough Pk.)
Chadbourn St. E14. . . . . 4D **67**
Chadd Grn. E13 . . . . 5C **54**
    (not continuous)
Chadston Ho. *N1*. *4D 49*
    (off Halton Rd.)
Chadswell *WC1* *2E 7*
    (off Cromer St.)
Chadwell St.
    EC1. . . . . 2C **62** (1C **8**)
Chadwick Av. SW19. . . . 5C **114**
Chadwick Cl. SW15 . . . . 5B **98**

Chadwick Rd. E11 . . . . . 1A **40**
    NW10 . . . . 5B **42**
    SE15 . . . . 5B **92**
Chadwick St.
    SW1 . . . . 4F **75** (5B **22**)
Chadwin Rd. E13 . . . . . . 4D **69**
Chadworth Ho. *EC1* *2F 9*
    (off Lever St.)
    N4 . . . . 3E **35**
Chagford St. NW1 . .3B **60** (4A **4**)
Chailey St. E5. . . . . 5E **37**
Chalbury Wlk. N1. . . . . . 1B **62**
Chalcot Cres. NW1. . . . . 5B **46**
Chalcot Gdns. NW3 . . . . 3B **46**
Chalcot M. SW16. . . . . . 3A **118**
Chalcot Rd. NW1 . . . . . . 4C **46**
Chalcot Sq. NW1 . . . . . . 4C **46**
    (not continuous)
Chalcroft Rd. SE13. . . . 3A **110**
Chaldon Rd. SW6. . . . . . 3A **86**
Chale Rd. SW2. . . . . 4A **104**
Chalfont Ct. *NW1* *4A 4*
    (off Baker St.)
Chalfont Ho. *SE16* *4D 79*
    (off Keetons Rd.)
Chalford *NW3* *3E 45*
    (off Finchley Rd.)
Chalford Rd. SE21 . . . . . 4F **119**
CHALK FARM **4C 46**
Chalk Farm Rd. NW1. . . 4C **46**
Chalk Hill Rd. W6. . . . . . 5F **71**
Chalk Rd. E13 . . . . 4D **69**
Chalkwell Ho. *E1* *5F 65*
    (off Pitsea St.)
Challenge Cl. NW10 . . . 5A **42**
Challenger Ho. *E14* . . . *1A 80*
    (off Victory Pl.)
Challice Way SW2 . . . . . 1B **118**
Challoner Cres. W14 . . . 1B **86**
Challoner St. W14 . . . . . 1B **86**
Chalmers Wlk. *SE17* . . . *2D 91*
    (off Hillingdon St.)
Chalsey Rd. SE4 . . . . . . 2B **108**
Chalton Dr. N2 . . . . 1F **31**
Chalton Ho. *NW1* *1B 6*
    (off Chalton St.)
Chalton St. NW1 . . 1E **61** (1B **6**)
    (not continuous)
Chamberlain Cotts. SE5. . 4F **91**
Chamberlain Ho. *E1*. . . *1E 79*
    (off Cable St.)
    NW1 . . . . 1C **6**
    SE1. . . . . *4B 24*
    (off Westminster Bri. Rd.)
Chamberlain St. NW1 . . 4B **46**
Chamberlayne Mans.
    NW10 . . . . *2F 57*
    (off Chamberlayne Rd.)
Chamberlayne Rd.
    NW10 . . . . 5E **43**
Chambers La. NW10 . . . 4D **43**
Chambers Rd. N7. . . . . . 1A **48**
Chambers St. SE16 . . . . 3C **78**
Chambers, The *SW10* . . *4E 87*
    (off Chelsea Harbour Dr.)
Chamber St. E1 . . . . 1B **78**
Chambers Wharf SE16. . 3C **78**
Chambon Pl. W6 . . . . . . 5C **70**
Chambord St.
    E2. . . . . 2B **64** (2F **11**)

Charlotte Rd.
EC2 . . . . 2A 64 (2D 11)
SW13 . . . . 4B 84
Charlotte Row SW4 . . . . 1E 103
Charlotte St. W1. . 4E 61 (5A 6)
Charlotte Ter. N1 . . . . 5B 48
Charlow Cl. SW6 . . . . 5E 87
CHARLTON 3F 97
Charlton Athletic F.C.
(Valley, The) 1E 97
Charlton Chu. La. SE7 . . 1E 97
Charlton Ct. E2. . . . . 5B 50
Charlton Dene SE7 . . . . . 3E 97
Charlton King's Rd. NW5. .2F 47
Charlton La. SE7 . . . . 5F 83
Charlton Lido 3F 97
Charlton Pk. La. SE7 . . . . 3F 97
Charlton Pk. Rd. SE7 . . . . 2F 97
Charlton Pl. N1 . . . . 1D 63
Charlton Rd. NW10 . . . . . 5A 42
SE3. . . . . 3C 96
SE7. . . . . 3C 96
Charlton Way SE3. . . . . . 4A 96
Charlwood Ho's. WC1 . . . . 2E 7
(off Midhope St.)
Charlwood Ho. SW1. . . . . 5F 75
(off Vauxhall Bri. Rd.)
Charlwood Pl. SW1 . . . . . 5E 75
Charlwood Rd. SW15. . . . 2F 99
Charlwood St. SW1 . . . . . 1E 89
(not continuous)
Charlwood Ter. SW15. . . . 2F 99
Charmans Ho. SW8 . . . . . 3A 90
(off Wandsworth Rd.)
Charminster Rd. SE9 . . 4F 125
Charmouth Ho. SW8 . . . . 3B 90
Charnock Ho. W12. . . . . 1D 71
(off White City Est.)
Charnock Rd. E5 . . . . 5D 37
Charnwood Gdns. E14 . . 5C 80
Charnwood St. E5 . . . . . . 4D 37
Charrington St. NW1 . . . . 1F 61
Charsley Rd. SE6. . . . . . 2D 123
Charter Ct. N4 . . . . 3C 34
Charterhouse 3D 63 (4E 9)
Charter Ho. WC2 . . . . 3E 15
(off Crown Ct.)
Charterhouse Bldgs.
EC1. . . . . 3E 63 (4E 9)
Charterhouse M.
EC1 . . . . 4D 63 (5E 9)
Charterhouse Rd. E8 . . 1C 50
Charterhouse Sq.
EC1 . . . . 4D 63 (5E 9)
Charterhouse St.
EC1 . . . . 4C 62 (1C 16)
Charteris Rd. N4 . . . . 3C 34
NW6 . . . . 5B 44
Charters Cl. SE19. . . . . . 5A 120
Chartes Ho. SE1. . . . . 5E 27
(off Stevens St.)
Chartfield Av. SW15. . . . 3D 99
Chartfield Sq. SW15. . . . 3F 99
Chartham Ct. SW9 . . . 1C 104
(off Canterbury Cres.)
Chartham Gro. SE27 . . 3D 119
Chartham Ho. SE1. . . . . . 5C 26
(off Weston St.)
Chart Ho. E14. . . . . 1D 95
(off Burrells Wharf Sq.)

Chartley Av. NW2 . . . . . . 5A 28
Chartridge SE17 . . . . 2F 91
(off Westmoreland Rd.)
Chart St. N1 . . . 2F 63 (1C 10)
Char Wood SW16. . . . . . 4C 118
Chase Cen., The NW10. . 2A 56
Chasefield Rd. SW17. . 4B 116
Chaseley St. E14 . . . . 5A 66
Chasemore Ho. SW6 . . . . 3A 86
(off Williams Cl.)
Chase Rd. NW10 . . . . 3A 56
Chase Rd. Trad. Est.
NW10. . . . . 3A 56
Chase, The E12 . . . . 1F 55
SW4 . . . . 1D 103
Chaston St. NW5 . . . . . . 2C 46
(off Grafton Ter.)
Chater Ho. E2 . . . . 2F 65
(off Roman Rd.)
Chatfield Rd. SW11 . . . . 1E 101
Chatham Cl. NW11 . . . . 1C 30
Chatham Pl. E9 . . . . 3E 51
Chatham Rd. SW11 . . 4B 102
Chatham St. SE17 . . . . . . 5F 77
Chatsworth Av.
BR1: Brom 4D 125
Chatsworth Ct. W8. . . . . 5C 72
(off Pembroke Rd.)
Chatsworth Est. E5 . . . . 1F 51
Chatsworth Ho. E16. . . . 1D 83
(off Wesley Av.)
Chatsworth Lodge W4 . . 1A 84
(off Bourne Pl.)
Chatsworth Pl. NW2. . . . 3E 43
Chatsworth Rd. E5 . . . . . 5E 37
E15 . . . . 2B 54
NW2 . . . . 3E 43
(not continuous)
Chatsworth Way SE27. . 3D 119
Chatterton M. N4 . . . . . . 5D 35
(off Chatterton Rd.)
Chatterton Rd. N4 . . . . . 5D 35
Chatto Rd. SW11 . . . . 3B 102
Chaucer Dr. SE1. . . . . 5B 78
Chaucer Ho. SW1. . . . . . . 1E 89
(off Churchill Gdns.)
Chaucer Mans. W14 . . . 2A 86
(off Queen's Club Gdns.)
Chaucer Rd. E7 . . . . 3C 54
E11. . . . . 1C 40
SE24. . . . . 3C 104
Chaucer Theatre 2F 19
(off Braham St.)
Chaucer Way SW19 . . . 5E 115
Chaulden Ho. EC1 . . . . . 2C 10
(off Cranwood St.)
Chauntler Cl. E16. . . . . . 5D 69
Cheadle Ct. NW8 . . . . . . 3F 59
(off Henderson Dr.)
Cheadle Ho. E14 . . . . 5B 66
(off Copenhagen Pl.)
Cheam St. SE15 . . . . 1E 107
Cheapside EC2. . 5E 63 (3A 18)
Chearsley SE17 . . . . 5E 77
(off Deacon Way)
Cheddington Ho. E2 . . . 5C 50
(off Whiston Rd.)
Chedworth Cl. E16. . . . . 5B 68
Cheesemans Ter. W14. . 1B 86
(not continuous)

Cheethams Rd. E12 . . . . . 5F 41
Chelford Rd.
BR1: Brom 5F 123
Chelmer Rd. E9 . . . . 2F 51
Chelmsford Cl. W6. . . . . . 2F 85
Chelmsford Ho. N7 . . . . 1B 48
(off Holloway Rd.)
Chelmsford Rd. E11 . . . 3F 39
E17. . . . . 1C 38
Chelmsford Sq. NW10. . 5E 43
CHELSEA 1A 88
Chelsea Bri SW1 . . . . . . 2D 89
SW8 . . . . 2D 89
Chelsea Bri. Bus. Cen.
SW8 . . . . 3D 89
Chelsea Bri. Rd. SW1 . . 1C 88
Chelsea Bri. Wharf
SW8 . . . . 2D 89
Chelsea Cloisters
SW3 . . . . 5A 74
Chelsea Cl. NW10 . . . . . 5A 42
Chelsea College of Art &
Design 1A 88
Chelsea Cres. NW2 . . . . 3B 44
SW10 . . . . 4E 87
Chelsea Emb. SW3 . . . . 2A 88
Chelsea Farm Ho. Studios
SW10 . . . . 2F 87
(off Milman's St.)
Chelsea F.C.
(Stamford Bridge). . . 3D 87
Chelsea Gdns. SW1. . . . 1C 88
Chelsea Ga. SW1. . . . . . 1C 88
(off Ebury Bri. Rd.)
Chelsea Harbour Design Cen.
SW10 . . . . 4E 87
(off Chelsea Harbour Dr.)
Chelsea Harbour Dr.
SW10 . . . . 4E 87
Chelsea Lodge SW3. . . . 2B 88
(off Tite St.)
Chelsea Mnr. Ct. SW3 . . 2A 88
Chelsea Mnr. Gdns.
SW3 . . . . 1A 88
Chelsea Mnr. St. SW3 . . 1A 88
Chelsea Pk. Gdns.
SW3 . . . . 2F 87
Chelsea Physic Garden
. . . . 2B 88
Chelsea Reach Twr.
SW10 . . . . 3F 87
(off Worlds End Est.)
Chelsea Sq. SW3 . . . . . . 1F 87
Chelsea Studios SW6 . . 3D 87
(off Fulham Rd.)
Chelsea Towers SW3. . . 2A 88
(off Chelsea Mnr. Gdns.)
Chelsea Village SW6. . . 3D 87
(off Fulham Rd.)
Chelsea Wharf SW10. . . 3F 87
(off Lots Rd.)
Chelsfield Gdns. SE26 . 3E 121
Chelsfield Ho. SE17. . . . 5A 78
(off Massinger St.)
Chelsham Rd. SW4 . . . . 1F 103
Cheltenham Gdns. E6. . 1F 69
Cheltenham Rd. E10 . . 1E 39
SE15 . . . . 2E 107
Cheltenham Ter. SW3 . . 1B 88
Chelverton Rd. SW15. . 2F 99

Cheyne Gdns. SW3 . . . . 2A 88
Cheyne M. SW3 . . . . 2A 88
Cheyne Pl. SW3 . . . . 2B 88
Cheyne Row SW3 . . . . . . 2A 88
Cheyne Wlk. NW4 . . . . . 1E 29
  SW10 . . . . 3F 87
  (not continuous)
Chichele Rd. NW2 . . . . . 2F 43
Chicheley St.
  SE1 . . . . 3B 76 (3A 24)
Chichester Cl. SE3 . . . . 3E 97
Chichester Ho. NW6. . . 1C 58
  SW9 . . . . 3C 90
  (off Brixton Rd.)
Chichester M. SE27 . . . 4C 118
Chichester Rents WC2 . 2B 16
Chichester Rd. E11 . . . 5A 40
  NW6 . . . . 1C 58
  W2 . . . . 4D 59
Chichester St. SW1 . . . 1E 89
Chichester Way E14 . . . 5F 81
Chicksand Ho. E1. . . . . 4C 64
  (off Chicksand St.)
Chicksand St. E1 . . . . . 4B 64
  (not continuous)
Chiddingstone SE13 . . . 3E 109
Chiddingstone St. SW6. . 5C 86
Chigwell Hill E1 . . . . . . 1D 79
Chilcot Cl. E14 . . . . 5D 67
Childebert Rd. SW17 . . 2D 117
Childeric Rd. SE14 . . . . 3A 94
Childerley St. SW6. . . . 4A 86
Childers St. SE8 . . . . . . 2A 94
Child La. SE10 . . . . 4B 82
CHILD'S HILL 5C 30
  (off Cricklewood La.)
Childs Hill Wlk. NW2. . 5B 30
Child's Pl. SW5 . . . . . . 5C 72
Child's St. SW5 . . . . . . 5C 72
Child's Wlk. SW5 . . . . . 5C 72
  (off Child's St.)
Chilham Ho.
  SE1. . . . . . . 4F 77 (5C 26)
  SE15 . . . . 2E 93
Chilham Rd. SE9 . . . . . 4F 125
Chilianwalla Memorial
  . . . . 2C 88
  (off Royal Hospital Chelsea)
Chillerton Rd. SW17 . . 5C 116
Chillingworth Rd. N7 . . 2C 48
Chiltern Ct. NW1 . . . . . 4A 4
  (off Baker St.)
  SE14 . . . . 3E 93
  (off Avonley Rd.)
Chiltern Gdns. NW2 . . . 5F 29
Chiltern Ho. SE17. . . . . 2F 91
  (off Portland St.)
Chiltern Rd. E3 . . . . . . 3C 66
Chiltern St. W1 . . 4C 60 (5B 4)
Chilthorne Cl. SE6 . . . 5B 108
Chilton Gro. SE8 . . . . . 5F 79
Chiltonian Ind. Est.
  SE12. . . . . 4B 110
Chilton St. E2 . . . . 3B 64
Chilver St. SE10 . . . . . . 1B 96
Chilworth Ct. SW19 . . . 1F 113
Chilworth M. W2 . . . . . . 5F 59
Chilworth St. W2 . . . . . . 5E 59
Chimney Ct. E1 . . . . . . 2D 79
  (off Brewhouse La.)

China Ct. E1. . . . . 2D 79
  (off Asher Way)
China M. SW2 . . . . 5B 104
China Wharf SE1 . . . . . 3C 78
Chinbrook Cres. SE12. . 3D 125
Chinbrook Rd. SE12. . . 3D 125
Ching Ct. WC2 . . . . 3D 15
  (off Monmouth St.)
Chingley Cl.
  BR1: Brom 5A 124
Chinnock's Wharf E14 . . 1A 80
  (off Narrow St.)
Chipka St. E14 . . . . 3E 81
  (not continuous)
Chipley St. SE14 . . . . . 2A 94
Chippendale Ho. SW1 . . 1D 89
  (off Churchill Gdns.)
Chippendale St. E5. . . . 5F 37
Chippenham Gdns.
  NW6 . . . . 2C 58
Chippenham M. W9. . . 3C 58
Chippenham Rd. W9 . . 3C 58
Chipperfield Ho. SW3 . . 1A 88
  (off Ixworth Pl.)
Chipstead Gdns. NW2 . . 4D 29
Chipstead St. SW6. . . . 4C 86
Chip St. SW4 . . . . 1F 103
Chisenhale Rd. E3 . . . . 1A 66
Chisholm Ct. W6 . . . . . 1C 84
Chisledon Wlk. E9 . . . . 3B 52
  (off Osborne Rd.)
Chisley Rd. N15. . . . . . 1A 36
Chiswell Sq. SE3 . . . . . 5D 97
Chiswell St.
  EC1 . . . . 4E 63 (5B 10)
CHISWICK 1A 84
Chiswick Comn. Rd.
  W4 . . . . 5A 70
Chiswick High Rd. W4 . 5A 70
  (not continuous)
Chiswick House 2A 84
Chiswick La. W4 . . . . . 1A 84
Chiswick La. Sth. W4 . . 2B 84
Chiswick Mall W4 . . . . . 2B 84
  W6 . . . . 2B 84
Chiswick Sq. W4 . . . . . 2A 84
Chiswick Wharf W4 . . . 2B 84
Chitty St. W1 . . . 4E 61 (5A 6)
Chivalry Rd. SW11. . . . 3A 102
Chobham Gdns. SW19 . . 2F 113
Chobham Rd. E15. . . . . 2F 53
Chocolate Studios N1 . . 1B 10
  (off Shepherdess Pl.)
Cholmeley Cres. N6. . . 2D 33
Cholmeley Lodge N6 . . 3D 33
Cholmeley Pk. N6 . . . . 3D 33
Cholmley Gdns. NW6. . 2C 44
Cholmondeley Av.
  NW10 . . . . 1C 56
Choppin's Ct. E1 . . . . . 2D 79
Chopwell Cl. E15 . . . . . 4F 53
Choumert Gro. SE15 . . 5C 92
Choumert M. SE15. . . . 5C 92
Choumert Rd. SE15 . . . 1B 106
Choumert Sq. SE15 . . . 5C 92
Chow Sq. E8 . . . . 2B 50
Chrisp Ho. SE10. . . . . . 2A 96
  (off Maze Hill)
Chrisp St. E14 . . . . 4D 67
  (not continuous)

Christchurch Av. NW6 . . 5F 43
Christchurch Ct. EC4 . . 2E 17
  (off Warwick La.)
Christ Church Ct. NW10. . 5A 42
Christchurch Hill NW3 . . 5F 31
Christchurch Ho.
  SW2 . . . . 1B 118
  (off Christchurch Rd.)
Christchurch Pas.
  NW3 . . . . 5E 31
Christchurch Pl. SW8. . 5F 89
Christchurch Rd. N8. . . 1A 34
  SW2 . . . . 1B 118
Christchurch Sq. E9 . . 5E 51
Christchurch St. SW3. . 2B 88
Christchurch Ter. SW3 . . 2B 88
  (off Christchurch St.)
Christchurch Way SE10. . 1A 96
Christian Cl. SE16 . . . . 2B 80
Christian Pl. E1 . . . . . . 5C 64
  (off Burslem St.)
Christian St. E1 . . . . . . 5C 64
Christie Ct. N19 . . . . . . 4A 34
Christie Ho. SE10. . . . . 1B 96
  (off Blackwall La.)
Christie Rd. E9. . . . . . . 3A 52
Christina Sq. N4 . . . . . 3D 35
Christina St.
  EC2 . . . . 3A 64 (3D 11)
Christopher Cl. SE16 . . 3F 79
Christopher Pl.
  NW1 . . . . 2F 61 (1C 6)
Christophers M. W11. . 2A 72
Christopher St.
  EC2 . . . . 3F 63 (4C 10)
Chryssell Rd. SW9. . . . 3C 90
Chubworthy St. SE14 . . 2A 94
Chudleigh Rd. NW6 . . . 4F 43
  SE4 . . . . 3B 108
Chudleigh St. E1. . . . . . 5F 65
Chulsa Rd. SE26 . . . . . 5D 121
Chumleigh St. SE5. . . . 2A 92
Church App. SE21 . . . . 3F 119
Church Av. E12 . . . . 5F 41
  NW1 . . . . 3D 47
Churchbury Rd. SE9. . . 5F 111
Church Cloisters EC3. . 5D 19
Church Cl. W8 . . . . 3D 73
Church Ct. SE16. . . . . . 3B 80
  (off Rotherhithe St.)
Church Cres. E9 . . . . . 4F 51
Churchcroft Cl. SW12. . 5C 102
Churchdown
  BR1: Brom 4A 124
CHURCH END. 3A 42
Church Entry EC4 . . . . 3E 17
Churchfield Mans. SW6. . 5B 86
  (off New Kings Rd.)
Churchfields SE10 . . . . 2E 95
Church Gth. N19. . . . . . 4F 33
  (off St John's Gro.)
Church Ga. SW6. . . . . . 1A 100
Church Grn. SW9 . . . . . 4C 90
Church Gro. SE13 . . . . 3D 109
Church Hill SW19. . . . . 5B 114
Church Ho. EC1 . . . . . . 3E 9
  (off Compton St.)
  SW1 . . . . 5C 22
  (off Gt. Smith St.)
Churchill Ct. N4 . . . . . . 2C 34

Churchill Gdns. SW1 . . . 1E **89**
(off Churchill Gdns., not cont.)
Churchill Gdns. Rd.
SW1 . . . . 1D **89**
Churchill Pl. E14 . . . . . . 2D **81**
Churchill Rd. E16 . . . . . . 5E **69**
NW2 . . . . 3D **43**
NW5 . . . . 1D **47**
Churchill Wlk. E9 . . . . . 2E **51**
Church La. E11 . . . . 3A **40**
SW17 . . . . 5B **116**
Churchley Rd. SE26 . . . 4D **121**
Church Mead SE5 . . . . . 3E **91**
(off Camberwell Rd.)
Churchmead Rd. NW10 . 3C **42**
Church Mt. N2 . . . . 1F **31**
Church Pas. EC2 . . . . . 2A **18**
(off Guildhall Yd.)
Church Path E11 . . . . . . 1C **40**
N5 . . . . 2D **49**
NW10 . . . . 4A **42**
SW14 . . . . 1A **98**
(not continuous)
Church Pl. W1 . . 1E **75** (5A **14**)
Church Ri. SE23 . . . . . . 2F **121**
Church Rd. E10 . . . . . . 3C **38**
E12 . . . . 2F **55**
N1 . . . . 3E **49**
N6 . . . . 1C **32**
NW10 . . . . 4A **42**
SW13 . . . . 5B **84**
SW19 . . . . 5A **114**
Church Rd. Almshouses
E10 . . . . 4D **39**
(off Church Rd.)
Church Rd. Ind. Est. E10 . 3C **38**
Church Row NW3 . . . . . 1E **45**
Church St. E15 . . . . 5A **54**
W2 . . . . 4F **59**
W4 . . . . 2B **84**
Church St. Est. NW8 . . . 3F **59**
(not continuous)
Church St. Nth. E15 . . . 5A **54**
Church St. Pas. E15 . . . 5A **54**
(off Church St.)
Church Ter. SE13 . . . . . 1A **110**
Church Va. SE23 . . . . . 2F **121**
Church Wlk. N6 . . . . . . 5C **32**
N16 . . . . 5F **35**
(not continuous)
NW2 . . . . 5B **30**
SW13 . . . . 4C **84**
SW15 . . . . 3D **99**
Churchward Ho. W14 . . 1B **86**
(off Ivatt Pl.)
Churchway NW1 . . 2F **61** (1C **6**)
(not continuous)
Churchwell Path E9 . . . 2E **51**
Churchyard Pas. SE5 . . 5F **91**
Churchyard Row SE11 . . 5D **77**
Churnfield N4 . . . . 4C **34**
Churston Av. E13 . . . . . 5D **55**
Churston Cl. SW2 . . . . 1C **118**
Churton Pl. SW1 . . . . . 5E **75**
Churton St. SW1 . . . . . 5E **75**
Chusan Pl. E14 . . . . . . 5B **66**
Chute Ho. SW9 . . . . . . 5C **90**
(off Stockwell Pk. Rd.)
Cibber Rd. SE23 . . . . . 2F **121**
Cicada Rd. SW18 . . . . . 4E **101**

Cicely Ho. NW8 . . . . . . 1F **59**
(off Cochrane St.)
Cicely Rd. SE15 . . . . . . 4C **92**
Cinderella Path NW11 . . 3D **31**
Cinderford Way
BR1: Brom 4A **124**
Cinnabar Wharf Central
E1 . . . . 2C **78**
(off Wapping High St.)
Cinnabar Wharf E. E1 . . 2C **78**
(off Wapping High St.)
Cinnabar Wharf W. E1 . . 2C **78**
(off Wapping High St.)
Cinnamon Cl. SE15 . . . . 3B **92**
Cinnamon Row SW11 . . 1E **101**
Cinnamon St. E1 . . . . . 2D **79**
Cinnamon Wharf SE1 . . 3B **78**
(off Shad Thames)
Circle, The NW2 . . . . . 5A **28**
SE1 . . . . 3F **27**
(off Queen Elizabeth St.)
Circus Lodge NW8 . . . . 2F **59**
(off Circus Rd.)
Circus M. W1 . . . . 4B **60**
(off Enford St.)
Circus Pl. EC2 . . 4F **63** (1C **18**)
Circus Rd. NW8 . . . . . . 2F **59**
Circus St. SE10 . . . . . . 3E **95**
Cirencester St. W2 . . . . 4D **59**
Cissbury Ho. SE26 . . . . 3C **120**
Cissbury Rd. N15 . . . . . 1F **35**
Citadel Pl. SE11 . . . . . . 1B **90**
Citizen Rd. N7 . . . . 1C **48**
Citrus Ho. SE8 . . . . 1B **94**
(off Alverton St.)
City Bus. Cen. SE16 . . . 4E **79**
City Central Est. EC1 . . . 2F **9**
(off Seward St.)
City Cross Bus. Pk.
SE10 . . . . 5A **82**
City Gdn. Row N1 . 1D **63** (1E **9**)
City Harbour E14 . . . . . 4D **81**
(off Selsdon Way)
City Hgts. SE1 . . . . 2E **27**
(off Weavers La.)
CITY OF LONDON
. . . . 5F **63** (3B **18**)
City of London Almshouses
SW9 . . . . 2B **104**
City of London Crematorium
E12 . . . . 5F **41**
City of Westminster College
. . . . 1E **75** (4B **14**)
City Pav. EC1 . . . . 5D **9**
(off Britton St.)
City Rd. EC1 . . . 1D **63** (1D **9**)
City Twr. EC2 . . . . 1B **18**
(off Basinghall St.)
City University . . 2D **63** (2D **9**)
City Vw. Ct. SE22 . . . . . 5C **106**
City Wall Apartments
EC1 . . . . 2F **9**
(off Seward St.)
Clabon M. SW1 . . . . . . 4B **74**
Clack St. SE16 . . . . 3E **79**
Clacton Rd. E6 . . . . 2F **69**
E17 . . . . 1A **38**
Claire Ct. NW2 . . . . 3A **44**
Claire Pl. E14 . . . . 4C **80**
Clairview Rd. SW16 . . . 5D **117**

Clairville Point SE23 . . . 3F **121**
(off Dacres Rd.)
Clancarty Rd. SW6 . . . . 5C **86**
Clandeboye Ho. E15 . . . 5B **54**
(off John St.)
Clandon Ho. SE1 . . . . . 4E **25**
(off Webber St.)
Clandon St. SE8 . . . . . . 5C **94**
Clanricarde Gdns. W2 . . 1C **72**
CLAPHAM 2E **103**
CLAPHAM COMMON . . 2F **103**
Clapham Comn. Nth. Side
SW4 . . . . 2B **102**
Clapham Comn. Sth. Side
SW4 . . . . 4D **103**
Clapham Comn. W. Side
SW4 . . . . 2B **102**
(not continuous)
Clapham Cres. SW4 . . . 2F **103**
Clapham High St.
SW4 . . . . 2F **103**
CLAPHAM JUNCTION . . 1A **102**
Clapham Junc. App.
SW11 . . . . 1A **102**
Clapham Mnr. Ct.
SW4 . . . . 1E **103**
Clapham Mnr. St.
SW4 . . . . 1E **103**
CLAPHAM PARK 5F **103**
Clapham Pk. Est.
SW4 . . . . 4F **103**
Clapham Pk. Rd.
SW4 . . . . 2E **103**
Clapham Pk. Ter.
SW4 . . . . 3A **104**
(off Kings Av.)
Clapham Rd. SW4 . . . . 1A **104**
Clapham Rd. Est.
SW4 . . . . 1A **104**
Clapton Comn. E5 . . . . 2B **36**
(not continuous)
CLAPTON PARK 1F **51**
Clapton Pk. Est. E5 . . . 1F **51**
Clapton Pas. E5 . . . . . . 2E **51**
Clapton Sq. E5 . . . . . . 2E **51**
Clapton Ter. N16 . . . . . 3C **36**
Clapton Way E5 . . . . . . 1C **50**
Clara Grant Ho. E14 . . . 4C **80**
(off Mellish St.)
Clara Nehab Ho. NW11 . 1B **30**
(off Leeside Cres.)
Clare Ct. WC1 . . . . 2E **7**
(off Judd St.)
Claredale Ho. E2 . . . . . 1D **65**
(off Claredale St.)
Claredale St. E2 . . . . . . 1C **64**
Clare Gdns. E7 . . . . 1C **54**
W11 . . . . 5A **58**
Clare La. N1 . . . . 4E **49**
Clare Lawn Av. SW14 . . 3A **98**
Clare Mkt. WC2 . . 5B **62** (3A **16**)
Clare M. SW6 . . . . 3D **87**
Claremont Cl. N1 . 1C **62** (1C **8**)
SW2 . . . . 1A **118**
Claremont Gro. W4 . . . . 3A **84**
Claremont Rd. E7 . . . . . 2D **55**
E11 . . . . 5F **39**
N6 . . . . 2E **33**
NW2 . . . . 2F **29**
W9 . . . . 1A **58**

Cleveland Row
  SW1 . . . . 2E **75** (2F **21**)
Cleveland Sq. W2. . . . . . . 5E **59**
Cleveland St.
  W1. . . . . 3D **61** (4E **5**)
Cleveland Ter. W2 . . . . . . 5E **59**
Cleveland Way E1. . . . . . 3E **65**
Cleveley Cl. SE7. . . . . . . 5F **83**
Cleveleys Rd. E5 . . . . . . 5D **37**
Cleverly Est. W12. . . . . . 2C **70**
Cleve Rd. NW6. . . . . . 4D **45**
Cleves Ho. E16. . . . . 1D **83**
  (off Southey M.)
Cleves Rd. E6 . . . . 5F **55**
Clewer Ct. E10 . . . . . . 3C **38**
  (off Leyton Grange Est.)
Cley Ho. SE4. . . . . 2F **107**
Clichy Est. E1 . . . . 4E **65**
Clichy Ho. E1 . . . . 4E **65**
  (off Stepney Way)
Clifden Rd. E5 . . . . 2E **51**
Cliffe Ho. SE10. . . . . . . 1B **96**
  (off Blackwall La.)
Clifford Ct. W2. . . . . . . 4D **59**
  (off Westbourne Pk. Vs.)
Clifford Dr. SW9. . . . . . 2D **105**
Clifford Gdns. NW10 . . 1E **57**
Clifford Haigh Ho. SW6. 3F **85**
Clifford Ho.
  BR3: Beck. 5D **123**
  (off Calverley Cl.)
  W14 . . . . 5B **72**
  (off Edith Vs.)
Clifford Rd. E16 . . . . . . 3B **68**
  N1. . . . . 5A **50**
Clifford's Inn Pas.
  WC2. . . . . . . 5C **62** (3B **16**)
Clifford St. W1 . . 1E **75** (5F **13**)
Clifford Way NW10. . . . 1B **42**
Cliff Rd. NW1 . . . . 3F **47**
Cliffsend Ho. SW9 . . . . 4C **90**
  (off Cowley Rd.)
Cliff Ter. SE8. . . . . 5C **94**
Cliffview Rd. SE13 . . . . 1C **108**
Cliff Vs. NW1 . . . . 3F **47**
Cliff Wlk. E16 . . . . 4B **68**
Clifton Av. W12. . . . . . . 2B **70**
Clifton Ct. N4 . . . . 4C **34**
  NW8 . . . . 3F **59**
  (off Maida Va.)
  SE15. . . . . 3D **93**
Clifton Cres. SE15 . . . . 3D **93**
Clifton Est. SE15 . . . . . 4D **93**
Clifton Gdns. N15. . . . . 1B **36**
  NW11 . . . . 1B **30**
  W4 . . . . 5A **70**
  (not continuous)
  W9 . . . . 3E **59**
Clifton Gro. E8 . . . . . . 3C **50**
Clifton Hill NW6. . . . . . 1D **59**
Clifton Ho. E2 . . . . 3F **11**
  (off Club Row)
  E11. . . . . 4A **40**
Clifton Pl. SE16 . . . . . . 3E **79**
  W2. . . . . 5F **59**
Clifton Ri. SE14 . . . . . . 3A **94**
  (not continuous)
Clifton Rd. E7 . . . . 3E **54**
  E16. . . . . 4A **68**
  N8. . . . . 1F **33**

Clifton Rd. NW10. . . . . 1C **56**
  SW19 . . . . 5F **113**
  W9 . . . . 3E **59**
Clifton St. EC2. . 3A **64** (4D **11**)
Clifton Ter. N4 . . . . 4C **34**
Clifton Vs. W9 . . . . 4E **59**
Cliftonville Ct. SE12. . 1C **124**
Clifton Wlk. W6 . . . . . . 5D **71**
  (off King Ed.)
Clifton Way SE15. . . . . 3D **93**
Climsland Ho.
  SE1 . . . . 2C **76** (1C **24**)
Clinch Ct. E16 . . . . 4C **68**
  (off Plymouth Rd.)
Clinger Ct. N1 . . . . 5A **50**
  (off Hobbs Pl. Est.)
Clink Exhibition, The . 1B **26**
Clink St. SE1 . . 2F **77** (1B **26**)
Clink Wharf SE1. . . . . . 1B **26**
  (off Clink St.)
Clinton Rd. E7 . . . . 1C **54**
  E3. . . . . 2A **66**
Clipper Cl. SE16 . . . . . 3F **79**
Clipper Ho. E14 . . . . . . 1E **95**
  (off Manchester Rd.)
Clipper Way SE13 . . . . 2E **109**
Clipstone M.
  W1 . . . . 4E **61** (5F **5**)
Clipstone St.
  W1. . . . . 4D **61** (5E **5**)
Clissold Ct. N4 . . . . . . 4E **35**
Clissold Cres. N16 . . . . 5F **35**
Clissold Leisure Cen. . 5F **35**
Clissold Rd. N16 . . . . . 5F **35**
Clitheroe Rd. SW9. . . . 5A **90**
Clitterhouse Cres.
  NW2 . . . . 3E **29**
Clitterhouse Rd. NW2 . 3E **29**
Clive Ct. W9 . . . . 3E **59**
  (off Maida Va.)
Cliveden Ho. E16 . . . . . 1C **82**
  (off Fitzwilliam M.)
Cliveden Pl. SW1. . . . . 5C **74**
Clive Ho. SE10 . . . . 2E **95**
  (off Haddo St.)
Clive Lloyd Ho. N15. . . 1E **35**
  (off Woodlands Pk. Rd.)
Clive Lodge NW4 . . . . 1F **29**
Clive Pas. SE21 . . . . . . 3F **119**
Clive Rd. SE21 . . . . 3F **119**
  SW19 . . . . 5A **116**
Cloak La. EC4 . . 1E **77** (4A **18**)
Clochar Ct. NW10 . . . . 5B **42**
Clock Ho. E3. . . . . 2E **67**
Clockhouse Cl. SW19. . 2E **113**
Clock Ho. Pde. E11 . . . 1D **41**
Clockhouse Pl. SW15. . 4A **100**
Clock Mus., The 2A **18**
Clock Pl. SE11 . . . . 5D **77**
  (off Newington Butts)
Clock Twr. M. N1 . . . . . 5E **49**
Clock Twr. Pl. N7 . . . . . 3A **48**
Cloister Rd. NW2. . . . . 5B **30**
Cloisters Bus. Cen.
  SW8 . . . . 3D **89**
  (off Battersea Pk. Rd.)
Cloisters, The 5D **23**
Cloisters, The E1 . . . . . 4F **11**
  SW9 . . . . 4C **90**
Clonbrock Rd. N16. . . . 1A **50**

Cloncurry St. SW6 . . . . 5F **85**
Clonmel Rd. SW6 . . . . 3B **86**
Clonmore St. SW18 . . . 1B **114**
Clorane Gdns. NW3 . . . 5C **30**
Close, The SE3. . . . . . . 5F **95**
Cloth Ct. EC1 . . . . 1E **17**
Cloth Fair EC1 . . 4D **63** (1E **17**)
Clothier St. E1. . 5A **64** (2E **19**)
Cloth St. EC1 . . . 4E **63** (5F **9**)
Cloudesdale Rd.
  SW17 . . . . 2D **117**
Cloudesley Pl. N1 . . . . 5C **48**
Cloudesley Rd. N1. . . . 5C **48**
  (not continuous)
Cloudesley Sq. N1 . . . . 5C **48**
Cloudesley St. N1 . . . . 5C **48**
Clova Rd. E7 . . . . 3B **54**
Clove Cres. E14 . . . . . . 1E **81**
Clove Hitch Quay
  SW11 . . . . 1E **101**
Clovelly Ho. W2. . . . . . . 5E **59**
  (off Hallfield Est.)
Clovelly Way E1 . . . . . . 5E **65**
Clover Cl. E11. . . . . 4F **39**
Clover M. SW3. . . . . 2B **88**
Clove St. E13 . . . . 3C **68**
Clowders Rd. SE6 . . . . 3B **122**
Cloysters Grn. E1 . . . . 2C **78**
Club Row E2 . . . 3B **64** (3F **11**)
Clunbury St. N1 . . . . . . 1F **63**
Cluny Est. SE1 . . 4A **78** (5D **27**)
Cluny M. SW5 . . . . 5C **72**
Cluny Pl. SE1 . . . 4A **78** (5D **27**)
Cluse Ct. N1 . . . . 1E **63**
  (off St Peters St.,
  not continuous)
Clutton St. E14. . . . . . . 4D **67**
Clyde Ct. NW1 . . . . 1F **61**
  (off Hampden Cl.)
Clyde Flats SW6. . . . . . 3B **86**
  (off Rhylston Rd.)
Clyde Pl. E10. . . . . 2D **39**
Clydesdale Ho. W11 . . . 5B **58**
  (off Clydesdale Rd.)
Clydesdale Rd. W11 . . 5B **58**
Clyde St. SE8 . . . . 2B **94**
Clyde Ter. SE23 . . . . . . 2E **121**
Clyde Va. SE23. . . . . . . 2E **121**
Clyde Wharf E16 . . . . . 2C **82**
Clynes Ho. E2 . . . . 2F **65**
  (off Knottisford St.)
Clyston St. SW8 . . . . . 5E **89**
Coach & Horses Yd.
  W1 . . . . 1E **75** (4E **13**)
Coach Ho. La. N5 . . . . 1D **49**
  SW19 . . . . 4F **113**
Coach Ho. M.
  SE1 . . . . 3A **78** (5D **27**)
  SE23 . . . . 4F **107**
Coach Ho. Yd. NW3 . . . 1E **45**
  (off Heath St.)
  SW18 . . . . 2D **101**
Coachmaker M. SW4 . . 1A **104**
  (off Fenwick Pl.)
Coach Yd. M. N19 . . . . 3A **34**
Coaldale Wlk. SE21 . . . 5E **105**
Coalecroft Rd. SW15 . . 2E **99**
Coalport Ho. SE11 . . . . 5C **76**
  (off Walnut Tree Wlk.)
Coates Av. SW18 . . . . . 4A **102**

Copenhagen St. N1 . . . . 5A 48
Cope Pl. W8 . . . . 4C 72
Copers Cope Rd.
  BR3: Beck. 5B 122
Cope St. SE16 . . . . 5F 79
Copford Wlk. N1 . . . . 5E 49
  (off Popham St.)
Copgate Path SW16 . . . . 5B 118
Copleston M. SE15 . . . . . 5B 92
Copleston Pas. SE5 . . . . . 5B 92
Copleston Rd. SE15 . . 1B 106
Copley Cl. SE17 . . . . 2E 91
Copley Pk. SW16 . . . . . 5B 118
Copley St. E1 . . . . 4F 65
Coppelia Rd. SE3 . . . . . 2B 110
Copperas St. SE8 . . . . . . 2D 95
Copperbeech Cl. NW3 . . 2F 45
Copperfield Ho. SE1 . . . . 3C 78
  (off Wolseley St.)
  W1 . . . . 5C 4
  (off Marylebone High St.)
  W11 . . . . 2F 71
  (off St Ann's Rd.)
Copperfield Rd. E3 . . . . 3A 66
Copperfield St.
  SE1 . . . . 3D 77 (3E 25)
Copper Mead Ho. NW2 . . 5E 29
Coppermill La. E17 . . . . . 1E 37
  (not continuous)
Copper Mill La. SW17 . . 4E 115
Copper Row SE1 . . . . 2F 27
Coppice Dr. SW15 . . . . . 4D 99
Coppock Cl. SW11 . . . . . 5A 88
Copse Cl. SE7 . . . . 2D 97
Copthall Av.
  EC2 . . . . 5F 63 (2C 18)
  (not continuous)
Copthall Bldgs. EC2 . . . 2C 18
Copthall Cl.
  EC2 . . . . 5F 63 (2B 18)
Copthorne Av. SW12 . . 5F 103
Coptic St. WC1 . . 4A 62 (1D 15)
Coral Ho. E1 . . . . 3A 66
  (off Harford St.)
Coral Row SW11 . . . . . . 1E 101
Coral St. SE1 . . 3C 76 (4C 24)
Coram Ho. W4 . . . . 1A 84
  (off Wood St.)
  WC1 . . . . 3D 7
Coram St. WC1 . . 3A 62 (4D 7)
Corbden Cl. SE15 . . . . . . 4B 92
Corbet Ct. EC3 . . 5F 63 (3C 18)
Corbet Ho. N1 . . . . 1C 62
  (off Barnsbury Est.)
Corbet Pl. E1 . . . 4B 64 (5F 11)
Corbett Ct. SE26 . . . . . . 4B 122
Corbett Ho. SW10 . . . . . 2E 87
  (off Cathcart Rd.)
Corbett Rd. E11 . . . . 1E 41
Corbetts La. SE16 . . . . . . 5E 79
  (not continuous)
Corbetts Pas. SE16 . . . . . 5E 79
  (off Corbetts La.)
Corbetts Wharf SE16 . . . 3D 79
  (off Bermondsey Wall E.)
Corbicum E11 . . . . 2A 40
Corbidge Ct. SE8 . . . . . . 2D 95
  (off Glaisher St.)
Corbiere Ho. N1 . . . . 5F 49
  (off De Beauvoir Est.)

Corbridge Cres. E2 . . . . . 1D 65
Corbyn St. N4 . . . . 3A 34
Corby Way E3 . . . . 3C 66
Cordelia Cl. SE24 . . . . . . 2D 105
Cordelia Ho. N1 . . . . 1A 64
  (off Arden Est.)
Cordelia St. E14 . . . . 5D 67
Cording St. E14 . . . . 4D 67
Cordwainers Ct. E8 . . . . 4D 51
  (off St Thomas's Sq.)
Cordwainers Wlk. E13 . . 1C 68
Cord Way E14 . . . . 4C 80
Cordwell Rd. SE13 . . . 3A 110
Corelli Ct. SW5 . . . . 5C 72
  (off W. Cromwell Rd.)
Corelli Rd. SE3 . . . . 5F 97
Corfe Ho. SW8 . . . . 3B 90
  (off Dorset Rd.)
Corfield St. E2 . . . . 2D 65
Coriander Av. E14 . . . . . . 5F 67
Corinne Rd. N19 . . . . 1E 47
Corker Wlk. N7 . . . . 4B 34
Cork Sq. E1 . . . . 2D 79
Cork St. W1 . . . 1E 75 (5F 13)
Cork St. M. W1 . . . . 5F 13
Cork Tree Ho. SE27 . . . . 5D 119
  (off Lakeview Rd.)
Corlett St. NW1 . . . . 4A 60
Cormont Rd. SE5 . . . . . . 4D 91
Cormorant Ct. SE8 . . . . . 2B 94
  (off Pilot Cl.)
Cormorant Rd. E7 . . . . . . 2B 54
Cornbury Ho. SE8 . . . . . 2B 94
  (off Evelyn St.)
Cornelia St. N7 . . . . 3B 48
Cornell Bldg. E1 . . . . 5C 64
  (off Coke St.)
Corner Fielde SW2 . . . . . 1B 118
Corner Grn. SE3 . . . . 5C 96
Corner Ho. St. WC2 . . . 1D 23
Corney Reach Way
  W4 . . . . 3A 84
Corney Rd. W4 . . . . 2A 84
Cornflower Ter. SE22 . . 4D 107
Cornford Gro. SW12 . . 2D 117
Cornhill EC3 . . . 5F 63 (3C 18)
Cornick Ho. SE16 . . . . . . 4D 79
  (off Slippers Pl.)
Cornish Ho. SE17 . . . . . . 2D 91
  (off Brandon Est.)
Cornmill La. SE13 . . . . . 1E 109
Cornmow Dr. NW10 . . . . 2B 42
Cornthwaite Rd. E5 . . . . 5E 37
Cornwall Av. E2 . . . . 2E 65
Cornwall Cres. W11 . . . . 5A 58
Cornwall Gdns. NW10 . . 3D 43
  SW7 . . . . 4D 73
Cornwall Gdns. Wlk.
  SW7 . . . . 4D 73
Cornwall Gro. W4 . . . . . 1A 84
Cornwallis Cl. SW8 . . . . 4A 90
  (off Lansdowne Grn.)
Cornwallis Ho. SE16 . . . 3D 79
  (off Cherry Garden St.)
  W12 . . . . 1D 71
  (off India Way)
Cornwallis Rd. N19 . . . . 4A 34
Cornwallis Sq. N19 . . . . 4A 34
Cornwall Mans. SW10 . . 3E 87
  (off Cremorne Rd.)

Cornwall Mans. W14 . . . 4F 71
  (off Blythe Rd.)
Cornwall M. Sth. SW7 . . 4E 73
Cornwall M. W. SW7 . . 4D 73
Cornwall Rd. N4 . . . . 2C 34
  N15 . . . . 1F 35
  SE1 . . . . 2C 76 (1B 24)
Cornwall Sq. SE11 . . . . . 1D 91
  (off Seaton Clo.)
Cornwall St. E1 . . . . 1D 79
Cornwall Ter.
  NW1 . . . . 3B 60 (4A 4)
Cornwall Ter. M. NW1 . . 4A 4
Corn Way E11 . . . . 5F 39
Cornwell Cres. E7 . . . . . . 1E 55
Cornwood Dr. E1 . . . . 5E 65
Corona Rd. SE12 . . . . . . 5C 110
Coronation Av. N16 . . . . 1B 50
Coronation Ct. E15 . . . . . 3B 54
  W10 . . . . 4E 57
  (off Brewster Gdns.)
Coronation Rd. E13 . . . . 2E 69
Coronet St. N1 . . 2A 64 (2D 11)
Corporation Row
  EC1 . . . . 3C 62 (3C 8)
Corporation St. E15 . . . . 1A 68
  N7 . . . . 2A 48
Corrance Rd. SW2 . . . . . 2A 104
Corringham Ct. NW11 . . 2C 30
Corringham Ho. E1 . . . . . 5F 65
  (off Pitsea St.)
Corringham Rd. NW11 . . 2C 30
Corringway NW11 . . . . . 2D 31
Corris Grn. NW9 . . . . 1A 28
Corry Dr. SW9 . . . . 2D 105
Corry Ho. E14 . . . . 1D 81
  (off Wade's Pl.)
Corsehill St. SW16 . . . . . 5E 117
Corsham St.
  N1 . . . . 2F 63 (2C 10)
Corsica St. N5 . . . . 3D 49
Corsley Way E9 . . . . 3B 52
  (off Osborne Rd.)
Cortayne Rd. SW6 . . . . . 5B 86
Cortis Rd. SW15 . . . . 4D 99
Cortis Ter. SW15 . . . . . . 4D 99
Corunna Rd. SW8 . . . . . 4E 89
Corunna Ter. SW8 . . . . . 4E 89
Corvette Sq. SE10 . . . . . 2F 95
Coryton Path W9 . . . . . . 3B 58
  (off Ashmore Rd.)
Cosbycote Av. SE24 . . . . 3E 105
Cosgrove Ho. E2 . . . . 5C 50
  (off Whiston Rd.)
Cosmo Pl. WC1 . . 4A 62 (5E 7)
Cosmur Cl. W12 . . . . 4B 70
Cossall Wlk. SE15 . . . . . 5D 93
Cossar M. SW2 . . . . 3C 104
Cosser St. SE1 . . 4C 76 (5B 24)
Costa St. SE15 . . . . 5C 92
Coston Wlk. SE4 . . . . . . 2F 107
Cosway Mans. NW1 . . . . 4A 60
  (off Shroton St.)
Cosway St. NW1 . . . . . . 4A 60
Cotall St. E14 . . . . 4C 66
Coteford St. SW17 . . . . 4B 116
Cotesbach Rd. E5 . . . . . . 5E 37
Cotes Ho. NW8 . . . . 3A 60
  (off Broadley St.)
Cotham St. SE17 . . . . . . 5E 77

Cotherstone Rd. SW2. . 1B 118
Cotleigh Rd. NW6 . . . . . . 4C 44
Cotman Cl. NW11. . . . . . 1E 31
  SW15 . . . . 4F 99
Cotman Ho. NW8 . . . . . . 1A 60
  (off Townshend Est.)
Cotswold Ct. EC1 . . . . 3F 9
Cotswold Gdns. E6 . . . . . 2F 69
  NW2 . . . . 4F 29
Cotswold Ga. NW2. . . . . . 3A 30
Cotswold M. SW11 . . . . . 4F 87
Cotswold St. SE27 . . . . 4D 119
Cottage Cl. E1. . . . . 3E 65
  (off Hayfield Pas.)
Cottage Grn. SE5 . . . . . . 3F 91
Cottage Gro. SW9 . . . . . 1A 104
Cottage Pl. SW3. . . . . . . 4A 74
Cottage St. E14 . . . . 1D 81
Cottage Wlk. N16. . . . . . . 5B 36
Cottesbrook St. SE14 . . . 3A 94
Cottesloe Ho. NW8. . . . . 3A 60
  (off Jerome Cres.)
Cottesloe M. SE1 . . . . . . 5C 24
  (off Emery St.)
Cottesloe Theatre 1A 24
  (in Royal National Theatre)
Cottesmore Ct. W8. . . . . 4D 73
  (off Stanford Rd.)
Cottesmore Gdns. W8 . . 4D 73
Cottingham Rd. SW8 . . . 3B 90
Cottington St. SE11 . . . . 1C 90
Cottle Way SE16. . . . . . . 3D 79
  (off Paradise St.)
Cotton Av. W3. . . . . 5A 56
Cotton Hill BR1: Brom. . 4E 123
Cotton Ho. SW2 . . . . . . 5A 104
Cotton Row SW11. . . . . . 1E 101
Cottons Cen.
  SE1 . . . . 2A 78 (1D 27)
Cotton's Gdns.
  E2. . . . . 2A 64 (1E 11)
Cottons La. SE1. . 2F 77 (1C 26)
Cotton St. E14 . . . . 1E 81
Cottrell Ct. SE10 . . . . . . 5B 82
Coulgate St. SE4 . . . . . 1A 108
Coulson St. SW3 . . . . . . 1B 88
Coulter Rd. W6 . . . . 4D 71
Councillor St. SE5 . . . . . 3E 91
Counter Ct. SE1 . . . . 2B 26
  (off Borough High St.)
Counter St. SE1. . 2A 78 (2D 27)
Countess Rd. NW5 . . . . . 2E 47
County Gro. SE5 . . . . . . 4E 91
County Hall Apartments
  SE1 . . . . 3F 23
County Hall (Former)
  . . . . 3B 78 (3F 23)
County St. SE1 . . . . 4E 77
Courland Gro. SW8. . . . . 4F 89
Courland St. SW8 . . . . . . 4F 89
Courtauld Ho. E2 . . . . . . 5C 50
  (off Goldsmiths Row)
Courtauld Institute Galleries
  . . . . 4F 15
Courtauld Rd. N19 . . . . . 3A 34
Courtenay Av. N6 . . . . . . 2A 32
Courtenay M. E17. . . . . . 1A 38
Courtenay Rd. E11 . . . . . 5B 40
Courtenay Sq. SE11 . . . . 1C 90
Courtenay St. SE11 . . . . 1C 90

Court Farm Rd. SE9 . . . . 2F 125
Courtfield Gdns. SW5 . . 5D 73
Courtfield Ho. EC1 . . . . . . 5B 8
  (off Baldwins Gdns.)
Courtfield M. SW5 . . . . . 5E 73
Courtfield Rd. SW7 . . . . 5E 73
Court Gdns. N7. . . . . 3C 48
  (not continuous)
Courthill Rd. SE13 . . . . . 2E 109
Courthope Ho. SE16. . . . 4E 79
  (off Lower Rd.)
  SW8 . . . . 3A 90
  (off Hartington Rd.)
Courthope Rd. NW3. . . . 1B 46
  SW19 . . . . 5A 114
Courtland Rd. E6 . . . . . . 5F 55
Courtlands Av. SE12 . . . 3D 111
Court La. SE21. . . . . 4A 106
Court La. Gdns. SE21. . 5A 106
Courtleigh NW11 . . . . . . 1B 30
Courtmead Cl. SE24. . . . 4E 105
Courtnell St. W2 . . . . . . 5C 58
Courtney Cl. N7 . . . . 2C 48
Courtney Ho. W14 . . . . . 4A 72
  (off Russell Rd.)
Courtney Rd. N7. . . . . . . 2C 48
Courtrai Rd. SE23 . . . . . 4A 108
Courtside N8. . . . . 1F 33
Court St. E1 . . . . 4D 65
Court Theatre 3B 72
  (in Holland Park)
Courtville Ho. W10 . . . . 2A 58
  (off Third Av.)
Courtyard, The E3 . . . . . 1C 66
  N1. . . . . 4B 48
  NW1 . . . . 4C 46
Courtyard Theatre 1E 7
  (off York Way)
Cousin La. EC4. . 1F 77 (5B 18)
Couthurst Rd. SE3 . . . . . 2D 97
Coutt's Cres. NW5 . . . . . 5C 32
Couzens Ho. E3 . . . . 4B 66
  (off Weatherley Cl.)
Covell Ct. SE8 . . . . 3C 94
COVENT GARDEN
  . . . . 1A 76 (4E 15)
Covent Garden . 1A 76 (4E 15)
Covent Gdn.
  WC2. . . . . 1A 76 (4E 15)
Coventry Cl. NW6. . . . . . 1C 58
Coventry Cross E3 . . . . . 3E 67
Coventry Hall SW16. . . . 5A 118
Coventry Rd. E1. . . . . . . 3D 65
Coventry St. W1 . 1F 75 (5B 14)
Coverdale Rd. NW2 . . . . 4F 43
  W12 . . . . 3D 71
Coverley Cl. E1 . . . . 4C 64
Coverley Point SE11 . . . 5B 76
  (off Tyers St.)
Coverton Rd. SW17 . . . . 5A 116
Covington Way SW16. . . 5B 118
  (not continuous)
Cowcross St.
  EC1. . . . . 4D 63 (5D 9)
Cowdenbeath Path N1 . . 5B 48
Cowden St. SE6 . . . . 4C 122
Cowdrey Rd. SW19 . . . . 5D 115
Cowick Rd. SW17 . . . . . 4B 116
Cowley La. E11 . . . . 5A 40

Cowley Rd. E11 . . . . 1D 41
  SW9 . . . . 4C 90
  (not continuous)
  SW14 . . . . 1A 98
  W3 . . . . 2B 70
Cowley St.
  SW1. . . . . 4A 76 (5D 23)
Cowling Cl. W11 . . . . 2A 72
Cowper Av. E6 . . . . 4F 55
Cowper Ho. SE17. . . . . . 1E 91
  (off Browning St.)
  SW1 . . . . 1F 89
  (off Aylesford St.)
Cowper Rd. N16. . . . . . . 2A 50
  SW19 . . . . 5E 115
Cowper's Ct. EC3 . . . . . . 3C 18
  (off Birchin La.)
Cowper St. EC2. . 3F 63 (3C 10)
Cowper Ter. W10 . . . . . . 4F 57
Cowthorpe Rd. SW8 . . . 4F 89
Cox Ho. W6 . . . . 2A 86
  (off Field Rd.)
Coxmount Rd. SE7 . . . . . 1F 97
Cox's Ct. E1 . . . . 1F 19
Coxson Way
  SE1. . . . . 3B 78 (4F 27)
Cox's Wlk. SE21. . . . . . 1C 120
Crabtree Cl. E2. . . . . 1B 64
Crabtree Ct. E15 . . . . . . 2D 53
Crabtree La. SW6. . . . . . 3E 85
  (not continuous)
Crabtree Wlk. SE15 . . . . 4B 92
  (off Peckham Rd.)
Crace St. NW1. . . 2F 61 (1B 6)
Craddock St. NW5 . . . . . 3C 46
Crafts Council & Gallery
  . . . . 1C 62
Cragie Ho. SE1. . . . . 5B 78
  (off Balaclava Rd.)
Craigerne Rd. SE3. . . . . 3D 97
Craignair Rd. SW2. . . . . 5C 104
Craig's Ct. SW1. . 2A 76 (1D 23)
Craik Ct. NW6 . . . . 1B 58
  (off Carlton Va.)
Crail Row SE17. . . . . 5F 77
Cramer St. W1. . 4C 60 (1C 12)
Crammond Cl. W6 . . . . . 2A 86
Crampton Ho. SW8 . . . . 4E 89
Crampton Rd. SE20 . . . . 5E 121
Crampton St. SE17 . . . . 5E 77
Cranberry La. E16 . . . . . 3A 68
Cranbourn All. WC2. . . . 4C 14
  (off Cranbourn St.)
Cranbourne Gdns.
  NW11 . . . . 1A 30
Cranbourne Pas. SE16. . 3D 79
Cranbourne Rd. E12. . . . 2F 55
  E15 . . . . 1E 53
Cranbourn Ho. SE16 . . . 3D 79
  (off Marigold St.)
Cranbourn St.
  WC2 . . . . 1F 75 (4C 14)
Cranbrook NW1 . . . . 5E 47
  (off Camden St.)
Cranbrook Est. E2. . . . . . 1F 65
Cranbrook Rd. SE8. . . . . 4C 94
  W4 . . . . 1A 84
Cranbrook St. E2 . . . . . . 1F 65
Cranbury Rd. SW6. . . . . 5D 87
Crandley Ct. SE8 . . . . . . 5A 80

Crane Ct. EC4 . . 5C **62** (3C **16**)
Crane Gro. N7 . . . . 3C **48**
Crane Ho. *E3* *1A 66*
    (off Roman Rd.)
SE15 . . . . 4B **92**
Crane Mead SE16 . . . . . . 5F **79**
Crane St. SE10 . . . . 1F **95**
SE15 . . . . 4B **92**
Cranfield Cl. SE27 . . . . 3E **119**
Cranfield Ct. *W1* *4A 60*
    (off Homer St.)
Cranfield Ho. WC1 . . . . . . 5D **7**
Cranfield Rd. SE4 . . 1B **108**
Cranfield Row SE1 . . . . . 5C **24**
Cranford Cotts. *E1* *1F 79*
    (off Cranford St.)
Cranford St. E1 . . . . 1F **79**
Cranford Way N8 . . . . . . 1B **34**
Cranhurst Rd. NW2 . . . . . 2E **43**
Cranleigh Ho's. *NW1* . . . *1E 61*
    (off Cranleigh St.)
Cranleigh M. SW11 . . . . . 5A **88**
Cranleigh St. NW1 . . . . . 1E **61**
CRANLEY GARDENS . . . 1D 33
Cranley Gdns. SW7 . . . . 1E **87**
Cranley M. SW7 . . . . 1E **87**
Cranley Pl. SW7 . . . . 5F **73**
Cranley Rd. E13 . . . . 4D **69**
Cranmer Ct. SW3 . . . . . . 5A **74**
SW4 . . . . 1F **103**
Cranmere Ct. SE5 . . . . . . 4E **91**
Cranmer Ho. *SW9* *3C 90*
    (off Brixton Rd.)
Cranmer Rd. E7 . . . . 1D **55**
SW9 . . . . 3C **90**
Cranmer Ter. SW17 . . . . 5F **115**
Cranmore Rd.
    BR1: Brom 3B **124**
Cranston Est. N1 . . . . . . 1F **63**
Cranston Rd. SE23 . . 1A **122**
Cranswick Rd. SE16 . . 1D **93**
Crantock Rd. SE6 . . . . . 2D **123**
Cranwell Cl. E3 . . . . 3D **67**
Cranwich Rd. N16 . . . . . 2F **35**
Cranwood St. EC1 . . . . . 2C **10**
Cranwood St.
    EC1 . . . . 2F **63** (2C **10**)
Cranworth Gdns. SW9 . . 4C **90**
Craster Rd. SW2 . . . . . 5B **104**
Crathie Rd. SE12 . . . . . 4D **111**
Craven Cl. N16 . . . . 2C **36**
Craven Ct. NW10 . . . . . . 5A **42**
Craven Gdns. SW19 . . 5C **114**
Craven Hill W2 . . . . 1E **73**
Craven Hill Gdns. W2 . . 1E **73**
    (not continuous)
Craven Hill M. W2 . . . . . 1E **73**
Craven Lodge *W2* *1E 73*
    (off Craven Hill)
Craven M. SW11 . . . . . 1C **102**
Craven Pk. NW10 . . . . . . 5A **42**
Craven Pk. M. NW10 . . 4A **42**
Craven Pk. Rd. N15 . . . . 1B **36**
NW10 . . . . 5A **42**
Craven Pas. *WC2* *1D 23*
    (off Craven St.)
Craven Rd. NW10 . . . . . . 5A **42**
W2 . . . . 1E **73**
Craven St. WC2 . . 2A **76** (1D **23**)
Craven Ter. W2 . . . . 1E **73**

Craven Wlk. N16 . . . . . . 2C **36**
Crawford Bldgs. *W1* . . . *4A 60*
    (off Homer St.)
Crawford Est. SE5 . . . . . 5E **91**
Crawford Mans. *W1* . . . *4A 60*
    (off Crawford St.)
Crawford Pas.
    EC1 . . . . 3C **62** (4C **8**)
Crawford Pl. W2 . . . . 5A **60**
Crawford Point E16 . . . . . 5B **68**
    (off Wouldham Rd.)
Crawford Rd. SE5 . . . . . . 4E **91**
Crawford St. W1 . . . . 4A **60**
Crawley Rd. E10 . . . . 3D **39**
Crawshay Ct. SW9 . . . . . 4C **90**
Crawthew Gro. SE22 . . 2B **106**
Crayford Cl. E6 . . . . 5F **69**
Crayford Ho. *SE1* *4C 26*
    (off Long La.)
Crayford Rd. N7 . . . . 1F **47**
Crayle Ho. *EC1* *3E 9*
    (off Malta St.)
Crealock St. SW18 . . . . 4D **101**
Creasy Est. SE1 . . . . . . 4A **78**
Crebor St. SE22 . . . . . . 4C **106**
Credenhill Ho. SE15 . . . 3D **93**
Credenhill St. SW16 . . 5E **117**
Crediton Hill NW6 . . . . . 2D **45**
Crediton Rd. E16 . . . . . . 5C **68**
NW10 . . . . 5F **43**
Credon Rd. E13 . . . . 1E **69**
SE16 . . . . 1D **93**
Creechurch La.
    EC3 . . . . . . 5A **64** (3E **19**)
    (not continuous)
Creechurch Pl. EC3 . . 3E **19**
Creed St. EC4 . . . . 3E **17**
Creed La. EC4 . . 5D **63** (3E **17**)
Creek Ho. *W14* *4A 72*
    (off Russell Rd.)
Creek Rd. SE8 . . . . 2C **94**
SE10 . . . . 2C **94**
Creekside SE8 . . . . 3D **95**
Creeland Gro. SE6 . . . . 1B **122**
Crefeld Cl. W6 . . . . 2A **86**
Creighton Av. E6 . . . . . . 1F **69**
Creighton Cl. W12 . . . . 1C **70**
Creighton Rd. NW6 . . . . 1F **57**
Cremer Bus. Cen. *E2* . . . *1F 11*
    (off Cremer St.)
Cremer Ho. *SE8* *3C 94*
    (off Deptford Chu. St.)
Cremer St. E2 . . 1B **64** (1F **11**)
Cremorne Est. SW10 . . 2F **87**
Cremorne Rd. SW10 . . 3E **87**
Creon Ct. *SW9* *3C 90*
    (off Caldwell St.)
Crescent EC3 . . 1B **78** (4F **19**)
Crescent Arc. *SE10* . . . *2E 95*
    (off Creek Rd.)
Crescent Ct. Bus. Cen.
    E16 . . . . 3F **67**
Crescent Gdns. SW19 . . 3C **114**
Crescent Gro. SW4 . . . 2E **103**
Crescent Ho. *EC1* *4F 9*
    (off Golden La. Est.)
SE8 . . . . 5D **95**
SE13 . . . . 5D **95**
Crescent La. SW4 . . . . . 2E **103**

Crescent Pl. SW3 . . . . . . 5A **74**
Crescent Rd. E6 . . . . . . 5E **55**
E10 . . . . 4D **39**
E13 . . . . 5C **54**
N8 . . . . 1F **33**
Crescent Row EC1 . . 3E **63** (4F **9**)
Crescent Stables
    SW15 . . . . 3A **100**
Crescent, The E17 . . . . . 1A **38**
NW2 . . . . 5D **29**
SW13 . . . . 5B **84**
SW19 . . . . 3C **114**
W3 . . . . 5A **56**
Crescent Way SE4 . . . . 1C **108**
Crescent Wharf *E16* . . . *3D 83*
    (off Nth. Woolwich Rd.)
Crescent Wood Rd.
    SE26 . . . . 3C **120**
Cresford Rd. SW6 . . . . . 4D **87**
Crespigny Rd. NW4 . . . . 1D **29**
Cressal Ho. *E14* *4C 80*
    (off Tiller Rd.)
Cresset Rd. E9 . . . . 3E **51**
Cresset St. SW4 . . . . . 1F **103**
Cressfield Cl. NW5 . . . . . 2C **46**
Cressida Rd. N19 . . . . . . 3E **33**
Cressingham Gdns. Est.
    SW2 . . . . 5C **104**
Cressingham Rd. SE13 . . 1E **109**
Cressington Cl. N16 . . 2A **50**
Cress M. BR1: Brom . . 5F **123**
Cresswell Gdns. SW5 . . 1E **87**
Cresswell Pk. SE3 . . . . 1B **110**
Cresswell Pl. SW10 . . 1E **87**
Cressy Ct. E1 . . . . 4E **65**
W6 . . . . 4D **71**
Cressy Ho's. *E1* *4E 65*
    (off Hannibal Rd.)
Cressy Pl. E1 . . . . 4E **65**
Cressy Rd. NW3 . . . . . . 2B **46**
Cresta Ho. *NW3* *4F 45*
    (off Finchley Rd.)
Crestfield St.
    WC1 . . . . 2A **62** (1E **7**)
Crest Rd. NW2 . . . . 4C **28**
Crestway SW15 . . . . . . 4C **98**
Creswick Wlk. E3 . . . . . 2C **66**
Crewdson Rd. SW9 . . . . 3C **90**
Crewe Pl. NW10 . . . . . . 2B **56**
Crewkerne Ct. SW11 . . *4F 87*
    (off Bolingbroke Wlk.)
Crews St. E14 . . . . 5C **80**
Crewys Rd. NW2 . . . . . . 4B **30**
SE15 . . . . 5D **93**
Crichton St. SW8 . . . . . . 5E **89**
Cricketers Ct. *SE11* . . . *5D 77*
    (off Kennington La.)
Cricketers M. SW18 . . 3D **101**
Cricketers Wlk. SE26 . . 5E **121**
Cricketfield Rd. E5 . . . . 1D **51**
Cricket La. BR3: Beck . . 5A **122**
Cricklade Av. SW2 . . . . 2A **118**
CRICKLEWOOD 5A 30
Cricklewood B'way.
    NW2 . . . . 5E **29**
Cricklewood La. NW2 . . 1F **43**
Cridland St. E15 . . . . . . 5B **54**
Crieff Rd. SW18 . . . . . . 4E **101**
Criffel Av. SW2 . . . . . . 2F **117**

Croydon Rd. E13 . . . . . . 3B **68**
Crozier Ho. SE3 . . . . . . 1D **111**
 SW8 . . . . *3B 90*
  (off Wilkinson St.)
Crozier Ter. E9 . . . . 2F **51**
Crucifix La.
 SE1 . . . . 3A **78** (3E **27**)
Cruden Ho. *SE5* *2D 91*
  (off Brandon Est.)
Cruden St. N1 . . . . 5D **49**
Cruikshank Ho. *NW8* . . . *1A 60*
  (off Townshend Est.)
Cruikshank Rd. E15 . . . . 1A **54**
Cruikshank St.
 WC1 . . . . 2C **62** (1B **8**)
Crummock Gdns. NW9 . . 1A **28**
Crusoe M. N16 . . . . 4F **35**
Crutched Friars
 EC3 . . . . 1A **78** (4E **19**)
Crutchley Rd. SE6 . . . . . 2A **124**
CRYSTAL PALACE 5B 120
Crystal Palace Mus. . . 5B 120
Crystal Palace National
  Sports Cen. 5C 120
Crystal Pal. Pde. SE19 . . 5B **120**
Crystal Pal. Pk. Rd.
 SE26 . . . . 5C **120**
Crystal Pal. Rd. SE22 . . 4B **106**
Crystal Ter. SE19 . . . . . 5F **119**
Crystal Vw. Ct.
 BR1: Brom 4F **123**
Crystal Wharf N1 . . . . . . 1D **63**
Cuba St. E14 . . . . 3C **80**
Cube Ho. SE1 . . 4B **78** (5F **27**)
Cubitt Ho. SW4 . . . . . . 4E **103**
Cubitt Steps E14 . . . . . . 2C **80**
Cubitt St. WC1 . . 2B **62** (2A **8**)
Cubitt's Yd. WC2 . . . . . . 4E **15**
Cubitt Ter. SW4 . . . . . . 1E **103**
CUBITT TOWN 5E 81
Cuddington *SE17* *5E 77*
  (off Deacon Way)
Cudham St. SE6 . . . . . . 5E **109**
Cudworth Ho. SW8 . . . . 4E **89**
Cudworth St. E1 . . . . . . 3D **65**
Cuff Cres. SE9 . . . . 4F **111**
Cuffley Ho. *W10* *4E 57*
  (off Sutton Way)
Cuff Point *E2* *1F 11*
  (off Columbia Rd.)
Culford Gdns. SW3 . . . . 5B **74**
Culford Gro. N1 . . . . 3A **50**
Culford Mans. SW3 . . . . 5B **74**
Culford M. N1 . . . . 3A **50**
Culford Rd. N1 . . . . 4A **50**
Culham Ho. *E2* *2F 11*
  (off Palissy St.)
Culling Rd. SE16 . . . . . . 4E **79**
Cullingworth Rd. NW10 . . 2C **42**
Culloden Cl. SE1 . . . . . . 1C **92**
Cullum St. EC3 . . 1A **78** (4D **19**)
Cullum Welch Ct. *N1* . . . *1C 10*
  (off Haberdasher St.)
Cullum Welch Ho. *EC1* . . *4F 9*
  (off Goswell Rd.)
Culmore Rd. SE15 . . . . . 3D **93**
Culmstock Rd. SW11 . . 3C **102**
Culpeper Ho. E14 . . . . . 5A **66**
Culpepper St. *SE11* *5C 76*
  (off Kennington Rd.)

Culross Bldgs. *NW1* *1A 62*
  (off Battle Bri. Rd.)
Culross Ho. *W10* *5F 57*
  (off Bridge Cl.)
Culross St. W1 . . 1C **74** (5B **12**)
Culverden Rd. SW12 . . 2E **117**
Culverhouse *WC1* *1F 15*
  (off Red Lion Sq.)
Culverhouse Gdns.
 SW16 . . . . 3B **118**
Culverley Rd. SE6 . . . . 1D **123**
Culvert Pl. SW11 . . . . . . 5C **88**
Culvert Rd. N15 . . . . . . 1A **36**
 SW11 . . . . 5B **88**
Culworth Ho. *NW8* *1A 60*
  (off Allitsen Rd.)
Culworth St. NW8 . . . . . 1A **60**
Culzean Cl. SE27 . . . . . 3D **119**
Cumberland Cl. E8 . . . . . 3B **50**
Cumberland St. *SW1* . . . *1D 89*
  (off Cumberland St.)
Cumberland Cres. W14 . . 5A **72**
  (not continuous)
Cumberland Gdns.
 WC1 . . . . 2C **62** (1B **8**)
Cumberland Ga.
 W1 . . . . 1B **74** (4A **12**)
Cumberland Ho. *E16* . . . *1C 82*
  (off Wesley Av.)
Cumberland Mans. *W1* . . *5B 60*
  (off George St.)
Cumberland Mkt.
 NW1 . . . . 2D **61** (1E **5**)
Cumberland Mills Sq.
 E14 . . . . 1F **95**
Cumberland Pk. Ind. Est.
 NW10 . . . . 2C **56**
Cumberland Pl.
 NW1 . . . . 2D **61** (1D **5**)
 SE6 . . . . 1B **124**
Cumberland Rd. E12 . . 1F **55**
 E13 . . . . 4D **69**
 SW13 . . . . 4B **84**
Cumberland St. SW1 . . . 1D **89**
Cumberland Ter.
 NW1 . . . . 1D **61** (1D **5**)
Cumberland Ter. M.
 NW1 . . . . 1D **5**
Cumbrian Gdns. NW2 . . 4F **29**
Cuming Mus. *5E 77*
  (off Walworth Rd.)
Cumming St. N1 . . 1B **62** (1A **8**)
Cumnor Cl. *SW9* *5B 90*
  (off Robsart St.)
Cunard Pl. EC3 . . 5A **64** (3E **19**)
Cunard Rd. NW10 . . . . . 2A **56**
Cunard Wlk. SE16 . . . . . 5F **79**
Cundy Rd. E16 . . . . 5E **69**
Cundy St. SW1 . . . . 5C **74**
Cunliffe St. SW16 . . . . 5E **117**
Cunningham Ho. *SE5* . . . *3F 91*
  (off Elmington Est.)
Cunningham Pl. NW8 . . . 3F **59**
Cupar Rd. SW11 . . . . . . 4C **88**
Cupola Cl. BR1: Brom . . 5D **125**
Cureton St. SW1 . . . . . . 5F **75**
Curlew Ho. *SE4* *2A 108*
  (off St Norbert Rd.)
 SE15 . . . . 4B **92**
Curlew St. SE1 . . 3B **78** (3F **27**)

Curnick's La. SE27 . . . . 4E **119**
Curran Ho. *SW3* *5A 74*
  (off Lucan Pl.)
Curricle St. W3 . . . . 2A **70**
Currie Hill Cl. SW19 . . . . 4B **114**
Currie Ho. *E14* *5F 67*
  (off Abbott Rd.)
Cursitor St.
 WC2 . . . . 5C **62** (2B **16**)
Curtain Pl. EC2 . . 3A **64** (3E **11**)
Curtain Rd. EC2 . . 3A **64** (2E **11**)
Curtis Dr. W3 . . . . 5A **56**
Curtis Fld. Rd. SW16 . . 4B **118**
Curtis Ho. *SE17* *1F 91*
  (off Morecambe St.)
Curtis St. SE1 . . . . 5B **78**
Curtis Way SE1 . . . . 5B **78**
Curve, The W12 . . . . . . 1C **70**
Curwen Av. E7 . . . . 1D **55**
Curwen Rd. W12 . . . . . . 3C **70**
Curzon Cl. *SW6* *4E 87*
  (off Imperial Rd.)
Curzon Cres. NW10 . . . . 4A **42**
Curzon Ga. W1 . . 2C **74** (2C **20**)
Curzon Sq. W1 . . 2C **74** (2C **20**)
Curzon St. W1 . . 2C **74** (2C **20**)
Custance Ho. *N1* *1B 10*
  (off Fairbank Est.)
Custance St.
 N1 . . . . 2F **63** (1B **10**)
CUSTOM HOUSE 5E 69
Custom Ho. Reach
 SE16 . . . . 3B **80**
Custom Ho. Wlk.
 EC3 . . . . 1A **78** (5D **19**)
Cutbush Ho. N7 . . . . . . 2F **47**
Cutcombe Rd. SE5 . . . . 5E **91**
Cuthbert Harrowing Ho.
 EC1 . . . . *4F 9*
  (off Golden La. Est.)
Cuthbert Ho. *W2* *4F 59*
  (off Hall Pl.)
Cuthbert St. W2 . . . . . . 4F **59**
Cuthill Wlk. SE5 . . . . . . 4F **91**
Cutlers Gdns. E1 . . . . . . 1E **19**
Cutlers Sq. E14 . . . . . . 5C **80**
Cutler St. E1 . . 5A **64** (2E **19**)
Cut, The E1 . . 1C **76** (3C **24**)
Cutty Sark 2E 95
Cutty Sark Gdns. SE10 . . 2E **95**
  (off King William Wlk.)
Cyclops M. E14 . . . . . . 5C **80**
Cygnet M. NW10 . . . . . 2A **42**
Cygnet St. E1 . . 3B **64** (3F **11**)
Cygnus Bus. Cen.
 NW10 . . . . 2B **42**
Cynthia St. N1 . . 1B **62** (1A **8**)
Cyntra Pl. E8 . . . . 4D **51**
Cypress Gdns. SE4 . . . . 3A **108**
Cypress Ho. SE14 . . . . . 4F **93**
 SE16 . . . . *3F 79*
  (off Woodland Cres.)
Cypress Pl. W1 . . 3E **61** (4A **6**)
Cyprus Cl. N4 . . . . 1D **35**
Cyprus Pl. E2 . . . . 1E **65**
Cyprus St. E2 . . . . 1E **65**
  (not continuous)
Cyrena Rd. SE22 . . . . . . 4B **106**
Cyril Mans. SW11 . . . . . 4B **88**

Darlington Ho. *SW8* *3F 89*
(off Hemans St.)
Darlington Rd. *SE2/* . . *5D 119*
Darnall Ho. *SE10* *4E 95*
(off Royal Hill)
Darnay Ho. *SE1* *4C 78*
Darnley Ho. *E14* *5A 66*
(off Camdenhurst St.)
Darnley Rd. *E9* *3E 51*
Darnley Ter. *W11* *2F 71*
Darrell Rd. *SE22* *3C 106*
Darren Cl. *N4* *2B 34*
Darsley Dr. *SW8* *4F 89*
Dartford Ho. *SE1* *5B 78*
(off Longfield Est.)
Dartford St. *SE17* *2E 91*
Dartington *NW1* *5E 47*
(off Plender St.)
Dartington Ho. *SW8* . . . *5F 89*
(off Union Gro.)
W2 . . . . *4D 59*
(off Senior St.)
Dartle Ct. *SE16* *3C 78*
(off Scott Lidgett Cres.)
Dartmoor Wlk. *E14* *5C 80*
(off Charnwood Gdns.)
Dartmouth Cl. *W11* . . . *5B 58*
Dartmouth Ct. *SE10* . . . *4E 95*
Dartmouth Gro. *SE10* . . *4E 95*
Dartmouth Hill *SE10* . . . *4E 95*
DARTMOUTH PARK **5D 33**
Dartmouth Pk. Av.
NW5 . . . . *5D 33*
Dartmouth Pk. Hill *N19* . *3D 33*
Dartmouth Pk. Rd.
NW5 . . . . *1D 47*
Dartmouth Pl. *SE23* . . . *2E 121*
W4 . . . . *2A 84*
Dartmouth Rd. *NW2* . . . *3F 43*
NW4 . . . . *1C 28*
SE23 . . . . *3D 121*
SE26 . . . . *3D 121*
Dartmouth Row *SE10* . . *5E 95*
Dartmouth St.
SW1 . . . . *3F 75* (4C 22)
Dartmouth Ter. *SE10* . . . *4F 95*
Dartrey Twr. *SW10* *3E 87*
(off World's End Est.)
Dartrey Wlk. *SW10* *3E 87*
Dart St. *W10* *2A 58*
Darville Rd. *N16* *5B 36*
Darwin Ct. *NW1* *5D 47*
SE17 . . . . *5F 77*
(off Barlow St.)
Darwin Ho. *SW1* *2E 89*
(off Grosvenor Rd.)
Darwin St. *SE17* *5F 77*
(not continuous)
Daryngton Ho. *SW8* . . . *3A 90*
(off Hartington Rd.)
Dashwood Rd. *N8* *1B 34*
Dassett Rd. *SE27* *5D 119*
Data Point Bus. Cen.
E16 . . . . *3F 67*
Datchelor Pl. *SE5* *4F 91*
Datchet Ho. *NW1* *1E 5*
(off Augustus St.)
Datchet Rd. *SE6* *2B 122*
Datchworth Ho. *N1* *4D 49*
(off Sutton Est., The)

Date St. *SE17* *1F 91*
Daubeney Rd. *F5* *1A 52*
Daubeney Twr. *SE8* . . . *1B 94*
(off Bowditch)
Dault Rd. *SW18* *4E 101*
Dauncey Ho. *SE1* *4D 25*
Davenant Rd. *N19* *4F 33*
Davenant St. *E1* *5C 64*
Davenport Ho. *SE11* . . . *5C 76*
(off Walnut Tree Wlk.)
Davenport Rd. *SE6* . . *4D 109*
Daventry Av. *E17* *1C 38*
Daventry St. *NW1* *4A 60*
Daver Ct. *SW3* *1A 88*
Davern Cl. *SE10* *5B 82*
Davey Cl. *N7* *3B 48*
Davey Rd. *E9* *4C 52*
Davey's Ct. *WC2* *4D 15*
Davey St. *SE15* *2B 92*
Davidge Ho. *SE1* *4C 24*
(off Coral St.)
Davidge St. *SE1* . . *3D 77* (4D 25)
David Ho. *E14* *4D 67*
(off Uamvar St.)
SW8 . . . . *3A 90*
(off Wyvil Rd.)
David Lee Point *E15* . . . *5A 54*
(off Leather Gdns.)
David Lloyd Leisure . . 2D 111
David M. *W1* . . . *4B 60* (5A 4)
Davidson Gdns. *SW8* . . *3A 90*
Davidson Terraces *E7* . . *2D 55*
(off Claremont Rd.,
not continuous)
David's Rd. *SE23* *1E 121*
David St. *E15* *3F 53*
Davies La. *E11* *4A 40*
Davies M. *W1* . . *1D 75* (4D 13)
Davies St. *W1* . . *5D 61* (3D 13)
Da Vinci Ct. *SE16* *1D 93*
(off Rossetti Rd.)
Davis Ho. *W12* *1D 71*
(off White City Est.)
Davis Rd. *W3* *2B 70*
Davis St. *E13* *1D 69*
Davisville Rd. *W12* *3C 70*
Dawes Ho. *SE17* *5F 77*
(off Orb St.)
Dawes Rd. *SW6* *3A 86*
Dawes St. *SE17* *1F 91*
Dawlish Av. *SW18* . . . *2D 115*
Dawlish Rd. *E10* *3E 39*
NW2 . . . . *3F 43*
Dawnay Gdns. *SW18* . *2F 115*
Dawnay Rd. *SW18* . . *2E 115*
Dawn Cres. *E15* *5F 53*
Dawpool Rd. *NW2* *4B 28*
Dawson Ho. *E2* *2E 65*
(off Sceptre Rd.)
Dawson Pl. *W2* *1C 72*
Dawson Rd. *NW2* *2E 43*
Dawson St. *E2* . . *1B 64* (1F 11)
Day Ho. *SE5* *3E 91*
(off Bethwin Rd.)
Daylesford Av. *SW15* . . *2C 98*
Daysbrook Rd. *SW2* . . *1B 118*
Dayton Gro. *SE15* *4E 93*
Deacon Ho. *SE11* *5B 76*
(off Black Prince Rd.)
Deacon M. *N1* *4F 49*

Deacon Rd. *NW2* *2C 42*
Deacon's Ri. *N2* *1F 31*
Deacon Way *SE17* *5E 77*
Deal Ho. *SE15* *2F 93*
(off Lovelinch La.)
Deal Porters Wlk. *SE16*. . *3F 79*
Deal Porters Way *SE16* . *4E 79*
Deal Rd. *SW17* *5C 116*
Deal's Gateway *SE10*. . *4C 94*
Deal St. *E1* *4C 64*
Dealtry Rd. *SW15* *2E 99*
Deal Wlk. *SW9* *3C 90*
Dean Abbott Ho. *SW1* . *5F 75*
(off Vincent St.)
Dean Bradley St. *SW1* . *4A 76*
Dean Cl. *E9* *2E 51*
SE16 . . . . *2F 79*
Dean Ct. *SW8* *3A 90*
(off Thorncroft St.)
Deancross St. *E1* *5E 65*
Deanery M. *W1* *1C 20*
Deanery Rd. *E15* *3A 54*
Deanery St.
W1 . . . . *2C 74* (1C 20)
Dean Farrar St.
SW1 . . . . . . *4F 75* (5C 22)
Dean Ho. *E1* *5E 65*
(off Tarling St.)
SE14 . . . . *3A 94*
(off New Cross Rd.)
Dean Rd. *NW2* *3E 43*
Dean Ryle St. *SW1* *5A 76*
Dean's Bldgs. *SE17* . . . *5F 77*
Dean's Ct. *EC4*. . *5D 63* (3E 17)
Deans Ga. Cl. *SE23* . . *3F 121*
Deanshanger Ho. *SE8* . *5F 79*
(off Chilton Gro.)
Dean's M. *W1* . . *5D 61* (2E 13)
Dean Stanley St.
SW1 . . . . *4A 76* (5D 23)
Deanston Wharf *E16* . . . *3D 83*
Dean St. *E7* *2C 54*
W1 . . . . *5F 61* (2B 14)
Dean's Yd. *SW1* *5C 22*
Dean Trench St.
SW1 . . . . *4A 76* (5D 23)
Deason St. *E15* *5E 53*
Deauville Ct. *SE16* *3F 79*
(off Eleanor Cl.)
SW4 . . . . *4E 103*
De Barowe M. *N5* *1D 49*
Debdale Ho. *E2* *5C 50*
(off Whiston Rd.)
De Beauvoir Ct. *N1*. . . . *4F 49*
(off Northchurch Rd.)
De Beauvoir Cres. *N1* . . *5A 50*
De Beauvoir Est. *N1*. . . *5A 50*
De Beauvoir Pl. *N1* . . . *3A 50*
De Beauvoir Rd. *N1*. . . *5A 50*
De Beauvoir Sq. *N1* . . . *4A 50*
DE BEAUVOIR TOWN . . **5A 50**
Debenham Ct. *E8*. *5C 50*
(off Pownall Rd.)
Debham Ct. *NW2* *5E 29*
Debnams Rd. *SE16* . . . *5E 79*
De Bruin Ct. *E14*. *1E 95*
(off Ferry St.)
Decima St. *SE1*. . *4A 78* (5D 27)
Deck Cl. *SE16*. *2F 79*
De Crespigny Pk. *SE5* . *5F 91*

Derby Rd. E7 . . . . 4F 55
E9 . . . . 5F 51
Derbyshire St. E2 . . . . . . 2C 64
(not continuous)
Derby St. W1 . . . . 2C 74 (2C 20)
Dereham Ho. SE4 . . . . . 2F 107
(off Frendsbury Rd.)
Dereham Pl.
EC2 . . . . 2A 64 (2E 11)
Derek Walcott Cl. SE24 . .3D 105
Dericote St. E8 . . . . .5D 51
Dering St. W1 . . 5D 61 (3D 13)
Dering Yd. W1 . . 5D 61 (3E 13)
Derinton Rd. SW17 . . . . 4B 116
Dermody Gdns. SE13 . . 3F 109
Dermody Rd. SE13 . . . . 3F 109
Deronda Est. SW2 . . . . 1D 119
Deronda Rd. SE24 . . . . 1D 119
Derrick Gdns. SE7 . . . . . 4E 83
Derry St. W8 . . . . 3D 73
Dersingham Rd. NW2 . . 5A 30
Derwent NW1 . . . . 2F 5
(off Robert St.)
Derwent Av. NW9 . . . . . . 1A 28
SW15 . . . . 4A 112
Derwent Ct. SE16 . . . . . . 3F 79
(off Eleanor Cl.)
Derwent Gro. SE22. . . . . 2B 106
Derwent Ho. E3 . . . . . . 3B 66
(off Southern Gro.)
SW7 . . . . .5E 73
(off Cromwell Rd.)
Derwent Ri. NW9 . . . . . . 1A 28
Derwent St. SE10 . . . . . . 1A 96
Desborough Cl. W2 . . . . 4D 59
Desborough Ho. W14. . . 2B 86
(off Nth. End Rd.)
Desenfans Rd. SE21 . .4A 106
Desford Rd. E16 . . . . 3A 68
Design Mus. 3B 78
Desmond St. SE14 . . . . 2A 94
Despard Rd. N19 . . . . . . 3E 33
Dethick Ct. E3 . . . . 5A 52
Detling Ho. SE17 . . . . . . 5A 78
(off Congreve St.)
Detling Rd. BR1: Brom. . 5C 124
Detmold Rd. E5 . . . . 4E 37
Devas St. E3 . . . . 3D 67
Devenay Rd. E15 . . . . . . 4B 54
Deventer Cres. SE22 . .3A 106
De Vere Gdns. W8 . . . . . 3E 73
Deverell St. SE1 . . 4F 77 (5B 26)
De Vere M. W8 . . . . 4E 73
(off De Vere Gdns.)
Devereux Ct. WC2 . . . . . 3B 16
Devereux La. SW13 . . . . 3D 85
Devereux Rd. SW11 . . . 4B 102
Devitt Ho. E14 . . . . 1D 81
(off Wade's Pl.)
Devizes St. N1 . . . . 5F 49
Devon Gdns. N4 . . . . . . 1D 35
Devonia Rd. N1 . . . . 1D 63
Devon Mans. SE1 . . . . . 3F 27
(off Tooley St.)
Devonport W2 . . . . 5A 60
Devonport M. W12 . . . . 3D 71
Devonport Rd. W12 . . . . 2D 71
(not continuous)
Devonport St. E1 . . . . . . 5F 65
Devons Est. E3 . . . . 2D 67

Devonshire Cl. E15 . . . . 1A 54
W1 . . . . 4D 61 (5D 5)
Devonshire Ct. E1 . . . . . 2E 65
(off Bancroft Rd.)
WC1 . . . . 5E 7
(off Boswell St.)
Devonshire Dr. SE10 . . . 3D 95
Devonshire Gro. SE15 . .2D 93
Devonshire Hall E9 . . . . 3E 51
(off Frampton Pk. Rd.)
Devonshire Ho. NW6 . . .3B 44
(off Kilburn High Rd.)
SE1 . . . . 5F 25
(off Bath Ter.)
SW1 . . . . .1F 89
(off Lindsay Sq.)
Devonshire M. SW10 . . .2F 87
(off Camera Pl.)
W4 . . . . 1A 84
Devonshire M. Nth.
W1 . . . . 4D 61 (5D 5)
Devonshire M. Sth.
W1 . . . . 4D 61 (5D 5)
Devonshire M. W.
W1 . . . . 3C 60 (4C 4)
Devonshire Pas. W4 . . . 1A 84
Devonshire Pl. NW2 . . . 5C 30
W8 . . . . 4D 73
W1 . . . . 3C 60 (4C 4)
Devonshire Pl. M.
W1 . . . . 4C 60 (4C 4)
Devonshire Pl. E16. . . . . 5D 69
E17 . . . . 1C 38
SE9 . . . . 2F 125
SE23 . . . . 1E 121
W4 . . . . 1A 84
Devonshire Row
EC2 . . . . 4A 64 (1E 19)
Devonshire Row M. W1 . .4E 5
Devonshire Sq.
EC2 . . . . 5A 64 (1E 19)
Devonshire St. W4 . . . . . 1A 84
W1 . . . . 4C 60 (5C 4)
Devonshire Ter. SE 5E 59
Devons Rd. E3 . . . . 2D 67
Devon St. SE15 . . . . . . 2D 93
Devon Wharf E14 . . . . . 4E 67
(off Leven Rd.)
De Walden Ho. NW8 . . . 1A 60
(off Allitsen Rd.)
De Walden St.
W1 . . . . 4C 60 (1C 12)
Dewar St. SE15 . . . . . . 1C 106
Dewberry Gdns. E6. . . . . 4F 69
Dewberry St. E14 . . . . . 4E 67
Dewey Rd. N1 . . . . 1C 62
Dewey St. SW17 . . . . . 5B 116
Dewhurst Rd. W14 . . . . . 4F 71
Dewsbury Rd. NW10 . . 2C 42
Dewsbury Ter. NW1 . . . 5D 47
D'Eynsford Rd. SE5 . . . . 4F 91
Dhonau Ho. SE1 . . . . . . 5B 78
(off Longfield Est.)
Diadem Ct. W1 . . . . . . 2B 14
Dial Wlk., The W8 . . . . . 3D 73
(off Broad Wlk., The)
Diamond St. SW17 . .3A 116
Diamond Ho. E3 . . . . . . 1A 66
(off Roman Rd.)
Diamond St. SE5 . . . . . 3A 92

Diamond Ter. SE10 . . . . 4E 95
Diamond Way SE8 . . . . 2C 94
Diana Cl. SE8 . . . . 2B 94
Diana Ho. SW13 . . . . . . 4B 84
Dibden Ho. SE5 . . . . . . 3A 92
Dibden St. N1 . . . . 5E 49
Dibdin Ho. NW6 . . . . . . 1D 59
Dicey Av. NW2 . . . . 1E 43
Dickens Est. SE1 . . . . . . 3C 78
SE16 . . . . 4C 78
Dickens House . .3B 62 (4A 8)
Dickens Ho. NW6 . . . . . 2C 58
(off Malvern Rd.)
NW8 . . . . 3F 59
(off Fisherton St.)
SE17 . . . . 1D 91
(off Doddington Gro.)
WC1 . . . . 3D 7
Dickens M. EC1 . . . . . . 5D 9
(off Turnmill St.)
Dickenson Ho. N8 . . . . 1B 34
Dickenson Rd. N8 . . . . 2A 34
Dickens Rd. E6 . . . . 1F 69
Dickens Sq.
SE1 . . . . 4E 77 (5A 26)
Dickens St. SW8 . . . . . . 5D 89
Dicksee Ho. NW8 . . . . . 3F 59
(off Lyons Pl.)
Dickson Ho. E1 . . . . . . 5D 65
(off Philpot St.)
Dickson Rd. SE9 . . . . . 1F 111
Digby Bus. Cen. E9 . . . . 3F 51
(off Digby Rd.)
Digby Cres. N4 . . . . 4E 35
Digby Mans. W6 . . . . . 1D 85
(off Hammersmith Bri. Rd.)
Digby Rd. E9 . . . . 3F 51
Digby St. E2 . . . . 2E 65
Diggon St. E1 . . . . 4F 65
Dighton Ct. SE17 . . . . . 2E 91
Dighton Rd. SW18 . . . . 3E 101
Dignum St. N1 . . . . 1C 62
Digswell St. N7 . . . . 3C 48
Dilhorne Cl. SE12 . . . . 3D 125
Dilke St. SW3 . . . . 2B 88
Dillwyn Cl. SE26 . . . . . 4A 122
Dilston Gro. SE16 . . . . . 5E 79
Dilton Gdns. SW15 . . . 1C 112
Dimes Pl. W6 . . . . 5D 71
Dimond Cl. E7 . . . . 1C 54
Dimsdale Wlk. E13 . . . . 1C 68
Dimson Cres. E3 . . . . . 2C 66
Dingle Gdns. E14 . . . . . 1C 80
Dingley La. SW16 . . . . 2F 117
Dingley Pl. EC1 . . 2E 63 (1A 10)
Dingley Rd. EC1 . . 2E 63 (2F 9)
Dingwall Gdns. NW11 . . 1C 30
Dingwall Rd. SW18 . . . 5E 101
Dinmont Est. E2 . . . . . . 1C 64
Dinmont Ho. E2 . . . . . . 1C 64
(off Pritchard's Rd.)
Dinmont St. E2 . . . . 1D 65
Dinmore Ho. E9 . . . . . . 5E 51
(off Templecombe Rd.)
Dinnington Ho. E1 . . . . 3D 65
(off Coventry Rd.)
Dinsdale Rd. SE3 . . . . . 2B 96
Dinsmore Rd. SW12 . . 5D 103
Dinton Ho. NW8 . . . . . . 3A 60
(off Lilestone St.)

Dinton Rd. SW19 . . . . . . 5F **115**
Dirleton Rd. E15. . . . . 5B **54**
Disbrowe Rd. W6 . . . . . . 2A **86**
Discovery Bus. Pk.
 SE16 . . . . 4C 78
 (off St James's Rd.)
Discovery Ho. *E14* 1E **81**
 (off Newby Pl.)
Discovery Wlk. E1 . . . . . 2D **79**
Disney Pl. SE1. . 3E **77** (3A **26**)
Disney St. SE1. . 3E **77** (3A **26**)
Disraeli Gdns. SW15 . . 2B **100**
Disraeli Rd. E7. . . . . 3C **54**
 SW15 . . . . 2A **100**
Diss St. E2 . . . . 2B **64** (1F **11**)
Distaff La. EC4. . 1E **77** (4F **17**)
Distillery La. W6 . . . . 1E **85**
Distillery Rd. W6 . . . . 1E **85**
Distin St. SE11 . . . . 5C **76**
Ditch All. SE10. . . . . 4D **95**
Ditchburn St. E14 . . . . . . 1E **81**
Dittisham Rd. SE9 . . . . . 4F **125**
Divisional Rd. E12 . . . . . 4F **41**
Divis Way *SW15* *4D 99*
 (off Dover Pk. Dr.)
Dixon Clark Ct. N1 . . . . . 3D **49**
Dixon Ho. *W10* *5F 57*
 (off Darfield Way)
Dixon Rd. SE14 . . . . . . 4A **94**
Dixon's All. SE16. . . . . . . 3D **79**
Dobree Av. NW10. . . . . . 4D **43**
Dobson Cl. NW6 . . . . 4F **45**
Dobson Ho. *SE5* *3F 91*
 (off Edmund St.)
 SE14 . . . . 2F 93
 (off John Williams Cl.)
Doby Ct. *EC4* *4A 18*
 (off Skinners La.)
Dock Cotts. *E1* *1E 79*
 (off Highway, The)
Dockers Tanner Rd. E14 . 4C **80**
Dockhead SE1 . . . . 3B **78**
Dockhead Wharf *SE1* . . . *4F 27*
 (off Shad Thames)
Dock Hill Av. SE16. . . . . 2F **79**
Docklands Sailing Cen.
 . . . . *4C 80*
Dockley Rd. SE16. . . . . . 4C **78**
Dockley Rd. Ind. Est.
 SE16 . . . . 4C 78
 (off Dockley Rd.)
Dock Offices *SE16* *4E 79*
 (off Surrey Quays Rd.)
Dock Rd. E16 . . . . 1B **82**
Dockside Rd. E16 . . . . . 1F **83**
Dock St. E1 . . . . 1C **78**
Doctor Johnson Av.
 SW17 . . . . 3D **117**
Doctors Cl. SE26 . . . . . . 5E **121**
Docwra's Bldgs. N1 . . . . 3A **50**
Dodbrooke Rd. SE27 . . 3C **118**
Dodd Ho. *SE16*. *5D 79*
 (off Rennie Est.)
Doddington Gro. SE17 . . 2D **91**
Doddington Pl. SE17 . . . 2D **91**
Dodson St. SE1 . . 3C **76** (4C **24**)
Dod St. E14 . . . . 5B **66**
Dog & Duck Yd. WC1 . . . 5F **7**
Doggett Rd. SE6. . . . . . 5C **108**
Dog Kennel Hill SE5 . . . 1A **106**

Dog Kennel Hill Est.
 SE22 . . . . 1A 106
 (off Albrighton Rd.)
Dog La. NW10 . . . . 1A **42**
Doherty Rd. E13. . . . . . . 3C **68**
Dolben Ct. SE8 . . . . 5B **80**
Dolben St. SE1 . 2D **77** (2D **25**)
 (not continuous)
Dolby Rd. SW6. . . . . 5B **86**
Dolland Ho. *SE11*. *1B 90*
 (off Newburn St.)
Dolland St. SE11 . . . . . . 1B **90**
Dollar Bay Ct. *E14* *3E 81*
 (off Lawn Ho. Clo)
DOLLIS HILL **4D 29**
Dollis Hill Av. NW2 . . . . . 5D **29**
Dollis Hill Est. NW2 . . . . 5C **28**
Dollis Hill La. NW2 . . . . . 1B **42**
Dolman Rd. W4 . . . . 5A **70**
Dolman St. SW4 . . . . . . 2B **104**
Dolphin Cl. SE16 . . . . . . 3F **79**
Dolphin Ct. NW11 . . . . . . 1A **30**
 SE8 . . . . 2B 94
 (off Wotton Rd.)
Dolphin Ho. SW18 . . . . 2D **101**
Dolphin La. E14 . . . . 1D **81**
Dolphin Sq. SW1 . . . . . . 1E **89**
 W4 . . . . 3A **84**
Dolphin Twr. *SE8* *2B 94*
 (off Abinger Gro.)
Dombey Ho. *SE1* *3C 78*
 (off Wolseley St.)
 W11. . . . . 2F 71
 (off St Ann's Rd.)
Dombey St.
 WC1 . . . . 4B **62** (5F **7**)
 (not continuous)
Domecq Ho. *EC1* *3E 9*
 (off Dallington St.)
Dome Hill Pk. SE26 . . 4B **120**
Domett Cl. SE5 . . . . 2F **105**
Domfe Pl. E5 . . . . 1E **51**
Domingo St. EC1 . . 3E **63** (3F **9**)
Dominica Cl. E6 . . . . 1F **69**
Dominion Ct. *E8. . . . . . . 4B 50*
 (off Middleton Rd.)
Dominion Ho. *E14* *1D 95*
 (off St Davids Sq.)
Dominion St.
 EC2 . . . . 4F **63** (5C **10**)
Dominion Theatre **2C 14**
 (off Tottenham Ct. Rd.)
Donald Hunter Ho. *E7* . . *2D 55*
 (off Post Office App., not cont.)
Donald Rd. E13 . . . . 5D **55**
Donaldson Rd. NW6 . . . . 5B **44**
Donato Dr. SE15. . . . . . . 2A **92**
Doncaster Gdns. N4 . . . 1E **35**
Donegal Ho. *E1* *3D 65*
 (off Cambridge Heath Rd.)
Donegal St. N1. . . . . 1B **62**
Doneraile Ho. *SW1* *1D 89*
 (off Ebury Bri. Rd.)
Doneraile St. SW6 . . . . . 5F **85**
Dongola Rd. E1 . . . . 4A **66**
 E13. . . . . 2D **69**
Dongola Rd. W. E13 . . . 2D **69**
Donkey All. SE22 . . . . . 5C **106**
Donkin Ho. *SE16* *5D 79*
 (off Rennie Est.)

Donmar Warehouse Theatre
 . . . . *3D 15*
 (off Earlham St.)
Donnatt's Rd. SE14 . . . . 4B **94**
Donne Ct. SE24 . . . . 4E **105**
Donne Ho. *E14*. *5C 66*
 (off Dod St.)
 SE14 . . . . 2F 93
 (off Samuel Cl.)
Donnelly Ct. *SW6* *3A 86*
 (off Dawes Rd.)
Donne Pl. SW3. . . . . 5A **74**
Donnington Ct. *NW1* . . . *1D 47*
 (off Castlehaven Rd.)
 NW10 . . . . 4D **43**
Donnington Mans.
 NW10 . . . . 5E 43
 (off Donnington Rd.)
Donnington Rd. NW10 . . 4D **43**
Donoghue Cotts. *E14*. . . *4A 66*
 (off Galsworthy Av.)
Donovan Ct. *SW10* *1F 87*
 (off Drayton Gdns.)
Donovan Ho. *E1* *1E 79*
 (off Cable St.)
Don Phelan Cl. SE5 . . . . 4F **91**
Doon St. SE1. . . 2C **76** (2B **24**)
Dora Ho. *E14* *5B 66*
 (off Rhodeswell Rd.)
 W11. . . . . 1F 71
 (off St Ann's Rd.)
Dorando Cl. W12. . . . . . 1D **71**
Doran Mnr. *N2* *1B 32*
 (off Gt. North Rd.)
Doran Wlk. E15 . . . . 4E **53**
Dora Rd. SW19 . . . . 5C **114**
Dora St. E14. . . . . 5B **66**
Dorchester Ct. *N1* *4A 50*
 (off Englefield Rd.)
 NW2 . . . . 5F **29**
 SE24 . . . . 3E **105**
Dorchester Dr. SE24. . . 3E **105**
Dorchester Gro. W4 . . . 1A **84**
Dorchester Ter. *NW2* . . . *5F 29*
 (off Gratton Ter.)
Dordrecht Rd. W3 . . . . . 2A **70**
Doreen Av. NW9. . . . . . . 3A **28**
Doreen Capstan Ho.
 E11 . . . . 5A 40
 (off Apollo Pl.)
Doria Rd. SW6 . . . . 5B **86**
Doric Ho. *E2* *1F 65*
 (off Mace St.)
Doric Way NW1 . . 2F **61** (1B **6**)
Doris Emmerton Ct.
 SW11 . . . . 2E **101**
Doris Rd. E7. . . . . 4C **54**
Dorking Cl. SE8 . . . . 2B **94**
Dorking Ho. SE1 . . 4F **77** (5C **26**)
Dorlcote Rd. SW18 . . . . 5A **102**
Dorman Way NW8 . . . . . 5F **45**
Dorma Trad. Pk. E10 . . . 3F **37**
Dormay St. SW18 . . . . . 3D **101**
Dormer Cl. E15 . . . . 3B **54**
Dormstone Ho. *SE17*. . . *5A 78*
 (off Beckway St.)
Dornberg Cl. SE3 . . . . . . 3C **96**
Dornberg Rd. SE3 . . . . . 3D **97**
Dorncliffe Rd. SW6 . . . . 5A **86**
Dorney NW3 . . . . 4A **46**

Dreadnought Wharf
SE10 . . . . 2D 95
(off Thames St.)
Dresden Cl. NW6 . . . . . 3D 45
Dresden Ho. *SE11 . . . . . 5B 76*
(off Lambeth Wlk.)
Dresden Rd. N19 . . . . . . 3E 33
Dressington Av. SE4. . . 4C 108
Drewery Ct. SE3. . . . . . 1A 110
Drewett Ho. *E1 . . . . 5C 64*
(off Christian St.)
Drew Ho. SW16 . . . . . . 3A 118
Drew Rd. E16 . . . . 2F 83
(not continuous)
Drewstead Rd. SW16 . . 2F 117
Driffield Rd. E3 . . . . . . 1A 66
Drill Hall Arts Cen. 5B 6
(off Chenies St.)
Drinkwater Ho. *SE5 . . . . 3F 91*
(off Picton St.)
Drive Mans. *SW6 . . . . . . 5A 86*
(off Fulham Rd.)
Drive, The N7 . . . . 3B 48
(not continuous)
NW10 . . . . 5B 42
NW11 . . . . 2A 30
SW6 . . . . 5A 86
Driveway, The *E17. . . . . 1D 39*
(off Hoe St.)
Dr Johnson's House 3C 16
(off Pemberton Row)
Droitwich Cl. SE26. . . . 3C 120
Dromore Rd. SW15 . . . 4A 100
Dron Ho. *E1 . . . . 4E 65*
(off Adelina Gro.)
Droop St. W10 . . . . 2F 57
Drovers Pl. SE15 . . . . . 3E 93
Druce Rd. SE21 . . . . . . 4A 106
Druid St. SE1 . . . 3A 78 (3E 27)
Drummond Cres.
NW1 . . . . 2F 61 (1B 6)
Drummond Ga. SW1 . . . 1F 89
Drummond Ho. *E2 . . . . . 1C 64*
(off Goldsmiths Row)
Drummond Rd. E11 . . . . 1E 41
SE16 . . . . 4D 79
Drummond St.
NW1 . . . . 3E 61 (3F 5)
Drum St. E1 . . . . 5B 64
Drury Ho. SW8 . . . . 4E 89
Drury La. WC2 . . 5A 62 (2E 15)
Drury Lane Theatre 3F 15
(off Catherine St.)
Drury Way NW10 . . . . . . 2A 42
Dryad St. SW15 . . . . . . 1F 99
Dryburgh Ho. *SW1 . . . . . 1D 89*
(off Abbots Mnr.)
Dryburgh Rd. SW15 . . . . 1D 99
Dryden Ct. SE11. . . . . . . 5D 77
Dryden Mans. *W14 . . . . 2A 86*
(off Queen's Club Gdns.)
Dryden Rd. SW19 . . . . . 5E 115
Dryden St. WC2 . . 5A 62 (3E 15)
Dryfield Wlk. SE8 . . . . . 2C 94
Drylands Rd. N8 . . . . . . 1A 34
Drysdale Ho. *N1 . . . . . . 1E 11*
(off Drysdale St.)
Drysdale Pl. N1 . . 2A 64 (1E 11)
Drysdale St.
N1 . . . . 2A 64 (1E 11)

Dublin Av. E8 . . . . 5C 50
Ducal St. E2 . . . . 2B 64
Du Cane Cl. W12 . . . . . . 5E 57
Du Cane Ct. SW17 . . . . 1C 116
Du Cane Rd. W12 . . . . . 5B 56
Ducavel Ho. SW2 . . . . . 1B 118
Duchess M. W1. . 4D 61 (1E 13)
Duchess of Bedford Ho.
W8 . . . . 3C 72
(off Duchess of Bedford's Wlk.)
Duchess of Bedford's Wlk.
W8 . . . . 3C 72
Duchess St. W1. . 4D 61 (1E 13)
Duchess Theatre 4F 15
(off Catherine St.)
Duchy St. SE1 . . 2C 76 (1C 24)
(not continuous)
Ducie St. SW4 . . . . 2B 104
Duckett M. N4 . . . . 1D 35
Duckett Rd. N4 . . . . 1C 34
Duckett St. E1 . . . . 3F 65
Duck La. W1 . . . . 3B 14
Du Cros Rd. W3 . . . . . . 2A 70
Dudden Hill La. NW10 . . 1B 42
Dudden Hill Pde. NW10 . 1B 42
Duddington Cl. SE9 . . . . 4F 125
Dudley Ct. *W1 . . . . 5B 60*
(off Up. Berkeley St.)
WC2 . . . . 5A 62 (2D 15)
Dudley Ho. *W2 . . . . 4F 59*
(off Nth. Wharf Rd.)
Dudley M. SW2 . . . . 4C 104
Dudley Rd. NW6 . . . . . . 1A 58
SW19 . . . . 5C 114
Dudley St. W2 . . . . 4F 59
Dudlington Rd. E5 . . . . . 4E 37
Dudmaston M. *SW3 . . . . 1F 87*
(off Fulham Rd.)
Dudrich M. *SE5 . . . . 3E 91*
(off Pitman St.)
Duffell Ho. SE11 . . . . . . 1B 90
(off Loughborough St.)
Dufferin Av. EC1 . . . . . . 4B 10
Dufferin St. EC1 . . . . . . 4B 10
(off Dufferin St.)
Dufferin St. EC1. . 3E 63 (4A 10)
Duff St. E14 . . . . 5D 67
Dufour's Pl. W1 . . 1E 61 (3A 14)
Dugard Way SE11 . . . . . 5D 77
Duke Humphrey Rd.
SE3 . . . . 4A 96
Duke of Wellington Pl.
SW1 . . . . 3C 74 (3C 20)
Duke of York Column
(Memorial) 2C 22
Duke of York Sq. SW3 . . 5B 74
Duke of York's Theatre. . 5D 15
(off St Martin's La.)
Duke of York St.
SW1 . . . . 2E 75 (1A 22)
Duke Rd. W4 . . . . 1A 84
Duke's Av. W4 . . . . 1A 84
Dukes Ct. SE13 . . . . . . 5E 95
SW14 . . . . 5A 84
Duke's Head Yd. N6 . . . 3D 33
Duke Shore Wharf E14. . 1B 80
Duke's Ho. *SW1 . . . . . . 5F 75*
(off Vincent St.)
Dukes La. W8 . . . . 3D 73

Duke's M. W1 . . . . 2C 12
Duke's Pl. EC3. . 5A 64 (3E 19)
Duke's Rd. WC1 . . 2F 61 (2C 6)
Dukesthorpe Rd.
SE26 . . . . 4F 121
Duke St. SW1 . . 2E 75 (1A 22)
W1 . . . . 5C 60 (2C 12)
Duke St. Hill
SE1 . . . . 2F 77 (1C 26)
Duke St. Mans. *W1 . . . . 3C 12*
(off Duke St.)
Duke's Yd. W1 . . 1C 74 (4C 12)
Dulas St. N4 . . . . 3B 34
Dulford St. W11 . . . . . . 1A 72
Dulka Rd. SW11 . . . . . . 3B 102
Dulverton NW1 . . . . 5E 47
(off Royal College St.)
Dulverton Mans. WC1 . . 4A 8
DULWICH 2A 120
Dulwich Bus. Cen.
SE23 . . . . 1F 121
Dulwich Comn. SE21 . . 1A 120
Dulwich Lawn Cl.
SE22 . . . . 3B 106
Dulwich Oaks Pl.
SE21 . . . . 3A 120
Dulwich Picture Gallery
. . . . 5F 105
Dulwich Ri. Gdns.
SE22 . . . . 3B 106
Dulwich Rd. SE24 . . . . . 3C 104
DULWICH VILLAGE . . . 5A 106
Dulwich Village SE21. . . 4F 105
Dulwich Wood Av.
SE19 . . . . 4A 120
Dulwich Wood Pk.
SE19 . . . . 4A 120
Dumain Ct. *SE11 . . . . . . 5D 77*
(off Opal St.)
Dumbarton Ct. SW2 . . . 4A 104
Dumbarton Rd. SW2 . . . 4A 104
Dumont Rd. N16 . . . . . . 5A 36
Dumpton Pl. NW1 . . . . . 4C 46
Dunbar Rd. E7 . . . . 3C 54
Dunbar St. SE27 . . . . . . 3E 119
Dunbar Wharf *E14 . . . . . 1B 80*
(off Narrow St.)
Dunboyne Rd. NW3 . . . . 2B 46
Dunbridge Ho. *SW15. . . 4B 98*
(off Highcliffe Dr.)
Dunbridge St. E2 . . . . . . 3C 64
Duncan Gro. W3. . . . . . 5A 56
Duncan Ho. *NW3 . . . . . 4B 46*
(off Fellows Rd.)
SW1 . . . . 1E 89
(off Dolphin Sq.)
Duncannon Ho. *SW1 . . . 1F 89*
(off Lindsay Sq.)
Duncannon St.
WC2 . . . . 1A 76 (5D 15)
Duncan Rd. E8 . . . . 5D 51
Duncan St. N1 . . . . 1D 63
Duncan Ter. N1 . . . . 1D 63
(not continuous)
Dunch St. E1 . . . . 5D 65
Duncombe Hill SE23 . . . 5A 108
Duncombe Rd. N19 . . . . 3F 33
Duncrievie Rd. SE13 . . . 4F 109
Dundalk Ho. *E1 . . . . 5E 65*
(off Clark St.)

Dundalk Rd. SE4 . . . . . . 1A 108
Dundas Rd. SE15 . . . . . . 5E 93
Dundee Ct. E1 . . . . 2D 79
  (off Wapping High St.)
Dundee Ho. W9 . . . . 2E 59
  (off Maida Va.)
Dundee Rd. E13 . . . . 1D 69
Dundee St. E1 . . . . 2D 79
Dundee Wharf E14 . . . . . 1B 80
Dundonald Ho. E14 . . . . . 3D 81
  (off Admirals Way)
Dundonald Rd. NW10 . . . . 5F 43
Dundry Ho. SE26 . . . . . . 3C 120
Dunedin Ho. E10 . . . . 5D 39
Dunelm Gro. SE27 . . . . . 3E 119
Dunelm St. E1 . . . . 5F 65
Dunfield Gdns. SE6 . . . . 5D 123
Dunfield Rd. SE6 . . . . . . 5D 123
  (not continuous)
Dunford Rd. N7 . . . . 1B 48
Dungarvan Av. SW15 . . . . 2C 98
Dunkeld Ho. E14 . . . . 5F 67
  (off Abbott Rd.)
Dunkery Rd. SE9 . . . . 4F 125
Dunkirk St. SE27 . . . . . . 4E 119
Dunlace Rd. E5 . . . . 1E 51
Dunlin Ho. SE16 . . . . 5F 79
  (off Tawny Way)
Dunloe Ct. E2 . . . . 1B 64
Dunloe St. E2 . . . . 1B 64
Dunlop Pl. SE16 . . . . 4B 78
Dunmore Point E2 . . . . . . 2F 11
  (off Gascoigne Pl.)
Dunmore Rd. NW6 . . . . . . 5A 44
Dunmow Ho. SE11 . . . . . 1B 90
  (off Newburn St.)
Dunmow Rd. E15 . . . . 1F 53
Dunmow Wlk. N1 . . . . . . 5E 49
  (off Popham St.)
Dunnage Cres. SE16 . . . . 5A 80
  (not continuous)
Dunnico Ho. SE17 . . . . . . 1A 92
  (off East St.)
Dunn's Pas. WC1 . . . . . . 2E 15
Dunn St. E8 . . . . 2B 50
Dunollie Pl. NW5 . . . . . . 2E 47
Dunollie Rd. NW5 . . . . . . 2E 47
Dunoon Gdns. SE23 . . . . 5F 107
Dunoon Ho. N1 . . . . 5B 48
  (off Bemerton Est.)
Dunoon Rd. SE23 . . . . . . 5E 107
Dunraven Rd. W12 . . . . . 2C 70
Dunraven St.
  W1 . . . . . . 1B 74 (4A 12)
Dunsany Rd. W14 . . . . . . 4F 71
Dunsford Way SW15 . . . . 4D 99
Dunsmure Rd. N16 . . . . . 3A 36
Dunstable M. W1 . . 4C 60 (5C 4)
Dunstan Ho's. E1 . . . . 4E 65
  (off Stepney Grn.)
Dunstan Rd. NW11 . . . . . 3B 30
Dunstan's Gro. SE22 . . . . 4D 107
Dunstan's Rd. SE22 . . . . 5C 106
Dunster Ct. EC3 . 1A 78 (4E 19)
Dunster Gdns. NW6 . . . . 4B 44
Dunster Ho. SE6 . . . . . . 3E 123
Dunsterville Way
  SE1 . . . . . . 3F 77 (4C 26)
Dunston Rd. E8 . . . . 5B 50
  SW11 . . . . 5C 88

Dunston St. E8 . . . . 5A 50
Dunton Ct. SE23 . . . . . . 2D 121
Dunton Rd. E10 . . . . 2D 39
  SE1 . . . . 1B 92
Duntshill Rd. SW18 . . . . 1D 115
Dunworth M. W11 . . . . . . 5B 58
Duplex Ride
  SW1 . . . . . . 3B 74 (4A 20)
Dupree Rd. SE7 . . . . 1D 97
Durand Gdns. SW9 . . . . . 4B 90
Durands Wlk. SE16 . . . . . 3B 80
Durant St. E2 . . . . 1C 64
Durban Ct. E7 . . . . 4F 55
Durban Ho. W12 . . . . 1D 71
  (off White City Est.)
Durban Rd. E15 . . . . 2A 68
  SE27 . . . . 4E 119
Durdans Ho. NW1 . . . . . . 4D 47
  (off Farrier St.)
Durell Ho. SE16 . . . . 3F 79
  (off Wolfe Cres.)
Durfey Ho. SE5 . . . . 3F 91
  (off Edmund St.)
Durford Cres. SW15 . . . . 1D 113
Durham Ct. NW6 . . . . . . 1C 58
  (off Kilburn Pk. Rd.)
Durham Hill
  BR1: Brom 4B 124
Durham Ho. St. WC2 . . . . 5E 15
Durham Pl. SW3 . . . . 1B 88
Durham Rd. E12 . . . . 1F 55
  E16 . . . . 3A 68
  N7 . . . . 4B 34
Durham Row E1 . . . . 4F 65
Durham St. SE11 . . . . . . 2B 90
Durham Ter. W2 . . . . 5D 59
Durham Yd. E2 . . . . 2D 65
Durley Rd. N16 . . . . 2A 36
Durlston Rd. E5 . . . . 4C 36
Durnford Ho. SE6 . . . . . . 3E 123
Durnford St. N15 . . . . . . 1A 36
  SE10 . . . . 2E 95
Durning Rd. SE19 . . . . . . 5F 119
Durnsford Av. SW19 . . . . 2C 114
Durnsford Rd. SW19 . . . . 2C 114
Durrell Rd. SW6 . . . . 4B 86
Durrels Ho. W14 . . . . 5B 72
  (off Warwick Gdns.)
Durrington Rd. E5 . . . . . . 1A 52
Durrington Twr. SW8 . . . . 5E 89
Durrisdeer Ho. NW2 . . . . 1B 44
  (off Lyndale)
Dursley Cl. SE3 . . . . 5E 97
Dursley Ct. SE15 . . . . . . 3A 92
  (off Lydney Cl.)
Dursley Gdns. SE3 . . . . . 4F 97
Dursley Rd. SE3 . . . . 5E 97
Durward St. E1 . . . . 4D 65
Durweston M. W1 . . . . . . 5A 4
Durweston St.
  W1 . . . . 4B 60 (1A 12)
Dutch Yd. SW18 . . . . 3C 100
Dutton St. SE10 . . . . 4E 95
Dye Ho. La. E3 . . . . 5C 52
Dyer's Bldgs.
  EC1 . . . . . . 4C 62 (1B 16)
Dyers Hall Rd. E11 . . . . . 3A 40
Dyers Hill Rd. E11 . . . . . 4F 39
Dyers La. SW15 . . . . 2D 99
Dylan Rd. SE24 . . . . 2D 105

Dylways SE5 . . . . 2F 105
Dymes Path SW19 . . . . . 2F 113
Dymock St. SE15 . . . . . . 3A 92
  (off Lydney Cl.)
Dymock St. SW6 . . . . . . 1D 101
Dyneley Rd. SE12 . . . . . . 3E 125
Dyne Rd. NW6 . . . . 4A 44
Dynevor Rd. N16 . . . . . . 5A 36
Dynham Rd. NW6 . . . . . . 4C 44
Dyott St. WC1 . . 5F 61 (2C 14)
Dysart St. EC2 . 3F 63 (4D 11)
Dyson Cl. NW2 . . . . 3E 29
Dyson Ho. SE10 . . . . 1B 96
  (off Blackwall La.)
Dyson Rd. E11 . . . . 1A 40
  E15 . . . . 3B 54

E

Eade Rd. N4 . . . . 2E 35
Eagle Cl. SE16 . . . . 1E 93
Eagle Ct. EC1 . . 4D 63 (5D 9)
Eagle Hill SE19 . . . . 5F 119
Eagle Ho. E1 . . . . 3D 65
  (off Headlam St.)
  N1 . . . . 1F 63
  (off Eagle Wharf Rd.)
Eagle Lodge NW11 . . . . . 2B 30
Eagle M. N1 . . . . 3A 50
Eagle Pl. SW10 . . . . 1E 87
  (off Rolandway)
  W1 . . . . 5A 14
Eagle St. WC1 . . 4B 62 (1F 15)
Eagle Wharf Ct. SE1 . . . . 2F 27
  (off Lafone St.)
Eagle Wharf E. E14 . . . . . 1A 80
  (off Narrow St.)
Eagle Wharf Rd. N1 . . . . . 1E 63
Eagle Wharf W. E14 . . . . 1A 80
  (off Narrow St.)
Ealdham Sq. SE9 . . . . . . 2E 111
Eamont Ct. NW8 . . . . 1A 60
  (off Eamont St.)
Eamont St. NW8 . . . . 1A 60
Eardley Cres. SW5 . . . . . 1C 86
Eardley Rd. SW16 . . . . . . 5E 117
Earldom Rd. SW15 . . . . . 2E 99
Earlham Ct. E11 . . . . 2B 40
Earlham Gro. E7 . . . . 2B 54
Earlham St.
  WC2 . . . . . . 5A 62 (3C 14)
Earl Ho. NW1 . . . . 3A 60
  (off Lisson Gro.)
Earlom Ho. WC1 . . . . 2B 8
  (off Margery St.)
EARL'S COURT 1C 86
Earl's Court Exhibition
  Building 1C 86
Earls Ct. Gdns. SW5 . . . . 5D 73
Earls Ct. Rd. W8 . . . . 4C 72
Earl's Ct. Sq. SW5 . . . . . 1D 87
Earlsferry Way N1 . . . . . . 4A 48
  (not continuous)
EARLSFIELD 1E 115
Earlsfield Rd. SW18 . . . . 1E 115
Earlsmead Rd. NW10 . . . . 2E 57
Earls Ter. W8 . . . . 4B 72
Earlsthorpe M. SW12 . . . . 4C 102
Earlsthorpe Rd. SE26 . . . . 4F 121

Edensor Rd. W4 . . . . . . 3A **84**
Edenvale St. SW6 . . . . . 5E **87**
Edgar Ho. *E9* *2A 52*
  (off Homerton Rd.)
  E11 . . . . 2C **40**
  SW8 . . . . *3A 90*
  (off Wyvil Rd.)
Edgar Kail Way SE22 . . 2A **106**
Edgarley Ter. SW6 . . . . 4A **86**
Edgar Rd. E3 . . . . 2D **67**
Edgcott Ho. *W10.* *4E 57*
  (off Sutton Way)
Edge Bus. Cen., The
  NW2 . . . . 4D **29**
Edgecombe Ho. SE5. . . 5A **92**
Edgecot Gro. N15 . . . . . 1A **36**
Edgehill Ho. SW9 . . . . . 5D **91**
Edgeley La. SW4 . . . . . 1F **103**
Edgeley Rd. SW4 . . . . . 1F **103**
Edgel St. SW18 . . . . . . 2D **101**
Edgepoint Cl. SE27 . . . 5D **119**
Edge St. W8 . . . . 2C **72**
Edgeworth Cl. NW4 . . . 1C **28**
Edgeworth Ho. *NW8.* . . . *5E 45*
  (off Boundary Rd.)
Edgeworth Rd. SE9. . . . 2E **111**
Edgson Ho. *SW1* *1D 89*
  (off Ebury Bri. Rd.)
Edgware Rd. NW2 . . . . 3D **29**
  W2 . . . . . . 3F **59** (3A **12**)
Edinburgh Cl. E2 . . . . . 1E **65**
Edinburgh Ct. *SE16.* . . . *2F 79*
  (off Rotherhithe St.)
Edinburgh Ga. SW1 . . . 3B **74**
Edinburgh Ho. *W9* *2D 59*
  (off Maida Va.)
Edinburgh Rd. E13 . . . 1D **69**
  E17 . . . . 1C **38**
  (not continuous)
Edington NW5 . . . . 3C **46**
Edison Bldg. E14 . . . . . 3C **80**
Edison Ct. SE10 . . . . . . 5B **82**
Edison Rd. N8 . . . . 1F **33**
Edis St. NW1 . . . . 5C **46**
Edith Brinson Ho. *E14* . *5F 67*
  (off Oban St.)
Edith Cavell Cl. N19. . . . 2A **34**
Edith Gro. SW10 . . . . . 2E **87**
Edith Ho. *W6* *1E 85*
  (off Queen Caroline St.)
Edithna St. SW9 . . . . . 1A **104**
Edith Neville Cotts.
  NW1 . . . . 1B **6**
  (off Doric Way)
Edith Ramsay Ho. *E1.* . *4A 66*
  (off Duckett St.)
Edith Rd. E6 . . . . 4F **55**
  E15 . . . . 2F **53**
  SW19 . . . . 5D **115**
  W14 . . . . 5A **72**
Edith Row SW6 . . . . . . 4D **87**
Edith St. E2 . . . . 1C **64**
Edith Summerskill Ho.
  SW6 . . . . *3B 86*
  (off Clem Attlee Est.)
Edith Ter. SW10 . . . . . . 3E **87**
Edith Vs. W14 . . . . 5B **72**
Edith Yd. SW10 . . . . . . 3E **87**
Edmeston Cl. E9 . . . . . . 3A **52**
Edmond Ct. SE14 . . . . . 4E **93**

Edmonton Ct. *SE16* *4E 79*
  (off Canada Est.)
Edmund Halley Way
  SE10 . . . . 3A **82**
Edmund Ho. SE17 . . . . 2D **91**
Edmundsbury Ct. Est.
  SW9 . . . . 2B **104**
Edmund St. SE5 . . . . . . 3F **91**
Ednam Ho. *SE15* *2C 92*
  (off Haymerle Rd.)
Edna St. SW11 . . . . . . 4A **88**
Edred Ho. *E9* *1A 52*
  (off Lindisfarne Way)
Edrich Ho. SW4 . . . . . . 4A **90**
Edric Ho. *SW1* *5F 75*
  (off Page St.)
Edric Rd. SE14 . . . . . . 3F **93**
Edward Bond Ho. *WC1* . *2E 7*
  (off Cromer St.)
Edward Cl. NW2 . . . . . . 1F **43**
Edward Ct. E16. . . . . . . 4C **68**
Edward Dodd Ho. *N1.* . . *1C 10*
  (off Haberdasher St.)
Edward Edward's Ho.
  SE1 . . . . 2D **25**
Edwardes Pl. W8 . . . . . 4B **72**
Edwardes Sq. W8 . . . . 4B **72**
Edward Ho. SE11 . . . . . 1B **90**
  (off Newburn St.)
Edward Mann Cl. *E1* . . . *5F 65*
  (off Caroline St.)
Edward VII Mans.
  NW10 . . . . *2F 57*
  (off Chamberlayne Rd.)
Edward M. N1 . . 2D **61** (1E **5**)
Edward Pl. SE8 . . . . . . 2B **94**
Edward Rd. E17 . . . . . . 1F **37**
Edward Robinson Ho.
  SE14 . . . . *3F 93*
  (off Reaston St.)
Edward's Cotts. N1 . . . 3D **49**
Edward's La. N16 . . . . . 4C **48**
Edwards M. N1. . . . . . . 4C **48**
  W1 . . . . 5C **60** (3B **12**)
Edward Sq. N1 . . . . 5B **48**
  SE16 . . . . 2A **80**
Edward St. E16. . . . . . . 3C **68**
  (not continuous)
  SE8 . . . . 3B **94**
  SE14 . . . . 3B **94**
Edward Temme Av. E15. 4B **54**
Edward Tyler Rd. SE12. . 2E **125**
Edwina Gdns. IG4: IIf . . 1F **41**
Edwin Ho. SE15 . . . . . . 3C **92**
Edwin's Mead E9 . . . . . 1A **52**
Edwin St. E1 . . . . 3E **65**
  E16 . . . . 4C **68**
Effie Pl. SW6 . . . . 3C **86**
Effie Rd. SW6 . . . . 3C **86**
Effingham Rd. SE12. . . 3A **110**
Effort St. SW17 . . . . . . 5A **116**
Effra Cl. SW19 . . . . . . 5D **115**
Effra Ct. *SW2* *3B 104*
  (off Brixton Hill)
Effra Pde. SW2. . . . . . . 3C **104**
Effra Rd. SW2 . . . . 2C **104**
  SW19 . . . . 5D **115**
Effra Rd. Retail Pk.
  SW2 . . . . 3C **104**
Egbert St. NW1 . . . . . . 5C **46**

Egbury Ho. SW15. . . . . *4B 98*
  (off Tangley Gro.)
Egerton Ct. E11. . . . . . . 2F **39**
Egerton Cres. SW3. . . . 5A **74**
Egerton Dr. SE10 . . . . . 4D **95**
Egerton Gdns. NW10 . . 5E **43**
  SW3 . . . . 5A **74**
Egerton Gdns. M. SW3. . 4A **74**
Egerton Pl. SW3. . . . . . 4A **74**
Egerton Rd. N16. . . . . . 2B **36**
Egerton Ter. SW3 . . . . . 4A **74**
Egham Cl. SW19 . . . . . 2A **114**
Egham Rd. E13 . . . . . . 4D **69**
Eglantine Rd. SW18. . . 3E **101**
Eglington Ct. SE17 . . . . 2E **91**
Egliston M. SW15 . . . . . 1E **99**
Egliston Rd. SW15. . . . . 1E **99**
Eglon M. NW1 . . . . 4B **46**
Egmont St. SE14. . . . . . 3F **93**
Egremont Ho. *SE13* *5D 95*
  (off Russett Way)
Egremont Rd. SE27 . . . 3C **118**
Egret Ho. *SE16.* *5F 79*
  (off Tawny Way)
Eider Cl. E7 . . . . 2B **54**
Eider Ct. *SE8* *2B 94*
  (off Pilot Cl.)
Eisenhower Dr. E6 . . . . 4F **69**
Elaine Gro. NW5 . . . . . 2C **46**
Elam Cl. SE5 . . . . 5D **91**
Elam St. SE5 . . . . 5D **91**
Elan Ct. E1 . . . . 4D **65**
Eland Ho. *SW1.* *4E 75*
  (off Bressenden Pl.)
Eland Rd. SW11 . . . . . . 1B **102**
Elba Pl. SE17 . . . . 5E **77**
Elbe St. SW6 . . . . 5E **87**
Elborough St. SW18. . . 1C **114**
Elbourne Ct. *SE16* *4F 79*
  (off Worgan St.)
Elbourn Ho. *SW3* *1A 88*
  (off Cale St.)
Elbury Dr. E16 . . . . 5C **68**
Elcho St. SW11 . . . . . . 3A **88**
Elcot Av. SE15 . . . . 3D **93**
Elder Av. N8 . . . . 1A **34**
Elderberry Gro. SE27 . . 4E **119**
Elderfield Ho. E14 . . . . 1C **80**
Elderfield Pl. SW17. . . . 4D **117**
Elderfield Rd. E5 . . . . . 1F **51**
Elderflower Way E15 . . 4A **54**
Elder Gdns. SE27 . . . . . 5E **119**
Elder Rd. SE27 . . . . 4E **119**
Elder St. E1 . . . 3B **64** (5F **11**)
  (not continuous)
Elderton Rd. SE26 . . . . 4A **122**
Elder Wlk. *N1.* *5D 49*
  (off Popham St.)
Elderwood Pl. SE27 . . . 5E **119**
Eldon Ct. NW6 . . . . 5C **44**
Eldon Gro. NW3 . . . . . . 2F **45**
Eldon Rd. W8. . . . . 4D **73**
Eldon St. EC2. . . 4F **63** (1C **18**)
Eldridge Ct. SE16. . . . . 4C **78**
Eleanor Cl. SE16 . . . . . 3F **79**
Eleanor Gro. SW13 . . . 1A **98**
Eleanor Ho. *W6* *1E 85*
  (off Queen Caroline Rd.)
Eleanor Rd. E8. . . . . . . 3D **51**
  E15 . . . . 3B **54**

Evangelist Rd. NW5 . . . . 1D **47**
Evans Cl. F8 . . . . 3B **50**
Evans Ho. SW8 . . . . 3F **89**
   (off Wandsworth Rd.)
W12 . . . . 1D **71**
   (off White City Est.)
Evans Rd. SE6 . . . . 2A **124**
Evanston Gdns. IG4: Ilf . . 1F **41**
Evelina Mans. SE5 . . . . . 3F **91**
Evelina Rd. SE15 . . . . . . 1E **107**
Evelyn Ct. E8 . . . . 1C **50**
N1 . . . . 1B **10**
   (off Evelyn Wlk., not cont.)
Evelyn Denington Ct.
N1 . . . . 4D **49**
   (off Sutton Est., The)
Evelyn Fox Ct. W10 . . . . 4E **57**
Evelyn Gdns. SW7 . . . . . 1E **87**
Evelyn Ho. SE14 . . . . 4A **94**
   (off Loring Rd.)
W12 . . . . 3B **70**
   (off Cobbold Rd.)
Evelyn Lowe Est. SE16 . . 4C **78**
Evelyn Mans. SW1 . . . . . 5F **21**
   (off Carlisle Pl.)
W14 . . . . 2A **86**
   (off Queen's Club Gdns.)
Evelyn Rd. E16 . . . . 2C **82**
SW19 . . . . 5D **115**
Evelyn St. SE8 . . . . 5A **80**
Evelyn Wlk. N1 . . 1F **63** (1B **10**)
Evelyn Yd. W1 . . 5F **61** (2B **14**)
Evenwood Cl. SW15 . . . . 3A **100**
Everard Ho. E1 . . . . 5C **64**
   (off Boyd St.)
Everatt Cl. SW18 . . . . . . 4B **100**
Everdon Rd. SW13 . . . . . 2C **84**
Everest Pl. E14 . . . . 4E **67**
Everett Ho. SE17 . . . . 1F **91**
   (off East St.)
Everilda St. N1 . . . . 5B **48**
Evering Rd. N16 . . . . 5B **36**
Everington St. W6 . . . . . . 2F **85**
   (not continuous)
Everitt Rd. NW10 . . . . . . 2A **56**
Everleigh St. N4 . . . . 3B **34**
Eve Rd. E11 . . . . 1A **54**
E15 . . . . 1A **68**
Eversholt St.
NW1 . . . . 1E **61** (1A **6**)
Evershot Rd. N4 . . . . 3B **34**
Eversleigh Rd. E6 . . . . . . 5F **55**
SW11 . . . . 1B **102**
Eversley Ho. E2 . . . . 2C **64**
   (off Gossett St.)
Eversley Pk. SW19 . . . . . 5D **113**
Eversley Rd. SE7 . . . . . . 2D **97**
Everthorpe Rd. SE15 . . 1B **106**
Everton Bldgs.
NW1 . . . . 2E **61** (2F **5**)
Evesham Ho. E2 . . . . 1E **65**
   (off Old Ford Rd.)
NW8 . . . . 5E **45**
   (off Abbey Rd.)
Evesham Rd. E15 . . . . . . 4B **54**
Evesham St. W11 . . . . . . 1F **71**
Evesham Wlk. SE5 . . . . . 5F **91**
SW9 . . . . 5C **90**
Evesham Way SW11 . . 1C **102**
Ewald Rd. SW6 . . . . 5B **86**

Ewart Pl. E3 . . . . 1B **66**
Ewart Rd. SE23 . . . . 5F **107**
Ewe Cl. N7 . . . . 3A **48**
Ewelme Rd. SE23 . . . . . . 1E **121**
Ewen Cres. SW2 . . . . . . 5C **104**
Ewen Ho. N1 . . . . 5B **48**
   (off Barnsbury Est.)
Ewer St. SE1 . . . 2E **77** (2F **25**)
Ewhurst Cl. E1 . . . . 4E **65**
Ewhurst Rd. SE4 . . . . . . 4B **108**
Exbury Ho. E9 . . . . 4E **51**
SW1 . . . . 1F **89**
   (off Rampayne St.)
Exbury Rd. SE6 . . . . 2C **122**
ExCeL 1D **83**
Excel Ct. WC2 . . . . 5C **14**
Excelsior Gdns. SE13 . . 1E **95**
Excelsior Ind. Est. SE15 . 2E **93**
Exchange Arc.
EC2 . . . . 4A **64** (5E **11**)
Exchange Bldg. E1 . . . . . 4F **11**
   (off Commercial St.)
Exchange Ct.
WC2 . . . . 1A **76** (5E **15**)
Exchange Ho. EC2 . . . . . 5E **11**
SW1 . . . . 5F **75**
   (off Vauxhall Bri. Rd.)
Exchange Mans. NW11 . 2B **30**
Exchange Pl.
EC2 . . . . 4A **64** (5D **11**)
Exchange Sq.
EC2 . . . . 4A **64** (5D **11**)
Exchange St. EC1 . 2E **63** (2F **9**)
Exeter Ct. NW6 . . . . 1C **58**
   (off Cambridge Rd.)
Exeter Ho. SE15 . . . . 2C **92**
   (off Friary Est.)
W2 . . . . 5E **59**
   (off Hallfield Est.)
Exeter Mans. NW2 . . . . . 3A **44**
Exeter M. NW6 . . . . 3D **45**
SW6 . . . . 3C **86**
Exeter Rd. E16 . . . . 4C **68**
E17 . . . . 1C **38**
NW2 . . . . 2A **44**
Exeter St. WC2 . . 1A **76** (4E **15**)
Exeter Way SE14 . . . . . . 3B **94**
Exford Gdns. SE12 . . . . 1D **125**
Exford Rd. SE12 . . . . . . 2D **125**
Exhibition Cl. W12 . . . . . 1E **71**
Exhibition Rd. SW7 . . . . 3F **73**
Exmoor Ho. E3 . . . . 1A **66**
   (off Gernon Rd.)
Exmoor St. W10 . . . . 3F **57**
Exmouth Ho. E14 . . . . . . 5D **81**
   (off Cahir St.)
EC1 . . . . 3B **8**
   (off Pine St.)
Exmouth Mkt.
EC1 . . . . 3C **62** (3B **8**)
Exmouth M. NW1 . 2E **61** (2A **6**)
Exmouth Pl. E8 . . . . 4D **51**
Exmouth Rd. E17 . . . . . . 1B **38**
Exmouth St. E1 . . . . 5E **65**
Exning Rd. E16 . . . . 3B **68**
Exonbury NW8 . . . . 5D **45**
   (off Abbey Rd.)
Exon St. SE17 . . . . 1A **92**
Export Ho. SE1 . . . . 4E **27**
   (off Tower Bri. Rd.)

Express Newspapers
SE1 . . . . 1D **25**
   (off Blackfriars Rd.)
Express Wharf E14 . . . . . 3C **80**
Exton St. SE1 . . 2C **76** (2B **24**)
Eyhurst Cl. NW2 . . . . . . 4C **28**
Eylewood Rd. SE27 . . . . 5E **119**
Eynella Rd. SE22 . . . . . . 5B **106**
Eynham Rd. W12 . . . . . . 5E **57**
Eynsford Ho. SE1 . . . . . . 4B **26**
   (off Crosby Row)
SE15 . . . . 2E **93**
SE17 . . . . 5A **78**
   (off Beckway St.)
Eyot Gdns. W6 . . . . 1B **84**
Eyot Grn. W4 . . . . 1B **84**
Eyre Ct. NW8 . . . . 1F **59**
Eyre St. Hill EC1 . . 3C **62** (4B **8**)
Eythorne Rd. SW9 . . . . . 4C **90**
Ezra St. E2 . . . . 2B **64**

Faber Gdns. NW4 . . . . . . 1C **28**
Fabian Rd. SW6 . . . . 3B **86**
Facade, The SE23 . . . . . 2E **121**
Factory Rd. E16 . . . . 2F **83**
Fairacres SW15 . . . . 2B **98**
Fairbairn Grn. SW9 . . . . 4D **91**
Fairbank Est. N1 . . 1F **63** (1B **10**)
Fairbridge Rd. N19 . . . . . 4F **33**
Fairburn Ct. SW15 . . . . . 3A **100**
Fairburn Ho. W14 . . . . . . 1B **86**
   (off Ivatt Pl.)
Fairby Ho. SE1 . . . . 5B **78**
   (off Longfield Est.)
Fairby Rd. SE12 . . . . 3D **111**
Faircharm Trad. Est.
SE8 . . . . 3D **95**
Fairchild Cl. SW11 . . . . . 5F **87**
Fairchild Ho. E9 . . . . 4E **51**
N1 . . . . 1D **11**
   (off Fanshaw St.)
Fairchild Pl. EC2 . . . . . . 4E **11**
Fairchild St. EC2 . 3A **64** (3E **11**)
Fairclough St. E1 . . . . . . 5C **64**
Fairdale Gdns. SW15 . . . 2D **99**
Fairfax Gdns. SE3 . . . . . 4E **97**
Fairfax Mans. NW3 . . . . 3E **45**
   (off Finchley Rd.)
Fairfax M. E16 . . . . 2D **83**
SW15 . . . . 2E **99**
Fairfax Pl. NW6 . . . . 4E **45**
W14 . . . . 4A **72**
Fairfax Rd. NW6 . . . . . . 4E **45**
W4 . . . . 4A **70**
Fairfield E1 . . . . 4E **65**
   (off Redman's Rd.)
NW1 . . . . 5E **47**
   (off Arlington Rd.)
Fairfield Av. NW4 . . . . . . 1D **29**
Fairfield Ct. NW10 . . . . . 5C **42**
Fairfield Dr. SW18 . . . . . 3D **101**
Fairfield Gdns. N8 . . . . . 1A **34**
Fairfield Gro. SE7 . . . . . 2F **97**
Fairfield Rd. E3 . . . . 1C **66**
N8 . . . . 1A **34**
Fairfield St. SW18 . . . . . 3D **101**

Fairfoot Rd. E3 . . . . 3C 66
Fairford SE6 . . . . 1C 122
Fairford Ho. SE11 . . . . . 5C 76
Fairhazel Gdns. NW6 . . . 3D 45
Fairhazel Mans. NW6 . . . 4E 45
 (off Fairhazel Gdns.)
Fairholme Rd. W14 . . . 1A 86
Fairholt Cl. N16 . . . . 3A 36
Fairholt Rd. N16 . . . . . . 3F 35
Fairholt St. SW7 . . . . 4A 74
Fairland Rd. E15 . . . . . . 3B 54
Fairlawn SE7 . . . . 3E 97
Fairlawn St. SE7 . . . . 3E 97
 (not continuous)
Fairlawn Mans. SE14 . . . 4F 93
Fairlawn Pk. SE26 . . . . . 5A 122
Fairlie Gdns. SE23 . . . . 5E 107
Fairlight Av. NW10 . . . . 1A 56
 (not continuous)
Fairlight Ct. NW10 . . . . . 1A 56
Fairlight Rd. SW17 . . . 4F 115
Fairlop Ct. E11 . . . . 3F 39
Fairlop Rd. E11 . . . . 2F 39
Fairmead Gdns. IG4: Ilf. . 1F 41
Fairmead Ho. E9 . . . . . . 1A 52
Fairmead Rd. N19 . . . . . 5F 33
Fairmile Av. SW16 . . . . 5F 117
Fairmount Rd. SW2 . . . . 4B 104
Fairstead Wlk. N1 . . . . . 5E 49
 (off Popham St.)
Fair St. SE1 . . . . 3A 78 (3E 27)
Fairthorn Rd. SE7 . . . . . 1C 96
Fairview Cl. SE26 . . . . . 5A 122
Fairview Ho. SW2 . . . . . 5B 104
Fairview Pl. SW2 . . . . . 5B 104
Fairview Rd. N15 . . . . . . 1B 36
Fairwall Ho. SE5 . . . . . . 4A 92
Fairway Cl. NW11 . . . . . 2E 31
Fairway Ct. SE16 . . . . . . 3F 79
 (off Christopher Cl.)
Fairways Bus. Pk. E10 . . 4A 38
Fairway, The W3 . . . . . . 5A 56
Fairweather Rd. N16 . . . 1C 36
Fairwyn Rd. SE26 . . . . . 4A 122
Fakruddin St. E1 . . . . . . 3C 64
Falcon WC1 . . . . 5E 7
 (off Old Gloucester St.)
Falconberg Ct.
 W1 . . . . 5F 61 (2C 14)
Falconberg M.
 W1 . . . . 5F 61 (2C 14)
Falcon Cl. SE1 . . . 2D 77 (1E 25)
Falcon Cl. EC4 . . 5C 62 (3C 16)
 N1 . . . . 1D 63
 (off City Garden Row)
Falconer Wlk. N7 . . . . . . 4B 34
Falconet Ct. E1 . . . . 2D 79
 (off Wapping High St.)
Falcon Gro. SW11 . . . . . 1A 102
Falcon Ho. E14 . . . . 1D 95
 (off St Davids Sq.)
Falcon La. SW11 . . . . . . 1A 102
Falcon Lodge W9 . . . . . . 4C 58
 (off Admiral Wlk.)
Falcon Pk. Ind. Est.
 NW10 . . . . 1A 42
Falcon Point
 SE1 . . . . 1D 77 (5E 17)
Falcon Rd. SW11 . . . . . . 5A 88
Falcon St. E13 . . . . 3B 68

Falcon Ter. SW11 . . . . . 1A 102
Falcon Way E14 . . . . . . 5D 81
Falconwood Ct. SE3 . . . . 5B 96
 (off Montpelier Row)
Falkirk Ct. SE16 . . . . 2F 79
 (off Rotherhithe St.)
Falkirk Ho. W9 . . . . 1D 59
 (off Maida Va.)
Falkirk St. N1 . . 1A 64 (1E 11)
Falkland Ho. SE6 . . . . . 4E 123
 W8 . . . . 4D 73
 W14 . . . . 1B 86
 (off Edith Vs.)
Falkland Pl. NW5 . . . . . . 2E 47
Falkland Rd. NW5 . . . . . 2E 47
Fallodon Ho. W11 . . . . . 4B 58
 (off Tavistock Cres.)
Fallow Ct. SE16 . . . . 1C 92
 (off Argyle Way)
Fallsbrook Rd. SW16 . . 5E 117
Falmouth Cl. SE12 . . . . 3B 110
Falmouth Gdns.
 IG4: Ilf 1F 41
Falmouth Ho. SE11 . . . . 1C 90
 (off Seaton Cl.)
 W2 . . . . 1A 74
 (off Clarendon Pl.)
Falmouth Rd.
 SE1 . . . . 4E 77 (5A 26)
Falmouth St. E15 . . . . . 2F 53
Falmouth Way E17 . . . . 1B 38
Falstaff Ct. SE11 . . . . . . 5D 77
 (off Opal St.)
Falstaff Ho. N1 . . . . 1A 64
 (off Arden East.)
Fambridge Cl. SE26 . . . . 4B 122
Fane Ho. E2 . . . . 5E 51
Fane St. W14 . . . . 2B 86
Fan Mus., The 3E 95
 (not continuous)
Fann St. EC2 . . . 3E 63 (4F 9)
Fanshaw St. N1 . . 1A 64 (1D 11)
Fanthorpe St. SW15 . . . 1E 99
Faraday Cl. N7 . . . . 3B 48
Faraday Ho. E14 . . . . . . 1B 80
 (off Brightlingsea Pl.)
 SE1 . . . . 4B 26
 (off Cole St.)
Faraday Lodge SE10 . . . 4B 82
Faraday Mans. W14 . . . . 2A 86
 (off Queen's Club Gdns.)
Faraday Mus. . . 1E 75 (5F 13)
Faraday Rd. E15 . . . . 3B 54
 SW19 . . . . 5C 114
 W10 . . . . 4A 58
Faraday Way SE18 . . . . . 4F 83
Fareham St.
 W1 . . . . 5F 61 (2B 14)
Faringford Rd. E15 . . . . 4A 54
Farjeon Ho. NW6 . . . . . . 4F 45
 (off Hilgrove Rd.)
Farjeon Rd. SE3 . . . . . . 4F 97
Farleigh Pl. N16 . . . . 1B 50
Farleigh Rd. N16 . . . . . . 1B 50
Farley Ct. NW1 . . . . 4B 4
 (off Allsop Pl.)
Farley Ho. SE26 . . . . . . 3D 121
Farley Rd. SE6 . . . . 5D 109
Farlington Pl. SW15 . . . 5D 99
Farlow Rd. SW15 . . . . . 1F 99

Farlton Rd. SW18 . . . . 1D 115
Farm Av. NW2 . . . . 5A 30
 SW16 . . . . 4A 118
Farm Cl. SW6 . . . . 3C 86
Farmcote Rd. SE12 . . . 1C 124
Farmdale Rd. SE10 . . . . 1C 96
Farmer Rd. E10 . . . . 3D 39
Farmer's Rd. SE5 . . . . . 3D 91
Farmer St. W8 . . . . 2C 72
Farmfield Rd.
 BR1: Brom 5A 124
Farmilo Rd. E17 . . . . 2B 38
Farm La. SW6 . . . . 2C 86
Farm La. Trad. Est.
 SW6 . . . . 2C 86
Farmleigh Ho. SW9 . . . 3D 105
Farm Pl. W8 . . . . 2C 72
Farm Rd. E12 . . . . 4F 41
 NW10 . . . . 5A 42
Farmstead Rd. SE6 . . . . 4D 123
Farm St. W1 . . . 1D 75 (5D 13)
Farm Wlk. NW11 . . . . . . 1B 30
Farnaby Ho. W10 . . . . . . 2B 58
 (off Bruckner St.)
Farnaby Rd. SE9 . . . . . . 2E 111
Farnan Rd. SW16 . . . . . 5A 118
Farncombe St. SE16 . . . 3C 78
Farndale Ct. SE18 . . . . . 3F 97
Farndale Ho. NW6 . . . . . 5D 45
 (off Kilburn Va.)
Farnell M. SW5 . . . . 1D 87
Farnham Ho. NW1 . . . . . 3A 60
 (off Harewood Av.)
Farnham Pl.
 SE1 . . . . 2D 77 (2E 25)
Farnham Royal SE11 . . . 1B 90
Farningham Ho. N4 . . . . 2F 35
Farnley Ho. SW8 . . . . . . 5F 89
Farnworth Ho. E14 . . . . 5F 81
 (off Manchester Rd.)
Faroe Rd. W14 . . . . 4F 71
Farquhar Rd. SE19 . . . . 5B 120
 SW19 . . . . 3C 114
Farrance St. E14 . . . . . . 5C 66
Farrell Ho. E1 . . . . 5E 65
 (off Ronald St.)
Farren Rd. SE23 . . . . . . 2A 122
Farrer Ho. SE8 . . . . 3C 94
Farriers Ho. EC1 . . . . . . 4A 10
 (off Errol St.)
Farriers M. SE15 . . . . . 1E 107
Farrier St. NW1 . . . . 4D 47
Farrier Wlk. SW10 . . . . . 2E 87
Farringdon La.
 EC1 . . . . 3C 62 (4C 8)
Farringdon Rd.
 EC1 . . . . 3C 62 (3B 8)
Farringdon St.
 EC4 . . . . 4D 63 (1D 17)
Farrins Rents SE16 . . . . 2A 80
Farrow La. SE14 . . . . . . 3E 93
Farrow Pl. SE16 . . . . 4A 80
Farthingale Wlk. E15 . . 4F 53
Farthing All. SE1 . . . . . . 3C 78
Farthing Flds. E1 . . . . . . 2D 79
Fashion & Textile Mus.
 . . . . 3A 78 (4E 27)
Fashion St. E1 . . 4B 64 (1F 19)
Fassett Rd. E8 . . . . 3C 50
Fassett Sq. E8 . . . . 3C 50

Faulkners All.
EC1 . . . . 4D **63** (5D **9**)
Faulkner St. SE14 . . . . . . 4E **93**
Faunce Ho. SE17 . . . . . . 2D **91**
  (off Doddington Gro.)
Faunce St. SE17 . . . . 1D **91**
Favart Rd. SW6 . . . . 4C **86**
Faversham Ho. NW1 . . . 5E **47**
  (off Bayham Pl.)
SE17 . . . . 1A **92**
  (off Kinglake St.)
Faversham Rd. SE6 . . 5B **108**
Fawcett Cl. SW11 . . . . . . 5F **87**
SW16 . . . . 5C **118**
Fawcett Est. E5 . . . . 3C **36**
Fawcett Rd. NW10 . . . . 4B **42**
Fawcett St. SW10 . . . . . . 2E **87**
Fawe Pk. M. SW15 . . . . 2B **100**
Fawe Pk. Rd. SW15 . . 2B **100**
Fawe St. E14 . . . . 4D **67**
Fawkham Ho. SE1 . . . . 5B **78**
  (off Longfield Est.)
Fawley Lodge E14 . . . . . 5E **81**
  (off Millennium Dr.)
Fawley Rd. NW6 . . . . 2D **45**
Fawnbrake Av. SE24 . . 3D **105**
Fawn Rd. E13 . . . . 1E **69**
Fawood Av. NW10 . . . . . 4A **42**
Faygate Rd. SW2 . . . . 2B **118**
Fayland Av. SW16 . . . . 5E **117**
Fazeley Ct. W9 . . . . 4C **58**
  (off Elmfield Way)
Fearnley Ho. SE5 . . . . . . 5A **92**
Fearon St. SE10 . . . . . . 1C **96**
Feathers Pl. SE10 . . . . . . 2F **95**
Featherstone Av. SE23 . 2D **121**
Featherstone St.
EC1 . . . . 3F **63** (3B **10**)
Featley Rd. SW9 . . . . . 1D **105**
Felbridge Cl. SW16 . . . 4C **118**
Felbridge Ho. SE22 . . 1A **106**
Felday Rd. SE13 . . . . . 4D **109**
Felden St. SW6 . . . . 4B **86**
Feldman Cl. N16 . . . . . . 3C **36**
Felgate M. W6 . . . . 5D **71**
Felix Av. N8 . . . . 1A **34**
Felixstowe Rd. NW10 . . 2D **57**
Felix St. E2 . . . . 1D **65**
Fellbrigg Rd. SE22 . . . 3B **106**
Fellbrigg St. E1 . . . . 3D **65**
Fellmongers Path SE1 . . 4F **27**
Fellows Ct. E2 . . 1B **64** (1F **11**)
  (not continuous)
Fellows Rd. NW3 . . . . . . 4F **45**
Felltram Way SE7 . . . . . 1C **96**
Felmersham Cl. SW4 . 2A **104**
Felsberg Rd. SW2 . . . . 4A **104**
Felsham M. SW15 . . . . 1F **99**
  (off Felsham Rd.)
Felsham Rd. SW15 . . . . 1E **99**
Felstead Gdns. E14 . . . 1E **95**
Felstead Rd. E9 . . . . . . 3B **52**
F11 . . . . 2C **40**
Felstead St. E9 . . . . 3B **52**
Felstead Wharf E14 . . . 1E **95**
Felsted Rd. E16 . . . . 5E **69**
Felton Ho. N1 . . . . 5F **49**
  (off Branch Pl.)
SE3 . . . . 2D **111**
Felton St. N1 . . . . 5F **49**

Fenchurch Av.
EC3 . . . . 5∧ **64** (3D **19**)
Fenchurch Bldgs.
EC3 . . . . 5A **64** (3E **19**)
Fenchurch Pl.
EC3 . . . . 5A **64** (4E **19**)
Fenchurch St.
EC3 . . . . 1A **78** (4D **19**)
Fen Ct. EC3 . . . . 5A **64** (4D **19**)
Fendall St. SE1 . 4A **78** (5E **27**)
  (not continuous)
Fendt Cl. E16 . . . . 5B **68**
Fenelon Pl. W14 . . . . . . 5B **72**
Fenham Rd. SE15 . . . . . 3C **92**
Fennel Cl. E16 . . . . 3A **68**
Fenner Cl. SE16 . . . . . . 5D **79**
Fenner Ho. E1 . . . . 2D **79**
  (off Watts St.)
Fenner Sq. SW11 . . . . . 1F **101**
Fenning St. SE1 . 3A **78** (3D **27**)
Fenn St. E9 . . . . 2F **51**
Fenstanton N4 . . . . 3B **34**
  (off Marquis Rd.)
Fen St. E16 . . . . 1B **82**
Fentiman Rd. SW8 . . . . . 2A **90**
Fenton Cl. E8 . . . . 3B **50**
SW9 . . . . 5B **90**
Fenton Ho. SE14 . . . . . . 3A **94**
Fentons Av. E13 . . . . 2D **69**
Fenton St. E1 . . . . 5D **65**
Fenwick Gro. SE15 . . . 1C **106**
Fenwick Pl. SW9 . . . . . 1A **104**
Fenwick Rd. SE15 . . . . 1C **106**
Ferdinand Ho. NW1 . . . 4C **46**
  (off Ferdinand Pl.)
Ferdinand Pl. NW1 . . . . 4C **46**
Ferdinand St. NW1 . . . . 4C **46**
Ferguson Cen., The
E17 . . . . 1A **38**
Ferguson Cl. E14 . . . . . . 5C **80**
Ferguson Dr. W3 . . . . . . 5A **56**
Ferguson Ho. SE10 . . . . 4E **95**
Fergus Rd. N5 . . . . 2D **49**
Fermain Ct. E. N1 . . . . . 5A **50**
  (off De Beauvoir Est.)
Fermain Ct. Nth. N1 . . . 5A **50**
  (off De Beauvoir Est.)
Fermain Ct. W. N1 . . . . 5A **50**
  (off De Beauvoir Est.)
Ferme Pk. Rd. N8 . . . . . 1A **34**
Fermor Rd. SE23 . . . . . 1A **122**
Fermoy Rd. W9 . . . . 3B **58**
Fernbank M. SW12 . . . 4D **103**
Fernbrook Cres. SE13 . 4A **110**
  (off Leahurst Rd.)
Fernbrook Rd. SE13 . . 3A **110**
Ferncliff Rd. E8 . . . . 2C **50**
Fern Cl. N1 . . . . 1A **64**
Fern Ct. SE14 . . . . 5F **93**
Ferncroft Av. NW3 . . . . . 5C **30**
Ferndale Rd. E7 . . . . . . 4D **55**
E11 . . . . 4A **40**
N15 . . . . 1B **36**
SW4 . . . . 2A **104**
SW9 . . . . 2A **104**
Ferndene Rd. SE24 . . . 2E **105**
Ferndown Lodge E14 . . 4E **81**
  (off Manchester Rd.)

Ferndown Rd. SE9 . . . 5F **111**
Fernhall Dr. IG4: Ilf. 1F **41**
Fernhead Rd. W9 . . . . . 1B **58**
Fernholme Rd. SE15 . . 3F **107**
Fernhurst Rd. SW6 . . . . 4A **86**
Fernlea Rd. SW12 . . . 1D **117**
Fernsbury St.
WC1 . . . . 2C **62** (2B **8**)
Fernshaw Cl. SW10 . . . . 2E **87**
Fernshaw Rd. SW10 . . . 2E **87**
Fernside NW11 . . . . 4C **30**
Fernside Rd. SW12 . . . 1B **116**
Ferns Rd. E15 . . . . 3B **54**
Fern St. E3 . . . . 3C **66**
Fernthorpe Rd. SW16 . . 5E **117**
Ferntower Rd. N5 . . . . . 2F **49**
Fern Wlk. SE1 . . . . 1C **92**
Fernwood Av. SW16 . . . 4F **117**
Ferranti Cl. SE18 . . . . . 4F **83**
Ferrers Rd. SW16 . . . . 5F **117**
Ferrey M. SW9 . . . . 5C **90**
Ferriby Cl. N1 . . . . 4C **48**
Ferrier Ind. Est.
SW18 . . . . 2D **101**
  (off Ferrier St.)
Ferrier Point E16 . . . . . 4C **68**
  (off Forty Acre La.)
Ferrier St. SW18 . . . . . 2D **101**
Ferrings SE21 . . . . 3A **120**
Ferris Rd. SE22 . . . . . . 2C **106**
Ferron Rd. E5 . . . . 5D **37**
Ferrybridge Ho. SE11 . . 4C **76**
  (off Lambeth Wlk.)
Ferry Ho. E5 . . . . 3D **37**
  (off Harrington Hill)
Ferry La. SW13 . . . . 2B **84**
Ferry Rd. SW13 . . . . 3C **84**
Ferry St. E14 . . . . 1E **95**
Festing Rd. SW15 . . . . . 1F **99**
Festival Ct. E8 . . . . 4B **50**
  (off Holly St.)
Fetter La. EC4 . . 5C **62** (3C **16**)
  (not continuous)
Fettes Ho. NW8 . . . . . . 1F **59**
  (off Wellington Rd.)
Ffinch St. SE8 . . . . 3C **94**
Field Cl. SW19 . . . . 3C **114**
WC1 . . . . 4B **62** (1A **16**)
Fieldgate Mans. E1 . . . 4C **64**
  (off Fieldgate St., not cont.)
Fieldgate St. E1 . . . . . . 4C **64**
Field Ho. NW6 . . . . 2F **57**
  (off Harvist Rd.)
Fieldhouse Rd. SW12 . . 1E **117**
Fielding Ho. NW6 . . . . . 2C **58**
W4 . . . . 2A **84**
  (off Devonshire Rd.)
Fielding M. SW13 . . . . . 2D **85**
  (off Jenner Pl.)
Fielding Rd. W4 . . . . . . 4A **70**
W14 . . . . 4F **71**
Fieldings, The SE23 . . 1E **121**
Fielding St. SE17 . . . . . 2E **91**
Field Point E7 . . . . 1C **54**
Field Rd. E7 . . . . 1B **54**
W6 . . . . 1A **86**
Fields Est. E8 . . . . 4C **50**
Fieldside Rd.
BR1: Brom 5F **123**
Field St. WC1 . . . 2B **62** (1F **7**)

Fleetfield WC1 . . . . 1E 7
(off Birkenhead St.)
Fleet Ho. E14 . . . . 1A 80
(off Victory Pl.)
Fleet Pl. EC4 . . . . 2D 17
(not continuous)
Fleet Rd. NW3 . . . . 2A 46
Fleet Sq. WC1 . . 2B 62 (2A 8)
Fleet St. EC4 . . 5C 62 (3B 16)
Fleet St. Hill E1 . . . . 3C 64
Fleetway WC1 . . . . 1E 7
(off Birkenhead St.)
Fleetway Bus. Cen.
NW2 . . . . 3B 28
Fleetwood Cl. E16 . . . . . 4F 69
Fleetwood Rd. NW10 . . 2C 42
Fleetwood St. N16 . . . . . 4A 36
Fleming Cl. W9 . . . . 3C 58
Fleming Cl. W2 . . . . 4F 59
(off St Marys Sq.)
Fleming Ho. N4 . . . . 3E 35
SE16 . . . . 3C 78
(off George Row)
Fleming Lodge W2 . . . . . 4C 58
(off Admiral Wlk.)
Fleming Rd. SE17 . . . . . 2D 91
Flempton Rd. E10 . . . . . 3A 38
Fletcher Bldgs. WC2 . . . 3E 15
(off Martlett Ct.)
Fletcher Ho. SE15 . . . . . 3E 93
(off Clifton Way)
Fletcher La. E10 . . . . . . 2E 39
Fletcher Path SE8 . . . . . 3C 94
Fletcher St. E1 . . . . 1C 78
Fletching Rd. E5 . . . . 5E 37
SE7 . . . . 2E 97
Fleur-de-Lis St.
E1 . . . . 3B 64 (4E 11)
Fleur Gates SW19 . . . . . 5F 99
Flimwell Cl.
BR1: Brom 5A 124
Flinders Ho. E1 . . . . 2D 79
(off Green Bank)
Flintmill Cres. SE3 . . . . . 5F 97
(not continuous)
Flinton St. SE17 . . . . 1A 92
Flint St. SE17 . . . . 5F 77
Flitcroft St. WC2 . . 5F 61 (3C 14)
Flitton Ho. N1 . . . . 4D 49
(off Sutton Est., The)
Flock Mill Pl. SW18 . . . 1D 115
Flockton St. SE16 . . . . . 3C 78
Flodden Rd. SE5 . . . . . . 4E 91
Flood St. SW3 . . . . 1A 88
Flood Wlk. SW3 . . . . 2A 88
Flora Cl. E14 . . . . 5D 67
Flora Gdns. W6 . . . . 5D 71
(off Albion Gdns.)
Floral Pl. N1 . . . . 2F 49
Floral St. WC2 . . 1A 76 (4D 15)
Florence Ct. E5 . . . . 5C 36
N1 . . . . 4D 49
(off Florence St.)
SW19 . . . . 5A 114
W9 . . . . 2E 59
(off Maida Va.)
Florence Ho. SE16 . . . . 1D 93
(off Rotherhithe New Rd.)
W11 . . . . 1F 71
(off St Ann's Rd.)

Florence Mans. NW4 . . 1D 29
(off Vivian Av.)
Florence Nightingale Mus.
. . . . 3B 76 (4F 23)
Florence Rd. E6 . . . . 5F 55
E13 . . . . 1C 68
N4 . . . . 2B 34
(not continuous)
SE14 . . . . 4B 94
SW19 . . . . 5D 115
Florence St. E16 . . . . . . 3B 68
N1 . . . . 4D 49
Florence Ter. SE14 . . . . 4B 94
SW15 . . . . 3A 112
Florence Way SW12 . . 1B 116
Flores Ho. E1 . . . . 4F 65
(off Shandy St.)
Florey Lodge W9 . . . . . . 4C 58
(off Admiral Wlk.)
Florfield Pas. E8 . . . . . . 3D 51
(off Florfield Rd.)
Florfield Rd. E8 . . . . 3D 51
Florian SE5 . . . . 4A 92
Florian Rd. SW15 . . . . . 2A 100
Florida St. E2 . . . . 2C 64
Florin Ct. SE1 . . . . 4F 27
(off Tanner St.)
Floris Pl. SW4 . . . . 1E 103
Floss St. SW15 . . . . 5E 98
Flower & Dean Wlk.
. . . . 4B 64 (1F 19)
Flowerpot Cl. N15 . . . . . 1B 36
Flowers Cl. NW2 . . . . . . 5C 28
Flowersmead SW17 . . . 2C 116
Flowers M. N19 . . . . 4E 33
Flower Wlk., The SW7 . . 3E 73
Floyd Rd. SE7 . . . . 1E 97
Fludyer St. SE13 . . . . . . 2A 110
Flynn Ct. E14 . . . . 1C 80
(off Garford St.)
Foley Ho. E1 . . . . 5E 65
(off Tarling St.)
Foley St. W1 . . 4E 61 (1F 13)
Folgate St. E1 . . 4A 64 (5E 11)
(not continuous)
Foliot Ho. N1 . . . . 1B 62
(off Priory Grn. Est.)
Foliot St. W3 . . . . 5B 56
Follett Ho. SW10 . . . . . . 3F 87
(off Worlds End Est.)
Follett St. E14 . . . . 5E 67
Follingham St. N1 . . . . . 1E 11
(off Drysdale Pl.)
Folly M. W11 . . . . 5B 58
Folly Wall E14 . . . . 3E 81
Fonda Ct. E14 . . . . 1C 80
(off Premiere Pl.)
Fontarabia Rd. SW11 . . 2C 102
Fontenelle Gdns. SE5 . . 4A 92
Fontenoy Ho. SE11 . . . . 5D 77
(off Kennington La.)
Fontenoy Rd. SW12 . . 2D 117
Fonthill M. N4 . . . . 4B 34
Fonthill Rd. N4 . . . . 3B 34
Fontley Way SW15 . . . . 5C 98
Footpath, The SW15 . . . 4C 98
Forber Ho. E2 . . . . 2E 65
(off Cornwall Av.)
Forbes Cl. NW2 . . . . 5C 28
Forbes St. E1 . . . . 5C 64

Forburg Rd. N16 . . . . . . 3C 36
Ford Cl. E3 . . . . 1A 66
Fordel Rd. SE6 . . . . 1E 123
Fordham St. E1 . . . . 5C 64
Fordingley Rd. W9 . . . . . 2B 58
Fordington Ho. SE26 . . 3C 120
Fordmill Rd. SE6 . . . . . 2C 122
Ford Rd. E3 . . . . 1B 66
Fords Pk. Rd. E16 . . . . . 4C 68
Ford Sq. E1 . . . . 4D 65
Ford St. E16 . . . . 5B 68
E3 . . . . 5A 52
Fordwych Rd. NW2 . . . . 1A 44
Fordyce Rd. SE13 . . . . . 4E 109
Foreign St. SE5 . . . . 5D 91
Foreland Ho. W11 . . . . . 1A 72
(off Walmer Rd.)
Foreshore SE8 . . . . 5B 80
Forest Bus. Pk. E10 . . . 2F 37
Forest Cl. E11 . . . . 1C 40
Forest Cft. SE23 . . . . . . 2D 121
Forest Dr. E12 . . . . 5F 41
E12 . . . . 5F 41
Forest Dr. E. E11 . . . . . 2F 39
Forest Dr. W. E11 . . . . . 2E 39
Forester Rd. SE15 . . . . 1D 107
FOREST GATE 2C 54
Forest Glade E11 . . . . . 1A 40
Forest Gro. E8 . . . . 3B 50
FOREST HILL 2E 121
Forest Hill Bus. Cen.
SE23 . . . . 2E 121
(off Clyde Va.)
Forest Hill Ind. Est.
SE23 . . . . 2E 121
Forest Hill Rd. SE22 . . 3D 107
Forestholme Cl. SE23 . . 2E 121
Forest La. E7 . . . . 2A 54
E15 . . . . 2A 54
Forest Lodge SE26 . . . . 3E 121
(off Dartmouth Rd.)
Forest Point E7 . . . . 2D 55
(off Windsor Rd.)
Fore St. EC2 . . 4E 63 (1A 18)
Fore St. Av. EC2 . . 4F 63 (1B 18)
Forest Rd. E7 . . . . 1C 54
E8 . . . . 3B 50
E11 . . . . 2F 39
Forest Side E7 . . . . 1D 55
Forest St. E7 . . . . 2C 54
Forest Vw. E11 . . . . 2B 40
Forest Vw. Av. E10 . . . . 1F 39
Forest Vw. Rd. E12 . . . 1F 55
Forest Way N19 . . . . . . 4E 33
Forfar Rd. SW11 . . . . . . 4C 88
Forge Pl. NW1 . . . . 3C 46
Forges Rd. E12 . . . . 4F 41
Forman Pl. N16 . . . . 1B 50
Formby Ct. N7 . . . . 2C 48
(off Morgan Rd.)
Formosa Ho. E1 . . . . 3A 66
(off Ernest St.)
Formosa St. W9 . . . . . . 3D 59
Formunt Cl. E16 . . . . . . 4B 68
Forres Gdns. NW11 . . . 1C 30
Forrester Path SE26 . . . 4E 121
Forset Cl. W2 . . . . 5A 60
(off Harrowby St.)
Forset St. W1 . . . . 5A 60
Forster Ho. BR1: Brom . . 4F 123

Forster Rd. E17 . . . . 1A 38
   SW12 . . . . 5A 104
Forston St. N1 . . . . 1E 63
Forsyth Gdns. SE17 . . . . 2D 91
Forsyth Ho. *E9* *4E 51*
   (off Frampton Pk. Rd.)
   SW1 . . . . *1E 89*
   (off Tachbrook St.)
Fortescue Av. E8 . . . . . . 4D 51
Fortess Gro. NW5 . . . . . . 2E 47
Fortess Rd. NW5 . . . . . . 2D 47
Fortess Wlk. NW5 . . . . . . 2D 47
Fortess Yd. NW5 . . . . . . 1D 47
Forthbridge Rd. SW11. . 2C 102
Fortis Cl. E16 . . . . 5E 69
Fortnam Rd. N19 . . . . . . 4F 33
Fort Rd. SE1 . . . . 5B 78
Fortrose Gdns. SW2. . . 1A 118
Fort St. E1 . . . . 4A 64 (1E 19)
   E16 . . . . 2D 83
Fortuna Cl. N7 . . . . 3B 48
Fortunegate Rd. NW10. . 5A 42
FORTUNE GREEN **1C 44**
Fortune Grn. Rd. NW6 . . 1C 44
Fortune Ho. *EC1* *4A 10*
   (off Fortune St.)
   SE11 . . . . *5C 76*
   (off Marylee Way)
Fortune St. EC1 . . 3E 63 (4A 10)
Fortune Theatre *3E 15*
   (off Russell St.)
Fortune Way NW10 . . . . 2C 56
Forty Acre La. E16 . . . . 4C 68
Forum Magnum Sq.
   SE1 . . . . *3A 24*
   (off York Rd.)
Forward Bus. Cen., The
   E16 . . . . 3F 67
Fosbrooke Ho. *SW8* . . . *3A 90*
   (off Davidson Gdns.)
Fosbury Ho. W2. . . . . . . 1D 73
Foscote M. W9. . . . . 3C 58
Foscote Rd. NW4 . . . . . . 1D 29
Foskett Rd. SW6 . . . . . . 5B 86
Fossdene Rd. SE7 . . . . . 1D 97
Fossil Rd. SE13 . . . . . . 1C 108
Foss Rd. SW17 . . . . . . 4F 115
Foster Ct. *E16* *1B 82*
   (off Tarling Rd.)
   NW1 . . . . *4E 47*
   (off Royal College St.)
Foster Ho. SE14 . . . . . . 4B 94
Foster La. EC2 . . 5E **63** (2F 17)
Foster Rd. E13 . . . . 3C 68
   W3 . . . . 1A 70
   W4 . . . . 1A 84
Foster's Way SW18 . . . . 1D 115
Fothergill Cl. E13 . . . . . . 1C 68
Foubert's Pl. W1. . 5E **61** (3F 13)
Foulden Rd. N16 . . . . . . 1B 50
Foulden Ter. N16 . . . . . . 1B 50
Foulis St. SW7 . . . . 1F 87
Foulser Rd. SW17 . . . . 3B 116
Founders Ct. EC2 . . . . . 2B 18
Founders Ho. *SW1* *1F 89*
   (off Aylesford St.)
Foundling Ct. *WC1* *3D 7*
   (off Brunswick Cen.)
Foundling Mus., The
   . . . . **3A 62** (3E **7**)

Foundry Cl. SE16 . . . . . . 2A 80
Foundry Ho. *E14* *4D 67*
   (off Morris Rd.)
Foundry M. NW1 . . . . 3A 6
Foundry Pl. SW18 . . . . 5D 101
Fountain Ct.
   EC4 . . . . . . 1C **76** (4B **16**)
   SE23 . . . . 2F 121
   SW1 . . . . *5D 75*
   (off Buckingham Pal. Rd.)
Fountain Dr. SE19 . . . . 4B 120
Fountain Grn. Sq. SE16. . 3C 78
Fountain Ho. NW6 . . . . . 4A 44
   W1 . . . . *1B 20*
   (off Park St.)
Fountain M. *N5* *1E 49*
   (off Highbury Grange)
   NW3 . . . . 3B 46
Fountain Pl. SW9 . . . . . . 4C 90
Fountain Rd. SW17 . . . . 5F 115
Fountain Sq. SW1 . . . . . 5D 75
Fountayne Rd. N16 . . . . 4C 36
Fount St. SW8 . . . . 3F 89
Fouracres NW1 . . . . *2F 5*
   (off Stanhope St.)
Fournier St. E1. . 4B **64** (5F **11**)
Four Seasons Cl. E3 . . . 1C 66
Fourth Av. W10 . . . . 3A 58
Fovant Ct. SW8 . . . . 5E 89
Fowey Cl. E1 . . . . 2D 79
Fowey Ho. *SE11*. *1C 90*
   (off Kennings Way)
Fowler Cl. SW11 . . . . . . 1F 101
Fowler Ho. *N15* *1F 35*
   (off South Gro.)
Fowler Rd. E7 . . . . 1C 54
   N1. . . . . 5D 49
Fowlers M. *N19* *4E 33*
   (off Holloway Rd.)
Fownes St. SW11. . . . . . 1A 102
Fox & Knot St. EC1. . . . . 5E 9
Foxberry Rd. SE4. . . . . 1A 108
Foxborough Gdns. SE4. . 3C 108
Foxbourne Rd. SW17. . 2C 116
Fox Cl. E1 . . . . 3E 65
   E16 . . . . 4C 68
Foxcombe Cl. E6 . . . . . . 1F 69
Foxcombe Rd. SW15 . . 1C 112
Foxcote SE5 . . . . 1A 92
Foxcroft *WC1* *1A 8*
   (off Penton Ri.)
Foxes Dale SE3 . . . . . . 1C 110
Foxfield *NW1* *5D 47*
   (off Arlington Rd.)
Foxglove St. W12. . . . . . 1B 70
Foxham Rd. N19. . . . . . . 5F 33
Foxhole Rd. SE9. . . . . . . 3F 111
Foxley Cl. E8 . . . . 2C 50
Foxley Rd. SW9. . . . . . . 3C 90
Foxley Sq. SW9. . . . . . . 4D 91
Foxmore St. SW11. . . . . 4B 88
Fox Rd. E16 . . . . 4B 68
Foxwell M. SE4 . . . . 1A 108
Foxwell St. SE4 . . . . . . 1A 108
Foxwood Rd. SE3. . . . . . 2B 110
Foyle Rd. SE3 . . . . 2B 96
Framfield Rd. N5. . . . . . . 2D 49
Framlingham Cl. E5 . . . . 4E 37
Frampton *NW1* *4F 47*
   (off Wrotham Rd.)

Frampton Ho. *NW8*. . . . *3F 59*
   (off Frampton St.)
Frampton Pk. Est. E9 . . . 4E 51
Frampton Pk. Rd. E9 . . . 3E 51
Frampton St. NW8 . . . . . 3F 59
Francemary Rd. SE4 . . 3C 108
Frances Ct. E17 . . . . 1C 38
Franche Ct. Rd. SW17. . 3E 115
Francis Barber Cl.
   SW16 . . . . 5B 118
Franciscan Rd. SW17. . 5B 116
Francis Chichester Way
   SW11 . . . . 4C 88
Francis Cl. E14. . . . . 5F 81
Francis Ct. EC1 . . . . 5D 9
   SE14 . . . . *2F 93*
   (off Myers La.)
Francis Ho. E17 . . . . 1B 38
   N1. . . . . *5A 50*
   (off Colville Est.)
Francis M. SE12. . . . . . 5C 110
Francis Rd. E10 . . . . 3E 39
Francis St. E15. . . . . 2A 54
   SW1 . . . . 5E **75** (5A **22**)
Francis Ter. N19 . . . . . . 5E 33
Francis Wlk. N1. . . . . . . 5B 48
Franconia Rd. SW4 . . . 3F 103
Frank Beswick Ho. *SW6.* *2B 86*
   (off Clem Attlee Ct.)
Frank Burton Cl. SE7 . . 1D 97
Frank Dixon Cl. SE21. . 5A 106
Frank Dixon Way SE21. . 1A 120
Frankfurt Rd. SE24. . . 3E 105
Frankham Ho. *SE8*. . . . *3C 94*
   (off Frankham St.)
Frankham St. SE8 . . . . . 3C 94
Frank Ho. *SW8*. *3A 90*
   (off Wyvil Rd.)
Frankland Cl. SE16 . . . . 4D 79
Frankland Rd. SW7 . . . . 4F 73
Franklin Bldg. E14 . . . . 3C 80
Franklin Cl. SE13. . . . . . 4D 95
   SE27. . . . . 3D 119
Franklin Ho. *E1* *2D 79*
   (off Watts St.)
Franklin Pl. SE10. . . . . . 4D 95
Franklin Sq. W14 . . . . . . 1B 86
Franklin's Row SW3. . . . 1B 88
Franklin St. E3. . . . . 2D 67
   N15. . . . . 1A 36
Franklyn Rd. NW10 . . . . 3B 42
Frank Soskice Ho. *SW6.* *2B 86*
   (off Clem Attlee Ct.)
Frank St. E13 . . . . 3C 68
Frank Whymark Ho.
   SE16 . . . . *3E 79*
   (off Rupack St.)
Fransfield Gro. SE26 . . 3D 121
Frans Hals Ct. E14. . . . . 4F 81
Franthorne Way SE6 . . 2D 123
Fraser Cl. E6. . . . . 5F 69
Fraser Ct. *E14* *1E 95*
   (off Ferry St.)
Fraser Rd. E17. . . . . 1D 39
Fraser St. W4. . . . . 1A 84
Frazier St. SE1 . . 3C **76** (4B 24)
Frean St. SE16. . . . . 4C 78
Frearson Ho. *WC1* *1A 8*
   (off Penton Ri.)
Freda Corbett Cl. SE15. . 3C 92

Frederica St. N7. . . . . . . 4B **48**
Frederick Charrington Ho.
E1 . . . . *3E* **65**
(off Wickford St.)
Frederick Cl. W2 . . . . . . 1B **74**
Frederick Ct. *SW3* *5B* **74**
(off Duke of York)
Frederick Cres. SW9 . . 3D **91**
Frederick Rd. SE17 . . . . 2D **91**
Frederick's Pl.
EC2. . . . . 5F **63** (3B **18**)
Frederick Sq. *SE16* *1A* **80**
(off Sovereign Cres.)
Frederick's Row
EC1 . . . . 2D **63** (1D **9**)
Frederick St.
WC1. . . . . 2B **62** (2F **7**)
Frederick Ter. E8 . . . . . 4B **50**
Frederic M. SW1 . . . . . 4A **20**
Frederic St. E17 . . . . . . 1A **38**
Fred Styles Ho. SE7 . . . 2E **97**
Fred White Wlk. N7 . . . 3A **48**
Freedom St. SW11 . . . . 5B **88**
Freegrove Rd. N7 . . . . . 2A **48**
(not continuous)
Freeling Ho. *NW8* *5F* **45**
(off Dorman Way)
Freeling St. N1 . . . . 4B **48**
(Carnoustie Dr.)
N1 . . . . 4A **48**
(Pembroke St.)
Freemantle St. SE17 . . . 1A **92**
Freemasons Rd. E16 . . . 4D **69**
Free Trade Wharf E1. . . 1F **79**
Freke Rd. SW11 . . . . . . 1C **102**
Fremantle Ho. *E1* *3D* **65**
(off Somerford St.)
Fremont St. E9 . . . . 5D **51**
(not continuous)
French Ordinary Ct. EC3. . 4E **19**
French Pl. E1 . . . 2A **64** (2E **11**)
Frendsbury Rd. SE4 . . 2A **108**
Frensham Dr. SW15. . . 3B **112**
(not continuous)
Frensham St. SE15 . . . . 2C **92**
Frere St. SW11 . . . . 5A **88**
Freshfield Av. E8 . . . . . 4B **50**
Freshfield Cl. SE13. . . 2F **109**
Freshford St. SW17 . . 3E **115**
Freshwater Cl. SW17 . 5C **116**
Freshwater Ct. *W1* *4A* **60**
(off Crawford St.)
Freshwater Rd. SW17. 5C **116**
Freston Rd. W10 . . . . . 1F **71**
Freswick Ho. *SE8* *5F* **79**
(off Chilton Gro.)
Freud Mus., The 3E **45**
Frewell Ho. *EC1* *5B* **8**
(off Bourne Est.)
Frewin Rd. SW18 . . . . 1F **115**
Friar M. SE27 . . . . 3D **119**
Friars Av. SW15 . . . . . 3B **112**
Friars Cl. SE1 . . . . 2E **25**
Friars Gdns. W3 . . . . . . 5A **56**
Friars Mead E14 . . . . . . 4E **81**
Friars Pl. La. W3 . . . . . 1A **70**
Friars Rd. E6 . . . . 5F **55**
Friar St. EC4 . . . 5D **63** (3E **17**)
Friars Way W3 . . . . 5A **56**
Friary Ct. SW1 . . . . 2A **22**

Friary Est. SE15 . . . . . . 2C **92**
(not continuous)
Friary Rd. SE15 . . . . . . 3C **92**
W3 . . . . 5A **56**
Friday St. EC4 . . 1E **77** (4F **17**)
Frideswide Pl. NW5. . . . 2E **47**
Friendly Pl. SE13. . . . . 4D **95**
Friendly St. SE8. . . . . . 5C **94**
Friendly St. M. SE8 . . . 5C **94**
Friendship Ho. *SE1* *3D* **77**
(off Belvedere Pl.)
Friend St. EC1 . . 2D **63** (1D **9**)
Friern Rd. SE22 . . . . . 5C **106**
Frigate Ho. *E14* *5E* **81**
(off Stebondale St.)
Frigate M. SE8 . . . . 2C **94**
Frimley Cl. SW19. . . . 2A **114**
Frimley St. *E1*. *3F* **65**
(off Frimley Way)
Frimley Way E1 . . . . . . 3F **65**
Frinstead Ho. *W10* . . . *1F* **71**
(off Freston Rd.)
Frinton Rd. E6 . . . . 2F **69**
N15. . . . . 1A **36**
Friston St. SW6 . . . . . . 5D **87**
Frith Ho. *NW8* *3F* **59**
(off Frampton St.)
Frith Rd. E11 . . . . 1E **53**
Frith St. W1 . . . 5F **61** (3B **14**)
Frithville Ct. *W12*. *2E* **71**
(off Frithville Gdns.)
Frithville Gdns. W12 . . 2E **71**
Frobisher Ct. SE10 . . . 2F **95**
(off Old Woolwich Rd.)
SE23. . . . . 2D **121**
W12 . . . . 3E **71**
(off Lime Gro.)
Frobisher Cres. EC2. . . . 5A **10**
(off Beech St.)
Frobisher Gdns. E10 . . 2D **39**
Frobisher Ho. *E1* 2D **79**
(off Watts St.)
SW1 . . . . 2D **89**
(off Dolphin Sq.)
Frobisher Pas. E14 . . . 2C **80**
Frobisher Pl. Pioneer Cen.
SE15. . . . . 4E **93**
Frobisher St. SE10. . . . 2A **96**
Frogley Rd. SE22. . . . 2B **106**
Frogmore SW18. . . . . 3C **100**
Frogmore Ind. Est. N5 . . 2E **49**
Frognal NW3 . . . . 1E **45**
Frognal Cl. NW3. . . . . . 2E **45**
Frognal Ct. NW3. . . . . . 3E **45**
Frognal Gdns. NW3 . . . 1E **45**
Frognal La. NW3 . . . . . . 2D **45**
Frognal Pde. NW3 . . . . 3E **45**
Frognal Ri. NW3 . . . . . . 5E **31**
Frognal Way NW3 . . . . 1E **45**
Froissart Rd. SE9 . . . . 3F **111**
Frome Ho. SE15. . . . . 2D **107**
Frome St. N1 . . . . 1E **63**
Frontenac NW10 . . . . . 4D **43**
Frostic Wlk. E1. . . . . . . 4C **64**
Froude St. SW8 . . . . . . 5D **89**
Fruiterers Pas. *EC4* . . . *5A* **18**
(off Queen St. Pl.)
Fryent Cres. NW9 . . . . 1A **28**
Fryent Flds. NW9 . . . . . 1A **28**
Fryent Gro. NW9 . . . . . 1A **28**

Fry Ho. E7. . . . . 4E **55**
Frying Pan All. E1 . . . . 1F **19**
Fry Rd. E6. . . . . 4F **55**
NW10. . . . . 5B **42**
Fulbeck Ho. *N7* *3B* **48**
(off Sutterton St.)
Fulbeck Rd. N19. . . . . . 1E **47**
Fulbourne St. E1 . . . . . 4D **65**
Fulbrook M. N19 . . . . . 1E **47**
Fulcher Ho. *N1*. *5A* **50**
(off Colville Est.)
SE8. . . . . 1B **94**
Fulford St. SE16. . . . . . 3D **79**
FULHAM **5A 86**
FULHAM BROADWAY . . **3C 86**
Fulham B'way. SW6. . . . 3C **86**
Fulham Ct. SW6. . . . . . 4C **86**
**Fulham F.C. Ground
(Craven Cottage). . . . 4F 85**
**Fulham F.C. (Loftus Road)
. . . . 2D 71**
Fulham High St. SW6 . . 5A **86**
Fulham Palace. **5A 86**
Fulham Pal. Rd. SW6 . . 1E **85**
W6 . . . . 1E **85**
Fulham Pk. Gdns. SW6 . 5B **86**
Fulham Pk. Rd. SW6 . . 5B **86**
Fulham Rd. SW3 . . . . . 1F **87**
SW6 . . . . 5A **86**
(not continuous)
SW10 . . . . 3D **87**
Fuller Cl. *E2*. *3C* **64**
(off Cheshire St.)
**Fuller's Griffin Brewery &
Vis. Cen.** **2B 84**
Fullerton Rd. SW18. . . 3D **101**
Fullwood's M.
N1 . . . . 2F **63** (1C **10**)
Fulmar Ho. *SE16* *5F* **79**
(off Tawny Way)
Fulmead St. SW6. . . . . 4D **87**
Fulmer Ho. *NW8* *3A* **60**
(off Mallory St.)
Fulmer Rd. E16 . . . . . . 4F **69**
Fulneck *E1* *4E* **65**
(off Mile End Rd.)
Fulready Rd. E10 . . . . . 1F **39**
Fulthorp Rd. SE3 . . . . . 5B **96**
Fulton M. *W2* *1E* **73**
(off Porchester Ter.)
Fulwood Pl.
WC1. . . . . 4B **62** (1A **16**)
Fulwood Wlk. SW19 . . 1A **114**
Furber St. W6 . . . . 4D **71**
Furley Ho. *SE15*. *3C* **92**
(off Peckham Pk. Rd.)
Furley Rd. SE15. . . . . . 3C **92**
Furlong Rd. N7. . . . . . . 3C **48**
Furmage St. SW18 . . . 5D **101**
Furneaux Av. SE27. . . 5D **119**
Furness Ho. *SW1*. *1D* **89**
(off Abbots Mnr.)
Furness Rd. NW10. . . . 1C **56**
SW6 . . . . 5D **87**
Furnival Mans. *W1*. . . . *1F* **13**
(off Wells St.)
Furnival St. EC4. . 5C **62** (2B **16**)
Furrow La. E9. . . . . 2E **51**
Fursecroft *W1*. *5B* **60**
(off George St.)

Garrick Av. NW11 . . . . . 1A **30**
Garrick Cl. SW18 . . . . . . 2E **101**
Garrick Ho. W4 . . . . 2A **84**
  W1 . . . . 2D **75** (2D **21**)
Garrick Ind. Est. NW9 . . 1B **28**
Garrick Rd. NW9 . . . 1B **28**
Garrick St.
  WC2 . . . . 1A **76** (4D **15**)
Garrick Theatre **5D 15**
  (off Charing Cross Rd.)
Garrick Yd. WC2 . . . . . 4D **15**
Garsdale Ter. W14 . . . . . 1B **86**
  (off Aisgill Av.)
Garsington M. SE4 . . . 1B **108**
Garson Ho. W2 . . . . . . 1F **73**
  (off Gloucester Ter.)
Garston Ho. N1 . . . . . . 4D **49**
  (off Sutton Est., The)
Garter Way SE16 . . . . . . 3F **79**
Garthorne Rd. SE23 . . 5F **107**
Garth Rd. NW2 . . . . . . 4B **30**
Gartmoor Gdns.
  SW19 . . . . 1B **114**
Garton Pl. SW18 . . . . 4E **101**
Gartons Way SW11 . . . 1E **101**
Garvary Rd. E16 . . . . . 5D **69**
Garway Rd. W2 . . . . . . 5D **59**
Gascoigne Pl.
  E2 . . . . 2B **64** (1F **11**)
  (not continuous)
Gascony Av. NW6 . . . . . 4C **44**
Gascoyne Ho. E9 . . . . . 4A **52**
Gascoyne Rd. E9 . . . . . 4F **51**
Gaselee St. E14 . . . . . . 2E **81**
  (off Baffin Way)
Gaskarth Rd. SW12 . . 4D **103**
Gaskell Rd. N6 . . . . . . 1B **32**
Gaskell St. SW4 . . . . . 5A **90**
Gaskin St. N1 . . . . . . 5D **49**
Gaspar Cl. SW5 . . . . . 5D **73**
  (off Courtfield Gdns.)
Gaspar M. SW5 . . . . . 5D **73**
Gassiot Rd. SW17 . . . 4B **116**
Gasson Ho. SE14 . . . . . 2F **93**
  (off John Williams Cl.)
Gastein Rd. W6 . . . . . . 2A **86**
Gastigny Ho. EC1 . . . . . 2A **10**
Gataker Ho. SE16 . . . . . 4D **79**
  (off Slippers Pl.)
Gataker St. SE16 . . . . . 4D **79**
Gatcombe Ho. SE22 . . 1A **106**
Gatcombe Rd. E16 . . . . 2C **82**
  N19 . . . . 5F **33**
Gateforth St. NW8 . . . . 3A **60**
Gate Hill Ct. W11 . . . . . 2B **72**
  (off Ladbroke Ter.)
Gatehouse Sq. SE1 . . . . 1A **26**
Gateley Ho. SE4 . . . . . . 2F **107**
  (off Coston Wlk.)
Gateley Rd. SW9 . . . . 1B **104**
Gate Lodge W9 . . . . . . 4C **58**
  (off Admiral Wlk.)
Gate M. SW7 . . . . 3A **74**
  (off Rutland Ga.)
Gatesborough St.
  EC2 . . . . . . 3A **64** (3D **11**)
Gates Ct. SE17 . . . . . . 1E **91**
Gatesden WC1 . . . 2A **62** (2F **7**)
Gateside Rd. SW17 . . . 3B **116**
Gate St. WC2 . . . . 5B **62** (2F **15**)

Gate Theatre, The 2C **72**
  (off Pembridge Rd.)
Gateway SE17 . . . . . . 2E **91**
Gateway Arc. N1 . . . . . 1D **63**
  (off Upper St.)
Gateway Ind. Est.
  NW10 . . . . 2B **56**
Gateway M. E8 . . . . . . 2B **50**
Gateway Rd. E10 . . . . . 5D **39**
Gateways, The SW3 . . . 5A **74**
  (off Sprimont Pl.)
Gathorne St. E2 . . . . . 1F **65**
Gatliff Cl. SW1 . . . . . . 1D **89**
  (off Ebury Bri. Rd.)
Gatliff Rd. SW1 . . . . . . 1D **89**
  (not continuous)
Gatonby St. SE15 . . . . . 4B **92**
Gattis Wharf N1 . . . . . . 1A **62**
  (off New Wharf Rd.)
Gatton Rd. SW17 . . . . 4A **116**
Gatwick Ho. E14 . . . . . 5B **66**
  (off Clemence St.)
Gatwick Rd. SW18 . . . 5B **100**
Gauden Cl. SW4 . . . . . 1F **103**
Gauden Rd. SW4 . . . . . 5F **89**
Gaugin Ct. SE16 . . . . . 1D **93**
  (off Stubbs Dr.)
Gaumont Ter. W12 . . . . 3E **71**
  (off Lime Gro.)
Gaunt St. SE1 . . . 4E **77** (5F **25**)
Gautrey Rd. SE15 . . . . 5E **93**
Gavel St. SE17 . . . . . . 5F **77**
Gaverick M. E14 . . . . . 5C **80**
Gavestone Cres.
  SE12 . . . . 5D **111**
Gavestone Rd. SE12 . . 5D **111**
Gaviller Pl. E5 . . . . . . 1D **51**
Gawber St. E2 . . . . . . 2E **65**
Gawsworth Cl. E15 . . . . 2B **54**
Gay Cl. NW2 . . . . 2D **43**
Gaydon Ho. W2 . . . . . . 4D **59**
  (off Bourne Ter.)
Gayfere St.
  SW1 . . . . 4A **76** (5D **23**)
Gayford Rd. W12 . . . . . 3B **70**
Gay Ho. N16 . . . . 2A **50**
Gayhurst SE17 . . . . . . 2F **91**
  (off Hopwood Rd.)
Gayhurst Ho. NW8 . . . . 3A **60**
  (off Mallory St.)
Gayhurst Rd. E8 . . . . . 4C **50**
Gaymead NW8 . . . . . . 5D **45**
  (off Abbey Rd.)
Gaynesford Rd. SE23 . . 2F **121**
Gay Rd. E15 . . . . 1F **67**
Gaysley Ho. SE11 . . . . . 5C **76**
  (off Hotspur St.)
Gay St. SW15 . . . . . . 1F **99**
Gayton Cres. NW3 . . . . 1F **45**
Gayton Rd. NW3 . . . . . 1F **45**
Gayville Rd. SW11 . . . 4B **102**
Gaywood Cl. SW2 . . . 1B **118**
Gaywood St.
  SE1 . . . . . . 4D **77** (5E **25**)
Gaza St. SE17 . . . . . . 1D **91**
Gaze Ho. E14 . . . . 5F **67**
  (off Blair St.)
Gean Ct. E11 . . . . 1F **53**
Geary Ho. N7 . . . . 2C **42**
Geary St. N7 . . . . 2B **48**

Gedling Pl. SE1 . . 4B **78** (5F **27**)
Geere Rd. E15 . . . . . . 5B **54**
Gees Ct. W1 . . . . 5C **60** (3C **12**)
Gee St. EC1 . . . . 3E **63** (3F **9**)
Geffrye Ct. N1 . . . . . . 1A **64**
Geffrye Est. N1 . . . . . . 1A **64**
Geffrye Mus. . . 1B **64** (1F **11**)
Geffrye St. E2 . . 1B **64** (1F **11**)
Geldart Rd. SE15 . . . . . 3D **93**
Geldeston Rd. E5 . . . . . 4C **36**
Gellatly Rd. SE14 . . . . . 5E **93**
Gemini Bus. Cen. E16 . . 3F **67**
Gemini Bus. Est. SE14 . . 1F **93**
Gemini Ct. E1 . . . . 1C **78**
  (off Vaughan Way)
General Wolfe Rd.
  SE10 . . . . 4F **95**
Geneva Ct. NW9 . . . . . 1B **28**
Geneva Dr. SW9 . . . . 2C **104**
Genoa Av. SW15 . . . . . 3E **99**
Genoa Ho. E1 . . . . 3F **65**
  (off Ernest St.)
Gentry Gdns. E13 . . . . . 3C **68**
Geoffrey Cl. SE5 . . . . . 5E **91**
Geoffrey Ct. SE4 . . . . . 5B **94**
Geoffrey Gdns. E6 . . . . 1F **69**
Geoffrey Ho. SE1 . . . . . 5C **26**
  (off Pardoner St.)
Geoffrey Jones Ct.
  NW10 . . . . 5C **42**
Geoffrey Rd. SE4 . . . . 1B **108**
Geographers' A-Z Shop
  . . . . 4C **62** (5B **8**)
George Beard Rd. SE8 . . 5B **80**
George Belt Ho. E2 . . . . 2F **65**
  (off Smart St.)
George Ct. WC2 . . . . . 5E **15**
George Downing Est.
  N16 . . . . 4B **36**
George Eliot Ho. SW1 . . 5E **75**
  (off Vauxhall Bri. Rd.)
George Elliston Ho.
  SE1 . . . . 1C **92**
  (off Old Kent Rd.)
George Eyre Ho. NW8 . . 1F **59**
  (off Cochrane St.)
George Gillett Ct. EC1 . . 3A **10**
George Inn Yd.
  SE1 . . . . . . 2F **77** (2B **26**)
George La. SE13 . . . . 4D **109**
George Lansbury Ho.
  NW10 . . . . 4A **42**
George Lindgren Ho.
  SW6 . . . . 3B **86**
  (off Clem Attlee Ct.)
George Loveless Ho. E2 . 1F **11**
  (off Diss St.)
George Lowe Ct. W2 . . 4D **59**
  (off Bourne Ter.)
George Mathers Rd.
  SE11 . . . . 5D **77**
George M. NW1 . . . . . 2A **6**
George Peabody Ct.
  NW1 . . . . 4A **60**
  (off Bell St.)
George Potter Ho.
  SW11 . . . . 5F **87**
  (off George Potter Way)
George Potter Way
  SW11 . . . . 5F **87**

Godbold Rd. E15 . . . . . . 3A 68
Goddard Pl. N19 . . . . 5E 33
Godfree Ct. *SE1* *3B 26*
  (off Long La.)
Godfrey Ho. EC1 . . . . 2B 10
Godfrey St. E15 . . . . 1E 67
  SW3 . . . . 1A 88
Goding St. SE11 . . . . 1A 90
Godley Rd. SW18 . . . . 1F 115
Godliman St.
  EC4 . . . . 5D 63 (3E 17)
Godman Rd. SE15 . . . . . 5D 93
Godolphin Ho. *NW3* *4A 46*
  (off Fellows Rd.)
Godolphin Pl. W3 . . . . . . 1A 70
Godolphin Rd. W12 . . . . 2D 71
  (not continuous)
Godstone Ho. *SE1* *5C 26*
  (off Pardoner St.)
Godwin Cl. N1 . . . . 1E 63
Godwin Cl. *NW1* *1E 61*
  (off Chalton St.)
Godwin Ho. NW6 . . . . . . *1D 59*
  (off Tollgate Gdns., not cont.)
Godwin Rd. E7 . . . . 1D 55
Goffers Ho. SE3 . . . . 4A 96
Golborne Gdns. W10 . . 3A 58
Golborne Ho. *W10* *3A 58*
  (off Adair Rd.)
Golborne M. W10 . . . . . . 4A 58
Golborne Rd. W10 . . . . . 4A 58
Goldcrest Cl. E16 . . . . . . 4F 69
Golden Cross M. *W11* . *5B 58*
  (off Portobello Rd.)
Golden Hinde Educational
  Mus. . . . 2F 77 (1B 26)
Golden Hind Pl. *SE8* . . *5B 80*
  (off Grove St.)
Golden La. EC1 . . 3E 63 (3F 9)
Golden La. Est.
  EC1 . . . . 3E 63 (4F 9)
Golden Plover Cl. E16 . . 5C 68
Golden Sq. W1 . . 1E 75 (4A 14)
Golden Yd. *NW3* *1E 45*
  (off Holly Mt.)
Golders Ct. NW11 . . . . . . 2B 30
Golders Gdns. NW11 . . . 2A 30
GOLDERS GREEN **1A 30**
Golders Green Crematorium
  NW11 . . . . 2C 30
Golders Grn. Cres.
  NW11 . . . . 2B 30
Golders Grn. Rd. NW11 . 1A 30
Golderslea NW11 . . . . . . 3C 30
Golders Mnr. Dr. NW11 . 1F 29
Golders Pk. Cl. NW11 . . 3C 30
Golders Way NW11 . . . . 2B 30
Goldhawk Ind. Est. W6 . . 4D 71
Goldhawk M. W12 . . . . . 3D 71
Goldhawk Rd. W6 . . . . . . 5B 70
Goldhurst Ter. NW6 . . . . 4D 45
Goldie Ho. N19 . . . . 2F 33
Golding St. E1 . . . . 5C 64
Golding Ter. E1 . . . . 5C 64
  SW11 . . . . 5C 88
Goldington Ct. *NW1* . . . *5F 47*
  (off Royal College St.)
Goldington Cres. NW1 . . 1F 61
Goldington St. NW1 . . . . 1F 61
Goldman Cl. E2 . . . . 3C 64

Goldmark Ho. SE3 . . . . 1D 111
Goldney Rd. W9 . . . . 3C 58
Goldsboro' Rd. SW8 . . . 4F 89
Goldsborough Ho. *E14* . *1D 95*
  (off St Davids Sq.)
Goldsmith Av. E12 . . . . . 3F 55
  NW9 . . . . 1A 28
Goldsmith Ct. *WC2* *2E 15*
  (off Stukeley St.)
Goldsmith Rd. E10 . . . . . 3C 38
  SE15 . . . . 4C 92
Goldsmith's Bldgs. W3 . 2A 70
Goldsmiths Cl. W3 . . . . . 2A 70
Goldsmith's Pl. *NW6* . . . *5D 45*
  (off Springfield La.)
Goldsmith's Row E2 . . . 1C 64
Goldsmith's Sq. E2 . . . . 1C 64
Goldsmith St.
  EC2 . . . . 5E 63 (2A 18)
Goldsworthy Gdns.
  SE16 . . . . 1E 93
Goldthorpe NW1 . . . . . . *5E 47*
  (off Camden St.)
Goldwell Ho. SE22 . . . . 1A 106
Goldwin Cl. SE14 . . . . . . 4E 93
Goldwing Cl. E16 . . . . . . 5C 68
Gollogly Ter. SE7 . . . . . . 1E 97
Gomm Rd. SE16 . . . . . . 4E 79
Gondar Gdns. NW6 . . . . 2B 44
Gonson St. SE8 . . . . 2D 95
Gonston Cl. SW19 . . . . 2A 114
Gonville St. SW6 . . . . . 1A 100
Gooch Ho. E5 . . . . 5D 37
  EC1 . . . . *5B 8*
  (off Portpool La.)
Goodall Ho. SE4 . . . . . . 2F 107
Goodall Rd. E11 . . . . 5E 39
Goodfaith Ho. *E14* *1D 81*
  (off Simpson's Rd.)
Goodge Pl. W1 . . 4E 61 (1A 14)
Goodge St. W1 . . 4E 61 (1A 14)
Goodhall St. NW10 . . . . 2B 56
  (not continuous)
Goodhart Pl. E14 . . . . . . 1A 80
Goodhope Ho. *E14* *1D 81*
  (off Poplar High St.)
Gooding Cl. N7 . . . . 3A 48
Gooding Ho. SE7 . . . . . . 1E 97
Goodman Cres. SW2 . . 2A 118
Goodman Rd. E10 . . . . . 2E 39
Goodman's Ct. E1 . . . . . 4F 19
Goodman's Stile E1 . . . . 5C 64
Goodmans Rd.
  EC3 . . . . 1B 78 (4F 19)
Goodrich Ct. W10 . . . . . . 5F 57
Goodrich Ho. *E9* *1E 65*
  (off Sewardstone Rd.)
Goodrich Rd. SE22 . . . . 4B 106
Goodson Rd. NW10 . . . . 4A 42
Goodson St. N1 . . . . 1C 62
Goodspeed Ho. *E14* . . . *1D 81*
  (off Simpson's Rd.)
Goodway Gdns. E14 . . . 5F 67
Goodwill Ho. *E14* *1D 81*
  (off Simpson's Rd.)
Goodwin Cl. SE16 . . . . . 4B 78
Goodwin Ho. W12 . . . . . 3C 70
Goodwins Ct.
  WC2 . . . . 1A 76 (4D 15)

Goodwin St. N4 . . . . 4C 34
Goodwood Cl. *W1* *5E 5*
  (off Devonshire St.)
Goodwood Ho. SE14 . . *4A 94*
  (off Goodwood St.)
Goodwood Rd. SE14 . . . 3A 94
Goodyear Pl. SE5 . . . . . . 2E 91
Goodyer Ho. *SW1* *1F 89*
  (off Tachbrook St.)
Goodyers Gdns. NW4 . . 1F 29
Goose Grn. Trad. Est.
  SE22 . . . . 2B 106
Gophir La. EC4 . . 1F 77 (4B 18)
Gopsall St. N1 . . . . 5F 49
Gordon Av. SW14 . . . . . 2A 98
Gordonbrock Rd. SE4 . . 3C 108
Gordon Cl. E17 . . . . 1C 38
  N19 . . . . 3E 33
Gordon Ct. W12 . . . . 5E 57
Gordondale Rd. SW19 . 2C 114
Gordon Gro. SE5 . . . . . . 5D 91
Gordon Ho. *E1* *1E 79*
  (off Glamis Rd.)
  SE10 . . . . *3D 95*
  (off Tarves Way)
Gordon Ho. Rd. NW5 . . 1C 46
Gordon Mans. *W14* . . . *4F 71*
  (off Addison Gdns.)
  WC1 . . . . *4B 6*
  (off Torrington Pl.)
Gordon Pl. W8 . . . . 3C 72
Gordon Rd. E11 . . . . 1C 40
  E15 . . . . 1E 53
  SE15 . . . . 5D 93
Gordon Sq. WC1 . 3F 61 (3B 6)
Gordon St. E13 . . . . 2C 68
  WC1 . . . . 3F 61 (3B 6)
Gorefield Ho. *NW6* *1C 58*
  (off Gorefield Pl.)
Gorefield Pl. NW6 . . . . . 1C 58
Gore Rd. E9 . . . . 5E 51
Gore St. SW7 . . . . 4E 73
Gorham Ho. *SE16* *3F 79*
  (off Wolfe Cres.)
Gorham Pl. W11 . . . . 1A 72
Goring St. EC3 . . . . 2E 19
Gorleston St. W14 . . . . . 5A 72
  (not continuous)
Gorse Cl. E16 . . . . 5C 68
Gorsefield Ho. *E14* *1C 80*
  (off E. India Dock Rd.)
Gorse Ri. SW17 . . . . . . 5C 116
Gorst Rd. NW10 . . . . 3A 56
  SW11 . . . . 4B 102
Gorsuch Pl. E2 . . 2B 64 (1F 11)
Gorsuch St. E2 . . 1B 64 (1F 11)
Gosberton St. SW12 . . 1B 116
Goslett Yd.
  WC2 . . . . 5F 61 (3C 14)
Gosling Ho. *E1* *1E 79*
  (off Sutton St.)
Gosling Way SW9 . . . . . 4C 90
GOSPEL OAK **1C 46**
Gospel Oak Est. NW5 . . 2B 46
Gosport Rd. E17 . . . . . . 1B 38
Gosset St. E2 . . . . 2B 64
Gosterwood St. SE8 . . . 2A 94
Goswell Pl. EC1 . . . . 2E 9
Goswell Rd. EC1 . 1D 63 (1D 9)

Grasmere Point *SE15* 3E **93**
  (off Old Kent Rd.)
Grasmere Rd. E13 . . . . . . 1C **68**
  SW16 . . . . 5B **118**
Grassmount SE23 . . . . . . 2D **121**
Gratton Rd. W14 . . . . 4A **72**
Gratton Ter. NW2 . . . . 5F **29**
Gravel La. E1 . . . 5B **64** (2F **19**)
Gravely Ho. *SE8* *5A 80*
  (off Chilton Gro.)
Gravenel Gdns. *SW17* . . *5A 116*
  (off Nutwell St.)
Graveney Rd. SW17 . . . . 4A **116**
Gravesend Rd. W12 . . . . . 1C **70**
Gray Ho. *SE17* *1E 91*
  (off King & Queen St.)
Grayling Cl. E16 . . . . 3A **68**
Grayling Rd. N16 . . . . 4F **35**
Grayling Sq. *E2* *2C 64*
  (off Nelson Gdns.)
Grayshott Rd. SW11 . . . . . 5C **88**
Gray's Inn . . . . **4B 62 (5A 8)**
Gray's Inn Bldgs. *EC1* . . . *4B 8*
  (off Rosebery Av.)
Gray's Inn Pl.
  WC1 . . . . 4B **62** (1A **16**)
Gray's Inn Rd.
  WC1 . . . . 2A **62** (1E **7**)
Gray's Inn Sq.
  WC1 . . . . 4B **62** (5B **8**)
Grayson Ho. EC1 . . . . 2A **10**
Gray St. SE1 . . . 3C **76** (4C **24**)
Gray's Yd. W1 . . . . 3C **12**
Grazebrook Rd. N16 . . . . . 4F **35**
Grazeley Ct. SE19 . . . . . . 5A **120**
Gt. Acre Ct. SW4 . . . . . . 2F **103**
Gt. Arthur Ho. *EC1* *4F 9*
  (off Golden La. Est.)
Gt. Bell All. EC2 . . 5F **63** (2B **18**)
Great Brownings SE21 . . 4B **120**
Gt. Castle St.
  W1 . . . . 5D **61** (2E **13**)
Gt. Central St. NW1 . . . . . 4B **60**
Gt. Central Way NW10 . . 1A **42**
Gt. Chapel St.
  W1 . . . . 5F **61** (2B **14**)
Gt. Chertsey Rd. W4 . . . . 4A **84**
Gt. Church La. W6 . . . . . . 5F **71**
Gt. College St.
  SW1 . . . . 4A **76** (5D **23**)
Great Cft. *WC1* *2E 7*
  (off Cromer St.)
Gt. Cross Av. SE10 . . . . . 3F **95**
  (not continuous)
Gt. Cumberland M.
  W1 . . . . 5B **60** (3A **12**)
Gt. Cumberland Pl.
  W1 . . . . 5B **60** (2A **12**)
Gt. Dover St.
  SE1 . . . . 3E **77** (4A **26**)
Gt. Eastern Bldgs. *E1* . . *4C 64*
  (off Fieldgate St.)
Gt. Eastern Ent. Cen.
  E14 . . . . 3D **81**
Gt. Eastern Rd. E15 . . . . 4F **53**
Gt. Eastern St.
  EC2 . . . . 2A **64** (2D **11**)
Gt. Eastern Wlk. EC2 . . . 1E **19**
Gt. Eastern Wharf
  SW11 . . . . 3A **88**

Greatfield Cl. N19 . . . . . 1E **47**
  SE4 . . . . 2C **108**
Gt. George St.
  SW1 . . . . 3F **75** (4C **22**)
Gt. Guildford Bus. Sq.
  SE1 . . . . 2F **25**
Gt. Guildford St.
  SE1 . . . . 2E **77** (1F **25**)
Great Hall Royal Hospital
  Chelsea **1B 88**
Greatham Wlk.
  SW15 . . . . 1C **112**
Gt. James St.
  WC1 . . . . 4B **62** (5F **7**)
Gt. Marlborough St.
  W1 . . . . 5E **61** (3F **13**)
Gt. Maze Pond
  SE1 . . . . 3F **77** (2C **26**)
  (not continuous)
Gt. Newport St.
  WC2 . . . . 1A **76** (4D **15**)
Gt. New St.
  EC4 . . . . 5C **62** (2C **16**)
Gt. North Rd. N2 . . . . . . 1B **32**
Greatorex Ho. *E1* *4C 64*
  (off Greatorex St.)
Greatorex St. E1 . . . . . . 4C **64**
Gt. Ormond St.
  WC1 . . . . 4A **62** (5E **7**)
Gt. Percy St.
  WC1 . . . . 2B **62** (1A **8**)
Gt. Peter St.
  SW1 . . . . 4F **75** (5B **22**)
Gt. Portland St.
  W1 . . . . 3D **61** (4E **5**)
Gt. Pulteney St.
  W1 . . . . 1E **75** (4A **14**)
Gt. Queen St.
  WC2 . . . . 5A **62** (3E **15**)
Gt. Russell St.
  WC1 . . . . 5F **61** (2C **14**)
Gt. St Helen's
  EC2 . . . . 5A **64** (2D **19**)
Gt. St Thomas Apostle
  EC4 . . . . 1E **77** (4A **18**)
Gt. Scotland Yd.
  SW1 . . . . 2A **76** (2D **23**)
Gt. Smith St.
  SW1 . . . . 4F **75** (5C **22**)
Great Spilmans SE22 . . 3A **106**
Gt. Suffolk St.
  SE1 . . . . 2D **77** (2E **25**)
Gt. Sutton St.
  EC1 . . . . 3D **63** (4E **9**)
Gt. Swan All.
  EC2 . . . . 5F **63** (2B **18**)
  (not continuous)
Gt. Titchfield St.
  W1 . . . . 3D **61** (4E **5**)
Gt. Tower St.
  EC3 . . . . 1A **78** (4D **19**)
Gt. Trinity La.
  EC4 . . . . 1E **77** (4A **18**)
Great Turnstile
  WC1 . . . . 4B **62** (1A **16**)
Gt. Western Rd. W9 . . . . 4B **58**
Gt. West Rd. W4 . . . . . . 1B **84**
  W6 . . . . 1B **84**
Gt. Winchester St.
  EC2 . . . . 5F **63** (2C **18**)

Gt. Windmill St.
  W1 . . . . 1F **75** (4B **14**)
Great Yd. SE1 . . . . 3E **27**
Greaves Cotts. E14 . . . . 4A **66**
Greaves Pl. SW17 . . . . . 4A **116**
Greaves Twr. *SW10* *3E 87*
  (off Worlds End Est.)
Grebe Cl. E7 . . . . 2B **54**
Grebe Ct. *E14* *3E 81*
  (off River Barge Cl.)
  SE8 . . . . *2B 94*
  (off Dorking Cl.)
Grecian Cres. SE19 . . . 5D **119**
Greek Ct. W1 . . 5F **61** (3C **14**)
Greek St. W1 . . . 5F **61** (3C **14**)
Greenacre Sq. SE16 . . . . 3F **79**
Grn. Arbour Ct. EC4 . . . . 2D **17**
Greenaway Gdns. NW3 . . 1D **45**
Greenaway Ho. *NW8* . . . *5E 45*
  (off Boundary Rd.)
  WC1 . . . . *2B 8*
  (off Fernsbury St.)
Green Bank E1 . . . . 2D **79**
Greenbay Rd. SE7 . . . . . 3F **97**
Greenberry St. NW8 . . . 1A **60**
Green Cl. E15 . . . . 5A **54**
  NW11 . . . . 2E **31**
Greencoat Mans. *SW1* . . *4E 75*
  (off Greencoat Row)
Greencoat Pl.
  SW1 . . . . 5E **75** (5A **22**)
Greencoat Row SW1 . . . 4E **75**
Greencourt Ho. *E1* *3F 65*
  (off Mile End Rd.)
Greencrest Pl. NW2 . . . . 5C **28**
Greencroft Cl. E6 . . . . . . 4F **69**
Greencroft Gdns. NW6 . . 4D **45**
Green Dale SE5 . . . . . . 2F **105**
  SE22 . . . . 3A **106**
Grn. Dale Cl. SE22 . . . . 3A **106**
Grn. Dragon Ct. SE1 . . . 1B **26**
Grn. Dragon Yd. E1 . . . . 4C **64**
Greene Ct. *SE14* *2F 93*
  (off Samuel Cl.)
Greene Ho. *SE1* *5B 26*
  (off Burbage Cl.)
Greenend Rd. W4 . . . . . 3A **70**
Greener Ho. SW4 . . . . . 1F **103**
Greenfell Mans. SE8 . . . 2D **95**
Greenfield Gdns. NW2 . . 4A **30**
Greenfield Rd. E1 . . . . . 4C **64**
  N15 . . . . 1A **36**
Greengate Lodge *E13* . . *1D 69*
  (off Hollybush St.)
Greengate St. E13 . . . . . 1D **69**
Greenham Cl.
  SE1 . . . . 3C **76** (4B **24**)
Greenham Ho. *E9* *5E 51*
  (off Templecombe Rd.)
Greenheath Bus. Cen.
  E2 . . . . *3D 65*
  (off Three Colts La.)
Greenhill NW3 . . . . 1F **45**
Greenhill Gro. E12 . . . . . 1F **55**
Greenhill Pk. NW10 . . . . 5A **42**
Greenhill Rd. NW10 . . . . 5A **42**
Greenhill's Rents
  EC1 . . . . 4D **63** (5D **9**)
Greenhills Ter. N1 . . . . . 3F **49**
Grn. Hundred Rd. SE15. . 2C **92**

Gwendolen Av. SW15 . . . . 2F **99**
Gwendolen St. SW15 . . . . 3F **99**
Gwendoline Av. E13 . . . . 5D **55**
Gwendwr Rd. W14 . . . . 1A **86**
Gwent Ct. SE16 . . . . 2F **79**
   (off Rotherhithe St.)
Gwilym Maries Ho. E2 . . 2D **65**
   (off Blythe St.)
Gwyn Cl. SW6 . . . . 3E **87**
Gwynne Cl. W4 . . . . 2B **84**
Gwynne Ho. E1 . . . . 4D **65**
   (off Turner St.)
  WC1 . . . . 2B **8**
   (off Lloyd Baker St.)
Gwynne Pl. WC1 . . 2B **62** (2A **8**)
Gwynne Rd. SW11 . . . . . 5F **87**
Gylcote Cl. SE5 . . . . . . 2F **105**

H

Haarlem Rd. W14 . . . . . . 4F **71**
Haberdasher Est.
  N1 . . . . 2F **63** (1C **10**)
Haberdasher Pl. N1 . . . 1C **10**
Haberdashers Ct.
  SE14 . . . . 1F **107**
Haberdasher St.
  N1 . . . . 2F **63** (1C **10**)
Habington Ho. SE5 . . . . . 3F **91**
   (off Notley St.)
Hackford Rd. SW9 . . . . . 4B **90**
Hackford Wlk. SW9 . . . . 4B **90**
Hackington Cres.
  BR3: Beck 5C **122**
HACKNEY **3D 51**
Hackney Gro. E8 . . . . . . 3D **51**
Hackney Rd. E2 . . 2B **64** (2F **11**)
HACKNEY WICK **3B 52**
HACKNEY WICK **3A 52**
Haddington Ct. SE10 . . 3D **95**
   (off Tarves Way)
Haddington Rd.
  BR1: Brom 3F **123**
Haddo Ho. SE10 . . . . . . 2D **95**
   (off Haddo St.)
Haddon Ct. W3 . . . . 1B **70**
Haddonfield SE8 . . . . . . 5F **79**
Haddon Hall St. SE1 . . 4F **77**
   (off Rephidim St.)
Haddo St. SE10 . . . . . . 2D **95**
Haden Ct. N4 . . . . 4C **34**
Hadfield Ho. E1 . . . . 5C **64**
   (off Ellen St.)
Hadleigh Cl. E1 . . . . 3E **65**
Hadleigh Ho. E1 . . . . . . 3E **65**
   (off Hadleigh Cl.)
Hadleigh St. E2 . . . . 2E **65**
Hadley Ct. N16 . . . . 3C **36**
Hadley Gdns. W4 . . . . . 1A **84**
Hadley St. NW1 . . . . 3D **47**
   (not continuous)
Hadlow Ho. SE17 . . . . . 1A **92**
   (off Kinglake St.)
Hadrian Est. E2 . . . . 1C **64**
Hadrian St. SE10 . . . . . 1A **96**
Hadstock Ho. NW1 . . . . . 1C **6**
   (off Ossulston St.)
Hadyn Pk. Ct. W12 . . . . 3C **70**
   (off Curwen Rd.)

Hadyn Pk. Rd. W12 . . . . 3C **70**
Hafer Rd. SW11 . . . . . . 2B **102**
Hafton Rd. SE6 . . . . 1A **124**
HAGGERSTON **4B 50**
Haggerston Rd. E8 . . . . 4B **50**
Hague St. E2 . . . . 2C **64**
Haig Ho. E2 . . . . 1C **64**
   (off Shipton St.)
Haig Rd. E. E13 . . . . 2E **69**
Haig Rd. W. E13 . . . . . . 2E **69**
Hailes St. SW19 . . . . . . 5E **115**
Hailsham Av. SW2 . . . . 2B **118**
Haimo Rd. SE9 . . . . 3F **111**
Hainault Rd. E11 . . . . . . 3E **39**
Haines St. SW8 . . . . 3E **89**
Hainford Cl. SE4 . . . . . . 2F **107**
Hainthorpe Rd. SE27 . . 3D **119**
Hainton Cl. E1 . . . . 5D **65**
Halberd M. E5 . . . . 4D **37**
Halcomb St. N1 . . . . . . 5A **50**
Halcrow St. E1 . . . . 4D **65**
Halcyon Wharf E1 . . . . . 2C **78**
   (off Hermitage Wall)
Haldane Pl. SW18 . . . . 1D **115**
Haldane Rd. E6 . . . . 2F **69**
  SW6 . . . . 3B **86**
Haldon Rd. SW18 . . . . . 4D **100**
Hale Ho. SW1 . . . . 1F **89**
   (off Lindsay Sq.)
Hale Path SE27 . . . . . . 4D **119**
Hale Rd. E6 . . . . 3F **69**
Hales Prior N1 . . . . 1F **7**
   (off Calshot St.)
Hales St. SE8 . . . . 3C **94**
Hale St. E14 . . . . 1D **81**
Halesworth Cl. E5 . . . . . 4E **37**
Halesworth Rd. SE13 . 1D **109**
Haley Rd. NW4 . . . . 1E **29**
Half Moon Ct. EC1 . . . . 1F **17**
Half Moon Cres. N1 . . . 1B **62**
   (not continuous)
Half Moon La. SE24 . . 4E **105**
Half Moon Pas. E1 . . . . 5B **64**
   (not continuous)
Half Moon St.
  W1 . . . . 2D **75** (1E **21**)
Halford Rd. E10 . . . . . . 1F **39**
  SW6 . . . . 2C **86**
Haliday Ho. N1 . . . . 3F **49**
   (off Mildmay St.)
Haliday Wlk. N1 . . . . . . 3F **49**
Halidon Cl. E9 . . . . 2E **51**
Halifax St. SE26 . . . . . 3D **121**
Haliwell Ho. NW6 . . . . . 5D **45**
   (off Mortimer Cres.)
Halkin Arc.
  SW1 . . . . 4B **74** (5A **20**)
   (not continuous)
Halkin M. SW1 . . 4C **74** (5B **20**)
Halkin Pl. SW1 . . 4C **74** (5B **20**)
Halkin St. SW1 . . 3C **74** (4C **20**)
Hallam Ct. W1 . . . . 5E **5**
   (off Hallam St.)
Hallam Ho. SW1 . . . . . . 1E **89**
   (off Churchill Gdns.)
Hallam M. W1 . . 4D **61** (5E **5**)
Hallam Rd. SW13 . . . . 1D **99**
Hallam St. W1 . . 3D **61** (4E **5**)
Hallane Ho. SE27 . . . . . 5E **119**
Hall Dr. SE26 . . . . 5E **121**

Halley Gdns. SE13 . . . . 2F **109**
Halley Ho. E2 . . . . 1C **64**
   (off Pritchards Rd.)
  SE10 . . . . 1B **96**
   (off Armitage Rd.)
Halley Rd. E7 . . . . 3E **55**
  E12 . . . . 3E **55**
Halley St. E14 . . . . 4A **66**
Hallfield Est. W2 . . . . . 5E **59**
   (not continuous)
Hall Ga. NW8 . . . . 2F **59**
Halliford St. N1 . . . . 4E **49**
Halliwell Ct. SE22 . . . 3C **106**
Halliwell Rd. SW2 . . . . 4B **104**
Hall Oak Wlk. NW6 . . . . 3B **44**
Hall Pl. W2 . . . . 3F **59**
   (not continuous)
Hall Rd. E15 . . . . 1F **53**
  NW8 . . . . 2E **59**
Hall St. EC1 . . . . 2D **63** (1E **9**)
Hallsville Rd. E16 . . . . . 5B **68**
Hallswelle Rd. NW11 . . 1B **30**
Hall, The SE3 . . . . 1C **110**
Hall Twr. W2 . . . . 4F **59**
   (off Hall Pl.)
Hall Vw. SE9 . . . . 2F **125**
Halpin Pl. SE17 . . . . . . 5F **77**
Halsbrook Rd. SE3 . . . 1E **111**
Halsbury Rd. W12 . . . . 2D **71**
Halsey M. SW3 . . . . 5B **74**
Halsey St. SW3 . . . . . . 5B **74**
Halsmere Rd. SE5 . . . . 4D **91**
Halstead Ct. E17 . . . . . 2B **38**
  N1 . . . . 1C **10**
   (off Fairbank Est.)
Halstead Rd. E11 . . . . . 1C **40**
Halston Cl. SW11 . . . . 4B **102**
Halstow Rd. NW10 . . . . 2F **57**
  SE10 . . . . 1B **96**
Halton Cross St. N1 . . . 5D **49**
Halton Mans. N1 . . . . . 4D **49**
Halton Pl. N1 . . . . 5E **49**
Halton Rd. N1 . . . . 4D **49**
Halyard Ho. E14 . . . . . . 4E **81**
Hamara Ghar E13 . . . . 5E **55**
Hambalt Rd. SW4 . . . . 3E **103**
Hambledon SE17 . . . . . 2F **91**
   (off Villa St.)
Hambledon Ct. SE22 . . 2A **106**
Hambledon Pl. SE21 . . 1A **120**
Hambledon Rd.
  SW18 . . . . 5B **100**
Hamble St. SW6 . . . . . 1D **101**
Hambley Ho. SE16 . . . . 5D **79**
   (off Camilla Rd.)
Hambridge Way SW2 . . 5C **104**
Hambro Rd. SW16 . . . . 5F **117**
Hamfrith Rd. E15 . . . . . 3B **54**
Hamilton Bldgs. EC2 . . 4E **11**
Hamilton Cl. NW8 . . . . . 2F **59**
  SE16 . . . . 3A **80**
Hamilton Ct. SE6 . . . . 1B **124**
  SW15 . . . . 1A **100**
  W9 . . . . 2F **59**
   (off Maida Va.)
Hamilton Gdns. NW8 . . 2E **59**
Hamilton Ho. E14 . . . . 1D **95**
   (off St Davids Sq.)
  E14 . . . . 1B **80**
   (off Victory Pl.)

Hans St. SW1 . . 4B 74 (5A 20)
Hanway Pl. W1 . . 5F 61 (2B 14)
Honway St. . . 5F 61 (2B 14)
Hanworth Ho. SE5 . . . . . 3D 91
    (not continuous)
Harad's Pl. E1 . . . . 1C 78
Harben Pde. NW3 . . . . . . 4E 45
    (off Finchley Rd.)
Harben Rd. NW6 . . . . . . 4E 45
Harberson Rd. E15 . . . 5B 54
  SW12 . . . . 1D 117
Harberton Rd. N19 . . . 3E 33
Harbet Rd. W2 . . . . 4F 59
Harbinger Rd. E14 . . . . 5D 81
Harbledown Ho. SE1 . . 4B 26
    (off Manciple St.)
Harbledown Rd. SW6 . . 4C 86
Harbord Cl. SE5 . . . . . . 5F 91
Harbord Ho. SE16 . . . . 5F 79
    (off Cope St.)
Harbord St. SW6 . . . . . 4F 85
Harborough Rd. SW16 . 4B 118
Harbour Av. SW10 . . . . 4E 87
Harbour Exchange Sq.
  E14 . . . . 3D 81
Harbour Quay E14 . . . . 2E 81
Harbour Rd. SE5 . . . . 1E 105
Harbour Yd. SW10 . . . . 4E 87
Harbridge Av. SW15 . . 5B 98
Harbut Rd. SW11 . . . . 2F 101
    (not continuous)
Harcombe Rd. N16 . . . 5A 36
Harcourt Bldgs. EC4 . . 4B 16
Harcourt Rd. E15 . . . . 1B 68
  SE4 . . . . 1B 108
Harcourt St. W1 . . . . . . 4A 60
Harcourt Ter. SW10 . . . 1D 87
Hardcastle Ho. SE14 . . 4A 94
    (off Loring Rd.)
Hardel Ri. SW2 . . . . . . 1D 119
Hardel Wlk. SW2 . . . . 5C 104
Harden Cl. SE7 . . . . . . 5F 83
Harden Ho. SE5 . . . . . . 5A 92
Harden's Manorway
  SE7 . . . . 4F 83
    (not continuous)
Harders Rd. SE15 . . . . 5D 93
Hardess St. SE24 . . . . 1E 105
Harding Cl. SE17 . . . . . 2E 91
Hardinge La. E1 . . . . . . 5E 65
    (not continuous)
Hardinge Rd. NW10 . . . 5D 43
Harding Ho. SW13 . . . . 2D 85
    (off Wyatt Dr.)
Hardington NW1 . . . . . 4C 46
    (off Belmont St.)
Hardman Rd. SE7 . . . . 1D 97
Hardwicke M. WC1 . . . . 2A 8
Hardwick Ho. NW8 . . . . 3A 60
    (off Lilestone St.)
Hardwick St.
  EC1 . . . . 2C 62 (2C 8)
Hardwicks Way SW18 . 3C 100
Hardwidge St.
  SE1 . . . . 3A 78 (3D 27)
Hardy Av. E16 . . . . 2C 82
Hardy Cl. SE16 . . . . . . 3F 79
Hardy Cotts. SE10 . . . . 2F 95
Hardy Ho. SW4 . . . . . 5E 103
Hardy Rd. SE3 . . . . 3B 96

Hare & Billet Rd. SE3 . . 4F 95
Hare Ct. EC4 . . . 5C 62 (3R 16)
Harecourt Rd. N1 . . . . . 3E 49
Haredale Rd. SE24 . . . 2E 105
Haredon Cl. SE23 . . . . 5F 107
Harefield M. SE4 . . . . 1B 108
Harefield Rd. SE4 . . . . 1B 108
Hare Marsh E2 . . . . 3C 64
Hare Pl. EC4 . . . . 3C 16
    (off Old Mitre Ct.)
Hare Row E2 . . . . 1D 65
Hare Wlk. N1 . . . . 1A 64
    (not continuous)
Harewood Av. NW1 . . . 3A 60
Harewood Pl.
  W1 . . . . 5D 61 (3E 13)
Harewood Row NW1 . . 4A 60
Harfield Gdns. SE5 . . 1A 106
Harfleur Ct. SE11 . . . . 5D 77
    (off Opal St.)
Harford Ho. SE5 . . . . . 2E 91
    (off Bethwin Rd.)
  W11 . . . . 4B 58
Harford St. E1 . . . . 3A 66
Hargood Rd. SE3 . . . . . 4E 97
Hargrave Mans. N19 . . 4F 33
Hargrave Pk. N19 . . . . 4E 33
Hargrave Pl. NW5 . . . . 2F 47
Hargrave Rd. N19 . . . . 4E 33
Hargreaves Ho. W12 . . 1D 71
    (off White City Est.)
Hargwyne St. SW9 . . . 1B 104
Haringey Pk. N8 . . . . . 1A 34
Harkness Ho. E1 . . . . . 5C 64
    (off Christian St.)
Harland Rd. SE12 . . . 1C 124
Harlequin Ct. NW10 . . 3A 42
    (off Mitchellbrook Way)
Harlescott Rd. SE15 . . 2F 107
HARLESDEN 1B 56
Harlesden Gdns. NW10 . 5B 42
Harlesden La. NW10 . . 5C 42
Harlesden Plaza NW10 . 1B 56
Harlesden Rd. NW10 . . 5C 42
Harleston Cl. E5 . . . . . 4E 37
Harley Ct. E11 . . . . . . 2C 40
Harleyford Ct. SE11 . . 2B 90
    (off Harleyford Rd.)
Harleyford Rd. SE11 . . 2B 90
Harleyford St. SE11 . . 2C 90
Harley Gdns. SW10 . . 1E 87
Harley Gro. E3 . . . . . . 2B 66
Harley Ho. E11 . . . . . . 2F 39
  NW1 . . . . 4C 4
Harley Pl. W1 . . 4D 61 (1D 13)
Harley Rd. NW3 . . . . . 4F 45
  NW10 . . . . 1A 56
Harley St. W1 . . 3D 61 (4D 5)
Harley Vs. NW10 . . . . 1A 56
Harling Ct. SW11 . . . . 5B 88
Harlinger St. SE18 . . . 4F 83
Harlowe Cl. E8 . . . . . . 5C 50
Harlow Ho. E8 . . . . . . 5B 50
    (off Clarissa St.)
Harlynwood SE5 . . . . . 3E 91
    (off Wyndham Rd.)
Harman Cl. NW2 . . . . . 5A 30
  SE1 . . . . 1C 92
Harman Dr. NW2 . . . . . 5A 30

Harmon Ho. SE8 . . . . . 5B 80
Harmont Ho. W1 . . . . . 1D 13
    (off Harley St.)
Harmony Cl. NW11 . . . 1A 30
Harmood Gro. NW1 . . . 4D 47
Harmood Ho. NW1 . . . 4D 47
    (off Harmood St.)
Harmood Pl. NW1 . . . . 4D 47
Harmood St. NW1 . . . . 3D 47
Harmsworth M. SE1 . . 4C 76
Harmsworth St. SE17 . 1D 91
Harold Ct. SE16 . . . . . 3F 79
    (off Christopher Cl.)
Harold Est. SE1 . . . . . 4A 78
Harold Gibbons Ct. SE7 . 2E 97
Harold Ho. E2 . . . . 1F 65
    (off Mace St.)
Harold Laski Ho. EC1 . . 2E 9
    (off Percival St.)
Harold Maddison Ho.
  SE17 . . . . 1D 91
    (off Penton Pl.)
Harold Pl. SE11 . . . . . 1C 90
Harold Rd. E11 . . . . . . 3A 40
  E13 . . . . 5D 55
  NW10 . . . . 2A 56
Haroldstone Rd. E17 . . 1F 37
Harold Wilson Ho.
  SW6 . . . . 2B 86
    (off Clem Attlee Ct.)
Harp All. EC4 . . 5D 63 (2D 17)
Harp Bus. Cen. NW2 . . 3C 28
    (off Apsley Way)
Harpenden Rd. E12 . . 4E 41
  SE27 . . . . 3D 119
Harpenmead Point
  NW2 . . . . 4B 30
Harper Ho. SW9 . . . . . 1D 105
Harper M. SW17 . . . . 3E 115
Harper Rd. SE1 . . 4E 77 (5A 26)
Harp Island Cl. NW10 . 4A 28
Harp La. EC3 . . 1A 78 (5D 19)
Harpley Sq. E1 . . . . . . 3E 65
Harpsden St. SW11 . . 4C 88
Harpur M. WC1 . . 4B 62 (5F 7)
Harpur St. WC1 . . 4B 62 (5F 7)
Harraden Rd. SE3 . . . . 4E 97
Harrier Av. E11 . . . . . 1D 41
Harriet Cl. E8 . . . . 5C 50
Harriet Ho. SW6 . . . . . 3D 87
    (off Wandon Rd.)
Harriet St.
  SW1 . . . . 3B 74 (4A 20)
Harriet Tubman Cl.
  SW2 . . . . 5B 104
Harriet Wlk.
  SW1 . . . . 3B 74 (4A 20)
HARRINGAY 1D 35
Harrington Cl. W10 . . . 2B 58
Harrington Gdns. SW7 . 5D 73
Harrington Hill E5 . . . 3D 37
Harrington Ho. NW1 . . 1F 5
    (off Harrington St.)
Harrington Rd. E11 . . . 3A 40
  SW7 . . . . 5F 73
Harrington Sq. NW1 . . 1E 61
Harrington St.
  NW1 . . . . 1E 61 (1F 5)
    (not continuous)
Harrington Way SE18 . . 4F 83

Haverstock Pl. N1. . . . . . . 1E *9*
(off Haverstock St.)
Haverstock St.
NW5 . . . . 2C **46**
Haverstock St.
N1 . . . . . . 1D **63** (1E *9*)
Havil St. SE5 . . . . 3A **92**
Havisham Ho. SE16 . . . 3C **78**
Hawarden Gro. SE24 . . 5E **105**
Hawarden Hill NW2 . . . 5C **28**
Hawbridge Rd. E11. . . . . 3F **39**
Hawes St. N1 . . . . 4D **49**
Hawgood St. E3 . . . . . . 4C **66**
Hawke Ho. E1. . . . . 3F **65**
(off Ernest St.)
Hawke Pl. SE16 . . . . . . 3F **79**
Hawke Rd. SE19. . . . . 5F **119**
Hawkesbury Rd. SW15. . 3D **99**
Hawkesfield Rd. SE23. . 2A **122**
Hawke Twr. SE14 . . . . . 2A **94**
Hawkins Ho. SE8 . . . . . 2C **94**
(off New King St.)
SW1 . . . . 2E **89**
(off Dolphin Sq.)
Hawkins Way SE6. . . . . 5C **122**
Hawkley Gdns. SE27 . . 2D **119**
Hawkshaw Cl. SW2 . . . 5A **104**
Hawkshead NW1. . . . . . . 1F **5**
Hawkshead Rd. NW10. . 4B **42**
W4 . . . . 3A **70**
Hawkslade Rd. SE15 . . 3F **107**
Hawksley Rd. N16 . . . . 5A **36**
Hawks M. SE10 . . . . . . 3E **95**
Hawksmoor Cl. E6 . . . . 5F **69**
Hawksmoor Ho. E14. . . . 4A **66**
(off Aston St.)
Hawksmoor M. E1 . . . . . 1D **79**
Hawksmoor Pl. E2 . . . 3C **64**
(off Cheshire St.)
Hawksmoor St. W6. . . . 2F **85**
Hawkstone Rd. SE16 . . 5E **79**
Hawkwell Wlk. N1 . . . . . 5E **49**
(off Maldon Cl.)
Hawkwood Mt. E5 . . . . 3D **37**
Hawley Cres. NW1 . . . . 4D **47**
Hawley M. NW1 . . . . . . 4D **47**
Hawley Rd. NW1 . . . . . 4D **47**
(not continuous)
Hawley St. NW1 . . . . . . 4D **47**
Hawstead Rd. SE6 . . . 4D **109**
Hawthorn Av. E3 . . . . . 5B **52**
Hawthorn Cres. SW17. . 5C **116**
Hawthorne Cl. N1. . . . . 3A **50**
Hawthorne Ho. SW1. . . 1E *89*
(off Churchill Gdns.)
Hawthorn Rd. NW10 . . . 4C **42**
Hawthorn Wlk. W10 . . . 3A **58**
Hawtrey Rd. NW3. . . . . 4A **46**
Hay Cl. E15. . . . . 4A **54**
Haycroft Gdns. NW10. . 5C **42**
Haycroft Rd. SW2. . . . 3A **104**
Hay Currie St. E14 . . . . 5D **67**
Hayday Rd. E16 . . . . . . 4C **68**
(not continuous)
Hayden's Pl. W11. . . . . 5B **58**
Haydon Pk. Rd.
SW19 . . . . 5C **114**
Haydons Rd. SW19 . . . 5D **115**
Haydon St. EC3. . 1B **78** (4F *19*)
Haydon Wlk. E1. . 5B **64** (3F *19*)
Haydon Way SW11. . . . 2F **101**

Hayes Ct. SE5. . . . . 3E **91**
(off Camberwell New Rd.)
Hayes Ct. SW2. . . . . . 1A **118**
Hayes Cres. NW11. . . . . 1B **30**
Hayes Gro. SE15 . . . . 1B **106**
Hayfield Pas. E1. . . . . . 3E **65**
Hayfield Yd. E1 . . . . . . 3E **65**
Haygarth Pl. SW19. . . . 5F **113**
Hay Hill W1 . . 1D **75** (5E *13*)
Hayles Bldgs. SE11 . . . 5D **77**
(off Elliotts Row)
Hayles St. SE11 . . . . . . 5D **77**
Hayling Cl. N16 . . . . . . 2A **50**
Haymans Point SE11 . . . 5B **76**
Hayman St. N1. . . . . . . 4D **49**
Haymarket
SW1 . . . . 1F **75** (5B *14*)
Haymarket Arc. SW1 . . . 5B *14*
Haymarket Theatre Royal
. . . . 5C *14*
(off Haymarket)
Haymerle Ho. SE15 . . . 2C **92**
(off Haymerle Rd.)
Haymerle Rd. SE15 . . . 2C **92**
Hayne Ho. W11 . . . . . . 2A *72*
(off Penzance Pl.)
Haynes Cl. SE3 . . . . . 1A **110**
Hayne St. EC1. . 4D **63** (5E *9*)
Hay's Galleria
SE1 . . . . . 2A **78** (1D *27*)
Hays La. SE1 . . 2A **78** (1D *27*)
Hay's M. W1. . . 2D **75** (1D *21*)
Hay St. E2 . . . . 5C **50**
Hayter Ct. E11 . . . . 4D **41**
Hayter Rd. SW2. . . . . 3A **104**
Hayton Cl. E8 . . . . 3B **50**
Hayward Ct. SW9. . . . . 5A **90**
(off Clapham Rd.)
Hayward Gdns. SW15 . . 4E **99**
Hayward's Pl.
EC1. . . . . . . 3D **63** (3D *9*)
Haywards Yd. SE4 . . . 3B **108**
(off Lindal Rd.)
Hazelbank Rd. SE6. . . 2F **123**
Hazelbourne Rd.
SW12 . . . . 4D **103**
Hazel Cl. N19. . . . . 4E **33**
SE15. . . . . 5C **92**
Hazeldean Rd. NW10. . . 4A **42**
Hazeldon Rd. SE4 . . . 3A **108**
Hazel Gro. SE26 . . . . . 4F **121**
Hazelhurst Ct. SE6. . . 5E **123**
(off Beckenham Hill Rd.)
Hazelhurst Rd. SW17. . 4E **115**
Hazellville Rd. N19 . . . 2F **33**
Hazelmere Ct. SW2. . . 1B **118**
Hazelmere Rd. NW6 . . . 5B **44**
Hazel Rd. E15 . . . . 2A **54**
NW10 . . . . 2D **57**
(not continuous)
Hazel Way SE1. . . . . . . 5B **78**
Hazelwood Cl. W5 . . . . 5A **28**
Hazelwood Ho. SE8 . . . 5A **80**
Hazelwood Rd. E17 . . . 1A **38**
Hazelwell Rd. SW15 . . . 3E **99**
Hazelwood Cl. E5. . . . . 5A **38**
Hazelwood Cres. W10 . . 3A **58**

Hazlewood Twr. W10 . . . 3A **58**
(off Golborne Gdns.)
Hazlitt M. W14. . . . . 4A **72**
Hazlitt Rd. W14 . . . . 4A **72**
Headbourne Ho.
SE1. . . . . 4F **77** (5C *26*)
Headcorn Rd.
BR1: Brom 5B **124**
Headfort Pl.
SW1 . . . . . . 3C **74** (4C *20*)
Headington Rd. SW18. . 2E **115**
Headlam Rd. SW4 . . . . 4F **103**
(not continuous)
Headlam St. E1. . . . . . . 3D **65**
Headley Cl. SE26 . . . . . 5E **121**
Head's M. W11 . . . . 5C **58**
Head St. E1. . . . . 5F **65**
(not continuous)
Heald St. SE14 . . . . . . 4C **94**
Healey Ho. SW9. . . . . . 3C **90**
Healey St. NW1 . . . . . . 3D **47**
Hearn's Bldgs. SE17. . . 5F **77**
Hearnshaw Ho. E14 . . . 4A **66**
(off Halley St.)
Hearn St. EC2 . . 3A **64** (4E *11*)
Hearnville Rd. SW12. . 1C **116**
Heath Brow NW3 . . . . . 5E **31**
Heath Cl. NW11. . . . . . 2D **31**
Heathcock Ct. WC2 . . . 5E *15*
(off Exchange Ct.)
Heathcote St.
WC1. . . . . . . 3B **62** (3F *7*)
Heathcroft NW11 . . . . . 3D **31**
Heath Dr. NW3. . . . . . . 1D **45**
Heathedge SE26 . . . . . 2D **121**
Heather Cl. N7. . . . . . . 5B **34**
SE13 . . . . 5F **109**
SW8 . . . . 1D **103**
Heather Gdns. NW11. . . 1A **30**
Heather Ho. E14. . . . . . 5E **67**
(off Dee St.)
Heatherley Ct. E5 . . . . 5C **36**
Heather Rd. NW2. . . . . 4B **28**
SE12 . . . . 2C **124**
Heather Wlk. W10 . . . . 3A **58**
Heatherwood Cl. E12 . . 4E **41**
Heathfield Av. SW18 . . 5F **101**
Heathfield Cl. E16 . . . . 4F **69**
Heathfield Gdns. NW11 . 1F **29**
SE3 . . . . 5A *96*
(off Baizdon Rd.)
SW18 . . . . 4F **101**
Heathfield Ho. SE3 . . . 5A **96**
Heathfield Pk. NW2 . . . 3E **43**
Heathfield Rd. SW18 . . 4E **101**
Heathfield Sq. SW18 . . 5F **101**
Heathfield St. W11 . . . . 1A *72*
(off Portland Rd.)
Heathgate NW11 . . . . . 1D **31**
Heathgate Pl. NW3 . . . 2B **46**
Heath Hurst Rd. NW3 . . 1A **46**
Heathland Rd. N16 . . . 3A **36**
Heath La. SE3. . . . . . . 5F **95**
(not continuous)
Heathlee Rd. SE3. . . . . 2B **110**
Heathmans Rd. SW6. . . 4B **86**
Heath Mead SW19 . . . 3F **113**
Heath Pas. NW3 . . . . . 4D **31**
Heathpool Ct. E1 . . . . . 3D **65**
Heath Ri. SW15 . . . . . . 4F **99**

Herbert Ho. *E1* 2F **19**
(off Old Castle St.)
Herbert M. SW2 . . . . . .4C **104**
Herbert Morrison Ho.
SW6 . . . . .2B **86**
(off Clem Attlee Ct.)
Herbert Rd. E12 . . . . . .1F **55**
E17 . . . . .2B **38**
NW9 . . . . .1C **28**
Herbert St. E13. . . . . .1C **68**
NW5 . . . . .3C **46**
Herbrand Est.
WC1. . . . . . . .3A **62** (3D **7**)
Herbrand St. WC1 . .3A **62** (3D **7**)
Hercules Ct. SE14 . . . . .2A **94**
Hercules PI. N7 . . . . . . .5A **34**
(not continuous)
Hercules Rd.
SE1 . . . . .4B **76** (5A **24**)
Hercules St. N7 . . . . . .5A **34**
Hercules Wharf *E14* . . .1A **82**
(off Orchard PI.)
Hercules Yd. N7 . . . . . .5A **34**
Hereford Bldgs. SW3 . . .2F **87**
(off Old Church St.)
Hereford Gdns. SE13 . .3A **110**
Hereford Ho. *NW6* 1C **58**
(off Carlton Va.)
SW3 . . . . .4A **74**
(off Old Brompton Rd.)
SW10 . . . . .3D **87**
(off Fulham Rd.)
Hereford M. W2 . . . . . .5C **58**
Hereford PI. SE14 . . . . .3B **94**
Hereford Retreat SE15 . .3C **92**
Hereford Rd. E11. . . . . .1D **41**
W2 . . . . .5C **58**
Hereford Sq. SW7 . . . . .5E **73**
Hereford St. E2 . . . . . . .3C **64**
Hereward Rd. SW17 . . .4B **116**
Heritage CI. SW9 . . . .1D **105**
Heritage Ct. *SE8*. 1F **93**
(off Trundley's Rd.)
Herlwyn Gdns. SW17. .4B **116**
Her Majesty's Theatre . . *1B* **22**
(off Haymarket)
Hermes CI. W9. . . . . . . .3C **58**
Hermes Ct. *SW9*. 4C **90**
(off Southey Rd.)
Hermes St. N1. . . .1C **62** (1B **8**)
Herm Ho. N1. . . . . .3E **49**
Hermiston Av. N8 . . . . .1A **34**
Hermitage Ct. *E1* 2C **78**
(off Knighten St.)
NW2 . . . . .5C **30**
Hermitage Gdns. NW2 . .5C **30**
Hermitage La. NW2 . . . .5C **30**
Hermitage Rd. N4 . . . . .2D **35**
SE19 . . . . .5F **119**
Hermitage Rooms *4A* **16**
(off Victoria Emb.)
Hermitage Row E8 . . . . .2C **50**
Hermitage St. W2. . . . . .4F **59**
Hermitage, The SE13 . . .5E **95**
SE23 . . . . .1E **121**
SW13 . . . . .4B **84**
Hermitage Wall E1. . . . .2C **78**
Hermitage Waterside
E1 . . . . .2C **78**
(off Thomas More St.)

Hermit PI. NW6 . . . . . .5D **45**
Hermit Rd. E16 . . . . . . .4B **68**
Hermit St. EC1 . . .2D **63** (1D **9**)
Herndon Rd. SW18 . . .3E **101**
Herne CI. NW10. . . . . . .2A **42**
HERNE HILL. **3E 105**
Herne Hill SE24 . . . . . .4E **105**
Herne Hill Ho. *SE24* . .4D **105**
(off Railton Rd.)
Herne Hill Rd. SE24. . .1E **105**
Herne Hill Stadium . . .**4F 105**
Herne PI. SE24 . . . . . .3D **105**
Heron CI. NW10. . . . . . .3A **42**
Heron Ct. *E14*. 4E **81**
(off New Union CI.)
Herondale Av. SW18 . .1F **115**
Heron Dr. N4 . . . . .4E **35**
Herongate Rd. E12. . . . .4E **41**
Heron Ho. E6 . . . . .4F **55**
NW8 . . . . .1A **60**
(off Barrow Hill Est.)
SW11 . . . . .3A **88**
(off Searles CI.)
Heron Ind. Est. E15 . . . .1D **67**
Heron PI. SE16. . . . . . . .2A **80**
W1 . . . . .2C **12**
(off Thayer St.)
Heron Quay E14 . . . . . .2C **80**
Heron Rd. SE24 . . . . . .2E **105**
Heron's Lea N6 . . . . . . .1B **32**
Herons, The E11 . . . . . .1B **40**
Herrick Ho. *SE5* 3F **91**
(off Elmington Est.)
Herrick Rd. N5 . . . . . . .5E **35**
Herrick St. SW1 . . . . . . .5F **75**
Herries St. W10 . . . . . . .1A **58**
Herringham Rd. SE7 . . .4E **83**
Hersant CI. NW10 . . . . .5C **42**
Herschell M. SE5 . . . . .1E **105**
Herschell Rd. SE23 . . .5A **108**
Hersham CI. SW15 . . . .5C **98**
Hertford Av. SW14 . . . . .3A **98**
Hertford PI. W1. . .3E **61** (4A **6**)
Hertford Rd. N1 . . . . . . .5A **50**
(not continuous)
Hertford St. W1. . .2D **75** (2D **21**)
Hertslet Rd. N7 . . . . . . .5B **34**
Hertsmere Rd. *E14* 1C **80**
(off Hertsmere Rd.)
Hertsmere Rd. E14 . . . .2C **80**
Hervey Rd. SE3 . . . . . . .4D **97**
Hesewall CI. SW4 . . . . .5E **89**
Hesketh PI. W11 . . . . . .1A **72**
Hesketh Rd. E7 . . . . . . .5C **40**
Heslop Rd. SW12. . . . .1B **116**
Hesper M. SW5 . . . . . . .5D **73**
Hesperus Ct. E14 . . . . . .5D **81**
Hesperus Cres. E14 . . . .5D **81**
Hessel St. E1 . . . . .5D **65**
Hestercombe Av. SW6 . .5A **86**
Hester Rd. SW11 . . . . . .3A **88**
Heston Ho. SE8 . . . . . . .4C **94**
Heston St. SE14. . . . . . .4C **94**
Hetherington Rd.
SW4 . . . . .2A **104**
Hethpool Ho. *W2* 3F **59**
(off Hall PI.)
Hetley Rd. W12 . . . . . . .2D **71**
Hevelius CI. SE10 . . . . .1B **96**

Hever Ho. *SE15* 2F **93**
(off Lovelinch CI.)
Heversham Ho. SE15. . .2E **93**
Hewer St. W10 . . . . . . .4F **57**
Hewett St. EC2. .3A **64** (4E **11**)
Hewison St. E3. . . . . . . .1B **66**
Hewlett Rd. N8 . . . . . . .1C **34**
Hewlett Ho. *SW8* 3D **89**
(off Havelock Ter.)
Hewlett Rd. E3 . . . . .1A **66**
Hexagon, The N6 . . . . . .3B **32**
Hexal Rd. SE6 . . . . . . .3A **124**
Hexham Rd. SE27 . . . . .2E **119**
Heybridge *NW1* 3D **47**
(off Lewis St.)
Heybridge Av. SW16 . . .5B **118**
Heybridge Way E10 . . . .2A **38**
Heydon Ho. *SE14* 4E **93**
(off Kender St.)
Heyford Av. SW8 . . . . . .3A **90**
Heyford Ter. SW8 . . . . . .3A **90**
Heygate St. SE17 . . . . . .5E **77**
Heylyn Sq. E3 . . . . .2B **66**
Heysham La. NW3. . . . . .5D **31**
Heysham Rd. N15 . . . . .1F **35**
Heythorp St. SW18 . . . .1B **114**
Heythrop College
(University of London)
. . . .*4D* **73**
(off Kensington Sq.)
Heywood Ho. *SE14*. 2F **93**
(off Myers La.)
Heyworth Rd. E5 . . . . . .1D **51**
E15. . . . . .2B **54**
Hibbert Ho. *E14* 4C **80**
(off Tiller Rd.)
Hibbert Rd. E17 . . . . . . .2B **38**
Hibbert St. SW11 . . . . .1F **101**
Hichisson Rd. SE15 . . .3E **107**
Hickes Ho. NW6 . . . . . .4F **45**
Hickin CI. SE7 . . . . .5F **83**
Hickin St. E14 . . . . .4E **81**
Hickleton *NW1* 5E **47**
(off Camden St.)
Hickling Ho. *SE16* 4D **79**
(off Slippers PI.)
Hickman CI. E16. . . . . . .4F **69**
Hickmore Wlk. SW4 . . .1F **103**
Hicks CI. SW11 . . . . . .1A **102**
Hicks St. SE8 . . . . .1A **94**
Hide PI. SW1 . . . . .5F **75**
Hider Ct. SE3 . . . . .3E **97**
Hides St. N7 . . . . .3B **48**
Hide Twr. *SW1* 5F **75**
(off Regency St.)
Higgins Ho. *N1*. 5A **50**
(off Colville St.)
Higginson Ho. *NW3* 4B **46**
(off Fellows Rd.)
Higgs Ind. Est. SE24 . .1D **105**
Highbank Way N8 . . . . .1C **34**
High Bri. SE10 . . . . .1F **95**
Highbridge Ct. *SE14*. . . .3E **93**
(off Farrow La.)
High Bri. Wharf *SE10*. . .1F **95**
(off High Bri.)
Highbrook Rd. SE3. . . .1F **111**
HIGHBURY **1D 49**
Highbury **5D 35**
Highbury Barn N5. . . . .1E **49**

Hollybush Pl. E2 . . . . . . 2D 65
Hollybush Steps NW3. . . 1E 45
 (off Holly Mt.)
Hollybush St. E13 . . . . . 2D 69
Holly Bush Va. NW3. . . . 1E 45
Hollybush Wlk. SW9 . . . 2D 105
Holly Cl. NW10. . . . . 4A 42
Hollycroft Av. NW3 . . . . 5C 30
Hollydale Rd. SE15 . . . . 4E 93
Holly Dene SE15 . . . . . . 4D 93
Hollydown Way E11 . . . . 5F 39
Holly Gro. SE15 . . . . 5B 92
Holly Hedge Ter. SE13. . 3F 109
Holly Hill NW3 . . . . 1E 45
Holly Ho. W10 . . . . 3A 58
 (off Hawthorn Wlk.)
Holly Lodge Gdns. N6 . . 4C 32
Holly Lodge Mans. N6 . . 4C 32
Holly M. SW10 . . . . 1E 87
 (off Drayton Gdns.)
Holly Mt. NW3 . . . . 1E 45
Hollymount Cl. SE10 . . . 4E 95
Holly Pk. N4 . . . . 2A 34
 (not continuous)
Holly Pk. Est. N4 . . . . . . 2B 34
Holly Pl. NW3. . . . . 1E 45
 (off Holly Berry La.)
Holly Rd. E11 . . . . 2B 40
 W4 . . . . 5A 70
Holly St. E8 . . . . 4B 50
Holly Ter. N6. . . . . 3C 32
Holly Tree Cl. SW19 . . . 1F 113
Holly Tree Ho. SE4. . . . 1B 108
 (off Brockley Rd.)
Holly Vw. Cl. NW4 . . . . . 1C 28
Holly Village N6 . . . . 4D 33
Holly Wlk. NW3 . . . . 1E 45
Hollywood M. SW10. . . . 2E 87
Hollywood Rd. SW10 . . . 2E 87
Holman Ho. E2 . . . . 2F 65
 (off Roman Rd.)
Holman Hunt Ho. W6. . . 1A 86
 (off Field Rd.)
Holman Rd. SW11 . . . . . 5F 87
Holmbrook NW1 . . . . 1E 61
 (off Eversholt St.)
Holmbury Ct. SW17 . . . 3B 116
Holmbury Ho. SE24 . . . 3D 105
Holmbury Vw. E5 . . . . . . 3D 37
Holmbush Rd. SW15 . . . 4A 100
Holmcote Gdns. N5 . . . . 2E 49
Holm Ct. SE12 . . . . 3D 125
Holmdale Gdns. NW4. . . 1F 29
Holmdale Rd. NW6 . . . . 2C 44
Holmdale Ter. N15. . . . . 2A 36
Holmdene Av. SE24 . . . 3E 105
Holmead Rd. SW6 . . . . . 3D 87
Holme Lacey Rd.
 SE12. . . . . 4B 110
Holmesdale Ho. NW6 . . 5C 44
 (off Kilburn Va.)
Holmesdale Rd. N6 . . . . 2D 33
Holmesley Rd. SE23 . . . 4A 108
Holmes Pl. SW10 . . . . . . 2E 87
Holmes Rd. NW5 . . . . . . 2D 47
Holmes Ter. SE1. . . . . . . 3B 24
Holmewood Gdns.
 SW2 . . . . 5B 104
Holmewood Rd. SW2. . . 5A 104
Holmfield Ct. NW3 . . . . . 2A 46

Holmleigh Rd. N16 . . . . 3A 36
Holmleigh Rd. Est. N16. . 3A 36
Holmoak Cl. SW15. . . . . 4B 100
Holm Oak M. SW4 . . . . . 3A 104
Holmsdale Ho. E14 . . . . 1D 81
 (off Poplar High St.)
Holmshaw Cl. SE26 . . . 4A 122
Holmside Rd. SW12 . . . 4C 102
Holmsley Ho. SW15. . . . 5B 98
 (off Tangley Gro.)
Holm Wlk. SE3 . . . . 5C 96
Holmwood Vs. SE7 . . . . 1C 96
Holne Chase N2 . . . . . . 1E 31
Holness Rd. E15 . . . . . . 3B 54
Holroyd Rd. SW15 . . . . . 2E 99
Holst Ct. SE1 . . . . 5B 24
 (off Westminster Bri. Rd.)
Holst Mans. SW13 . . . . . 2E 85
Holsworthy Sq. WC1 . . . 4A 8
Holt Ct. E15 . . . . 2E 53
Holt Ho. SW2. . . . . 4C 104
Holton St. E1 . . . . 3F 65
Holwood Pl. SW4 . . . . . . 2F 103
Holybourne Av. SW15 . . 5C 98
Holyhead Cl. E3 . . . . 2C 66
Holyoake Ct. SE16 . . . . 3B 80
Holyoak Rd. SE11 . . . . . 5D 77
Holyport Rd. SW6 . . . . . 3F 85
Holyrood M. E16 . . . . . . 2C 82
 (off Badminton M.)
Holyrood St.
 SE1 . . . . 2A 78 (2D 27)
Holywell Cen. 3D 11
 (off New Nth. Pl.)
Holywell Cl. SE3 . . . . . . 2C 96
 SE16. . . . . 1D 93
Holywell La.
 EC2 . . . . 3A 64 (3E 11)
Holywell Row
 EC2 . . . . 3A 64 (4D 11)
Homecroft Rd. SE26. . . 5E 121
Homefield Cl. SW16 . . . 3A 118
Homefield Ho. SE23 . . . 3F 121
Homefield Rd. SW19 . . . 5F 113
 W4 . . . . 5B 70
Homefield St.
 N1 . . . . 1A 64 (1D 11)
Homeleigh Rd. SE15 . . 3F 107
Home Pk. Rd. SW19 . . . 4B 114
Homer Dr. E14 . . . . 5C 80
Home Rd. SW11 . . . . 5A 88
Homer Rd. E9. . . . . 3A 52
Homer Row W1 . . . . 4A 60
Homer St. W1 . . . . 4A 60
HOMERTON 2F 51
Homerton Gro. E9 . . . . . 2F 51
Homerton High St. E9 . . 2F 51
Homerton Rd. E9 . . . . . . 2A 52
Homerton Row E9 . . . . . 2E 51
Homerton Ter. E9. . . . . . 3E 51
 (not continuous)
Homesdale Cl. E11 . . . . 1C 40
Homestall Rd. SE22. . . . 3E 107
Homestead Pk. NW2 . . . 5B 28
Homestead Rd. SW6 . . . 3B 86
Homewoods SW12. . . . . 5E 103
Homildon Ho. SE26 . . . . 3C 120
Honduras St. EC1. . . . . 3E 63 (3F 9)
Honeybourne Rd. NW6 . . 2D 45
Honeybrook Rd. SW12. . 5E 103

Honey La. EC2 . . . . 3A 18
Honeyman Cl. NW6 . . . . 4F 43
 (not continuous)
Honeywell Rd. SW11. . . 4B 102
Honeywood Rd. NW10. . 1B 56
Honiton Gdns. SE15. . . . 5E 93
 (off Gibbon Rd.)
Honiton Rd. NW6 . . . . . . 1B 58
Honley Rd. SE6 . . . . 5D 109
HONOR OAK 4E 107
Honor Oak Crematorium
 SE23 . . . . 3A 108
HONOR OAK PARK . . . 5A 108
Honor Oak Pk. SE23. . . 4E 107
Honor Oak Ri. SE23. . . . 4E 107
Honor Oak Rd. SE23 . . . 1E 121
Hood Cl. EC4 . . . . 3C 16
Hood Ho. SE5. . . . . 3F 91
 (off Elmington Est.)
 SW1 . . . . 1F 89
 (off Dolphin Sq.)
Hooke Ho. E3 . . . . 1A 66
 (off Gernon Rd.)
Hookham Ct. SW8 . . . . . 4F 89
Hooks Cl. SE15 . . . . 4D 93
Hooper Rd. E16 . . . . 5C 68
Hooper's Ct.
 SW3. . . . . 3B 74 (4A 20)
Hooper Sq. E1 . . . . 5C 64
 (off Hooper St.)
Hooper St. E1 . . . . 5C 64
Hoop La. NW11 . . . . 2B 30
 (not continuous)
Hope Cl. N1 . . . . 3E 49
 SE12. . . . . 3D 125
Hope Ct. NW10. . . . . 2F 57
 (off Chamberlayne Rd.)
Hopedale Rd. SE7 . . . . . 2D 97
Hopefield Av. NW6 . . . . 1A 58
Hope St. SW11 . . . . 1F 101
Hopewell St. E1 . . . . 4B 64
Hopewell St. SE5 . . . . . 3F 91
Hopewell Yd. SE5. . . . . . 3F 91
 (off Hopewell St.)
Hope Wharf SE16. . . . . . 3E 79
Hop Gdns.
 WC2. . . . . 1A 76 (5D 15)
Hopgood St. W12 . . . . . 2E 71
Hopkins Ho. E14 . . . . . . 5C 66
 (off Canton St.)
Hopkins M. E15 . . . . 5B 54
Hopkinsons Pl. NW1 . . . 5C 46
Hopkins St.
 W1 . . . . 5E 61 (3A 14)
Hopping La. N1 . . . . 3D 49
Hop St. SE10 . . . . 5B 82
Hopton Rd. SW16 . . . . . 5A 118
Hopton's Gdns. SE1 . . . 1E 25
Hopton St.
 SE1 . . . . 2D 77 (1E 25)
Hopwood Cl. SW17 . . . 3E 115
Hopwood Rd. SE17 . . . . 2F 91
Hopwood Wlk. E8. . . . . . 4C 50
Horace Rd. E7 . . . . 1D 55
Horatio Cl. SE16. . . . . . . 2E 79
 (off Rotherhithe St.)
Horatio Ho. E2 . . . . 1B 64
 (off Horatio St.)
 W6. . . . . 1F 85
 (off Fulham Pal. Rd.)

Horatio Pl. *E14* 2E **81**
(off Preston's Rd.)
Horatio St. *E2* 1B **64**
Horbury Cres. W11. . . . . . 1C **72**
Horbury M. W11. . . . . 1B **72**
Horder Rd. SW6 . . . . 4A **86**
Hordle Prom. E. SE15 . . 3B **92**
Hordle Prom. Sth. *SE15* . .3B **92**
(off Quarley Way)
Horizon Bldg. *E14* 1C **80**
(off Hertsmere Rd.)
E14 . . . . .1C **80**
(off Hertsmere Rd.)
Horizon Way SE7 . . . . 5D **83**
Horle Wlk. SW9 . . . . 5D **91**
Horley Rd. SE9 . . . . 4F **125**
Hormead Rd. W9 . . . . 3B **58**
Hornbeam Cl. SE11 . . . .5C **76**
Hornblower Cl. SE16 . . . 4A **80**
Hornby Cl. NW3 . . . . 4F **45**
Hornby Ho. *SE11* 2C **90**
(off Clayton St.)
Horncastle Cl. SE12. . .5C **110**
Horncastle Rd. SE12 . 5C **110**
Horndean Cl. SW15 . . . 1C **112**
Horner Ho. *N1* 5A **50**
(off Whitmore Est.)
Horne Way SW15 . . . . . . 5E **85**
Hornfair Rd. SE7 . . . . 2E **97**
Horniman Dr. SE23 . . . . 1D **121**
Horniman Mus. **1D 121**
Horn La. SE10 . . . . 1C **96**
(not continuous)
Horn Link Way SE10. . . . .5C **82**
HORN PARK **3D 111**
Horn Pk. Cl. SE12 . . . . . 3D **111**
Hornpark La. SE12. . . 3D **111**
HORNSEY **1C 34**
Hornsey La. N6 . . . . 3D **33**
Hornsey La. Est. N19 . . . 2F **33**
Hornsey La. Gdns. N6 . .2E **33**
Hornsey Ri. N19 . . . . 2F **33**
Hornsey Ri. Gdns. N19. . 2F **33**
Hornsey Rd. N7 . . . . 3A **34**
N19. . . . . .3A **34**
Hornsey St. N7 . . . . 2B **48**
HORNSEY VALE **1B 34**
Hornshay St. SE15 . . . . . 2E **93**
Hornton Ct. *W8* 3C **72**
(off Kensington High St.)
Hornton Pl. W8 . . . . 3D **73**
Hornton St. W8 . . . . 3C **72**
Horsa Rd. SE12 . . . . 5E **111**
Horse & Dolphin Yd. W1 . .4C **14**
Horseferry Pl. SE10 . . . . 2E **95**
Horseferry Rd. E14. . . 1A **80**
SW1 . . . . . . 4F **75** (5B **22**)
Horseferry Rd. Est. SW1 . .5B **22**
Horseguards Av.
SW1. . . . . .2A **76** (2D **23**)
Horse Guards Parade
. . . . **2A 76 (2D 23)**
Horse Guards Rd.
SW1 . . . . 2F **75** (2C **22**)
Horsell Rd. N5 . . . . 2C **48**
(not continuous)
Horselydown La.
SE1. . . . . 3B **78** (3F **27**)
Horselydown Mans. SE1 . .3F **27**
(off Lafone St.)

Horsemongers M. SE1. . 4A **26**
Horse Ride SW1. . 2E **75** (2B **22**)
Horseshoe Cl. E14 . . . . . 1E **95**
NW2. . . . . .4D **29**
Horseshoe Wharf *SE1* . .1B **26**
(off Clink St.)
Horse Yd. *N1* 5D **49**
(off Essex Rd.)
Horsfeld Gdns. SE9 . . . . 3F **111**
Horsfeld Rd. SE9 . . . . . . 3F **111**
Horsfield Ho. *N1* 4E **49**
(off Northampton St.)
Horsford Rd. SW2 . . . . . 3B **104**
Horsley St. SE17 . . . . 2F **91**
Horsman Ho. *SE5*. 2E **91**
(off Bethwin Rd.)
Horsman St. SE5 . . . . 2E **91**
Horsmonden Rd. SE4. . 3B **108**
Hortensia Ho. *SW10* . . .3E **87**
(off Hortensia Rd.)
Hortensia Rd. SW10 . . 3E **87**
Horton Av. NW2 . . . . 1A **44**
Horton Ho. SE15. . . . . . . 2E **93**
SW8 . . . . .3B **90**
W6 . . . . .1A **86**
(off Field Rd.)
Horton Rd. E8 . . . . 3D **51**
Horton St. SE13 . . . . . . 1D **109**
Horwood Ho. *E2*. 2D **65**
(off Pott St.)
NW8 . . . . .3A **60**
(off Paveley St.)
Hosack Rd. SW17 . . . . . 2C **116**
Hoser Av. SE12 . . . . 2C **124**
Hosier La.
EC1 . . . . 4D **63** (1D **17**)
Hoskins Cl. E16 . . . . 5E **69**
Hoskins St. SE10 . . . . . . 1F **95**
Hospital Rd. E9 . . . . 2F **51**
Hospital Way SE13. . . .4F **109**
Hotham Rd. SW15 . . . . . 1E **99**
Hotham St. E15 . . . . 5A **54**
Hothfield Pl. SE16 . . . . . . 4E **79**
Hotspur St. SE11 . . . . . . 5C **76**
Houghton Cl. E8 . . . . 3B **50**
Houghton St.
WC2. . . . . 5B **62** (3A **16**)
(not continuous)
Houndsditch
EC3 . . . . .5A **64** (2E **19**)
Houseman Way SE5. . . . 3F **91**
Houses of Parliament
. . . . **4A 76 (5E 23)**
Houston Rd. SE23 . . . . . 2A **122**
Hove Av. E17 . . . . 1B **38**
Hoveden Rd. NW2 . . . . . 2A **44**
Hove St. *SE15* 3E **93**
(off Culmore Rd.)
Howard Cl. NW2 . . . . 1A **44**
Howard Ho. *E16*. 1D **83**
(off Wesley Av.)
SE8. . . . . .1B **94**
(off Evelyn St.)
SW1 . . . . .1E **89**
(off Dolphin Sq.)
SW9. . . . . .1D **105**
(off Barrington Rd.)
Howard Ho. W1 . . . . .4E **5**
(off Cleveland St.)
Howard M. N5 . . . . 1D **49**

Howard Rd. E11 . . . . 5A **40**
N15. . . . . .1A **36**
N16. . . . . .1F **49**
NW2. . . . . .1F **43**
Howard's La. SW15 . . . . 2D **99**
Howards Rd. E13 . . . . . . 2C **68**
Howarth Ct. *E15* 2E **53**
(off Clays La.)
Howbury Rd. SE15. . . 1E **107**
Howden St. SE15 . . . . . 1C **106**
Howell Cl. E10 . . . . 2D **39**
Howell Wlk. SE17 . . . . . . 5D **77**
Howick Pl.
SW1. . . . . . . 4E **75** (5A **22**)
Howie St. SW11 . . . . 3A **88**
Howitt Cl. N16 . . . . 1A **50**
NW3 . . . . .3A **46**
Howitt Rd. NW3 . . . . 3A **46**
Howland Est. SE16 . . . . . 4E **79**
Howland Ho. SW16 . . . 3A **118**
Howland M. E.
W1 . . . . 4E **61** (5A **6**)
Howland St. W1. . 4E **61** (5F **5**)
Howland Way SE16 . . . 3A **80**
Howlett's Rd. SE24 . . . . 4E **105**
Howley Pl. W2 . . . . 4E **59**
Howsman Rd. SW13 . . . 2C **84**
Howson Rd. SE4 . . . . . . 2A **108**
How's St. E2 . . . . 1B **64**
HOXTON **1A 64**
Hoxton Hall Theatre . . **1A 64**
(off Hoxton Rd.)
Hoxton Mkt. N1 . . . . 2D **11**
Hoxton Sq. N1. . 2A **64** (2D **11**)
Hoxton St. N1 . . 5A **50** (2E **11**)
Hoylake Rd. W3. . . . . 5A **56**
Hoyland Cl. SE15. . . . . . 3D **93**
Hoyle Rd. SW17. . . . . . . 5A **116**
Hoy St. E16 . . . . 5B **68**
Hubbard Rd. SE27 . . . . . 4E **119**
Hubbard St. E15. . . . . . . 5A **54**
Huberd Ho. *SE1* 5C **26**
(off Manciple St.)
Hubert Gro. SW9 . . . . . . 1A **104**
Hubert Ho. *NW8*. 3A **60**
(off Ashbridge St.)
Hubert Rd. E6. . . . . 2F **69**
Hucknall Ct. *NW8* 3F **59**
(off Cunningham Pl.)
Huddart St. E3 . . . . 4B **66**
(not continuous)
Huddleston Cl. E2 . . . . . 1E **65**
Huddlestone Rd. E7. . . . 1B **54**
NW2 . . . . .3D **43**
Huddleston Rd. N7. . . . . 5E **33**
Hudson Cl. W12. . . . . . . 1D **71**
Hudson Ct. *E14* 1C **94**
(off Maritime Quay)
Hudson's Pl. *SW1* 5D **75**
(off Bridge Pl.)
Huggin Ct. EC4 . . . . 4F **17**
Huggin Hill
EC4 . . . . .1E **77** (4A **18**)
Huggins Pl. SW2 . . . . . . 1B **118**
Hughan Rd. E15 . . . . 2F **53**
Hugh Astor Ct. *SE1*. . . .5E **25**
(off Keyworth St.)
Hugh Dalton Av. SW6 . . .2B **86**
Hughenden Ho. *NW8* . . .3A **60**
(off Jerome Cres.)

Ifor Evans Pl. E1 . . . . 3F 65
Ightham Ho. SE17 . . . . . . 5A 78
(off Comus Pl.)
Ilbert St. W10 . . . . 2F 57
Ilchester Gdns. W2 . . . . . 1D 73
Ilchester Pl. W14 . . . . 4B 72
Ildersly Gro. SE21 . . . . . 2F 119
Ilderton Rd. SE16 . . . . . . 1E 93
Ilderton Wharf SE15 . . . . 2E 93
(off Rollins St.)
Ilex Rd. NW10 . . . . 3B 42
Ilex Way SW16 . . . . 5C 118
Ilford Ho. N1 . . . . 3F 49
(off Dove Rd.)
Ilfracombe Flats SE1 . . . 3A 26
(off Marshalsea Rd.)
Ilfracombe Rd.
BR1: Brom 3B 124
Iliffe St. SE17 . . . . 1D 91
Iliffe Yd. SE17 . . . . 1D 91
(off Crampton St.)
Ilkeston Ct. E5 . . . . 1F 51
(off Overbury St.)
Ilkley Rd. E16 . . . . 4E 69
Ilminster Gdns. SW11 . . 2A 102
Imani Mans. SW11 . . . . . . 5F 87
Imber St. N1 . . . . 5F 49
Imperial Av. N16 . . . . 1A 50
Imperial College 4F 73
Imperial Coll. Rd. SW7 . . 4F 73
Imperial Ct. N6 . . . . 1E 33
NW8 . . . . 1A 60
(off Prince Albert Rd.)
SE11 . . . . 1C 90
Imperial Ho. E14 . . . . 1B 80
(off Victory Pl.)
E3 . . . . 2A 66
(off Grove Rd.)
Imperial M. E6 . . . . 1F 69
Imperial Pde. EC4 . . . . . . 3D 17
(off New Bri. St.)
Imperial Rd. SW6 . . . . . . 4D 87
Imperial Sq. SW6 . . . . . . 4D 87
Imperial St. E3 . . . . 2E 67
Imperial War Mus.
. . . . 4C 76 (5C 24)
Imre Cl. W12 . . . . 2D 71
Inchmery Rd. SE6 . . . . . 2D 123
Independent Pl. E8 . . . . . 2B 50
Independents Rd. SE3 . . 1B 110
Inderwick Rd. N8 . . . . 1B 34
Indescon Ct. E14 . . . . 3C 80
India Pl. WC2 . . . . 4F 15
India St. EC3 . . . 5B 64 (3F 19)
India Way W12 . . . . 1D 71
Indigo M. E14 . . . . 1E 81
N16 . . . . 5F 35
Indus Rd. SE7 . . . . 3E 97
Infirmary St. SW3 . . . . . . 2B 88
(off West Rd.)
Ingal Rd. E13 . . . . 3C 68
Ingate Pl. SW8 . . . . 4D 89
Ingatestone Rd. E12 . . . . 3E 41
Ingelow Ho. W8 . . . . 3D 73
(off Holland St.)
Ingelow Rd. SW8 . . . . . . 5D 89
Ingersoll Rd. W12 . . . . . . 2D 71
Ingestre Pl. W1 . . 1E 61 (3A 14)
Ingestre Rd. E7 . . . . 1C 54
NW5 . . . . 1D 47

Ingham Rd. NW6 . . . . 1C 44
Inglebert St. EC1 . . 2C 62 (1D 8)
Ingleborough St. SW9 . . 5C 90
Ingleby Rd. N7 . . . . 5A 34
Inglefield Sq. E1 . . . . 2D 79
(off Prusom St.)
Inglemere Rd. SE23 . . . . 3F 121
Inglesham Wlk. E9 . . . . . 3B 52
Ingleside Gro. SE3 . . . . . 2B 96
Inglethorpe St. SW6 . . . . 4F 85
Ingleton St. SW9 . . . . 5C 90
Inglewood Cl. E14 . . . . . . 5C 80
Inglewood Rd. NW6 . . . . 2C 44
Inglis St. SE5 . . . . 4D 91
Ingoldisthorpe Gro.
SE15 . . . . 2B 92
Ingram Av. NW11 . . . . 2E 31
Ingram Cl. SE11 . . . . 5B 76
Ingram Ho. E3 . . . . 5A 52
Ingrave St. SW11 . . . . . . 1F 101
Ingrebourne Ho.
BR1: Brom 5F 123
(off Brangbourne Rd.)
NW8 . . . . 4F 59
(off Broadley St.)
Ingress St. W4 . . . . 1A 84
Inigo Jones Rd. SE7 . . . . 3F 97
Inigo Pl. WC2 . . . . 4D 15
Inkerman Rd. NW5 . . . . . 3D 47
Inkerman Ter. W8 . . . . . . 4C 72
(off Allen St.)
Inman Rd. NW10 . . . . 5A 42
SW18 . . . . 5E 101
Inner Circ. NW1 . . 2C 60 (2B 4)
Inner Pk. Rd. SW19 . . 1F 113
Inner Temple Hall 3B 16
Inner Temple La.
EC4 . . . . 5C 62 (3B 16)
Innes Gdns. SW15 . . . . . 4D 99
Innis Ho. SE17 . . . . 1A 92
(off East St.)
Inniskilling Rd. E13 . . . . 1E 69
Innis St. SE15 . . . . 3A 92
**Inn of Court &
City Yeomanry Mus.** . . 1A 16
(off Chancery La.)
Innovation Cen., The
E14 . . . . 3E 81
(off Marsh Wall)
Inskip Cl. E10 . . . . 4D 39
Institute for English Studies
. . . . 4F 61 (5C 6)
Institute of Classical Studies
. . . . 4F 61 (3B 6)
**Institute of Commonwealth
Studies** 5D 7
(off Russell Sq.)
Institute of Contemporary Arts
. . . . 2C 22
Institute of Germanic Studies
. . . . 5D 7
(off Russell Sq.)
**Institute of Historical
Research** 4F 61 (5C 6)
**Institute of Latin American
Studies** 3F 61 (3C 6)
Institute of Romance Studies
. . . . 4F 61 (5C 6)
**Institute of United States
Studies** 4F 61 (5C 6)

Institute Pl. E8 . . . . 2D 51
Integer Gdns. E11 . . . . . . 2F 39
International Ho. E1 . . . . 5F 19
(off St Katharine's Way)
Inver Cl. E5 . . . . 4E 37
Inver Ct. W2 . . . . 5D 59
Inverforth Cl. NW3 . . . . . 4E 31
Invergarry Ho. W9 . . . . . 1D 59
(off Carlton Va.)
Inverine Rd. SE7 . . . . 1D 97
Inverness Ct. SE6 . . . . . 1B 124
Inverness Gdns. W8 . . . . 2D 73
Inverness M. W2 . . . . 1D 73
Inverness Pl. W2 . . . . 1D 73
Inverness St. NW1 . . . . . 5D 47
Inverness Ter. W2 . . . . . . 5D 59
Inverton Rd. SE15 . . . . . . 2F 107
Invicta Plaza
SE1 . . . . 2D 77 (1D 25)
Invicta Rd. SE3 . . . . 3C 96
Inville Rd. SE17 . . . . 1F 91
Inville Wlk. SE17 . . . . 1F 91
Inwen Ct. SE8 . . . . 1A 94
Inwood Ct. NW1 . . . . 4E 47
(off Rochester Sq.)
Inworth St. SW11 . . . . . . 5A 88
Inworth Wlk. N1 . . . . 5E 49
(off Popham St.)
Iona Cl. SE6 . . . . 5C 108
Ion Ct. E2 . . . . 1C 64
Ionian Bldg. E14 . . . . 1A 80
Ionian Ho. E1 . . . . 3F 65
(off Duckett St.)
Ion Sq. E2 . . . . 1C 64
Ipsden Bldgs. SE1 . . . . . 2C 24
Ipswich Ho. SE4 . . . . 3F 107
Ireland Yd.
EC4 . . . . 5D 63 (3E 17)
Irene Rd. SW6 . . . . 4C 86
Ireton St. E3 . . . . 3C 66
Iris Ct. SE14 . . . . 4E 93
(off Briant St.)
Iron Bri. Cl. NW10 . . . . . . 2A 42
Iron Bri. Ho. NW1 . . . . . . 4B 46
Iron Mill Pl. SW18 . . . . . 4D 101
Iron Mill Rd. SW18 . . . . . 4D 101
Ironmonger La.
EC2 . . . . 5E 63 (3A 18)
Ironmonger Pas. EC1 . . . 2A 10
(off Ironmonger Row)
Ironmonger Row
EC1 . . . . 2E 63 (2A 10)
Ironmongers Pl. E14 . . . . 5C 80
Ironside Cl. SE16 . . . . . . 3F 79
Ironside Ho. E9 . . . . 1A 52
Irvine Ho. E14 . . . . 4D 67
(off Uamvar St.)
N7 . . . . 3B 48
(off Caledonian Rd.)
Irving Gro. SW9 . . . . 5B 90
Irving Ho. SE17 . . . . 1D 91
(off Doddington Gro.)
Irving Mans. W14 . . . . . . 2A 86
(off Queen's Club Gdns.)
Irving M. N1 . . . . 3E 49
Irving Rd. W14 . . . . 4F 71
Irving St. WC2 . . 1F 75 (5C 14)
Irving Way NW9 . . . . 1C 28
Irwell Est. SE16 . . . . 4E 79
Irwin Gdns. NW10 . . . . . . 5D 43

Isabella Ho. *SE11* 1D **91**
   (off Othello Clo.)
  W6 . . . . .1E **85**
   (off Queen Caroline St.)
Isabella Rd. E9 . . . . .2E **51**
Isabella St.
  SE1 . . . . .2D **77** (2D **25**)
Isabel St. SW9 . . . . .4B **90**
Isambard M. E14 . . . . . . .4E **81**
Isambard Pl. SE16 . . . . .2E **79**
Isel Way SE22 . . . . .3A **106**
Isis Cl. SW15 . . . . .2E **99**
Isis Ho. *NW8* 3F **59**
   (off Church St. Est.)
Isis St. SW18 . . . . .2E **115**
Island Row E14 . . . . . . .5B **66**
Isleden Ho. *N1* 5E **49**
   (off Prebend St.)
Isledon Rd. N7 . . . . .5C **34**
ISLEDON VILLAGE . . .**5C 34**
Isley Ct. SW8 . . . . .5E **89**
ISLINGTON **4D 49**
Islington Grn. N1 . . . . . .5D **49**
Islington High St. N1 . .1C **62**
   (not continuous)
Islington Pk. M. N1 . . . .4D **49**
Islington Pk. St. N1 . . . .4C **48**
Islip St. NW5 . . . . .2E **47**
Ismailia Rd. E7 . . . . .4D **55**
Isom Cl. E13 . . . . .2D **69**
Ivanhoe Ho. *E3* 1A **66**
   (off Grove Rd.)
Ivanhoe Rd. SE5 . . . . .1B **106**
Ivatt Pl. W14 . . . . .1B **86**
Iveagh Cl. E9 . . . . .5F **51**
Iveagh Ct. EC3 . . . . .3F **19**
Iveagh Ho. SW9 . . . . . . .5D **91**
  SW10 . . . . .3E **87**
   (off King's Rd.)
Ive Farm Cl. E10 . . . . . .4C **38**
Ive Farm La. E10 . . . . . .4C **38**
Iveley Rd. SW4 . . . . .5E **89**
Iverna Ct. W8 . . . . .4C **72**
Iverna Gdns. W8 . . . . . .4C **72**
Iverson Rd. NW6 . . . . . .3B **44**
Ives Rd. E16 . . . . .4A **68**
Ives St. SW3 . . . . .5A **74**
Ivestor Ter. SE23 . . . . .5E **107**
Ivimey St. E2 . . . . .2C **64**
Ivinghoe Ho. N7 . . . . . . .2F **47**
Ivor Ct. N8 . . . . .1A **34**
  NW1 . . . . .3A **4**
   (off Gloucester Pl.)
Ivories, The *N1* 4E **49**
   (off Northampton St.)
Ivor Pl. NW1 . . . .3B **60** (4A **4**)
Ivor St. NW1 . . . . .4E **47**
Ivorydown
  BR1: Brom 4C **124**
Ivory Ho. E1 . . . . .2B **78**
Ivory Sq. SW11. . . . . . .1E **101**
Ivybridge Ct. *NW1* 4D **47**
   (off Lewis St.)
Ivybridge La.
  WC2 . . . . . . .1A **76** (5E **15**)
Ivychurch La. SE17 . . . .1B **92**
Ivy Cotts. E14 . . . . .1E **81**
Ivy Ct. *SE16* 1D **93**
   (off Argyle Way)
Ivydale Rd. SE15 . . . . .1F **107**

Ivyday Gro. SW16 . . . . .3B **118**
Ivy Gdns. N8. . . . . .1A **34**
Ivymount Rd. SE27 . . . .3C **118**
Ivy Rd. E16. . . . . .5C **68**
  E17 . . . . .1C **38**
  NW2 . . . . .1E **43**
  SE4 . . . . .2B **108**
  SW17 . . . . .5A **116**
Ivy St. N1 . . . . .1A **64**
Ixworth Pl. SW3 . . . . . . .1A **88**

Jacaranda Gro. E8 . . . . .4B **50**
Jack Clow Rd. E15. . . . . .1A **68**
Jack Dash Ho. *E14*. . . .3E **81**
   (off Lawn Ho. Cl.)
Jack Dash Way E6 . . . . .3F **69**
Jackman Ho. *E1*. 2D **79**
   (off Watts St.)
Jackman M. NW2. . . . . . .5A **28**
Jackman St. E8 . . . . .5D **51**
Jackson Cl. E9 . . . . .4E **51**
Jackson Ct. E7 . . . . .3D **55**
Jackson Rd. N7 . . . . .1B **48**
Jacksons La. N6. . . . . . . .2C **32**
Jack Walker Ct. N5 . . . .1D **49**
Jacobin Lodge N7 . . . . . .2A **48**
Jacobs Ho. *E13* 2E **69**
   (off New City Rd.)
Jacob St. SE1. . . . . .3C **78**
Jacob's Well M.
  W1. . . . . .4C **60** (1C **12**)
Jacotts Ho. *W10*. 3E **57**
   (off Sutton Way)
Jacqueline Creft Ter.
  N6. . . . . .1C **32**
   (off Grange Rd.)
Jade Cl. E16. . . . . .5F **69**
  NW2 . . . . .2F **29**
Jade Ter. NW6 . . . . .4E **45**
Jaffray Rd. SE27 . . . . .4D **119**
Jaggard Way SW12 . . .5B **102**
Jagger Ho. *SW11*. 4B **88**
   (off Rosenau Rd.)
Jago Wlk. SE5 . . . . .3F **91**
Jamaica Rd.
  SE1. . . . . . . .3B **78** (4F **27**)
  SE16. . . . . .3B **78**
Jamaica St. E1 . . . . .5E **65**
James Anderson Ct.
  E2 . . . . .1A **64**
   (off Kingsland Rd.)
James Av. NW2 . . . . . . .2E **43**
James Boswell Cl.
  SW16 . . . . .4B **118**
James Brine Ho. *E2* . .2B **64**
   (off Ravenscroft St.)
James Campbell Ho.
  E2 . . . . .1E **65**
   (off Old Ford Rd.)
James Cl. E13 . . . . .1C **68**
  NW11 . . . . .1A **30**
James Collins Cl. W9 . .3B **58**
James Ct. *N1* 5E **49**
   (off Raynor Pl.)
James Docherty Ho.
  E2. . . . . .1D **65**
   (off Patriot Sq.)

James Hammett Ho.
  E2 . . . . .2B **64**
   (off Ravenscroft St.)
James Ho. *E1*. 3A **66**
   (off Solebay St.)
  SE16 . . . . .3F **79**
   (off Wolfe Cres.)
James Joyce Wlk.
  SE24 . . . . .2D **105**
James La. E10 . . . . .2E **39**
  E11 . . . . .2F **39**
James Lind Ho. *SE8* . .5B **80**
   (off Grove St.)
James Middleton Ho.
  E2 . . . . .2D **65**
   (off Middleton St.)
Jameson Ct. *E2* 1E **65**
   (off Russia La.)
Jameson Ho. *SE11*. . . .1B **90**
   (off Glasshouse Wlk.)
Jameson Lodge N6 . . . .1E **33**
Jameson St. W8. . . . . . . .2C **72**
James Stewart Ho.
  NW6 . . . . .4B **44**
James St. W1 . .5C **60** (3C **12**)
  WC2 . . . . . . .1A **76** (3E **15**)
James Stroud Ho. *SE17*. .1E **91**
   (off Bronti Cl.)
James Ter. *SW14*. 1A **98**
   (off Church Path)
Jamestown Rd. NW1. . .5D **47**
Jamestown Way E14 . .1F **81**
Jamuna Cl. E14 . . . . .4A **66**
Jane Austen Hall *E16* .2D **83**
   (off Wesley Av.)
Jane Austen Ho. *SW1* .1E **89**
   (off Churchill Gdns.)
Jane St. E1. . . . . .5D **65**
Janet St. E14 . . . . .4C **80**
Janeway Pl. SE16 . . . . . .3D **79**
Janeway St. SE16 . . . . . .3C **78**
Jansen Wlk. SW11 . . . .1F **101**
Janson Cl. E15. . . . . .2A **54**
  NW10 . . . . .5A **28**
Janson Rd. E15 . . . . .2A **54**
Japan Cres. N4 . . . . .3B **34**
Jardine Rd. E1 . . . . .1F **79**
Jarman Ho. *E1* 4E **65**
   (off Jubilee St.)
  SE16 . . . . .5F **79**
   (off Hawkstone Rd.)
Jarrett Cl. SW2 . . . . . . .1D **119**
Jarrow Rd. SE16 . . . . . . .5E **79**
Jarrow Way E9 . . . . .1B **52**
Jarvis Rd. SE22 . . . . . . .2A **106**
Jasmin Cl. SE12. . . . . . .4B **110**
Jasmine Ct. SW19 . . . .5C **114**
Jasmin Lodge *SE16* . .1D **93**
   (off Sherwood Gdns.)
Jason Ct. *SW9*. 4C **90**
   (off Southey Rd.)
  W1 . . . . .2C **12**
Jasper Pas. SE19. . . . . .5B **120**
Jasper Rd. E16. . . . . .5F **69**
  SE19. . . . . .5B **120**
Jasper Wlk. N1 . . . . .1B **10**
Java Wharf SE1 . . . . . . .3F **27**
Jay M. SW7 . . . . .3E **73**
Jean Darling Ho. *SW10*. .2F **87**
   (off Milman's St.)

Jean Pardies Ho. *E1* **4E 65**
  (off Jubilee St.)
Jebb Av. SW2 . . . . **4A 104**
  (not continuous)
Jebb St. E3 . . . . **1C 66**
Jedburgh Rd. E13 . . . . . **2E 69**
Jedburgh St. SW11 . . **2C 102**
Jeddo M. W3 . . . . **3B 70**
Jeddo Rd. W12 . . . . **3B 70**
Jefferson Bldg. E14 . . **3C 80**
Jeffrey Row SE12 . . . **3D 111**
Jeffrey's Pl. NW1 . . . . **4E 47**
Jeffreys Rd. SW4 . . . . **5A 90**
Jeffrey's St. NW1 . . . . **4E 47**
Jeger Av. E2 . . . . **5B 50**
Jeken Rd. SE9 . . . . **2E 111**
Jelf Rd. SW2 . . . . **3C 104**
Jellicoe Ho. *E2* **1C 64**
  (off Ropley St.)
NW1 . . . . **3D 61 (4E 5)**
Jellicoe Rd. E13 . . . . . **3C 68**
Jemotts Ct. SE14 . . . . . **2F 93**
  (off Myers La.)
Jenkinson Ho. *E2* **2F 65**
  (off Usk St.)
Jenkins Rd. E13 . . . . . . **3D 69**
Jenner Av. W3 . . . . **4A 56**
Jenner Ho. *SE3* **2A 96**
  (off Restell Cl.)
WC1 . . . . **3E 7**
  (off Hunter St.)
Jenner Pl. SW13 . . . . . **2D 85**
Jenner Rd. N16 . . . . . . **5B 36**
Jennifer Ho. SE11 . . . . **5C 76**
  (off Reedworth St.)
Jennifer Rd.
  BR1: Brom **3B 124**
Jenningsbury Ho. *SW3* . **1A 88**
  (off Marlborough St.)
Jennings Ho. SE10 . . . . **1F 95**
  (off Old Woolwich Rd.)
Jennings Rd. SE22 . . **4B 106**
Jenny Hammond Cl.
  E11 . . . . **5B 40**
Jephson Ct. SW4 . . . . **5A 90**
Jephson Ho. *SE17* **2D 91**
  (off Doddington St.)
Jephson Rd. E7 . . . . . . **4E 55**
Jephson St. SE5 . . . . . **4F 91**
Jephtha Rd. SW18 . . . **4C 100**
Jepson Ho. *SW6* **4D 87**
  (off Pearscroft Rd.)
Jerdan Pl. SW6 . . . . . . **3C 86**
Jeremiah St. E14 . . . . . **5D 67**
Jeremy Bentham Ho.
  E2 . . . . **2C 64**
  (off Mansford St.)
Jermyn St. SW1 . . **2E 75 (1F 21)**
Jerningham Ct. SE14 . . **4A 94**
Jerningham Rd. SE14 . . **5A 94**
Jerome Cres. NW8 . . . . **3A 60**
Jerome Ho. *NW1* **4A 60**
  (off Lisson Gro.)
SW7 . . . . **5F 73**
  (off Glendower Pl.)
Jerome St. E1 . . **3B 64 (5F 11)**
Jerrard St. SE13 . . . . . **1D 109**
Jerrold St. N1 . . **1A 64 (1E 11)**

Jersey Ho. N1 . . . . **3E 49**
Jersey Rd. E11 . . . . **3F 39**
  E16 . . . . **5E 69**
  N1 . . . . **3E 49**
Jersey St. E2 . . . . **2D 65**
Jerusalem Pas.
  EC1 . . . . **3D 63 (4D 9)**
Jervis Bay Ho. *E14* **5F 67**
  (off Blair St.)
Jervis Ct. *SE10* **4E 95**
  (off Blissett St.)
W1 . . . . **3E 13**
Jerviston Gdns. SW16 . **5C 118**
Jessam Av. E5 . . . . **3D 37**
Jessel Ho. *SW1* **5F 75**
  (off Page St.)
WC1 . . . . **2D 7**
  (off Judd St.)
Jessel Mans. *W14* **2A 86**
  (off Queen's Club Gdns.)
Jesse Rd. E10 . . . . **3E 39**
Jessica Rd. SW18 . . . **4E 101**
Jessie Blythe La. N19 . . **2A 34**
Jessie Wood Ct. *SW9* . . **3C 90**
  (off Caldwell St.)
Jesson Ho. *SE17* **5F 77**
  (off Orb St.)
Jessop Ct. N1 . . . . **1D 63**
Jessop Rd. SE24 . . . . . **2D 105**
Jessop Sq. *E14* **2C 80**
  (off Heron Quay)
Jevington Way SE12 . . **1D 125**
Jewry St. EC3 . . **5B 64 (3F 19)**
Jew's Row SW18 . . . . . **2D 101**
Jews' Wlk. SE26 . . . . . **4D 121**
Jeymer Av. NW2 . . . . . **2D 43**
Jeypore Pas. SW18 . . **4E 101**
Jeypore Rd. SW18 . . . **5E 101**
Jim Griffiths Ho. *SW6* . **2B 86**
  (off Clem Attlee Ct.)
Joan Cres. SE9 . . . . . . **5F 111**
Joanna Ho. *W6* **1E 85**
  (off Queen Caroline St.)
Joan St. SE1 . . **2D 77 (2D 25)**
Jocelin Ho. *N1* **5B 48**
  (off Barnsbury Est.)
Jocelyn St. SE15 . . . . . **4C 92**
Jockey's Flds.
  WC1 . . . . **4B 62 (5A 8)**
Jodane St. SE8 . . . . . . **5B 80**
Jodrell Rd. E3 . . . . **5B 52**
Joe Hunte Ct. SE27 . . **5D 119**
Johanna St. SE1 . **3C 76 (4B 24)**
John Adam St.
  WC2 . . . . **1A 76 (5E 15)**
John Aird Ct. *W2* **4F 59**
  (off Howley Pl., not cont.)
John Archer Way
  SW18 . . . . **4F 101**
John Ashby Cl. SW2 . . **4A 104**

John Baird Ct. SE26 . . . **4E 121**
John Barker Ct. *NW6* . . **4A 44**
  (off Brondesbury Pk.)
John Barnes Wlk. E15 . . **3B 54**
John Betts' Ho. W12 . . **4B 70**
John Brent Ho. *SE8* . . . **5F 79**
  (off Bush Rd.)
John Buck Ho. NW10 . . **5B 42**
John Campbell Rd.
  N16 . . . . **2A 50**
John Carpenter St.
  EC4 . . . . **1D 77 (4D 17)**
John Cartwright Ho.
  E2 . . . . **2D 65**
  (off Old Bethnal Grn. Rd.)
John Drinkwater Cl.
  E11 . . . . **2B 40**
John Felton Rd. SE16 . . **3C 78**
John Fielden Ho. *E2* . . **2D 65**
  (off Canrobert St.)
John Fisher St. E1 . . . . **1C 78**
John Harrison Way
  SE10 . . . . **4B 82**
John Islip St. SW1 . . . . **5F 75**
John Kennedy Ct. *N1* . . **3F 49**
  (off Newington Grn. Rd.)
John Kennedy Ho.
  SE16 . . . . **5F 79**
  (off Rotherhithe Old Rd.)
John Knight Lodge
  SW6 . . . . **3C 86**
John McDonald Ho.
  E14 . . . . **4E 81**
  (off Glengall Gro.)
John McKenna Wlk.
  SE16 . . . . **4C 78**
John Masefield Ho.
  N15 . . . . **1F 35**
  (off Fladbury Rd.)
John Maurice Cl. SE17 . **5F 77**
John Parker Sq.
  SW11 . . . . **1F 101**
John Parry Ct. *N1* **1A 64**
  (off Hare Wlk.)
John Penn Ho. SE14 . . **3B 94**
  (off Amersham Va.)
John Penn St. SE13 . . . **4D 95**
John Pound Ho. SW18 . **5D 101**
John Prince's St.
  W1 . . . . **5D 61 (2E 13)**
John Pritchard Ho. *E1* . **3C 64**
  (off Buxton St.)
John Ratcliffe Ho. *NW6* . **2C 58**
  (off Chippenham Gdns.)
John Rennie Wlk. E1 . . **1D 79**
John Roll Way SE16 . . **4C 78**
John Ruskin St. SE5 . . **3D 91**
John Scurr Ho. *E14* . . . **5A 66**
  (off Ratcliffe La.)
John Silkin La. SE8 . . . **1F 93**
John's M. WC1 . . **3B 62 (4A 8)**
John Smith Av. SW6 . . **3B 86**
John Smith M. E14 . . . **1F 81**
Johnson Cl. E8 . . . . . . **5C 50**
Johnson Ho. *E2* **2C 64**
  (off Roberta St.)
NW1 . . . . **1E 61**
  (off Cranleigh St.)

Johnson Ho. *NW3* *4B 46*
(off Adelaide Rd.)
SW1 . . . . *5C 74*
(off Cundy St.)
SW8 . . . . *3F 89*
(off Wandsworth Rd.)
Johnson Lodge *W2*. . . . *4C 58*
(off Admiral Wlk.)
Johnson Mans. *W14* . . . 2A *86*
(off Queen's Club Gdns.)
Johnson's Ct.
EC4 . . . . 5C *62* (3C 16)
Johnson's Pl. SW1 . . . . 1E *89*
Johnson St. E1 . . . . 1E *79*
John Spencer Sq. N1 . . . 3D *49*
John's Pl. E1 . . . . 5D *65*
Johnston Cl. SW9. . . . . 4B *90*
Johnstone Ho. *SE13*. . . *1F 109*
(off Belmont Hill)
Johnston Ter. NW2 . . . . . 5F *29*
John Strachey Ho. *SW6*. . 2B *86*
(off Clem Attlee Ct.)
John St. E15 . . . . 5B *54*
WC1 . . . . .3B *62* (4A *8*)
John Strype Ct. E10 . . . 3D *39*
John Trundle Ct. EC2 . . . 5F *9*
John Trundle Highwalk
EC2 . . . . .5F *9*
(off Beech St.)
John Tucker Ho. *E14* . . . *4C 80*
(off Mellish St.)
John Wesley Highwalk
EC1 . . . . .1F *17*
(off Barbican)
John Wheatley Ho.
SW6 . . . . .2B *86*
(off Clem Attlee Ct.)
John Williams Cl. SE14. . 2F *93*
John Woolley Cl. SE13. . 2A 110
Joiners Arms Yd. SE5. . . 4F *91*
Joiners Pl. N5. . . . . 1F *49*
Joiner St. SE1 . . 2F *77* (2C *26*)
Joiners Yd. *N1* 1E *7*
(off Caledonia St.)
Jonathan St. SE11 . . . . 1B *90*
Jones Ho. *E14*. 5F *67*
(off Blair St.)
Jones M. SW15 . . . . . . 2A *100*
Jones Rd. E13 . . . . 3D *69*
Jones St. W1 . . 1D *75* (5D *13*)
Jonson Ho. *SE1* 5C *26*
(off Burbage Cl.)
Jordan Ho. *N1*. 5F *49*
(off Colville St.)
SE4 . . . . 2F *107*
(off St Norbert Rd.)
Jordans Ho. *NW8* 3F *59*
(off Capland St.)
Joscoyne Ho. *E1* 5D *65*
(off Philpot St.)
Joseph Conrad Ho. *SW1*. . 5E *75*
(off Tachbrook St.)
Joseph Ct. *N15*. 1A *36*
(off Amhurst Pk.)
N16. . . . . 2A *36*
(off Amhurst Pk.)
Joseph Gdns. SE18. . . . 4F *83*
Joseph Hardcastle Cl.
SE14 . . . . .3F *93*
Josephine Av. SW2 . . . 3B *104*

Joseph Irwin Ho. *E14*. . . 1B *80*
(off Gill St.)
Joseph Lister Ct. E7. . . . 4C *54*
Joseph Powell Cl.
SW12 . . . . .4D 103
Joseph Priestley Ho.
E2. . . . . .2D *65*
(off Canrobert St.)
Joseph Ray Rd. E11. . . . 4A *40*
Joseph St. E3. . . . . 3B *66*
Joseph Trotter Cl. EC1 . . 2C *8*
Joshua St. E14 . . . . 5E *67*
Joslings Cl. W12 . . . . . . 1C *70*
Josseline Ct. *E3*. 1A *66*
(off Ford St.)
Joubert St. SW11. . . . . 5B *88*
Jowett St. SE15 . . . . . . 3B *92*
Jowitt Ho. *E2* 2F *65*
(off Morpeth St.)
Joyce Page Cl. SE7 . . . . 2F *97*
Joyce Wlk. SW2. . . . . . 4C *104*
Jubb Powell Ho. N15. . . 1A *36*
Jubilee Bldgs. NW8 . . . . 5F *45*
Jubilee Cl. NW9. . . . . . . 1A *28*
Jubilee Cres. E14. . . . . . 4E *81*
Jubilee Ho. *SE11*. *5C 76*
(off Reedworth St.)
WC1 . . . . .3F *7*
Jubilee Mans. *E1*. 5E *65*
(off Jubilee St.)
Jubilee Pl. SW3 . . . . . . 1A *88*
Jubilee St. E1. . . . . 5E *65*
Jubilee, The SE10 . . . . 3D *95*
Jubilee Walkway
SE1 . . . . 1D *77* (5E *17*)
Jubilee Yd. SE1 . . . . . . 3F *27*
Judd St. WC1 . . 2A *62* (2D *7*)
Jude St. E16. . . . . 5B *68*
Judges Wlk. NW3. . . . . 5E *31*
Juer Ho. *SW11*. *3A 88*
(off Juer St.)
Juer St. SW11 . . . . *3A 88*
Julia Garfield M. E16 . . 2D *83*
Julian Pl. E14 . . . . 1D *95*
Julian Taylor Path
SE23. . . . . .2D *121*
Juliet Ho. *N1* 1A *64*
(off Arden Est.)
Juliette Rd. E13. . . . . . . 1C *68*
Julius Nyerere Cl. *N1* . . 5B *48*
(off Copenhagen St.)
Junction App. SE13 . . 1E *109*
SW11 . . . . 1A *102*
Junction Av. NW10. . . . 3E *57*
Junction M. W2 . . . . . . 5A *60*
Junction Pl. W2 . . . . . . 5F *59*
(off Praed St.)
Junction Rd. E13 . . . . . 1D *69*
N19. . . . . .1E *47*
Juniper Ct. *W8*. 4D *73*
(off St Mary's Pl.)
Juniper Cres. NW1. . . . 4C *46*
Juniper Ho. SE15 . . . . . 3E *93*
W10 . . . . .3A *58*
(off Fourth Av.)
Juniper St. E1. . . . . 1E *79*
Juno Ct. *SW9*. *3C 90*
(off Caldwell St.)
Juno Way SE14. . . . . . . 2F *93*

Juno Way Ind. Est.
SE14 . . . . .2F *93*
Jupiter Ct. *SW9* *3C 90*
(off Caldwell St.)
Jupiter Ho. *E14* *1D 95*
(off St Davids Sq.)
Jupiter Way N7 . . . . 3B *48*
Jupp Rd. E15 . . . . 4F *53*
Jupp Rd. W. E15. . . . . . 5F *53*
Jura Ho. *SE16*. *5F 79*
(off Plough Way)
Jurston Ct. SE1 . . . . . . 4C *24*
Justice Wlk. *SW3*. 2A *88*
(off Lawrence St.)
Jutland Cl. N19 . . . . 3A *34*
Jutland Ho. SE5 . . . . . . 5E *91*
Jutland Rd. E13 . . . . . . 3C *68*
SE6. . . . . .5E 109
Juxon St. SE11 . . . . . . 5B *76*
JVC Bus. Pk. NW2 . . . . 3C *28*

Kilburn Priory NW6 . . . . 5D **45**
Kilburn Sq. NW6 . . . . 5C **44**
Kilburn Va. NW6 . . . . 5D **45**
Kilburn Va. Est. *NW6*. . . *5D* **45**
   (off Kilburn Va.)
Kildare Gdns. W2. . . . . . . 5C **58**
Kildare Rd. E16 . . . . 4C **68**
Kildare Ter. W2 . . . . 5C **58**
Kildare Wlk. E14 . . . . 5C **66**
Kildoran Rd. SW2 . . . . . . 3A **104**
Kilgour Rd. SE23 . . . . . . 4A **108**
Kilkie St. SW6 . . . . 5E **87**
Killarney Rd. SW18 . . . . 4E **101**
Killearn Rd. SE6 . . . . . . 1F **123**
Killick St. N1 . . . . . 1B **62** (1F **7**)
Killieser Av. SW2 . . . . . 2A **118**
Killip Cl. E16 . . . . 5B **68**
Killoran Ho. *E14*. *4E* **81**
   (off Galbraith St.)
Killowen Rd. E9 . . . . 3F **51**
Killyon Rd. SW8 . . . . 5E **89**
Killyon Ter. SW8 . . . . 5E **89**
Kilmaine Rd. SW6 . . . . . 3A **86**
Kilmarsh Rd. W6 . . . . . . 5E **71**
Kilmington Rd. SW13 . . 2C **84**
Kilmore Ho. *E14*. *5D* **67**
   (off Vesey Path)
Kilmorie Rd. SE23 . . . . 1A **122**
Kilmuir Ho. *SW1* *5C* **74**
   (off Bury St.)
Kiln Ct. *E14* *1B* **80**
   (off Newell St.)
Kilner Ho. *E16* *4D* **69**
   (off Freemasons Rd.)
SE11. . . . . *2C* **90**
   (off Clayton St.)
Kilner St. E14 . . . . 4C **66**
Kiln M. SW17 . . . . 5F **115**
Kiln Pl. NW5. . . . . 2C **46**
Kilravock St. W10 . . . . . 2A **58**
Kimbell Gdns. SW6 . . . . 4A **86**
Kimbell Pl. SE3 . . . . 2E **111**
Kimberley Av. E6 . . . . . . 1F **69**
SE15. . . . . 5D **93**
Kimberley Gdns. N4. . . . 1D **35**
Kimberley Ho. *E14*. *4E* **81**
   (off Galbraith St.)
Kimberley Rd. E11 . . . . . 4F **39**
E16 . . . . 3B **68**
NW6 . . . . 5A **44**
SW9 . . . . 5A **90**
Kimber Rd. SW18 . . . . . 5C **100**
Kimble Ho. *NW8* *3A* **60**
   (off Lilestone St.)
Kimble Rd. SW19 . . . . . . 5F **115**
Kimbolton Cl. SE12 . . . . 4B **110**
Kimbolton Ct. *SW3*. *5A* **74**
   (off Fulham Rd.)
Kimbolton Row *SW3* . . . *5A* **74**
   (off Fulham Rd.)
Kimmeridge Rd. SE9 . . . 4F **125**
Kimpton Rd. SE5 . . . . . . 4F **91**
Kinburn St. SE16 . . . . . . 3F **79**
Kincaid Rd. SE15 . . . . . . 3D **93**
Kincardine Gdns. *W9*. . . *3C* **58**
   (off Harrow Rd.)
Kinder Ho. *N1*. *1F* **63**
   (off Cranston Est.)
Kindersley Ho. *E1* *5C* **64**
   (off Pinchin St.)

Kinder St. E1 . . . . 5D **65**
Kinefold Ho. N7 . . . . 3A **48**
Kinfauns Rd. SW2 . . . . 2C **118**
King Alfred Av. SE6 . . . 4C **122**
   (not continuous)
King & Queen St. SE17. . 1E **91**
King & Queen Wharf
SE16. . . . . 1F **79**
King Arthur Cl. SE15 . . . 3E **93**
King Charles Ct. *SE17*. . *2D* **91**
   (off Royal Rd.)
King Charles Ho. *SW6*. . *3D* **87**
   (off Wandon Rd.)
King Charles I Island
SW1. . . . . 1D **23**
King Charles's Ct.
SE10. . . . . *2E* **95**
   (off Park Row)
King Charles St.
SW1. . . . . 3F **75** (3C **22**)
King Charles Ter. *E1* . . . *1D* **79**
   (off Sovereign Cl.)
King Charles Wlk.
SW19 . . . . 1A **114**
King Ct. E10. . . . . 2D **39**
King David La. E1 . . . . . 1E **79**
Kingdon Ho. *E14* *4E* **81**
   (off Galbraith St.)
Kingdon Rd. NW6 . . . . . . 3C **44**
King Edward Bldg.
EC1 . . . . 5D **63** (2F **17**)
King Edward Mans.
E8. . . . . *5D* **51**
   (off Mare St.)
King Edward III M.
SE16. . . . . 3D **79**
King Edward M. SW13. . 4C **84**
King Edward Rd. E10 . . 3E **39**
King Edwards Mans.
SW6 . . . . *3C* **86**
   (off Fulham Rd.)
King Edward's Rd. E9 . . 5D **51**
King Edward St.
EC1. . . . . 5E **63** (2F **17**)
King Edward Wlk.
SE1 . . . . 4C **76** (5C **24**)
Kingfield St. E14 . . . . . . 5E **81**
Kingfisher Av. E11 . . . . . 1D **41**
Kingfisher Ct. *E14* *3E* **81**
   (off River Barge Cl.)
SW19 . . . . 2F **113**
Kingfisher M. SE13 . . . . 2C **108**
Kingfisher Sq. *SE8*. *2B* **94**
   (off Clyde St.)
Kingfisher Way NW10 . . 3A **42**
King Frederick IX Twr.
SE16. . . . . 4B **80**
King George Av. E16 . . . 5E **69**
King George VI Memorial
. . . . 2F **75** (2B **22**)
King George St. SE10 . . 3E **95**
Kingham Cl. SW18. . . . . 5E **101**
W11. . . . . *3A* **72**
   (off Holland Pk. Av.)
King Henry's Reach W6. . 2E **85**
King Henry's Rd. NW3 . . 4A **46**
King Henry St. N16 . . . . 2A **50**
King Henry's Wlk. N1. . . 3A **50**
King Henry Ter. E1 . . . . . 1D **79**
   (off Sovereign Cl.)

Kinghorn St.
EC1. . . . . 4E **63** (1F **17**)
King Ho. W12. . . . . 5D **57**
King James Ct. SE1 . . . . 4E **25**
King James St.
SE1 . . . . 3D **77** (4E **25**)
King John Ct.
EC2 . . . . 3A **64** (3E **11**)
King John St. E1. . . . . . . 4F **65**
King John's Wlk. SE9 . . 1F **125**
SE9 . . . . 5F **111**
   (not continuous)
Kinglake Est. SE17. . . . . 1A **92**
Kinglake St. SE17 . . . . . 1A **92**
   (not continuous)
Kingly Ct. W1. . . . . 4A **14**
Kingly St. W1. . . 5E **61** (3F **13**)
Kingsand Rd. SE12 . . . . 2C **124**
Kings Arms Ct. E1 . . . . . 4C **64**
Kings Arms Yd.
EC2. . . . . 5F **63** (2B **18**)
Kings Av. BR1: Brom . . 5B **124**
SW4 . . . . 5F **103**
SW12 . . . . 1F **117**
King's Bench St.
SE1 . . . . 3D **77** (3E **25**)
King's Bench Wlk.
EC4 . . . . 5C **62** (3C **16**)
Kingsbridge Ct. *E14*. . . . *4C* **80**
   (off Dockers Tanner Rd.)
NW1. . . . . *4D* **47**
   (off Castlehaven Rd.)
Kingsbridge Rd. W10. . 5E **57**
Kingsbury Rd. N1. . . . . . 3A **50**
NW9 . . . . 1A **28**
Kingsbury Ter. N1 . . . . . 3A **50**
Kingsbury Trad. Est.
NW9 . . . . 1A **28**
Kingsclere Cl. SW15 . . . 5C **98**
Kingscliffe Gdns.
SW19 . . . . 1B **114**
Kings Cl. E10. . . . . 2D **39**
Kings Coll. Ct. NW3. . . . 4A **46**
King's College London
Chelsea Campus. . . . **1F 87**
Strand Campus
   . . . . **1B 76 (4A 16)**
Waterloo Campus . . . **2B 24**
King's College London
Dental Institute **5F 91**
Kings Coll. Rd. NW3. . . . 4A **46**
King's College School of
Medicine & Dentistry
   . . . . **5E 91**
Kings College University
Hampstead Campus
   . . . . **1C 44**
Kingscote St.
EC4 . . . . 1D **77** (4D **17**)
King's Ct. E13 . . . . 5D **55**
Kings Ct. *N7*. *4B* **48**
   (off Caledonian Rd.)
NW8. . . . . *5B* **46**
   (off Prince Albert Rd.)
King's Ct. SE1 . . 3D **77** (3E **25**)
Kings Ct. W6 . . . . 5C **70**
Kings Ct. Nth. SW3 . . . . 1A **88**
Kingscourt Rd. SW16. . 3F **117**
Kings Ct. Sth. *SW3* *1A* **88**
   (off King's Rd.)

King's Cres. N4 . . . . 5E **35**
Kings Cres. Est. N4 . . . . 4E **35**
Kingscroft SW4 . . . . 4A **104**
Kingscroft Rd. NW2 . . . . 3B **44**
KING'S CROSS . . 1A **62** (1E **7**)
King's Cross Bri. WC1 . . . 1E **7**
King's Cross Rd.
  WC1 . . . . 2B **62** (1F **7**)
Kingsdale Gdns. W11 . . . 2F **71**
Kingsdown Av. W3 . . . . . 1A **70**
Kingsdown Cl. SE16 . . . 1D **93**
  (off Masters Dr.)
  W10 . . . . 5F **57**
Kingsdown Ho. E8 . . . . . 2C **50**
Kingsdown Rd. E11 . . . . 5A **40**
  N19 . . . . 4A **34**
Kingsfield Ho. SE9 . . . . 3F **125**
Kingsford St. NW5 . . . . 2B **46**
King's Gdns. NW6 . . . . . 4C **44**
Kings Gth. M. SE23 . . . 2E **121**
Kingsgate Est. N1 . . . . . 3A **50**
Kingsgate Ho. SW9 . . . . 4C **90**
Kingsgate Mans. WC1 . . 1F **15**
  (off Red Lion Sq.)
Kingsgate Pde. SW1 . . . 5A **22**
Kingsgate Pl. NW6 . . . . 4C **44**
Kingsgate Rd. NW6 . . . . 4C **44**
Kingsground SE9 . . . . . 5F **111**
King's Gro. SE15 . . . . . 3D **93**
  (not continuous)
Kings Hall Leisure Cen.
  . . . . 2E **51**
Kingshall M. SE13 . . . 1E **109**
Kings Head Pas. SW4 . . 2F **103**
  (off Clapham Pk. Rd.)
Kings Head Theatre . . 5D **49**
  (off Upper St.)
King's Head Yd.
  SE1 . . . . . . 2F **77** (2B **26**)
Kingshill SE17 . . . . 5E **77**
Kingshold Rd. E9 . . . . . 4E **51**
Kingsholm Gdns. SE9 . . 2F **111**
Kings Ho. SW8 . . . . . . 3A **90**
  (off Sth. Lambeth Rd.)
Kingshurst Rd. SE12 . . 5C **110**
Kings Keep SW15 . . . . . 3F **99**
KINGSLAND 3A **50**
Kingsland NW8 . . . . 5A **46**
Kingsland Grn. E8 . . . . . 3A **50**
Kingsland High St. E8 . . 3B **50**
Kingsland Pas. E8 . . . . . 3A **50**
Kingsland Rd.
  E2 . . . . 2A **64** (2E **11**)
  E13 . . . . 2E **69**
Kingsland Shop. Cen.
  E8 . . . . 3B **50**
Kingslawn Cl. SW15 . . . 3D **99**
Kingsley Cl. NW4 . . . . . 1E **29**
Kingsley Flats SE1 . . . . 5A **78**
  (off Old Kent Rd.)
Kingsley Ho. SW3 . . . . . 2F **87**
  (off Beaufort St.)
Kingsley Mans. W14 . . . 2A **86**
  (off Greyhound Rd.)
Kingsley M. E1 . . . . 1D **79**
  W8 . . . . 4D **73**
Kingsley Pl. N6 . . . . 2C **32**
Kingsley Rd. E7 . . . . . . 4C **54**
  NW6 . . . . 5B **44**
  SW19 . . . . 5D **115**

Kingsley St. SW11 . . . 1B **102**
Kingsley Way N2 . . . . . . 1E **31**
Kings Mall W6 . . . . 5E **71**
Kingsmead Av. NW9 . . . 2A **28**
Kingsmead Cl. N6 . . . . 2F **33**
Kingsmead Ho. E9 . . . . 1A **52**
Kingsmead Rd. SW2 . . 2C **118**
King's Mead Way E9 . . . 1A **52**
Kingsmere Cl. SW15 . . 1F **99**
Kingsmere Pl. N16 . . . . 3F **35**
Kingsmere Rd. SW19 . . 2F **113**
King's M. SW4 . . . . 3A **104**
  WC1 . . . . 3B **62** (4A **8**)
Kingsmill NW8 . . . . 1F **59**
  (off Kingsmill Ter.)
Kingsmill Ho. SW3 . . . . 1A **88**
  (off Marlborough St.)
Kingsmill Ter. NW8 . . . . 1F **59**
Kingsnorth Ho. W10 . . . 5F **57**
Kings Pde. NW10 . . . . . 5E **43**
  W12 . . . . 4C **70**
Kings Pas. E11 . . . . 2A **40**
King's Pl. SE1 . . 3E **77** (4F **25**)
King Sq. EC1 . . . . 2E **63** (2F **9**)
King's Quay SW10 . . . . 4E **87**
  (off Chelsea Harbour Dr.)
Kings Reach Twr. SE1 . . 1C **24**
Kingsridge SW19 . . . . 2A **114**
King's Rd. E6 . . . . 5E **55**
Kings Rd. E11 . . . . 2A **40**
  NW10 . . . . 4D **43**
King's Rd. SW3 . . . . . . 2F **87**
  SW6 . . . . 3D **87**
  SW10 . . . . 3D **87**
Kings Rd. SW14 . . . . . 1A **98**
  SW19 . . . . 5C **114**
King's Scholars' Pas.
  SW1 . . . . 4E **75**
  (off Carlisle Pl.)
King Stairs Cl. SE16 . . 3D **79**
King's Ter. NW1 . . . . . . 5E **47**
Kingsthorpe Rd. SE26 . . 4F **121**
Kingston By-Pass
  SW15 . . . . 4A **112**
Kingston Ho. NW6 . . . . 4A **44**
Kingston Ho. E. SW7 . . 3A **74**
  (off Prince's Ga.)
Kingston Ho. Nth. SW7 . 3A **74**
  (off Prince's Ga.)
Kingston Ho. Sth. SW7 . 3A **74**
  (off Ennismore Gdns.)
Kingston Rd. SW15 . . 2C **112**
  SW19 . . . . 2C **112**
Kingston Sq. SE19 . . . 5F **119**
Kingston University
  Kingston Hill 5A **112**
Kingston University
  (Roehampton Vale Cen.)
  . . . . 3B **112**
KINGSTON VALE 4A **112**
Kingston Va. SW15 . . . 4A **112**
Kingstown St. NW1 . . . 5C **46**
  (not continuous)
King St. E13 . . . . 3C **68**
  EC2 . . . . 5E **63** (3A **18**)
  SW1 . . . . 2E **75** (2A **22**)
  W6 . . . . 5C **70**
  WC2 . . . . 1A **76** (4D **15**)
King St. Cloisters W6 . . 5D **71**
  (off King St.)

Kings Wlk. Shop. Cen.
  SW3 . . . . 1B **88**
Kingswater Pl. SW11 . . 3A **88**
Kingsway Mans. WC1 . . 1F **15**
  (off Red Lion Sq.)
Kingsway Pl. EC1 . . . . . 3C **8**
  (off Corporation Row)
Kingswear Rd. NW5 . . . 5D **33**
Kingswood E2 . . . . 1E **65**
  (off Cyprus St.)
Kingswood Av. NW6 . . . 5A **44**
Kingswood Cl. SW8 . . . 3A **90**
Kingswood Ct. NW6 . . . 4C **44**
  (off W. End La.)
Kingswood Dr. SE19 . . 4A **120**
Kingswood Est. SE21 . . 4A **120**
Kingswood Pl. SE13 . . 2A **110**
Kingswood Rd. E11 . . . 2A **40**
  SE20 . . . . 5E **121**
  SW2 . . . . 4A **104**
Kings Yd. E9 . . . . 3C **52**
  E15 . . . . 3C **52**
  SW15 . . . . 1E **99**
  (off Lwr. Richmond Rd.)
Kingthorpe Ter. NW10 . 3A **42**
Kington Ho. NW6 . . . . . 5D **45**
  (off Mortimer Cres.)
Kingward Ho. E1 . . . . . 4C **64**
  (off Hanbury St.)
Kingweston Cl. NW2 . . 5A **30**
King William La. SE10 . 1A **96**
King William's Ct.
  SE10 . . . . 2F **95**
  (off Park Row)
King William St.
  EC4 . . . . 5F **63** (3C **18**)
King William Wlk.
  SE10 . . . . 2E **95**
  (not continuous)
Kingwood Rd. SW6 . . . 4A **86**
Kinloch Dr. NW9 . . . . . 2A **28**
Kinloch St. N7 . . . . 5B **34**
Kinnaird Av.
  BR1: Brom 5B **124**
Kinnear Rd. W12 . . . . . 3B **70**
Kinnerton Pl. Nth.
  SW1 . . . . 4A **20**
Kinnerton Pl. Sth. SW1 . 4A **20**
Kinnerton St.
  SW1 . . . . 3C **74** (4B **20**)
Kinnoul Rd. W6 . . . . . . 2A **86**
Kinross Ct. SE6 . . . . . 1B **124**
  (off Cumberland Pl.)
Kinsale Rd. SE15 . . . . 1C **106**
Kinsella Gdns. SW19 . . 5D **113**
Kinsham Ho. E2 . . . . . . 3C **64**
  (off Ramsey St.)
Kintore Way SE1 . . . . . 5B **78**
Kintyre Ct. SW2 . . . . . 5A **104**
Kintyre Ho. E14 . . . . . . 2E **81**
  (off Coldharbour)
Kinveachy Gdns. SE7 . . 1F **97**
Kinver Rd. SE26 . . . . . 4E **121**
Kipling Dr. SW19 . . . . . 5F **115**
Kipling Est.
  SE1 . . . . 3F **77** (4C **26**)
Kipling Ho. E16 . . . . . . 1D **83**
  (off Southampton M.)

Kipling Ho. *SE5* 3F *91*
(off Elmington Est.)
Kipling St. SE1. . 3F 77 (4C 26)
Kippington Dr. SE9 . . . . 1F *125*
Kirby Est. SE16 . . . . 4D 79
Kirby Gro. SE1. . 3A 78 (3D 27)
Kirby St. EC1 . . . . 4C 62 (5C 8)
Kirkdale SE26 . . . . 2D 121
Kirkdale Cnr. SE26 . . . . 4E 121
Kirkdale Rd. E11 . . . . 3A 40
Kirkeby Ho. *EC1* 5B 8
(off Leather La.)
Kirkland Ho. *E14* 1D *95*
(off St Davids Sq.)
E14 . . . . 1D *95*
(off Westferry Rd.)
Kirkland Wlk. E8 . . . . 3B 50
Kirkman Pl. W1 . . . . 1B 14
Kirkmichael Rd. E14 . . . . 5E 67
Kirk Rd. E17 . . . . 1B 38
Kirkside Rd. SE3 . . . . 2C 96
Kirkstall Gdns. SW2. . . 1A 118
Kirkstall Rd. SW2 . . . . 1F 117
Kirkstead Ct. E5 . . . . . . 1F 51
Kirkstone *NW1* 1F 5
(off Harrington St.)
Kirk St. WC1 . . . . 4F 7
Kirkwall Pl. E2 . . . . 2E 65
Kirkwood Pl. NW1 . . . . . 4C 46
Kirkwood Rd. SE15 . . . . 5D 93
Kirtley Ho. SW8 . . . . 4E 89
Kirtley Rd. SE26 . . . . . 4A 122
Kirtling St. SW8 . . . . 3E 89
Kirton Cl. W4 . . . . 5A 70
Kirton Gdns. E2. . 2B 64 (2F 11)
(not continuous)
Kirton Lodge SW18 . . . 4D 101
Kirton Rd. E13 . . . . 1E 69
Kirwyn Way SE5. . . . . . . 3D 91
Kitcat Ter. E3 . . . . 2C 66
Kitchener Rd. E7 . . . . . . 3D 55
Kite Pl. *E2* 2C *64*
(off Lampern Sq.)
Kite Yd. *SW11* 4B *88*
(off Cambridge Rd.)
Kitson Rd. SE5 . . . . 3F 91
SW13 . . . . 4C 84
Kittiwake Ct. *SE8* 2B *94*
(off Abinger Gro.)
Kitto Rd. SE14 . . . . 5F 93
Kiver Rd. N19 . . . . 4F 33
Klea Av. SW4 . . . . 4E 103
Klein's Wharf *E14*. 4C *80*
(off Westferry Rd.)
Knapdale Cl. SE23 . . . . 2D 121
Knapmill Rd. SE6 . . . . . 2C 122
Knapmill Way SE6 . . . . 2D 123
Knapp Cl. NW10 . . . . . . 3A 42
Knapp Rd. E3 . . . . 3C 66
Knapton M. SW17 . . . . 5C 116
Knaresborough Dr.
SW18 . . . . 1D 115
Knaresborough Pl. SW5. . 5D 73
Knatchbull Rd. NW10. . . 5A 42
SE5. . . . . 5D 91
Knebworth Ho. SW8 . . . 5F 89
Knebworth Rd. N16 . . . 1A 50
Kneller Rd. SE4 . . . . . . 2A 108
Knighten St. E1 . . . . 2D 79
Knighthead Point E14. . . 3C 80

Knight Ho. *SE17*. 5A *78*
(off Tatum St.)
Knightland Rd. E5 . . . . . 4D 37
Knightleas Ct. NW2 . . . . 3E 43
Knighton Pk. Rd. SE26. . 5F 121
Knighton Rd. E7. . . . . . . 5C 40
Knightrider Ct. EC4 . . . . 4E 17
Knightrider St.
EC4 . . . . 5D 63 (4E 17)
Knights Arc. *SW1*. 4A *20*
(off Knightsbridge)
KNIGHTSBRIDGE 3A 74
Knightsbridge
SW7. . . . . 3B 74 (4A 20)
Knightsbridge Ct. SW1. . 4A 20
Knightsbridge Grn.
SW1 . . . . 3B 74
(not continuous)
Knights Cl. E9. . . . . 2E 51
Knights Ct. BR1: Brom. . 3B 124
Knights Hill SE27. . . . . 5D 119
Knight's Hill Sq. SE27. . 4D 119
Knights Ho. *SW8* 3A *90*
(off Sth. Lambeth Rd.)
Knight's Rd. E16 . . . . . . 3C 82
Knight's Wlk. SE11. . . . . 5D 77
(not continuous)
Knightswood Ct. N6 . . . 2F 33
Knivet Rd. SW6 . . . . 2C 86
Knobs Hill Rd. E15 . . . . 5D 53
Knockholt Rd. SE9 . . . . 3F 111
Knoll Ho. *NW8* 1E *59*
(off Carlton Hill)
Knoll Rd. SW18 . . . . . . 3E 101
Knollys Cl. *SW16*. 3C *118*
(off Tavistock Pl.)
Knolly's Ho. WC1. . . . . . 3D 7
Knollys Rd. SW16 . . . . 3B 118
Knottisford St. E2 . . . . . 2E 65
Knotts Grn. M. E10 . . . . 1D 39
Knotts Grn. Rd. E10. . . . 1D 39
Knowlden Ho. *E1* 1E *79*
(off Cable St.)
Knowle Cl. SW9 . . . . . . 1C 104
Knowles Hill Cres.
SE13 . . . . 3F 109
Knowles Wlk. SW4. . . . . 1E 103
Knowlton Ho. *SW9*. 4C *90*
(off Cowley Rd.)
Knowsley Rd. SW11 . . . 5B 88
Knox Ct. SW4 . . . . 5A 90
Knox Rd. E7 . . . . 3B 54
Knox St. NW1 . . . 4B 60 (5A 4)
Knoyle St. SE14 . . . . . . 2A 94
Kohat Rd. SW19 . . . . . 5D 115
Kossuth St. SE10 . . . . . 1A 96
Kotree Way SE1 . . . . . . 5C 78
Kramer M. SW5 . . . . 1C 86
Kreedman Wlk. E8 . . . . 2C 50
Krupnik Pl. EC2 . . . . . . 2E 11
Kubrick Bus. Est. *E7* . . . 1D *55*
(off Station App.)
Kuhn Way E7 . . . . 2C 54
Kylemore Cl. E6 . . . . . . 1F 69
Kylemore Rd. NW6 . . . . 4C 44
Kylestrome Ho. *SW1*. . . 5C *74*
(off Cundy St.)
Kynance M. SW7. . . . . . 4D 73
Kynance Pl. W8 . . . . 4E 73
Kynaston Av. N16. . . . . . 5B 36

Kynaston Rd.
BR1: Brom 5C 124
N16. . . . . 5A 36
Kyrle Rd. SW11 . . . . . . 4C 102
Kyverdale Rd. N16. . . . . 2B 36

Laburnum Cl. SE15 . . . . 3E 93
Laburnum Ct. E2 . . . . . . 5B 50
SE16 . . . . 3E *79*
(off Albion St.)
Laburnum St. E2 . . . . . . 5B 50
SE16 . . . . 3E *79*
(off Albion St.)
La Caye Apartments
E14 . . . . 5F *81*
(off Glenaffric Av.)
Lacey Wlk. E3 . . . . 1C 66
Lacine Ct. *SE16* 3F *79*
(off Christopher Cl.)
Lackington St.
EC2. . . . . 4F 63 (5C 10)
Lackland Ho. *SE1*. 1B *92*
(off Rowcross St.)
Lacland Ho. *SW10* 3F *87*
(off Worlds End Est.)
Lacon Ho. *WC1*. 5F 7
(off Theobalds Rd.)
Lacon Rd. SE22 . . . . . . 2C 106
Lacy Rd. SW15. . . . . 2F 99
(not continuous)
Ladas Rd. SE27 . . . . . . 4E 119
Ladbroke Cres. W11 . . . 5A 58
Ladbroke Gdns. W11. . . 1B 72
Ladbroke Gro. W10 . . . 3F 57
Ladbroke Gro. Ho. *W11*. . 1B *72*
(off Ladbroke Gro.)
Ladbroke M. W11 . . . . . 2A 72
Ladbroke Rd. W11 . . . . 2B 72
Ladbroke Sq. W11 . . . . 1B 72
Ladbroke Ter. W11. . . . . 1B 72
Ladbroke Wlk. W11 . . . . 2B 72
Ladlands SE22 . . . . 5C 106
Ladycroft Rd. SE13 . . . 1D 109
Lady Dock Wlk. SE16 . . 3A 80
Lady Margaret Rd.
NW5 . . . . 2E 47
Lady Micos Almshouses
E1 . . . . 5E *65*
(off Aylward St.)
Ladyship Ter. SE22 . . . 5C 106
Ladysmith Av. E6 . . . . . 1F 69
Ladysmith Rd. E16. . . . . 2B 68
Lady Somerset Rd.
NW5 . . . . 1D 47
LADYWELL 3D 109
Ladywell Cl. SE4 . . . . . 3C 108
Ladywell Hgts. SE4 . . . 4B 108
Ladywell Rd. SE13. . . . . 3C 108
Ladywell St. E15 . . . . . . 5B 54
Lafone St. SE1. . 3B 78 (3F 27)
Lagado M. SE16 . . . . . . 2F 79
Laing Ho. SE5 . . . . 3E 91
Lainson St. SW18 . . . . 5C 100
Lairdale Cl. SE21 . . . . . 1E 119
Laird Ho. *SE5*. 3E *91*
(off Redcar St.)
Lairs Cl. N7 . . . . 2A 48

Landward Ct. *W1* *5A 60*
(off Harrowby St.)
Lane Cl. NW2 . . . . 5D 29
Lane End SW15 . . . . 4F 99
Lanercost Cl. SW2 . . . 2C 118
Lanercost Rd. SW2 . . . 2C 118
Lanesborough Ct. *N1* . . *2A 64*
(off Fanshaw St.)
Lanesborough Pl. SW1 . 3C 20
Lane, The NW8 . . . . 1E 59
SE3 . . . . 1C 110
Laneway SW15 . . . . 3D 99
Laney Ho. *EC1* *5B 8*
(off Leather La.)
Lanfranc Rd. E3 . . . . . . 1A 66
Lanfrey Pl. W14 . . . . . . 1B 86
Langbourne Av. N6 . . . . 4C 32
Langbourne Ct. E17 . . . 1A 38
Langbourne Mans. N6 . . 4C 32
Langbourne Pl. E14 . . . 1D 95
Langbrook Rd. SE3 . . . 1F 111
Langdale *NW1* *1F 5*
(off Stanhope St.)
Langdale Cl. SE17 . . . . 2E 91
Langdale Ho. *SW1* *1E 89*
(off Churchill Gdns.)
Langdale Rd. SE10 . . . . 3E 95
Langdale St. E1 . . . . . . 5D 65
Langdon Ct. *EC1* *1E 9*
(off City Rd.)
NW10 . . . . 5A 42
Langdon Ho. E14 . . . . . 5E 67
Langdon Pk. Rd. N6 . . . 2E 33
Langdon Way SE1 . . . . 5C 78
Langford Cl. E8 . . . . 2C 50
NW8 . . . . 1E 59
Langford Ct. *NW8* *1E 59*
(off Abbey Rd.)
Langford Grn. SE5 . . . 1A 106
Langford Ho. SE8 . . . . . 2C 94
Langford Pl. NW8 . . . . . 1E 59
Langford Rd. SW6 . . . . 5D 87
Langham Mans. *SW5* . *1D 87*
(off Earl's Ct. Sq.)
Langham Pl. W4 . . . . . . 2A 84
W1 . . . . 4D 61 (1E 13)
Langham St.
W1 . . . . 4D 61 (1E 13)
Langholm Cl. SW12 . . . 5F 103
Langhorne Ct. *NW8* . . . *4F 45*
(off Dorman Way)
Lang Ho. *SW8* *3A 90*
(off Hartington Rd.)
Langland Gdns. NW3 . . 2D 45
Langland Ho. *SE5* *3F 91*
(off Edmund St.)
Langler Rd. NW10 . . . . 1E 57
Langley Ct.
WC2 . . . . 1A 76 (4D 15)
Langley Cres. E11 . . . . 2E 41
Langley Dr. E11 . . . . . . 2D 41
Langley La. SW8 . . . . . 2B 90
Langley Mans. *SW8* . . . *2B 90*
(off Langley La.)
Langley St.
WC2 . . . . 5A 62 (3D 15)
Langmead St. SE27 . . . 4D 119
Langmore Ho. *E1* *5C 64*
(off Stutfield St.)
Langport Ho. SW9 . . . . 5D 91

Langroyd Rd. SW17 . . . 2B 116
Langside Av. SW15 . . . 2C 98
Langston Hughes Cl.
SE24 . . . . 2D 105
Lang St. E1 . . . . 3E 65
Langthorn Ct.
EC2 . . . . 5F 63 (3B 18)
Langthorne Ct.
SE6: Brom 4E 123
Langthorne Rd. E11 . . . 5E 39
Langthorne St. SW6 . . . 3F 85
Langton Cl. WC1 . 3B 62 (3A 8)
Langton Ho. *SE11* *5B 76*
(off Lambeth Wlk.)
Langton Pl. SW18 . . . . 1C 114
Langton Ri. SE23 . . . . . 5D 107
Langton Rd. NW2 . . . . . 5E 29
SW9 . . . . 3D 91
Langton St. SW10 . . . . 2E 87
Langton Way SE3 . . . . . 4B 96
Langtry Pl. SW6 . . . . . . 2C 86
Langtry Rd. NW8 . . . . . 5D 45
Langtry Wlk. NW8 . . . . 5D 45
Lanhill Rd. W9 . . . . 3C 58
Lanier Rd. SE13 . . . . . 4F 109
Lannoy Point SW6 . . . . *3A 86*
(off Pellant Rd.)
Lanrick Ho. *E14* *5F 67*
(off Lanrick Rd.)
Lanrick Rd. E14 . . . . . . 5F 67
Lansbury Est. E14 . . . . 5D 67
Lansbury Gdns. E14 . . . 5F 67
Lanscombe Wlk. SW8 . . 4A 90
Lansdell Ho. *SW2* *4C 104*
(off Tulse Hill)
Lansdowne Ct. *W11* . . . *1A 72*
(off Lansdowne Ri.)
Lansdowne Cres. W11 . 1A 72
Lansdowne Dr. E8 . . . . 3C 50
Lansdowne Gdns.
SW8 . . . . 4A 90
Lansdowne Grn. Est.
SW8 . . . . 4A 90
Lansdowne Gro. NW10 . 1A 42
Lansdowne Hill SE27 . . 3D 119
Lansdowne La. SE7 . . . 2F 97
Lansdowne M. SE7 . . . 1F 97
W11 . . . . 2B 72
Lansdowne Pl.
SE1 . . . . 4F 77 (5C 26)
Lansdowne Ri. W11 . . . 1A 72
Lansdowne Rd. E11 . . . 4B 40
E17 . . . . 1C 38
W11 . . . . 1A 72
Lansdowne Row
W1 . . . . 2D 75 (1E 21)
Lansdowne Ter.
WC1 . . . . 3A 62 (4E 7)
Lansdowne Wlk. W11 . . 2B 72
Lansdowne Way SW8 . . 4F 89
Lansdowne Wood Cl.
SE27 . . . . 3D 119
Lansdowne Workshops
SE7 . . . . 1E 97
Lansdun Rd. E7 . . . . . . 4E 55
Lantern Cl. SW15 . . . . . 2C 98
Lanterns Ct. E14 . . . . . 4C 80
Lant Ho. *SE1* *4F 25*
(off Toulmin St.)
Lant St. SE1 . . . 3E 77 (3F 25)

Lanvanor Rd. SE15 . . . 5E 93
Lanyard Ho. SE8 . . . . . 5B 80
Lapford Cl. W9 . . . . 3B 58
Lapse Wood Wlk.
SE23 . . . . 1D 121
Lapwing Twr. *SE8* *2B 94*
(off Taylor Cl.)
Lapworth Ct. *W2* *4D 59*
(off Chichester Rd.)
Lara Cl. SE13 . . . . 4E 109
Larch Av. W3 . . . . 2A 70
Larch Cl. E13 . . . . 3D 69
N19 . . . . 4E 33
SE8 . . . . 2B 94
SW12 . . . . 2D 117
Larch Ct. *W9* *4C 58*
(off Admiral Wlk.)
Larch Ho. *SE16* *3E 79*
(off Ainsty Est.)
W10 . . . . *3A 58*
(off Rowan Wlk.)
Larch Rd. E10 . . . . 4C 38
NW2 . . . . 1E 43
Larcom St. SE17 . . . . . 5E 77
Larden Rd. W3 . . . . 2A 70
Larissa St. SE17 . . . . . 1F 91
Larkbere Rd. SE26 . . . 4A 122
Larkhall La. SW4 . . . . . 5F 89
Larkhall Ri. SW4 . . . . . 1E 103
Lark Row E2 . . . . 5E 51
Larkspur Cl. E6 . . . . . . 4F 69
Larnach Rd. W6 . . . . . . 2F 85
Larpent Av. SW15 . . . . 3E 99
Lascelles Cl. E11 . . . . . 4F 39
Lascelles Ho. *NW1* . . . *3A 60*
(off Harewood Av.)
Lassell St. SE10 . . . . . 1F 95
Lasseter Pl. SE3 . . . . . 2A 96
Latchmere Pas. SW11 . 5A 88
Latchmere Rd. SW11 . . 5B 88
Latchmere St. SW11 . . 5B 88
Latham Ct. *W14* *5C 72*
(off W. Cromwell Rd.)
Latham Ho. *E1* *5F 65*
(off Chudleigh St.)
Latimer Ho. E9 . . . . 3F 51
W11 . . . . *1B 72*
(off Kensington Pk. Rd.)
Latimer Pl. W10 . . . . . . 5E 57
Latimer Rd. E7 . . . . 1D 55
N15 . . . . 1A 36
W10 . . . . 4E 57
(not continuous)
Latona Ct. *SW9* *3C 90*
(off Caldwell St.)
Latona Rd. SE15 . . . . . 2C 92
Lattimer Pl. W4 . . . . . . 3A 84
Latymer Ct. W6 . . . . . . 5F 71
Lauderdale Ho. *SW9* . . *4C 90*
(off Gosling Way)
Lauderdale Mans. *W9* . *2D 59*
(off Lauderdale Rd.,
not continuous)
Lauderdale Pl. *EC2* *5F 9*
(off Beech St.)
Lauderdale Rd. W9 . . . 2D 59
Lauderdale Twr. EC2 . . . 5F 9
Laud St. SE11 . . . . 1B 90
Launcelot Rd.
BR1: Brom 4C 124

Leconfield Ho. SE5 . . . . 2A 106
Leconfield Rd. N5. . . . . . 1F 49
Leda Ct. SW9. . . . . 3C 90
(off Caldwell St.)
Ledam Ho. EC1 . . . . 5B 8
(off Bourne Est.)
Ledbury Ho. SE22 . . . . 1A 106
W11 . . . . 5B 58
(off Colville Rd.)
Ledbury M. Nth. W11. . . . 1C 72
Ledbury M. W. W11. . . . . 1C 72
Ledbury Rd. W11. . . . . . 5B 58
Ledbury St. SE15 . . . . . 3C 92
LEE 4C 110
Lee Bri. SE13 . . . . 1E 109
Lee Chu. St. SE13 . . . . 2A 110
Lee Conservancy Rd. E9. . 2B 52
Lee Ct. SE13. . . . . 2F 109
(off Lee High Rd.)
Leeds Pl. N4. . . . . 3B 34
Leefern Rd. W12 . . . . . . 3C 70
Leegate SE12 . . . . 3B 110
LEE GREEN 3B 110
Lee High Rd. SE12. . . . . 1E 109
SE13. . . . . 1E 109
Lee Ho. EC2 . . . . 1A 18
(off Monkwell Sq.)
Leeke St. WC1. . . . . . 2B 62 (1F 7)
Leeland Way NW10 . . . . . 1B 42
Lee Pk. SE3 . . . . 2B 110
Leerdam Dr. E14. . . . . . . 4E 81
Lee Rd. SE3 . . . . 1B 110
Lees Ct. W1 . . . . 4B 12
(off Lees Pl.)
Leeside Ct. SE16 . . . . . . 2F 79
(off Rotherhithe St.)
Leeside Cres. NW11 . . . . 1A 30
Leeson Rd. SE24 . . . . . 2C 104
Lees Pl. W1. . . . . 1C 74 (4B 12)
Lee St. E8 . . . . 5B 50
Lee Ter. SE3 . . . . 1A 110
Lee Valley Ice Cen. 4F 37
Leeward Ct. E1. . . . . . . 1C 78
Leeward Gdns. SW19. . . . 5A 114
Leeway SE8 . . . . 1B 94
Leewood Cl. SE12 . . . . . 4B 110
Lefevre Wlk. E3 . . . . 5B 52
Leff Ho. NW6 . . . . 5A 44
Lefroy Ho. SE1 . . . . 4F 25
(off Southwark Bri. Rd.)
Lefroy Rd. W12 . . . . 3B 70
Legard Rd. N5 . . . . 5D 35
Legatt Rd. SE9 . . . . 3F 111
Leggatt Rd. E15 . . . . . . 1E 67
Legge St. SE13. . . . . . . 3E 109
Leghorn Rd. NW10. . . . . 1B 56
Legion Cl. N1 . . . . 4C 48
Legion Ter. E3 . . . . 5B 52
Leicester Ct. W9 . . . . . . 4C 58
(off Elmfield Way)
WC2 . . . . 4C 14
Leicester Flds. WC2. . . . . 5C 14
Leicester Ho. SW9. . . . . 1D 105
(off Loughborough Rd.)
Leicester Pl.
WC2 . . . . . . 1F 75 (4C 14)
Leicester Rd. E11 . . . . . 1D 41
NW10. . . . . 4A 42
Leicester Sq.
WC2 . . . . . . 1F 75 (5C 14)

Leicester St.
WC2 . . . . 1F 75 (4C 14)
Leigham Av. SW16 . . . . 3A 118
Leigham Cl. SW16. . . . . 3B 118
Leigham Ct. Rd.
SW16 . . . . 2A 118
Leigham Hall Pde.
SW16 . . . . 3A 118
(off Streatham High Rd.)
Leigham Va. SW2 . . . . . 3B 118
SW16 . . . . 3B 118
Leigh Gdns. NW10. . . . . 1E 57
Leigh Orchard Cl.
SW16 . . . . 3B 118
Leigh Pl. EC1 . . 4C 62 (5B 8)
Leigh Rd. E10. . . . . 2E 39
N5. . . . . 1D 49
Leigh St. WC1. . . . . 2A 62 (2D 7)
Leighton Cres. NW5. . . . . 2E 47
Leighton Gdns. NW10 . . . 1D 57
Leighton Gro. NW5 . . . . . 2E 47
Leighton Ho. SW1 . . . . . 5F 75
(off Herrick St.)
Leighton Mans. W14 . . . . 2A 86
(off Greyhound Rd.)
Leighton Pl. NW5. . . . . . 2E 47
Leighton Rd. NW5 . . . . . 2E 47
Leila Parnell Pl. SE7 . . . . 2E 97
Leinster Gdns. W2. . . . . . 5E 59
Leinster M. W2 . . . . 1E 73
Leinster Pl. W2 . . . . 5E 59
Leinster Sq. W2. . . . . . . 5C 58
(not continuous)
Leinster Ter. W2. . . . . . . 1E 73
Leithcote Gdns.
SW16 . . . . 4B 118
Leithcote Path SW16. . . . 3B 118
Leith Mans. W9 . . . . 2D 59
(off Grantully Rd.)
Lelita Cl. SE8 . . . . 5C 50
Leman Pas. E1. . . . . 5C 64
(off Leman St.)
Leman St. E1. . . . . 5B 64
Le May Av. SE12 . . . . . 3D 125
Lemmon Rd. SE10. . . . . 2A 96
Lemna Rd. E11 . . . . 2B 40
Le Moal Ho. E1 . . . . 4E 65
(off Stepney Way)
Lemsford Cl. N15. . . . . . 1C 36
Lemsford Ct. N4 . . . . . . 4E 35
Lemuel St. SW18. . . . . . 4E 101
Lena Gdns. W6. . . . . . . 4E 71
Lenanton Steps E14. . . . . 3C 80
(off Manilla St.)
Lendal Ter. SW4. . . . . . . 1F 103
Len Freeman Pl. SW6 . . . 2B 86
Lenham Ho. SE1 . . . . . . 4C 26
(off Staple St.)
Lenham Rd. SE12 . . . . . 2B 110
Lennard Rd. SE20 . . . . . 5F 121
Lennon Rd. NW2 . . . . . . 2E 43
Lennox Gdns. NW10 . . . . 1B 42
SW1 . . . . 4B 74
Lennox Gdns. M. SW1. . . 4B 74
Lennox Lewis Cen. E5 . . . 4E 37
(off Theydon Rd.)
Lennox Rd. E17. . . . . . . 1B 38
N4. . . . . 4B 34

Lens Rd. E7 . . . . 4E 55
Lenthall Ho. SW1 . . . . . . 1E 89
(off Churchill Gdns.)
Lenthall Rd. E8 . . . . 4C 50
Lenthorp Rd. SE10. . . . . 5B 82
Lentmead Rd.
BR1: Brom 3B 124
Len Williams Ct. NW6 . . . 1C 58
Leof Cres. SE6 . . . . 5D 123
Leonard Ct. WC1. . 3F 61 (3C 6)
Leonard Rd. E7 . . . . 1C 54
Leonard St. EC2. . 3F 63 (3C 10)
Leonora Ho. W9. . . . . . . 3E 59
(off Lanark Rd.)
Leontine Cl. SE15 . . . . . 3C 92
Leopards Ct. EC1. . . . . . . 5B 8
Leopold Av. SW19 . . . . . 5B 114
Leopold Bldgs. E2 . . . . . 1F 11
(off Columbia Rd.)
Leopold Rd. E17. . . . . . . 1C 38
NW10 . . . . 4A 42
SW19 . . . . 4B 114
Leopold St. E3 . . . . 4B 66
Leopold Ter. SW19. . . . . 5B 114
Leo St. SE15 . . . . 3D 93
Leo Yd. EC1 . . . . 4E 9
Leppoc Rd. SW4. . . . . . 3F 103
Leroy St. SE1. . . . . 5A 78
Lerry Cl. W14. . . . . 2B 86
Lescombe Cl. SE23 . . . . 3A 122
Lescombe Rd. SE23. . . . 3A 122
Leslie Prince Ct. SE5 . . . 3F 91
Leslie Rd. E11 . . . . 1E 53
E16. . . . . 5D 69
Lessar Av. SW4 . . . . . . 4E 103
Lessingham Av. SW17. . . 4B 116
Lessing St. SE23 . . . . . 5A 108
Lester Av. E15 . . . . 3A 68
Leswin Pl. N16. . . . . 5B 36
Leswin Rd. N16 . . . . 5B 36
Letchford Gdns. NW10. . . 2C 56
Letchford M. NW10 . . . . . 2C 56
Letchmore Ho. W10. . . . . 3E 57
(off Sutton Way)
Letchworth St. SW17. . . . 4B 116
Lethbridge Cl. SE13 . . . . 4E 95
Letterstone Rd. SW6 . . . . 3B 86
Lettice St. SW6 . . . . 4B 86
Lett Rd. E15 . . . . 4F 53
Lettsom St. SE5 . . . . . . 5A 92
Lettsom Wlk. E13. . . . . . 1C 68
Leucha Rd. E17 . . . . . . 1A 38
Levana Cl. SW19 . . . . . 1A 114
Levant Ho. E1. . . . . 3F 65
(off Ernest St.)
Leverhurst Ho. SE27 . . . 5E 119
Levendale Rd. SE23 . . . . 2A 122
Levenhurst Way SW4. . . . 5A 90
Leven Rd. E14 . . . . 4E 67
Leverett St. SW3 . . . . . . 5A 74
Leverington Pl. N1. . . . . 2C 10
Leverson St. SW16 . . . . 5E 117
Leverstock Ho. SW3 . . . . 1A 88
(off Cale St.)
Lever St. EC1 . . . 2D 63 (2E 9)
Leverton Pl. NW5. . . . . . 2E 47
Leverton St. NW5. . . . . . 2E 47
Levison Way N19 . . . . . 3F 33
Levita Ho. NW1 . . . . 1C 6
(not continuous)

Lewesdon Cl. SW19 . . . . 1F **113**
Lewes Ho. SE1 . . . . 3E **27**
(off Druid St.)
SE15 . . . . 2C **92**
(off Friary Est.)
Leweston Pl. N16 . . . . 2B **36**
Lewey Ho. E3 . . . . 3B **66**
(off Joseph St.)
Lewin Rd. SW14 . . . . 1A **98**
SW16 . . . . 5F **117**
Lewis Ct. SE16 . . . . 1D **93**
(off Stubbs Dr.)
Lewis Gro. SE13 . . . . 2E **109**
LEWISHAM **1E 109**
Lewisham Bus. Cen.
SE14 . . . . 2F **93**
Lewisham Cen. SE13 . . 2E **109**
Lewisham Crematorium
SE6 . . . . 2B **124**
Lewisham Hgts. SE23 . . 1E **121**
Lewisham High St.
SE13 . . . . 4D **109**
Lewisham Hill SE13 . . . . 5E **95**
Lewisham Model Mkt.
SE13 . . . . 2E **109**
(off Lewisham High St.)
Lewisham Pk. SE13 . . . 3E **109**
Lewisham Rd. SE13 . . . 4D **95**
Lewisham St.
SW1 . . . . 3F **75** (4C **22**)
(not continuous)
Lewisham Way SE4 . . . . 4B **94**
SE14 . . . . 4B **94**
Lewis Ho. E14 . . . . 2E **81**
(off Coldharbour)
Lewis Pl. E8 . . . . 2C **50**
Lewis Silkin Ho. SE15 . . 2E **93**
(off Lovelinch Cl.)
Lewis St. NW1 . . . . 3D **47**
(not continuous)
Lexham Gdns. W8 . . . . . 5C **72**
Lexham Gdns. M. W8 . . 4D **73**
Lexham M. W8 . . . . 5C **72**
Lexham Wlk. W8 . . . . . . 4D **73**
Lexington Apartments
EC1 . . . . 3F **63** (3C **10**)
Lexington St. W1 . . 1E **75** (4A **14**)
Lexton Gdns. SW12 . . . . 1F **117**
Leybourne Ho. E14 . . . . 5B **66**
SE15 . . . . 2E **93**
Leybourne Rd. E11 . . . . . 3B **40**
NW1 . . . . 4D **47**
Leybourne St. NW1 . . . . 4D **47**
Leybridge Ct. SE12 . . . 3C **110**
Leyden Mans. N19 . . . . . 2A **34**
Leyden St. E1 . . . 4B **64** (1F **19**)
Leydon Cl. SE16 . . . . . . 2F **79**
Leyes Rd. E16 . . . . 1F **83**
Leyland Ho. E14 . . . . 1D **81**
(off Hale St.)
Leyland Rd. SE12 . . . . . 3C **110**
Leylang Rd. SE14 . . . . . 3F **93**
Leys Ct. SW9 . . . . 5C **90**
Leysdown Ho. SE17 . . . . 1A **92**
(off Madron St.)
Leysfield Rd. W12 . . . . . 4C **70**
Leyspring Rd. E11 . . . . . . 3B **40**
LEYTON **4E 39**
Leyton Bus. Cen. E10. . . 4C **38**
Leyton Ct. SE23 . . . . . . 1E **121**

Leyton Grange Est. E10. . 4C **38**
Leyton Grn. Rd. E10. . . . . 1E **39**
Leyton Grn. Twr. E10 . . . . 1E **39**
(off Leyton Grn. Rd.)
Leyton Ind. Village E10. . 2F **37**
Leyton Leisure Lagoon. . 2E **39**
Leyton Orient F.C.
(Matchroom Stadium)
. . . . 4D **39**
Leyton Pk. Rd. E10 . . . . . 5E **39**
Leyton Rd. E15. . . . . 2E **53**
LEYTONSTONE **5A 40**
Leytonstone Ho. E11 . . . 2B **40**
(off Hanbury Dr.)
Leytonstone Rd. E15 . . . 1A **54**
Leyton Way E11 . . . . 2A **40**
Leywick St. E15 . . . . 1A **68**
Liardet St. SE14 . . . . . . 2A **94**
Liberia Rd. N5 . . . . 3D **49**
Liberty M. SW12 . . . . . . 4D **103**
Liberty St. SW9 . . . . 4B **90**
Libra Rd. E13 . . . . 1C **68**
E3 . . . . 1B **66**
Library Mans. W12 . . . . . . 3E **71**
(off Pennard Rd.)
Library Pde. NW10 . . . . . 5A **42**
(off Craven Pk. Rd.)
Library Pl. E1. . . . . 1D **79**
Library St. SE1. . 3D **77** (5D **25**)
Lichfield Rd. E6 . . . . 2F **69**
E3 . . . . 2A **66**
NW2 . . . . 1A **44**
Lickey Ho. W14 . . . . 2B **86**
(off Nth. End Rd.)
Lidcote Gdns. SW9 . . . . 5B **90**
Liddell Gdns. NW10 . . . . 1E **57**
Liddell Rd. NW6 . . . . 3C **44**
Liddington Rd. E15 . . . . 5B **54**
Liddon Rd. E13 . . . . 2D **69**
Liden Cl. E17 . . . . 2B **38**
Lidfield Rd. N16. . . . . 1F **49**
Lidgate Rd. SE15 . . . . . . 3B **92**
Lidiard Rd. SW18 . . . . . 2E **115**
Lidyard Rd. N19 . . . . 3E **33**
Liffords Pl. SW13 . . . . . . 5B **84**
Lifford St. SW15 . . . . 2F **99**
Lighter Cl. SE16 . . . . 5A **80**
Lighterman Ho. E14 . . . . 1E **81**
Lighterman M. E1 . . . . . . 5F **65**
Lightermans Rd. E14 . . . 3C **80**
Lightermans Wlk.
SW18 . . . . 2C **100**
Light Horse Ct. SW3 . . . 1C **88**
(off Royal Hospital Rd.)
Ligonier St. E2. . 3B **64** (3F **11**)
Lilac Ct. E13. . . . . 5E **55**
Lilac Ho. SE4 . . . . 1C **108**
Lilac Pl. SE11 . . . . 5B **76**
Lilac St. W12 . . . . 1C **70**
Lilburne Ho. SE9 . . . . . . 3F **111**
Lilestone Ho. NW8 . . . . . . 3F **59**
(off Frampton St.)
Lilestone St. NW8 . . . . . 3A **60**
Lilford Ho. SE5. . . . . 5E **91**
Lilford Rd. SE5 . . . . 5D **91**
Lilian Barker Cl. SE12. . 3C **110**
Lilian Cl. N16. . . . . 5A **36**
Lilley Cl. E1 . . . . 2C **78**
Lillian Rd. SW13 . . . . . . 2C **84**

Lillie Mans. SW6 . . . . . . 2A **86**
(off Lillie Rd.)
Lillie Rd. SW6 . . . . 2A **86**
Lillieshall Rd. SW4 . . . 1D **103**
Lillie Yd. SW6 . . . . 2C **86**
Lillington Gdns. Est.
SW1 . . . . 5E **75**
(off Vauxhall Bri. Rd.)
Lilliput Ct. SE12. . . . . . 3D **111**
Lily Cl. W14 . . . . 5F **71**
(not continuous)
Lily Nichols Ho. E16. . . . 2F **83**
(off Connaught Rd.)
Lily Pl. EC1 . . . . . . 4C **62** (5C **8**)
Lily Rd. E17 . . . . 1C **38**
Lilyville Rd. SW6. . . . . . . 4B **86**
Limberg Ho. SE8 . . . . . . 5B **80**
Limborough Ho. E14 . . . 4C **66**
(off Thomas Rd.)
Limburg Rd. SW11 . . . 2A **102**
Limeburner La.
EC4 . . . . 5D **63** (3D **17**)
Lime Cl. E1 . . . . 2C **78**
Lime Ct. E11 . . . . 4A **40**
(off Trinity Cl.)
E17 . . . . 1E **39**
Lime Gro. W12 . . . . 3E **71**
Limeharbour E14 . . . . . . 4D **81**
LIMEHOUSE **5B 66**
Limehouse C'way. E14. . 1B **80**
Limehouse Ct. E14. . . . . 5C **66**
Limehouse Cut E14 . . . . 4D **67**
(off Morris Rd.)
Limehouse Flds. Est.
E14 . . . . 4A **66**
Limehouse Link E14 . . . 5A **66**
Lime Kiln Dr. SE7 . . . . . 2D **97**
Limerick Cl. SW12 . . . . 5E **103**
Limerston St. SW10. . . . 2E **87**
Limes Av. NW11 . . . . . . 2A **30**
SW13 . . . . 5B **84**
Limes Ct. NW6 . . . . 4A **44**
(off Brondesbury Pk.)
Limes Fld. Rd. SW14 . . 1A **98**
Limesford Rd. SE15 . . 2F **107**
Limes Gdns. SW18 . . . 4C **100**
Limes Gro. SE13 . . . . . 2E **109**
Limes, The SW18 . . . . 4C **100**
W2 . . . . 1C **72**
Lime St. EC3 . . 1A **78** (4D **19**)
Lime St. Pas.
EC3 . . . . 5A **64** (3D **19**)
Limes Wlk. SE15 . . . . . 2E **107**
Limetree Cl. SW2 . . . . . 1B **118**
Limetree Ter. SE6 . . . . 1B **122**
Limetree Wlk. SW17 . . 5C **116**
Lime Wlk. E15 . . . . 5A **54**
Limpsfield Av. SW19 . . 2F **113**
Linacre Cl. SE15 . . . . . 1D **107**
Linacre Ct. W6 . . . . 1F **85**
Linacre Rd. NW2 . . . . . . 3D **43**
Linale Ho. N1 . . . . 1B **10**
Linberry Wlk. SE8 . . . . . 5B **80**
Linchmere Rd. SE12 . . 5B **110**
Lincoln Av. SW19 . . . . . 3F **113**
Lincoln Ct. N16. . . . . 2F **35**
SE12 . . . . 3E **125**
Lincoln Ho.
SW3 . . . . 3B **74** (4A **20**)
SW9 . . . . 3C **90**

Lincoln M. NW6 . . . . . 5B **44**
  SE21 . . . . 2F **119**
Lincoln Rd. E7 . . . . . . 3F **55**
  E13 . . . . 3D **69**
Lincolns Inn Flds.
  WC2 . . . . 5B **62** (2F **15**)
Lincoln's Inn Hall
  . . . . 5B **62** (2A **16**)
Lincoln St. E11 . . . . . . 4A **40**
  SW3 . . . . 5B **74**
Lincombe Rd.
  BR1: Brom 3B **124**
Lindal Rd. SE4 . . . . . . 3B **108**
Linden Av. NW10 . . . . 1F **57**
Linden Ct. W12 . . . . . . 2E **71**
Linden Gdns. W2 . . . . 1C **72**
  W4 . . . . 1A **84**
Linden Gro. SE15 . . . 1D **107**
  SE26 . . . . 5E **121**
Linden Ho. SE8 . . . . . . 2B **94**
    (off Abinger Gro.)
  SE15 . . . . 1D **107**
Linden Lea N2 . . . . 1E **31**
Linden M. N1 . . . . 2F **49**
  W2 . . . . 1C **72**
Linden Wlk. N19 . . . . . 4E **33**
Lindfield Gdns. NW3 . . 2D **45**
Lindfield St. E14 . . . . . 5C **66**
Lindisfarne Way E9 . . . 1A **52**
Lindley Est. SE15 . . . . 3C **92**
Lindley Ho. E1 . . . . 4E **65**
    (off Lindley St.)
  SE15 . . . . 3C **92**
    (off Peckham Pk. Rd.)
Lindley Rd. E10 . . . . . . 4E **39**
Lindley St. E1 . . . . 4E **65**
Lindop Ho. E1 . . . . 3A **66**
    (off Mile End Rd.)
Lindore Rd. SW11 . . . 2B **102**
Lindo St. SE15 . . . . . . 5E **93**
Lindrop St. SW6 . . . . . 5E **87**
Lindsay Sq. SW1 . . . . . 1F **89**
Lindsell St. SE10 . . . . . 4E **95**
Lindsey M. N1 . . . . 4E **49**
Lindsey St.
  EC1 . . . . 4D **63** (5E **9**)
Lind St. SE8 . . . . 5C **94**
Lindway SE27 . . . . . . 5D **119**
Linfield WC1 . . . . 2F **7**
    (off Sidmouth St.)
Linford St. SW8 . . . . . . 4E **89**
Lingard Ho. E14 . . . . . . 4E **81**
    (off Marshfield St.)
Lingards Rd. SE13 . . . . 2E **109**
Lingfield Ho. SE1 . . . . . 4E **25**
Lingfield Rd. SW19 . . . 5F **113**
Lingham St. SW9 . . . . . 5A **90**
Ling Rd. E16 . . . . 4C **68**
Lings Coppice SE21 . . 2F **119**
Lingwell Rd. SW17 . . . 3A **116**
Lingwood Rd. E5 . . . . . 2C **36**
Linhope St. NW1 . . . . . 3B **60**
Linkenholt Mans.
  W6 . . . . 5B **70**
    (off Stamford Brook Av.)
Link Ho. E3 . . . . 1D **67**
  W10 . . . . 5F **57**
    (off Kingsdown Cl.)
Link Rd. E1 . . . . 1C **78**
  E12 . . . . 4F **41**

Links Rd. NW2 . . . . . . 4B **28**
Link St. E9 . . . . 3E **51**
Linksview N2 . . . . 1B **32**
    (off Gt. North Rd.)
Links Yd. E1 . . . . 4B **64**
    (off Spelman St.)
Linkway N4 . . . . 2E **35**
Linkwood Wlk. NW1 . . 4F **47**
Linley Sambourne House
  . . . . 4C **72**
    (off Stafford Ter.)
Linnell Cl. NW11 . . . . . 1D **31**
Linnell Dr. NW11 . . . . . 1D **31**
Linnell Ho. E1 . . . . 5F **11**
    (off Folgate St.)
Linnell Rd. SE5 . . . . . . 5A **92**
Linnet M. SW12 . . . . . 5C **102**
Linom Rd. SW4 . . . . . 2A **104**
Linscott Rd. E5 . . . . . . 1E **51**
Linsey Ct. E10 . . . . 3C **38**
    (off Grange Rd.)
Linsey St. SE16 . . . . . . 5C **78**
    (not continuous)
Linslade Ho. E2 . . . . . . 5C **50**
  NW8 . . . . 3A **60**
    (off Paveley St.)
Linstead St. NW6 . . . . 4C **44**
Linstead Way SW18 . . 5A **100**
Lintaine Cl. W6 . . . . . . 2A **86**
Linthorpe Rd. N16 . . . 2A **36**
Linton Cl. SE7 . . . . 1E **97**
Linton Gdns. E6 . . . . . . 5F **69**
Linton Gro. SE27 . . . . 5D **119**
Linton Ho. E14 . . . . . . 4C **66**
    (off St Paul's Way)
Linton St. N1 . . . . 5E **49**
    (not continuous)
Linver Rd. SW6 . . . . . . 5C **86**
Linwood Cl. SE5 . . . . . 5B **92**
Lion Cl. SE4 . . . . 4C **108**
Lion Ct. E1 . . . . 1F **79**
    (off Highway, The)
  N1 . . . . 5B **48**
    (off Copenhagen St.)
  SE1 . . . . 2E **27**
Lionel Gdns. SE9 . . . . 3F **111**
Lionel Mans. W14 . . . . 4F **71**
    (off Haarlem Rd.)
Lionel M. W10 . . . . 4A **58**
Lionel Rd. SE9 . . . . . . 3F **111**
Lion Gate M. SW18 . . . 5C **100**
Lion Mills E2 . . . . 1C **64**
Lions Cl. SE9 . . . . 3F **125**
Lion Yd. SW4 . . . . 2F **103**
Liphook Cres.
  SE23 . . . . 5E **107**
Lipton Rd. E1 . . . . 5F **65**
Lisburne Rd. NW3 . . . . 1B **46**
Lisford St. SE15 . . . . . 4B **92**
Lisgar Ter. W14 . . . . . . 5B **72**
Liskeard Gdns. SE3 . . . 4C **96**
Liskeard Ho. SE11 . . . . 1C **90**
    (off Kennings Way)
Lisle Cl. SW17 . . . . . . 4D **117**
Lisle Ct. NW2 . . . . 5A **30**
Lisle St. WC2 . . 1F **75** (4C **14**)
Lismore SW19 . . . . . . 5B **114**
    (off Woodside)
Lismore Cir. NW5 . . . . 2C **46**
Lismore Ho. SE15 . . . . 1D **107**

Lismore Wlk. N1 . . . . . 3E **49**
    (off Clephane Rd. Nth.)
  N1 . . . . 3F **49**
    (off Clephane Rd.)
Lissenden Gdns. NW5 . 1C **46**
    (not continuous)
Lissenden Mans. NW5 . 1C **46**
Lisson Grn. Est. NW8 . . 3A **60**
    (off Tresham Cres.)
LISSON GROVE 4A **60**
Lisson Gro. NW1 . . . . . 3A **60**
  NW8 . . . . 3F **59**
Lisson Ho. NW1 . . . . . . 4A **60**
    (off Lisson St.)
Lisson St. NW1 . . . . . . 4A **60**
Lister Cl. W3 . . . . 4A **56**
Listergate Ct. SW15 . . . 2E **99**
Lister Ho. E1 . . . . 4C **64**
  SE3 . . . . 2A **96**
    (off Restell Cl.)
Lister Lodge W2 . . . . . . 4C **58**
    (off Admiral Wlk.)
Lister M. N7 . . . . 1B **48**
Lister Rd. E11 . . . . 3A **40**
Liston Rd. SW4 . . . . . . 1E **103**
Listowel Cl. SW9 . . . . . 3C **90**
Listria Pk. N16 . . . . . . 4A **36**
Litcham Ho. E1 . . . . . . 2F **65**
    (off Longnor Rd.)
Litchfield Av. E15 . . . . 3A **54**
Litchfield Ct. E17 . . . . 1C **38**
Litchfield Gdns. NW10 . 3C **42**
Litchfield St.
  WC2 . . . . 1F **75** (4C **14**)
Litchfield Way NW11 . . 1E **31**
Lithos Rd. NW3 . . . . . . 3D **45**
Lit. Albany St. NW1 . . . 3D **61**
    (off Longford St.)
  NW1 . . . . 2E **5**
Little Angel Theatre . . . 5D **49**
    (off Cross St.)
Lit. Argyll St.
  W1 . . . . 5E **61** (3F **13**)
Lit. Boltons, The SW5 . . 1D **87**
  SW10 . . . . 1D **87**
Little Bornes SE21 . . . 4A **120**
Littlebourne SE13 . . . . 5A **110**
Little Britain
  EC1 . . . . 4D **63** (1E **17**)
Little Brownings SE23 . 2D **121**
Littlebury Rd. SW4 . . . 1F **103**
Lit. Chester St.
  SW1 . . . . 4D **75** (5D **21**)
Little Cloisters
  SW1 . . . . 4A **76** (5D **23**)
Lit. College La. EC4 . . . 4B **18**
    (off College St.)
Lit. College St.
  SW1 . . . . 4A **76** (5D **23**)
Littlecombe SE7 . . . . . 2D **97**
Littlecombe Cl. SW15 . . 4F **99**
Littlecote Cl. SW19 . . . 5A **100**
Lit. Dean's Yd. SW1 . . . 5D **23**
Little Dimocks SW12 . . 2D **117**
Lit. Dorrit Ct.
  SE1 . . . . 3E **77** (3A **26**)
Lit. Edward St.
  NW1 . . . . 2D **61** (1E **5**)
Lit. Essex St. WC2 . . . . 4B **16**
Littlefield Cl. N19 . . . . . 1E **47**

Louvaine Rd. SW11 . . . 2F **101**
Lovat Cl. NW2 . . . . 5B **28**
Lovat La. EC3 . . 1A **78** (4D **19**)
   (not continuous)
Lovatt Ct. SW12 . . . . . . 1D **117**
Lovegrove St. SE1 . . . . 1C **92**
Lovegrove Wlk. E14 . . 2E **81**
Lovelace Ho. E8 . . . . . . 5B **50**
   (off Haggerston Rd.)
Lovelace Rd. SE21 . . . 2E **119**
Love La. EC2 . . 5E **63** (2A **18**)
Lovelinch Cl. SE15 . . . . 2E **93**
Lovell Ho. E8 . . . . 5C **50**
   (off Shrubland Rd.)
Lovell Pl. SE16 . . . . 4A **80**
Loveridge M. NW6 . . . . 3B **44**
Loveridge Rd. NW6 . . . 3B **44**
Lovers Wlk. SE10 . . . . . 2F **95**
Lovers' Wlk. W1 . .2C **74** (1B **20**)
Love Wlk. SE5 . . . . 5F **91**
Low Cross Wood La.
   SE21 . . . . 3B **120**
Lowden Rd. SE24 . . . . 2D **105**
Lowder Ho. E1 . . . . 2D **79**
   (off Wapping La.)
Lowe Av. E16 . . . . 4C **68**
Lowell Ho. SE5 . . . . 3E **91**
   (off Wyndham Est.)
Lowell St. E14 . . . . 5A **66**
Lwr. Addison Gdns. W14. .3A **72**
Lwr. Belgrave St.
   SW1 . . . . 4D **75** (5D **21**)
LOWER CLAPTON 1D **51**
Lwr. Clapton Rd. E5. . . 5D **37**
Lwr. Clarendon Wlk.
   W11 . . . . 5A **58**
   (off Clarendon Rd.)
Lwr. Common Sth.
   SW15 . . . . 1D **99**
Lwr. Grosvenor Pl.
   SW1 . . . . 4D **75** (5E **21**)
LOWER HOLLOWAY . . . 2B **48**
Lwr. James St.
   W1 . . . . 1E **75** (4A **14**)
Lwr. John St.
   W1 . . . . 1E **75** (4A **14**)
Lwr. Lea Crossing E14 . .1A **82**
Lower Mall W6 . . . . 1E **85**
   (off Hammersmith Bri. Rd.)
W6 . . . . 1D **85**
   (not continuous)
Lower Marsh
   SE1 . . . . 3C **76** (4B **24**)
Lwr. Merton Ri. NW3 . . 4A **46**
Lwr. Richmond Rd.
   SW15 . . . . 1D **99**
Lower Rd. SE1. . 3C **76** (3B **24**)
   SE16 . . . . 3E **79**
   (not continuous)
Lwr. Sloane St. SW1 . . 5C **74**
LOWER SYDENHAM . . 4F **121**
Lwr. Sydenham Ind. Est.
   SE26 . . . . 5B **122**
Lower Ter. NW3 . . . . . . 5E **31**
   SE27 . . . . 5D **119**
   (off Woodcote Pl.)
Lwr. Thames St.
   EC3 . . . . 1F **77** (5C **18**)
Lowerwood Ct. W11. . . 5A **58**
   (off Westbourne Pk. Rd.)

Lowestoft Cl. E5 . . . . . . 4E **37**
   (off Mundford Rd.)
Loweswater Ho. E3 . . . 3B **66**
Lowfield Rd. NW6 . . . . 4C **44**
Low Hall La. E17 . . . . . 1A **38**
Low Hall Mnr. Bus. Cen.
   E17 . . . . 1A **38**
Lowman Rd. N7 . . . . . . 1B **48**
Lowndes Cl. SW1 . . . . 4C **74**
Lowndes Ct.
   SW1 . . . . 4B **74** (5A **20**)
   W1 . . . . 3F **13**
Lowndes Pl. SW1 . . . . 4C **74**
Lowndes Sq.
   SW1 . . . . 3B **74** (4A **20**)
Lowndes St.
   SW1 . . . . 4C **74** (5A **20**)
Lowood Ho. E1 . . . . 1E **79**
   (off Bewley St.)
Lowood St. E1 . . . . 1D **79**
Lowry Ct. SE16 . . . . 1D **93**
   (off Stubbs Dr.)
Lowther Gdns. SW7 . . . 3F **73**
Lowther Hill SE23 . . . . 5A **108**
Lowther Ho. E8 . . . . 5B **50**
   (off Clarissa St.)
   SW1 . . . . 1E **89**
   (off Churchill Gdns.)
Lowther Rd. N7 . . . . . . 2C **48**
   SW13 . . . . 4B **84**
Loxford Av. E6 . . . . 1F **69**
Loxham St. WC1. . 2A **62** (2E **7**)
Loxley Cl. SE26 . . . . . . 5F **121**
Loxley Rd. SW18 . . . . . 1F **115**
Loxton Rd. SE23 . . . . . 1F **121**
Lubbock Ho. E14 . . . . . . 1D **81**
   (off Poplar High St.)
Lubbock St. SE14 . . . . . 3E **93**
Lucan Ho. N1 . . . . 5F **49**
   (off Colville Est.)
Lucan Pl. SW3 . . . . 5A **74**
Lucas Av. E13 . . . . 5D **55**
Lucas Cl. NW10 . . . . . . 4C **42**
Lucas Ct. SE26 . . . . . . 5A **122**
   SW11 . . . . 4C **88**
Lucas Sq. NW11 . . . . . . 1C **30**
Lucas St. SE8 . . . . 4C **94**
Lucerne M. W8 . . . . 2C **72**
Lucerne Rd. N5 . . . . . . 1D **49**
Lucey Rd. SE16 . . . . . . 4C **78**
Lucey Way SE16 . . . . . 4C **78**
   (not continuous)
Lucien Rd. SW17 . . . . . 4C **116**
   SW19 . . . . 2D **115**
Lucorn Cl. SE12 . . . . . 4B **110**
Lucy Brown Ho. SE1 . . 2A **26**
Ludgate B'way.
   EC4 . . . . 5D **63** (3D **17**)
Ludgate Cir.
   EC4 . . . . 5D **63** (3D **17**)
Ludgate Hill
   EC4 . . . . 5D **63** (3D **17**)
Ludgate Sq.
   EC4 . . . . 5D **63** (3E **17**)
Ludlow St. EC1 . . 3E **63** (3F **9**)
Ludovick Wlk. SW15 . . . 2A **98**
Ludwick M. SE14 . . . . . 3A **94**
Luffman Rd. SE12 . . . . 3D **125**
Lugard Ho. W12 . . . . . . 2D **71**

Lugard Rd. SE15 . . . . . 5D **93**
Luke Ho. E1 . . . . 5D **65**
   (off Tillman St.)
Luke St. EC2 . . 3A **64** (3D **11**)
Lukin St. E1 . . . . 5E **65**
Lullingstone Ho. SE15 . .2E **93**
   (off Lovelinch Cl.)
Lullingstone La. SE13. .4F **109**
Lulot Gdns. N19 . . . . . . 4D **33**
Lulworth NW1 . . . . 4F **47**
   (off Wrotham Rd.)
   SE17 . . . . 1F **91**
   (off Portland St.)
Lulworth Ct. N1 . . . . 4A **50**
   (off St Peter's Way)
Lulworth Ho. SW8 . . . . 3B **90**
Lulworth Rd. SE9 . . . . 2F **125**
   SE15. . . . . 5D **93**
Lumiere Bldg., The E7. . 2F **55**
   (off Romford Rd.)
Lumiere Ct. SW17 . . . 2C **116**
Lumley Ct. WC2. . .1A **76** (5E **15**)
Lumley Flats SW1 . . . . . 1C **88**
   (off Holbein Pl.)
Lumley St. W1. . 5C **60** (3C **12**)
Lumsdon NW8 . . . . 5D **45**
   (off Abbey Rd.)
Lund Point E15. . . . . . . 5E **53**
Lundy Wlk. N1 . . . . 3E **49**
Lunham Rd. SE19 . . . . 5A **120**
Luntley Pl. E1. . . . . 4C **64**
Lupin Cl. SW2 . . . . 2D **119**
Lupin Point SE1 . . . . . . 3B **78**
   (off Abbey St.)
Lupton Cl. SE12 . . . . . 3D **125**
Lupton St. NW5 . . . . . . 1E **47**
   (not continuous)
Lupus St. SW1. . . . . . . 1D **89**
Luralda Gdns. E14 . . . 1F **95**
Lurgan Av. W6 . . . . 2F **85**
Lurline Gdns. SW11. . . 4C **88**
Luscombe Way SW8 . . 3A **90**
Lushington Rd. NW10 . .1D **57**
   SE6. . . . . 4D **123**
Lushington Ter. E8 . . . . 2C **50**
   (off Wayland Av.)
Luther King Cl. E17 . . .1B **38**
Luton Ho. E13 . . . . 3C **68**
   (off Luton Rd.)
Luton Pl. SE10 . . . . 3E **95**
Luton Rd. E13 . . . . 3C **68**
Luton St. NW8 . . . . 3F **59**
Lutton Ter. NW3 . . . . . . 1E **45**
   (off Lakis Cl.)
Luttrell Av. SW15. . . . . 3D **99**
Lutwyche Rd. SE6 . . . . 2B **122**
Lutyens Ho. SW1 . . . . . . 1E **89**
   (off Churchill Gdns.)
Luxborough Ho. W1. . . .5B **4**
   (off Luxborough St.)
Luxborough St.
   W1 . . . . 4C **60** (5B **4**)
Luxborough Twr. W1 . . 5B **4**
Luxemburg Gdns. W6. . .5F **71**
Luxfield Rd. SE9. . . . . . 1F **125**
Luxford St. SE16. . . . . . 5F **79**
Luxmore St. SE4 . . . . . 4B **94**
Luxor St. SE5 . . . . 1E **105**
Lyall Av. SE21 . . . . 4A **120**
Lyall M. SW1 . . 4C **74** (5B **20**)

Lyall M. W. SW1 . . . . 4C 74
Lyall St. SW1 . . . 4C 74 (5B 20)
Lyal Rd. E3 . . . . 1A 66
Lycett Pl. W12 . . . . 3C 70
Lyceum Theatre 4F 15
Lydden Gro. SW18 . . . . . 5D 101
Lydden Rd. SW18 . . . . . . 5D 101
Lydford NW1 . . . . 5E 47
(off Royal College St.)
Lydford Cl. N16 . . . . 2A 50
(off Pellerin Rd.)
Lydford Rd. N15 . . . . 1F 35
NW2 . . . . 3E 43
W9 . . . . 3B 58
Lydhurst Av. SW2 . . . . . . 2B 118
Lydney Cl. SE15 . . . . 3A 92
SW19 . . . . 2A 114
Lydon Rd. SW4 . . . . 1E 103
Lyford Rd. SW18 . . . . 5F 101
Lyford St. SE7 . . . . 5F 83
Lygon Ho. E2 . . . . 2B 64
(off Gosset St.)
SW6 . . . . 4A 86
(off Fulham Pal. Rd.)
Lygon Pl. SW1 . . 4D 75 (5D 21)
Lyham Cl. SW2 . . . . 4A 104
Lyham Rd. SW2 . . . . 3A 104
Lyly Ho. SE1 . . . . 5C 26
(off Burbage Cl.)
Lyme Farm Rd. SE12 . . 2C 110
Lyme Gro. E9 . . . . 4E 51
Lyme Gro. Ho. E9 . . . . 4E 51
(off Lyme Gro.)
Lymer Av. SE19 . . . . 5B 120
Lyme St. NW1 . . . . 4E 47
Lyme Ter. NW1 . . . . 4E 47
Lyminge Gdns. SW18 . . 1A 116
Lymington Lodge E14 . . . . 4F 81
(off Schooner Cl.)
Lymington Rd. NW6 . . . . . 3D 45
Lympstone Gdns. SE15 . . 3C 92
Lynch Cl. SE3 . . . . 5B 96
Lynch Wlk. SE8 . . . . 2B 94
(off Dacca St.)
Lyncott Cres. SW4 . . . . . 2D 103
Lyncourt SE3 . . . . 5F 95
Lyncroft Gdns. NW6 . . . . . 2C 44
Lyncroft Mans. NW6 . . . . . 2C 44
Lyndale NW2 . . . . 1B 44
Lyndale Av. NW2 . . . . 5B 30
Lyndale Cl. SE3 . . . . 2B 96
Lynde Ho. SW4 . . . . 1F 103
Lyndhurst Cl. NW10 . . . . . 5A 28
Lyndhurst Ct. NW8 . . . . . . 5F 45
(off Finchley Rd.)
Lyndhurst Dr. E10 . . . . 2E 39
Lyndhurst Gdns. NW3 . . . 2F 45
Lyndhurst Gro. SE15 . . . . 5A 92
Lyndhurst Lodge E14 . . . . 5F 81
(off Millennium Dr.)
Lyndhurst Rd. NW3 . . . . . . 2F 45
Lyndhurst Sq. SE15 . . . . . 4B 92
Lyndhurst Ter. NW3 . . . . . 2F 45
Lyndhurst Way SE15 . . . . 4B 92
Lyneham Wlk. E5 . . . . 2A 52
Lynette Av. SW4 . . . . 4D 103
Lym M. E3 . . . . 2B 66
N16 . . . . 1A 50
Lynmouth Rd. E17 . . . . . . 1A 38
N16 . . . . 3B 36

Lynne Cl. SE23 . . . . 5B 108
Lynn Ho. SE15 . . . . 2D 93
(off Friary Est.)
Lynn M. E11 . . . . 4A 40
Lynn Rd. E11 . . . . 4A 40
SW12 . . . . 5D 103
Lynsted Gdns. SE9 . . . . . . 1F 111
Lynton Cl. NW10 . . . . 2A 42
Lynton Est. SE1 . . . . 5C 78
Lynton Ho. W2 . . . . 5E 59
(off Hallfield Est.)
Lynton Mans. SE1 . . . . 5B 24
(off Kennington Rd.)
Lynton Rd. N8 . . . . 1F 33
(not continuous)
NW6 . . . . 1B 58
SE1 . . . . 5B 78
Lynwood Rd. SW17 . . . . . 3B 116
Lyon Ho. NW8 . . . . 3A 60
(off Broadley St.)
Lyon Ind. Est. NW2 . . . . . . 4D 29
Lyons Pl. NW8 . . . . 3F 59
Lyon St. N1 . . . . 4B 48
Lyons Wlk. W14 . . . . 5A 72
Lyric M. SE26 . . . . 4E 121
Lyric Rd. SW13 . . . . 4B 84
Lyric Theatre 4B 14
(off Shaftesbury Av.)
Lysander Gro. N19 . . . . 3F 33
Lysander Ho. E2 . . . . 1D 65
(off Temple St.)
Lysander M. N19 . . . . 3E 33
Lysia Ct. SW6 . . . . 3F 85
(off Lysia St.)
Lysias Rd. SW12 . . . . 4D 103
Lysia St. SW6 . . . . 3F 85
Lysons Wlk. SW15 . . . . 2C 98
Lytcott Gro. SE22 . . . . 3A 106
Lytham St. SE17 . . . . 1F 91
Lyttelton Cl. NW3 . . . . 4A 46
Lyttelton Ho. E9 . . . . 4E 51
(off Well St.)
Lyttelton Rd. E10 . . . . 5D 39
Lyttelton Theatre 1A 24
(in Royal National Theatre)
Lytton Cl. N2 . . . . 1F 31
Lytton Gro. SW15 . . . . 3F 99
Lytton Rd. E11 . . . . 2A 40
Lyveden Rd. SE3 . . . . 3D 97

M

Mabledon Ct. WC1 . . . . 2C 6
(off Mabledon Pl.)
Mabledon Pl.
WC1 . . . . 2F 61 (2C 6)
Mablethorpe Rd. SW6 . . . 3A 86
Mabley St. E9 . . . . 2A 52
Macarthur Cl. E7 . . . . 3C 54
Macarthur Ter. SE7 . . . . . . 2F 97
Macartney Ho. SE10 . . . . . 3F 95
(off Chesterfield Wlk.)
SW9 . . . . 4C 90
(off Gosling Way)
Macaulay Ct. SW4 . . . . . 1D 103
Macaulay Rd. E6 . . . . 1F 69
SW4 . . . . 1D 103
Macaulay Sq. SW4 . . . . . 2D 103
McAuley Cl. SE1 . . 4C 76 (5B 24)

Macauley M. SE13 . . . . 4E 95
Macbeth Ho. N1 . . . . 1A 64
Macbeth St. W6 . . . . 1D 85
McCall Cl. SW4 . . . . 5A 90
McCall Cres. SE7 . . . . 1F 97
McCall Ho. N7 . . . . 1A 48
Macclesfield Ho. EC1 . . . . 2F 9
(off Central St.)
Macclesfield Rd.
EC1 . . . . 2E 63 (1F 9)
Macclesfield St.
W1 . . . . 1F 75 (4C 14)
McCoid Way SE1 . . 3E 77 (4F 25)
McCrone M. NW3 . . . . 3F 45
McCullum Rd. E3 . . . . 5B 52
McDermott Cl. SW11 . . . . 1A 102
McDermott Rd. SE15 . . . . 1C 106
Macdonald Rd. E7 . . . . 1C 54
N19 . . . . 4E 33
McDowall Cl. E16 . . . . 4B 68
McDowall Rd. SE5 . . . . 4E 91
Macduff Rd. SW11 . . . . . . 4C 88
Mace Cl. E1 . . . . 2D 79
Mace Gateway E16 . . . . . . 1C 82
Mace St. E2 . . . . 1F 65
McEwen Way E15 . . . . 5F 53
Macey St. SE10 . . . . 2E 95
(off Thames St.)
Macfarlane Rd. W12 . . . . . 2E 71
Macfarren Pl.
NW1 . . . . 3C 60 (4C 4)
McGlashon Ho. E1 . . . . 3C 64
(off Hunton St.)
McGrath Rd. E15 . . . . 2B 54
McGregor Ct. N1 . . . . 1E 11
McGregor Ho. E16 . . . . . . 4E 69
McGregor Rd. W11 . . . . . . 5B 58
Machell Rd. SE15 . . . . 1E 107
McIndoe Ct. N1 . . . . 5F 49
(off Sherborne St.)
McIntosh Ho. SE16 . . . . . . 5E 79
(off Millender Wlk.)
Macintosh Ho. W1 . . . . 5C 4
(off Beaumont St.)
Mackay Ho. W12 . . . . 1D 71
(off White City Est.)
Mackay Rd. SW8 . . . . 1D 103
McKay Trad. Est. W10 . . 3A 58
Mackennal St. NW8 . . . . . 1A 60
Mackenzie Cl. W12 . . . . . . 1D 71
Mackenzie Ho. NW2 . . . . . 5C 28
Mackenzie Rd. N7 . . . . . . 3B 48
Mackenzie Wlk. E14 . . . . . 2C 80
McKerrell Rd. SE15 . . . . . . 4C 92
Mackeson Rd. NW3 . . . . . . 1B 46
Mackie Rd. SW2 . . . . 5C 104
Mackintosh La. E9 . . . . 2F 51
Macklin St.
WC2 . . . . 5A 62 (2E 15)
Mackonochie Ho. EC1 . . . 5B 8
(off Baldwins Gdns.)
Mackrow Wlk. E14 . . . . 1E 81
Mack's Rd. SE16 . . . . 5C 78
Mackworth Ho. NW1 . . . . . 1F 5
(off Augustus St.)
Mackworth St.
NW1 . . . . 2E 61 (1F 5)
Maclaren M. SW15 . . . . . . 2E 99
Maclean Rd. SE23 . . . . . . 4A 108
McLeod Ct. SE22 . . . . 1C 120

Malyons Rd. SE13 . . . . 4D 109
Malyons Ter. SE13 . . . 3D 109
Managers St. E14 . . . . . . 2E 81
Manaton Cl. SE15 . . . 1D 107
Manbey Gro. E15 . . . . . 3A 54
Manbey Pk. Rd. E15 . . 3A 54
Manbey Rd. E15 . . . . . . 3A 54
Manbey St. E15 . . . . . . 3A 54
Manbre Rd. W6 . . . . 2E 85
Manchester Ct. E16 . . . 5D 69
(off Garvary Rd.)
Manchester Dr. W10 . . . 3A 58
Manchester Gro. E14 . . 1E 95
Manchester Ho. SE17. . 1E 91
Manchester M. W1. . . . 1B 12
Manchester Rd. E14. . . 1E 95
N15. . . . . 1F 35
Manchester Sq.
W1. . . . . 5C 60 (2B 12)
Manchester St.
W1. . . . . 4C 60 (1B 12)
Manchuria Rd. SW11. . 4C 102
Manciple St.
SE1. . . . . 3F 77 (4B 26)
Mandalay Rd. SW4 . . . 3E 103
Mandarin Ct. NW10 . . . 3A 42
(off Mitchellbrook Way)
SE8. . . . . 2B 94
Mandarin St. E14 . . . . . 1C 80
Mandela Cl. W12. . . . . . 1D 71
Mandela Ho. E2 . . . . . . 2F 11
(off Virginia Rd.)
SE5. . . . . 5D 91
Mandela Rd. E16 . . . . . 5C 68
Mandela St. NW1. . . . . 5E 47
SW9 . . . . 3C 90
(not continuous)
Mandela Way SE1 . . . . 5A 78
Mandeville Cl. SE3 . . . 3B 96
Mandeville Ho. SE1. . . 1B 92
(off Rolls Rd.)
SW4 . . . . 3E 103
Mandeville M. SW4 . . . 2F 103
Mandeville Pl.
W1. . . . . 5C 60 (2C 12)
Mandeville St. E5. . . . . 5A 38
Mandrake Rd. SW17 . . 3B 116
Mandrake Way E15 . . . 4A 54
Mandrell Rd. SW2 . . . 3A 104
Manette St. W1. . 5F 61 (3C 14)
Manfred Rd. SW15. . . 3B 100
Manger Rd. N7 . . . . 3A 48
Manilla St. E14 . . . . . . 3C 80
Man in the Moon Theatre
. . . . 2F 87
(off King's Rd.)
Manitoba Ct. SE16 . . . . 3E 79
(off Canada Est.)
Manley Ct. N16 . . . . . . 5B 36
Manley Ho. SE11 . . . . . 5C 76
Manley St. NW1. . . . . . 5C 46
Manneby Prior N1 . . . . 1A 8
(off Cumming St.)
Manningford Cl.
EC1. . . . . 2D 63 (1D 9)
Manningtree Cl. SW19 . .1A 114
Manningtree St. E1. . . . 5C 64
Manny Shinwell Ho.
SW6 . . . . 2B 86
(off Clem Attlee Ct.)

Manor Av. E7 . . . . 1E 55
SE4 . . . . 5B 94
Manor Brook SE3 . . . . 2C 110
Manor Ct. E10 . . . . 3D 39
N2. . . . . 1B 32
(off Aylmer Rd.)
SW2 . . . . 3B 104
SW6 . . . . 4D 87
SW16 . . . . 3A 118
Manor Est. SE16 . . . . . 5D 79
Manorfield Cl. N19. . . . 1E 47
(off Fulbrook M.)
Manor Flds. SW15 . . . . 4F 99
Manor Gdns. N7. . . . . . 5A 34
SW4 . . . . 5E 89
(off Larkhall Ri.)
. . . . 1A 84
Manor Gro. SE15 . . . . . 2E 93
Manorhall Gdns. E10. . 3C 38
Manor Ho. NW1. . . . . . 4A 60
(off Marylebone Rd.)
Manor Ho. Ct. W9 . . . . 3E 59
(off Warrington Gdns.)
Mnr. House Dr. NW6 . . 4F 43
Mnr. House Gdn. E11 . . 1D 41
Manor La. SE13 . . . . . 3A 110
Manor La. Ter. SE13 . . 2A 110
Manor M. NW6. . . . . . . 1C 58
(off Cambridge Av.)
SE4 . . . . 5B 94
Manor Mt. SE23 . . . . . 1E 121
Manor Pde. N16. . . . . . 4B 36
NW10 . . . . 1B 56
(off High St. Harlesden)
MANOR PARK 1F 55
Manor Pk. SE13 . . . . . 2F 109
Manor Park Crematorium
E7 . . . . 1E 55
Mnr. Park Pde. SE13 . 2F 109
(off Lee High Rd.)
Mnr. Park Rd. E12 . . . . 1F 55
(not continuous)
NW10 . . . . 5B 42
Manor Pl. SE17 . . . . . . 1D 91
Manor Rd. E10 . . . . . . 2C 38
E15 . . . . 1A 68
E16 . . . . 3A 68
N16 . . . . 4F 35
Manor Way SE3 . . . . . 2B 110
Manresa Rd. SW3 . . . . 1A 88
Mansard Beeches
SW17 . . . . 5C 116
Mansell St. E1. . 5B 64 (3F 19)
Mansel Rd. SW19 . . . 5A 114
Manse Rd. N16 . . . . . . 5B 36
Mansfield Ct. E2 . . . . . 5B 50
(off Whiston Rd.)
Mansfield Hgts. N2 . . 1A 32
Mansfield M.
W1. . . . . 4D 61 (1D 13)
Mansfield Pl. NW3. . . . 1E 45
Mansfield Rd. E11. . . . 1D 41
NW3 . . . . 2B 46
Mansfield St.
W1. . . . . 4D 61 (1D 13)
Mansford St. E2. . . . . . 1C 64
Mansion Cl. SW9. . . . . 4C 90
(not continuous)
Mansion Cottage
Vis. Info. Cen. 3A 32

Mansion Gdns. NW3 . . 5D 31
Mansion House
. . . . 5F 63 (3B 18)
Mansion Ho. Pl.
EC4. . . . . 5F 63 (3B 18)
Mansion Ho. St. EC2 . . 3B 18
Mansions, The SW5 . . 1D 87
Manson M. SW7. . . . . . 5F 73
Manson Pl. SW7. . . . . . 5F 73
Manston NW1. . . . . 4E 47
(off Agar Gro.)
Manstone Rd. NW2 . . . 2A 44
Manston Ho. W14 . . . . 4A 72
(off Russell Rd.)
Mantilla Rd. SW17 . . . 4C 116
Mantle Rd. SE4 . . . . . 1A 108
Mantle Way E15 . . . . . 4A 54
Mantua St. SW11. . . . . 1F 101
Mantus Cl. E1. . . . . 3E 65
Mantus Rd. E1 . . . . 3E 65
Manville Gdns. SW17 . 3D 117
Manville Rd. SW17 . . 2C 116
Manwood Rd. SE4 . . . 3B 108
Manygates SW12. . . . . 2D 117
Mapesbury M. NW4. . . 1C 28
NW9 . . . . 1C 28
Mapesbury Rd. NW2 . . 4A 44
Mapeshill Pl. NW2. . . . 3E 43
Mapes Ho. NW6. . . . . . 4A 44
Mape St. E2 . . . . 3D 65
Maple Av. W3. . . . . 2A 70
Maple Cl. N16 . . . . 1C 36
SW4 . . . . 4F 103
Maple Ct. SE6 . . . . 1D 123
Maplecroft Cl. E6 . . . . 5F 69
Mapledene Est. E8. . . . 4C 50
Mapledene Rd. E8 . . . . 4B 50
Maple Ho. SE8. . . . . . . 3B 94
(off Idonia St.)
Maple Leaf Sq. SE16 . . 3F 79
Maple Lodge W8 . . . . . 4D 73
(off Abbots Wlk.)
Maple M. NW6. . . . . . . 1D 59
SW16 . . . . 5B 118
Maple Pl. W1 . . . 3E 61 (5A 6)
Maple Rd. E11 . . . . 1A 40
Maples Pl. E1 . . . . 4D 65
Maplestead Rd. SW2. . 5B 104
Maple St. W1 . . . 4E 61 (5F 5)
Mapleton Cres. SW18. . 4D 101
Mapleton Rd. SW18. . . 4C 100
(not continuous)
Maple Wlk. W10. . . . . . 2F 57
Maplin Rd. E16 . . . . . . 5C 68
Maplin St. E3. . . . . 2B 66
Mapperley Cl. E11 . . . . 1B 40
Marathon Ho. NW1 . . . 5A 4
(off Marylebone Rd.)
Marban Rd. W9 . . . . . . 2B 58
Marble Arch 4A 12
MARBLE ARCH
. . . . 1B 74 (4A 12)
Marble Arch W1. . 1B 74 (4A 12)
Marble Arch Apartments
W1 . . . . 5B 60
(off Harrowby St.)
Marble Dr. NW2 . . . . . . 3F 29
Marble Ho. W9. . . . . . . 3B 58
Marble Quay E1 . . . . . . 2C 78
Marbrook Ct. SE12. . . 3E 125

Matcham Rd. E11 . . . . . 5A **40**
Matchroom Stadium 4D **39**
Matham Gro. SE22 . . . . . 2B **106**
Matheson Lang Ho. SE1 . 4B **24**
Matheson Rd. W14 . . . . . 5B **72**
Mathews Pk. Av. E15 . . . 3B **54**
Mathews Yd.
  WC2 . . . . 5A **62** (3D **15**)
Mathieson Ct. SE1 . . . . . 4E **25**
  (off King James St.)
Mathison Ho. SW10 . . . . 3E **87**
  (off Coleridge Gdns.)
Matilda Ho. E1 . . . . 2C **78**
  (off St Katherine's Way)
Matilda St. N1 . . . . 5B **48**
Matisse Ct. EC1 . 3F **63** (3B **10**)
Matlock Cl. SE24 . . . . . . 2E **105**
Matlock Ct. SE5 . . . . 2F **105**
Matlock Rd. E10 . . . . 1E **39**
Matlock St. E14 . . . . 5A **66**
Maton Ho. SW6 . . . . 3B **86**
  (off Estcourt Rd.)
Matrimony Pl. SW4 . . . . . 5E **89**
Matson Ho. SE16 . . . . . . 4D **79**
Matthew Cl. W10 . . . . . . 3F **57**
Matthew Parker St.
  SW1 . . . . 3F **75** (4C **22**)
Matthews Ho. E14 . . . . . 4C **66**
  (off Burgess St.)
Matthews St. SW11 . . . . 5B **88**
Matthias Rd. N16 . . . . . . 2A **50**
Mattison Rd. N4 . . . . 1C **34**
Maude Ho. E2 . . . . 1C **64**
  (off Ropley St.)
Maude Rd. SE5 . . . . 4A **92**
Maud Gdns. E13 . . . . . . 5B **54**
Maudlins Grn. E1 . . . . . . 2C **78**
Maud Rd. E10 . . . . 5E **39**
  E13 . . . . 1B **68**
Maud St. E16 . . . . 4B **68**
Maud Wilkes Cl. NW5 . . . 2E **47**
Mauleverer Rd. SW2 . . . 3A **104**
Maundeby Wlk. NW10 . . . 3A **42**
Maunsel St. SW1 . . . . . . 5F **75**
Mauretania Bldg. E1 . . . 1F **79**
  (off Jardine Rd.)
Maurice Bishop Ter. N6 . 1C **32**
  (off View Rd.)
Maurice Drummond Ho.
  SE10 . . . . 4D **95**
  (off Catherine Gro.)
Maurice St. W12 . . . . . . 5D **57**
Mauritius Rd. SE10 . . . . 5A **82**
Maury Rd. N16 . . . . 4C **36**
Maverton Rd. E3 . . . . . . 5C **52**
Mavis Wlk. E6 . . . . 4F **69**
  (off Greenwich Cres.)
Mavor Ho. N1 . . . . 5B **48**
  (off Barnsbury Est.)
Mawbey Ho. SE1 . . . . . . 1B **92**
Mawbey Pl. SE1 . . . . 1B **92**
Mawbey Rd. SE1 . . . . . . 1B **92**
Mawbey St. SW8 . . . . . . 3A **90**
Mawdley Ho. SE1 . . . . . . 4D **25**
Mawson Ho. EC1 . . . . . . 5B **8**
  (off Baldwins Gdns.)
Mawson La. W4 . . . . 2B **84**
Maxden Ct. SE15 . . . . . . 1B **106**
Maxilla Wlk. W10 . . . . . . 5F **57**
  (off Westway)

Maxted Rd. SE15 . . . . . 1B **106**
Maxwell Ct. SE22 . . . . . 1C **120**
  SW4 . . . . 3F **103**
Maxwell Rd. SW6 . . . . . 3D **87**
Maya Cl. SE15 . . . . 5D **93**
Mayall Rd. SE24 . . . . . . 3D **105**
Maybourne Cl. SE26 . . . 5D **121**
Maybury Ct. W1 . . . . . . 1C **12**
  (off Marylebone St.)
Maybury Gdns. NW10 . . 3D **43**
Maybury M. N6 . . . . 2E **33**
Maybury Rd. E13 . . . . . 3E **69**
Maybury St. SW17 . . . . 5A **116**
Mayday Gdns. SE3 . . . . 5F **97**
Maydew Ho. SE16 . . . . . 5E **79**
  (off Abbeyfield Est.)
Maydwell Ho. E14 . . . . . 4C **66**
  (off Thomas Rd.)
Mayerne Rd. SE9 . . . . . 3F **111**
Mayeswood Rd. SE12 . . 4E **125**
MAYFAIR 1D **75** (5D **13**)
Mayfair M. NW1 . . . . . . 4B **46**
  (off Regents Pk. Rd.)
Mayfair Pl. W1 . . 2D **75** (1E **21**)
Mayfield Av. W4 . . . . . . 5A **70**
Mayfield Cl. E8 . . . . 3B **50**
  SW4 . . . . 3F **103**
Mayfield Gdns. NW4 . . . 1F **29**
Mayfield Ho. E2 . . . . . . 1D **65**
  (off Cambridge Heath Rd.)
Mayfield Rd. E8 . . . . . . 4B **50**
  E13 . . . . 3B **68**
  N8 . . . . 1B **34**
  W12 . . . . 3A **70**
Mayfield Rd. Flats N8 . . 1B **34**
Mayflower Cl. SE16 . . . . 5F **79**
Mayflower Rd. SW9 . . . 1A **104**
Mayflower St. SE16 . . . . 3E **79**
Mayford NW1 . . . . 1E **61**
  (not continuous)
Mayford Cl. SW12 . . . . . 5B **102**
Mayford Rd. SW12 . . . . 5B **102**
Maygood St. N1 . . . . . . 1C **62**
Maygrove Rd. NW6 . . . . 3B **44**
Mayhew Ct. SE5 . . . . . . 2F **105**
Mayhill Rd. SE7 . . . . . . 2D **97**
Maylands Ho. SW3 . . . . 5A **74**
  (off Elystan St.)
Maynard Cl. SW6 . . . . . 3D **87**
Maynard Rd. E17 . . . . . 1E **39**
Maynards Quay E1 . . . . 1E **79**
Mayne Ct. SE26 . . . . . . 5D **121**
Mayo Ho. E1 . . . . 4E **65**
  (off Lindley St.)
Mayola Rd. E5 . . . . 1E **51**
Mayo Rd. NW10 . . . . . . 3A **42**
Mayow Rd. SE23 . . . . . 4F **121**
  SE26 . . . . 4F **121**
May Rd. E13 . . . . 1C **68**
May's Bldgs. M. SE10 . . 3E **95**
May's Ct. SE10 . . . . 3F **95**
Mays Ct. WC2 . 1A **76** (5D **15**)
Maysoule Rd. SW11 . . . 2F **101**
Mayston M. SE10 . . . . . 1C **96**
  (off Ormiston Rd.)
May St. W14 . . . . 1B **86**
Mayton St. N7 . . . . 5B **34**
May Tree Ho. SE4 . . . . . 1B **108**
  (off Wickham Rd.)
Maytree Wlk. SW2 . . . . 2C **118**

Mayville Est. N16 . . . . . 2A **50**
Mayville Rd. E11 . . . . . . 4A **40**
May Wlk. E13 . . . . 1D **69**
Mayward Ho. SE5 . . . . . 4A **92**
  (off Peckham Rd.)
May Wynne Ho. E16 . . . 1D **83**
  (off Murray Sq.)
Maze Hill SE3 . . . . 2A **96**
  SE10 . . . . 2A **96**
Maze Hill Lodge SE10 . . 2F **95**
  (off Park Vista)
Mazenod Av. NW6 . . . . 4C **44**
M.C.C. Cricket Mus. & Tours
  . . . . 2F **59**
Mead Cl. NW1 . . . . 3C **46**
Meadcroft Rd. SE11 . . . 2D **91**
  (not continuous)
Meader Ct. SE14 . . . . . 3F **93**
Mead Ho. W11 . . . . 2B **72**
  (off Ladbroke Rd.)
Meadowbank NW3 . . . . 4B **46**
Meadow Bank SE3 . . . . 1B **110**
Meadowbank Cl. SW6 . . 3E **85**
Meadowbank Rd. NW9 . 2A **28**
Meadow Cl. E9 . . . . 2B **52**
  SE6 . . . . 5C **122**
Meadowcourt Rd. SE3 . 2B **110**
Meadow La. SE12 . . . . . 3D **125**
Meadow M. SW8 . . . . . 2B **90**
Meadow Pl. SW8 . . . . . 3A **90**
  W4 . . . . 3A **84**
Meadow Rd. SW8 . . . . . 3B **90**
Meadow Row SE1 . . . . 4E **77**
Meadows Cl. E10 . . . . . 4C **38**
Meadowside SE9 . . . . . 2E **111**
Meadowside Leisure Cen.
  . . . . 2E **111**
Meadowsweet Cl. E16 . . 4F **69**
Meadowview Rd. SE6 . . 5B **122**
Mead Path SW17 . . . . . 4E **115**
Mead Pl. E9 . . . . 3E **51**
Mead Row SE1 . 4C **76** (5B **24**)
Meads Ct. E15 . . . . 3B **54**
Meadway NW11 . . . . . . 1C **30**
Meadway Cl. NW11 . . . 1D **31**
Meadway Ct. NW11 . . . 1D **31**
Meadway Ga. NW11 . . . 1C **30**
Meadway, The SE3 . . . . 5F **95**
Meakin Est. SE1 . 4A **78** (5D **27**)
Meanley Rd. E12 . . . . . 1F **55**
Meard St. W1 . . 5F **61** (3B **14**)
  (not continuous)
Meath Rd. E15 . . . . 1B **68**
Meath St. SW11 . . . . . . 4D **89**
Mechanic's Path SE8 . . 3C **94**
  (off Deptford High St.)
Mecklenburgh Pl.
  WC1 . . . . 3B **62** (3F **7**)
Mecklenburgh Sq.
  WC1 . . . . 3B **62** (3F **7**)
Mecklenburgh St.
  WC1 . . . . 3B **62** (3F **7**)
Medburn St. NW1 . . . . . 1F **61**
Medebourne Cl. SE3 . . 1C **110**
Mede Ho. BR1: Brom. . 5D **125**
  (off Pike Cl.)
Medfield St. SW15 . . . . 5C **98**
Medhurst Cl. E3 . . . . . . 1A **66**
  (not continuous)

Merriam Av. E9. . . . . . . 3B **52**
Merrick Sq. SE1. . 4F **77** (5B **26**)
Merriman Rd. SE3 . . . . . . 4E **97**
Merrington Rd. SW6 . . . 2C **86**
Merritt Rd. SE4 . . . . . . 3B **108**
Merritt's Bldgs. EC2. . . 4D **11**
Merrivale NW1 . . . . 5E **47**
(off Camden St.)
Merrow St. SE17. . . . . . . 1F **91**
Merrow Wlk. SE17 . . . . 1F **91**
Merryfield SE3 . . . . 5B **96**
Merryfield Ho. SE9 . . . 3E **125**
(off Grove Pk. Rd.)
Merryweather Ct. N19 . . 5E **33**
Merryfields Way SE6. . 5D **109**
Merthyr Ter. SW13. . . . . 2D **85**
Merton Av. W4 . . . . 5B **70**
Merton La. N6 . . . . 4B **32**
Merton Mans. SE8 . . . . 4C **94**
(off Brookmill Rd.)
Merton Ri. NW3 . . . . 4A **46**
(not continuous)
Merton Rd. E17 . . . . 1E **39**
SW18 . . . . 4C **100**
Mertoun Ter. W1. . . . . . 4B **60**
(off Seymour Pl.)
Merttins Rd. SE15 . . . 3F **107**
Meru Cl. NW5. . . . . 1C **46**
Mervan Rd. SW2 . . . . . 2C **104**
Messent Rd. SE9 . . . . . 3E **111**
Messina Av. NW6. . . . . 4C **44**
Messiter Ho. N1 . . . . 5B **48**
(off Barnsbury Est.)
Meteor St. SW11 . . . . . 2C **102**
Methley St. SE11 . . . . . 1C **90**
Methwold Rd. W10. . . . 4F **57**
Metro Bus. Cen., The
SE26 . . . . 5B **122**
Metro Central Hgts.
SE1 . . . . 5F **25**
Metropolis SE11. . . . . . 4D **77**
(off Oswin St.)
Metropolitan Bus. Cen.
N1 . . . . 4A **50**
(off Enfield Rd.)
Metropolitan Cl. E14 . . 4C **66**
Metropolitan Wharf E1 . 2E **79**
Mews St. E1 . . . . 2C **78**
Mews, The IG4: Ilf 1F **41**
N1 . . . . 5E **49**
SE22 . . . . 3C **106**
Mexborough NW1. . . . . 5E **47**
Mexfield Rd. SW15 . . . 3B **100**
Meymott St.
SE1 . . . . 2D **77** (2D **25**)
Meynell Cres. E9 . . . . . 4F **51**
Meynell Gdns. E9. . . . . 4F **51**
Meynell Rd. E9 . . . . 4F **51**
Meyrick Ho. E14 . . . . . . 4C **66**
(off Burgess St.)
Meyrick Rd. NW10 . . . . 3C **42**
SW11 . . . . 1F **101**
Miah Ter. E1 . . . . 2C **78**
Miall Wlk. SE26 . . . . . 4A **122**
Micawber Ct. N1 . . . . . . 1A **10**
(off Windsor Ter.)
Micawber Ho. SE16 . . . 3C **78**
(off Llewellyn St.)
Micawber St.
N1 . . . . 2E **63** (1A **10**)

Michael Cliffe Ho. EC1 . . 2D **9**
Michael Faraday Ho.
SE17. . . . . 1A **92**
(off Beaconsfield Rd.)
Michael Manley Ind. Est.
SW8 . . . . 5E **89**
(off Clyston St.)
Michael Rd. E11 . . . . . . 3B **40**
SW6. . . . . 4D **87**
Michaels Cl. SE13 . . . . 2A **110**
Michael Stewart Ho.
SW6 . . . . 2B **86**
(off Clem Attlee Ct.)
Michelangelo Ct.
SE16. . . . . 1D **93**
(off Stubbs Dr.)
Micheldever Rd. SE12. . 4A **110**
Michelle Ct. W3 . . . . . . 1A **70**
Michelson Ho. SE11 . . 5B **76**
(off Black Prince Rd.)
Michigan Ho. E14 . . . . 4C **80**
Mickledore NW1 . . . . 1A **6**
(off Ampthill Est.)
Micklethwaite Rd. SW6. . 2C **86**
Middle Dene NW7 . . . . 5F **45**
Middlefield NW8 . . . . . . 5F **45**
Middle La. N8 . . . . 1A **34**
Middle La. M. N8. . . . . . 1A **34**
Middle Pk. Av. SE9. . . . 4F **111**
Middle Rd. E13 . . . . 1C **68**
Middle Row W10 . . . . . 3A **58**
Middlesex County Cricket Club
(Lord's Cricket Ground)
. . . . 2F **59**
Middlesex Ct. W4 . . . . . 1B **84**
Middlesex Filter Beds
Nature Reserve. 5F **37**
Middlesex Pas. EC1 . . . 1E **17**
Middlesex Pl. E9 . . . . . . 3E **51**
(off Elsdale St.)
Middlesex St.
E1. . . . . 4A **64** (1E **19**)
Middlesex University
(Nth. End Rd.) 3D **31**
Middlesex University
(Archway Campus, The)
. . . . 3E **33**
Middlesex Wharf E5 . . . 4E **37**
Middle St. EC1. . . 4E **63** (5F **9**)
Middle Temple Hall . . . 4B **16**
(off Middle Temple La.)
Middle Temple La.
EC4 . . . . 5C **62** (3B **16**)
Middleton Bldgs. W1 . . 1F **13**
Middleton Dr. SE16 . . . 3F **79**
Middleton Gro. N7 . . . . 2A **48**
Middleton Ho. E8 . . . . . 4C **50**
SE1 . . . . 5B **26**
(off Burbage Cl.)
SW1 . . . . 5F **75**
(off Causton St.)
Middleton M. N7 . . . . . . 2A **48**
Middleton Rd. E8 . . . . . 4B **50**
NW11 . . . . 2C **30**
Middleton St. E2 . . . . . . 2D **65**
Middleton Way SE13 . . 2F **109**
Middleway NW11. . . . . . 1D **31**
Middle Yd. SE1. . 2A **78** (1D **27**)
Midford Pl. W1 . . 3E **61** (4A **6**)
Midhope Ho. WC1 . . . . . 2E **7**
(off Midhope St.)

Midhope St.
WC1 . . . . 2A **62** (2E **7**)
Midhurst SE26 . . . . 5E **121**
Midhurst Ho. E14. . . . . 5B **66**
(off Salmon La.)
Midhurst Way E5 . . . . . 1C **50**
Midland Cres. NW3 . . . 3E **45**
Midland Pde. NW6 . . . . 3D **45**
Midland Pl. E14 . . . . . . 1E **95**
Midland Rd. E10 . . . . . . 2E **39**
NW1 . . . . 1F **61** (1C **6**)
Midland Ter. NW2 . . . . . 5F **29**
NW10 . . . . 3A **56**
(not continuous)
Midmoor Rd. SW12 . . 1E **117**
Midship Cl. SE16 . . . . . 2F **79**
Midship Point E14 . . . . 3C **80**
(off Quarterdeck, The)
Midstrath Rd. NW10 . . 1A **42**
Midway Ho. EC1 . . . . . . 1D **9**
Midwood Cl. NW2 . . . . 5D **29**
Mighell Av. IG4: Ilf 1F **41**
Milborne Gro. SW10 . . 1E **87**
Milborne St. E9 . . . . . . 3E **51**
Milborough Cres.
SE12. . . . . 4A **110**
Milcote St. SE1. . 3D **77** (4D **25**)
Mildenhall Rd. E5 . . . . 1E **51**
Mildmay Av. N1 . . . . . . 3F **49**
Mildmay Gro. Nth. N1 . . 2F **49**
Mildmay Gro. Sth. N1 . . 2F **49**
Mildmay Pk. N1 . . . . . . 2F **49**
Mildmay Pl. N16 . . . . . 2A **50**
Mildmay Rd. N1 . . . . . . 2F **49**
Mildmay St. N1 . . . . . . 3F **49**
MILE END 3B **66**
Mile End Pl. E1. . . . . . . 3F **65**
Mile End Rd. E1. . . . . . 4E **65**
Miles Bldgs. NW1 . . . . 4A **60**
(off Penfold Pl.)
Miles Ct. E1 . . . . 5D **65**
(off Tillman St.)
Miles Ho. SE10 . . . . 1A **96**
(off Tuskar St.)
Miles Pl. NW8 . . . . 4F **59**
(off Broadley St.)
Miles St. SW8 . . . . 2A **90**
(not continuous)
Miles St. Bus. Est.
SW8 . . . . 2A **90**
Milfoil St. W12. . . . . 1C **70**
Milford La. WC2 . .1C **76** (4A **16**)
Milford M. SW16 . . . . . 3B **118**
Milford Towers SE6 . . . 5D **109**
Milk St. BR1: Brom . . . 5D **125**
EC2 . . . . 5E **63** (3A **18**)
Milkwell Yd. SE5 . . . . . 4E **91**
Milkwood Rd. SE24 . . . 3D **105**
Milk Yd. E1 . . . . 1E **79**
Millais Ho. SW1 . . . . . . 5A **76**
(off Marsham St.)
Millais Rd. E11 . . . . 1E **53**
Millard Cl. N16 . . . . 2A **50**
Millard Ho. SE8 . . . . . . 1B **94**
(off Leeway)
Millbank SW1 . . 4A **76** (5D **23**)
Millbank Ct. SW1 . . . . . 5A **76**
(off John Islip St.)
Millbank Twr. 5A **76**
Millbank Way SE12 . . . 3C **110**

Millbrook Ho. *SE15* 2C 92
(off Peckham Pk. Rd.)
Millbrook Pas. SW9 . . . 1D 105
Millbrook Pl. *NW1* 1E 61
(off Hampstead Rd.)
Millbrook Rd. SW9 . . . 1D 105
Mill Ct. E10 . . . . 5E 39
Millcroft Ho. *SE6* 4E 123
(off Melfield Gdns.)
Millender Wlk. SE16 . . . 5E 79
Millenium Village
SE10 . . . . 4B 82
Millennium Bridge
. . . . 1D 77 (5F 17)
Millennium Bus. Cen.
NW2 . . . . 4D 29
Millennium Cl. E16 . . . 5D 69
Millennium Dome 2A 82
Millennium Dr. E14 . . . 5F 81
Millennium Pl. E2 . . . . 1D 65
Millennium Sq. SE1 . . . 3B 78
Millennium Way SE10 . . 3A 82
Miller Rd. SW19 . . . . 5F 115
Miller's Av. E8 . . . . . . 2B 50
Miller's Ct. W4 . . . . . . 1B 84
Millers Mdw. Cl. SE3 . . 3B 110
Miller's Ter. E8 . . . . . . 2B 50
Miller St. NW1 . . . . . . 1E 61
(not continuous)
Millers Way W6 . . . . . 3E 71
Millers Wharf Ho. *E1* . . 2C 78
(off St Katherine's Way)
Miller Wlk.
SE1 . . . . 2C 76 (2C 24)
Millfield N4 . . . . 4C 34
Millfield La. N6 . . . . . 3A 32
(not continuous)
Millfield Pl. N6 . . . . . . 4C 32
Millfields Rd. E5 . . . . 1E 51
Mill Gdns. SE26 . . . . 3D 121
Millgrove St. SW11 . . . 4C 88
Millharbour E14 . . . . . 3D 81
Mill Hill SW13 . . . . . . 5C 84
Mill Hill Rd. SW13 . . . . 5C 84
Millhouse Pl. SE27 . . 4D 119
Millicent Rd. E10 . . . . 3B 38
Milligan St. E14 . . . . 1B 80
Millington Ho. N16 . . . 5F 35
Mill La. NW6 . . . . 2B 44
Millman M. WC1 . . 3B 62 (4F 7)
Millman Pl. *WC1* 4A 8
(off Millman St.)
Millman St.
WC1 . . . . 3B 62 (4F 7)
Millmark Gro. SE14 . . . 5A 94
MILL MEADS 1F 67
Mill Pl. E14 . . . . 5A 66
Mill Pond Cl. SW8 . . . . 3F 89
Millpond Est. SE16 . . . 3D 79
Mill Rd. E16 . . . . 2D 83
Mill Row N1 . . . . 5A 50
Mills Ct. EC2 . . . . 3D 11
Mills Gro. E14 . . . . . . 5E 67
Millshot Cl. SW6 . . . . 4E 85
Mills Ho. *SW8* 4E 89
(off Thessaly Rd.)
Millstream Ho. *SE16* . . 3D 79
(off Jamaica Rd.)
Millstream Rd.
SE1 . . . . 3B 78 (4F 27)

Mill St. SE1 . . . . 3B 78
W1 . . . . 1D 75 (4F 13)
MILLWALL 5D 81
Millwall Dock Rd. E14 . . 4C 80
Millwall F.C. (Den, The)
. . . . 1E 93
Millwood St. W10 . . . . 4A 58
Mill Yd. E1 . . . . 1C 78
Milman Rd. NW6 . . . . 1F 57
Milman's St. SW10 . . . 2F 87
Milne Gdns. SE9 . . . . 3F 111
Milner Pl. N1 . . . . 5C 48
Milner Rd. E15 . . . . . 2A 68
Milner Sq. N1 . . . . . . 4D 49
Milner St. SW3 . . . . . 5B 74
Milo Gdns. SE22 . . . . 4B 106
Milo Rd. SE22 . . . . . 4B 106
Milroud Ho. *E1* 4F 65
(off Stepney Grn.)
Milroy Wlk.
SE1 . . . . 2D 77 (1D 25)
Milson Rd. W14 . . . . 4F 71
Milstead Ho. E5 . . . . . 2D 51
Milton Av. E6 . . . . 4F 55
N6 . . . . 2E 33
Milton Cl. N2 . . . . 1E 31
SE1 . . . . 5B 78
Milton Ct. EC2 . . 4F 63 (5B 10)
SE14 . . . . 2B 94
SW18 . . . . 3C 100
Milton Ct. Highwalk
EC2 . . . . 4F 63
(off Silk St.)
Milton Ct. Rd. SE14 . . . 2A 94
Milton Gdn. Est. N16 . . 1F 49
Milton Gro. N16 . . . . . 1F 49
Milton Ho. *E2* 2E 65
(off Roman Rd.)
SE5 . . . . 3F 91
(off Elmington Est.)
Milton Mans. W14 . . . . 2A 86
(off Queen's Club Gdns.)
Milton Pk. N6 . . . . . . 2E 33
Milton Pl. E5 . . . . 1C 50
N7 . . . . 2C 48
(off Eastwood Cl.)
Milton Rd. N6 . . . . . . 2E 33
NW9 . . . . 2C 28
SE24 . . . . 3D 105
SW19 . . . . 5E 115
Milton St.
EC2 . . . . 4F 63 (5B 10)
Milverton Ho. SE23 . . 3A 122
Milverton Rd. NW6 . . . 4E 43
Milverton St. SE11 . . . 1C 90
Milward Wlk. E1 . . . . . 4D 65
Mimosa Lodge NW10 . . 2B 42
Mimosa St. SW6 . . . . 4B 86
Minard Rd. SE6 . . . . 5A 110
Mina Rd. SE17 . . . . . 1A 92
Minchin Ho. *E14* . . . 5C 66
(off Dod St.)
Mincing La.
EC3 . . . . 1A 78 (4D 19)
Minehead Rd. SW16 . . 5B 118
Minera M. SW1 . . . . . 5C 74
Minerva Cl. SW9 . . . . 3C 90
(not continuous)
Minerva Rd. NW10 . . . 2A 56
Minerva St. E2 . . . . . 1D 65

Minerva Wlk.
EC1 . . . . 5D 63 (2E 17)
Minet Av. NW10 . . . . . 1A 56
Minet Gdns. NW10 . . . 1A 56
Minet Rd. SW9 . . . . . 5D 91
Minford Gdns. W14 . . . 3F 71
Minford Ho. *W14* . . . 3F 71
(off Minford Gdns.)
Mingard Wlk. N7 . . . . 4B 34
Ming St. E14 . . . . 1C 80
Miniver Pl. EC4 . . . . . 4A 18
Minnow St. SE17 . . . . 5A 78
Minnow Wlk. SE17 . . . 5A 78
Minories EC3 . . 5B 64 (3F 19)
Minshill St. SW8 . . . . 4F 89
Minson Rd. E9 . . . . . . 5F 51
Minstead Gdns. SW15 . . 5B 98
Minster Ct. EC3 . . . . . 4E 19
Minster Pavement EC3 . . 4E 19
Minster Rd. NW2 . . . . 2A 44
Mint Bus. Pk. E16 . . . 4D 69
Mintern St. N1 . . . . . 1F 63
Minton Ho. SE11 . . . . 5C 76
(off Walnut Tree Wlk.)
Minton M. NW6 . . . . . 3D 45
Mint St. SE1 . . . 3E 77 (3F 25)
Mirabel Rd. SW6 . . . . 3B 86
Miranda Cl. E1 . . . . . 4E 65
Miranda Rd. N19 . . . . 3E 33
Mirfield St. SE7 . . . . . 5F 83
Mirror Path SE9 . . . . 3E 125
Missenden *SE17* . . . 1F 91
(off Roland Way)
Missenden Ho. *NW8* . . 3A 60
(off Jerome Cres.)
Mission Pl. SE15 . . . . 4C 92
Mission, The E14 . . . . 5B 66
(off Commercial Rd.)
Mistral SE5 . . . . 4A 92
Mitali Pas. E1 . . . . . . 5C 64
(not continuous)
Mitcham Ho. SE5 . . . . 4E 91
Mitcham La. SW16 . . 5E 117
Mitcham Rd. E6 . . . . . 2F 69
SW17 . . . . 5B 116
Mitchellbrook Way
NW10 . . . . 3A 42
Mitchell Ho. *W12* . . . 1D 71
(off White City Est.)
Mitchell's Pl. *SE21* . . 4A 106
(off Aysgarth Rd.)
Mitchell St. EC1 . . 3E 63 (3F 9)
(not continuous)
Mitchell Wlk. *E6* 4F 69
(off Neats Ct. Rd.)
Mitchison Rd. N1 . . . . 3F 49
Mitford Rd. N19 . . . . . 4A 34
Mitre Bri. Ind. Pk.
NW10 . . . . 3D 57
Mitre Ct. EC2 . . . . . . 2A 18
Mitre Rd. E15 . . . . . . 1A 68
SE1 . . . . 3C 76 (3C 24)
Mitre Sq. EC3 . . 5A 64 (3E 19)
Mitre St. EC3 . . 5A 64 (3E 19)
Mitre, The E14 . . . . . . 1B 80
Mitre Way NW10 . . . . 3D 57
W10 . . . . 3D 57
Mitre Yd. SW3 . . . . . . 5A 74
Moat Dr. E13 . . . . 1E 69
Moatfield NW6 . . . . . . 4A 44

Mothers Sq. *E5* *1D 51*
(off Hana M.)
Motley Av. EC2 . . . . 4D 11
Motley St. SW8 . . . . 5E 89
MOTTINGHAM **2F 125**
Mottingham Gdns.
SE9 . . . . 1F 125
Mottingham La. SE9. . . 1E 125
Mottingham Rd. SE9 . . 2F 125
Moules Ct. SE5. . . . . 3E 91
Moulins Rd. E9. . . . . 4E 51
Moulsford Ho. N7 . . . . . 2F 47
Moundfield Rd. N16. . . 1C 36
Mounsey Ho. *W10* *2A 58*
(off Third Av.)
Mountacre Cl. SE26 . . . 4B 120
Mt. Adon Pk. SE22. . . . 5C 106
Mountague Pl. E14. . . . 1E 81
Mountain Ho. SE11 . . . 5B 76
Mt. Angelus Rd. SW15. 5B 98
Mt. Ash Rd. SE26. . . . . 3D 121
Mountbatten Cl. SE19. . 5A 120
Mountbatten Cl. *SE16* . . *2E 79*
(off Rotherhithe St.)
Mountbatten Ho. *N6*. . . *2C 32*
(off Hillcrest)
Mountbatten M.
SW18 . . . . 5E 101
Mt. Carmel Chambers
W8 . . . . *3C 72*
(off Dukes La.)
Mount Ct. SW15. . . . . . . 1A 100
Mountearl Gdns.
SW16 . . . . 3B 118
Mt. Ephraim La.
SW16 . . . . 3F 117
Mt. Ephraim Rd.
SW16 . . . . 3F 117
Mountfield Cl. SE6 . . . . 5F 109
Mountford Rd. E8. . . . . 2C 50
Mountford St. E1 . . . . . 5C 64
Mountfort Cres. N1. . . . 4C 48
Mountfort Ter. N1 . . . . . 4C 48
Mount Gdns. SE26 . . . . 3D 121
Mountgrove Rd. N5 . . . 5D 35
Mountjoy Cl. *EC2* *1A 18*
(off Beech St.)
Mountjoy Ho. EC2. . . . . 1F 17
Mount Lodge N6. . . . . . 1E 33
Mount Mills EC1. . 2D 63 (2E 9)
Mt. Nod Rd. SW16. . . . 3B 118
Mount Pleasant SE27 . . 4E 119
WC1. . . . . 3C 62 (4B 8)
Mt. Pleasant Cres. N4 . . 3B 34
Mt. Pleasant Hill E5. . . 4D 37
Mt. Pleasant La. E5. . . 3D 37
Mt. Pleasant Rd. NW10. . 4E 43
SE13. . . . . 4D 109
Mt. Pleasant Vs. N4. . . 2B 34
Mount Rd. NW2 . . . . . . 5D 29
NW4 . . . . 1C 28
SW19. . . . . 2C 114
Mount Row W1. . 1D 75 (5D 13)
Mountsfield Ct. SE13 . . 4F 109
Mounts Pond Rd. SE3. . 5F 95
(not continuous)
Mount Sq., The NW3 . . 5E 31
Mount St. W1 . . 1C 74 (5B 12)
Mount St. M.
W1. . . . . 1D 75 (5D 13)

Mount Ter. E1. . . . . 4D 65
Mount, The E5 . . . . 4D 37
(Alcester Cres.)
E5. . . . . 4D 37
(Muston Rd.)
NW3. . . . . 5E 31
Mount Vernon NW3 . . . 1E 45
Mountview Cl. NW11. . . 3D 31
Mount Vw. Rd. N4 . . . . 2A 34
Mount Vs. SE27. . . . . . 3D 119
Mowatt Cl. N19. . . . . . . 4F 33
Mowbray Rd. NW6. . . . 4A 44
Mowlem St. E2 . . . . 1D 65
Mowll St. SW9. . . . . 3C 90
Moxon Cl. E13 . . . . 1B 68
Moxon St. W1 . . 4C 60 (1B 12)
Moye Cl. E2 . . . . 1C 64
Moyers Rd. E10 . . . . . . 2E 39
Moylan Rd. W6 . . . . 2A 86
Moyle Ho. *SW1* *1E 89*
(off Churchill Gdns.)
Moyne Ho. SW9. . . . . . 3D 105
Moyser Rd. SW16 . . . . 5D 117
Mozart St. W10 . . . . . . 2B 58
Mozart Ter. SW1. . . . . . 5C 74
Mudlarks Blvd. SE10 . . 4B 82
Mudlarks Way SE7. . . . 4C 82
SE10. . . . . 4B 82
(not continuous)
Muir Dr. SW18 . . . . 4A 102
Muirfield W3 . . . . 5A 56
Muirfield Cl. SE16. . . . . 1D 93
Muirfield Cres. E14 . . . 4D 81
Muirkirk Rd. SE6 . . . . . 1E 123
Muir Rd. E5 . . . . 1C 50
Mulberry Bus. Cen.
SE16 . . . . 3F 79
Mulberry Cl. NW3. . . . . 1F 45
SE7 . . . . 2F 97
SE22. . . . . 3C 106
SW3 . . . . 2F 87
SW16 . . . . 4E 117
Mulberry Ct. *E11* *1F 53*
(off Langthorne Rd.)
EC1. . . . . *2E 9*
(off Tompion St.)
Mulberry Ho. E2. . . . . . 2E 65
(off Victoria Pk. Sq.)
SE8. . . . . 2B 94
Mulberry Housing
Co-operative SE1. . . 1C 24
Mulberry M. SE14 . . . . 4B 94
Mulberry Pl. *E14* *1E 81*
(off Clove Cres.)
W6 . . . . 1C 84
Mulberry Rd. E8. . . . . . 4B 50
Mulberry St. E1 . . . . . . 5C 64
Mulberry Wlk. SW3 . . . 2F 87
Mulgrave Rd. NW10 . . 1B 42
SW6 . . . . 2B 86
Mulkern Rd. N19 . . . . . 3F 33
Mullen Twr. *WC1* *4B 8*
(off Mount Pleasant)
Muller Rd. SW4 . . . . . . 4F 103
Mullet Gdns. E2. . . . . . 2C 64
Mulletsfield *WC1* *2E 7*
(off Cromer St.)
Mullins Path SW14 . . . 1A 98
Mull Wlk. N1 . . . . *3E 49*
(off Clephane Rd.)

Mull Wlk. *N1* *3F 49*
(off Marquess Rd. Nth.)
Mulready Ho. *SW1*. . . . *5A 76*
(off Marsham St.)
Mulready St. NW8 . . . . 3A 60
Multi Way W3 . . . . 3A 70
Multon Ho. E9 . . . . 4E 51
Multon Rd. SW18. . . . . 5F 101
Mulvaney Way
SE1. . . . . 3F 77 (4C 26)
(not continuous)
Mumford Ct.
EC2 . . . . 5E 63 (2A 18)
Mumford Rd. SE24 . . . 3D 105
Muncaster Rd. SW11. . 3B 102
Muncies M. SE6. . . . . . 2E 123
Mundania Rd. SE22. . . 4D 107
Munday Ho. *SE1* *5B 26*
(off Deverell St.)
Munday Rd. E16. . . . . . 1C 82
Munden St. W14 . . . . . 5A 72
Mundford Rd. E5 . . . . . 4E 37
Mund St. W14 . . . . 1B 86
Mundy Ho. W10. . . . . . 2A 58
Mundy St. N1 . . 2A 64 (1D 11)
Munnings Ho. *E16*. . . . *1D 83*
(off Portsmouth M.)
Munro Ho. SE1 . 3C 76 (4B 24)
Munro M. W10. . . . . . . 4A 58
(not continuous)
Munro Ter. SW10 . . . . . 3F 87
Munro Way E5 . . . . 1C 50
Munster Cl. SW6 . . . . . 5B 86
Munster M. SW6 . . . . . 3A 86
Munster Rd. SW6. . . . . 3A 86
Munster Sq. NW1. . 2D 61 (2E 5)
Munton Rd. SE17 . . . . . 5E 77
Murchison Rd. E10. . . . 4E 39
Murdoch Ho. *SE16*. . . . *4F 79*
(off Moodkee St.)
Murdock Cl. E16. . . . . . 5B 68
Murdock St. SE15 . . . . 2D 93
Murfett Cl. SW19 . . . . 2A 114
Muriel Ct. E10 . . . . 2D 39
Muriel St. N1 . . . . 1B 62
(not continuous)
Murillo Rd. SE13 . . . . . 2F 109
Murphy Ho. *SE1* *5E 25*
(off Borough Rd.)
Murphy St. SE1 . 3C 76 (4B 24)
Murray Gro. N1. . 1E 63 (1A 10)
Murray M. NW1 . . . . . . 4F 47
Murray Rd. SW19. . . . . 5F 113
Murray Sq. E16 . . . . . . 5C 68
Murray St. NW1 . . . . . . 4E 47
Murray Ter. NW3 . . . . . 1E 45
Mursell Est. SW8. . . . . 4B 90
Musard Rd. W6 . . . . . . 2A 86
Musbury St. E1. . . . . . . 5E 65
Muscal *W6* *2A 86*
(off Field Rd.)
Muscatel Pl. SE5 . . . . . 4A 92
Muschamp Rd. SE15 . . 1B 106
Muscovy St. EC3 . .1A 78 (4D 19)
Museum Chambers
WC1 . . . . *1D 15*
(off Bury Pl.)
Mus. in Dockland 1C 80
Museum La. *SW7*. *4F 73*
(off Exhibition Rd.)

N

Newhaven Gdns. SE9 . . 2F **111**
Newhaven La. E16 . . . . . . 3B **68**
Newick Rd. E5 . . . . 1D **51**
NEWINGTON **4E 77**
Newington Barrow Way
N7 . . . . 5B **34**
Newington Butts SE11 . . 5D **77**
Newington C'way.
SE1 . . . . 4D **77** (5E **25**)
Newington Ct. Bus. Cen.
SE1 . . . . 5F **25**
Newington Grn. N16 . . . . 2F **49**
Newington Grn. Mans.
N16 . . . . 2F **49**
Newington Grn. Rd. N1 . . 3F **49**
Newington Ind. Est.
SE17 . . . . 5E **77**
(off Crampton St.)
New Inn B'way.
EC2 . . . . 3A **64** (3E **11**)
New Inn Pas. WC2 . . . . . 3A **16**
New Inn Sq. EC2 . . . . . . 3E **11**
New Inn St. EC2 . . 3A **64** (3E **11**)
New Inn Yd.
EC2 . . . . 3A **64** (3E **11**)
New Jubilee Wharf E1 . . 2E **79**
(off Wapping Wall)
New Kent Rd. SE1 . . . . . . 4E **77**
New Kings Rd. SW6 . . . . 5B **86**
New King St. SE8 . . . . . . 2C **94**
Newland Ct. EC1 . . . . 2B **10**
Newland Ho. SE14 . . . . . 2F **93**
(off John Williams Cl.)
NEWLANDS **3F 107**
Newlands NW1 . . . . 1F **5**
(off Harrington St.)
Newlands Pk. SE26 . . 5E **121**
Newlands Quay E1 . . . . 1E **79**
New London St. EC3 . . 4E **19**
New London Theatre . . **2E 15**
(off Drury La.)
New Lydenburg Commercial
Est. SE7 . . . . 4E **83**
New Lydenburg St. SE7 . 4E **83**
Newlyn NW1 . . . . 5E **47**
(off Plender St.)
Newman Pas.
W1 . . . . 4E **61** (1A **14**)
Newman Rd. E13 . . . . . . 2D **69**
Newman's Ct. EC3 . . . . 3C **18**
Newman's Row
WC2 . . . . 4B **62** (1A **16**)
Newman St.
W1 . . . . 4E **61** (1A **14**)
Newman Yd.
W1 . . . . 5E **61** (2B **14**)
Newmarket Grn. SE9 . . 5F **111**
Newmill Ho. E3 . . . . 3E **67**
New Mt. St. E15 . . . . 4F **53**
Newnes Path SW15 . . 2D **99**
Newnham Ter.
SE1 . . . . 4C **76** (5B **24**)
New Nth. Pl.
EC2 . . . . 3A **64** (3D **11**)
New Nth. Rd.
N1 . . . . 4E **49** (1C **10**)
New Nth. St.
WC1 . . . . 4B **62** (5F **7**)
Newnton Cl. N4 . . . . 2F **35**
(not continuous)

New Orleans Wlk. N19 . . 2F **33**
New Oxford St.
WC1 . . . . 5F **61** (2C **14**)
New Pk. Pde. SW2 . . . 5A **104**
(off New Pk. Rd.)
New Pk. Rd. SW2 . . . 1F **117**
New Pl. Sq. SE16 . . . . . . 4D **79**
New Plaistow Rd. E15 . . 5A **54**
Newport Av. E13 . . . . . . 3D **69**
E14 . . . . 1F **81**
Newport Ct.
WC2 . . . . 1F **75** (4C **14**)
Newport Ho. E3 . . . . 2A **66**
(off Strahan Rd.)
Newport Pl.
WC2 . . . . 1F **75** (4C **14**)
Newport Rd. E10 . . . . . . 4E **39**
SW13 . . . . 4C **84**
Newport St. SE11 . . . . . 5B **76**
New Priory Ct. NW6 . . . . 4C **44**
(off Mazenod Av.)
Newquay Ho. SE11 . . . . 1C **90**
Newquay Rd. SE6 . . . . 2D **123**
New Quebec St.
W1 . . . . 5B **60** (3A **12**)
New Ride SW7 . . . . 3A **74**
New River Ct. N5 . . . . . . 1E **49**
New River Head
EC1 . . . . 2C **62** (1C **8**)
New River Wlk. N1 . . . . 3E **49**
New River Way N4 . . . . 2F **35**
New Rd. E1 . . . . 4D **65**
E12 . . . . 4F **41**
N8 . . . . 1A **34**
New Rochford St. NW5 . . 2B **46**
New Row
WC2 . . . . 1A **76** (4D **15**)
New Spitalfields Mkt.
E10 . . . . 5D **39**
New Spring Gdns. Wlk.
SE1 . . . . 1A **90**
SE11 . . . . 1A **90**
New Sq. WC2 . . . 5C **62** (2B **16**)
New Sq. Pas. WC2 . . . 2B **16**
Newstead Rd. SE12 . . 5B **110**
Newstead Way SW19 . . 4F **113**
New St. EC2 . . . 4A **64** (1E **19**)
New St. Hill
BR1: Brom 5D **125**
New St. Sq.
EC4 . . . . 5C **62** (2C **16**)
Newton Cl. E17 . . . . 1A **38**
Newton Gro. W4 . . . . . . 5A **70**
Newton Ho. E1 . . . . 1D **79**
(off Cornwall St.)
NW8 . . . . 1F **59**
(off Abbey Rd.)
Newton Mans. W14 . . 2A **86**
(off Queen's Club Gdns.)
Newton Pl. E14 . . . . 5C **80**
Newton Point E16 . . . . . 5B **68**
(off Clarkson Rd.)
Newton Rd. E15 . . . . . . 2F **53**
NW2 . . . . 1E **43**
W2 . . . . 5D **59**
Newton St.
WC2 . . . . 5A **62** (2E **15**)
Newton's Yd. SW18 . . 3C **100**
New Twr. Bldgs. E1 . . . . 2D **79**
Newtown St. SW11 . . . . 4D **89**

New Turnstile WC1 . . . . . 1F **15**
New Union Cl. E14 . . . . . 4E **81**
New Union St.
EC2 . . . . 4F **63** (1B **18**)
New Wanstead E11 . . . . 1B **40**
New Wharf Rd. N1 . . . . . 1A **62**
New Zealand Way W12 . . 1D **71**
Niagra Cl. N1 . . . . 1E **63**
Niagra Ct. SE16 . . . . . . 4E **79**
(off Canada Est.)
Nicholas Ct. W4 . . . . 2A **84**
(off Corney Reach Way)
Nicholas La.
EC4 . . . . 1F **77** (4C **18**)
(not continuous)
Nicholas M. W4 . . . . 2A **84**
Nicholas Pas. EC4 . . . . 3C **18**
Nicholas Rd. E1 . . . . . . 3E **65**
Nicholas Stacey Ho.
SE7 . . . . 1D **97**
(off Frank Burton Cl.)
Nicholay Rd. N19 . . . . . 3F **33**
Nicholl Ho. N4 . . . . 3E **35**
Nicholsfield Wlk. N7 . . 3B **48**
Nicholls Point E13 . . . . . 5C **54**
(off Park Gro.)
Nicholl St. E2 . . . . 5C **50**
Nichols Cl. N4 . . . . 3C **34**
(off Osborne Rd.)
Nichol's Ct. E2 . . . . 1F **11**
(off Cremer St.)
Nicholson Ho. SE17 . . . 1F **91**
Nicholson St.
SE1 . . . . 2D **77** (2D **25**)
Nickleby Ho. SE16 . . . . 3C **78**
(off George Row)
Nickols Wlk. SW18 . . 2D **101**
Nicoll Ct. NW10 . . . . . . 5A **42**
Nicoll Pl. NW4 . . . . 1D **29**
Nicoll Rd. NW10 . . . . . . 5A **42**
Nicosia Rd. SW18 . . 5A **102**
Niederwald Rd. SE26 . . 4A **122**
Nigel Ho. EC1 . . . . 5B **8**
(off Portpool La.)
Nigel Playfair Av. W6 . . 5D **71**
Nigel Rd. E7 . . . . 2E **55**
SE15 . . . . 1C **106**
Nigeria Rd. SE7 . . . . . . 3E **97**
Nightingale Ct. E14 . . . . 3E **81**
(off Ovex Cl.)
N4 . . . . 4B **34**
(off Tollington Pk.)
SW6 . . . . 4D **87**
(off Maltings Pl.)
Nightingale Gro.
SE13 . . . . 3F **109**
Nightingale Ho. E1 . . . . 2C **78**
(off Thomas More St.)
N1 . . . . 5A **50**
(off Wilmer Gdns.)
W12 . . . . 5E **57**
(off Du Cane Rd.)
Nightingale La. E11 . . . . 1D **41**
SW12 . . . . 5B **102**
Nightingale Lodge W9 . . 4C **58**
(off Admiral Wlk.)
Nightingale M. E11 . . . 1C **40**
E3 . . . . 1F **65**
SE11 . . . . 5D **77**
Nightingale Pl. SW10 . . 2E **87**

Nightingale Rd. E5 . . . . . 5D 37	Norland Ho. W11 . . . . . . 2F 71	Nth. Carriage Dr. W2 . . 1A 74
NW10 . . . . 1B 56	(off Queensdale Cres.)	(off Bayswater Rd.)
Nightingale Sq. SW12 . . 5C 102	Norland Pl. W11 . . . . . . 2A 72	Northchurch SE17 . . . . . 1F 91
Nightingale Wlk.	Norland Rd. W11 . . . . . . 2F 71	(not continuous)
SW4 . . . . 4D 103	(off Queensdale Cres.)	Northchurch Rd. N1 . . . . 4F 49
Nile Cl. N16 . . . . 5B 36	Norland Sq. W11 . . . . . . 2A 72	(not continuous)
Nile Rd. E13 . . . . 1E 69	Norland Sq. Mans.	Northchurch Ter. N1 . . . 4A 50
Nile St. N1 . . . 2E 63 (1A 10)	W11 . . . . 2A 72	Nth. Circular Rd.
Nile Ter. SE15 . . . . 1B 92	(off Norland Sq.)	NW2 . . . . 5A 28
Nimegen Way SE22 . . 3A 106	Norley Va. SW15 . . . . . 1C 112	NW4 . . . . 2E 29
Nimrod Ho. E16 . . . . . . 4D 69	Norlington Rd. E10 . . . . 3E 39	NW10 . . . . 2A 42
(off Vanguard Cl.)	E11 . . . . 3E 39	Nth. Colonnade, The
Nimrod Pas. N1 . . . . . . 3A 50	Normanby Cl. SW15 . . . 3B 100	E14 . . . . 2C 80
Nimrod Rd. SW16 . . . . 5D 117	Normanby Rd. NW10 . . . 1B 42	Northcote M. SW11 . . . . 2A 102
Nina Mackay Cl. E15 . . 5A 54	Norman Ct. N4 . . . . 2C 34	Northcote Rd. NW10 . . . 4A 42
NINE ELMS 3E 89	NW10 . . . . 4C 42	SW11 . . . . 3A 102
Nine Elms La. SW8 . . . . 3E 89	Normand Gdns. W14 . . . 2A 86	North Ct. SE24 . . . . . . 1D 105
Nirvana Apartments	(off Greyhound Rd.)	SW1 . . . . 5D 23
N1 . . . . 5D 49	Normand M. W14 . . . . . 2A 86	(off Gt. Peter St.)
(off Islington Grn.)	Normand Rd. W14 . . . . . 2B 86	W1 . . . . 4E 61 (5A 6)
Nita Ct. SE12 . . . . 1C 124	Normandy Cl. SE26 . . . 3A 122	North Cres. E16 . . . . . . 3F 67
Niton St. SW6 . . . . 3F 85	Normandy Ho. E14 . . . . . 3E 81	WC1 . . . . 4F 61 (5B 6)
Nobel Ho. SE5 . . . . 5E 91	(off Plevna St.)	Northcroft Ct. W12 . . . . 3C 70
Noble Ct. E1 . . . . 1D 79	Normandy Rd. SW9 . . . . 4C 90	North Crofts SE23 . . . . 1D 121
Noblefield Hgts. N2 . . . 1A 32	Normandy Ter. E16 . . . . 5D 69	Nth. Cross Rd. SE22 . . . 3B 106
Noble M. N16 . . . . 5F 35	Norman Gro. E3 . . . . . . 1A 66	Northdene Gdns. N15 . . 1B 36
(off Albion Rd.)	Norman Ho. SW8 . . . . . . 3A 90	Northdown St. N1 . . 1A 62 (1F 7)
Noble St. EC2 . . 5E 63 (2F 17)	(off Wyvil Rd.)	North Dr. SW16 . . . . . . 4E 117
Noel Coward Ho. SW1 . . 5E 75	Normanhurst Rd.	NORTH END 4E 31
(off Vauxhall Bri. Rd.)	SW2 . . . . 2B 118	North End NW3 . . . . . . 4E 31
Noel Ho. NW6 . . . . 4F 45	Norman Rd. E11 . . . . . . 4F 39	Nth. End Av. NW3 . . . . . 4E 31
(off Harben Rd.)	SE10 . . . . 3D 95	(not continuous)
Noel Rd. E6 . . . . 3F 69	Norman St. EC1 . 2E 63 (2A 10)	Nth. End Cres. W14 . . . 5B 72
N1 . . . . 1D 63	Normanton Av. SW19 . . 2C 114	Nth. End Ho. W14 . . . . 5A 72
Noel St. W1 . . 5E 61 (3A 14)	Normanton St. SE23 . . . 2F 121	Nth. End Pde. W14 . . . . 5A 72
Noel Ter. SE23 . . . . . . 2E 121	Normington Cl. SW16 . . 5C 118	(off Nth. End Rd.)
Nolan Way E5 . . . . 1C 50	Norrice Lea N2 . . . . 1F 31	Nth. End Rd. NW11 . . . . 3C 30
Norbiton Rd. E14 . . . . . 5B 66	Norris Ho. E9 . . . . 5E 51	W14 . . . . 5A 72
Norbroke St. W12 . . . . . 1B 70	(off Handley Rd.)	Nth. End Way NW3 . . . . 4E 31
Norburn St. W10 . . . . . 4A 58	N1 . . . . 5A 50	Northern Rd. E13 . . . . . 1D 69
Norcombe Ho. N19 . . . . 5F 33	(off Colville Est.)	Northesk Ho. E1 . . . . . . 3D 65
(off Wedmore St.)	SE8 . . . . 1B 94	(off Tent St.)
Norcott Rd. N16 . . . . . . 4C 36	(off Grove St.)	Nth. Eyot Gdns. W6 . . . 1B 84
Norcroft Gdns. SE22 . . 5C 106	Norris St. SW1 . 1F 75 (5B 14)	Northey St. E14 . . . . . . 1A 80
Norden Ho. E2 . . . . 2D 65	Norroy Rd. SW15 . . . . . 2F 99	Northfield Ho. SE15 . . . 2C 92
(off Pott St.)	Norstead Pl. SW15 . . . 2C 112	Northfield Rd. N16 . . . . 2A 36
Norfolk Av. N15 . . . . . . 1B 36	Nth. Access Rd. E17 . . . 1F 37	Northfields SW18 . . . . . 2C 100
Norfolk Cres. W2 . . . . . 5A 60	NORTH ACTON 4A 56	Northfields Prospect Bus. Cen.
Norfolk Ho. SE3 . . . . . . 2A 96	Nth. Acton Rd. NW10 . . 1A 56	SW18 . . . . 2C 100
(off Restell Cl.)	Northampton Gro. N1 . . 2E 49	Northfleet Ho. SE1 . . . . 3B 26
SE8 . . . . 4C 94	Northampton Pk. N1 . . . 3E 49	(off Tennis St.)
SW1 . . . . 5F 75	Northampton Rd.	Nth. Flock St. SE16 . . . 3C 78
(off Page St.)	EC1 . . . . 3C 62 (3C 8)	Nth. Flower Wlk. W2 . . 1E 73
Norfolk Ho. Rd. SW16 . 3F 117	Northampton Row EC1 . . 3C 8	(off Lancaster Wlk.)
Norfolk Mans. SW11 . . . 4B 88	Northampton Sq.	North Gdn. E14 . . . . . . 2B 80
(off Prince of Wales Dr.)	EC1 . . . . 2D 63 (2D 9)	North Ga. NW8 . . . . . . 1A 60
Norfolk M. W10 . . . . . . 4B 58	Northampton St. N1 . . . 4E 49	(off Prince Albert Rd.)
(off Blagrove Rd.)	Nth. Audley St.	Northgate Dr. NW9 . . . . 1A 28
Norfolk Pl. W2 . . . . 5F 59	W1 . . . . 5C 60 (3B 12)	Northgate Ho. E14 . . . . 1C 80
(not continuous)	North Av. NW10 . . . . . . 2E 57	(off E. India Dock Rd.)
Norfolk Rd. NW8 . . . . . 5F 45	North Bank NW8 . . . . . 2A 60	Nth. Gower St.
NW10 . . . . 4A 42	Nth. Birkbeck Rd. E11 . . 5F 39	NW1 . . . . 2E 61 (2A 6)
Norfolk Row SE1 . . . . . 5B 76	North Block SE1 . . . . . . 3A 24	North Gro. N6 . . . . 2C 32
(not continuous)	(off York Rd.)	N15 . . . . 1F 35
Norfolk Sq. W2 . . . . . . 5F 59	Nth. Boundary Rd. E12 . 5F 41	North Hill N6 . . . . 1B 32
Norfolk Sq. M. W2 . . . . 5F 59	Northbourne Rd. SW4 . . 3F 103	Nth. Hill Av. N6 . . . . . . 1C 32
(off London St.)	Nth. Branch Av. NW10 . 2E 57	North Ho. SE8 . . . . 1B 94
Norfolk St. E7 . . . . 2C 54	Northbrook Rd. SE13 . . 3A 110	Northiam WC1 . . . . 2E 7
Norfolk Ter. W6 . . . . . . 1A 86	Northburgh St.	(off Cromer St.)
Norgrove St. SW12 . . . . 5C 102	EC1 . . . . 3D 63 (4E 9)	Northiam St. E9 . . . . . . 5D 51

Northington St.
WC1 . . . . 3B 62 (4A 8)
NORTH KENSINGTON . . 4F 57
Northlands St. SE5 . . . . . 5E 91
Northleach Ct. SE15 . . . . 2A 92
(off Birdlip Cl.)
North Lodge E16 . . . . . . 1D 83
(off Wesley Av.)
Nth. Lodge Cl. SW15 . . . . 3F 99
North M. WC1 . . . 3B 62 (4A 8)
Northolme Rd. N5 . . . . . . 1E 49
Northover BR1: Brom . . 3B 124
North Pl. SW18 . . . . 3C 100
Nth. Pole Rd. W10 . . . . . 4E 57
Northport St. N1 . . . . . . 5F 49
North Ride W2 . . . . 1A 74
North Ri. W2 . . . . 5A 60
North Rd. N6 . . . . 2C 32
N7 . . . . 3A 48
SW19 . . . . 5E 115
North Row W1 . . 1B 74 (4A 12)
Nth. Row Bldgs. W1 . . . . 4B 12
(off Northe Row)
North Several SE3 . . . . . 5F 95
Nth. Side Wandsworth Comm.
SW18 . . . . 3F 101
North Sq. NW11 . . . . . . 1C 30
Northstead Rd. SW2 . . . 2C 118
North St. E13 . . . . 1D 69
SW4 . . . . 1E 103
North St. Pas. E13 . . . . . 1D 69
Nth. Tenter St. E1 . . . . . . 5B 64
North Ter. SW3 . . . . 4A 74
Northumberland All.
EC3 . . . . 5A 64 (3E 19)
(not continuous)
Northumberland Av. E12 . . 3E 41
WC2 . . . . . 2A 76 (1D 23)
Northumberland Ho.
SW1 . . . . 1D 23
(off Northumberland Av.)
Northumberland Pl. W2 . . 5C 58
Northumberland Rd.
E17 . . . . 2C 38
Northumberland St.
WC2 . . . . . . 2A 76 (1D 23)
Northumbria St. E14 . . . . 5C 66
Nth. Verbena Gdns. W6 . . 1C 84
Northview N7 . . . . 5A 34
North Vw. SW19 . . . . 5E 113
Nth. View Cres. NW10 . . 1B 42
North Vs. NW1 . . . . 3F 47
North Wlk. W8 . . . . 1D 73
(off Bayswater Rd.)
Northway NW11 . . . . 1D 31
Northway Rd. SE5 . . . . . 1E 105
Northways Pde. NW3 . . . . 4F 45
(off College Cres., not cont.)
Nth. Western Commercial
Cen. NW1 . . . . 4A 48
Northwest Pl. N1 . . . . . . 1C 62
North Wharf E14 . . . . 2E 81
(off Coldharbour)
Nth. Wharf Rd. W2 . . . . . 4F 59
Northwick Cl. NW8 . . . . . 3F 59
Northwick Ho. W9 . . . . . . 3E 59
(off St John's Wood Rd.)
Northwick Ter. NW8 . . . . 3F 59
Northwold Rd. E5 . . . . . . 4B 36
N16 . . . . 4B 36

Northwood Est. E5 . . . . . 4C 36
Northwood Ho. SE27 . . . . 4E 119
Northwood Rd. N6 . . . . . . 2D 33
SE23 . . . . 1B 122
Northwood Way SE19 . . 5F 119
Nth. Woolwich Rd.
E16 . . . . 2B 82
Nth. Worple Way
SW14 . . . . 1A 98
Norton Folgate
EC2 . . . . . . 4A 64 (5E 11)
Norton Folgate Ho's.
E1 . . . . 5F 11
(off Puma Ct.)
Norton Ho. E2 . . . . 1F 65
(off Mace St.)
E1 . . . . 5D 65
(off Bigland St.)
SW1 . . . . 4F 75
(off Arneway St.)
SW9 . . . . 5B 90
(off Aytoun Rd.)
Norton Rd. E10 . . . . 3B 38
Norway Ga. SE16 . . . . . . 4A 80
Norway Pl. E14 . . . . 5B 66
Norway St. SE10 . . . . . . 2D 95
Norway Wharf E14 . . . . . 5B 66
(off Norway Pl.)
Norwich Ho. E14 . . . . . . 5D 67
(off Cordelia St.)
Norwich Rd. E7 . . . . 2C 54
Norwich St.
EC4 . . . . . . 5C 62 (2B 16)
Norwood Cl. NW2 . . . . . . 5A 30
Norwood High St.
SE27 . . . . 3D 119
Norwood Ho. E14 . . . . . . 1D 81
(off Poplar High St.)
NORWOOD NEW TOWN
. . . . 5E 119
Norwood Pk. Rd. SE27 . . 5E 119
Norwood Rd. SE24 . . . . . 1D 119
SE27 . . . . 2D 119
Notley St. SE5 . . . . 3F 91
Notting Barn Rd. W10 . . . 3F 57
Nottingdale Sq. W11 . . . . 2A 72
Nottingham Av. E16 . . . . 4E 69
Nottingham Ct.
WC2 . . . . . . 5A 62 (3D 15)
Nottingham Ho. WC2 . . . 3D 15
(off Shorts Gdns.)
Nottingham Pl.
W1 . . . . 4C 60 (4B 4)
Nottingham Rd. E10 . . . . 1E 39
SW17 . . . . 1B 116
Nottingham St.
W1 . . . . 4C 60 (5B 4)
Nottingham Ter. NW1 . . . 4B 4
NOTTING HILL 1B 72
Notting Hill Ga. W11 . . . . 2C 72
Nottingwood Ho. W11 . . 1A 72
(off Clarendon Rd.)
Nova Bldg. E14 . . . . 5C 80
Novello St. SW6 . . . . . . 4C 86
Novel Sq. SE10 . . . . 5B 82
Nowell Rd. SW13 . . . . . . 2C 84
Noyna Rd. SW17 . . . . . . 3B 116
Nubia Way
BR1: Brom 3A 124
Nuding Cl. SE13 . . . . . . 1C 108

Nuffield Lodge N6 . . . . . 1E 33
W2 . . . . 4C 58
(off Admiral Wlk.)
Nugent Rd. N19 . . . . 3A 34
Nugent Ter. NW8 . . . . . . 1E 59
Nun Ct. EC2 . . . . 2B 18
NUNHEAD 1D 107
Nunhead Cres. SE15 . . 1D 107
Nunhead Est. SE15 . . . 2D 107
Nunhead Grn. SE15 . . . 1D 107
Nunhead Gro. SE15 . . . 1D 107
Nunhead La. SE15 . . . . 1D 107
Nunhead Pas. SE15 . . . 1C 106
Nursery Cl. SE4 . . . . 5B 94
SW15 . . . . 2F 99
Nursery La. E2 . . . . 5B 50
E7 . . . . 3C 54
W10 . . . . 4E 57
Nursery Rd. E9 . . . . 3E 51
E12 . . . . 4F 41
SW9 . . . . 2B 104
Nutbourne St. W10 . . . . . 2A 58
Nutbrook St. SE15 . . . . 1C 106
Nutcroft Rd. SE15 . . . . . . 3D 93
Nutfield Rd. E15 . . . . 1E 53
NW2 . . . . 5C 28
SE22 . . . . 2B 106
Nutford Pl. W1 . . . . 5B 60
Nuthurst Av. SW2 . . . . . 2B 118
Nutley Ter. NW3 . . . . 3E 45
Nutmeg Cl. E16 . . . . 3A 68
Nutmeg La. E14 . . . . 5F 67
Nuttall St. N1 . . . . 1A 64
Nutter La. E11 . . . . 1E 41
Nutt St. SE15 . . . . 3B 92
Nutwell St. SW17 . . . . . 5A 116
Nye Bevan Est. E5 . . . . . 5F 37
Nye Bevan Ho. SW6 . . . . 3B 86
(off St Thomas's Way)
Nynehead St. SE14 . . . . 3A 94
Nyon Gro. SE6 . . . . 2B 122
Nyssa Ct. E15 . . . . 2A 68
(off Teasel Way)
Nyton Cl. N19 . . . . 3A 34

O

Oak Apple Ct. SE12 . . . 1C 124
Oakbank Gro. SE24 . . . 2E 105
Oakbrook Cl.
BR1: Brom 4D 125
Oakbury Rd. SW6 . . . . . 5D 87
Oak Cott. Cl. SE6 . . . . . 1B 124
Oak Ct. SE15 . . . . 3B 92
(off Sumner Rd.)
Oak Cres. E16 . . . . 4A 68
Oakcroft Rd. SE13 . . . . . 5F 95
Oakdale Rd. E7 . . . . 4D 55
E11 . . . . 4F 39
N4 . . . . 1E 35
SE4 . . . . 1E 107
SE15 . . . . 1E 107
SW16 . . . . 5A 118
Oakdene SE15 . . . . 4D 93
Oakden St. SE11 . . . . . . 5C 76
Oake Ct. SW15 . . . . 3A 100
Oakeford Ho. W14 . . . . . 4A 72
(off Russell Rd.)
Oakend Ho. N4 . . . . 2F 35

Oakeshott Av. N6 . . . . . . 4C **32**
Oakey La. SE1 . . 4C **76** (5B **24**)
Oakfield Ct. N8 . . . . 2A **34**
NW11 . . . . 2F **29**
Oakfield Gdns. SE19 . . 5A **120**
(not continuous)
Oakfield Ho. E3 . . . . 4C **66**
(off Gale St.)
Oakfield Rd. E6 . . . . 5F **55**
N4 . . . . 1C **34**
SW19 . . . . 3F **113**
Oakfields Rd. NW11 . . . 1A **30**
Oakfield St. SW10 . . . . 2C **87**
Oakford Rd. NW5 . . . . . . 1E **47**
Oak Gro. NW2 . . . . 1A **44**
Oakhall Ct. E11 . . . . 1D **41**
Oak Hall Rd. E11 . . . . . . 1D **41**
Oakham Cl. SE6 . . . . . . 2B **122**
Oakham Ho. W10 . . . . . . 3E **57**
(off Sutton Way)
Oakhill Av. NW3 . . . . . . 1D **45**
Oakhill Ct. SE23 . . . . . 4E **107**
Oak Hill Pk. NW3 . . . . . . 1D **45**
Oak Hill Pk. M. NW3 . . 1E **45**
Oakhill Pl. SW15 . . . . . 3C **100**
Oak Hill Rd. SW15 . . . . 3B **100**
Oak Hill Way NW3 . . . . . 1E **45**
Oak Ho. W10 . . . . 3A **58**
(off Sycamore Wlk.)
Oakhurst Gro. SE22 . . 2C **106**
Oakington Rd. W9 . . . . . 3C **58**
Oakington Way N8 . . . . 2A **34**
Oakland Rd. E15 . . . . . . 1F **53**
Oaklands Ct. NW10 . . . . 5A **42**
(off Nicoll Rd.)
Oaklands Est. SW4 . . . . 4E **103**
Oaklands Gro. W12 . . . . 2C **70**
Oaklands M. NW2 . . . . . 1F **43**
(off Oaklands Rd.)
Oaklands Pas. NW2 . . . . 1F **43**
(off Oaklands Rd.)
Oaklands Pl. SW4 . . . . 2E **103**
Oaklands Rd. NW2 . . . . 1F **43**
Oak La. E14 . . . . 1B **80**
Oakley Cres. EC1 . . . . . 1D **63**
Oakley Dr. SE13 . . . . . . 4F **109**
Oakley Gdns. SW3 . . . . 2A **88**
Oakley Ho. SW1 . . . . 5B **74**
Oakley Pl. SE1 . . . . 1B **92**
Oakley Rd. N1 . . . . 4F **49**
Oakley Sq. NW1 . . . . . . 1E **61**
Oakley St. SW3 . . . . 2A **88**
Oakley Wlk. W6 . . . . 2F **85**
Oakley Yd. E2 . . . . 3B **64**
Oak Lodge E11 . . . . 1C **40**
W8 . . . . 4D **73**
(off Chantry Sq.)
Oakmead Rd. SW12 . . . 1C **116**
Oak Pk. Gdns. SW19 . . 1F **113**
Oak Pk. M. N16 . . . . . . 5B **36**
Oak Pl. SW18 . . . . 3D **101**
Oakridge La.
BR1: Brom 5F **123**
Oakridge Rd.
BR1: Brom 4F **123**
Oaks Av. SE19 . . . . 5A **120**
Oaksford Av. SE26 . . . 3D **121**
Oakshade Rd.
BR1: Brom 4F **123**
Oakshaw Rd. SW18 . . 5D **101**

Oakshott Ct.
NW1 . . . . 1F **61** (1B **6**)
(not continuous)
Oaks, The NW6 . . . . 4F **43**
(off Brondesbury Pk.)
NW10 . . . . 4D **43**
Oak St. E14 . . . . 3E **81**
(off Stewart St.)
Oak Tree Gdns.
BR1: Brom 5D **125**
Oak Tree Ho. W9 . . . . . . 3C **58**
(off Shirland Rd.)
Oak Tree Rd. NW8 . . . . 2A **60**
Oakview Lodge NW11 . . 2B **30**
(off Beechcroft Av.)
Oakview Rd. SE6 . . . . . 5D **123**
Oak Village NW5 . . . . . 1C **46**
Oak Vs. NW11 . . . . 1B **30**
(off Hendon Pk. Row)
Oak Way W3 . . . . 2A **70**
Oakwood Bus. Pk.
NW10 . . . . 3A **56**
Oakwood Ct. E6 . . . . . . 5F **55**
W14 . . . . 4B **72**
Oakwood Dr. SE19 . . . 5F **119**
Oakwood La. W14 . . . . 4B **72**
Oakworth Rd. W10 . . . . 4E **57**
Oast Ct. E14 . . . . 1B **80**
(off Newell St.)
Oast Lodge W4 . . . . 3A **84**
(off Corney Reach Way)
Oatfield Ho. N15 . . . . . . 1A **36**
(off Perry Ct.)
Oat La. EC2 . . . 5E **63** (2A **18**)
Oatwell Ho. SW3 . . . . . 1A **88**
(off Marlborough St.)
Oban Cl. E13 . . . . 3E **69**
Oban Ho. E14 . . . . 5F **67**
(off Oban St.)
Oban Rd. E13 . . . . 2E **69**
Oban St. E14 . . . . 5F **67**
Oberon Ho. N1 . . . . 1A **64**
(off Arden Est.)
Oberstein Rd. SW11 . . 2F **101**
Oborne Cl. SE24 . . . . . 3D **105**
O'Brien Ho. E2 . . . . 2F **65**
(off Roman Rd.)
Observatory Gdns. W8 . . 3C **72**
Observatory M. E14 . . . 5F **81**
Occupation Rd. SE17 . . 1E **91**
Ocean Est. E1 . . . . 3F **65**
(Ernest St.)
E1 . . . . 4A **66**
(Masters St.)
Ocean Music Venue . . . *3D **51***
(off Mare St.)
Ocean St. E1 . . . . 4F **65**
Ocean Wharf E14 . . . . . 3B **80**
Ockbrook E1 . . . . 4E **65**
(off Hannibal Rd.)
Ockendon M. N1 . . . . . . 3F **49**
Ockendon Rd. N1 . . . . . 3F **49**
Ockley Rd. SW16 . . . . 4A **118**
Octagon Arc.
EC2 . . . . . 4A **64** (1D **19**)
Octagon Ct. SE16 . . . . . 2F **79**
(off Rotherhithe St.)
Octavia Ho. SW1 . . . . . . 4F **75**
(off Medway St.)
W10 . . . . 3A **58**

Octavia St. SW11 . . . . . 4A **88**
Octavius St. SE8 . . . . . . 3C **94**
Odeon Cinema
Shaftesbury Av. 3C **14**
(off Tottenham Ct. Rd.)
. . . . *1B **14***
Odeon Ct. E16 . . . . 4C **68**
NW10 . . . . 5A **42**
(off St Albans Rd.)
Odessa Rd. E7 . . . . 5B **40**
NW10 . . . . 1C **56**
Odessa St. SE16 . . . . . 3B **80**
Odette Duval Ho. E1 . . . 4E **65**
(off Stepney Way)
Odger St. SW11 . . . . 5B **88**
Odhams Wlk.
WC2 . . . . . . 5A **62** (3E **15**)
Odin Ho. SE5 . . . . 5E **91**
O'Donnell Ct.
WC1 . . . . 3A **62** (3E **7**)
Odontological Mus., The
Royal College of Surgeons
. . . . *2A **16***
(off Lincoln's Inn Flds.)
O'Driscoll Ho. W12 . . . 5D **57**
Offa's Mead E9 . . . . 1B **52**
Offenbach Ho. E2 . . . . . 1F **65**
(off Mace St.)
Offerton Rd. SW4 . . . . . 1E **103**
Offham Ho. SE17 . . . . . . 5A **78**
(off Beckway St.)
Offley Rd. SW9 . . . . 3C **90**
Offord Rd. N1 . . . . 4B **48**
Offord St. N1 . . . . 4B **48**
Ogilvie Ho. E1 . . . . 5F **65**
(off Stepney C'way.)
Oglander Rd. SE15 . . . 2B **106**
Ogle St. W1 . . . . 4E **61** (5F **5**)
O'Gorman Ho. SW10 . . 3E **87**
(off King's Rd.)
Ohio Rd. E13 . . . . 3B **68**
Oil Mill La. W6 . . . . 1C **84**
Okeburn Rd. SW17 . . . 5C **116**
Okehampton Rd. NW10 . . 5E **43**
Olaf St. W11 . . . . 1F **71**
Oldacre M. SW12 . . . . 5C **102**
Old Bailey EC4 . . 5D **63** (3E **17**)
Old Bailey
(Central Criminal Court)
. . . . 5D **63** (2E **17**)
Old Barge Ho. All. SE1 . . 1C **76**
(off Barge Ho. St.)
SE1 . . . . 5C **16**
Old Barrack Yd.
SW1 . . . . 3C **74** (4B **20**)
(not continuous)
Old Barrowfield E15 . . 5A **54**
Old Bellgate Wharf
E14 . . . . 4B **80**
Old Bethnal Grn. Rd.
E2 . . . . 2C **64**
Old Billingsgate Mkt.
EC3 . . . . 5D **19**
Old Billingsgate Wlk.
EC3 . . . . . . 1A **78** (5D **19**)
Old Bond St.
W1 . . . . 1E **75** (5F **13**)
Old Brewer's Yd.
WC2 . . . . . . 5A **62** (3D **15**)
Old Brewery M. NW3 . . 1F **45**

Paul Ho. E14 . . . . 1F **81**
Pauls Ho. E3 . . . . 4B **66**
    (off Timothy Rd.)
Paul St. E15 . . . . 5A **54**
  EC2 . . . . 3F **63** (4C **10**)
Paul's Wlk. EC4 . . 1E **77** (4E **17**)
Paultons Sq. SW3 . . . . 2F **87**
Paultons St. SW3 . . . . 2F **87**
Pauntley St. N19 . . . . 3E **33**
Pavan Ct. E2 . . . . 2E **65**
    (off Sceptre Rd.)
Paveley Dr. SW11 . . . . 3A **88**
Paveley Ho. N1 . . . . 1B **62**
    (off Priory Grn. Est.)
Paveley St. NW8 . . . . 2A **60**
Pavement, The E11 . . . . . . 3E **39**
    (off Hainault Rd.)
  SW4 . . . . 2E **103**
Pavilion NW8 . . . . 2F **59**
Pavilion Ct. NW6 . . . . 2C **58**
    (off Stafford Rd.)
Pavilion Rd.
  SW1 . . . . 4B **74** (4A **20**)
Pavilion Sq. SW17 . . . . . . 3B **116**
Pavilion St.
  SW1 . . . . 4B **74** (5A **20**)
    (off Wood La.)
Pavilion Ter. W12 . . . . 5E **57**
    (off Wood La.)
Pavilion, The SW8 . . . . . . 3F **89**
Pawsey Cl. E13 . . . . 5D **55**
Paxton Ct. SE12 . . . . 3E **125**
  SE26 . . . . 4A **122**
    (off Adamsrill Rd.)
Paxton Pl. SE27 . . . . 4A **120**
Paxton Rd. SE23 . . . . 3A **122**
  W4 . . . . 2A **84**
Paxton Ter. SW1 . . . . 2D **89**
Paymal Ho. E1 . . . . 4E **65**
    (off Stepney Way)
Payne Ho. N1 . . . . 5B **48**
    (off Barnsbury Est.)
Paynell Ct. SE3 . . . . 1A **110**
Payne Rd. E3 . . . . 1D **67**
Paynesfield Av. SW14 . . 1A **98**
Payne St. SE8 . . . . 3B **94**
Paynes Wlk. W6 . . . . 2A **86**
Peabody Av. SW1 . . . . . . 1D **89**
Peabody Bldgs. E1 . . . . . 1C **78**
    (off John Fisher St.)
  EC1 . . . . 4A **10**
    (off Roscoe St.)
  SW3 . . . . 2A **88**
    (off Lawrence St.)
Peabody Cl. SE10 . . . . . . 4D **95**
  SW1 . . . . 1D **89**
Peabody Ct. EC1 . . . . 4A **10**
    (off Roscoe St.)
  SE5 . . . . 4F **91**
    (off Kimpton Rd.)
Peabody Est. E2 . . . . 1D **65**
    (off Minerva St.)
  E1 . . . . 1F **79**
    (off Glamis Pl.)
  EC1 . . . . 4C **8**
    (off Farringdon La.)
  EC1 . . . . 4A **10**
  (off Whitecross St., not cont.)
  N1 . . . . 5E **49**
  SE1 . . . . 2C **76** (2C **24**)
    (Duchy St.)

Peabody Est.
  SE1 . . . . 2E **77** (2F **25**)
    (Gt. Guildford St.)
  SE1 . . . . 3A **26**
    (Mint St.)
  SE24 . . . . 5D **105**
  SW1 . . . . 5E **75**
    (off Vauxhall Bri. Rd.)
  SW3 . . . . 2A **88**
  SW6 . . . . 2C **86**
    (off Lillie Rd.)
  SW11 . . . . 1A **102**
  W6 . . . . 1E **85**
  W10 . . . . 4E **57**
Peabody Hill SE21 . . . . . 1D **119**
Peabody Sq.
  SE1 . . . . 3D **77** (4D **25**)
    (not continuous)
Peabody Twr. EC1 . . . . . . 4A **10**
    (off Golden La.)
Peabody Trust SE17 . . . . . 5F **77**
Peabody Yd. N1 . . . . 5E **49**
Peace Pagoda 2B **88**
Peachey Edwards Ho.
  E2 . . . . 2D **65**
    (off Teesdale St.)
Peach Gro. E11 . . . . 5F **39**
Peach Rd. W10 . . . . 2F **57**
Peachum Rd. SE3 . . . . . . 2B **96**
Peachwalk M. E3 . . . . . . 1F **65**
Peacock St. SE17 . . . . . . 5D **77**
Peacock Theatre 3F **15**
    (off Portugal St.)
Peacock Wlk. E16 . . . . . . 5D **69**
    (off Mortlake Rd.)
  N6 . . . . 2D **33**
Peacock Yd. SE17 . . . . . . 1D **91**
    (off Iliffe St.)
Peak Hill SE26 . . . . 4E **121**
Peak Hill Av. SE26 . . . . . . 4E **121**
Peak Hill Gdns. SE26 . . . 4E **121**
Peak Ho. N4 . . . . 3E **35**
    (off Woodberry Down Est.)
Peak, The SE26 . . . . 3E **121**
Pearcefield Av.
  SE23 . . . . 1E **121**
Pear Cl. SE14 . . . . 3A **94**
Pear Ct. SE15 . . . . 3B **92**
    (off Thruxton Way)
Pearcroft Rd. E11 . . . . . . 4F **39**
Peardon St. SW8 . . . . . . 5D **89**
Pearfield Rd. SE23 . . . . . 3A **122**
Pearl Cl. NW2 . . . . 2F **29**
Pearl St. E1 . . . . 2D **79**
Pearman St.
  SE1 . . . . 4C **76** (5C **24**)
Pear Pl. SE1 . . . . 3C **76** (3B **24**)
Pear Rd. E11 . . . . 5F **39**
Pearscroft Ct. SW6 . . . . . 4D **87**
Pearscroft Rd. SW6 . . . . . 4D **87**
Pearse St. SE15 . . . . 2A **92**
Pearson Cl. SE5 . . . . 4E **91**
    (off Camberwell New Rd.)
Pearson M. SW4 . . . . . 1F **103**
    (off Slievemore Cl.)
Pearson's Av. SE14 . . . . 4C **94**
Pearson St. E2 . . . . 1B **64**
Peartree SE26 . . . . 5A **122**
Peartree Av. SW17 . . . . . 3E **115**
Pear Tree Cl. E2 . . . . 5B **50**

Pear Tree Ct.
  EC1 . . . . 3C **62** (4C **8**)
Pear Tree Ho. SE4 . . . . . 1B **108**
Peartree La. E1 . . . . 1E **79**
Pear Tree St. EC1 . . 3E **63** (3D **9**)
Peartree Way SE10 . . . . . 5C **82**
Peary Ho. NW10 . . . . . . 4A **42**
Peary Pl. E2 . . . . 2E **65**
Peckarmans Wood
  SE26 . . . . 3C **120**
Peckett Sq. N5 . . . . 1E **49**
Peckford Pl. SW9 . . . . . . 5C **90**
PECKHAM 4C **92**
Peckham Gro. SE15 . . . . . 3A **92**
Peckham High St. SE15 . . 4C **92**
Peckham Hill St. SE15 . . . 3C **92**
Peckham Pk. Rd. SE15 . . . 3C **92**
Peckham Rd. SE5 . . . . . . 4A **92**
  SE15 . . . . 4A **92**
Peckham Rye SE15 . . . . . 1C **106**
Peckham Sq. SE15 . . . . . 4C **92**
Pecks Yd. E1 . . . . 5F **11**
    (off Hanbury St.)
Peckwater St. NW5 . . . . . 2E **47**
Pedlar's Wlk. N7 . . . . . . 2B **48**
Pedley St. E1 . . . . 3B **64**
Pedro St. E5 . . . . 5F **37**
Pedworth Gdns. SE16 . . . 5E **79**
Peek Cres. SW19 . . . . . . 5F **113**
Peel Gro. E2 . . . . 1E **65**
    (not continuous)
Peel Pas. W8 . . . . 2C **72**
    (off Peel St.)
Peel Pct. NW6 . . . . 1C **58**
Peel St. W8 . . . . 2C **72**
Peerless St.
  EC1 . . . . 2F **63** (2B **10**)
Pegasus Cl. N16 . . . . . . 1F **49**
Pegasus Ct. NW10 . . . . . 2D **57**
    (off Trenmar Gdns.)
Pegasus Ho. E1 . . . . 3F **65**
    (off Beaumont Sq.)
Pegasus Pl. SE11 . . . . . . 2C **90**
  SW6 . . . . 4C **86**
Pegley Gdns. SE12 . . . . . 2C **124**
Pekin Cl. E14 . . . . 5C **66**
    (off Pekin St.)
Pekin St. E14 . . . . 5C **66**
Peldon Wlk. N1 . . . . 5D **49**
    (off Popham St.)
Pelham Cl. SE5 . . . . 1A **106**
Pelham Ct. SW3 . . . . 5A **74**
    (off Fulham Rd.)
Pelham Cres. SW7 . . . . . 5A **74**
Pelham Ho. W14 . . . . . . 5B **72**
    (off Mornington Av.)
Pelham Pl. SW7 . . . . 5A **74**
Pelham St. SW7 . . . . 5F **73**
Pelican Est. SE15 . . . . . . 4B **92**
Pelican Ho. SE8 . . . . 5B **80**
Pelican Pas. E1 . . . . 3E **65**
Pelican Wlk. SW9 . . . . . . 2D **105**
Pelican Wharf E1 . . . . . . 2E **79**
    (off Wapping Wall)
Pelier St. SE17 . . . . 2E **91**
Pelinore Rd. SE6 . . . . . . 2A **124**
Pella Ho. SE11 . . . . 1B **90**
Pellant Rd. SW6 . . . . 3A **86**
Pellatt Rd. SE22 . . . . 3B **106**
Pellerin Rd. N16 . . . . 2A **50**

Portman St.
  W1 . . . . 5C **60** (3B **12**)
Portman Towers
  W1 . . . . 5B **60** (2A **12**)
Port Meers Cl. E17. . . . 1B **38**
Portnall Rd. W9 . . . . . 1B **58**
Portobello Ct. Est.
  W11 . . . . 5B **58**
Portobello M. W11 . . . . 1C **72**
Portobello Rd. W10 . . . 4A **58**
  W11 . . . . 5B **58**
Portobello Road Market
  . . . . **4A 58**
Portpool La. EC1. . 4C **62** (5B **8**)
Portree St. E14 . . . . . 5F **67**
Portsdown Av. NW11 . . 1B **30**
Portsdown M. NW11 . . 1B **30**
Portsea Hall W2 . . . . . 5B **60**
  (off Portsea Pl.)
Portsea M. W2 . . . . . . 5A **60**
  (off Portsea Pl.)
Portsea Pl. W2. . . . . . 5A **60**
Portslade M. SW8 . . . . 5E **89**
Portsmouth M. E16 . . . 2D **83**
Portsmouth Rd. SW15 . . 5D **99**
Portsmouth St.
  WC2 . . . . . 5B **62** (3F **15**)
Portsoken St.
  EC3 . . . . 1B **78** (4F **19**)
Portswood Pl. SW15 . . 4B **98**
Portugal St.
  WC2 . . . . . 5B **62** (3F **15**)
Portway E15 . . . . 5B **54**
Portway Gdns. SE18 . . . 3F **97**
Pory Ho. SE11 . . . . . . 5B **76**
Poseidon Ct. E14 . . . . 5C **80**
  (off Homer Dr.)
Postern, The EC2 . . . . 1A **18**
Post Office App. E7 . . . 2D **55**
Post Office Ct. EC4 . . . 3C **18**
  (off Barbican)
Post Office Way SW8 . . 3F **89**
Potier St. SE1 . . 4F **77** (5C **26**)
Potterne Cl. SW19 . . . . 5F **99**
Potters Flds.
  SE1 . . . . 2A **78** (2E **27**)
Potter's La. SW16. . . . 5F **117**
Potters Lodge E14 . . . . 1E **95**
  (off Manchester Rd.)
Potters Rd. SW6 . . . . . 5E **87**
Pottery La. W11 . . . . . 2A **72**
Pottery St. SE16. . . . . 3D **79**
Pott St. E2 . . . . 2D **65**
Poulton Cl. E8 . . . . . . 3D **51**
Poultry EC2 . . . . 5F **63** (3B **18**)
Pound La. NW10 . . . . . 3C **42**
Pound Pk. Rd. SE7 . . . 5F **83**
Pountney Rd. SW11 . . 1C **102**
Povey Ho. SE17 . . . . . 5A **78**
  (off Tatum St.)
Powell Rd. E5 . . . . . . 5D **37**
Powell's Wlk. W4 . . . . 2A **84**
Powergate Bus. Pk.
  NW10 . . . . 2A **56**
Powerscroft Rd. E5. . . . 1E **51**
Powis Ct. W11 . . . . . . 5B **58**
  (off Powis Gdns.)
Powis Gdns. NW11 . . . 2B **30**
  W11 . . . . 5B **58**
Powis M. W11 . . . . . . 5B **58**

Powis Pl. WC1 . . . 3A **62** (4E **7**)
Powis Rd. E3 . . . . 2D **67**
Powis Sq. W11 . . . . . . 5B **58**
  (not continuous)
Powis Ter. W11 . . . . . . 5B **58**
Powlett Ho. NW1 . . . . . 3D **47**
  (off Powlett Pl.)
Powlett Pl. NW1 . . . . . 4C **46**
  (not continuous)
Pownall Rd. E8 . . . . . . 5B **50**
Powster Rd.
  BR1: Brom 5C **124**
Poynders Ct. SW4 . . . . 4E **103**
Poynders Gdns. SW4 . . 5E **103**
Poynders Rd. SW4 . . . 4E **103**
Poynings Rd. N19 . . . . 5E **33**
Poynter Ho. NW8 . . . . 3F **59**
  (off Fisherton St.)
  W11 . . . . 2F **71**
  (off Queensdale Cres.)
Poyntz Rd. SW11 . . . . 5B **88**
Poyser St. E2 . . . . 1D **65**
Praed M. W2 . . . . 5F **59**
Praed St. W2 . . . . 5F **59**
Pragel St. E13 . . . . . . 1E **69**
Pragnell Rd. SE12 . . . 2D **125**
Prague Pl. SW2 . . . . . 3A **104**
Prah Rd. N4 . . . . 4C **34**
Prairie St. SW8 . . . . . 5C **88**
Pratt M. NW1 . . . . 5E **47**
Pratt St. NW1 . . . . . . 5E **47**
Pratt Wlk. SE11 . . . . . 5B **76**
Prayle Gro. NW2 . . . . 3F **29**
Preachers Ct. EC1 . . . . 5E **9**
Prebend Gdns. W6. . . . 5B **70**
  (not continuous)
Prebend Mans. W4 . . . 5B **70**
  (off Chiswick High Rd.)
Prebend St. N1. . . . . . 5E **49**
Precinct, The N1 . . . . . 5E **49**
  (not continuous)
Premier Cnr. W9 . . . . . 1B **58**
Premiere Pl. E14 . . . . . 1C **80**
Premier Ho. N1 . . . . . 4D **49**
  (off Waterloo Ter.)
Premier Pl. SW15 . . . 2A **100**
Prendergast Rd. SE3 . . 1A **110**
Prentice Ct. SW19 . . . 5B **114**
Prentis Rd. SW16 . . . . 4F **117**
Prentiss Ct. SE7 . . . . . 5F **83**
Presburg St. E5 . . . . . 5F **37**
Prescot St. E1 . . . . . . 1B **78**
Prescott Ho. SE5 . . . . 2D **91**
  (off Hillingdon St.)
Prescott Pl. SW4 . . . . 1F **103**
Presentation M. SW2 . . 2B **118**
President Dr. E1 . . . . . 2D **79**
President Ho.
  EC1 . . . . 2D **63** (2E **9**)
President Quay E1 . . . . 2B **78**
  (off St Katherine's Way)
President St. EC1 . . . . 1F **9**
Press Ho. NW10 . . . . . 5A **28**
Press Rd. NW10 . . . . . 5A **28**
Prestage Way E14 . . . . 1E **81**
Prestbury Rd. E7 . . . . . 4E **55**
Prested Rd. SW11 . . . 2A **102**
Preston Cl. SE1 . . . . . 5A **78**
Preston Dr. E11 . . . . . 1E **41**
Preston Gdns. NW10 . . 3B **42**

Preston Ho. SE1 . . . . . 5F **27**
  (off Stanworth St.)
  SE17 . . . . 5A **78**
  (off Preston Cl.)
Preston Pl. NW2 . . . . . 3C **42**
Preston Rd. E11. . . . . . 1A **40**
  SE19 . . . . 5D **119**
Preston's Rd. E14. . . . . 1E **81**
Preston St. E2. . . . . . . 1F **65**
Prestwich Ter. SW4 . . . 3E **103**
Prestwood Ho. SE16 . . 4D **79**
  (off Drummond Rd.)
Prestwood St. N1 . . . . 1E **63**
Pretoria Rd. E11. . . . . . 3F **39**
  E16 . . . . 3B **68**
  SW16 . . . . 5D **117**
Priam Ho. E2 . . . . 1D **65**
  (off Old Bethnal Grn. Rd.)
Price Cl. SW17 . . . . . 3B **116**
Price' Ct. SW11 . . . . . 1F **101**
Price Ho. N1 . . . . 5E **49**
  (off Britannia Row)
Price's St. SE1 . . 2D **77** (2E **25**)
Price's Yd. N1 . . . . . . 5B **48**
Prichard Ct. N7 . . . . . 3B **48**
Prideaux Pl. W3. . . . . 1A **70**
  WC1 . . . . 2B **62** (1A **8**)
Prideaux Rd. SW9 . . . . 1A **104**
Priestfield Rd. SE23 . . 3A **122**
Priestley Cl. N16 . . . . . 2B **36**
Priestley Ho. EC1 . . . . 3A **10**
Priestley Way NW2 . . . 3C **28**
Priest's Bri. SW14 . . . . 1A **98**
Priest's Ct. EC2. . . . . . 2F **17**
Prima Rd. SW9 . . . . . 3C **90**
Prime Meridian Line . . 3F **95**
Primrose Cl. SE6 . . . . 5E **123**
Primrose Ct. SW12. . . 5F **103**
Primrose Gdns. NW3 . . 3A **46**
PRIMROSE HILL **5C 46**
Primrose Hill
  EC4 . . . . 5C **62** (3C **16**)
Primrose Hill Ct. NW3 . . 4B **46**
Primrose Hill Rd. NW3 . 4B **46**
Primrose Hill Studios
  NW1 . . . . 5C **46**
Primrose Mans. SW11. . 4C **88**
Primrose M. NW1 . . . . 4B **46**
  (off Sharpleshall St.)
  SE3 . . . . 3C **96**
Primrose Rd. E10 . . . . 3D **39**
Primrose Sq. E9. . . . . . 4E **51**
Primrose St.
  EC2 . . . . 4A **64** (5D **11**)
Primrose Wlk. SE14. . . 3A **94**
Primula St. W12 . . . . . 5C **56**
Prince Albert Ct. NW8 . 5B **46**
  (off Prince Albert Rd.)
Prince Albert Rd. NW1. . 2A **60**
  NW8 . . . . 2A **60**
Prince Arthur M. NW3 . . 1E **45**
Prince Arthur Rd.
  NW3 . . . . 2E **45**
Prince Charles Dr.
  NW4 . . . . 2E **29**
Prince Charles Rd.
  SE3 . . . . 5B **96**
Prince Consort Rd.
  SW7 . . . . 4E **73**
Princedale Rd. W11. . . 2A **72**

Provost Rd. NW3 . . . . . 4B 46
Provost St. N1 . . 1F 63 (1B 10)
Prowse Pl. NW1 . . . . . . 4E 47
Prudent Pas. EC2 . . . . . 2A 18
Prusom's Island E1 . . . 2E 79
(off Cinnamon St.)
Prusom St. E1 . . . . 2D 79
Pryors, The NW3 . . . . . 5F 31
Pudding La.
EC3. . . . . . . 1F 77 (5C 18)
Pudding Mill La. E15. . . 5D 53
Puddle Dock
EC4 . . . . 1D 77 (4E 17)
(not continuous)
Pugin Ct. N1 . . . . 4C 48
(off Liverpool Rd.)
Pulborough Rd. SW18 . . 5B 100
Pulford Rd. N15 . . . . . . 1F 35
Pulham Ho. SW8 . . . . . 3B 90
(off Dorset Rd.)
Pullen's Bldgs. SE17 . . . 1D 91
(off Iliffe St.)
Pullman Ct. SW2 . . . . . 1A 118
Pullman Gdns. SW15. . . 4E 99
Pullman M. SE12 . . . . 3D 125
Pulross Rd. SW9 . . . . . 1B 104
Pulteney Cl. E3 . . . . 5B 52
Pulteney Ter. N1 . . . . . . 5B 48
(not continuous)
Pulton Ho. SE4 . . . . . . 2A 108
(off Turnham Rd.)
Pulton Pl. SW6 . . . . 3C 86
Puma Ct. E1 . . . . 4B 64 (5F 11)
Pump Ct. EC4 . . 5C 62 (3B 16)
Pump Ho. Cl. SE16. . . . . 3E 79
Pumping Sta. Rd. W4 . . 3A 84
Pump La. SE14 . . . . 3E 93
Punderson's Gdns. E2 . . 2D 65
Purbeck Dr. NW2 . . . . . 4F 29
Purbeck Ho. SW8 . . . . . 3B 90
(off Bolney St.)
Purbrook Est.
SE1 . . . . . . 3A 78 (4E 27)
Purbrook St.
SE1 . . . . . . 4A 78 (5E 27)
Purcell Cres. SW6 . . . . . 3F 85
(off Milman's St.)
Purcell Ho. SW10. . . . . . 2F 87
(off Milman's St.)
Purcell Mans. W14 . . . . . 2A 86
(off Queen's Club Gdns.)
Purcell M. NW10 . . . . . . 4A 42
Purcell Room 1A 24
(off Waterloo Rd.)
Purcell St. N1. . . . . 1A 64
Purchese St.
NW1 . . . . . . 1F 61 (1C 6)
Purdon Ho. SE15 . . . . . . 4C 92
(off Peckham High St.)
Purdy St. E3 . . . . 3D 67
Purelake M. SE13 . . . . . 1F 109
(off Marischal Rd.)
Purley Av. NW2 . . . . . . 4A 30
Purley Pl. N1 . . . . 4D 49
Purneys Rd. SE9. . . . . . 2F 111
Purser Ho. SW2 . . . . . . 4C 104
(off Tulse Hill)
Pursers Cross Rd.
SW6 . . . . 4B 86
(not continuous)
Purves Rd. NW10. . . . . . 2D 57

Pusey Ho. E14 . . . . 5C 66
(off Saracen St.)
Puteaux Ho. E2. . . . . . . 1F 65
(off Mace St.)

PUTNEY **2F 99**
Putney Bri. SW6. . . . . . 1A 100
SW15 . . . . 1A 100
Putney Bri. App. SW6. . . 1A 100
Putney Bri. Rd. SW15. . . 2A 100
SW18 . . . . 2A 100
Putney Comn. SW15 . . . 1E 99
Putney Exchange Shop. Cen.
SW15 . . . . 2F 99
PUTNEY HEATH **4E 99**
Putney Heath SW15. . . . 5D 99
Putney Heath La.
SW15 . . . . 4F 99
Putney High St. SW15 . . 2F 99
Putney Hill SW15 . . . . . 5F 99
(not continuous)
Putney Pk. Av. SW15. . . 2C 98
Putney Pk. La. SW15. . . 2D 98
(not continuous)
PUTNEY VALE **3C 112**
Putney Vale Crematorium
SW15 . . . . 2C 112
Putney Wharf SW15 . . . 1A 100
Pylon Trad. Est. E16 . . . 3A 68
Pymers Mead SE21 . . . . 1E 119
Pynfolds SE16 . . . . 3D 79
Pynnersmead SE24 . . . . 3E 105
Pyrford Ho. SW9 . . . . . 2D 105
Pyrland Rd. N5. . . . . 2F 49
Pyrmont Gro. SE27 . . . . 3D 119
Pytchley Rd. SE22 . . . . 1A 106

Quadrangle Cl. SE1 . . . . 5A 78
Quadrangle, The E15. . . 3A 54
SE24 . . . . 3E 105
SW6 . . . . 3A 86
SW10 . . . . 4E 87
W2 . . . . 5A 60
W12 . . . . 5D 57
(off Du Cane Rd.)
Quadrant Arc. W1 . . . . . 5A 14
Quadrant Gro. NW5 . . . . 2B 46
Quadrant Ho. SE1 . . . . . 1D 25
Quadrant, The W10 . . . . 2F 57
Quaggy Wlk. SE3 . . . . . 2C 110
Quain Mans. W14 . . . . . 2A 86
(off Queen's Club Gdns.)
Quainton St. NW10 . . . . 5A 28
Quaker Ct. E1 . . . . 4F 11
(off Quaker St.)
EC1. . . . . 3B 10
Quakers Pl. E7 . . . . 2F 55
Quaker St. E1 . . 3B 64 (4F 11)
Quality Ct. WC2 . . . . . . 2B 16
Quantock Gdns. NW2 . . 4F 29
Quantock Ho. N16 . . . . . 3B 36
Quarley Way SE15. . . . . 3B 92
Quarrendon St. SW6 . . . 5C 86
Quarry Rd. SW18 . . . . . 4E 101
Quarterdeck, The E14 . . 3C 80
Quarter Mile La. E10. . . 1D 53
Quastel Ho. SE1 . . . . . . 4B 26
(off Long La.)

Quay Ho. E14 . . . . 3C 80
(off Admirals Way)
Quayside Cotts. E1. . . . . 2C 78
(off Mew St.)
Quayside Ct. SE16 . . . . . 2F 79
(off Abbotshade Rd.)
Quayside Ho. E14 . . . . . 2B 80
Quay Vw. Apartments
E14 . . . . 4C 80
(off Arden Cres.)
Quebec Ct. E14 . . . . . . 5C 66
Quebec M. W1. . 5B 60 (3A 12)
Quebec Way SE16 . . . . . 3F 79
Quebec Way Ind. Est.
SE16 . . . . 3A 80
Quedgeley Ct. SE15. . . . 2B 92
(off Ebley Cl.)
Queen Alexandra Mans.
WC1 . . . . 2D 7
(off Bidborough St.)
Queen Alexandra's Ct.
SW19 . . . . 5B 114
Queen Anne Ho. E16 . . . 1C 82
(off Hardy Av.)
Queen Anne M.
W1 . . . . 4D 61 (1E 13)
Queen Anne Rd. E9 . . . . 3F 51
Queen Anne's Ct. SE10. . 1F 95
(off Park Row)
Queen Anne's Gdns. W4. . 4A 70
Queen Anne's Ga.
SW1 . . . . 3F 75 (4B 22)
Queen Anne's Gro. W4. . 4A 70
Queen Anne St.
W1. . . . . . . 5D 61 (2D 13)
Queen Anne's Wlk. WC1. . 4E 7
Queen Anne Ter. E1 . . . . 1D 79
(off Sovereign Cl.)
Queen Caroline St. W6. . 1E 85
(not continuous)
Queen Catherine Ho.
SW6 . . . . 3D 87
(off Wandon Rd.)
Queen Elizabeth Bldgs.
EC4. . . . . 4B 16
Queen Elizabeth Hall . . . 2B 76 (1A 24)
Queen Elizabeth Ho.
SW12 . . . . 5C 102
Queen Elizabeth II
Conference Cen.
. . . . 3F 75 (4C 22)
Queen Elizabeth's Cl.
N16 . . . . 4F 35
Queen Elizabeth's Coll.
SE10 . . . . 3E 95
Queen Elizabeth St.
SE1 . . . . 3A 78 (3E 27)
Queen Elizabeth's Wlk.
N16 . . . . 3F 35
Queen Elizabeth Wlk.
SW13 . . . . 4C 84
(not continuous)
Queenhithe EC4. . 1E 77 (4A 18)
Queen Isabella Way
EC1 . . . . 2E 17
(off King Edward St.)
Queen Margaret Flats
E2 . . . . 2D 65
(off St Jude's Rd.)

Raphael Ct. *SE16*. 1D **93**
   (off Stubbs Dr.)
Raphael St. SW7 . . . . 3B **74**
Rapley Ho. *E2* 2C **64**
   (off Turin St.)
Rashleigh Ct. SW8. . . . . . 5D **89**
Rashleigh Ho. *WC1* 2D **7**
   (off Thanet St.)
Rastell Av. SW2 . . . . 2F **117**
Ratcliffe Cl. SE12. . . . . . 5C **110**
Ratcliffe Ct. *SE1* 4A **26**
   (off Gt. Dover St.)
Ratcliffe Cross St. E1. . . . 5F **65**
Ratcliffe Ho. E14 . . . . . . 5A **66**
Ratcliffe La. E14 . . . . 5A **66**
Ratcliffe Orchard E1 . . . . 1F **79**
Ratcliff Rd. E7 . . . . 2E **55**
Rathbone Ho. *E16* 5B **68**
   (off Rathbone St.)
  NW6 . . . . 5C **44**
Rathbone Mkt. E16. . . . . . 4B **68**
Rathbone Pl. W1. .4F **61** (1B 14)
Rathbone Point *E5* 1C **50**
   (off Nolan Way)
Rathbone St. E16 . . . . . . 4B **68**
  W1 . . . . 4E **61** (1A 14)
Rathcoole Gdns. N8 . . . . 1B **34**
Rathfern Rd. SE6 . . . . . . 1B **122**
Rathgar Rd. SW9 . . . . . 1D **105**
Rathmell Dr. SW4 . . . . . . 4F **103**
Rathmore Rd. SE7 . . . . . . 1D **97**
Rattray Ct. SE6. . . . . 2B **124**
Rattray Rd. SW2 . . . . . . 2C **104**
Raul Rd. SE15 . . . . 5C **92**
Raveley St. NW5 . . . . 1E **47**
   (not continuous)
Ravenet St. SW11 . . . . . . 4D **89**
   (not continuous)
Ravenfield Rd. SW17. . . . 3B **116**
Ravenhill Rd. E13 . . . . . . 1E **69**
Raven Ho. *SE16* 5F **79**
   (off Tawny Way)
Ravenna Rd. SW15 . . . . . 3F **99**
Raven Row E1 . . . . 4D **65**
   (not continuous)
Ravensbourne Ct. SE6. . 5C **108**
Ravensbourne Ho.
  BR1: Brom 5F **123**
  NW8 . . . . 4A **60**
   (off Broadley St.)
Ravensbourne Mans.
  SE8 . . . . 2C **94**
   (off Berthon St.)
Ravensbourne Pk.
  SE6 . . . . 5C **108**
Ravensbourne Pk. Cres.
  SE6 . . . . 5B **108**
Ravensbourne Pl.
  SE13 . . . . 5D **95**
Ravensbourne Rd.
  SE6 . . . . 5B **108**
Ravensbury Rd.
  SW18 . . . . 2C **114**
Ravensbury Ter.
  SW18 . . . . 2D **115**
Ravenscar *NW1* 5E **47**
   (off Bayham St.)
Ravenscar Rd.
  BR1: Brom 4A **124**
Ravenscourt Av. W6. . . . 5C **70**

Ravenscourt Gdns. W6. . 5C **70**
Ravenscourt Pk. W6 . . . . 4C **70**
Ravenscourt Pk. Mans.
  W6 . . . . 4D **71**
   (off Paddenswick Rd.)
Ravenscourt Pl. W6. . . . . 5D **71**
Ravenscourt Rd. W6 . . . . 5D **71**
   (not continuous)
Ravenscourt Sq. W6 . . . . 4C **70**
Ravenscroft Av. NW11. . 2B **30**
Ravenscroft Cl. E16 . . . . 4C **68**
Ravenscroft Rd. E16 . . . . 4C **68**
Ravenscroft St. E2 . . . . . 1B **64**
Ravensdale Rd. N16 . . . . 2B **36**
Ravensdon St. SE11 . . . . 1C **90**
Ravenshaw St. NW6 . . . . 2B **44**
Ravenslea Rd. SW12. . 5B **102**
Ravensleigh Gdns.
  BR1: Brom 5D **125**
Ravensmede Way W4 . . 5B **70**
Ravens M. SE12. . . . . . . 3C **110**
Ravenstone SE17. . . . . . . 1A **92**
Ravenstone Rd. NW9. . . . 1B **28**
Ravenstone St. SW12 . 1C **116**
Ravens Way SE12 . . . . . 3C **110**
Ravenswood Rd.
  SW12 . . . . 5D **103**
Ravensworth Rd. *SW6* . . 3C **86**
   (off Fulham Rd.)
Ravensworth Rd. NW10. . 2D **57**
Ravent Rd. SE11 . . . . . . 5B **76**
Ravey St. EC2. . 3A **64** (3D 11)
Rav Pinter Cl. N16. . . . . 2A **36**
Rawalpindi Ho. E16 . . . . 3B **68**
Rawchester Ct. SW18. . 1B **114**
Rawlings St. SW3 . . . . . 5B **74**
Rawlinson Ct. NW2 . . . . 2E **29**
Rawlinson Ho. *SE13*. . 2F **109**
   (off Mercator Rd.)
Rawlinson Point *E16* . . 4B **68**
   (off Fox Rd.)
Rawreth Wlk. *N1* 5E **49**
   (off Basire St.)
Rawson St. SW11 . . . . . . 4C **88**
   (not continuous)
Rawstone Wlk. E13 . . . . 1C **68**
Rawstorne Pl.
  EC1 . . . . 2D **63** (1D **9**)
Rawstorne St.
  EC1 . . . . 2D **63** (1D **9**)
Rayburne Ct. W14 . . . . . 4A **72**
Raydon St. N19 . . . . 4D **33**
Rayford Av. SE12 . . . . . 5B **110**
Ray Gunter Ho. *SE17*. . 1D **91**
   (off Marsland Cl.)
Ray Ho. *N1*. 5A **50**
   (off Colville Est.)
Rayleigh Rd. E16. . . . . . 2D **83**
Raymede Towers *W10* . . 4F **57**
   (off Treverton St.)
Raymond Bldgs.
  WC1. . . . . . . 4B **62** (5A **8**)
Raymond Cl. SE26 . . . . . 5E **121**
Raymond Revuebar . . . **4B 14**
   (off Walkers Cl.)
Raymond Rd. E13 . . . . . . 5E **55**
  SW19 . . . . 5A **114**
Raymouth Ho. *SE16*. . . . 5E **79**
   (off Raymouth Rd.)
Raymouth Rd. SE16. . . . 5D **79**

Raynald Ho. SW16. . . . . 3A **118**
Rayne Ho. *W9* 3D **59**
   (off Delaware Rd.)
Rayner Ct. *W12* 3E **71**
   (off Bamborough Gdns.)
Rayners Rd. SW15. . . . . 3A **100**
Rayner Towers E10 . . . . 2C **38**
   (off Albany Rd.)
Raynes Av. E11 . . . . 2E **41**
Raynham *W2* 5A **60**
   (off Norfolk Cres.)
Raynham Ho. *E1*. 3F **65**
   (off Harpley Sq.)
Raynham Rd. W6. . . . . . 5D **71**
Raynor Pl. N1. . . . . 4E **49**
Ray St. EC1. . . . . . 3C **62** (4C **8**)
Ray St. Bri. EC1. . . . . . . 4C **8**
Ray Wlk. N7. . . . . 4B **34**
Reachview Cl. NW1 . . . . 4E **47**
Read Ct. E17 . . . . 1C **38**
Reade Ho. *SE10*. 2F **95**
   (off Trafalgar Gro.)
Reade Wlk. NW10 . . . . . 4A **42**
Read Ho. *SE11*. 2C **90**
   (off Clayton St.)
Reading Ho. *SE15* 2C **92**
   (off Friary Est.)
  W2 . . . . 5E **59**
   (off Hallfield Est.)
Reading La. E8 . . . . 3D **51**
Reapers Cl. NW1 . . . . . . 5F **47**
Reardon Ho. *E1* 2D **79**
   (off Reardon St.)
Reardon Path E1 . . . . . . 2D **79**
   (not continuous)
Reardon St. E1. . . . . 2D **79**
Reaston St. SE14 . . . . . . 3F **93**
Reckitt Rd. W4 . . . . 1A **84**
Record St. SE15. . . . . . . 2E **93**
Recovery St. SW17 . . . . 5A **116**
Recreation Rd. SE26 . . . 4F **121**
Rector St. N1 . . . . 5E **49**
Rectory Cres. E11 . . . . . 1E **41**
   (not continuous)
Rectory Fld. Cres. SE7. . 3E **97**
Rectory Gdns. SW4 . . . . 1E **103**
Rectory Gro. SW4 . . . . . 1E **103**
Rectory La. SW17 . . . . . 5C **116**
Rectory Orchard SW19. .4A **114**
Rectory Rd. E8. . . . . 1C **50**
  N16. . . . . 4B **36**
  SW13 . . . . 5C **84**
Rectory Sq. E1 . . . . 4F **65**
Reculver Ho. *SE15*. 2E **93**
   (off Lovelinch Cl.)
Reculver Rd. SE16 . . . . . 1F **93**
Red Anchor Cl. SW3. . . . 2F **87**
Redan Pl. W2. . . . . 5D **59**
Redan St. W14 . . . . 4F **71**
Redan Ter. SE5 . . . . 5D **91**
Redberry Gro. SE26. . . . 3E **121**
Redbourne Ho. *E14* . . . 5B **66**
   (off Norbiton Rd.)
Redbourn Ho. *W10*. . . . 3E **57**
   (off Sutton Way)
REDBRIDGE **1F 41**
Redbridge Gdns. SE5. . . 3A **92**
Redbridge La. E.
  IG4: Ilf 1F **41**
Redbridge La. W. E11. . 1D **41**

Rigeley Rd. NW10 . . . . . 2C **56**
Rigg App. E10 . . . . 3F **37**
Rigge Pl. SW4 . . . . 2F **103**
Riggindale Rd. SW16 . . 5F **117**
Riley Ho. SW10 . . . . 3F **87**
(off Riley St.)
Riley Rd. SE1 . . 4B **78** (5E **27**)
Riley St. SW10 . . . . 2F **87**
Rill Ho. SE5 . . . . 3F **91**
(off Harris St.)
Rinaldo Rd. SW12 . . . 5D **103**
Ringcroft St. N7 . . . . 2C **48**
Ringford Rd. SW18 . . 3B **100**
Ring Ho. E1 . . . . 1E **79**
(off Sage St.)
Ringlet Cl. E16 . . . . 4D **69**
Ringmer Av. SW6 . . . . . . 4A **86**
Ringmer Gdns. N19 . . . . 4A **34**
Ringmore Ri. SE23 . . . 5D **107**
Ring Rd. W12 . . . . 2E **71**
Ringsfield Ho. SE17 . . . . 1E **91**
(off Bronti Cl.)
Ringstead Rd. SE6 . . . 5D **109**
Ring, The W2 . . . 1F **73** (4A **12**)
(not continuous)
Ringwood Gdns. E14 . . . 5C **80**
SW15 . . . . 1C **112**
Ringwood Rd. E17 . . . . 1B **38**
Ripley Gdns. SW14 . . . 1A **98**
Ripley Ho. SW1 . . . . 2E **89**
(off Churchill Gdns.)
Ripley M. E11 . . . . 1A **40**
Ripley Rd. E16 . . . . 5E **69**
Ripon Gdns. IG1: Ilf . . . 1F **41**
Ripplevale Gro. N1 . . . . 4B **48**
Risborough SE17 . . . . . . 5E **77**
Risborough Ho. NW8 . . 3A **60**
(off Mallory St.)
Risborough St.
SE1 . . . . 3D **77** (3E **25**)
Risdon Ho. SE16 . . . . . . 3E **79**
(off Risdon St.)
Risdon St. SE16 . . . . 4E **79**
Riseholme Ct. E9 . . . . . 3B **52**
Riseldine Rd. SE23 . . . 4A **108**
Rise, The E11 . . . . 1C **40**
NW10 . . . . 1A **42**
Risinghill St. N1 . . . . . . 1B **62**
Rising Sun Ct. EC1 . . . . . 5E **9**
Rita Rd. SW8 . . . . 2A **90**
Ritches Rd. N15 . . . . . . 1E **35**
Ritchie Ho. E14 . . . . 5F **67**
(off Blair St.)
N19 . . . . 3F **33**
SE16 . . . . 4E **79**
(off Howland Est.)
Ritchie St. N1 . . . . 1C **62**
Ritherdon Rd. SW17 . . 2C **116**
Ritson Ho. N1 . . . . 5B **48**
(off Barnsbury Est.)
Ritson Rd. E8 . . . . 3C **50**
Rivaz Pl. E9 . . . . 3E **51**
Riven Ct. W2 . . . . 5D **59**
(off Inverness Ter.)
Riverbank Rd.
BR1: Brom 3C **124**
River Barge Cl. E14 . . . 3E **81**
River Cl. E11 . . . . 1E **41**
River Ct. SE1 . . 1D **77** (5D **17**)
Rivercourt Rd. W6 . . . . 5D **71**

Riverdale SE13 . . . . 2E **109**
Riverdale Dr. SW18 . . . 1D **115**
Riverdale Shop. Cen.
SE13 . . . . 1E **109**
Riverfleet WC1 . . . . 1E **7**
(off Birkenhead St.)
River Ho. SE26 . . . . 3D **121**
Rivermead Ct. SW6 . . 1B **100**
Rivermead Ho. E9 . . . . . 2A **52**
River Pk. Trad. Est. E14. 4B **80**
River Pl. N1 . . . . 4E **49**
Riversdale Rd. N5 . . . . 5D **35**
Riverside NW4 . . . . 2D **29**
SE7 . . . . 4D **83**
(not continuous)
WC1 . . . . 1E **7**
(off Birkenhead St.)
Riverside Bus. Cen.
SW18 . . . . 1D **115**
Riverside Cl. E5 . . . . 3E **37**
Riverside Ct. SE3 . . . . . 2B **110**
SW8 . . . . 2F **89**
Riverside Dr. NW11 . . . 1A **30**
W4 . . . . 3A **84**
Riverside Gdns. W6 . . . 1D **85**
Riverside Ho. N1 . . . . . . 4E **49**
(off Canonbury St.)
Riverside Mans. E1 . . . . 2E **79**
(off Milk Yd.)
Riverside Rd. E15 . . . . . 1E **67**
N15 . . . . 1C **36**
SW17 . . . . 4D **115**
Riverside Wlk. SE10 . . . 4A **82**
(Morden Wharf Rd.)
SE10 . . . . 3F **81**
(Tunnel Av.)
SW6 . . . . 1A **100**
W4 . . . . 2B **84**
(off Chiswick Wharf)
Riverside Workshops
SE1 . . . . 1A **26**
(off Park St.)
River St. EC1 . . 2C **62** (1B **8**)
River Ter. W6 . . . . 1E **85**
WC2 . . . . 5F **15**
Riverton Cl. W9 . . . . . . 2B **58**
Riverview Gdns.
SW13 . . . . 2D **85**
Riverview Hgts. SE16 . . 3C **78**
(off Bermondsey Wall W.)
Riverview Pk. SE6 . . . . 2C **122**
River Wlk. W6 . . . . 3E **85**
River Way SE10 . . . . 4B **82**
Rivet Ho. SE1 . . . . 1B **92**
(off Coopers Rd.)
Rivington Bldgs.
EC2 . . . . 2A **64** (2D **11**)
Rivington Ct. NW10 . . . 5C **42**
Rivington Pl.
EC2 . . . . 2A **64** (2E **11**)
Rivington St.
EC2 . . . . 2A **64** (2D **11**)
Rivington Wlk. E8 . . . . . 5C **50**
Rixon St. N7 . . . . 5C **34**
Roach Rd. E3 . . . . 4C **52**
Roads Pl. N19 . . . . 4A **34**
Roan St. SE10 . . . . 2E **95**
Robert Adam St.
W1 . . . . 5C **60** (2B **12**)
Roberta St. E2 . . . . 2C **64**

Robert Bell Ho. SE16 . . 5C **78**
(off Rouel Rd.)
Robert Burns M. SE24. . 3D **105**
Robert Cl. W9 . . . . 3E **59**
Robert Dashwood Way
SE17 . . . . 5E **77**
Robert Gentry Ho. W14 . 1A **86**
(off Gledstanes Rd.)
Robert Jones Ho. SE16 . . 5C **78**
(off Rouel Rd.)
Robert Keen Cl. SE15 . . 4C **92**
Robert Lowe Cl. SE14 . . 3F **93**
Robert Owen Ho. SW6 . . 4F **85**
Robert Runcie Ct. SW9 . 2B **104**
Roberts Cl. SE16 . . . . . . 3F **79**
Roberts Ct. N1 . . . . 5D **49**
(off Essex Rd.)
NW10 . . . . 3A **42**
Roberts M. SW1 . .4C **74** (5B **20**)
Robertson Rd. E15 . . . . 5E **53**
Robertson St. SW8 . . . 1D **103**
Roberts Pl. EC1 . . 3C **62** (3C **8**)
Robert St. NW1 . . 2D **61** (2E **5**)
WC2 . . . . 1A **76** (5E **15**)
Robert Sutton Ho. E1 . . 5E **65**
(off Tarling St.)
Robeson St. E3 . . . . 4B **66**
Robin Ct. E14 . . . . 3E **81**
SE16 . . . . 5C **78**
Robin Cres. E6 . . . . 4F **69**
Robin Gro. N6 . . . . 4C **32**
ROBIN HOOD 3A **112**
Robin Hood Gdns. E14 . . 1E **81**
(off Woolmore St., not cont.)
Robin Hood La. E14 . . . 1E **81**
SW15 . . . . 3A **112**
Robin Hood Rd. SW19 . . 5C **112**
Robin Hood Way SW15 . 3A **112**
Robin Ho. NW8 . . . . 1A **60**
(off Barrow Hill Est.)
Robinia Cres. E10 . . . . . 4D **39**
Robins Ct. SE12 . . . . . . 3E **125**
Robinscroft M. SE10 . . 4E **95**
Robinson Cl. E11 . . . . . . 5A **40**
Robinson Ct. N1 . . . . 5D **49**
(off St Mary's Path)
Robinson Ho. E14 . . . . . 4C **66**
(off Selsey St.)
W10 . . . . 5F **57**
(off Bramley Rd.)
Robinson Rd. E2 . . . . . . 1E **65**
SW17 . . . . 5A **116**
Robinson St. SW3 . . . . 2B **88**
Robinwood Pl. SW15. . 4A **112**
Robsart St. SW9 . . . . . . 5B **90**
Robson Av. NW10 . . . . . 4C **42**
Robson Cl. E6 . . . . 5F **69**
Robson Rd. SE27 . . . . . 3D **119**
Roby Ho. EC1 . . . . 3F **9**
(off Mitchell St.)
Rochdale Rd. E17 . . . . . 2C **38**
Rochdale Way SE8 . . . . 3C **94**
Roche Ho. E14 . . . . 1B **80**
(off Beccles St.)
Rochelle Cl. SW11 . . . . 2F **101**
Rochelle St. E2 . . 2B **64** (2F **11**)
(not continuous)
Rochemont Wlk. E8 . . . . 5C **50**
(off Pownell Rd.)
Rochester Av. E13 . . . . . 5E **55**

Rookstone Rd. SW17 . . 5B **116**
Rook Wlk. E6 . . . . 5F **69**
Rookwood Rd. N16 . . . . 2B **36**
Roosevelt Memorial
. . . . **1C 74 (4C 12)**
Rootes Dr. W10 . . . . 4F **57**
Ropemaker Rd. SE16 . . . 3A **80**
Ropemaker's Flds.
E14 . . . . 1B **80**
Ropemaker St.
EC2 . . . . 4F **63** (5B **10**)
Roper La. SE1 . . 3A **78** (4E **27**)
Ropers Orchard SW3 . . 2A **88**
(off Danvers St.)
Ropers Wlk. SW2 . . . . . 5C **104**
Ropery Bus. Pk. SE7 . . . 5E **83**
Ropery St. E3 . . . . 3B **66**
Rope St. SE16 . . . . 5A **80**
Rope Wlk. Gdns. E1 . . . 5C **64**
Ropewalk M. E8 . . . . 4C **50**
(off Middleton Rd.)
Ropley St. E2 . . . . 1C **64**
Rosa Alba M. N5 . . . . . . 1E **49**
Rosalind Ho. N1 . . . . 1A **64**
(off Arden Ho.)
Rosaline Rd. SW6 . . . . . 3A **86**
Rosaline Ter. SW6 . . . . . 3A **86**
(off Rosaline Rd.)
Rosamond St. SE26 . . . 3D **121**
Rosary Gdns. SW7 . . . . . 5E **73**
Rosaville Rd. SW6 . . . . . 3B **86**
Roscoe St. EC1 . . 3E **63** (4A **10**)
(not continuous)
Roscoe St. Est.
EC1 . . . . 3E **63** (4A **10**)
Rose All. EC2 . . . . 1E **19**
(off Bishopsgate)
SE1 . . . . 2E **77** (1A **26**)
Rose & Crown Ct. EC2 . . 2A **18**
Rose & Crown Yd.
SW1 . . . . 2E **75** (1A **22**)
Rosebank SW6 . . . . 3E **85**
Rosebank Gdns. E3 . . . . 1B **66**
Rosebank Rd. E17 . . . . . 1D **39**
Rosebank Wlk. NW1 . . . . 4F **47**
Roseberry Gdns. N4 . . . 1D **35**
Roseberry Pl. E8 . . . . . . 3B **50**
Roseberry St. SE1 . . . . . 5D **79**
Rosebery Av. E12 . . . . . . 3F **55**
EC1 . . . . 3C **62** (4B **8**)
Rosebery Ct. EC1 . . . . 4B **8**
(off Rosebery Av.)
Rosebery Gdns. N8 . . . . 1A **34**
Rosebery Ho. E2 . . . . 1E **65**
(off Sewardstone Rd.)
Rosebery Rd. SW2 . . . . 4A **104**
Rosebery Sq. EC1 . . . . 4B **8**
Rosebury Rd. SW6 . . . . . 5D **87**
Rose Bush Ct. NW3 . . . . 2B **46**
Rose Ct. E8 . . . . 4B **50**
(off Richmond Rd.)
E1 . . . . 1F **19**
SE8 . . . . 5F **79**
Rosecroft Av. NW3 . . . . . 5C **30**
Rosecroft Gdns. NW2 . . . 5C **28**
Rosedale Ct. N5 . . . . 1D **49**
Rosedale Ho. N16 . . . . . 3F **35**
Rosedale Rd. E7 . . . . . . 2E **55**
Rosedale Ter. W6 . . . . . . 4D **71**
(off Dalling Rd.)

Rosedene NW6 . . . . 5F **43**
(not continuous)
Rosedene Av. SW16 . . . 3B **118**
Rosedene Ter. E10 . . . . . 4D **39**
Rosedew Rd. W6 . . . . . . 2F **85**
Rosefield Gdns. E14 . . . 1C **80**
Roseford Ct. W12 . . . . . . 3F **71**
(off Shepherd's Bush Grn.)
Rosehart M. W11 . . . . . . 5C **58**
Rosehill Rd. SW18 . . . . . 4E **101**
Roseleigh Av. N5 . . . . . . 1D **49**
Rosemary Ct. SE8 . . . . . 2B **94**
(off Dorking Cl.)
Rosemary Dr. E14 . . . . . . 5F **67**
IG4: Ilf 1F **41**
Rosemary Ho. N1 . . . . . . 5F **49**
(off Branch Pl.)
Rosemary Rd. SE15 . . . . 3B **92**
SW17 . . . . 3E **115**
Rosemary St. N1 . . . . . . 5F **49**
Rosemead NW9 . . . . 2B **28**
Rosemont Rd. NW3 . . . . . 3E **45**
Rosemoor St. SW3 . . . . . 5B **74**
Rosemount Point SE23 . . 3F **121**
Rosenau Cres. SW11 . . . 4B **88**
Rosenau Rd. SW11 . . . . 4A **88**
Rosendale Rd. SE24 . . . 5E **105**
Roseneath Rd. SW11 . . . 4C **102**
Rosenthal Rd. SE6 . . . . 5C **108**
Rosenthorpe Rd. SE15 . . 3F **107**
Roserton St. E14 . . . . . . 3E **81**
Rose Sq. SW7 . . . . 1F **87**
Rose St. EC4 . . . 5D **63** (2E **17**)
WC2 . . . . 1A **76** (4D **15**)
(not continuous)
Rosethorn Cl. SW12 . . . 5F **103**
Rosetta Cl. SW8 . . . . . . 3A **90**
(off Kenchester Clo.)
Roseveare Rd. SE12 . . . 4E **125**
Rose Way SE12 . . . . 3C **110**
Roseway SE21 . . . . 4F **105**
Rosewood Ct. E11 . . . . . 1F **53**
Rosewood Gdns. SE13 . . 5E **95**
Rosewood Ho. SW8 . . . . 2B **90**
Rosewood Sq. W12 . . . . 5C **56**
Rosher Cl. E15 . . . . 4F **53**
Roshni Ho. SW17 . . . . . 5A **116**
Rosina St. E9 . . . . 3F **51**
Roskell Rd. SW15 . . . . . . 1F **99**
Roslin Ho. E1 . . . . 1F **79**
(off Brodlove La.)
Roslin Way
BR1: Brom 5C **124**
Rosmead Rd. W11 . . . . . 1A **72**
Rosoman Pl. EC1 . . 3C **62** (3C **8**)
Rosoman St.
EC1 . . . . 2C **62** (2C **8**)
Ross Ct. E5 . . . . 1D **51**
(off Napoleon Rd.)
Rosscourt Mans. SW1 . . 5E **21**
(off Buckingham Pal. Rd.)
Rossdale Rd. SW15 . . . . 2E **99**
Rosse M. SE3 . . . . 4D **97**
Rossendale St. E5 . . . . . 4D **37**
Rossendale Way NW1 . . 5E **47**
Rossetti Ct. WC1 . . . . 5B **6**
(off Ridgmount Pl.)
Rossetti Ho. SW1 . . . . . . 5F **75**
(off Erasmus St.)
Rossetti M. NW8 . . . . . . 5F **45**

Rossetti Rd. SE16 . . . . . 1D **93**
Ross Ho. E1 . . . . 2D **79**
(off Prusom St.)
Rossington St. E5 . . . . . 4C **36**
Rossiter Rd. SW12 . . . . 1D **117**
Rosslyn Av. SW13 . . . . . 1A **98**
Rosslyn Hill NW3 . . . . . . 1F **45**
Rosslyn Mans. NW6 . . . . 4E **45**
(off Goldhurst Ter.)
Rosslyn Pk. M. NW3 . . . . 2F **45**
Rossmore Cl. NW1 . . . . . 3A **60**
(off Rossmore Rd.)
Rossmore Ct. NW1 . . . . . 3B **60**
Rossmore Rd. NW1 . . . . 3A **60**
Ross Way SE9 . . . . 1F **111**
Rostella Rd. SW17 . . . . 4F **115**
Rostrevor Av. N15 . . . . . 1B **36**
Rostrevor M. SW6 . . . . . 4B **86**
Rostrevor Rd. SW6 . . . . 4B **86**
SW19 . . . . 5C **114**
Rotary St. SE1 . . 4D **77** (5D **25**)
Rothay NW1 . . . . 1E **5**
(off Albany St.)
Rothbury Hall SE10 . . . . 5A **82**
Rothbury Rd. E9 . . . . 4B **52**
Rotheley Ho. E9 . . . . 4E **51**
(off Balcorne St.)
Rotherfield Ct. N1 . . . . . . 4F **49**
(off Rotherfield St., not cont.)
Rotherfield St. N1 . . . . . . 4E **49**
Rotherham Wlk. SE1 . . . 2D **25**
ROTHERHITHE **3E 79**
Rotherhithe New Rd.
SE16 . . . . 1D **93**
Rotherhithe Old Rd.
SE16 . . . . 5F **79**
Rotherhithe St. SE16 . . . 3E **79**
Rotherhithe Tunnel
SE16 . . . . 2F **79**
Rother Ho. SE15 . . . . . . 2D **107**
Rotherwick Ho. E1 . . . . . 1C **78**
(off Thomas More St.)
Rotherwick Rd. NW11 . . 2C **30**
Rotherwood Rd. SW15 . . 1F **99**
Rothery St. N1 . . . . 5D **49**
(off St Marys Path)
Rothesay Ct. SE6 . . . . . 2B **124**
(off Cumberland Pl.)
SE11 . . . . 2C **90**
(off Harleyford St.)
SE12 . . . . 3D **125**
Rothley Ct. NW8 . . . . 3F **59**
(off St John's Wood Rd.)
Rothsay Rd. E7 . . . . 4E **55**
Rothsay St.
SE1 . . . . 4A **78** (5D **27**)
Rothsay Wlk. E14 . . . . . . 5C **80**
(off Charnwood Gdns.)
Rothschild St. SE27 . . . 4D **119**
Roth Wlk. N7 . . . . 4B **34**
Rothwell St. NW1 . . . . . . 5B **46**
Rotten Row NW3 . . . . . . 3E **31**
SW7 . . . . 3A **74** (3A **20**)
Rotterdam Dr. E14 . . . . . 4E **81**
Rouel Rd. SE16 . . . . 4C **78**
(Dockley Rd.)
SE16 . . . . 5C **78**
(Southwark Pk. Rd.)
Roundacre SW19 . . . . . 2F **113**

Rucklidge Pas. *NW10* . . . *1B 56*
  (off Rucklidge Av.)
Rudall Cres. NW3 . . . . 1F 45
Rudbeck Ho. *SE15* *3C 92*
  (off Peckham Pk. Rd.)
Ruddington Cl. E5 . . . . . . 1A 52
Rudge Ho. *SE16* *4C 78*
  (off Jamaica Rd.)
Rudgwick Ter. NW8 . . . . 5A 46
Rudloe Rd. SW12 . . . . . 5E 103
Rudolf Pl. SW8 . . . . 2A 90
Rudolph Rd. E13 . . . . . . 1B 68
  NW6 . . . . 1C 58
Rufford St. N1 . . . . 5A 48
Rufus Ho. *SE1* *5F 27*
  (off Abbey St.)
Rufus St. N1 . . . 2A 64 (2D 11)
Rugby Mans. *W14* *5A 72*
  (off Bishop King's Rd.)
Rugby Rd. W4 . . . . 3A 70
Rugby St. WC1 . . 3B 62 (4F 7)
Rugg St. E14 . . . . 1C 80
Rugless Ho. *E14* *3E 81*
  (off E. Ferry Rd.)
Rugmere *NW1* *4C 46*
  (off Ferdinand St.)
Ruislip St. SW17 . . . . . 4B 116
Rumball Ho. *SE5* *3A 92*
  (off Harris St.)
Rumbold Rd. SW6 . . . . . 3D 87
Rum Cl. E1 . . . . 1E 79
Rumford Ho. *SE1* *5F 25*
  (off Tiverton St.)
Rumsey M. N4 . . . . 5D 35
Rumsey Rd. SW9 . . . . . 1B 104
Runacres Ct. SE17 . . . . 1E 91
Runbury Circ. NW9 . . . . 4A 28
Runcorn Pl. W11 . . . . . . 1A 72
Rundell Cres. NW4 . . . . 1D 29
Rundell Twr. SW8 . . . . . 4B 90
Runnymede Ct. SW15 . . 1C 112
Runnymede Ho. E9 . . . . 1A 52
Rupack St. SE16 . . . . . . 3E 79
Rupert Ct. W1 . . 1F 75 (4B 14)
Rupert Gdns. SW9 . . . . 5D 91
Rupert Ho. SE11 . . . . . . 5C 76
Rupert Rd. N19 . . . . 5F 33
  (not continuous)
  NW6 . . . . 1B 58
  W4 . . . . 4A 70
Rupert St. W1 . . 1F 75 (4B 14)
Rusbridge Cl. E8 . . . . . . 2C 50
Ruscoe Rd. E16 . . . . . . 5B 68
Rusham Rd. SW12 . . . . 4B 102
Rush Common M. SW2 . 5B 104
Rushcroft Rd. SW2 . . . . 2C 104
Rushcutters Ct. *SE16* . . . *5A 80*
  (off Boat Lifter Way)
Rushey Grn. SE6 . . . . . 5D 109
Rushey Mead SE4 . . . . 3C 108
Rushford Rd. SE4 . . . . . 4B 108
Rushgrove Pde. NW9 . . . 1A 28
Rush Hill M. *SW11* *1C 102*
  (off Rush Hill Rd.)
Rush Hill Rd. SW11 . . . 1C 102
Rushmead E2 . . . . 2D 65
Rushmere Pl. SW19 . . . 5F 113
Rushmore Cres. E5 . . . . 1F 51
Rushmore Ho. *W14* *4A 72*
  (off Russell Rd.)

Rushmore Rd. E5 . . . . . 1E 51
  (not continuous)
Rusholme Gro. SE19 . . 5A 120
Rusholme Rd. SW15 . . . 4F 99
Rushton Ho. SW8 . . . . . 5F 89
Rushton St. N1 . . . . 1F 63
Rushworth St.
  SE1 . . . . 3D 77 (3E 25)
Ruskin Av. E12 . . . . 3F 55
Ruskin Cl. NW11 . . . . . . 1D 31
Ruskin Ct. *SE5* *1F 105*
  (off Champion Hill)
Ruskin Ho. *SW1* *5F 75*
  (off Herrick St.)
Ruskin Mans. *W14* *2A 86*
  (off Queen's Club Gdns.)
Ruskin Pk. Ho. SE5 . . 1F 105
Ruskin Wlk. SE24 . . . . 3E 105
Rusper Cl. NW2 . . . . . . 5E 29
Rusper Ct. SW9 . . . . . . 5A 90
  (off Clapham Rd.)
Russell Cl. SE7 . . . . 3E 97
  W4 . . . . 2B 84
Russell Ct. E10 . . . . 2D 39
  SE15 . . . . *5D 93*
  (off Heaton Rd.)
  SW1 . . . . 2A 22
  SW16 . . . . 5B 118
  WC1 . . . . 4D 7
Russell Flint Ho. *E16* . . . *1D 83*
  (off Pankhurst Av.)
Russell Gdns. NW11 . . . 1A 30
  W14 . . . . 4A 72
Russell Gdns. M. W14 . 3A 72
Russell Gro. SW9 . . . . . 3C 90
Russell Ho. *E14* *5C 66*
  (off Saracen St.)
  SW1 . . . . *1E 89*
  (off Cambridge St.)
Russell Lodge *SE1* *5B 26*
  (off Spurgeon St.)
Russell Pde. *NW11* *1A 30*
  (off Golders Grn. Rd.)
Russell Pl. NW3 . . . . . . 2A 46
  SE16 . . . . 4A 80
Russell Rd. E10 . . . . . . 1D 39
  E16 . . . . 5C 68
  N8 . . . . 1F 33
  N15 . . . . 1A 36
  NW9 . . . . 1B 28
  W14 . . . . 4A 72
Russell's Footpath
  SW16 . . . . 5A 118
Russell Sq. WC1 . 4A 62 (4D 7)
Russell St.
  WC2 . . . . 1A 76 (4E 15)
Russell Yd. SW15 . . . . 2A 100
Russet Cres. N7 . . . . . . 2B 48
Russett Way SE13 . . . . 5D 95
Russia Ct. EC2 . . . . 2A 18
Russia Dock Rd. SE16 . 2A 80
Russia La. E2 . . . . 1E 65
Russia Row
  EC2 . . . . 5E 63 (3A 18)
Russia Wlk. SE16 . . . . . 3A 80
Rusthall Av. W4 . . . . . . 5A 70
Rustic Wlk. *E16* *5D 69*
  (off Lambert Rd.)
Ruston M. W11 . . . . 5A 58
Ruston Rd. SE18 . . . . . . 4F 83

Ruston St. E3 . . . . 5B 52
Rust Sq. SE5 . . . . 3F 91
Rutford Rd. SW16 . . . . 5A 118
Ruth Ct. E3 . . . . 1A 66
Rutherford Ho. *E1* *3D 65*
  (off Brady St.)
Rutherford St. SW1 . . . 5F 75
Ruth Ho. *W10* *3A 58*
  (off Kensal Rd.)
Ruthin Cl. NW9 . . . . . . 1A 28
Ruthin Rd. SE3 . . . . . . 2C 96
Ruthven St. E9 . . . . 5F 51
Rutland Ct. SE5 . . . . . . 2F 105
  SW7 . . . . *3A 74*
  (off Rutland Gdns.)
Rutland Gdns. N4 . . . . . 1D 35
  SW7 . . . . 3A 74
Rutland Gdns. M. SW7 . 3A 74
Rutland Ga. SW7 . . . . . 3A 74
Rutland Ga. M. *SW7* . . . *3A 74*
  (off Rutland Ga.)
Rutland Gro. W6 . . . . . . 1D 85
Rutland Ho. *W8* *4D 73*
  (off Marloes Rd.)
Rutland M. NW8 . . . . . . 5D 45
Rutland M. E. *SW7* *4A 74*
  (off Ennismore St.)
Rutland M. Sth. *SW7* . . *4A 74*
  (off Ennismore St.)
Rutland M. W. *SW7* . . . *4A 74*
  (off Rutland Ga.)
Rutland Pk. NW2 . . . . . 3E 43
  SE6 . . . . 2B 122
Rutland Pk. Gdns.
  NW2 . . . . *3E 43*
  (off Rutland Pk.)
Rutland Pk. Mans.
  NW2 . . . . *3E 43*
Rutland Pl. EC1 . . 3D 63 (5E 9)
Rutland Rd. E7 . . . . 4F 55
  E9 . . . . 5F 51
  E17 . . . . 1C 38
Rutland St. SW7 . . . . . . 4A 74
Rutland Wlk. SE6 . . . . 2B 122
Rutley Cl. SE17 . . . . . . 2D 91
Rutt's Ter. SE14 . . . . . . 4F 93
Ruvigny Gdns. SW15 . . 1F 99
Ryan Cl. SE3 . . . . 2D 111
Rycott Path SE22 . . . . 5C 106
Ryculff Sq. SE3 . . . . . . 5B 96
Rydal Gdns. NW9 . . . . . 1A 28
  SW15 . . . . 5A 112
Rydal Rd. SW16 . . . . . . 4F 117
Rydal Water NW1 . 2E 61 (2F 5)
Rydens Ho. *SE9* *3E 125*
  (off Gro. Park Rd.)
Ryder Cl. BR1: Brom . 5D 125
Ryder Ct. E10 . . . . 4D 39
  SW1 . . . . 1A 22
Ryder Dr. SE16 . . . . . . 1D 93
Ryder Ho. *E1* *3E 65*
  (off Colebert Av.)
Ryder M. E9 . . . . 2E 51
Ryder's Ter. NW8 . . . . . 1E 59
Ryder St. SW1 . . 2E 75 (1A 22)
Ryder Yd. SW1 . . 2E 75 (1A 22)
Ryde Va. Rd. SW12 . . . 2E 117
Rydons Cl. SE9 . . . . . . 1F 111
Rydon St. N1 . . . . 5E 49
Rydston Cl. N7 . . . . 4A 48

Ryecotes Mead SE21 . . . 1A **120**
Ryecroft Lodge SW16 . . . 5D **119**
Ryecroft Rd. SE13 . . . . 3E **109**
  SW16 . . . . 5C **118**
Ryecroft St. SW6 . . . . . . 4D **87**
Ryedale SE22 . . . . 4D **107**
Ryefield Path SW15 . . . 1C **112**
Ryefield Rd. SE19 . . . . . 5E **119**
Rye Hill Pk. SE15 . . . . . 2E **107**
Rye Ho. *SE16* *3E 79*
  (off Swan Rd.)
  SW1 . . . . *1D 89*
  (off Ebury Bri. Rd.)
Ryelands Cres. SE12 . . . 4E **111**
Rye La. SE15 . . . . 4C **92**
Rye Pas. SE15 . . . . 1C **106**
Rye Rd. SE15 . . . . 2F **107**
Rye Wlk. SW15 . . . . 3F **99**
Ryfold Rd. SW19 . . . . . 3C **114**
Rylandes Rd. NW2 . . . . . 5C **28**
Ryland Rd. NW5 . . . . 3D **47**
Rylett Cres. W12 . . . . . . 3B **70**
Rylett Rd. W12 . . . . 3B **70**
Rylston Rd. SW6 . . . . . . 2B **86**
Rymer St. SE24 . . . . . . 4D **105**
Rysbrack St.
  SW3 . . . . 4B **74** (5A **20**)

S

Sabbarton St. E16 . . . . . . 5B **68**
Sabella Ct. E3 . . . . 1B **66**
Sabine Rd. SW11 . . . . . 1B **102**
Sable St. N1 . . . . 4D **49**
Sach Rd. E5 . . . . 4D **37**
Sackville Ho. SW16 . . . 3A **118**
Sackville St. W1 . . 1E **75** (5A **14**)
Saddlers M. SW8 . . . . . . 4A **90**
Saddle Yd. W1 . . 2D **75** (1D **21**)
Sadler Ho. *EC1* *1C 8*
  (off Spa Grn. Est.)
Sadler's Wells Theatre
  . . . . **2C 62 (1C 8)**
Saffron Av. E14 . . . . 1F **81**
Saffron Cl. NW11 . . . . . . 1B **30**
Saffron Ct. *E15* *2A 54*
  (off Maryland Pk.)
Saffron Hill EC1 . . 4C **62** (5C **8**)
Saffron St. EC1 . . 4C **62** (5C **8**)
Saffron Wharf *SE1* *3B 78*
  (off Shad Thames)
Sage St. E1 . . . . 1E **79**
Sage Way WC1 . . . . 2F **7**
Saigasso Cl. E16 . . . . . . 5F **69**
Sail Ct. *E14* *1F 81*
  (off Newport Av.)
Sailmakers Ct. SW6 . . . . 5E **87**
Sail St. SE11 . . . . 5B **76**
Sainfoin Rd. SW17 . . . . 2C **116**
Sainsbury Rd. SE19 . . . 5A **120**
St Agnes Cl. E9 . . . . 5E **51**
St Agnes Pl. SE11 . . . . . 2C **90**
St Agnes Well EC1 . . . . . 3C **10**
St Aidan's Rd. SE22 . . . 4D **107**
St Alban's Av. W4 . . . . . . 4A **70**
St Alban's Cl. NW11 . . . . 3C **30**
St Albans Ct. *EC2* *1A 18*
  (off Wood St.)
St Alban's Gro. W8 . . . . 4D **73**

St Alban's La. NW11 . . . 3C **30**
St Albans Mans. *W8* *4D 73*
  (off Kensington Ct. Pl.)
St Alban's Pl. N1 . . . . 5D **49**
St Albans Rd. NW5 . . . . 5C **32**
  NW10 . . . . 5A **42**
St Alban's St.
  SW1 . . . . 1F **75** (5B **14**)
  (not continuous)
St Albans Ter. W6 . . . . . . 2A **86**
St Albans Vs. NW5 . . . . . 5C **32**
St Alfege Pas. SE10 . . . . 2E **95**
St Alfege Rd. SE7 . . . . . . 2F **97**
St Alphage Gdn.
  EC2 . . . . 4E **63** (1A **18**)
  (not continuous)
St Alphage Highwalk
  EC2 . . . . 1A **18**
St Alphage Ho. EC2 . . . . 1B **18**
St Alphonsus Rd. SW4 . . 2E **103**
St Amunds Cl. SE6 . . . . 4C **122**
St Andrews Chambers
  W1 . . . . *1A 14*
  (off Wells St.)
St Andrew's Cl. NW2 . . . 5D **29**
St Andrews Cl. SE16 . . . 1D **93**
St Andrew's Ct. SW18 . . 2E **115**
St Andrew's Gro. N16 . . . 3F **35**
St Andrew's Hill
  EC4 . . . . 1D **77** (4E **17**)
  (not continuous)
St Andrews Mans. *W1* . . *1B 12*
  (off Dorset St.)
  W14 . . . . *2A 86*
  (off St Andrews Rd.)
St Andrew's M. N16 . . . . 3A **36**
  SE3 . . . . 3C **96**
St Andrews M. SW12 . . . 1F **117**
St Andrew's Pl.
  NW1 . . . . 3D **61** (3E **5**)
St Andrew's Rd. E11 . . . . 1A **40**
St Andrew's Rd. E12 . . . . 4F **41**
St Andrew's Rd. E13 . . . . 2D **69**
  NW10 . . . . 3D **43**
  NW11 . . . . 1B **30**
  W3 . . . . 1A **70**
  W14 . . . . 2A **86**
St Andrews Sq. W11 . . . 5A **58**
St Andrew St.
  EC1 . . . . 4C **62** (1C **16**)
St Andrews Way E3 . . . . . 3D **67**
St Andrew's Wharf SE1 . . 3B **78**
St Anne's Cl. N6 . . . . 5C **32**
St Anne's Ct. NW6 . . . . . 5A **44**
  W1 . . . . 5F **61** (3B **14**)
St Anne's Flats *NW1* *1B 6*
  (off Doric Way)
St Anne's Pas. E14 . . . . . 5B **66**
St Anne's Rd. E11 . . . . . . 4F **39**
St Anne's Row E14 . . . . . 5B **66**
St Anne's Trad. Est. *E14* . . *5B 66*
  (off St Anne's Row)
St Anne St. E14 . . . . 5B **66**
St Ann's Cres. SW18 . . . 4D **101**
St Ann's Gdns. NW5 . . . . 3C **46**
St Ann's Hill SW18 . . . . 3D **101**
St Ann's Ho. *WC1* *2B 8*
  (off Margery St.)
St Ann's La.
  SW1 . . . . 4F **75** (5C **22**)

St Ann's Pk. Rd.
  SW18 . . . . 4E **101**
St Ann's Pas. SW13 . . . . 1A **98**
St Ann's Rd. N15 . . . . . . 1D **35**
  SW13 . . . . 5B **84**
  W11 . . . . 1F **71**
St Ann's St.
  SW1 . . . . 4F **75** (5C **22**)
St Ann's Ter. NW8 . . . . . . 1F **59**
St Ann's Vs. W11 . . . . . . 2F **71**
St Anselm's Pl.
  W1 . . . . 1D **75** (4D **13**)
St Anthony's Cl. E1 . . . . 2C **78**
  SW17 . . . . 2A **116**
St Anthony's Flats *NW1* . . *1F 61*
  (off Aldenham St.)
St Antony's Rd. E7 . . . . . 4D **55**
St Asaph Rd. SE4 . . . . . 1F **107**
St Aubins Ct. N1 . . . . 5F **49**
St Aubyn's Av. SW19 . . . 5B **114**
St Augustine's Ho. *NW1* . . *1B 6*
  (off Werrington St.)
St Augustine's Mans.
  SW1 . . . . *5E 75*
  (off Bloomburg St.)
St Augustine's Path N5 . . 1E **49**
St Augustine's Rd. NW1 . . 4F **47**
St Austell Rd. SE13 . . . . 5E **95**
St Barnabas Cl. SE22 . . 3A **106**
St Barnabas Rd. E17 . . . 1C **38**
St Barnabas St. SW1 . . . 1C **88**
St Barnabas Ter. E9 . . . . 2F **51**
St Barnabas Vs. SW8 . . . 4A **90**
St Bartholomew's Cl.
  SE26 . . . . 4D **121**
**St Bartholomew's
  Hospital Mus.** **1E 17**
St Benedict's Cl.
  SW17 . . . . 5C **116**
St Benet's Cl. SW17 . . . 2A **116**
St Benet's Pl.
  EC3 . . . . 1F **77** (4C **18**)
St Bernard's Cl. SE27 . . . 4F **119**
St Bernards Ho. E14 . . . . *4E 81*
  (off Galbraith St.)
St Bernard's Rd. E6 . . . . 5F **55**
St Botolph Row
  EC3 . . . . 5B **64** (3F **19**)
St Botolph St.
  EC3 . . . . 5B **64** (2F **19**)
St Brelades Ct. N1 . . . . . 5A **50**
St Bride's Av. EC4 . . . . . 3D **17**
St Bride's Church
  . . . . **5D 63 (3D 17)**
St Bride's Crypt Mus. . . **3D 17**
St Bride's Pas. EC4 . . . . 3D **17**
St Bride St.
  EC4 . . . . 5D **63** (2D **17**)
St Catherine's Cl.
  SW17 . . . . 2A **116**
St Catherine's Ct. W4 . . . 4A **70**
St Catherine's Dr. SE14 . . 5F **93**
St Catherines M. SW3 . . 5B **74**
St Catherines Twr. E10 . . 2D **39**
St Chad's Pl.
  WC1 . . . . 2A **62** (1E **7**)
St Chad's St.
  WC1 . . . . 2A **62** (1E **7**)
  (not continuous)
St Charles Pl. W10 . . . . . 4A **58**

St James St. W6 . . . . . . 1E **85**
St James's Wlk.
EC1 . . . . 3D **63** (3D **9**)
St James Ter. SW12 . . . 1C **116**
ST JOHN'S 5C **94**
St John's Av. NW10 . . . 5B **42**
SW15 . . . . 3F **99**
St Johns Chu. Rd. E9 . . 2E **51**
St John's Cl. SW6 . . . . . 3C **86**
St John's Ct. E1 . . . . 2D **79**
  (off Scandrett St.)
N4 . . . . 4D **35**
N5 . . . . 1D **49**
SE13 . . . . 5E **95**
W6 . . . . 5D **71**
  (off Glenthorne Rd.)
St John's Cres. SW9 . . 1C **104**
St Johns Dr. SW18 . . . . 1D **115**
St John's Est. N1 . . . . . 1F **63**
SE1 . . . . 3F **27**
St John's Gdns. W11 . . 1A **72**
St John's Gate 4D **9**
St John's Gro. N19 . . . . 4E **33**
SW13 . . . . 5B **84**
St John's Hill SW11 . . . 3F **101**
St John's Hill Gro.
SW11 . . . . 2F **101**
St John's Ho. E14 . . . . . 5E **81**
  (off Pier St.)
St Johns Ho. SE17 . . . . 2F **91**
  (off Lytham St.)
St John's La.
EC1 . . . . 3D **63** (4D **9**)
St John's M. W11 . . . . . 5C **58**
St John's Pk. SE3 . . . . . 3B **96**
St John's Pk. Mans.
N19 . . . . 5E **33**
St John's Path EC1 . . . . 4D **9**
St Johns Pathway
SE23 . . . . 1E **121**
St John's Pl. EC1 . . 3D **63** (4D **9**)
St John's Rd. E16 . . . . . 5C **68**
N15 . . . . 1A **36**
NW11 . . . . 1B **30**
SW11 . . . . 2A **102**
St John's Sq.
EC1 . . . . 3D **63** (4D **9**)
St John's Ter. E7 . . . . . 3D **55**
SW15 . . . . 3A **112**
  (off Kingston Va.)
W10 . . . . 3F **57**
St John St. EC1 . . 1C **62** (1C **8**)
St John's Vs. SE8 . . . . . 5C **94**
St John's Vs. N19 . . . . . 4F **33**
W8 . . . . 4D **73**
St John's Way N19 . . . . 4E **33**
ST JOHN'S WOOD 1F **59**
St John's Wood Ct.
NW8 . . . . 2F **59**
  (off St John's Wood Rd.)
St John's Wood High St.
NW8 . . . . 1F **59**
St John's Wood Pk.
NW8 . . . . 5F **45**
St John's Wood Rd.
NW8 . . . . 3F **59**
St John's Wood Ter.
NW8 . . . . 1F **59**
St Joseph's Cl. W10 . . . 4A **58**
St Josephs Ct. SE7 . . . 2D **97**

St Joseph's Flats NW1 . . 1B **6**
  (off Drummond Cres.)
St Joseph's Ho. W6 . . . . 5F **71**
  (off Brook Grn.)
St Joseph's St. SW8 . . 4D **89**
St Joseph's Va. SE3 . . 1F **109**
St Jude's Rd. E2 . . . . . 1D **65**
St Jude St. N1 . . . . 2A **50**
St Julian's St. SW16 . . 4C **118**
St Julian's Farm Rd.
SE27 . . . . 4C **118**
St Julian's Rd. NW6 . . . 5C **44**
St Katharine Docks
. . . . 2C **78** (5F **19**)
St Katharine's Pier E1 . . 1F **27**
  (off St Katharine's Way)
St Katharine's Pct. NW1 . .1D **61**
St Katharine's Way
E1 . . . . 2B **78** (1F **27**)
  (not continuous)
St Katherine's Row EC3 . . 4E **19**
St Katherines Wlk. W11 . .2F **71**
  (off St Ann's Rd.)
St Kilda's Rd. N16 . . . . 3F **35**
St Kitts Ter. SE19 . . . . 5A **120**
St Laurence Cl. NW6 . . 5F **43**
St Lawrence Cotts. E14 . .2E **81**
  (off St Lawrence St.)
St Lawrence Ct. N1 . . . 4F **49**
St Lawrence Ho. SE1 . . 5E **27**
  (off Purbrook St.)
St Lawrence St. E14 . . . 2E **81**
St Lawrence Ter. W10 . . 4A **58**
St Lawrence Way SW9 . . 4C **90**
St Leonard M. N1 . . . . . 1A **64**
St Leonard's Ct. N1 . . . 1C **10**
St Leonard's Rd. E14 . . 4D **67**
  (not continuous)
NW10 . . . . 3A **56**
St Leonards Sq. NW5 . . 3C **46**
St Leonard's St. E3 . . . 2D **67**
St Leonard's Ter. SW3 . . 1B **88**
St Loo Av. SW3 . . . . . . 2A **88**
St Louis Rd. SE27 . . . . 4F **119**
St Lucia Dr. E15 . . . . . 5B **54**
ST LUKE'S 3E **63** (3A **10**)
St Luke's Av. SW4 . . . . 2F **103**
St Luke's Cl. EC1 . .3E **63** (3A **10**)
St Lukes Ct. E10 . . . . . 2D **39**
  (off Capworth St.)
St Luke's Est.
EC1 . . . . 2F **63** (2B **10**)
St Luke's M. W11 . . . . . 5B **58**
St Luke's Rd. W11 . . . . 4B **58**
St Luke's Sq. E16 . . . . . 5B **68**
St Luke's St. SW3 . . . . 1A **88**
St Luke's Yd. W9 . . . . . 1B **58**
  (not continuous)
St Margarets Cl. EC2 . . 2B **18**
  (off Lothbury)
St Margarets Ct.
SE1 . . . . 2E **77** (2A **26**)
SW15 . . . . 2D **99**
St Margaret's Cres.
SW15 . . . . 3D **99**
St Margaret's Gro. E11 . . 5B **40**
St Margaret's La. W8 . . 4D **73**
St Margaret's Pas.
SE13 . . . . 1A **110**
  (not continuous)

St Margaret's Rd. E12 . . 4E **41**
NW10 . . . . 2E **57**
St Margarets Rd. SE4 . . 2B **108**
  (not continuous)
St Margaret St.
SW1 . . . . 3A **76** (4D **23**)
St Mark's Cl. SE10 . . . . 3E **95**
St Marks Cl. SW6 . . . . . 4C **86**
St Marks Ct. E10 . . . . . 2D **39**
  (off Capworth St.)
NW8 . . . . 1E **59**
  (off Abercorn Pl.)
St Mark's Cres. NW1 . . 5C **46**
St Mark's Ga. E9 . . . . . 4B **52**
St Mark's Gro. SW10 . . 3D **87**
St Mark's Ho. SE17 . . . 2F **91**
  (off Lytham St.)
St Marks Ind. Est. E16 . . 2F **83**
St Mark's Pl. SW19 . . 5B **114**
W11 . . . . 5A **58**
St Mark's Ri. E8 . . . . . . 2B **50**
St Mark's Rd. W10 . . . . 4F **57**
St Mark's Sq. NW1 . . . 5C **46**
St Mark St. E1 . . . . 5B **64**
St Martin-in-the-Fields Church
. . . . 5D **15**
St Martin's Almshouses
NW1 . . . . 5E **47**
St Martin's Av. E6 . . . . 1F **69**
St Martin's Cl. NW1 . . . 5E **47**
St Martins Ct. N1 . . . . . 5A **50**
  (off De Beauvoir Est.)
St Martin's Ct.
WC2 . . . . 1A **76** (4D **15**)
St Martins Est. SW2 . . 1C **118**
St Martin's La.
WC2 . . . . 1A **76** (4D **15**)
St Martin's le-Grand
EC1 . . . . 5E **63** (2F **17**)
St Martin's Pl.
WC2 . . . . 1A **76** (5D **15**)
St Martin's Rd. SW9 . . 5B **90**
St Martin's St.
WC2 . . . . 1F **75** (5C **14**)
  (not continuous)
St Martin's Theatre 4D **15**
  (off West St.)
St Martins Way SW17 . . 3E **115**
St Mary Abbot's Ct. W14 . .4B **72**
  (off Warwick Gdns.)
St Mary Abbot's Pl. W8 . . 4B **72**
St Mary Abbot's Ter.
W14 . . . . 4B **72**
St Mary at Hill
EC3 . . . . 1A **78** (5D **19**)
St Mary Axe
EC3 . . . . 5A **64** (3D **19**)
St Marychurch St. SE16 . .3E **79**
St Mary Graces Ct. E1 . . 1B **78**
St Marylebone Cl.
NW10 . . . . 5A **42**
St Mary le-Park Ct.
SW11 . . . . 3A **88**
  (off Parkgate Rd.)
St Mary Newington Cl.
SE17 . . . . 1A **92**
  (off Surrey Sq.)
St Mary's Av. E11 . . . . 2D **41**
St Mary's Cl. SE7 . . . . 3F **97**
W6 . . . . 4B **70**

Shepherdess Pl.
N1 . . . . 2E **63** (1A **10**)
Shepherdess Wlk.
N1 . . . . 1E **63** (1A **10**)
Shepherd Ho. *E14* *5D 67*
(off Annabel Cl.)
Shepherd Mkt.
W1 . . . . 2D **75** (1D **21**)
SHEPHERD'S BUSH. . . . 3E 71
Shepherd's Bush Grn.
W12 . . . . 3E **71**
Shepherd's Bush Mkt.
W12 . . . . 3E **71**
(not continuous)
Shepherd's Bush Pl.
W12 . . . . 3F **71**
Shepherd's Bush Rd.
W6 . . . . 5E **71**
Shepherd's Cl. N6 . . . . 1D **33**
Shepherds Ct. *W12*. . . . *3F 71*
(off Shepherd's Bush Grn.)
Shepherd's Hill N6. . . . 1D **33**
Shepherds La. E9 . . . . . 4E **51**
Shepherd's Path *NW3*. . *2F 45*
(off Lyndhurst Rd.)
Shepherds Pl.
W1 . . . . 1C **74** (4B **12**)
Shepherd St.
W1 . . . . 2D **75** (2D **21**)
Shepherds Wlk. NW2. . . 4C **28**
Shepherd's Wlk. NW3 . . 2F **45**
(not continuous)
Sheppard Dr. SE16. . . . 1D **93**
Sheppard Ho. *E2* *1C 64*
(off Warner Pl.)
SW2 . . . . 1C **118**
Sheppard St. E16 . . . . . 3B **68**
Shepperton Rd. N1 . . . . 5E **49**
Sheppey Wlk. *N1* *4E 49*
(off Church Rd.)
Shepton Ho's. *E2* *2E 65*
(off Welwyn St.)
Sherard Ct. N7 . . . . 5A **34**
Sherard Ho. *E9*. *4E 51*
(off Frampton Pk. Rd.)
Sheraton Ho. *SW1* *2D 89*
(off Churchill Gdns.)
Sheraton St. W1. . 5F **61** (3B **14**)
Sherborne Ho. SW1. . . . 1D **89**
SW8 . . . . *3B 90*
(off Bolney St.)
Sherborne La.
EC4. . . . . 1F **77** (4B **18**)
Sherborne St. N1 . . . . . 5F **49**
Sherboro Rd. N15 . . . . . 1B **36**
Sherbrooke Ho. *E2*. . . . *1E 65*
(off Bonner Rd.)
Sherbrooke Rd. SW6 . . . 3A **86**
Shere Ho. SE1 . . . . 5B **26**
Sherfield Gdns. SW15 . . 4B **98**
Sheridan Bldgs. *WC2*. . *3E 15*
(off Martlett Ct.)
Sheridan Ct. *NW6*. *4E 45*
(off Belsize Rd.)
Sheridan Ho. *E1* *5E 65*
(off Tarling St.)
SE11 . . . . *5C 76*
(off Wincott St.)
Sheridan M. E11 . . . . . 1D **41**
Sheridan Pl. SW13. . . . 1B **98**

Sheridan Rd. E7. . . . . . 5B **40**
Sheridan St. E1. . . . . . 5D **65**
Sheridan Wlk. NW11 . . 1C **30**
Sheringham NW8 . . . . . 5F **45**
Sheringham Ho. *NW1* . . *4A 60*
(off Lisson St.)
Sheringham Rd. N7 . . . 3B **48**
Sherington Rd. SE7. . . . 2D **97**
Sherlock Ct. *NW8*. *5F 45*
(off Dorman Way)
Sherlock Holmes Mus. . . 4A 4
Sherlock M. W1. . 4C **60** (5B **4**)
Shernhall St. E17 . . . . . 1E **39**
Sherrard Rd. E7 . . . . . . 3E **55**
E12 . . . . 3E **55**
Sherren Ho. E1. . . . . . . 3E **65**
Sherrick Grn. Rd. NW10. . 2D **43**
Sherriff Rd. NW6 . . . . . 3C **44**
Sherrin Rd. E10 . . . . . . 1D **53**
Sherston Ct. *SE17* *5D 77*
(off Newington Butts)
WC1 . . . . 2B **8**
Sherwin Ho. *SE11* *2C 90*
(off Kennington Rd.)
Sherwin Rd. SE14 . . . . 4F **93**
Sherwood NW6 . . . . . . 4A **44**
Sherwood Cl. SW13. . . 1D **99**
Sherwood Ct. SW11. . . 1E **101**
W1 . . . . *4B 60*
(off Bryanston St.)
Sherwood Gdns. E14 . . 5C **80**
SE16 . . . . 1C **92**
Sherwood St.
W1 . . . . 1E **75** (4A **14**)
Shetland Rd. E3 . . . . . . 1B **66**
Shifford Path SE23. . . . 3F **121**
Shillaker Ct. W3. . . . . . 2B **70**
Shillibeer Pl. *W1* *4A 60*
(off York St.)
Shillingford St. N1. . . . 4D **49**
Shillingstone Ho. *W14*. *4A 72*
(off Russell Rd.)
Shinfield St. W12. . . . . 5E **57**
Ship & Mermaid Row
SE1. . . . . 3F **77** (3C **26**)
Shipka Rd. SW12. . . . 1D **117**
Shiplake Ho. *E2* *2F 11*
(off Arnold Cir.)
Shipman Rd. E16. . . . . 5D **69**
SE23 . . . . 2F **121**
Ship St. SE8. . . . . 4C **94**
Ship Tavern Pas.
EC3 . . . . 1A **78** (4D **19**)
Shipton Ho. *E2*. *1B 64*
(off Shipton St.)
Shipton St. E2 . . . . 1B **64**
Shipway Ter. N16. . . . . 5B **36**
Shipwright Rd. SE16 . . 3A **80**
Shipwright Yd.
SE1 . . . . 2A **78** (2D **27**)
Ship Yd. E14 . . . . 1D **95**
Shirburn Ct. SE23. . . . 5E **107**
Shirebrook Rd. SE3 . . . 1F **111**
Shirehall Cl. NW4 . . . . 1F **29**
Shirehall Gdns. NW4 . . 1F **29**
Shirehall La. NW4 . . . . 1F **29**
Shirehall Pk. NW4 . . . . 1F **29**
Shire Pl. SW18 . . . . . . 5E **101**
Shirland M. W9 . . . . . . 2B **58**
Shirland Rd. W9 . . . . . 2B **58**

Shirlbutt St. E14 . . . . . 1D **81**
Shirley Gro. SW11. . . . 1C **102**
Shirley Ho. *SE5* *3F 91*
(off Picton St.)
Shirley Ho. Dr. SE7 . . . 3E **97**
Shirley Rd. E15 . . . . . . 4A **54**
W4 . . . . 3A **70**
Shirley St. E16. . . . . . . 5B **68**
Shirlock Rd. NW3 . . . . 1B **46**
Shobroke Cl. NW2 . . . . 5E **29**
Shoe La. EC4 . . 5C **62** (2C **16**)
Shooters Hill Rd. SE3 . . 4A **96**
SE3 . . . . 3E **97**
SE10 . . . . 4F **95**
SE18 . . . . 3E **97**
Shoot Up Hill NW2. . . . 2A **44**
Shore Bus. Cen. E9 . . . 4E **51**
SHOREDITCH . . 2A 64 (1D 11)
Shoreditch Ct. *E8*. . . . *4B 50*
(off Queensbridge Rd.)
Shoreditch High St.
E1. . . . . 3A **64** (4E **11**)
Shoreham Cl. SW18 . . 3D **101**
Shore Ho. SW8 . . . . . . 1D **103**
Shore M. *E9*. *4E 51*
(off Shore Rd.)
Shore Pl. E9 . . . . 4E **51**
Shore Rd. E9 . . . . 4E **51**
Shorncliffe Rd. SE1 . . . 1B **92**
Shorndean St. SE6. . . . 1E **123**
Shorrold's Rd. SW6 . . . 3B **86**
Shortcroft Mead Ct.
NW10. . . . . *2C 42*
(off Cooper Rd.)
Shorter St. EC3 . . . . . . 1B **78**
Shortlands W6 . . . . 5F **71**
Shortlands Rd. E10 . . . 2D **39**
Short Rd. E11. . . . . 4A **40**
W4 . . . . 2A **84**
Shorts Gdns.
WC2. . . . . 5A **62** (3D **15**)
Short St. SE1. . . 3C **76** (3C **24**)
Short Wall E15 . . . . . . 2E **67**
Short Way SE9 . . . . . . 1F **111**
Shottendane Rd. SW6 . . 4C **86**
Shottery Cl. SE9 . . . . . 3F **125**
Shottfield Av. SW14. . . 2A **98**
Shottsford *W11* *5C 58*
(off Ledbury Rd.)
Shoulder of Mutton All.
E14 . . . . 1A **80**
Shouldham St. W1. . . . 4A **60**
Shrewsbury Ct. EC1. . . 4A **10**
Shrewsbury Cres.
NW10. . . . . 5A **42**
Shrewsbury Ho. *SW8*. . *2B 90*
(off Meadow Rd.)
Shrewsbury M. *W2* . . . *4C 58*
(off Chepstow Rd.)
Shrewsbury Rd. E7. . . . 2F **55**
W2 . . . . 5C **58**
Shrewsbury St. W10 . . 3E **57**
Shroffold Rd.
BR1: Brom 4A **124**
Shropshire Pl.
WC1. . . . . 3E **61** (4B **6**)
Shroton St. NW1 . . . . . 4A **60**
Shrubbery Cl. N1 . . . . . 5E **49**
Shrubbery Rd. SW16. . 4A **118**
Shrubbery, The E11. . . 1D **41**

Sth. Worple Av. SW14 . . 1A **98**
Sth. Worple Way
   SW14 . . . . 1A **98**
Southwyck Ho. SW9 . . . . 2D **105**
Sovereign Cl. E1 . . . . 1D **79**
Sovereign Cres. SE16 . . 1A **80**
Sovereign Ho. E1 . . . . . . 3D **65**
   (off Cambridge Heath Rd.)
Sovereign M. E2 . . . . 1B **64**
Spa Ct. SW16 . . . . 4B **118**
Spafield St.
   EC1 . . . . 3C **62** (3B **8**)
Spa Grn. Est.
   EC1 . . . . 2D **63** (1C **8**)
Spalding Ho. SE4 . . . . . 2A **108**
Spalding Rd. NW4 . . . . . . 2E **29**
   SW17 . . . . 5D **117**
Spanby Rd. E3 . . . . 3C **66**
Spaniards Cl. NW11 . . . . . 3F **31**
Spaniards End NW3 . . . . 3E **31**
Spaniards Rd. NW3 . . . . 4E **31**
Spanish Pl.
   W1 . . . . 5C **60** (2C **12**)
Spanish Rd. SW18 . . . . 3E **101**
Sparke Ter. E16 . . . . 5B **68**
   (off Clarkson Rd.)
Spa Rd. SE16 . . 4B **78** (5F **27**)
Sparrick's Row
   SE1 . . . . 3F **77** (3C **26**)
Sparrow Ho. E1 . . . . 3E **65**
   (off Cephas Av.)
Sparsholt Rd. N19 . . . . . 3B **34**
Sparta St. SE10 . . . . 4E **95**
Speaker's Corner
   . . . . 1B **74** (4A **12**)
Speakman Ho. SE4 . . . 1A **108**
   (off Arica Rd.)
Spearman Ho. E14 . . . . . 5C **66**
   (off Up. North St.)
Spear M. SW5 . . . . 5C **72**
Spears Rd. N19 . . . . 3A **34**
Spectacle Works E13 . . 2E **69**
Spedan Cl. NW3 . . . . 5E **31**
Speechly M. E8 . . . . 2B **50**
Speed Highwalk EC2 . . . 4E **63**
   (off Silk St.)
Speed Ho. EC2 . . . . 5A **10**
   (off Silk St.)
Speedwell St. SE8 . . . . . 3C **94**
Speedy Pl. WC1 . . . . 2D **7**
Speke's Monument . . . 2E **73**
Speldhurst Rd. E9 . . . . . 4F **51**
   W4 . . . . 4A **70**
Spellbrook Wlk. N1 . . . . . 5E **49**
Spelman Ho. E1 . . . . 4C **64**
   (off Spelman St.)
Spelman St. E1 . . . . 4C **64**
   (not continuous)
Spence Cl. SE16 . . . . . . 3B **80**
Spencer Dr. N2 . . . . 1E **31**
Spencer House **2F 21**
Spencer Ho. NW4 . . . . . 1D **29**
Spencer Mans. W14 . . . 2A **86**
   (off Queen's Club Gdns.)
Spencer M. SW9 . . . . . . 4B **90**
   (off Sth. Lambeth Rd.)
   W6 . . . . 2A **86**
SPENCER PARK **3F 101**
Spencer Pk. SW18 . . . 3F **101**
Spencer Pl. N1 . . . . 4D **49**

Spencer Ri. NW5 . . . . . . 1D **47**
Spencer Rd. E6 . . . . 5F **55**
   N8 . . . . 1B **34**
   (not continuous)
   SW18 . . . . 2F **101**
Spencer St.
   EC1 . . . . 2D **63** (2D **9**)
Spencer Wlk. NW3 . . . . . 1E **45**
   (off Perrin's Ct.)
   NW3 . . . . 1F **45**
   SW15 . . . . 2F **99**
Spenlow Ho. SE16 . . . . . 4C **78**
   (off Jamaica Rd.)
Spenser Gro. N16 . . . . . 2A **50**
Spenser M. SE21 . . . . . 2F **119**
Spenser Rd. SE24 . . . . 3D **105**
Spenser St.
   SW1 . . . . 4E **75** (5A **22**)
Spensley Wlk. N16 . . . . . 5F **35**
Spert St. E14 . . . . 1A **80**
Spey St. E14 . . . . 4E **67**
Spezia Rd. NW10 . . . . . . 1C **56**
Spice Ct. E1 . . . . 1C **78**
Spice Quay Hgts. SE1 . . 2B **78**
Spicer Cl. SW9 . . . . 5D **91**
Spindrift Av. E14 . . . . . . 5C **80**
Spinnaker Ho. E14 . . . . . 3C **80**
   (off Byng St.)
Spinney Gdns. SE19 . . 5B **120**
Spinney, The SW13 . . . 3D **85**
   SW16 . . . . 3E **117**
Spire Ho. W2 . . . . 1E **73**
   (off Lancaster Ga.)
Spirit Quay E1 . . . . 2C **78**
SPITALFIELDS . . **4B 64** (5F **11**)
Spital Sq. E1 . . . 4A **64** (5E **11**)
Spital St. E1 . . . . 4C **64**
Spital Yd. E1 . . . 4A **64** (5E **11**)
Splendour Wlk. SE16 . . . 1E **93**
   (off Verney Rd.)
Spode Ho. SE11 . . . . . . 5B **24**
Spode Wlk. NW6 . . . . . . 2D **45**
Sportsbank St. SE6 . . . 5E **109**
Spratt Hall Rd. E11 . . . . 1C **40**
Spriggs Ho. N1 . . . . 4D **49**
   (off Canonbury Rd.)
Sprimont Pl. SW3 . . . . . 1B **88**
Springall St. SE15 . . . . . 3D **93**
Springalls Wharf SE16 . . 3D **78**
   (off Bermondsey Wall W.)
Springbank Rd. SE13 . . 4F **109**
Springbank Wlk. NW1 . . 4F **47**
Spring Ct. NW6 . . . . 3B **44**
Springdale M. N16 . . . . . 1F **49**
Springdale Rd. N16 . . . . 1F **49**
Springfield E5 . . . . 3D **37**
Springfield Ct. NW3 . . . . 4A **46**
   (off Eton Av.)
Springfield Gdns. E5 . . . 3D **37**
   NW9 . . . . 1A **28**
Springfield Gro. SE7 . . . 2E **97**
Springfield La. NW6 . . . . 5D **45**
Springfield Rd. SE26 . . 3D **121**
   (not continuous)
Springfield Rd. E15 . . . . 2A **68**
   E17 . . . . 1B **38**
   NW8 . . . . 5E **45**
   SE26 . . . . 5D **121**
   SW19 . . . . 5B **114**
Springfield Wlk. NW6 . . 5D **45**

Spring Gdns. N5 . . . . . . 2E **49**
   SW1 . . . . 2F **75** (1C **22**)
   (not continuous)
Spring Hill E5 . . . . 2C **36**
   SE26 . . . . 4E **121**
Springhill Cl. SE5 . . . . . 1F **105**
Spring Ho. WC1 . . . . 2B **8**
Spring La. E5 . . . . 2D **37**
Spring M. W1 . . 4B **60** (5A **4**)
Spring Pk. Dr. N4 . . . . . 3E **35**
Spring Pas. SW15 . . . . . 1F **99**
Spring Path NW3 . . . . . . 2F **45**
Spring Pl. NW5 . . . . 2D **47**
Springrice Rd. SE13 . . . 4F **109**
Spring St. W2 . . . . 5F **59**
Spring Tide Cl. SE15 . . . 4C **92**
Spring Va. Ter. W14 . . . 4F **71**
Spring Wlk. E1 . . . . 4C **64**
Springwater WC1 . . . . . . 5F **7**
Springwell Av. NW10 . . 5B **42**
Springwell Cl. SW16 . . 4B **118**
Springwell Rd.
   SW16 . . . . 4C **118**
Sprowston M. E7 . . . . . . 3C **54**
Sprowston Rd. E7 . . . . . 2C **54**
Spruce Ho. SE16 . . . . . . 3F **79**
   (off Woodland Cres.)
Sprules Rd. SE4 . . . . . . 5A **94**
Spurgeon St.
   SE1 . . . . 4F **77** (5B **26**)
Spurling Rd. SE22 . . . . 2B **106**
Spur Rd. SE1 . . 3C **76** (3B **24**)
   SW1 . . . . 3E **75** (4F **21**)
Spurstowe Rd. E8 . . . . . 3D **51**
Spurstowe Ter. E8 . . . . . 3D **51**
Square Rigger Row
   SW11 . . . . 1E **101**
Square, The E10 . . . . . . 5E **39**
   W6 . . . . 1E **85**
Squarey St. SW17 . . . . 3E **115**
Squire Gdns. NW8 . . . . . 2F **59**
   (off Grove End Rd.)
Squires Ct. SW4 . . . . . . 4A **90**
   SW19 . . . . 4C **114**
Squires Mt. NW3 . . . . . . 5F **31**
Squirrels, The SE13 . . 1F **109**
Squirries St. E2 . . . . 2C **64**
Stables Gallery & Arts Cen.
   . . . . **5C 28**
Stables Mkt., The
   NW1 . . . . 4D **47**
Stables M. SE27 . . . . . 5E **119**
Stables Way SE11 . . . . 1C **90**
Stable Way W10 . . . . . . 5E **57**
Stable Yd. SW1 . . . . 3F **21**
   SW15 . . . . 1E **99**
Stable Yd. Rd.
   SW1 . . . . 3E **75** (3A **22**)
   (not continuous)
Stableyard, The SW9 . . 5B **90**
Stacey Cl. E10 . . . . 1F **39**
Stacey St. N7 . . . . 5C **34**
   WC2 . . . . 5F **61** (3C **14**)
Stack Ho. SW1 . . . . 5C **74**
   (off Cundy St.)
Stackhouse St. SW3 . . 5A **20**
Stacy Path SE5 . . . . 3A **92**
Stadium Rd. E. NW4 . . . 2D **29**
Stadium St. SW10 . . . . 3E **87**
Staffa Rd. E10 . . . . 3A **38**

Stafford Cl. E17 . . . . . . 1B **38**
(not continuous)
NW6 . . . . 2C **58**
Stafford Ct. SW8 . . . . . 3A **90**
Stafford Cripps Ho. E2 . . 2E **65**
(off Globe Rd.)
SW6 . . . . 2B **86**
(off Clem Attlee Ct.)
Stafford Mans. SW1 . . . . 5F **21**
(off Stafford Pl.)
SW4 . . . . 2A **104**
SW11 . . . . 3B **88**
(off Albert Bri. Rd.)
W14 . . . . 4F **71**
(off Haarlem Rd.)
Stafford Pl. SW1 . . 4E **75** (5F **21**)
Stafford Rd. E7 . . . . . . 4E **55**
E3 . . . . 1B **66**
NW6 . . . . 2C **58**
Staffordshire St. SE15 . . 4C **92**
Stafford St. W1 . . 2E **75** (1F **21**)
Stafford Ter. W8 . . . . . . 4C **72**
Staff St. EC1 . . 2F **63** (2C **10**)
STAG LANE 2B **112**
Stag La. SW15 . . . . . . 3B **112**
Stag Pl. SW1 . . 4E **75** (5F **21**)
Stainer Ho. SE3 . . . . . . 2E **111**
Stainer St. SE1 . 2F **77** (2C **26**)
Staining La.
EC2 . . . . 5E **63** (2A **18**)
Stainsbury St. E2 . . . . . 1E **65**
Stainsby Pl. E14 . . . . . 5C **66**
Stainsby Rd. E14 . . . . . 5C **66**
Stainton Rd. SE6 . . . . . 4F **109**
Stalbridge Flats W1 . . . 3C **12**
(off Lumley St.)
Stalbridge St. NW1 . . . 4A **60**
Stalham St. SE16 . . . . . 4D **79**
Stamford Bridge **3D 87**
Stamford Brook Arches
W6 . . . . 5C **70**
Stamford Brook Av. W6 . 4B **70**
Stamford Brook Gdns.
W6 . . . . 4B **70**
Stamford Brook Mans.
W6 . . . . 5B **70**
(off Goldhawk Rd.)
Stamford Brook Rd. W6 . 4B **70**
Stamford Cl. NW3 . . . . . 5E **31**
(off Heath St.)
Stamford Ct. W6 . . . . . 5C **70**
Stamford Ga. SW6 . . . . 3D **87**
Stamford Gro. E. N16 . . 3C **36**
Stamford Gro. W. N16 . . 3C **36**
STAMFORD HILL **3B 36**
Stamford Hill N16 . . . . 4B **36**
Stamford Lodge N16 . . 2B **36**
Stamford Rd. E6 . . . . . 5F **55**
N1 . . . . 4A **50**
Stamford St.
SE1 . . . . 2C **76** (2B **24**)
Stamp Pl. E2 . . 1B **64** (1F **11**)
Stanard Cl. N16 . . . . . 2A **36**
Stanborough Pas. E8 . . 3B **50**
Stanbridge Rd. SW15 . . 1E **99**
Stanbury Ct. NW3 . . . . 3A **46**
Stanbury Rd. SE15 . . . . 5D **93**
(not continuous)
Standard Pl. EC2 . . . . . 2E **11**
Standard Rd. NW10 . . . 3A **56**

Standen Rd. SW18 . . . . 5B **100**
Standish Ho. SE3 . . . . . 2D **111**
(off Elford Cl.)
W6 . . . . 5C **70**
(off St Peter's Gro.)
Standish Rd. W6 . . . . . 5C **70**
Standlake Point SE23 . . 3F **121**
Stane Pas. SW16 . . . . . 5A **118**
Stanesgate Ho. SE15 . . 3C **92**
(off Friary Est.)
Stane Way SE18 . . . . . 3F **97**
Stanfield Ho. NW8 . . . . 3F **59**
(off Frampton St.)
Stanfield Rd. E3 . . . . . 1A **66**
Stanford Ct. SW6 . . . . . 4D **87**
Stanford Pl. SE17 . . . . . 5A **78**
Stanford Rd. W8 . . . . . 4D **73**
Stanford St. SW1 . . . . . 5F **75**
Stangate SE1 . . . . 5A **24**
Stanhope Cl. SE16 . . . . 3F **79**
Stanhope Gdns. N4 . . . 1D **35**
N6 . . . . 1D **33**
SW7 . . . . 5E **73**
Stanhope Ga.
W1 . . . . 2C **74** (2C **20**)
Stanhope Ho. SE8 . . . . 3B **94**
SW1 . . . . 2B **74**
Stanhope Pl. W2 . . . . . 1B **74**
Stanhope Rd. E17 . . . . 1D **39**
N6 . . . . 1D **33**
Stanhope Row
W1 . . . . 2D **75** (2D **21**)
Stanhope St. NW1 . .1E **61** (1F**5**)
Stanhope Ter. W2 . . . . . 1F **73**
Stanier Cl. W14 . . . . . . 1B **86**
Stanier Ho. SW6 . . . . . 5C **86**
(off Adolphus St.)
Stanlake M. W12 . . . . . 2E **71**
Stanlake Rd. W12 . . . . 2E **71**
Stanlake Vs. W12 . . . . 2E **71**
Stanley Bldgs. NW1 . . . 1A **62**
(off Stanley Pas.)
Stanley Cl. SW8 . . . . . 2B **90**
Stanley Cohen Ho. EC1 . . 4F **9**
(off Golden La. Est.)
Stanley Cres. W11 . . . . 1B **72**
Stanley Gdns. NW2 . . . 2E **43**
W3 . . . . 3A **70**
W11 . . . . 1B **72**
Stanley Gdns. M. W11 . . 1B **72**
(off Kensington Pk. Rd.)
Stanley Gro. SW8 . . . . 5C **88**
Stanley Holloway Ho.
E16 . . . . 5C **68**
(off Coolfin Rd.)
Stanley Ho. E14 . . . . . 5C **66**
(off Saracen St.)
Stanley Pas. NW1 . . . . 1A **62**
Stanley Rd. E10 . . . . . 1D **39**
E12 . . . . 2F **55**
E15 . . . . 5F **53**
NW9 . . . . 2C **28**
Stanley St. SE8 . . . . . 3B **94**
Stanley Ter. N19 . . . . . 4A **34**
Stanmer St. SW11 . . . . 4A **88**
Stanmore Pl. NW1 . . . . 5D **47**
Stanmore Rd. E11 . . . . 3B **40**

Stanmore St. N1 . . . . . 5B **48**
Stannard Cotts. E1 . . . . 3E **65**
(off Fox Cl.)
Stannard M. E8 . . . . . . 3C **50**
(off Stannard Rd.)
Stannard Rd. E8 . . . . . 3C **50**
Stannary Pl. SE11 . . . . 1C **90**
Stannary St. SE11 . . . . 2C **90**
Stansbury Ho. W10 . . . 2A **58**
(off Beethoven St.)
Stansfeld Rd. E6 . . . . . 4F **69**
Stansfield Rd. SE1 . . . . 5B **78**
(off Balaclava Rd.)
Stansfield Rd. SW9 . . . 1B **104**
Stanstead Gro. SE6 . . . 1B **122**
Stanstead Rd. E11 . . . . 1D **41**
SE6 . . . . 1A **122**
SE23 . . . . 1F **121**
Stanswood Gdns. SE5 . . 3A **92**
Stanthorpe Cl. SW16 . . 5A **118**
Stanthorpe Rd. SW16 . . 5A **118**
Stanton Ho. SE10 . . . . 2E **95**
(off Thames St.)
SE16 . . . . 3B **80**
(off Rotherhithe St.)
Stanton Rd. SE26 . . . . 4B **122**
SW13 . . . . 5B **84**
Stanton Sq. SE26 . . . . 4B **122**
Stanton Way SE26 . . . . 4B **122**
Stanway St. N1 . . . . . . 1A **64**
Stanwick Rd. W14 . . . . 5B **72**
Stanworth St.
SE1 . . . . 4B **78** (4F **27**)
Stanyhurst SE23 . . . . . 1A **122**
Staplefield Cl. SW2 . . . 1A **118**
Stapleford Cl. SW19 . . 5A **100**
Staplehurst Rd. SE13 . . 3F **109**
Staple Inn WC1 . . . . . . 1B **16**
Staple Inn Bldgs.
WC1 . . . . 4C **62** (1B **16**)
Staples Cl. SE16 . . . . . 2A **80**
STAPLES CORNER . . . 3D **29**
Staples Cnr. Bus. Pk.
NW2 . . . . 3D **29**
Staple St. SE1 . 3F **77** (4C **26**)
Stapleton Hall Rd. N4 . . 3B **34**
Stapleton Ho. E2 . . . . . 2D **65**
(off Ellsworth St.)
Stapleton Rd. SW17 . . . 3C **116**
Star All. EC3 . . . . 4E **19**
Starboard Way E14 . . . 4C **80**
Starcross St.
NW1 . . . . 2E **61** (2A **6**)
Starfield Rd. W12 . . . . 3C **70**
Star La. E16 . . . . 3A **68**
Starling Ho. NW8 . . . . 1A **60**
(off Barrow Hill Est.)
Star Pl. E1 . . . . 1C **78**
Star Rd. W14 . . . . 2B **86**
Star St. W2 . . . . 5A **60**
Star Yd. WC2 . . 5C **62** (2B **16**)
Statham Gro. N16 . . . . 1F **49**
Statham Ho. SW8 . . . . 4E **89**
(off Wadhurst Rd.)
Station App. E7 . . . . . . 1D **55**
NW10 . . . . 2B **56**
SE3 . . . . 1D **111**
SE12 . . . . 4C **110**
(off Burnt Ash Hill)

Station App. SE26 . . . . . 5B **122**
(Lower Sydenham Stat.)
SE26 . . . . 4E **121**
(Sydenham Stat.)
SW6 . . . . 1A **100**
SW16 . . . . 5F **117**
Station App. Rd.
SE1 . . . . 3C **76** (4A **24**)
Station Av. SW9 . . . . . . 1D **105**
Station Cres. SE3 . . . . . 1C **96**
Stationer's Hall Ct.
EC4 . . . . 5D **63** (3E **17**)
Station Pde. NW2 . . . . . . 3E **43**
SW12 . . . . 1C **116**
Station Pas. SE15 . . . . . . 4E **93**
Station Path E8 . . . . 3D **51**
(off Graham Rd.)
SW6 . . . . 1B **100**
Station Pl. N4 . . . . 4C **34**
Station Ri. SE27 . . . . . . 2D **119**
Station Rd. E7 . . . . 1C **54**
E12 . . . . 1F **55**
E17 . . . . 1A **38**
N19 . . . . 5E **33**
NW4 . . . . 1C **28**
NW10 . . . . 1B **56**
SE13 . . . . 1E **109**
SE20 . . . . 5E **121**
SW13 . . . . 5B **84**
Station Ter. NW10 . . . . . . 1F **57**
SE5 . . . . 4E **91**
Station Ter. M. SE3 . . . . 1C **96**
Station Way SE15 . . . . . 5C **92**
Staton Ct. E10 . . . . 2D **39**
(off Kings Cl.)
Staunton Ho. SE17 . . . . . 5A **78**
(off Tatum St.)
Staunton St. SE8 . . . . . . 2B **94**
Staveley NW1 . . . . 1F **5**
(off Varndell St.)
Staveley Cl. E9 . . . . 2F **51**
N7 . . . . 1A **48**
SE15 . . . . 4D **93**
Staveley Gdns. W4 . . . . . 4A **84**
Staveley Rd. W4 . . . . . . 3A **84**
Staverton Rd. NW2 . . . . . 4E **43**
Stave Yd. Rd. SE16 . . . . 2A **80**
Stavordale Rd. N5 . . . . . 1D **49**
Stayner's Rd. E1 . . . . . . 3F **65**
Steadman Ct. EC1 . . . . . 3A **10**
(off Old St.)
Stead St. SE17 . . . . 5F **77**
Stean St. E8 . . . . 5B **50**
Stebbing Ho. W11 . . . . . 2F **71**
(off Queensdale Cres.)
Stebondale St. E14 . . . . 5E **81**
Stedham Pl. WC1 . . . . . . 2D **15**
(off New Oxford St.)
Steedman St. SE17 . . . . 5E **77**
Steele Ho. E15 . . . . . . 1A **68**
(off Eve Rd.)
Steele Rd. E11 . . . . 1A **54**
Steele's M. Nth. NW3 . . 3B **46**
Steele's M. Sth. NW3 . . 3B **46**
Steele's Rd. NW3 . . . . . 3B **46**
Steele's Studios NW3 . . 3B **46**
Steel's La. E1 . . . . 5E **65**
Steelyard Pas. EC4 . . . . 5B **18**
Steen Way SE22 . . . . . . 3A **106**
Steep Hill SW16 . . . . . . 3F **117**

Steeple Cl. SW6 . . . . 5A **86**
SW19 . . . . 5A **114**
Steeple Ct. E1 . . . . 3D **65**
Steeple Wlk. N1 . . . . . . 5E **49**
(off New Nth Rd.)
Steerforth St. SW18 . . . 2E **115**
Steers Way SE16 . . . . . . 3A **80**
Stelfox Ho. WC1 . . . . 1A **8**
(off Penton Ri.)
Stella Rd. SW17 . . . . . 5B **116**
Stellman Cl. E5 . . . . 5C **36**
Stephan Cl. E8 . . . . 5C **50**
Stephendale Rd. SW6 . . 1D **101**
Stephen Fox Ho. W4 . . . 1A **84**
(off Chiswick La.)
Stephen M. W1 . . 4F **61** (1B **14**)
Stephen Pl. SW4 . . . . . . 1E **103**
Stephens Ct. E16 . . . . . . 3B **68**
SE4 . . . . 1A **108**
Stephenson Ho.
SE1 . . . . 4E **77** (5F **25**)
Stephenson Rd. E17 . . . 1A **38**
Stephenson St. E16 . . . 3A **68**
NW10 . . . . 2A **56**
Stephenson Way
NW1 . . . . 3E **61** (3A **6**)
Stephen's Rd. E15 . . . . 5A **54**
Stephen St. W1 . . 4F **61** (1B **14**)
STEPNEY 4F **65**
Stepney C'way. E1 . . . . . 5F **65**
Stepney City Apartments
E1 . . . . 4E **65**
Stepney Grn. E1 . . . . . . 4E **65**
Stepney Grn. Ct. E1 . . . . 4F **65**
(off Stepney Grn.)
Stepney High St. E1 . . . 4F **65**
Stepney Way E1 . . . . . . 4D **65**
Sterling Cl. NW10 . . . . . 4C **42**
Sterling Gdns. SE14 . . . . 2A **94**
Sterling Ho. SE3 . . . . . . 2D **111**
Sterling St. SW7 . . . . . . 4A **74**
Sterndale Rd. W14 . . . . 4F **71**
Sterne St. W12 . . . . 3F **71**
Sternhall La. SE15 . . . . 1C **106**
Sternhold Av. SW2 . . . . 2F **117**
Sterry St. SE1 . . 3F **77** (4B **26**)
Steucers La. SE23 . . . . 1A **122**
Steve Biko La. SE6 . . . . 4C **122**
Steve Biko Lodge E13 . . 1C **68**
(off London Rd.)
Steve Biko Rd. N7 . . . . . 5C **34**
Stevedore St. E1 . . . . . . 2D **79**
Stevenage Rd. SW6 . . . . 3F **85**
Stevens Av. E9 . . . . 3E **51**
Stevens Cl.
BR3: Beck 5C **122**
Stevenson Cres. SE16 . . 1C **92**
Stevenson Ho. NW8 . . . 5E **45**
(off Boundary Rd.)
Stevens St. SE1 . . 4A **78** (5E **27**)
Steventon Rd. W12 . . . . 1B **70**
Steward St. E1 . . 4A **64** (5E **11**)
(not continuous)
Stewart Rd. E15 . . . . . . 1F **53**
Stewart's Gro. SW3 . . . . 1F **87**
Stewart's Rd. SW8 . . . . 3E **89**
Stewart St. E14 . . . . . . 3E **81**
Stew La. EC4 . . 1E **77** (4F **17**)
Stifford Ho. E1 . . . . 4E **65**
(off Stepney Way)

Stileman Ho. E3 . . . . 4B **66**
(off Ackroyd Dr.)
Stillingfleet Rd. SW13 . . 2C **84**
Stillington St. SW1 . . . . . 5E **75**
Stillness Rd. SE23 . . . . 4A **108**
Stirling Rd. E13 . . . . . . 1D **69**
SW9 . . . . 5A **90**
Stockbeck NW1 . . . . 1A **6**
(off Ampthill Est.)
Stock Exchange
. . . . 5F **63** (3C **18**)
Stockfield Rd. SW16 . . 3B **118**
Stockholm Ho. E1 . . . . . 1C **78**
(off Swedenborg Gdns.)
Stockholm Rd. SE16 . . . 1E **93**
Stockholm Way E1 . . . . 2C **78**
Stockhurst Cl. SW15 . . . 5E **85**
Stockleigh Hall NW8 . . . 1A **60**
(off Prince Albert Rd.)
Stock Orchard Cres. N7 . 2B **48**
Stock Orchard St. N7 . . 2B **48**
Stocks Pl. E14 . . . . 1B **80**
Stock St. E13 . . . . 1C **68**
Stockton Ho. E2 . . . . . . 2D **65**
(off Ellsworth St.)
STOCKWELL 5B **90**
Stockwell Av. SW9 . . . . 1B **104**
Stockwell Gdns. SW9 . . 4B **90**
Stockwell Gdns. Est.
SW9 . . . . 5A **90**
Stockwell Grn. SW9 . . . 5B **90**
Stockwell Grn. Ct. SW9 . 5B **90**
Stockwell La. SW9 . . . . 5B **90**
Stockwell M. SW9 . . . . . 5B **90**
Stockwell Pk. Cres.
SW9 . . . . 5B **90**
Stockwell Pk. Est.
SW9 . . . . 5B **90**
Stockwell Pk. Rd. SW9 . 4B **90**
Stockwell Pk. Wlk.
SW9 . . . . 1C **104**
Stockwell Rd. SW9 . . . . 5B **90**
Stockwell St. SE10 . . . . 2E **95**
Stockwell Ter. SW9 . . . . 4B **90**
Stoddart Ho. SW8 . . . . . 2B **90**
Stofield Gdns. SE9 . . . . 3F **125**
Stoford Cl. SW19 . . . . . 5A **100**
Stokenchurch St. SW6 . . 4D **87**
STOKE NEWINGTON . . . 5B **36**
Stoke Newington Chu. St.
N16 . . . . 5F **35**
Stoke Newington Comn.
N16 . . . . 4B **36**
Stoke Newington High St.
N16 . . . . 5B **36**
Stoke Newington Rd.
N16 . . . . 2B **50**
Stoke Pl. NW10 . . . . . . 2B **56**
Stokesley St. W12 . . . . 5B **56**
Stokes Rd. E6 . . . . 3F **69**
Stoll Cl. NW2 . . . . 5E **29**
Stoms Path SE6 . . . . . 5C **122**
(off Maroons Way)
Stondon Ho. E15 . . . . . 5B **54**
(off John St.)
Stondon Pk. SE23 . . . . 4A **108**
Stondon Wlk. E6 . . . . . . 1F **69**
Stonebridge Rd. N15 . . 1B **36**
Stone Bldgs. WC2 . . . . . 1A **16**
Stone Cl. SW4 . . . . 5E **89**

Stuart Twr. *W9* 2E **59**
(off Maida Va.)
Stubbs Dr. SE16 . . . . . . .1D **93**
Stubbs Ho. *E2*. 2F **65**
(off Bonner St.)
SW1 . . . . .5F **75**
(off Erasmus St.)
Stubbs Point E13 . . . . . . .3C **68**
Stucley Pl. NW1 . . . . .4D **47**
Studdridge St. SW6 . . . . .5C **86**
(not continuous)
Studd St. N1 . . . . .5D **49**
Studholme Ct. NW3 . . . . . .1C **44**
Studholme St. SE15 . . . . .3D **93**
Studio Pl. SW1 . . . . .4A **20**
Studland *SE17* 1F **91**
(off Portland St.)
Studland Ho. *E14* 5A **66**
(off Aston St.)
Studland Rd. SE26 . . . . . .5F **121**
Studland St. W6 . . . . .5D **71**
Studley Cl. E5 . . . . .2A **52**
Studley Ct. *E14* 1F **81**
(off Jamestown Way)
Studley Dr. IG4: Ilf 1F **41**
Studley Est. SW4 . . . . . . .4A **90**
Studley Rd. E7 . . . . .3D **55**
SW4 . . . . .4A **90**
Stukeley Rd. E7 . . . . .2E **55**
Stukeley St.
WC2 . . . . .5A **62** (2E **15**)
Stumps Hill La.
BR3: Beck 5C **122**
Stunell Ho. *SE14* 2F **93**
(off John Williams Cl.)
Sturdee Ho. *E2*. 1C **64**
(off Horatio St.)
Sturdy Ho. *E3*. 1A **66**
(off Gernon Rd.)
Sturdy Rd. SE15 . . . . .5D **93**
Sturgeon Rd. SE17 . . . . . .1E **91**
Sturgess Av. NW4 . . . . . .2D **29**
Sturge St. SE1 . . .3E **77** (3F **25**)
Sturmer Way N7 . . . . .2B **48**
Sturminster Ho. *SW8*. . . .3B **90**
(off Dorset Rd.)
Sturry St. E14 . . . . .5D **67**
Sturt St. N1 . . . .1E **63** (1A **10**)
Stutfield St. E1 . . . . .5C **64**
Styles Gdns. SW9 . . . . . .1D **105**
Styles Ho. SE1 . . . . .3D **25**
Sudbourne Rd. SW2 . . . . .3A **104**
Sudbrooke Rd. SW12. . . .4B **102**
Sudbury Ct. *SW8* 4F **89**
(off Allen Edwards Dr.)
Sudbury Cres.
BR1: Brom 5C **124**
Sudbury Ho. SW18. . . . . .3D **101**
Sudeley St. N1 . . . . .1D **63**
Sudlow Rd. SW18 . . . . . .3C **100**
Sudrey St. SE1. .3E **77** (4F **25**)
Suffield Ho. *SE17*. 1D **91**
(off Berryfield Rd.)
Suffolk Ct. E10 . . . . .2C **38**
Suffolk La.
EC4. . . . . .1F **77** (4B **18**)
Suffolk Pl.
SW1 . . . . .2F **75** (1C **22**)
Suffolk Rd. E13 . . . . .2C **68**
N15 . . . . .1F **35**

Suffolk Rd. NW10 . . . . . . .4A **42**
SW13 . . . . .3B **84**
Suffolk St. E7 . . . . .1C **54**
SW1 . . . . .1F **75** (5C **14**)
Sugar Bakers Ct. EC3. . . .3E **19**
Sugar Ho. La. E15 . . . . . .1E **67**
Sugar Loaf Wlk. E2 . . . . .2E **65**
Sugar Quay EC3 . . . . .5E **19**
Sugar Quay Wlk.
EC3 . . . . .1A **78** (5E **19**)
Sugden Rd. SW11 . . . . . .1C **102**
Sugden St. *SE5*. 2F **91**
(off Depot St.)
Sulby Ho. *SE4* 2A **108**
(off Turnham Rd.)
Sulgrave Gdns. W6 . . . . . .3E **71**
Sulgrave Rd. W6 . . . . .4E **71**
Sulina Rd. SW2 . . . . .5A **104**
Sulivan Ct. W6. . . . . .5C **86**
Sulivan Ent. Cen.
SW6 . . . . .1D **101**
Sulivan Rd. SW6 . . . . . . .1C **100**
Sulkin Ho. *E2* 2F **65**
(off Knottisford St.)
Sullivan Av. E16 . . . . .4F **69**
Sullivan Cl. SW11 . . . . . .1A **102**
Sullivan Ct. N16. . . . . .2B **36**
Sullivan Ho. *SE11* 5B **76**
(off Vauxhall St.)
SW1 . . . . .2D **89**
(off Churchill Gdns.)
Sullivan Rd. SE11 . . . . . . .5C **76**
Sultan St. SE5 . . . . .3E **91**
Sumatra Rd. NW6 . . . . . .2C **44**
Sumburgh Rd. SW12 . .4C **102**
Summercourt Rd. E1 . . . .5E **65**
Summerfield Av. NW6 . . .1A **58**
Summerfield St. SE12 . .5B **110**
Summerhouse Rd. N16 . .4A **36**
Summerley St. SW18. . .2D **115**
Summersby Rd. N6 . . . .1D **33**
Summerskill Cl. SE15. .1D **107**
Summers St.
EC1 . . . . .3C **62** (4B **8**)
SUMMERSTOWN 3E **115**
Summerstown SW17 . . .3E **115**
Summit Av. NW9 . . . . . . .1A **28**
Summit Cl. NW2 . . . . .2A **44**
Summit Est. N16 . . . . . . .2C **36**
Sumner Av. SE15 . . . . . . .4B **92**
Sumner Bldgs. SE1 . . . . .1F **25**
Sumner Ct. SW8 . . . . . . .3A **90**
Sumner Est. SE15 . . . . . .3B **92**
Sumner Ho. *E3*. 4D **67**
(off Watts Gro.)
Sumner Pl. SW7 . . . . .5F **73**
Sumner Pl. M. SW7 . . . . .5F **73**
Sumner Rd. SE15. . . . . . .2B **92**
(not continuous)
Sumner St.
SE1 . . . . .2D **77** (1E **25**)
Sumpter Cl. NW3 . . . . . . .3E **45**
Sunbeam Cres. W10 . . . .3E **57**
Sunbeam Rd. NW10 . . . .3A **56**
Sunbury Av. SW14 . . . . .2A **98**
Sunbury Av. Pas. SW14. .2A **98**
Sunbury Ho. *E2*. 2F **11**
(off Swanfield St.)
SE14 . . . . .2F **93**
(off Myers La.)

Sunbury La. SW11 . . . . .4F **87**
(not continuous)
Sunbury Workshops *E2*. .2F **11**
(off Swanfield St.)
Sun Ct. EC3 . . . . .3C **18**
Suncroft Pl. SE26. . . . . . .3E **121**
Sunderland Ct. SE22 . . .5C **106**
Sunderland Mt. SE23 . .2F **121**
Sunderland Rd. SE23 . .1F **121**
Sunderland Ter. W2. . . . .5D **59**
Sunderland Way E12 . . .4F **41**
Sundew Av. W12 . . . . . . .1C **70**
Sundew Cl. W12 . . . . . . .1C **70**
Sundorne Rd. SE7 . . . . . .1E **97**
Sundra Wlk. E1 . . . . .3F **65**
SUNDRIDGE. 5D **125**
Sundridge Ho. *E9*. 4F **51**
(off Church Cres.)
Sunfields Pl. SE3 . . . . . . .3D **97**
SUN-IN-THE-SANDS . . .3D **97**
Sun La. SE3 . . . . .3D **97**
Sunlight Cl. SW19 . . . . . .5E **115**
Sunlight Sq. E2 . . . . .2D **65**
Sunningdale Av. W3 . . . .1A **70**
Sunningdale Cl. SE16 . .1D **93**
Sunningdale Gdns. *W8*. .4C **72**
(off Stratford Rd.)
Sunninghill Rd. SE13 . .5D **95**
Sunningdale Rd. SE12 . .3D **111**
Sunnydene St. SE26 . .4A **122**
Sunnyhill Cl. E5 . . . . .1A **52**
Sunnyhill Rd. SW16. . .4A **118**
Sunnymead Rd. NW9. . .2A **28**
SW15 . . . . .3D **99**
Sunnyside NW2 . . . . .5B **30**
SW19 . . . . .5A **114**
Sunnyside Ho's. *NW2* . .5B **30**
(off Sunnyside)
Sunnyside Pas. SW19 . .5A **114**
Sunnyside Rd. E10. . . . . .3C **38**
N19. . . . . .2F **33**
Sun Pas. *SE16*. 4C **78**
(off Old Jamaica Rd.)
Sunray Av. SE24. . . . . . .2F **105**
Sun Rd. W14 . . . . .1B **86**
Sunset Rd. SE5 . . . . .2E **105**
Sun St. EC2 . . . .4F **63** (5C **10**)
(not continuous)
Sun St. Pas.
EC2 . . . . .4A **64** (1D **19**)
Sun Wlk. E1 . . . . .1B **78**
Sunwell Cl. SE15. . . . . . .4D **93**
Sun Wharf *SE8*. 3D **95**
(off Creekside)
Surma Cl. E1 . . . . .3D **65**
Surrendale Pl. W9 . . . . . .3C **58**
Surrey Canal Rd. SE15. .2E **93**
Surrey County Cricket Club
(Oval Cricket Ground)
. . . . .2B **90**
Surrey Gdns. N4. . . . . . . .1E **35**
Surrey Gro. SE17 . . . . . .1A **92**
Surrey Ho. *SE16*. 2F **79**
(off Rotherhithe St.)
Surrey La. SW11 . . . . . . .4A **88**
Surrey La. Est. SW11 . .4A **88**
Surrey M. SE27 . . . . .4A **120**
Surrey Mt. SE23. . . . . . . .1D **121**
Surrey Quays Rd.
SE16 . . . . .4E **79**

Surrey Quays Shop. Cen.
SE16 . . . . 4F 79
Surrey Rd. SE15 . . . . . . 3F 107
Surrey Row SE1 . . 3D 77 (3D 25)
Surrey Sq. SE17 . . . . . . 1A 92
Surrey Steps WC2 . . . . . 4A 16
(off Surrey St.)
Surrey St. E13 . . . . 2D 69
WC2 . . . . . . 1B 76 (4A 16)
Surrey Ter. SE17 . . . . . . 1A 92
Surrey Water Rd. SE16 . . 2F 79
Surridge Ct. SW9 . . . . . . 5A 90
(off Clapham Rd.)
Surr St. N7 . . . . 2A 48
Susan Constant Ct. E14 . . 1F 81
(off Newport Av.)
Susannah St. E14 . . . . . 5D 67
Susan Rd. SE3 . . . . 5D 97
Sussex Cl. N19 . . . . 4A 34
Sussex Ct. SE10 . . . . . . 2E 95
(off Roan St.)
Sussex Gdns. N4 . . . . . . 1E 35
N6 . . . . 1B 32
W2 . . . . 1F 73
Sussex Ga. N6 . . . . 1B 32
Sussex Lodge W2 . . . . . . 5F 59
(off Sussex Pl.)
Sussex Mans. SW7 . . . . . 5F 73
(off Old Brompton Rd.)
WC2 . . . . 4E 15
(off Maiden La.)
Sussex M. SE6 . . . . 5C 108
Sussex M. E. W2 . . . . . . 5F 59
(off Clifton Pl.)
Sussex M. W. W2 . . . . . . 1F 73
Sussex Pl. NW1 . . 3B 60 (3A 4)
W2 . . . . 5F 59
W6 . . . . 1E 85
Sussex Sq. W2 . . . . 1F 73
Sussex St. E13 . . . . 2D 69
SW1 . . . . 1D 89
Sussex Way N19 . . . . . . 3F 33
(not continuous)
Sutcliffe Cl. NW11 . . . . . 1D 31
Sutcliffe Pk. Athletics Track
. . . . 3E 111
Sutherland Av. W9 . . . . . 3C 58
Sutherland Ct. N16 . . . . . 5F 35
W9 . . . . 3C 58
(off Marylands Rd.)
Sutherland Gdns.
SW14 . . . . 1A 98
Sutherland Gro. SW18 . . 4A 100
Sutherland Ho. W8 . . . . . 4D 73
Sutherland Pl. W2 . . . . . 5C 58
Sutherland Point E5 . . . . 5D 37
(off Brackenfield Cl.)
Sutherland Rd. E3 . . . . . 1B 66
W4 . . . . 2A 84
Sutherland Row W1 . . . . 1D 89
Sutherland Sq. SE17 . . . 1E 91
Sutherland St. SW1 . . . . 1D 89
Sutherland Wlk. SE17 . . . 1E 91
Sutlej Rd. SE7 . . . . 3E 97
Sutterton St. N7 . . . . . . 3B 48
Sutton Ct. Rd. E13 . . . . . 2E 69
Sutton Est. EC1 . . . . . . 2C 10
W10 . . . . 4E 57
Sutton Est., The N1 . . . . 4D 49
SW3 . . . . 1A 88

Sutton Pl. E9 . . . . 2E 51
Sutton Rd. E13 . . . . 3B 68
Sutton Row W1 . . 5F 61 (2C 14)
Sutton Sq. E9 . . . . 2E 51
Sutton St. E1 . . . . 1E 79
Sutton's Way
EC1 . . . . 3E 63 (4A 10)
Sutton Wlk.
SE1 . . . . 2B 76 (2A 24)
Sutton Way W10 . . . . . . 3E 57
Swaby Rd. SW18 . . . . . . 1E 115
Swaffield Rd. SW18 . . . . 5D 101
Swains La. N6 . . . . 3C 32
Swainson Rd. W3 . . . . . 3B 70
Swain St. NW8 . . . . 3A 60
(off Tresham Cres.)
Swallands Rd. SE6 . . . . . 3C 122
(not continuous)
Swallow Cl. SE14 . . . . . . 4F 93
Swallow Ct. SE12 . . . . . 5C 110
W9 . . . . 4C 58
(off Admiral Wlk.)
Swallow Dr. NW10 . . . . . 3A 42
Swallowfield Rd. SE7 . . . 1D 97
Swallow Gdns. SW16 . . . 5F 117
Swallow Ho. NW8 . . . . . 1A 60
(off Barrow Hill Est.)
Swallow Pas. W1 . . . . . . 3E 13
(off Swallow Pl.)
Swallow Pl. W1 . . 5D 61 (3E 13)
Swallow St.
W1 . . . . 1E 75 (5A 14)
Swanage Ct. N1 . . . . . . 4A 50
(off Hertford Rd.)
Swanage Ho. SW8 . . . . . 3B 90
(off Dorset Rd.)
Swanage Rd. SW18 . . . . 4E 101
Swan App. E6 . . . . 4F 69
Swanbourne SE17 . . . . . 5E 77
(off Wansey St.)
Swanbourne Ho. NW8 . . . 3A 60
(off Capland St.)
Swan Cen., The
SW17 . . . . 3D 115
Swan Ct. E14 . . . . 5B 66
(off Agnes St.)
SW3 . . . . 1A 88
SW6 . . . . 3C 86
(off Fulham Rd.)
Swandon Way SW18 . . 3D 101
Swanfield St.
E2 . . . . 2B 64 (2F 11)
Swan Ho. N1 . . . . 4F 49
(off Oakley Rd.)
Swan La. EC4 . . 1F 77 (5C 18)
Swanley Ho. SE17 . . . . . 1A 92
(off Kinglake Est.)
Swan Mead
SE1 . . . . 4A 78 (5D 27)
Swan M. SW6 . . . . 4B 86
SW9 . . . . 5B 90
Swanne Ho. SE10 . . . . . 3E 95
(off Gloucester Cir.)
Swan Pas. E1 . . . . 1B 78
(off Royal Mint Pl.)
Swan Pl. SW13 . . . . 5B 84
Swan Rd. SE16 . . . . 3E 79
SE18 . . . . 4F 83
Swanscombe Ho. W11 . . . 2F 71
(off St Ann's Rd.)

Swanscombe Point E16 . . 4B 68
(off Clarkson Rd.)
Swanscombe Rd. W4 . . . 1A 84
W11 . . . . 2F 71
Swan St. SE1 . . . 4E 77 (5A 26)
Swansland Gdns. SW19 . . 1F 113
Swan Wlk. SW3 . . . . . . 2B 88
Swanwick Cl. SW15 . . . . 5B 98
Swan Yd. N1 . . . . 3D 49
Swathling Ho. SW15 . . . . 4B 98
(off Tunworth Cres.)
Swaton Rd. E3 . . . . 3C 66
Swedeland Ct. E1 . . . . . 1E 19
Swedenborg Gdns. E1 . . 1D 79
Sweden Ga. SE16 . . . . . 4A 80
Swedish Quays SE16 . . . 4A 80
(not continuous)
Sweeney Cres.
SE1 . . . . 3B 78 (4F 27)
Swell Ct. E17 . . . . 1C 38
Swete St. E13 . . . . 1C 68
Sweyn Pl. SE3 . . . . 5C 96
Swift Lodge W9 . . . . . . 3C 58
(off Admiral Wlk.)
Swiftsden Way
BR1: Brom 5A 124
Swift St. SW6 . . . . 4B 86
Swinbrook Rd. W10 . . . . 4A 58
Swinburne Ct. SE5 . . . . 2F 105
(off Basingdon Way)
Swinburne Ho. E2 . . . . . 2E 65
(off Roman Rd.)
Swinburne Rd. SW15 . . . 2C 98
Swindon St. W12 . . . . . 2D 71
Swinford Gdns. SW9 . . 1D 105
Swingfield Ho. E9 . . . . . 5E 51
(off Templecombe Rd.)
Swinley Ho. NW1 . . . . . 1E 5
(off Redhill St.)
Swinnerton St. E9 . . . . . 2A 52
Swinton Pl. WC1 . . 2B 62 (1F 7)
Swinton St. WC1 . . 2B 62 (1F 7)
Swiss Cen. WC2 . . . . . 5B 14
Swiss Ct. WC2 . . . . . . 5C 14
SWISS COTTAGE 4F 45
Swiss Ter. NW6 . . . . . . 4F 45
Switch Ho. E14 . . . . . . 1F 81
Sybil M. N4 . . . . 1D 35
Sybil Phoenix Cl. SE8 . . 1F 93
Sybil Thorndike Casson Ho.
SW5 . . . . 1C 86
(off Old Brompton Rd.)
Sybourn St. E17 . . . . . . 2B 38
Sycamore Av. E3 . . . . . 5B 52
Sycamore Cl. E16 . . . . . 3A 68
W3 . . . . 2A 70
Sycamore Ct. E7 . . . . . 3C 54
NW6 . . . . 5C 44
(off Bransdale Cl.)
Sycamore Gdns. W6 . . . 3D 71
Sycamore Gro. SE6 . . . . 4E 109
Sycamore Ho. SE16 . . . . 3F 79
(off Woodland Cres.)
W6 . . . . 3D 71
Sycamore Lodge W8 . . . 4D 73
(off Stone Hall Pl.)
Sycamore M. SW4 . . . . 1E 103
Sycamore Rd. SW19 . . . 5E 113
Sycamore St. EC1 . . 3E 63 (4F 9)
Sycamore Wlk. W10 . . . 3A 58

Sydcote SE21 . . . . 1E **119**	Taeping St. E14 . . . . 5D **81**	Tanfield Av. NW2 . . . . . . 1B **42**
SYDENHAM **4E 121**	Taffrail Ho. E14 . . . . . . 1D **95**	Tangley Gro. SW15 . . . . 4B **98**
Sydenham Av. SE26. . . 5D **121**	(off Burrells Wharf Sq.)	Tangmere WC1 . . . . 2F **7**
Sydenham Cotts.	Taft Way E3 . . . . 2D **67**	(off Sidmouth St.)
SE12 . . . . 2E **125**	Tailor Ho. WC1 . . . . 4E **7**	Tanhurst Ho. SW2 . . . . 5B **104**
Sydenham Hill SE23 . . 1D **121**	(off Colonnade)	(off Redlands Way)
SE26 . . . . 1D **121**	Tailworth St. E1 . . . . 4C **64**	Tankerton Ho's. WC1 . . . . 2E **7**
Sydenham Pk. SE26 . . . 3E **121**	(off Chicksand St.)	(off Tankerton St.)
Sydenham Pk. Mans.	Tait Ct. E3 . . . . 5B **52**	Tankerton St.
SE26 . . . . 3E **121**	(off St Stephen's Rd.)	WC1 . . . . 2A **62** (2E **7**)
(off Sydenham Pk.)	SW8 . . . . 4A **90**	Tankridge Rd. NW2 . . . . 4D **29**
Sydenham Pk. Rd.	(off Lansdowne Grn.)	Tanner Ho. SE1 . . . . 4E **27**
SE26 . . . . 3E **121**	Tait Ho. SE1 . . . . 2C **24**	(off Tanner St.)
Sydenham Pl. SE27 . . . 3D **119**	(off Greet St.)	Tanneries, The E1 . . . . . 3E **65**
Sydenham Ri. SE23 . . . 2D **121**	Takhar M. SW11 . . . . 5A **88**	(off Cephas Av.)
Sydenham Rd. SE26. . . 4E **121**	Talacre Rd. NW5 . . . . . . 3C **46**	Tanner Point E13 . . . . . . 5C **54**
Sydmons Ct. SE23 . . . 5E **107**	Talbot Ct. EC3 . . . . 4C **18**	(off Pelly Rd.)
Sydner M. N16 . . . . 1B **50**	Talbot Cres. NW4 . . . . . . 1C **28**	Tanner's Hill SE8 . . . . . . 4B **94**
Sydner Rd. N16 . . . . 1B **50**	Talbot Gro. Ho. W11 . . . 5A **58**	Tanner St. SE1. . 3A **78** (4E **27**)
Sydney Cl. SW3 . . . . . . 5F **73**	(off Lancaster Rd.)	(not continuous)
Sydney Gro. NW4 . . . . . 1E **29**	Talbot Ho. E14 . . . . 5D **67**	Tannington Ter. N5. . . . . 5D **35**
Sydney M. SW3 . . . . . . 5F **73**	(off Girauld St.)	Tannsfeld Rd. SE26 . . . 5F **121**
Sydney Pl. SW7 . . . . . . 5F **73**	Talbot Pl. SE3 . . . . 5A **96**	Tansley Cl. N7 . . . . 2F **47**
Sydney Rd. E11 . . . . 1D **41**	Talbot Rd. E7 . . . . 1C **54**	Tanswell St.
Sydney St. SW3 . . . . . . 1A **88**	N6 . . . . 1C **32**	SE1 . . . . 3C **76** (4B **24**)
Sylvan Gro. NW2 . . . . . 1F **43**	SE22 . . . . 2A **106**	Tantallon Rd. SW12. . . 1C **116**
SE15 . . . . 2D **93**	W11 . . . . 5B **58**	Tant Av. E16 . . . . 5B **68**
Sylvan Rd. E7 . . . . 3D **55**	(not continuous)	Tanza Rd. NW3 . . . . 1B **46**
E17 . . . . 1C **38**	Talbot Sq. W2 . . . . 5F **59**	Tapley Ho. SE1 . . . . 3C **78**
Sylvester Path E8 . . . . . 3D **51**	Talbot Wlk. NW10 . . . . . 3A **42**	(off Wolseley St.)
Sylvester Rd. E8 . . . . . . 3D **51**	W11 . . . . 5A **58**	Taplow SE17 . . . . 1F **91**
E17 . . . . 2B **38**	Talbot Yd. SE1 . . 2F **77** (2B **26**)	(off Thurlow St.)
Sylvia Ct. N1 . . . . 1F **63**	Talcott Path SW2 . . . . . 1C **118**	Taplow Ho. E2 . . . . 2F **11**
Symes M. NW1 . . . . 1E **61**	Talfourd Pl. SE15 . . . . . . 4B **92**	(off Palissy St.)
Symington Ho. SE1 . . . 5B **26**	Talfourd Rd. SE5 . . . . . . 4B **92**	Taplow St. N1 . . 1E **63** (1A **10**)
(off Deverell St.)	Talgarth Mans. W14 . . . . 1A **86**	Tappesfield Rd. SE15. . 1E **107**
Symington M. E9 . . . . . 2F **51**	(off Talgarth Rd.)	Tapp St. E1 . . . . 3D **65**
Symister M. N1 . . . . 2D **11**	Talgarth Rd. W6 . . . . 1F **85**	Tara M. N8 . . . . 1A **34**
Symons St. SW3 . . . . . . 5B **74**	W14 . . . . 1F **85**	Taranto Ho. E1 . . . . 4F **65**
Symphony M. W10 . . . . 2A **58**	Talgarth Wlk. NW9 . . . . . 1A **28**	(off Master's St.)
Syon Lodge SE12 . . . . . 5C **110**	Talia Ho. E14 . . . . 4E **81**	Tarbert Rd. SE22 . . . . . 3A **106**
Syringa Ho. SE4 . . . . . . 1B **108**	(off Manchester Rd.)	Tarbert Wlk. E1 . . . . 1E **79**
	Talina Cen. SW6 . . . . . . 4E **87**	Tariff Cres. SE8 . . . . 5B **80**
	Talisman Sq. SE26. . . . 4C **120**	Tarleton Gdns. SE23 . . 2D **121**
	Tallack Rd. E10 . . . . 3B **38**	Tarling Ho. E1 . . . . 5D **65**
T	Talleyrand Ho. SE5 . . . . 5E **91**	(off Tarling St.)
	(off Lilford Rd.)	Tarling Rd. E16 . . . . 5B **68**
Tabard Ct. E14 . . . . 5E **67**	Tallis Cl. E16 . . . . 5D **69**	Tarling St. E1 . . . . 5D **65**
(off Lodore St.)	Tallis Gro. SE7 . . . . 2D **97**	Tarling St. Est. E1 . . . . . 5E **65**
Tabard Gdn. Est.	Tallis St. EC4. . 1C **76** (4C **16**)	Tarns, The NW1 . . . . 1F **5**
SE1 . . . . 4F **77** (4B **26**)	Tallis Vw. NW10 . . . . 3A **42**	(off Varndell St.)
(off Manciple St.)	Talmage Cl. SE23 . . . . 5E **107**	Tarn St. SE1 . . . 4E **77** (5F **25**)
Tabard Ho. SE1 . . . . 5C **26**	Talma Rd. SW2 . . . . . . 2C **104**	Tarplett Ho. SE15 . . . . . 2E **93**
(off Manciple St.)	Talwin St. E3 . . . . 2D **67**	(off John Williams Cl.)
Tabard St. SE1 . . 3E **77** (3A **26**)	Tamar Cl. E3 . . . . 5B **52**	Tarquin Ho. SE26. . . . . 4C **120**
Tabernacle Av. E13 . . . . 3C **68**	Tamar Ho. E14 . . . . 3E **81**	(off High Level Dr.)
Tabernacle St.	(off Plevna St.)	Tarragon Cl. SE14 . . . . . 3A **94**
EC2 . . . . 2F **63** (4C **10**)	SE11 . . . . 1C **90**	Tarragon Gro. SE26 . . . 5F **121**
Tableer Av. SW4 . . . . . . 3E **103**	(off Kennington La.)	Tarranbrae NW6 . . . . . . 4A **44**
Tabley Rd. N7 . . . . 1A **48**	Tamarind Ct. W8 . . . . . . 4D **73**	Tarrant Ho. E2 . . . . 2E **65**
Tabor Rd. W6 . . . . 4D **71**	(off Stone Hall Gdns.)	(off Roman Rd.)
Tachbrook Est. SW1 . . . 1F **89**	Tamarind Yd. E1 . . . . . . 2C **78**	Tarrant Pl. W1 . . . . 4B **60**
Tachbrook M. SW1 . . . . 5E **75**	(off Kennet St.)	Tarrington Cl. SW16. . . 3F **117**
Tachbrook St. SW1. . . . 5E **75**	Tamarisk Sq. W12 . . . . . 1B **70**	Tartan Ho. E14 . . . . 5C **67**
(not continuous)	Tamar St. SE7 . . . . 4F **83**	(off Dee St.)
Tack M. SE4 . . . . 1C **108**	Tamplin Ho. W10 . . . . . . 2B **58**	Tarver Rd. SE17 . . . . . . 1D **91**
Tadema Ho. NW8 . . . . . . 3F **59**	(off Dowland St.)	Tarves Way SE10 . . . . . 3D **95**
(off Penfold St.)	Tamworth N7 . . . . 3A **48**	Tasker Ho. E14 . . . . 4B **66**
Tadema Rd. SW10 . . . . . 3E **87**	Tamworth St. SW6 . . . . . 2C **86**	(off Wallwood St.)
Tadmor St. W12 . . . . . . 2F **71**	Tancred Rd. N4 . . . . 2D **35**	Tasker Rd. NW3 . . . . . . 2B **46**
Tadworth Ho. SE1. . . . . 4D **25**		
Tadworth Rd. NW2 . . . . 4C **28**		

Tasman Ct. E14 . . . . 5D 81
(off Westferry Rd.)
Tasman Ho. E1 . . . . 2D 79
(off Clegg St.)
Tasman Rd. SW9 . . . . . . 1A 104
Tasman Wlk. E16 . . . . . . 5F 69
Tasso Rd. W6 . . . . 2A 86
Tasso Yd. W6 . . . . 2A 86
(off Tasso Rd.)
Tatchbury Ho. SW15 . . . 4B 98
(off Tunworth Cres.)
Tate Britain **5A 76**
Tate Ho. E2 . . . . 1F 65
(off Mace St.)
Tate Modern . . . 2D 77 (1E 25)
Tatham Pl. NW8 . . . . . . 1F 59
Tatnell Rd. SE23 . . . . . . 4A 108
Tatsfield Ho. SE1 . . . . . 5C 26
(off Pardoner St.)
Tatton Cres. N16 . . . . . . 2B 36
Tatum St. SE17 . . . . 5F 77
Tauheed Cl. N4 . . . . 4E 35
Taunton Ho. W2 . . . . . . 5E 59
(off Hallfield Est.)
Taunton M. NW1 . . . . . . 3B 60
Taunton Pl. NW1 . . . . . . 3B 60
Taunton Rd. SE12 . . . . . 3A 110
Taverners Cl. W11 . . . . . 2A 72
Taverners Cl. E3 . . . . . . 2A 66
(off Grove Rd.)
Taverner Sq. N5 . . . . . . 1E 49
Tavern La. SW9 . . . . 5C 90
Tavern Quay SE16 . . . . . 5A 80
Tavistock Cl. N16 . . . . . 2A 50
Tavistock Ct. WC1 . . . . . 3C 6
(off Tavistock Sq.)
Tavistock Cres. W11 . . . 4B 58
(not continuous)
Tavistock Ho. WC1 . .3F 61 (3C 6)
Tavistock M. W11 . . . . . 5B 58
Tavistock Pl. WC1 . .3A 62 (3D 7)
Tavistock Rd. E7 . . . . . . 1B 54
E15 . . . . 3B 54
N4 . . . . 1F 35
NW10 . . . . 1B 56
W11 . . . . 5B 58
(not continuous)
Tavistock Sq.
WC1 . . . . 3F 61 (3C 6)
Tavistock St.
WC2 . . . . 1A 76 (4E 15)
(not continuous)
Tavistock Ter. N19 . . . . . 5F 33
Tavistock Twr. SE16 . . . 4A 80
Taviton St. WC1 . . . 3F 61 (3B 6)
Tavy Cl. SE11 . . . . 1C 90
(off White Hart St., not cont.)
Tawny Way SE16 . . . . . . 5F 79
Taybridge Rd. SW11 . . 1C 102
Tay Bldgs. SE1 . . . . 5D 27
Tayburn Cl. E14 . . . . . . 5E 67
Tayler Ct. NW8 . . . . . . 5F 45
Taylor Cl. SE8 . . . . 2B 94
Taylor Ct. E15 . . . . 2E 53
Taylors Grn. W3 . . . . . . 5A 56
Taylors La. NW10 . . . . 4A 42
Taylor's La. SE26 . . . . . 4D 121
Taymount Grange SE23 .2E 121
Taymount Ri. SE23 . . . 2E 121
Tayport Cl. N1 . . . . 4A 48

Tayside Ct. SE5 . . . . . . 2F 105
Teak Cl. SE16 . . . . 2A 80
Tealby Ct. N7 . . . . 2B 48
(off George's Rd.)
Teal Cl. E16 . . . . 4F 69
Teal Ct. SE8 . . . . 2B 94
(off Abinger Gro.)
Teale St. E2 . . . . 1C 64
Teal St. SE10 . . . . 4B 82
Teasel Way E15 . . . . . . 2A 68
Tea Trade Wharf SE1 . . 3B 78
(off Shad Thames)
Ted Roberts Ho. E2 . . . 1D 65
(off Parmiter St.)
Tedworth Gdns. SW3 . . 1B 88
Tedworth Sq. SW3 . . . . 1B 88
Teesdale Cl. E2 . . . . . . 1C 64
Teesdale Rd. E11 . . . . . 1B 40
Teesdale St. E2 . . . . . . 1D 65
Teesdale Yd. E2 . . . . . . 1D 65
(off Teesdale St.)
Tee, The W3 . . . . 5A 56
Teignmouth Cl. SW4 . . 2F 103
Teignmouth Rd. NW2 . . 2F 43
Telecom Tower, The
. . . . 4E 61 (5F 5)
Telegraph Hill NW3 . . . 5D 31
Telegraph Pas. SW2 . . 5A 104
Telegraph Pl. E14 . . . . 5D 81
Telegraph Quarters
SE10 . . . . 1F 95
(off Park Row)
Telegraph Rd. SW15 . .5D 99
Telegraph St.
EC2 . . . . 5F 63 (2B 18)
Telemann Sq. SE3 . . . 2D 111
Telephone Pl. SW6 . . . 2B 86
Telfer Ho. EC1 . . . . . . 2E 9
(off Lever St.)
Telferscot Rd. SW12 . . 1F 117
Telford Av. SW2 . . . . . 1F 117
Telford Cl. E17 . . . . . . 2A 38
Telford Ho. SE1 . . . . . 5F 25
(off Tiverton St.)
Telford Rd. NW9 . . . . . 1C 28
W10 . . . . 4A 58
Telfords Yd. E1 . . . . . . 1C 78
Telford Ter. SW1 . . . . . 2E 89
Telford Way W3 . . . . . 4A 56
Tell Gro. SE22 . . . . . . 2B 106
Tellson Av. SE18 . . . . . 4F 97
Temair Ho. SE10 . . . . . 3D 95
(off Tarves Way)
Temeraire St. SE16 . . . 3E 79
Tempelhof Av. NW4 . . 2E 29
Temperley Rd. SW12 . .5C 102
Templar Ct. NW8 . . . . . 2F 59
(off St John's Wood Rd.)
Templar Ho. NW2 . . . . 3B 44
Templars Av. NW11 . . . 1B 30
Templars Ho. E15 . . . . 2D 53
Templar St. SE5 . . . . . 5D 91
Temple EC4 . . . . 4B 16
Temple Bar **3B 16**
Temple Chambers EC4. . 4C 16
Temple Cl. E11 . . . . . . 2A 40
Templecombe Rd. E9 . . 5E 51
Temple Cl. E1 . . . . 4F 65
(off Rectory Sq.)

Temple Ct. SW8 . . . . . . 3A 90
(off Thorncroft St.)
Temple Dwellings E2. . . 1D 65
(off Temple St.)
TEMPLE FORTUNE 1B 30
Temple Fortune Hill
NW11 . . . . 1C 30
Temple Fortune La.
NW11 . . . . 1B 30
Temple Fortune Pde.
NW11 . . . . 1B 30
Temple Gdns. EC4 . . . . 4B 16
(off Middle Temple La.)
NW11 . . . . 1B 30
Temple Gro. NW11 . . . 1C 30
Temple La. EC4. . 5C 62 (3C 16)
Templemead Cl. W3 . . 5A 56
Templemead Ho. E9 . . 1A 52
Temple Mill La. E10 . . 1D 53
(not continuous)
E15 . . . . 1E 53
TEMPLE MILLS 1D 53
Temple Mills E10 . . . . 5E 39
Temple of Mithras (remains)
. . . . 3B 18
(off Queen Victoria St.)
Temple Pl. WC2. . 1B 76 (4A 16)
Temple Rd. E6 . . . . . . 5F 55
NW2 . . . . 1E 43
Temple St. E2 . . . . . . 1D 65
Templeton Cl. N15 . . . 1F 35
N16 . . . . 2A 50
Templeton Pl. SW5 . . . 5C 72
Templeton Rd. N15 . . . 1F 35
Temple W. M. SE11 . . 5D 25
Templewood Av. NW3 . 5D 31
Templewood Gdns.
NW3 . . . . 5D 31
Templewood Point NW2. .4B 30
(off Granville Rd.)
Tenbury Cl. E7 . . . . . . 2F 55
Tenbury Ct. SW12 . . . 1F 117
Tenby Ho. W2 . . . . . . 5E 59
(off Hallfield Est.)
Tenby Mans. W1 . . . . 5C 4
(off Nottingham St.)
Tench St. E1 . . . . 2D 79
Tenda Rd. SE16 . . . . . 5D 79
Tenham Av. SW2 . . . . 1F 117
Tenison Ct. W1. . 1E 75 (4F 13)
Tenison Way SE1. .2B 76 (2A 24)
Tenniel Cl. W2 . . . . . . 1E 73
Tennis St. SE1. . 3F 77 (3B 26)
Tennyson Av. E11. . . . 2C 40
E12 . . . . 4F 55
Tennyson Ct. SW6 . . . 4E 87
(off Imperial Rd.)
Tennyson Ho. SE17 . . 1E 91
(off Browning St.)
Tennyson Mans. W14. .2B 86
(off Queen's Club Gdns.)
Tennyson Rd. E10 . . . 3D 39
E15 . . . . 4A 54
E17 . . . . 1B 38
NW6 . . . . 5B 44
(not continuous)
SW19 . . . . 5E 115
Tennyson St. SW8 . . . 5D 89
Tenterden Ho. SE17 . . 1A 92
(off Surrey Gro.)

Tilleard Ho. *W10* 2A **58**
  (off Herries St.)
Tiller Leisure Cen., The . .4C **80**
Tiller Rd. E14 . . . . 4C **80**
Tillett Sq. SE16 . . . . 3A **80**
Tillet Way E2 . . . . 2C **64**
Tilling Rd. NW2 . . . . 3E **29**
Tillings Cl. SE5 . . . . 4E **91**
Tillman St. E1 . . . . 5D **65**
Tilloch St. N1 . . . . 4B **48**
Tillotson Ct. *SW8* 3F **89**
  (off Wandsworth Rd.)
Tilney Ct. EC1 . . 3E **63** (3A **10**)
Tilney Gdns. N1 . . . . 3F **49**
Tilney St. W1. . . 2C **74** (1C **20**)
Tilson Cl. SE5 . . . . 3A **92**
Tilson Gdns. SW12 . . . . 5A **104**
Tilson Ho. SW2 . . . . 5A **104**
Tilston Cl. E11 . . . . 5B **40**
Tilton St. SW6 . . . . 2A **86**
Timberland Cl. SE15 . . . . 3C **92**
Timberland Rd. E1. . . . . . 5D **65**
Timber Mill Way SW4 . . 1F **103**
Timber Pond Rd. SE16 . . 2F **79**
Timber St. EC1 . . 3E **63** (3F **9**)
Timberwharf Rd. N16. . 1C **36**
Timber Wharves Est.
  E14 . . . . 5C **80**
  (off Copeland Dr.)
Timbrell Pl. SE16 . . . . . . 2B **80**
Time Sq. E8 . . . . 2B **50**
Timor Ho. *E1* 3A **66**
  (off Duckett St.)
Timothy Cl. SW4 . . . . . . 3E **103**
Timothy Rd. E3 . . . . 4B **66**
Timsbury Wlk. SW15 . . 1C **112**
Tindal St. SW9 . . . . 4D **91**
Tinderbox All. SW14 . . 1A **98**
Tinniswood Cl. N5 . . . . . 2C **48**
Tinsley Rd. E1 . . . . 4E **65**
Tintagel Cres. SE22 . . . . 2B **106**
Tintagel Gdns. SE22. . . . 2B **106**
Tintern Cl. SW15 . . . . . . 3A **100**
Tintern Ho. *NW1* 1E **5**
  (off Augustus St.)
  SW1 . . . . 5D **75**
  (off Abbots Mnr.)
Tintern Path *NW9* 1A **28**
  (off Fryent Gro.)
Tintern St. SW4 . . . . . . 2A **104**
Tinto Rd. E16 . . . . 3C **68**
Tinworth St. SE1 . . . . . . 1A **90**
  SE11 . . . . 1A **90**
Tipthorpe Rd. SW11 . . . 1C **102**
Tiptree *NW1* 4D **47**
  (off Castlehaven Rd.)
Tisbury Ct. W1 . . . . 4B **14**
Tisdall Pl. SE17 . . . . 5F **77**
Tissington Ct. SE16 . . . . 5E **79**
Titan Bus. Est. *SE8*. . . . 3C **94**
  (off Ffinch St.)
Titchborne Row W2 . . . . 5A **60**
Titchfield Rd. NW8 . . . . 5A **46**
Titchwell Rd. SW18 . . 1F **115**
Tite St. SW3 . . . . 1B **88**
Titmuss St. W12 . . . . 3E **71**
Tiverton Rd. N15. . . . . . . 1F **35**
  NW10 . . . . 5F **43**
Tiverton St. SE1 . . 4E **77** (5F **25**)
Tivoli Ct. SE16 . . . . 2B **80**

Tivoli Gdns. SE18 . . . . . . 5F **83**
  (not continuous)
Tivoli Rd. N8 . . . . 1F **33**
  SE27 . . . . 5E **119**
Tobacco Dock E1 . . . . . . 1D **79**
Tobacco Quay E1 . . . . . . 1D **79**
Tobago St. E14 . . . . 3C **80**
Tobin Cl. NW3 . . . . 4A **46**
Toby La. E1 . . . . 3A **66**
Todds Wlk. N7 . . . . 4B **34**
Tokenhouse Yd.
  EC2. . . . . 5F **63** (2B **18**)
Token Yd. SW15. . . . . . . 2A **100**
Toland Sq. SW15 . . . . . . 3C **98**
Tolchurch *W11* 5B **58**
  (off Dartmouth Clo.)
Tolford Rd. E5 . . . . 2D **51**
Tollbridge Cl. W10. . . . . 3A **58**
Tollet St. E1 . . . . 3F **65**
Tollgate Dr. SE21 . . . . . . 2A **120**
Tollgate Gdns. NW6. . . . 1D **59**
Tollgate Ho. *NW6*. 1D **59**
  (off Tollgate Gdns.)
Tollgate Rd. E6. . . . . 4E **69**
  E16 . . . . 4E **69**
Tollhouse Way N19 . . . . 4E **33**
Tollington Pk. N4 . . . . . . 4B **34**
Tollington Pl. N4 . . . . . . 4B **34**
Tollington Rd. N7 . . . . . . 1B **48**
Tollington Way N7 . . . . . 5A **34**
Tolmers Sq. NW1 . . 3E **61** (3A **6**)
  (not continuous)
Tolpaide Ho. *SE11* 5C **76**
  (off Hotspur St.)
Tolpuddle Av. *E13*. 5E **55**
  (off Queens Rd.)
Tolpuddle St. N1 . . . . . . 1C **62**
Tom Groves Cl. E15 . . . . 2F **53**
Tom Hood Cl. E15. . . . . . 2F **53**
Tom Jenkinson Rd. E16. . 2C **82**
Tomkyns Ho. *SE11*. 5C **76**
  (off Distin St.)
Tomlin's Gro. E3 . . . . 2C **66**
Tomlinson Cl. E2 . . . . . . 2B **64**
Tomlins Ter. E14 . . . . 5A **66**
Tomlins Wlk. N7. . . . . . . 4B **34**
Tom Nolan Cl. E15. . . . . 1A **68**
Tompion Ho. *EC1* 2E **9**
  (off Percival St.)
Tompion St. EC1. . 2D **63** (2D **9**)
  (not continuous)
Tom Smith Cl. SE10. . . . 2A **96**
Tomson Ho. *SE1* 5F **27**
  (off Riley Rd.)
Tom Williams Ho. *SW6*. . 2B **86**
  (off Clem Attlee Ct.)
Tonbridge Ho's. *WC1*. . . 2D **7**
  (off Tonbridge St.)
Tonbridge St.
  WC1. . . . . 2A **62** (1D **7**)
Tonbridge Wlk. WC1 . . . 1D **7**
Toneborough *NW8*. 5D **45**
  (off Abbey Rd.)
Tonsley Hill SW18 . . . . . 3D **101**
Tonsley Pl. SW18 . . . . . . 3D **101**
Tonsley Rd. SW18 . . . . . 3D **101**
Tonsley St. SW18 . . . . . . 3D **101**
Tony Cannell M. E3 . . . . 2B **66**
Took's Ct. WC2 . . 5C **62** (2B **16**)

Tooley St. SE1. . 2F **77** (1C **26**)
Toomy Cen. *E16*. 1D **83**
  (off Evelyn Rd.)
TOOTING 5A **116**
TOOTING BEC 3B **116**
Tooting Bec Gdns.
  SW16 . . . . 4F **117**
  (not continuous)
Tooting Bec Rd. SW16. . 4D **117**
  SW17 . . . . 3C **116**
Tooting B'way. SW17. . 5A **116**
TOOTING GRAVENEY . . 5B **116**
Tooting Gro. SW17. . . . . 5A **116**
Tooting High St. SW17. . 5A **116**
Tooting Mkt. SW17 . . . . 4B **116**
Topaz Wlk. NW2 . . . . . . 2F **29**
Topham Ho. *SE10*. 3E **95**
  (off Prior St.)
Topham St. EC1 . 3C **62** (3B **8**)
Topley St. SE9 . . . . 2E **111**
Topmast Point E14 . . . . 3C **80**
Topp Wlk. NW2 . . . . 4E **29**
Topsfield Cl. N8 . . . . 1F **33**
Topsfield Pde. *N8* 1A **34**
  (off Tottenham La.)
Topsfield Rd. N8 . . . . . . 1A **34**
Topsham Rd. SW17 . . . . 3B **116**
Torbay Ct. NW1 . . . . 4D **47**
Torbay Mans. *NW6* 5B **44**
  (off Willesden La.)
Torbay Rd. NW6 . . . . . . 4B **44**
Torbay St. NW1 . . . . 4D **47**
Tor Ct. W8 . . . . 3C **72**
Torcross Dr. SE23 . . . . . 2E **121**
Tor Gdns. W8 . . . . 3C **72**
Tor Ho. N6 . . . . 1D **33**
Tornay Ho. *N1* 1B **62**
  (off Priory Grn. Est.)
Torney Ho. E9 . . . . 4E **51**
Torquay St. W2 . . . . 4D **59**
Torrance Cl. SE7 . . . . . . 2F **97**
Torrens Ct. SE5. . . . . 1F **105**
Torrens Rd. E15 . . . . 3B **54**
  SW2 . . . . 3B **104**
Torrens Sq. E15 . . . . 3B **54**
Torrens St. EC1 . . . . 1C **62**
Torres Sq. E14 . . . . 1C **94**
Torrey Dr. SW9. . . . . 5C **90**
Torriano Av. NW5. . . . . . 2F **47**
Torriano Cotts. NW5. . . . 2E **47**
Torriano M. NW5 . . . . . . 2E **47**
Torridge Gdns. SE15 . . 2E **107**
Torridon Ho. *NW6* 1D **59**
  (off Randolph Gdns.)
Torridon Rd. SE6 . . . . . . 5F **109**
Torrington Ct. *SE26* . . . 5C **120**
  (off Crystal Pal. Pk. Rd.)
Torrington Pl. E1 . . . . . . 2C **78**
  WC1. . . . . 4F **61** (5B **6**)
Torrington Sq.
  WC1. . . . . 3F **61** (4C **6**)
Tortington Ho. *SE15*. . . 3C **92**
  (off Friary Est.)
Torwood Rd. SW15 . . . . 3C **98**
Tothill Ho. *SW1* 5F **75**
  (off Page St.)
Tothill St. SW1. . 3F **75** (4C **22**)
Tottan Ter. E1 . . . . 5F **65**
Tottenhall *NW1* 4C **46**
  (off Ferdinand St.)

U

Vineyard Cl. SE6 . . . . . 1C **122**
Vineyard Hill Rd.
  SW19 . . . . 4B **114**
Vineyard M. EC1 . . . . . . 3C **8**
Vineyard Wlk.
  EC1 . . . . 3C **62** (3B **8**)
Viney Rd. SE13 . . . . . 1D **109**
Vining St. SW9 . . . . . . 2C **104**
Vinopolis, City of Wine
  . . . . 2F **77** (1B **26**)
Vintners Ct. EC4 . 1E **77** (5A **18**)
Vintners Hall *4A 18*
  (off Up. Thames St.)
Vintner's Pl.
  EC4 . . . . 1E **77** (4A **18**)
Viola Sq. W12 . . . . 1B **70**
Violet Cl. E16 . . . . 3A **68**
  SE8 . . . . 2B **94**
Violet Hill NW8 . . . . . . 1E **59**
Violet Hill Ho. NW8 . . . *1E 59*
  (off Violet Hill, not continuous)
Violet Rd. E17 . . . . 1C **38**
  E3 . . . . 3D **67**
Violet St. E2 . . . . 3D **65**
V.I.P. Trading Est. SE7 . . 5E **83**
Virgil Pl. W1 . . . . 4B **60**
Virgil St. SE1 . . 4B **76** (5A **24**)
Virginia Ct. SE16 . . . . . *3F 79*
  (off Eleanor Cl.)
  WC1 . . . . 3C **6**
  (off Burton St.)
Virginia Ho. E14 . . . . . . *1E 81*
  (off Newby Pl.)
Virginia Rd.
  E2 . . . . 2B **64** (2F **11**)
Virginia St. E1 . . . . 1C **78**
Virginia Wlk. SW2 . . . . 4B **104**
Viscount Ct. W2 . . . . . . *5C 58*
  (off Pembridge Vs.)
Viscount St.
  EC1 . . . . 3E **63** (4F **9**)
Vista Dr. IG4: Ilf 1F **41**
Vista, The SE9 . . . . . . 4F **111**
Vittoria Ho. N1 . . . . 5B **48**
  (off High Rd.)
Vivian Av. NW4 . . . . . . 1D **29**
Vivian Comma Cl. N4 . . 5D **35**
Vivian Mans. NW4 . . . . *1D 29*
  (off Vivian Av.)
Vivian Rd. E3 . . . . 1A **66**
Vivian Sq. SE15 . . . . . 1D **107**
Vixen M. E8 . . . . *4B 50*
  (off Haggerston Rd.)
Vogans Mill SE1 . . . . . . 3B **78**
Vogler Ho. E1 . . . . *1E 79*
  (off Cable St.)
Vollasky Ho. E1 . . . . . . *4C 64*
  (off Daplyn St.)
Voltaire Rd. SW4 . . . . . 1F **103**
Volt Av. NW10 . . . . 2A **56**
Voluntary Pl. E11 . . . . . 1C **40**
Vorley Rd. N19 . . . . . . 4E **33**
Voss St. E2 . . . . 2C **64**
Voyager Bus. Est.
  SE16 . . . . *4C 78*
  (off Spa Rd.)
Vulcan Rd. SE4 . . . . . . 5B **94**
Vulcan Sq. E14 . . . . . . 5D **81**
Vulcan Ter. SE4 . . . . . . 5B **94**
Vulcan Way N7 . . . . . . 3B **48**

Vyner Rd. W3 . . . . 1A **70**
Vyner St. E2 . . . . 5D **51**

W

W12 Shop. Cen. W12. . . 3F **71**
Wadding St. SE17 . . . . . 5F **77**
Waddington Rd. E15 . . . 2F **53**
Waddington St. E15 . . . 3F **53**
Wade Ho. SE1 . . . . *3C 78*
  (off Parkers Row)
Wadeson St. E2 . . . . . . 1D **65**
Wade's Pl. E14 . . . . . . 1D **81**
Wadham Gdns. NW3 . . 5A **46**
Wadham Rd. SW15 . . . 2A **100**
Wadhurst Rd. SW8 . . . . 4E **89**
  W4 . . . . 4A **70**
Wadley Rd. E11 . . . . . . 2A **40**
Wager St. E3 . . . . 3B **66**
Waghorn Rd. E13 . . . . . 5E **55**
Waghorn St. SE15 . . . 1C **106**
Wagner St. SE15 . . . . . 3E **93**
Wainford Cl. SW19 . . . . 5F **99**
Wainwright Ho. E1 . . . . *2E 79*
  (off Garnet St.)
Waite Davies Rd.
  SE12 . . . . 5B **110**
Waite St. SE15 . . . . . . 2B **92**
Waithman St. EC4 . . . . 3D **17**
  (off Apothecary St.)
Wakefield Ct. SE26 . . . 5E **121**
Wakefield Gdns. IG1: Ilf . . 1F **41**
Wakefield Ho. SE15 . . . 4C **92**
Wakefield M.
  WC1 . . . . . . 2A **62** (2E **7**)
Wakefield Rd. N15 . . . . 1B **36**
Wakefield St. E6 . . . . . 5F **55**
  WC1 . . . . . . 3A **62** (2E **7**)
Wakeford Cl. SW4 . . . . 3E **103**
Wakeham St. N1 . . . . . 3F **49**
Wakehurst Rd. SW11 . . 3A **102**
Wakeling St. E14 . . . . . 5A **66**
Wakelin Ho. N1 . . . . . . *4D 49*
  (off Sebbon St.)
  SE23 . . . . 5A **108**
  (off Brockley Pk.)
Wakelin Rd. E15 . . . . . 1A **68**
Wakeman Ho. NW10 . . *2F 57*
  (off Wakeman Rd.)
Wakeman Rd. NW10 . . 2E **57**
Wakley St. EC1. . 2D **63** (1D **9**)
Walberswick St. SW8 . . 3A **90**
Walbrook EC4 . . 1F **77** (4B **18**)
  (not continuous)
Walbrook Wharf EC4 . . 5A **18**
  (off Bell Wharf La.)
Walburgh St. E1 . . . . . . 5D **65**
Walcorde Av. SE17 . . . . 5E **77**
Walcot Gdns. SE11 . . . *5C 76*
  (off Kennington Rd.)
Walcot Sq. SE11 . . . . . 5C **76**
Walcott St. SW1 . . . . . 5E **75**
Waldeck Gro. SE27 . . . 3D **119**
Waldemar Av. SW6 . . . 4A **86**
Waldemar Rd. SW19 . . 5C **114**
Walden Cl. SW8 . . . . . 4F **89**
Walden Ho. SW1 . . . . . *5C 74*
  (off Pimlico Rd.)
Waldenshaw Rd. SE23. . 1E **121**

Walden St. E1 . . . . 5D **65**
Waldo Cl. SW4 . . . . . . 3E **103**
Waldo Ho. NW10 . . . . . *2D 57*
  (off Waldo Rd.)
Waldo Rd. NW10 . . . . . 2C **56**
  (not continuous)
Waldram Cres. SE23 . . 1E **121**
Waldram Pk. Rd. SE23. . 1F **121**
Waldram Pl. SE23 . . . . 1E **121**
Waldron M. SW3 . . . . . 2F **87**
Waldron Rd. SW18 . . . 3E **115**
Walerand Rd. SE13 . . . 5E **95**
Waleran Flats SE1 . . . . 5A **78**
Wales Cl. SE15 . . . . . . 3D **93**
Wales Farm Rd. W3 . . . 4A **56**
Waley St. E1 . . . . 4A **66**
Walford Ho. E1. . . . . . . 5C **64**
Walford Rd. N16 . . . . . 1A **50**
WALHAM GREEN . . . **4C 86**
Walham Grn. Ct. SW6. . 3D **87**
  (off Waterford Rd.)
Walham Gro. SW6 . . . . 3C **86**
Walham Yd. SW6. . . . . 3C **86**
Walker Ho. NW1 . 1F **61** (1B **6**)
Walker's Ct. W1 . . . . . . 4B **14**
Walkerscroft Mead
  SE21 . . . . 1E **119**
Walkers Pl. SW15 . . . . 2A **100**
Walkinshaw Ct. N1 . . . . *4E 49*
  (off Rotherfield St.)
Wallace Collection
  . . . . 5C **60** (2C **12**)
Wallace Ct. NW1 . . . . . *4A 60*
  (off Old Marylebone Rd.)
Wallace Ho. N7 . . . . . . *3B 48*
  (off Caledonian Rd.)
Wallace Rd. N1 . . . . . . 3E **49**
Wallace Way N19. . . . . *4F 33*
  (off St John's Way)
Wallbutton Rd. SE4 . . . 5A **94**
Wallcote Av. NW2. . . . . 3F **29**
Wall Ct. N4 . . . . *3B 34*
  (off Stroud Grn. Rd.)
Waller Rd. SE14 . . . . . . 4F **93**
Waller Way SE10. . . . . 3D **95**
Wallflower St. W12 . . . 1B **70**
Wallgrave Rd. SW5 . . . 5D **73**
Wallingford Av. W10 . . 4F **57**
Wallis All. SE1 . . . . 3A **26**
Wallis Cl. SW11 . . . . . 1F **101**
Wallis Ho. SE14 . . . . . . 4A **94**
Wallis Rd. E9 . . . . 3B **52**
Wallis's Cotts. SW2 . . . 5A **104**
Wallorton Gdns. SW14. . 2A **98**
Wallside EC2 . . . . 1A **18**
Wall St. N1 . . . . 3F **49**
Wallwood Rd. E11 . . . . 2F **39**
Wallwood St. E14 . . . . 4B **66**
Walmer Ho. W10 . . . . . *5F 57*
  (off Bramley Rd.)
Walmer Pl. W1 . . . . *4B 60*
  (off Walmer St.)
Walmer Rd. W10 . . . . . 5E **57**
  W11 . . . . 1A **72**
Walmer St. W1 . . . . . . 4B **60**
Walm La. NW2. . . . . . . 3E **43**
Walney Wlk. N1 . . . . . . 3E **49**
Walnut Cl. SE8 . . . . . . 2B **94**
Walnut Ct. W8 . . . . *4D 73*
  (off St Mary's Ga.)

Weavers Ter. *SW6* **2C 86**
(off Micklethwaite Rd.)
Weaver St. E1 . . . . 3C **64**
Weavers Way NW1 . . . . . 5F **47**
Weaver Wlk. SE27 . . . . 4E **119**
Webb Cl. W10 . . . . 3E **57**
Webber Row SE1 . . . . . . 5C **24**
SE1 . . . . 3D **77**
Webber St.
SE1 . . . . 3C **76** (3C **24**)
Webb Est. E5 . . . . 2C **36**
Webb Gdns. E13 . . . . 3C **68**
Webb Ho. SW8 . . . . 3F **89**
Webb Pl. NW10 . . . . 2B **56**
Webb Rd. SE3 . . . . 2B **96**
Webb's Rd. SW11 . . . . . 2B **102**
Webb St. SE1 . . 4A **78** (5D **27**)
Webheath NW6 . . . . 4B **44**
Webster Rd. E11 . . . . 5E **39**
SE16 . . . . 4C **78**
Weddell Ho. E1 . . . . 3F **65**
(off Duckett St.)
Wedderburn Rd. NW3 . . . 2F **45**
Wedgewood Ho. SW1 . . . 1D **89**
(off Churchill Gdns.)
Wedgewood M.
W1 . . . . 5F **61** (3C **14**)
Wedgwood Ho. E2 . . . . . 2F **65**
(off Warley St.)
SE11 . . . . 4C **76**
(off Lambeth Wlk.)
Wedgwood Wlk. NW6 . . 2D **45**
(off Dresden Cl.)
Wedlake St. W10 . . . . 3A **58**
Wedmore Ct. N19 . . . . . . 4F **33**
Wedmore Gdns. N19 . . . . 4F **33**
Wedmore M. N19 . . . . . . 5F **33**
Wedmore St. N19 . . . . . . 5F **33**
Weech Rd. NW6 . . . . 1C **44**
Weedington Rd. NW5 . . . 2C **46**
Weedon Ho. W12 . . . . . . 5C **56**
Weekley Sq. SW11 . . . 1F **101**
Weigall Rd. SE12 . . . . . 3C **110**
Weighhouse St.
W1 . . . . 5C **60** (3C **12**)
Weimar St. SW15 . . . . . 1A **100**
Weir Rd. SW12 . . . . 5E **103**
SW19 . . . . 3D **115**
Weir's Pas.
NW1 . . . . 2F **61** (1C **6**)
Weiss Rd. SW15 . . . . 1F **99**
Welbeck Av.
BR1: Brom 4C **124**
Welbeck Ct. W14 . . . . . . 5B **72**
(off Addison Bri. Pl.)
Welbeck Ho. W1 . . . . . . 2D **13**
(off Welbeck St.)
Welbeck Rd. E6 . . . . 2F **69**
Welbeck St. W1 . . 4C **60** (1C **12**)
Welbeck Way
W1 . . . . 5D **61** (2D **13**)
Welby Ho. N19 . . . . 2F **33**
Welby St. SE5 . . . . 4D **91**
Welcome Ct. E17 . . . . . . 2C **38**
(off Boundary Rd.)
Welfare Rd. E15 . . . . 4A **54**
Welford Cl. E5 . . . . 5F **37**
Welford Ct. NW1 . . . . . . 4D **47**
(off Castlehaven Rd.)
SW8 . . . . 5E **89**

Welford Ct. W9 . . . . 4C **58**
(off Elmfield Way)
Welford Pl. SW19 . . . . . 4A **114**
Welham Rd. SW17 . . . 5C **116**
Welland Ct. SE6 . . . . . . 2B **122**
(off Oakham Cl.)
Welland Ho. SE15 . . . . 2E **107**
Welland St. SE10 . . . . . 2E **95**
Wellby Ct. E13 . . . . 5E **55**
Well Cl. SW16 . . . . 4B **118**
Wellclose Sq. E1 . . . . . . 1C **78**
Wellclose St. E1 . . . . . . 1C **78**
E3 . . . . 1A **66**
(off Driffield Rd)
Wellcome Cen. for
Medical Science **3B 6**
Well Cott. Cl. E11 . . . . . . 1E **41**
Well Ct. EC4 . . . . 5E **63** (3A **18**)
(not continuous)
Weller Ho. SE16 . . . . . . 3C **78**
(off George Row)
Wellers Ct. N1 . . 1A **62** (1D **7**)
Weller St. SE1 . . 3E **77** (3F **25**)
Welles Ct. E14 . . . . 1C **80**
(off Premiere Pl.)
Wellesley Av. W6 . . . . . . 4D **71**
Wellesley Cl. SE7 . . . . . . 1E **97**
Wellesley Ct. NW2 . . . . . 4C **28**
W9 . . . . 2E **59**
(off Maida Va.)
Wellesley Ho. NW1 . . . . . 2C **6**
(off Wellesley Pl.)
SW1 . . . . 1D **89**
(off Ebury Bri. Rd.)
Wellesley Mans. W14 . . 1B **86**
(off Edith Vs.)
Wellesley Pl.
NW1 . . . . 2F **61** (2B **6**)
NW5 . . . . 2C **46**
Wellesley Rd. E11 . . . . . 1C **40**
E17 . . . . 1C **38**
NW5 . . . . 2C **46**
Wellesley St. E1 . . . . 4F **65**
Wellesley Ter.
N1 . . . . 2E **63** (1A **10**)
Wellfield Rd. SW16 . . . 4A **118**
Wellfield Wlk. SW16 . . 5B **118**
(not continuous)
Wellfit St. SE24 . . . . . . 1D **105**
Wellgarth Rd. NW11 . . . 3D **31**
Wellington Arch **3C 20**
Wellington Av. N15 . . . . 1B **36**
Wellington Bldgs. SW1 . 1C **88**
Wellington Ct. SE14 . . . 4F **93**
W11 . . . . 5C **58**
(off Wellington Rd.)
SW1 . . . . 3B **74**
(off Knightsbridge)
SW6 . . . . 4D **87**
(off Maltings Pl.)
Wellington Est. E2 . . . . . 1E **65**
Wellington Gdns. SE7 . . 2E **97**
Wellington Gro. SE10 . . 3F **95**
Wellington Ho. E16 . . . . 1C **82**
(off Pepys Cres.)
NW3 . . . . 3B **46**
(off Eton Rd.)
Wellington Mans. E10 . . 3C **38**

Wellington M. N7 . . . . . 3B **48**
(off Roman Way)
SE7 . . . . 2E **97**
SE22 . . . . 2C **106**
SW16 . . . . 3F **117**
Wellington Monument . . **3C 20**
Wellington Mus.
. . . . **3C 74** (3C **20**)
Wellington Pk. Est.
NW2 . . . . 3C **28**
Wellington Pas. E11 . . . 1C **40**
(off Wellington Rd.)
Wellington Pl. NW8 . . . . 2F **59**
Wellington Rd. E7 . . . . . 1B **54**
E10 . . . . 3A **38**
E11 . . . . 1C **40**
NW8 . . . . 1F **59**
NW10 . . . . 2F **57**
SW19 . . . . . . 2C **114**
Wellington Row E2 . . . . . 2C **64**
Wellington Sq. SW3 . . . 1B **88**
Wellington St.
WC2 . . . . 1B **76** (4F **15**)
Wellington Ter. E1 . . . . . 2D **79**
W11 . . . . 1C **72**
Wellington Way E3 . . . . . 2C **66**
Wellmeadow Rd.
SE13 . . . . 4A **110**
(not continuous)
Well Pl. NW3 . . . . 5F **31**
Well Rd. NW3 . . . . 5F **31**
Wells Ct. NW6 . . . . 1C **58**
(off Cambridge Av.)
Wells Gdns. IG1: Ilf 2F **41**
Wells Ho. BR1: Brom . . 5D **125**
(off Pike Cl.)
EC1 . . . . 1C **8**
(off Spa Grn. Est.)
SE16 . . . . 4E **79**
(off Howland Est.)
Wells Ho. Rd. NW10 . . . 4A **56**
Wells M. W1 . . 4E **61** (1A **14**)
Wells Pk. Rd. SE26 . . . . 3C **120**
Wells Pl. SW18 . . . . 5E **101**
Wells Ri. NW8 . . . . 5B **46**
Wells Rd. W12 . . . . 3E **71**
Wells Sq. WC1 . . 2B **62** (2F **7**)
Wells St. W1 . . . 4E **61** (1F **13**)
Wells Ter. N4 . . . . 4C **34**
Well St. E9 . . . . 4E **51**
E15 . . . . 3A **54**
Wells Way SE5 . . . . 2F **91**
SW7 . . . . 4F **73**
Wells Yd. N7 . . . . 2C **48**
Well Wlk. NW3 . . . . 1F **45**
Welsford St. SE1 . . . . . . 5C **78**
(not continuous)
Welsh Cl. E13 . . . . 2C **68**
Welsh Ho. E1 . . . . 2D **79**
(off Wapping La.)
Welshpool Ho. E8 . . . . . . 5C **50**
(off Welshpool St.)
Welshpool St. E8 . . . . . . 5C **50**
Welshside NW9 . . . . 1A **28**
(off Ruthin Cl.)
Welshside Wlk. NW9 . . . 1A **28**
Welstead Ho. E1 . . . . . . 5D **65**
(off Cannon St. Rd.)
Welstead Way W4 . . . . . 5B **70**
Weltje Rd. W6 . . . . 5C **70**

Wharf Rd. E15 . . . . 5F **53**
N1. . . . . .1E **63** (1F **9**)
(Angel)
N1. . . . . .1A **62**
(King's Cross)
NW1 . . . . .5F **47**
Wharfside Rd. E16. . . . .4A **68**
Wharf St. E16. . . . . .4A **68**
Wharf, The
EC3 . . . . .2B **78** (1E **27**)
Wharf Vw. Ct. E14 . . . . .5E **67**
(off Athol Sq.)
Wharton Cl. NW10 . . . . .3A **42**
Wharton Cotts.
WC1. . . . . .2C **62** (2B **8**)
(off Maltby St.)
Wharton Ho. SE1 . . . . . .5F **27**
(off Maltby St.)
Wharton St. WC1. .2B **62** (2A **8**)
Whateley Rd. SE22 . . . .3B **106**
Whatman Ho. E14 . . . . . .5B **66**
(off Wallwood St.)
Whatman Rd. SE23 . . . .5F **107**
Wheatland Ho. SE22 . . .1A **106**
Wheatlands Rd. SW17. . .3C **116**
Wheatley Ho. SW15. . . . .5C **98**
(off Ellisfield Dr)
Wheatley St. W1. .4C **60** (1C **12**)
Wheat Sheaf Cl. E14. . . .5D **81**
Wheatsheaf La. SW6 . . . .3E **85**
SW8 . . . . .3A **90**
(not continuous)
Wheatsheaf Ter. SW6. . . .3B **86**
Wheatstone Rd. W10 . . . .4A **58**
Wheeler Gdns. N1 . . . . . .5A **48**
(off Outram Pl.)
Wheel Ho. E14 . . . . .1D **95**
(off Burrells Wharf Sq.)
Wheelwright St. N7 . . . . .4B **48**
Wheler Ho. E1 . . . . .4F **11**
(off Quaker St.)
Wheler St. E1 . .3B **64** (4F **11**)
Whellock Rd. W4 . . . . . .4A **70**
Whetstone Pk.
WC2 . . . . .5B **62** (2F **15**)
Whewell Rd. N19. . . . . . .4A **34**
Whidborne Bldgs. WC1 . . .2E **7**
(off Whidborne St.)
Whidborne Cl. SE8. . . . .5C **94**
Whidborne St.
WC1. . . . . .2A **62** (2E **7**)
(not continuous)
Whinfell Cl. SW16 . . . . .5F **117**
Whinyates Rd. SE9. . . . .1F **111**
Whipps Cross E17. . . . . .1F **39**
Whipps Cross Rd. E11 . . .1F **39**
(not continuous)
Whiskin St. EC1. .2D **63** (2D **9**)
Whistler M. SE15 . . . . . .3B **92**
Whistlers Av. SW11 . . . . .3F **87**
Whistler St. N5 . . . . .2D **49**
Whistler Twr. SW10 . . . . .3E **87**
(off Worlds End Est.)
Whistler Wlk. SW10 . . . . .3F **87**
Whiston Ho. N1 . . . . .4D **49**
(off Richmond Gro.)
Whiston Rd. E2 . . . . .1B **64**
Whitbread Rd. SE4. . . . .2A **108**
Whitburn Rd. SE13 . . . .2D **109**
Whitby Ct. N7 . . . . .1A **48**

Whitby Ho. NW8. . . . . . .5E **45**
(off Boundary Rd.)
Whitby St. E1. . .3B **64** (3F **11**)
(not continuous)
Whitcher Cl. SE14 . . . . .2A **94**
Whitcher Pl. NW1 . . . . . .3E **47**
Whitchurch Ho. W10 . . . .5F **57**
(off Kingsdown Cl.)
Whitchurch Rd. W11 . . . .1F **71**
Whitcomb Ct. SW1 . . . . .5C **14**
(off Whitcomb St.)
Whitcomb St.
WC2 . . . . .1F **75** (5C **14**)
Whiteadder Way E14. . . .5D **81**
Whitear Wlk. E15 . . . . . .3F **53**
Whitebeam Cl. SW9 . . . . .3B **90**
White Bear Pl. NW3 . . . . .1F **45**
White Bear Yd. EC1. . . . . .4B **8**
(off Clerkenwell Rd.)
Whitechapel High St.
E1. . . . . .5B **64** (2F **19**)
Whitechapel Rd. E1. . . . .4C **64**
White Chu. La. E1 . . . . . .5C **64**
White Chu. Pas. E1 . . . . .5C **64**
(off White Chu. La.)
Whitecross Pl.
EC2. . . . . .4F **63** (5C **10**)
Whitecross St.
EC1 . . . . .3E **63** (3A **10**)
Whitefield Av. NW2 . . . . .3E **29**
Whitefield Cl. SW18 . . . .4A **100**
Whitefoot La.
BR1: Brom 4E **123**
Whitefoot Ter.
BR1: Brom 3A **124**
Whitefriars St.
EC4 . . . . .5C **62** (3C **16**)
Whitehall SW1. .2A **76** (2D **23**)
Whitehall Ct.
SW1. . . . . .2A **76** (2D **23**)
(not continuous)
Whitehall Gdns. SW1 . . .2D **23**
Whitehall Pk. N19 . . . . . .3E **33**
Whitehall Pl. E7. . . . . . . .2C **54**
SW1. . . . . .2A **76** (2D **23**)
Whitehall Theatre 1D **23**
(off Whitehall)
White Hart Ct. E2 . . . . . .1D **19**
White Hart La. NW10. . . . .3B **42**
SW13 . . . . .1A **98**
White Hart St.
EC4 . . . . .5D **63** (3E **17**)
SE11. . . . . .1C **90**
White Hart Yd.
SE1. . . . . .2F **77** (2B **26**)
Whitehaven St. NW8 . . . .3A **60**
Whitehead Cl. SW18 . . . .5E **101**
Whiteheads Gro. SW3 . . .5A **74**
White Heather Ho. WC1. . .2E **7**
(off Cromer St.)

White Horse All. EC1. . . . .5D **9**
White Horse La. E1 . . . . .3F **65**
Whitehorse M.
SE1. . . . . .4C **76** (5C **24**)
White Horse Rd. E1 . . . .4A **66**
(not continuous)
White Horse St.
W1. . . . . .2D **75** (2E **21**)
White Horse Yd.
EC2. . . . . .5F **63** (2B **18**)
White Ho. SW4 . . . . .5F **103**
(off Clapham Pk. Est.)
SW11 . . . . .4F **87**
Whitehouse Est. E10 . . . .1E **39**
White Ho., The NW1 . . . . .3E **5**
White Kennett St.
E1. . . . . .5A **64** (2E **19**)
Whitelands Ho. SW3 . . . .1B **88**
(off Cheltenham Ter.)
Whitelegg Rd. E13. . . . . .1B **68**
Whiteley Rd. SE19. . . . . .5F **119**
Whiteleys Cen. W2 . . . . .5D **59**
Whiteley's Cotts. W14 . . .5B **72**
White Lion Ct. EC3 . . . . .3D **19**
SE15 . . . . .2E **93**
White Lion Hill
EC4 . . . . .1D **77** (4E **17**)
White Lion St. N1 . . . . . .1C **62**
White Lodge Cl. N2 . . . . .1F **31**
White Lyon Ct. EC2. . . . . .5F **9**
White Post La. E9 . . . . . .4B **52**
White Post St. SE15 . . . . .3E **93**
White Rd. E15 . . . . .4A **54**
White's Grounds
SE1 . . . . .3A **78** (4E **27**)
White's Grounds Est.
SE1 . . . . .3E **27**
White's Row E1. . .4B **64** (1F **19**)
Whites Sq. SW4 . . . . . . .2F **103**
Whitestone La. NW3 . . . . .5E **31**
Whitestone Wlk. NW3 . . . .5E **31**
Whiteswan M. W4 . . . . . .1A **84**
Whitethorn Ho. E1 . . . . . .2E **79**
(off Prusom St.)
Whitethorn Pas. E3 . . . . .3C **66**
(off Whitethorn St.)
Whitethorn St. E3. . . . . .4C **66**
White Tower, The . .1B **78** (5F **19**)
(in Tower of London, The)
Whitfield Ho. NW1 . . . . . .3A **60**
(off Salisbury St.)
Whitfield Pl. W1. . . . . .4F **5**
Whitfield Rd. E6. . . . . . . .4E **55**
SE3 . . . . .4F **95**
Whitfield St. W1. .3E **61** (4F **5**)
Whitgift Ho. SE11 . . . . . .5B **76**
Whitgift St. SE11 . . . . . . .5B **76**
Whitley Ho. SW1 . . . . . . .2E **89**
(off Churchill Gdns.)
Whitlock Dr. SW19. . . . . .5A **100**
Whitman Ho. E2 . . . . . . .2E **65**
(off Cornwall Av.)
Whitman Rd. E3 . . . . . . .3A **66**
Whitmore Est. N1. . . . . . .5A **50**
Whitmore Gdns. NW10. . .1E **57**
Whitmore Ho. N1. . . . . . .5A **50**
(off Whitmore Est.)
Whitmore Rd. N1. . . . . . .5A **50**
Whitnell Way SW15. . . . .3E **99**

Woburn Ct. *SE16* 1D **93**
   (off Masters Dr.)
Woburn M. WC1 . . 3F **61** (4C **6**)
Woburn Pl. WC1 . . 3A **62** (4D **7**)
Woburn Sq.
  WC1 . . . . 3F **61** (4C **6**)
Woburn Wlk.
  WC1 . . . . 2F **61** (2C **6**)
Wodehouse Av. SE5 . . . 4B **92**
Woking Cl. SW15 . . . . . 2B **98**
Wolcot Ho. *NW1* 1A **6**
   (off Aldenham St.)
Wolfe Cres. SE7 . . . . . . 1F **97**
  SE16 . . . . 3F **79**
Wolfe Ho. *W12* 1D **71**
   (off White City Est.)
Wolffe Gdns. E15 . . . . . 3B **54**
Wolfington Rd. SE27 . . 4D **119**
Wolfram Cl. SE13 . . . 3A **110**
Wolftencroft Cl.
  SW11 . . . . 1A **102**
Wollaston Cl. SE1 . . . . . 5E **77**
Wollett Ct. *NW1* *4E 41*
   (off St Pancras Way)
Wolseley Av. SW19 . . 2C **114**
Wolseley Rd. E7 . . . . . 4D **55**
  N8 . . . . 1F **33**
Wolseley St. SE1 . . . . . 3C **78**
Wolsey Ct. NW6 . . . . . . 4E **45**
  SW11 . . . . *4A 88*
   (off Westbridge Rd.)
Wolsey M. NW5 . . . . . . 3E **47**
Wolsey Rd. N1 . . . . 2F **49**
Wolsey St. E1 . . . . 4E **65**
Wolverley St. E2 . . . . . . 2D **65**
Wolverton SE17 . . . . . . 1A **92**
   (not continuous)
Wolverton Gdns. W6 . . 5F **71**
Womersley Rd. N8 . . . . 1B **34**
Wontner Cl. N1 . . . . 4E **49**
Wontner Rd. SW17 . . . 2B **116**
Woodall Cl. E14 . . . . . . 1D **81**
Woodbank Rd.
  BR1: Brom 3B **124**
Woodbastwick Rd.
  SE26 . . . . 5F **121**
Woodberry Down N4 . . 2E **35**
Woodberry Down Est.
  N4 . . . . 3E **35**
   (Woodberry Down)
  N4 . . . . 2E **35**
   (Woodberry Gro.)
Woodberry Gro. N4 . . . 2E **35**
Woodbine Pl. E11 . . . . . 1C **40**
Woodbine Ter. E9 . . . . . 3E **51**
Woodborough Rd.
  SW15 . . . . 2D **99**
Woodbourne Av.
  SW16 . . . . 3F **117**
Woodbourne Cl.
  SW16 . . . . 3A **118**
Woodbridge Cl. N7 . . . . 4B **34**
  NW2 . . . . 5C **28**
Woodbridge Ho. E11 . . 3B **40**
Woodbridge St.
  EC1 . . . . 3D **63** (3D **9**)
   (not continuous)
Woodburn Cl. NW4 . . . 1F **29**
Woodbury Ho. SE26 . . 3C **120**
Woodbury St. SW17 . . 5A **116**

Woodchester Sq. W2 . . 4D **59**
Woodchurch Rd. NW6 . . 4C **44**
Wood Cl. E2 . . . . 3C **64**
  NW9 . . . . 2A **28**
Woodcock Ho. *E14* *4C 66*
   (off Burgess St.)
Woodcocks E16 . . . . . . 4E **69**
Woodcombe Cres.
  SE23 . . . . 1E **121**
Woodcote Ho. *SE8* *2B 94*
   (off Prince St.)
Woodcote Pl. SE27 . . . 5D **119**
Woodcote Rd. E11 . . . . 2C **40**
Woodcote Vs. *SE27* . . . *5E 119*
   (off Woodcote Pl.)
Woodcroft M. SE8 . . . . . 5A **80**
Wood Dene *SE15* *4D 93*
   (off Queen's Rd.)
Wood Dr. BR7: Chst . . 5F **125**
Woodend SE19 . . . . . . 5E **119**
Wooder Gdns. E7 . . . . . 1C **54**
Woodfall Rd. N4 . . . . . . 4C **34**
Woodfall St. SW3 . . . . . 1B **88**
Woodfarrs SE5 . . . . . . 2F **105**
Woodfield Av. SW16 . . 3F **117**
Woodfield Gro. SW16 . . 3F **117**
Woodfield Ho. *SE23* . . *3F 121*
   (off Dacres Rd.)
Woodfield La. SW16 . . 3F **117**
Woodfield Pl. W9 . . . . . 3B **58**
Woodfield Rd. W9 . . . . . 4B **58**
Woodford Ct. *W14* *3F 71*
   (off Shepherd's Bush Grn.)
Woodford Rd. E7 . . . . . 5D **41**
Woodger Rd. W12 . . . . 3E **71**
Woodget Cl. E6 . . . . 5F **69**
Woodgrange Rd. E7 . . . 2D **55**
Woodhall *NW1* *2F 5*
   (off Robert St.)
Woodhall Av. SE21 . . . 3B **120**
Woodhall Dr. SE21 . . . 3B **120**
Woodham Rd. SE6 . . . . 3E **123**
Woodhatch Cl. E6 . . . . . 4F **69**
Woodhayes Rd. SW19 . . 5E **113**
Woodheyes Rd. NW10 . . 2A **42**
Woodhouse Gro. E12 . . 3F **55**
Woodhouse Rd. E11 . . . 5B **40**
Woodland Cl. SE19 . . . 5A **120**
Woodland Ct. *E11* *1C 40*
   (off New Wanstead)
Woodland Cres. SE10 . . 2A **96**
  SE16 . . . . 3F **79**
Woodland Hill SE19 . . 5A **120**
Woodland M. SW16 . . 3A **118**
Woodland Rd. SE19 . . 5A **120**
Woodlands NW11 . . . . . 1A **30**
Woodlands Art Gallery . 2C **96**
Woodlands Av. E11 . . . 3D **41**
Woodlands Cl. NW11 . . 1A **30**
Woodlands Ct. *NW10* . . *5F 43*
   (off Wrentham Av.)
  SE23 . . . . 5D **107**
Woodlands Ga. SW15 . . 3B **100**
Woodlands Gro. SE10 . . 1A **96**
Woodlands Ho. NW6 . . 4A **44**
Woodlands Pk. Rd.
  N15 . . . . 1D **35**
  SE10 . . . . 2A **96**
   (not continuous)

Woodlands Rd. E11 . . . 4A **40**
  SW13 . . . . 1B **98**
Woodlands St. SE13 . . 5F **109**
Woodlands, The N5 . . . 1E **49**
  SE13 . . . . 5F **109**
Woodland St. E8 . . . . . 3B **50**
Woodlands Way
  SW15 . . . . 3B **100**
Woodland Ter. SE7 . . . . 5F **83**
Woodland Wlk.
  BR1: Brom 4F **123**
   (not continuous)
  NW3 . . . . 2A **46**
  SE10 . . . . 1A **96**
Wood La. N6 . . . . 1D **33**
  NW9 . . . . 2A **28**
  W12 . . . . 5E **57**
Woodlawn Cl. SW15 . . 3B **100**
Woodlawn Rd. SW6 . . . 3F **85**
Woodlea Rd. N16 . . . . . 5A **36**
Woodleigh Gdns.
  SW16 . . . . 3A **118**
Woodmans Gro. NW10 . 2B **42**
Woodman's M. W12 . . . 4D **57**
Woodmere Cl. SW11 . . 1C **102**
Woodnook Rd. SW16 . . 5D **117**
Woodpecker Rd. SE14 . . 2A **94**
Wood Point *E16* *4C 68*
   (off Fife Rd.)
Woodquest Av. SE24 . . 3E **105**
Woodriffe Rd. E11 . . . . 2F **39**
Woodrush Cl. SE14 . . . 3A **94**
Wood's Bldgs. *E1* *4D 65*
   (off Winthrop St.)
Woodseer St. E1 . . . . . 4B **64**
Woodsford *SE17* *1F 91*
   (off Portland St.)
Woodsford Sq. W14 . . . 3A **72**
Woodside SW19 . . . . . 5B **114**
Woodside Av. N6 . . . . . 1B **32**
Woodside Cl. E12 . . . . . 3E **41**
Woodside M. SE22 . . . 3B **106**
Woodside Rd. E13 . . . . 3E **69**
Woods M. W1 . . 1C **74** (4B **12**)
Woodsome Rd. NW5 . . 5C **32**
Woods Pl. SE1 . 4A **78** (5E **27**)
Woodspring Rd.
  SW19 . . . . 2A **114**
Woods Rd. SE15 . . . . . 4D **93**
Woodstock Av. NW11 . . 2A **30**
Woodstock Ct. SE11 . . 1B **90**
  SE12 . . . . 4C **110**
Woodstock Gro. W12 . . 3F **71**
Woodstock M. W1 . . . . 1C **12**
Woodstock Rd. E7 . . . . 4E **55**
  N4 . . . . 3C **34**
  NW11 . . . . 2B **30**
  W4 . . . . 5A **70**
Woodstock St.
  W1 . . . . 5D **61** (3D **13**)
Woodstock Ter. E14 . . . 1D **81**
Wood St. E16 . . . . 1D **83**
  EC2 . . . . 5E **63** (2A **18**)
  W4 . . . . 1A **84**
Woodsyre SE26 . . . . . 4B **120**
Wood Ter. NW2 . . . . . . 5D **29**
Woodthorpe Rd. SW15 . 2D **99**
Wood Va. N10 . . . . 1E **33**
  SE23 . . . . 1D **121**
Wood Va. Est. SE23 . . 5E **107**

Woodvale Wlk. SE27 . . 5E **119**
Woodvale Way NW11 . . . 5F **29**
Woodview Cl. N4 . . . . . . 2D **35**
SW15 . . . . 4A **112**
Woodville SE3 . . . . 3D **97**
Woodville Cl. SE12 . . . 3C **110**
Woodville Gdns. NW2 . . 2F **29**
Woodville Ho. SE1 . . . . . 5F **27**
 (off Grange Wlk.)
Woodville Rd. E11 . . . . . 3B **40**
 N16 . . . . 2A **50**
 NW6 . . . . 1B **58**
 NW11 . . . . 2F **29**
Woodward Av. NW4 . . . 1C **28**
Woodwarde Rd. SE22 . . 4A **106**
Woodwell St. SW18 . . . 3E **101**
Wood Wharf SE10 . . . . . 2E **95**
Wood Wharf Bus. Pk.
 E14 . . . . 2D **81**
Woodyard Cl. NW5 . . . . 2C **46**
Woodyard La. SE21 . . . 5A **106**
Woodyates Rd. SE12 . . 4C **110**
Woolacombe Rd. SE3 . . 4E **97**
Woolcombes Ct. SE16 . . 2F **79**
 (off Princes Riverside Rd.)
Wooler St. SE17 . . . . . . 1F **91**
Woolf M. WC1 . . . . 3C **6**
 (off Burton Pl.)
Woolgar M. N16 . . . . 2A **50**
 (off Gillett St.)
Woollaston Rd. N4 . . . . 1D **35**
Woolley Ho. SW9 . . . . 1D **105**
 (off Loughborough Rd.)
Woollon Ho. E1 . . . . 5E **65**
 (off Clark St.)
Woolmead Av. NW4 . . . 2C **28**
Woolmore St. E14 . . . . . 1E **81**
Woolneigh St. SW6 . . . 1D **101**
Woolridge Way E9 . . . . 4E **51**
Woolstaplers Way
 SE16 . . . . 4C **78**
Woolstone Rd. SE23 . . 2A **122**
Woolwich Chu. St.
 SE18 . . . . 4F **83**
Woolwich Dockyard Ind. Est.
 SE18 . . . . 4F **83**
Woolwich Rd. SE7 . . . . 1C **96**
 SE10 . . . . 1B **96**
Wooster Gdns. E14 . . . 5F **67**
Wooster Pl. SE1 . . . . . . 5F **77**
 (off Searles Rd.)
Wootton St.
 SE1 . . . . 2C **76** (2C **24**)
Worcester Cl. NW2 . . . 5D **29**
Worcester Ct. W9 . . . . . 4C **58**
 (off Elmfield Way)
Worcester Dr. W4 . . . . . 3A **70**
Worcester Ho. SE11 . . 5B **24**
 SW9 . . . . 3C **90**
 (off Cranmer Rd.)
 W2 . . . . 5E **59**
 (off Hallfield Est.)
Worcester M. NW6 . . . 3D **45**
Worcester Rd. SW19 . . 5B **114**
Wordsworth Av. E12 . . . 4F **55**
Wordsworth Ho. NW6 . . 2C **58**
 (off Stafford Rd.)
Wordsworth Pl. NW3 . . 2B **46**
Wordsworth Rd. N16 . . 1A **50**
 SE1 . . . . 5B **78**

Worfield St. SW11 . . . . . 3A **88**
Worgan St. SE11 . . . . . 1B **90**
 SE16 . . . . 5F **79**
Worland Rd. E15 . . . . . 4A **54**
Worlds End Est. SW10 . . 3F **87**
World's End Pas. SW10 . . 3F **87**
 (off Worlds End Est.)
World's End Pl. SW10 . . 3F **87**
 (off Worlds End Est.)
Worlidge St. W6 . . . . . . 1E **85**
Worlingham Rd. SE22 . . 2B **106**
Wormholt Rd. W12 . . . . 1C **70**
Wormwood St.
 EC2 . . . . 5A **64** (2D **19**)
 (not continuous)
Wornington Rd. W10 . . 3A **58**
 (not continuous)
Wornum Ho. W10 . . . . . 1A **58**
 (off Kilburn La.)
Woronzow St. NW8 . . . 5F **45**
Worple Rd. SW20 . . . . 5B **114**
Worple Rd. M. SW19 . . 5B **114**
Worple St. SW14 . . . . . 1A **98**
Worship St.
 EC2 . . . . 3F **63** (4C **10**)
Worslade Rd. SW17 . . . 4F **115**
Worsley Bri. Rd.
 BR3: Beck 5C **122**
 SE26 . . . . 4B **122**
Worsley Gro. E5 . . . . . . 1C **50**
Worsley Ho. SE23 . . . . 2E **121**
Worsley Rd. E11 . . . . . . 1A **54**
Worsopp Dr. SW4 . . . . 3E **103**
Worth Gro. SE17 . . . . . . 1F **91**
Worthing Cl. E15 . . . . . 5A **54**
Worthington Ho. EC1 . . 1C **8**
 (off Myddelton Pas.)
Wortley Rd. E6 . . . . 4F **55**
Wotton Ct. E14 . . . . 1F **81**
 (off Jamestown Way)
Wotton Rd. NW2 . . . . . 5E **29**
 SE8 . . . . 2B **94**
Wouldham Rd. E16 . . . 5B **68**
Wragby Rd. E11 . . . . . . 5A **40**
Wrayburn Ho. SE16 . . . 3C **78**
 (off Llewellyn St.)
Wray Cres. N4 . . . . 4A **34**
Wren Av. NW2 . . . . 2E **43**
Wren Cl. E16 . . . . 5B **68**
Wren Ho. E3 . . . . 1A **66**
 (off Gernon Rd.)
 SW1 . . . . 1F **89**
 (off Aylesford St.)
Wren Landing E14 . . . . 2C **80**
Wrenn Ho. SW13 . . . . . 2E **85**
Wren Rd. SE5 . . . . 4F **91**
Wren's Pk. Ho. E5 . . . . 4D **37**
Wren St. WC1 . . . 3B **62** (3A **8**)
Wrentham Av. NW10 . . 1F **57**
Wrenthorpe Rd.
 BR1: Brom 4A **124**
Wrestlers Ct. EC3 . . . . 2D **19**
Wrexham Rd. E3 . . . . . 1C **66**
Wricklemarsh Rd. SE3 . . 5D **97**
 (not continuous)
Wrigglesworth St.
 SE14 . . . . 3F **93**
Wright Cl. SE13 . . . . . . 2F **109**
Wright Rd. N1 . . . . 3A **50**
Wrights Grn. SW4 . . . . 2F **103**

Wright's La. W8 . . . . 4D **73**
Wright's Rd. E3 . . . . 1B **66**
 (not continuous)
Wrotham Ho. SE1 . . . . . 5C **26**
 (off Law St.)
Wrotham Rd. NW1 . . . . 4E **47**
Wrottesley Rd. NW10 . . 1C **56**
Wroughton Rd. SW11 . . 3B **102**
Wroxton Rd. SE15 . . . . 5E **93**
Wulfstan St. W12 . . . . . 4B **56**
 (not continuous)
Wyatt Cl. SE16 . . . . 3B **80**
Wyatt Dr. SW13 . . . . . . 2D **85**
Wyatt Ho. NW8 . . . . 3F **59**
 (off Frampton St.)
 SE3 . . . . 5B **96**
Wyatt Pk. Rd. SW2 . . . 2A **118**
Wyatt Rd. E7 . . . . 3C **54**
 N5 . . . . 5E **35**
Wybert St. NW1 . . 3E **61** (3F **5**)
Wycherley Cl. SE3 . . . . 3B **96**
Wychcombe Studios
 NW3 . . . . 3B **46**
Wychwood End N6 . . . . 2E **33**
Wychwood Way SE19 . . 5F **119**
Wyclif Ct. EC1 . . . . 2D **9**
 (off Wyclif St.)
Wycliffe Rd. SW11 . . . . 5C **88**
Wyclif St. EC1 . . . 2D **63** (2D **9**)
Wycombe Gdns. NW11 . . 4C **30**
Wycombe Ho. NW8 . . . 3A **60**
 (off Grendon St.)
Wycombe Pl. SW18 . . . 4E **101**
Wycombe Sq. W8 . . . . 2B **72**
Wydeville Mnr. Rd.
 SE12 . . . . 4D **125**
Wye St. SW11 . . . . 5F **87**
Wyfold Rd. SW6 . . . . . . 3A **86**
Wykeham Ct. NW4 . . . . 1E **29**
 (off Wykeham Rd.)
Wykeham Rd. NW4 . . . 1E **29**
Wyke Rd. E3 . . . . 4C **52**
Wyldes Cl. NW11 . . . . . 3E **31**
Wyleu St. SE23 . . . . . . 5A **108**
Wyllen Cl. E1 . . . . 3E **65**
Wymans Way E7 . . . . . 1E **55**
Wymering Mans. W9 . . 2C **58**
 (off Wymering Rd., not cont.)
Wymering Rd. W9 . . . . 2C **58**
Wymond St. SW15 . . . 1E **99**
Wynan Rd. E14 . . . . . . 1D **95**
Wyndcliff Rd. SE7 . . . . 2D **97**
Wyndham Cres. N19 . . 5E **33**
Wyndham Deedes Ho.
 E2 . . . . 1C **64**
 (off Hackney Rd.)
Wyndham Est. SE5 . . . 3E **91**
Wyndham Ho. E14 . . . . 3D **81**
 (off Marsh Wall)
Wyndham M. W1 . . . . . 4B **60**
Wyndham Pl.
 W1 . . . . 4B **60** (1A **12**)
Wyndham Rd. E6 . . . . . 4F **55**
 SE5 . . . . 3E **91**
Wyndhams Ct. E8 . . . . . 4B **50**
 (off Celandine Dr.)
Wyndhams Theatre . . . 4D **15**
 (off St Martin's La.)
Wyndham St. W1 . . . . . 4B **60**
Wyndham Yd. W1 . . . . 4B **60**

HOSPITALS and HOSPICES
covered by this atlas.

N.B. Where Hospitals and Hospices are not named on the map,
the reference given is for the road in which they are situated.

ATHLONE HOUSE 3B **32**
Hampstead Lane
LONDON
N6 4RX
Tel: 020 83485231

BARNES HOSPITAL 1A **98**
South Worple Way
LONDON
SW14 8SU
Tel: 020 88784981

BELVEDERE DAY HOSPITAL 5C **42**
341 Harlesden Road
LONDON
NW10 3RX
Tel: 020 84593562

BLACKHEATH BMI HOSPITAL, THE . . .1B **110**
40-42 Lee Terrace
LONDON
SE3 9UD
Tel: 020 83187722

BOLINGBROKE HOSPITAL 3A **102**
Bolingbroke Grove
LONDON
SW11 6HN
Tel: 020 72237411

BRITISH HOME & HOSPITAL FOR
INCURABLES 5D **119**
Crown Lane
LONDON
SW16 3JB
Tel: 020 86708261

CAMDEN MEWS DAY HOSPITAL 4E **47**
1-5 Camden Mews
LONDON
NW1 9DB
Tel: 020 75304780

CHARING CROSS HOSPITAL 2F **85**
Fulham Palace Road, LONDON
W6 8RF
Tel: 020 88461234

CHELSEA & WESTMINSTER HOSPITAL
. . . . .2E **87**
369 Fulham Road, LONDON
SW10 9NH
Tel: 020 87468000

CHILDREN'S HOSPITAL, THE (LEWISHAM)
. . . . .3D **109**
Lewisham University Hospital
Lewisham High Street
LONDON
SE13 6LH
Tel: 020 83333000

CROMWELL HOSPITAL, THE 5D **73**
162-174 Cromwell Road
LONDON
SW5 0TU
Tel: 020 74602000

EASTMAN DENTAL HOSPITAL &
DENTAL INSTITUTE, THE 3B **62** (3F **7**)
256 Gray's Inn Road
LONDON
WC1X 8LD
Tel: 020 79151000

EDENHALL MARIE CURIE CENTRE 2F **45**
11 Lyndhurst Gardens
LONDON
NW3 5NS
Tel: 020 78533400

ELIZABETH GARRETT ANDERSON &
OBSTETRIC HOSPITAL, THE
. . . . .3E **61** (4A **6**)
Huntley Street
LONDON
WC1E 6DH
Tel: 020 73803501

FLORENCE NIGHTINGALE DAY HOSPITAL
. . . . .4A **60**
1B Harewood Row
LONDON
NW1 6SE
Tel: 020 77259940

FLORENCE NIGHTINGALE HOSPITAL
. . . . .4A **60**
11-19 Lisson Grove
LONDON
NW1 6SH
Tel: 020 75357700

GAINSBOROUGH CLINIC 4C **76** (5C **24**)
22 Barkham Terrace, LONDON
SE1 7PW
Tel: 020 79285633

GORDON HOSPITAL 5F **75**
Bloomburg Street
LONDON
SW1V 2RH
Tel: 020 87468733

GREAT ORMOND STREET HOSPITAL FOR
CHILDREN 3A **62** (4E **7**)
Great Ormond Street
LONDON
WC1N 3JH
Tel: 020 74059200

GUY'S HOSPITAL 2F **77** (2B **26**)
St Thomas Street
LONDON
SE1 9RT
Tel: 020 79555000

GUY'S NUFFIELD HOUSE 3F **77** (3B **26**)
Newcomen Street
LONDON
SE1 1YR
Tel: 020 79554257

HAMMERSMITH & NEW QUEEN
CHARLOTTE'S HOSPITAL 5C **56**
Du Cane Road
LONDON
W12 0HS
Tel: 020 83831000

HARLEY STREET CLINIC, THE
. . . . .4D **61** (5D **5**)
35 Weymouth Street
LONDON
W1G 8BJ
Tel: 020 79357700

HEART HOSPITAL, THE 4C **60** (1C **12**)
16-18 Westmoreland Street
LONDON
W1G 8PH
Tel: 020 75738888

HIGHGATE PRIVATE HOSPITAL 1B **32**
17 View Road
LONDON
N6 4DJ
Tel: 020 83414182

HOMERTON UNIVERSITY HOSPITAL . . .2F **51**
Homerton Row, LONDON
E9 6SR
Tel: 020 85105555

HOSPITAL FOR TROPICAL DISEASES
. . . . .3E **61** (4A **6**)
Mortimer Market
Capper Street
LONDON
WC1E 6AU
Tel: 020 73879300

HOSPITAL OF ST JOHN & ST ELIZABETH
. . . . .1F **59**
60 Grove End Road
LONDON
NW8 9NH
Tel: 020 78064000

KING EDWARD VII'S HOSPITAL
SISTER AGNES 4C **60** (5C **4**)
5-10 Beaumont Street
LONDON
W1G 6AA
Tel: 020 74864411

KING'S COLLEGE HOSPITAL 5F **91**
Denmark Hill
LONDON
SE5 9RS
Tel: 020 77374000

KING'S COLLEGE HOSPITAL,
DULWICH 2A **106**
East Dulwich Grove
LONDON
SE22 8PT
Tel: 020 77374000

LAMBETH HOSPITAL 1A **104**
108 Landor Road
LONDON
SW9 9NT
Tel: 020 74116100

LATIMER DAY HOSPITAL 4E **61** (5F **5**)
40 Hanson Street
LONDON
W1W 6UL
Tel: 020 73809187

LEWISHAM UNIVERSITY HOSPITAL . .3D **109**
Lewisham High Street
LONDON
SE13 6LH
Tel: 020 83333000

LISTER HOSPITAL, THE 1D **89**
Chelsea Bridge Road
LONDON
SW1W 8RH
Tel: 020 77303417

LONDON BRIDGE HOSPITAL
. . . . .2F **77** (1C **26**)
27 Tooley Street
LONDON
SE1 2PR
Tel: 020 74073100

LONDON CHEST HOSPITAL 1E **65**
Bonner Road
LONDON
E2 9JX
Tel: 020 73777000

LONDON CLINIC, THE 3C **60** (4C **4**)
20 Devonshire Place
LONDON
W1G 6BW
Tel: 020 79354444

LONDON FOOT HOSPITAL 3E **61** (4F **5**)
33 & 40 Fitzroy Square
LONDON
W1P 6AY
Tel: 020 75304500

LONDON INDEPENDENT BMI HOSPITAL, THE
. . . . .4F **65**
1 Beaumont Square
LONDON
E1 4NL
Tel: 020 77802400

LONDON LIGHTHOUSE 5A **58**
111-117 Lancaster Road
LONDON
W11 1QT
Tel: 020 77921200

LONDON WELBECK HOSPITAL
. . . . .4C **60** (1C **12**)
27 Welbeck Street
LONDON
W1G 8EN
Tel: 020 72242242

MAUDSLEY HOSPITAL, THE 5F **91**
Denmark Hill
LONDON
SE5 8AZ
Tel: 020 87776611

MIDDLESEX HOSPITAL, THE . . .4E **61** (1A **14**)
Mortimer Street
LONDON
W1T 3AA
Tel: 020 76368333

MILDMAY MISSION HOSPITAL
. . . . .2B **64** (2F **11**)
Hackney Road
LONDON
E2 7NA
Tel: 020 76136300

MILE END HOSPITAL 3F **65**
Bancroft Road
LONDON
E1 4DG
Tel: 020 73777000

MOORFIELDS EYE HOSPITAL
. . . . .2F **63** (2B **10**)
162 City Road
LONDON
EC1V 2PD
Tel: 020 72533411

NATIONAL HOSPITAL FOR NEUROLOGY &
NEUROSURGERY, THE 3A **62** (4E **7**)
Queen Square
LONDON
WC1N 3BG
Tel: 020 78373611

NEWHAM GENERAL HOSPITAL 3E **69**
Glen Road
LONDON
E13 8SL
Tel: 020 74764000

PARKSIDE HOSPITAL 3F **113**
53 Parkside
LONDON
SW19 5NX
Tel: 020 89718000

PLAISTOW HOSPITAL 1E **69**
Samson Street
LONDON
E13 9EH
Tel: 020 85866200

PORTLAND HOSPITAL FOR WOMEN &
CHILDREN, THE 3D **61** (4E **5**)
209 Great Portland Street
LONDON
W1N 6AH
Tel: 020 75804400

PRINCESS GRACE HOSPITAL . . .3C **60** (4B **4**)
42-52 Nottingham Place
LONDON
W1U 5NY
Tel: 020 74861234

PRINCESS GRACE HOSPITAL ANNEXE
. . . . .4C **60** (5C **4**)
29-31 Devonshire Street
LONDON
W1G 6PU
Tel: 020 74861234

PRINCESS LOUISE HOSPITAL 4F **57**
St Quintin Avenue
LONDON
W10 6DL
Tel: 020 89690133

QUEEN MARY'S HOUSE 5E **31**
23 East Heath Road
LONDON
NW3 1DU
Tel: 020 74314111

QUEEN MARY'S UNIVERSITY HOSPITAL
. . . . .4C **98**
Roehampton Lane
LONDON
SW15 5PN
Tel: 020 87896611

RICHARD HOUSE CHILDREN'S HOSPICE
.................................1F **83**
Richard House Drive,
LONDON
E16 3RG
Tel: 020 75110222

ROEHAMPTON PRIORY HOSPITAL 2B **98**
Priory Lane
LONDON
SW15 5JJ
Tel: 020 88768261

ROYAL BROMPTON HOSPITAL 1A **88**
Sydney Street
LONDON
SW3 6NP
Tel: 020 73528121

ROYAL BROMPTON HOSPITAL (ANNEXE)
.................................1F **87**
Fulham Road
LONDON
SW3 6HP
Tel: 020 73528121

ROYAL FREE HOSPITAL, THE 2A **46**
Pond Street
LONDON
NW3 2QG
Tel: 020 77940500

ROYAL HOSPITAL FOR NEURO-DISABILITY
.................................4A **100**
West Hill
LONDON
SW15 3SW
Tel: 020 87804500

ROYAL LONDON HOMOEOPATHIC
HOSPITAL, THE 4A **62** (5E **7**)
Great Ormond Street
LONDON
WC1N 3HR
Tel: 020 78378833

ROYAL LONDON HOSPITAL 4D **65**
Whitechapel Road
LONDON
E1 1BB
Tel: 020 73777000

ROYAL MARSDEN HOSPITAL
(FULHAM), THE 1F **87**
Fulham Road
LONDON
SW3 6JJ
Tel: 020 73528171

ROYAL NATIONAL ORTHOPAEDIC HOSPITAL
(OUTPATIENTS) 3D **61** (4E **5**)
45-51 Bolsover Street
LONDON
W1W 5AQ
Tel: 020 73875070

ROYAL NATIONAL THROAT, NOSE &
EAR HOSPITAL 2B **62** (1F **7**)
330 Gray's Inn Road
LONDON
WC1X 8DA
Tel: 020 79151300

ST ANDREW'S HOSPITAL 3D **67**
Devas Street
LONDON
E3 3NT
Tel: 020 74764000

ST ANN'S HOSPITAL 1E **35**
St Ann's Road
LONDON
N15 3TH
Tel: 020 84426000

ST BARTHOLOMEW'S HOSPITAL
.................................4D **63** (1E **17**)
West Smithfield
LONDON
EC1A 7BE
Tel: 020 73777000

ST CHARLES HOSPITAL 4F **57**
Exmoor Street
LONDON
W10 6DZ
Tel: 020 89692488

ST CHRISTOPHER'S HOSPICE 5E **121**
51-59 Lawrie Park Road
LONDON
SE26 6DZ
Tel: 020 87789252

ST CLEMENT'S HOSPITAL 2B **66**
2A Bow Road
LONDON
E3 4LL
Tel: 020 73777000

ST GEORGE'S HOSPITAL (TOOTING)
.................................5F **115**
Blackshaw Road
LONDON
SW17 0QT
Tel: 020 86721255

ST JOHN'S HOSPICE 1F **59**
Hospital of St John & St Elizabeth,
60 Grove End Road
LONDON
NW8 9NH
Tel: 020 78064040

ST JOSEPH'S HOSPICE 5D **51**
Mare Street
LONDON
E8 4SA
Tel: 020 85256000

ST LUKE'S HOSPITAL FOR THE CLERGY
................................3E **61** (4F **5**)
14 Fitzroy Square
LONDON
W1T 6AH
Tel: 020 73884954

ST MARY'S HOSPITAL 5F **59**
Praed Street
LONDON
W2 1NY
Tel: 020 77256666

ST PANCRAS HOSPITAL 5F **47**
4 St Pancras Way
LONDON
NW1 0PE
Tel: 020 75303500

ST THOMAS' HOSPITAL
................................4B **76** (5F **23**)
Lambeth Palace Road
LONDON
SE1 7EH
Tel: 020 79289292

SPRINGFIELD UNIVERSITY HOSPITAL
................................3A **116**
61 Glenburnie Road
LONDON
SW17 7DJ
Tel: 020 86826000

TRINITY HOSPICE 2D **103**
30 Clapham Common North Side
LONDON
SW4 0RN
Tel: 020 77871000

UNIVERSITY COLLEGE HOSPITAL
................................3E **61** (4A **6**)
Gower Street
LONDON
WC1E 6AU
Tel: 020 73879300

WELLINGTON HOSPITAL, THE 2F **59**
8a Wellington Place
LONDON
NW8 9LE
Tel: 020 75865959

WESTERN OPHTHALMIC HOSPITAL ...4B **60**
153 Marylebone Road
LONDON
NW1 5QH
Tel: 020 78866666

WHIPPS CROSS UNIVERSITY HOSPITAL
................................1F **39**
Whipps Cross Road
LONDON
E11 1NR
Tel: 020 85395522

WHITTINGTON HOSPITAL 4E **33**
Highgate Hill
LONDON
N19 5NF
Tel: 020 72723070

WILLESDEN COMMUNITY HOSPITAL
................................4C **42**
Harlesden Road
LONDON
NW10 3RY
Tel: 020 84518017

RAIL, CROYDON TRAMLINK, DOCKLANDS LIGHT RAILWAY AND LONDON UNDERGROUND STATIONS

with their map square reference

A

Acton Central (Rail) 2A **70**
Aldgate East (Tube) 5B **64** (2F **19**)
Aldgate (Tube) 5B **64** (3F **19**)
All Saints (DLR) 1D **81**
Angel (Tube) 1C **62**
Archway (Tube) 4E **33**
Arsenal (Tube) 5C **34**

B

Baker Street (Tube) 3B **60** (4A **4**)
Balham (Rail & Tube) 1C **116**
Bank (DLR & Tube) 5F **63** (3B **18**)
Barbican (Rail & Tube) 4E **63** (5F **9**)
Barnes (Rail) 1C **98**
Barnes Bridge (Rail) 5B **84**
Barons Court (Tube) 1A **86**
Battersea Park (Rail) 3D **89**
Bayswater (Tube) 1D **73**
Beckenham Hill (Rail) 5E **123**
Bellingham (Rail) 3D **123**
Belsize Park (Tube) 2A **46**
Bermondsey (Tube) 4C **78**
Bethnal Green (Rail) 3D **65**
Bethnal Green (Tube) 2E **65**
Blackfriars (Rail & Tube) 1D **77** (4D **17**)
Blackheath (Rail) 1B **110**
Blackwall (DLR) 1E **81**
Bond Street (Tube) 5D **61** (3D **13**)
Borough (Tube) 3E **77** (4A **26**)
Bow Church (DLR) 2C **66**
Bow Road (Tube) 2C **66**
Brent Cross (Tube) 2F **29**
Brixton (Rail & Tube) 2C **104**
Brockley (Rail) 1A **108**
Bromley-by-Bow (Tube) 2D **67**
Brondesbury (Rail) 4B **44**
Brondesbury Park (Rail) 5A **44**

C

Caledonian Road (Tube) 3B **48**
Caledonian Road & Barnsbury (Rail)
. . . . .4B **48**
Cambridge Heath (Rail) 1D **65**
Camden Road (Rail) 4E **47**

Camden Town (Tube) 5D **47**
Canada Water (Tube) 3E **79**
Canary Wharf (DLR) 2C **80**
Canary Wharf (Tube) 2D **81**
Canning Town (Rail, DLR & Tube) . . .5A **68**
Cannon Street (Rail & Tube) . . .1F **77** (4B **18**)
Canonbury (Rail) 2E **49**
Catford Bridge (Rail) 5C **108**
Catford (Rail) 5C **108**
Chalk Farm (Tube) 4C **46**
Chancery Lane (Tube) 4C **62** (1B **16**)
Charing Cross (Rail & Tube)
. . . . .2A **76** (1D **23**)
Charlton (Rail) 1E **97**
City Thameslink (Rail) 5D **63** (2D **17**)
Clapham Common (Tube) 2E **103**
Clapham High Street (Rail) 1F **103**
Clapham Junction (Rail) 1A **102**
Clapham North (Tube) 1A **104**
Clapham South (Tube) 4D **103**
Clapton (Rail) 4D **37**
Covent Garden (Tube) 1A **76** (4E **15**)
Cricklewood (Rail) 1F **43**
Crofton Park (Rail) 3B **108**
Crossharbour & London Arena (DLR)
. . . . .4D **81**
Crouch Hill (Rail) 2B **34**
Custom House for ExCel (Rail & DLR)
. . . . .1D **83**
Cutty Sark for Maritime Greenwich (DLR)
. . . . .2E **95**

D

Dalston Kingsland (Rail) 2A **50**
Denmark Hill (Rail) 5F **91**
Deptford (Rail) 3C **94**
Deptford Bridge (DLR) 4C **94**
Devons Road (DLR) 3D **67**
Dollis Hill (Tube) 2C **42**
Drayton Park (Rail) 1C **48**

E

Earl's Court (Tube) 5D **73**
Earlsfield (Rail) 1E **115**
East Acton (Tube) 5B **56**
East Dulwich (Rail) 2A **106**
East India (DLR) 1F **81**

Index to Stations